Gender and American Law

The Impact of the Law on the Lives of Women

Series Editor

Karen J. Maschke

GARLAND PUBLISHING, INC.
New York & London
1997

Contents of the Series

The Legal Response to Violence Against Women

Edited with introductions by

Karen J. Maschke

GARLAND PUBLISHING, INC.

New York & London

1997

Library of Congress Cataloging-in-Publication Data

The legal response to violence against women / edited with introductions by Karen J. Maschke.

p. cm. — (Gender and American law ; 5)

Includes bibliographical references.

ISBN 0-8153-2519-3 (alk. paper)

1. Women—Crimes against—United States. 2. Violent crimes—United States. 3. Abused women—Legal status, laws, etc.—United States. 4. Abused wives—Legal status, laws, etc.—United States. I. Maschke, Karen J. II. Series.

KF9304.L44 1997

345.73'025—dc21 96-39890

CIP

Printed on acid-free, 250-year-life paper

Manufactured in the United States of America

Contents

Series Introduction

From colonial times to the present, the law has been used to both expand and contract the rights of women. Over the last two decades, a body of literature has emerged that examines the ways in which the law has had an impact on the lives of women in the United States. The topics covered in this series include the historical development of women's legal rights, matters surrounding reproduction, sexuality and the family, equal employment opportunity, educational equity, violence against women, pornography, sex work, hate speech, and developments in feminist legal thought. The articles represent multidisciplinary approaches in examining women's experiences with the law and provide theoretical insights about the nature of gender equality.

A unifying theme in these articles is that women have been constructed historically as "different," and that this characterization "has had implications in regard to the way in which women are understood as objects and subjects of law" (Fineman 1992, p. 1). Biological differences between women and men and assumptions about the different "nature" of women and men have provided the basis for legal restrictions on women's ownership of property, guardianship of their children, ability to control their reproduction, and access to the workplace and educational institutions.

Even though women have more legal rights now than at any other time in history, many of the articles show that the law can both eradicate and reinforce women's subordination. Nineteenth-century child custody law is a telling example. While "judges granted women new legal power in family affairs," they also placed "severe limits on married women's overall legal rights" (Grossberg 1983, p. 235). On the one hand, by claiming the authority to determine which parent should be granted custody, judges dismantled the practice of fathers possessing unquestioned domain over matters of child custody and guardianship. Yet judges also "ensured that women's domestic powers did not translate into extensive external political and economic authority" (Grossberg 1983, p. 237).

The limitations of legal reform are also revealed by contemporary attempts to achieve gender equality. For example, in the 1970s many local governments adopted comparable worth wage policies. Such policies were "designed to correct historically discriminatory wages of female- and minority-dominated jobs" (Evans and Nelson 1989, p. 172). However, when some local communities were forced to raise women's wages to correct discriminatory practices, they eliminated or modified various jobs and social programs. Many of these programs, such as after school latchkey programs, were developed in response to the needs of two-paycheck and female-headed families. "In other words," note Evans and Nelson, "local governments are reacting to comparable worth with threats to renege on the emerging social commitment to policies addressing what have been traditionally defined as *women's* problems" (Evans and Nelson 1989, p. 183).

Other articles provide additional evidence of how legal reforms may actually disadvantage women in ways that are unanticipated. Furthermore, they reveal the problems in employing the model of equality as a basis for achieving gender justice. The emerging "difference theories" in feminist legal thought focus on the ways in which women and men live "gendered lives," and the ways in which legal and social institutions are shaped and operate according to gendered constructs (Fineman 1992).

The articles in this series also show how the law affects women in different ways. Women of color, poor women, and single mothers may experience the power of the law in ways that are different from the experiences of white, middle-class women. Poverty reform discourses are laden with images of single mothers as "bad" and often lump these women together "with drug addicts, criminals, and other socially-defined 'degenerates' in the newly-coined category of 'underclass'" (Fineman 1992, p. 283). Consequently, current welfare policies are not designed so much to help single mothers as they are to punish them for their bad behavior.

Several authors show how in the legal matters concerning male violence against women, "the experiences of women of color are frequently the product of intersecting patterns of racism and sexism" (Crenshaw 1991, p. 1243). These authors contend that theories of gender oppression must acknowledge the intersection of race and sex, the ways in which women have contributed to the social construction of race, and the oppression of black women. They also point out that the analyses of the law's role in women's oppression must take account of the intersectional identities of women and of how the law responds to, reinforces, and stigmatizes those identities.

The articles in this series bring together an outstanding selection from a growing body of work that examines how the law treats women and gender difference. They represent some of the most intriguing theoretical writing on the subject and reflect the strong multidisciplinary character of contemporary research on women and the legal order.

Notes

Cited works are contained in volumes five, three, seven, and two, respectively.

Crenshaw, Kimberle. 1991. Mapping the Margins: Intersectionality, Identity Politics, and Violence Against Women of Color. *Stanford Law Review* 43:1241–99.

Evans, Sara M. and Barbara J. Nelson. 1989. Comparable Worth: The Paradox of Technocratic Reform. *Feminist Studies* 15:171–90.

Fineman, Martha. 1992. Feminist Theory in Law: The Difference it Makes. *Columbia Journal of Gender and Law* 2:1–23.

Grossberg, Michael. 1983. Who Gets the Child? Custody, Guardianship, and the Rise of a Judicial Patriarchy in Nineteenth-Century America. *Feminist Studies* 9:235–60.

Volume Introduction

According to federal statistics, on average every year, women experience 572,032 violent victimizations by someone with whom they are intimate (Bachman 1994, p. 6). Another study found that "over six million women are beaten every year in the United States" (Strauss 1991, p. 30). Data collected between 1987 and 1991 indicated "that every year nearly 133,000 women age 12 or older were victims of rape or attempted rape." More than half of the rape victims knew the perpetrator (Bachman 1994, p. 11).

Although violence is a stark reality in the lives of many women, police, prosecutors, and judges often continue to downplay or ignore the extent to which women are victims of violent attacks. Many men are never arrested, prosecuted, or incarcerated for the violence they commit against women (Stalans and Lurigio 1995). Moreover, women are often blamed for causing the violence and thus are doubly victimized by a legal system that fails to protect or believe them.

The legal system's response to rape reveals how women can be victimized by the very system that was designed to protect victims of crime. Historically, the rape victim's behavior prior to the rape, her behavior during the assault, and her relationship to the perpetrator was often taken into consideration by legal officials in deciding whether a "real" rape occurred (Donat and D'Emilio 1992; Estrich 1987). Until the 1970s, the law in most states recognized that a rape occurred only when "a man forced a women to have sexual intercourse under the threat of bodily injury, she resisted strenuously, and there was outside corroboration" (Epstein and Langenbahn 1994, p. 7). In the 1970s, many states passed comprehensive rape reform legislation that shifted the emphasis from the victim's behavior to that of the perpetrator's and eliminated the resistance and corroboration requirements (Donat and D'Emilio 1992). Laws enacted over the past two decades have redefined rape by 1) including sexual penetration other than penile-vaginal penetration and oral and anal sodomy, 2) making rape gender-neutral, 3) recognizing that submission can be obtained by the perpetrator by using threats rather than force, 4) including marital rape as a crime, and 5) grading crimes of sexual assault according to whether there was sexual penetration and aggravating conditions (Epstein and Langenbaum 1994).

These rape law reforms have had an important impact on the legal system's response to rape and its view of rape victims. However, deeply ingrained stereotypical views of rape victims continue to shape the legal system's response to rape. For example, in 1989 a Florida jury acquitted a rape defendant because they felt the woman was asking for sex based on the clothing she was wearing when attacked (Crenshaw 1991). Moreover, many rape cases never even make it to court. Lisa Frohmann's study indicates that prosecutors regularly make decisions not to file cases because of biases in the organizational context of complaint filing. She found that prosecutors actively look for "'holes' or problems that will make the victim's version of 'what happened' unbelievable or not convincing beyond a reasonable doubt." The case is therefore defined as "unconvictable," and the prosecutor decides not to file charges (Frohman 1991, p. 214).

Cultural myths and stereotypes concerning race have also played a role in the legal system's response to rape. The dominant conceptualization of rape in this country is that of a black offender and white victim. Lynchings of black men accused of rape were used to control and discipline the black community, and "the casting of all Black men as potential threats to the sanctity of white womanhood" is a construct that has never been completely dispelled (Crenshaw 1991, p. 1267; Wriggins 1983). Black women during the slave era who were raped by white men, especially their white masters, could not count on the legal system to protect them from their victimizers (Crenshaw 1991; Wriggins 1983). Nor can black women count on legal protection today. As Kimberle Crenshaw points out, "Black women who are raped are racially discriminated against because their rapists, whether Black or white, are less likely to be charged with rape, and when charged and convicted, are less likely to receive significant jail time than the rapists of white women" (Crenshaw 1991, p. 1277).

Women who are victims of domestic violence often experience many of the same problems with the legal system as do victims of rape. Under English legal doctrine, a man was permitted "to beat his wife with a stick, as long as the stick was no thicker than his thumb" (Sherman, no date, p. 1). Today, men who use violence against women can be prosecuted for engaging in criminal behavior. Yet police, prosecutors, and judges are often reluctant to intervene in what they consider to be a "family matter."

In most domestic violence incidents the police are often the first legal officials who come into contact with a victim and offender. Their response to domestic violence sends a message about how such incidents will be dealt with by the law enforcement community. Traditionally, police officers have been reluctant to arrest offenders, choosing instead to walk them around the block or drive them to a friend's house to "cool off." The message given to the batterer is that nothing will happen to him; the message given to the victim is that the police will not protect her.

Although most states now have pro-arrest or mandatory arrest laws, many police officers are still reluctant to take domestic violence offenders into custody. Studies of police response to domestic violence suggest that domestic violence training may be a crucial factor in police officer's attitudes about domestic violence and in whether they implement arrest statutes (Buchanan and Perry 1985; Ferraro 1989; Mignon and Holmes 1995). Leadership from the police chief and the response from other criminal justice officials can also affect whether police officials implement or ignore domestic violence arrest laws (Ferraro 1989). When the police do arrest batterers, there is no guarantee that the prosecutor will file charges, that the offender will be convicted, or that he will be punished. Moreover, there is no conclusive evidence that arrest and prosecution will deter offenders from repeating the violence. Yet despite the unproven efficacy of arrest laws, many victims' advocates contend that without these measures, domestic violence would no longer be treated as a crime. Consequently, women would once again be without legal protection from the men who abuse them (Lerman 1992).

Although men who commit acts of domestic violence may never be held accountable for their actions, women who use violence against their abusers are often arrested, prosecuted, and convicted. This is particularly true for battered women who kill their abusers. Several studies have shown that these women "are routinely convicted and sentenced to long prison terms" (Developments 1993, p. 1575). In the mid-1970s, courts began to accept expert testimony on what is known as the "battered woman syndrome." This syndrome is based on a "pattern of responses and perceptions presumed to be characteristic of women who have been subjected to continuous physical abuse by their mate" (Schuller and Vidmar 1992, p. 273–74). Expert testimony on the battered woman syndrome is used within a claim of self-defense to show that the defendant had a reasonable belief that she was in imminent danger of being killed or seriously injured by her abuser, "even when she has killed her abuser in a seemingly nonconfrontational setting" (Developments 1993, 1580).

Recent studies of the battered woman's syndrome have focused on the problem of employing expert testimony that reinforces stereotypical views of women as passive, helpless victims while at the same time trying to explain why it was reasonable for the woman to kill her abuser (Schneider 1992). As Sharon Allard has shown, this is particularly problematic when the woman is black. Because black women have been portrayed by the "omnipresent images of the hostile Sapphire, the wanton Jezebel, and the strong and assertive Sojourner Truth," Allard contends that the battered woman syndrome fails as a theory for black women who have killed their abusers (Allard 1991, 196, 206).

Violence against women is a serious social problem that affects the family, the workplace, and the community. Although reforms have made the legal system more responsive to the victims of domestic violence and rape, the reforms do not adequately protect women from male violence. Nor do they hold all men accountable for their violent behavior. Thus, greater attention should be given to asking why the legal system often ignores women's victimization and how society as a whole can take steps to protect women from male violence.

Notes

Articles marked with an asterisk (*) are included in this volume.

*Allard, Sharon Angella. 1991. Rethinking Battered Woman Syndrome: A Black Feminist Perspective. *UCLA Women's Law Journal* 1:191–207.

Bachman, Ronet. 1991. Violence Against Women. U.S. Department of Justice. Bureau of Justice Statistics. Washington, D.C.: GPO.

Buchanan, Dale R. and Patricia A. Perry. 1985. Attitudes of Police Recruits Toward Domestic Disturbances: An Evaluation of Family Crisis Intervention Training. *Journal of Criminal Justice* 13:561–72.

*Crenshaw, Kimberle. 1991. Mapping the Margins: Intersectionality, Identity Politics, and Violence Against Women of Color. *Stanford Law Review* 43:1241–99.

Developments in the Law. 1993. Legal Responses to Domestic Violence. *Harvard Law Review* 1498–1620.

*Donat, Patricia L.N. and John D'Emilio. 1992. A Feminist Redefinition of Rape and Sexual Assault: Historical Foundations and Change. *Journal of Social Issues* 48:9–22.
Epstein, Joel and Stacia Langenbahn. 1994. The Criminal Justice and Community Response to Rape. U.S. Department of Justice. National Institute of Justice. Washington, D.C.: GPO.
Estrich, Susan. 1987. *Real Rape*. Cambridge: Harvard University Press.
*Ferraro, Kathleen J. 1989. Policing Woman Battering. *Social Problems* 35:61–74.
*Frohmann, Lisa. 1991. Discrediting Victims' Allegations of Sexual Assault: Prosecutorial Accounts of Case Rejections. *Social Problems* 38:213–26.
Lerman, Lisa G. 1992. The Decontextualization of Domestic Violence. *Journal of Criminal Law and Criminology* 83:217–40.
Mignon, Sylvia I. and William M. Holmes. 1995. Police Response to Mandatory Arrest Laws. *Crime and Delinquency* 41:430–42.
Schneider, Elizabeth M. 1992. Particularity and Generality: Challenges of Feminist Theory and Practice in Work on Woman-Abuse. *New York University Law Review* 67:520–68.
Schuller, Regina A. and Neil Vidmar. 1992. Battered Woman Syndrome Evidence in the Courtroom: A Review of the Literature. *Law and Human Behavior* 16:273–311.
Sherman, Lawrence. no date. Domestic Violence. Department of Justice. National Institute of Justice. Washington, D.C.: GPO.
*Stalans, Loretta J. and Arthur J. Lurigio. 1995. Responding to Domestic Violence Against Women. *Crime and Delinquency* 41:387–98.
Strauss, Murray. 1991. Conceptualization and Measurement of Battering: Implications for Public Policy. In *Woman Battering: Policy Responses,* edited by M. Steinman. Cincinnati: Anderson.
*Wriggins, Jennifer. 1983. Rape, Racism, and the Law. *Harvard Women's Law Journal* 6:103–41.

RAPE, RACISM, AND THE LAW

JENNIFER WRIGGINS*

INTRODUCTION

The history of rape in this country has focused on the rape of white women by Black men. From a feminist perspective, two of the most damaging consequences of this selective blindness are the denials that Black women are raped and that all women are subject to pervasive and harmful sexual coercion of all kinds.

This Note examines the historical legacy of the racist social meaning of rape and its consequences. Part I describes the history of the legal and societal focus on punishing Black men when the rape of white women is claimed. Part II discusses the denial of the rape of Black women. Part III argues that the narrow focus on one racial combination of rape obscures the significance of the sexual coercion

---

*Student, Harvard Law School.

Acknowledgments. Dozens of people contributed to the making of this Note, and the author is indebted to each of them. Among those who helped in ways the author especially appreciates are: Nia Burnette, Lisa Biow, George Chauncey, Jr., Rhonda Copelon, Christopher Edley, Jr., Karen A. Getman, Geraldine Hines, Muhammed Kenyatta, Mary Ann Kopydlowski, Catharine A. MacKinnon, Judy Miles, Stephanie Y. Moore, Lori J. Nelson, Lynn Paltrow, Jane Schacter, Robin Wiener, and Mary Whisner. Without their support, advice, and criticisms, this Note could not have been written. Special thanks are due to Mary Ellen Roy for her patient editing. Responsibility for the views expressed herein lies with the author.

The word "Black" is capitalized in this Note when used to denote someone's race. The reason for this has been well stated by Catharine MacKinnon:

> Black is conventionally (I am told) regarded as a color rather than a racial or national designation, hence is not usually capitalized. I do not regard Black as merely a color of skin pigmentation, but as a heritage, an experience, a cultural and personal identity, the meaning of which becomes specifically stigmatic and/or glorious and/or ordinary under specific social conditions. It is as much socially created as, and at least in the American context no less specifically meaningful or definitive than, any linguistic, tribal, or religious ethnicity, all of which are conventionally recognized by capitalization.

MacKinnon, *Feminism, Marxism, Method, and the State: An Agenda for Theory*, 7 SIGNS 515, 516 (1982). While a parallel argument could support the capitalization of "white," such a usage would resonate with a long tradition of dominance by whites and is hence rejected.

all women face. Part IV argues that feminists must go beyond traditional rape reform measures to stop sexual coercion.

PART I: THE NARROW FOCUS ON BLACK OFFENDER/WHITE VICTIM RAPE

There are many different kinds of rape.[1] Its victims[2] are of all races,[3] and its perpetrators are of all races.[4] Yet the kind of rape

[1] By "rape" this Note refers not to the legal definition of rape or sexual assault, but rather to "any attempted or completed sexual act that is forced on an individual against his or her will." Bowker, *Rape and Other Sexual Assaults*, WOMEN AND CRIME IN AMERICA 180, 180 (L. Bowker ed. 1981). The term thus includes a wide range of situations, from a stranger assaulting a woman in a dark alley to a husband forcing sex on his wife, regardless of whether penetration is involved or the act is illegal. The term "illegal rape" refers to situations where the imposition of sex is prohibited by law.

This Note addresses only the rape of women by men. Besides being the most prevalent and widely-studied kind of rape, it is also an important manifestation of, and means of perpetuating, male dominance. This Note argues that the treatment of this kind of rape by the legal system also serves as a weapon of white dominance.

[2] Rape statistics are notoriously unreliable. An initial problem with them is that they report only activity which the law defines as rape. Illegal rape is not necessarily the only or most harmful sex forced on victims. *See* MacKinnon, *Feminism, Marxism, Method, and the State: Toward Feminist Jurisprudence* 8 SIGNS (forthcoming 1983); Comment, *Rape and Rape Laws: Sexism in Society and Law*, 61 CAL. L. REV. 919, 941 (1973).

A second major problem with rape statistics is that underreporting even of illegal rape renders them inaccurate. It is likely that Black women underreport more than white women, especially if the woman's assailant is white. *See infra* note 122. A recent estimate is that only one in two illegal rapes is reported. Bowker, *Women as Victims: An Examination of the Results of L.E.A.A.'s National Crime Survey Program*, in WOMEN AND CRIME IN AMERICA, *supra* note 1, at 158-64.

A third problem is that police often decide not to pursue rape complaints which may be valid, especially if the complainant is Black, so these complaints may not appear in police "reported rape" figures. Chappell, Geis, Schafer & Siegel, *A Comparative Study of Forcible Rape Offenses Known to the Police in Boston and Los Angeles*, in FORCIBLE RAPE 227, 235 (D. Chappell, R. Geis & G. Geis eds. 1977).

More accurate figures may be derived from victim surveys which involve interviewing a random sample of citizens in a particular area concerning their victimization. It is from such surveys that the estimated ratios of actual to reported rapes are derived. However, this method has in some circumstances been found to underestimate the crime committed against Blacks. Hood & Sparks, *Citizens Attitudes and Police Practice in Reporting Offenses*, in VICTIMOLOGY 167 (I. Drapkin & E. Viano eds. 1974).

[3] This Note focuses on rape between white and Black people in this country. It does not deal with rape involving other people of color for several reasons. First, most of what has been written about race and rape focuses exclusively on Black/white issues. (Exceptions include J. WILLIAMS & K. HOLMES, THE SECOND ASSAULT (1981) [hereinafter cited as THE SECOND ASSAULT]; AEGIS, March-Apr. 1979 (special issue entitled *Violence Against Women and Race*); Chu & Torres, *Rape: It Can't Happen to Me!*, BRIDGE: AN ASIAN AMERICAN PERSPECTIVE, Spring 1979.) Second, critics of feminist rape literature have primarily addressed its failure to combat the myth of the Black rapist and to recognize the differences between the vulnerability of white and Black women as rape victims. *See infra* note 183. This Note attempts to begin to correct these failures. A remaining failure is commentators' neglect of rape as it affects other people of color.

[4] *See infra* text accompanying notes 121-232.

that has been treated most seriously throughout this nation's history has been the illegal forcible rape of a white woman by a Black man.[5] The selective acknowledgement of Black accused/white victim rape was especially pronounced during slavery and through the first half of the twentieth century.[6] Today a powerful legacy remains that permeates thought about rape and race.[7]

Slavery

During the slavery period, statutes in many jurisdictions provided the death penalty or castration for rape when the convicted man was Black or mulatto and the victim white.[8] These extremely harsh penalties were frequently imposed.[9] In addition, mobs occasionally broke into jails and courtrooms and lynched slaves alleged to have raped white women,[10] prefiguring Reconstruction mob behavior.[11]

In contrast to the harsh penalties imposed on Black offenders, courts occasionally released a defendant accused of raping a white woman when the evidence was inconclusive as to whether he was

---

[5] *See* Mann & Selva, *The Sexualization of Racism: The Black as Rapist and White Justice*, 3 W. J. Black Studies 168 (1979); *see also infra* text accompanying notes 8–80.

[6] *See infra* text accompanying notes 8–63.

[7] *See infra* text accompanying notes 64–80.

[8] *See, e.g.*, Alabama Code of 1852 (death penalty for rape of a white woman by a slave or free Black); Mississippi 1857 Statute (death penalty for attempted carnal connection with or rape of a white female under fourteen by a slave); Tennessee 1858 Law (death by hanging for rape of a free white woman by a slave or free Black); Missouri 1825 Statute (castration for rape or attempted rape by a Black or mulatto); Arkansas Code of 1838 (death penalty for assault with intent to commit rape by a Black or mulatto). Bienen, *Rape III—National Developments in Rape Reform Legislation*, 6 Women's Rights L. Rep. 170, 173 n.14 (1980). Although the last two states appear to provide strong sanctions for the rape of a Black woman by a Black man, the case law demonstrates that the claims of Black women were ignored. *See infra* text accompanying notes 93-96. Although concentrated in the South, statutes distinguishing between the races for sexual crimes were enacted in other states as well. *See, e.g.*, Pennsylvania Code of 1700 (death penalty for rape of a white woman by a Black man); Kansas Compilation of 1855 (castration at his own expense for rape or attempted rape of a white woman by a Black or mulatto). Bienen, *supra*, at 173 n.14; *see also* Burns, *Race Discrimination—Law and Race in America*, in The Politics of Law 89 (D. Kairys ed. 1982).

[9] Dennis, a slave, v. State, 5 Ark. 230 (1843); State v. Joshua, a slave, 15 La. Ann. 118 (1860); State v. Bill, 8 Rob. 527 (La. 1844); Isham v. State, 33 Tenn. (1 Sneed) 111 (1853); Ellick v. State, 31 Tenn. (1 Swan) 325 (1851); Commonwealth v. Watts (4 Leigh) 672 (1833); Thompson v. Commonwealth, 31 Va. (4 Leigh) 652 (1833). 1-3 Judicial Cases Concerning American Slavery and the Negro (H. Catterall ed. 1926-1932); *see* M. Hindus, Prison and Plantation: Crime, Justice and Authority in Massachusetts and South Carolina 1767–1878, at 150–61 (1980); K. Stampp, The Peculiar Institution 210–11 (1956).

[10] K. Stampp, *supra* note 9, at 190–91.

[11] *See infra* text accompanying notes 26–40.

Black or mulatto.[12] The rape of Black women by white or Black men, on the other hand, was legal;[13] indictments were sometimes dismissed for failing to allege that the victim was white.[14] In those states where it was illegal for white men to rape white women, statutes provided less severe penalties for the convicted white rapist than for the convicted Black one.[15] In addition, common-law rules both defined rape narrowly[16] and made it a difficult crime to prove.[17]

During slavery, then, the legal system treated seriously only one racial combination of rape—rape involving a Black offender and a white victim. This selective recognition continued long after slavery ended.

The Post-Civil War Period

After the Civil War, state legislatures made their rape statutes race-neutral,[18] but the legal system treated rape in much the same way

[12] Thurman v. State, 18 Ala. 276 (1850); Dick, a slave, v. State, 30 Miss. 631 (1856).

[13] S. Brownmiller, Against Our Will 176 (1975); Evans, *Rape, Race, and Research*, in Blacks and Criminal Justice 75, 79 (C. Owens & J. Bell eds. 1977); *see* W. Bowers, Executions in America 173 (1974); A. L. Higginbotham, In the Matter of Color 282 (1978); Blackwell, *Social and Legal Dimensions of Interracial Liaisons*, in The Black Male in America 219, 225 (D. Wilkinson & R. Taylor eds. 1977) [hereinafter cited as The Black Male]; *infra* notes 89-96 and accompanying text.

[14] State v. Charles, a slave, 1 Fla. 298 (1847); Commonwealth v. Jerry Mann, 4 Va. (Va. Cas.) 210 (1820); George, a slave, v. State, 37 Miss. 316 (1859); *see infra* text accompanying notes 93-96.

[15] *See, e.g.*, Virginia Code of 1819 and 1823 Law (death penalty for rape or attempted rape of a white woman by a slave, Black, or mulatto and term of 10-21 years for rape by a white man); Kentucky 1802 Code (death penalty for rape of a white woman by a slave and term of years for rape by a white man). Bienen, *supra* note 8, at 173 n.14; Georgia Penal Code of 1816 (death penalty for rape or attempted rape of a free white woman by a slave or free person of color and term of not more than 20 years for rape or attempted rape by a white man) No. 380 §§ 33-34; No. 508 and 509, § 2; Georgia Acts of 1816 § 1, Compilation of the Laws of Georgia 804 (Lamar ed. 1821), *cited in* Amicus Brief of Women's Legal Defense Fund and Equal Rights Advocates at 17, Coker v. Georgia, 433 U.S. 584 (1977).

[16] For example, rape by one's husband and rape not involving penetration by the penis were not defined as "rape." *See* H. Feild & L. Bienen, Jurors and Rape 154, 163 (1980) [hereinafter cited as Jurors]; MacKinnon, *Violence Against Women: A Perspective,* Aegis, Jan. 1982 51, 53; MacKinnon, *supra* note 2; Comment, *supra* note 2, at 925-26.

[17] The two most important rules were those allowing admission of evidence of the sexual history of the victim and requiring extensive corroborating evidence of the rape. Berger, *Man's Trial, Woman's Tribulation,* 77 Colum. L. Rev. 1, 15-20 (1977); Note, *The Victim in a Forcible Rape Case: A Feminist View,* 11 Am. Crim. L. Rev. 335, 336 (1973); Comment, *supra* note 2, at 919; *see infra* text accompanying notes 140-163. Such rules were relaxed when the defendant was Black. *See infra* text accompanying notes 145-151.

[18] A compilation of all post-Civil War state legislation enacted prior to 1917 that mentioned race contained no rape statutes. F. Johnson, The Development of State Legislation Concerning the Free Negro (1918). Such race-specific legislation included many anti-

as it had before the war. Black women raped by white or Black men had no hope of recourse through the legal system.[19] White women raped by white men faced traditional common-law barriers that protected most rapists from prosecution.[20]

Allegations of rape involving Black offenders and white victims were treated with heightened virulence. This was manifested in two ways. The first response was lynching, which peaked near the end of the nineteenth century.[21] The second, from the early twentieth century on, was the use of the legal system as a functional equivalent of lynching, as illustrated by mob coercion of judicial proceedings,[22] special doctrinal rules,[23] the language of opinions,[24] and the markedly disparate numbers of executions for rape between white and Black defendants.[25]

Lynching

Between 1882 and 1946 at least 4715 persons were lynched, about three-quarters of whom were Black.[26] Although lynching tapered off after the early 1950s, occasional lynch-like killings persist to this day.[27] The influence of lynching extended far beyond the numbers

---

miscegenation statutes. *Id.* at 8–10, 62–207. These statutes, providing criminal penalties for interracial marriage, were declared unconstitutional only quite recently, in Loving v. Virginia, 388 U.S. 1 (1967), and McLaughlin v. Florida, 379 U.S. 184 (1964).

For thorough general discussions of miscegenation see D. Bell, Race, Racism and American Law 53–81 (1980); Applebaum, *Miscegenation Statutes: A Constitutional and Social Problem*, 53 Geo. L.J. 49 (1964). For a more specific historical discussion, see J. Johnston, Race Relations in Virginia and Miscegenation in the South 1776-1860 (1970).

[19] *See infra* text accompanying notes 101–112.

[20] *See supra* note 16.

[21] A. Raper, The Tragedy of Lynching 1–2 (1933); C. Woodward, The Strange Career of Jim Crow 43 (1974); Note, *Constitutionality of Proposed Federal Anti-Lynching Legislation*, 34 Va. L. Rev. 944 (1948).

[22] *See infra* text accompanying notes 37–50.

[23] *See infra* text accompanying notes 51–55.

[24] *See infra* text accompanying notes 56–58.

[25] *See infra* text accompanying notes 59–63.

[26] A. Rose, The Negro in America 185 (1948) (citing a Tuskegee Institute study). A study by the NAACP found the number of lynchings acknowledged by white officials between 1882 and 1927 to be 4951, with approximately 70% of the victims being Black. White, *A Statement of Fact* [*on Lynching*], in A Documentary History of the Negro People in the United States 1910–1932, at 610 (H. Aptheker ed. 1973) [hereinafter cited as Documentary History].

[27] In March 1981, in Mobile, Alabama, a 19-year-old Black man was beaten, strangled to death, and left hanging from a tree by a rope tied in a noose. N.Y. Times, Mar. 23, 1981, at A12, col. 6. There were suggestions by people in the community that he was killed for socializing with white women, or that he was mistaken for a Black co-worker who was married to a white woman. *Id.*, Mar. 26, 1981, at A16, col. 6. Three white men were arrested for the murder but later released when a grand jury failed to return indictments. *Id.*, July 28, 1981, at A12, col. 6.

of Black people[28] murdered because accounts of massive white crowds torturing, burning alive, and dismembering their victims[29] created a widespread sense of terror in the Black community.[30]

The most common justification for lynching was the claim that a Black man had raped a white woman.[31] The thought of this particular crime aroused in many white people an extremely high level of mania and panic. One white woman, the wife of an ex-Congressman, stated in 1898, "If it needs lynching to protect woman's dearest possession from human beasts, then I say lynch a thousand times a week if necessary."[32] The quote resonates with common stereotypes that Black male sexuality is wanton and bestial,[33] and that Black men are wild, criminal[34] rapists of white women.[35]

---

[28] Black women were not spared the violence of lynchings. The NAACP study, discussed in White, *supra* note 26, found that of the 4951 people lynched, 76 were Black women. *Id.* at 610. Vivid first person accounts of the lynchings of Black women document that no gentleness was accorded them on account of their sex. *See* G. LERNER, BLACK WOMEN IN WHITE AMERICA 161–63 (1972); Katz, *The Negro Woman and the Law*, in 2 FREEDOMWAYS 289 (1962); DOCUMENTARY HISTORY, *supra* note 26, at 142.

[29] *See* A. RAPER, *supra* note 21, at 141–44, 420–21; I. WELLS, *Lynching Bee*, in A RED RECORD: LYNCHINGS IN THE UNITED STATES 1892-1893-1894 (1895), *reprinted in* JUSTICE DENIED: THE BLACK MAN IN WHITE AMERICA 196 (W. Chace & P. Collier eds. 1970).

[30] A. ROSE, *supra* note 26, at 186-87; Hall, *"The Mind that Burns in Each Body": Women, Rape, and Racial Violence*, in POWERS OF DESIRE: THE POLITICS OF SEXUALITY (A. Snitow, C. Stansell & S. Thompson eds. forthcoming 1983); Hernton, *The Negro Male*, in THE BLACK MALE, *supra* note 13, at 244–46.

[31] A. ROSE, *supra* note 26, at 185; C. WOODWARD, *supra* note 21, at 43; Hall, *supra* note 30; Reynolds, *The Remedy for Lynch Law*, 7 YALE L.J. 20, 20 (1897–98) (quoting an article that refers to the lynching of a Black man for the alleged rape of a white woman as "the usual crime").

[32] Reynolds, *supra* note 31, at 20.

[33] Day, *The Hidden Fear*, in THE BLACK MALE, *supra* note 13, at 193, 197–98. The assumption made by whites that Blacks have bestial sexuality has deep historical roots. *See* W. JORDAN, WHITE OVER BLACK: AMERICAN ATTITUDES TOWARD THE NEGRO 1550–1812, at 32–40, 151 (1968). In a culture with a somatophobic heritage such as ours, the association of any group with physicality or sexuality is in itself degrading. For discussions of this phenomenon as it relates to women, see S. DE BEAUVOIR, THE SECOND SEX 182–84 (1952); S. GRIFFIN, WOMEN AND NATURE (1978); Ortner, *Is Female to Male as Nature is to Culture?*, in WOMAN, CULTURE AND SOCIETY 67 (M. Rosaldo & L. Lamphere eds. 1974); Spelman, *Woman as Body: Ancient and Contemporary Views*, 8 FEMINIST STUDIES 109, 119 (1982).

[34] The association of Black men with criminality extends back at least to the nineteenth century. A. ROSE, *supra* note 26, at 303. White criminals often capitalized on and perpetuated this stereotype by dying their faces black before committing crimes. *Id.* at 304; Johnson, *The Negro and Crime*, in THE SOCIOLOGY OF CRIME AND DELINQUENCY 419, 422 (M. Wolfgang, L. Santz & N. Johnston eds. 2d ed. 1970). The alleged propensity of Black men to rape white women can be seen partly as a manifestation of the criminality stereotype. In 1933, Arthur Raper made this link in trying to explain lynching: "[A]ccording to the popular estimate, all Negroes are essentially alike and are inclined to commit certain crimes, chief of which is the rape of white women." A. RAPER, *supra* note 21, at 50; *see* A. ROSE, *supra* note 26, at 305. Note that "all Negroes" refers only to Black men; Black women are left out of this formulation.

[35] In the United States the myth of Black male sexuality includes the characterization of the Black male as rapist of white women. *See, e.g.*, E. GENOVESE, ROLL JORDAN ROLL: THE

Many whites accepted lynching as an appropriate punishment for a Black man accused of raping a white woman. The following argument made to the jury by defense counsel in a 1907 Louisiana case illustrates this acceptance:

> Gentlemen of the jury, this man, a nigger, is charged with breaking into the house of a white man in the nighttime and assaulting his wife, with the intent to rape her. Now, don't you know that, if this nigger had committed such a crime, he never would have been brought here and tried; that he would have been lynched, and if I were there I would help pull on the rope.[36]

The Legal System's Treatment: "Legal Lynching"

It is doubtful whether the legal system better protected the rights of a Black man accused of raping a white woman than did the mob.[37] Contemporary legal literature used the term "legal lynching"

WORLD THE SLAVES MADE 336 (1976); G. LERNER, *supra* note 28, at 193; Mann & Selva, *supra* note 5, at 169–70; Schmidt, *Principle and Prejudice: The Supreme Court and Race in the Progressive Era. Part 1: The Heyday of Jim Crow*, 82 COLUM. L. REV. 3, 444, 454 (1982).

[36] State v. Petit, 119 La. 1013, 1016, 44 So. 848, 849 (1907) (quoting defense counsel). The argument also reveals much about the way the legal system defined the rape of white women. The house where the alleged rape took place belonged not to the victim but to "a white man" and she was "his wife." A Black woman would not have received such protection from the legal system and a white woman did only because she belonged to a white man. These dynamics are discussed *infra* text accompanying notes 143–166. Also, note that the jury here is accurately addressed by the defense counsel as "gentlemen," *i.e.*, it consists entirely of white men, probably landowners. *See, e.g.*, Day v. Commonwealth, 43 Va. (2 Gratt.) 562 (1845); 44 Va. (3 Gratt.) 629 (1846) (new trial for free mulatto defendant convicted of rape of white woman because of evidence that one juror was not a landowner in the county where the trial was held).

[37] The district attorney responded to the defense's claim in the *Petit* case, discussed *supra* note 36, by arguing that a legal system controlled by whites made lynching unnecessary because it had the same result:

> During the reconstruction days, when we had negro domination in this state, the Kuklux Klans were organized and the best people of the state shouldered their guns for the protection of our white people. During those days white people were thrown into jail and tried by negro justices of the peace and negro juries. Now we have no more negro domination, but *a government by the white people, and hence no necessity for lynching*. . . . [T]he fact that this negro is given a fair trial is no reason why you should believe him innocent.

119 La. at 1016, 44 So. at 849 (quoting the district attorney) (emphasis added). Although the defendant claimed the district attorney's argument was prejudicial, the Supreme Court of Louisiana affirmed the conviction, commenting: "While this discussion of matters outside of the record was highly improper, and should have been, in its inception, repressed by the trial judge, we fail to perceive in the remarks of the district attorney any appeal to racial prejudice for the purpose of influencing the jury." *Id.* at 1017, 44 So. at 849.

to describe the legal system's treatment of Black men.[38] Well past the first third of the twentieth century, courts were often coerced by violent mobs, which threatened to execute the defendant themselves unless the court convicted him.[39] Such mobs often did lynch the defendant if the judicial proceedings were not acceptable to them.[40] A contemporary authority on lynching commented in 1934 that "the local sentiment which would make a lynching possible would insure a conviction in the courts."[41] Even if the mob was not overtly pressuring for execution, a Black defendant accused of raping a white woman faced a hostile, racist legal system.[42] State court submission to mob pressure is well illustrated by the most famous series of cases about interracial rape, the Scottsboro cases of the 1930s.[43] Eight young Black men were convicted of what the Alabama Supreme Court called "a most foul and revolting crime,"[44] which was the rape of "two defenseless white girls."[45] The defendants were summarily sentenced to death based on minimal and dubious evidence, having been denied effective assistance of counsel.[46] The Alabama Supreme Court upheld the convictions in opinions demonstrating relentless determination to hold the defendants guilty regardless of strong evidence that mob pressure had influenced the verdicts and the weak evidence presented against the defendants. In one decision, that court affirmed the trial court's denial of a change of venue on the grounds that the mobs' threats of harm were not imminent enough although the National Guard had been called out to protect the defendants from mob executions.[47] The U.S. Supreme Court later recognized

---

[38] Chadbourn, *infra* note 39, at 332.

[39] A. Raper, *supra* note 21, at 143; Chadbourn, *Plan for Survey of Lynching and the Judicial Process*, 9 N.C. L. Rev. 330, 332–33 (1931); *see* Thompson v. State, 117 Ala. 67, 23 So. 676 (1898) (change of venue granted for Black defendant accused of rape because threats of mob violence threatened defendant's imminent death or would pressure jury into convicting); *see also* R. Wilkins, Rape: A Case History of Murder, Terror and Injustice Visited Upon a Negro Community (1949).

[40] Chadbourn, *supra* note 39, at 331.

[41] Chadbourn, *Lynching and the Law*, 20 A.B.A.J. 71 (1934).

[42] Burns, *Black People and the Tyranny of American Law*, 407 Annals, Spring 1973, at 156, 159–60.

[43] Patterson v. State, 224 Ala. 531, 141 So. 195 (1932); Powell v. State, 224 Ala. 540, 141 So. 201 (1932); Weems v. State, 224 Ala. 524, 141 So. 215 (1932).

[44] Powell v. State, 224 Ala. 540, 544, 141 So. 201, 204 (1932).

[45] *Id.* at 548, 141 So. at 207.

[46] Powell v. Alabama, 287 U.S. 45, 71 (1932).

[47] Patterson v. State, 224 Ala. 531, 534, 141 So. 195, 196 (1932); Powell v. State, 224 Ala. 540, 545–46, 141 So. 201, 205–06 (1932).

that the proceedings had in fact taken place in an atmosphere of "tense, hostile, and excited public sentiment."[48] After a lengthy appellate process, including three favorable Supreme Court rulings,[49] all of the Scottsboro defendants were released, having spent a total of 104 years in prison.[50]

In addition, courts applied special doctrinal rules to Black defendants accused of the rape or attempted rape of white women.[51] One such rule allowed juries to consider the race of the defendant and victim in drawing factual conclusions as to the defendant's intent in attempted rape cases. If the accused was Black and the victim white, the jury was entitled to draw the inference, based on race alone, that he intended to rape her. One court wrote, "In determining the question of intention, the jury may consider social conditions and customs founded upon racial differences, such as that the prosecutrix was a white woman and defendant was a Negro man."[52] The "social conditions and customs founded upon racial differences" which the jury was to consider included the assumption that Black men always and only want to rape white women,[53] and that a white woman would never consent to sex with a Black man.[54]

---

[48] Powell v. Alabama, 287 U.S. 45, 51 (1932); *see also* C. NORRIS & S. WASHINGTON, THE LAST OF THE SCOTTSBORO BOYS 19-25 (1979).

[49] Norris v. Alabama, 294 U.S. 587 (1935) (systematic and arbitrary exclusion of Blacks from jury lists resulting in exclusion of Blacks from juries constitutes denial of Fourteenth Amendment due process rights); Patterson v. Alabama, 294 U.S. 600 (1935) (state Supreme Court must consider defendants' claim of systematic exclusion of Blacks from juries despite defendants' failure to file timely bill of exceptions in light of Supreme Court's decision on identical facts in Norris v. Alabama that such claims have merit); Powell v. Alabama, 287 U.S. 45 (1932) (defendant accused of capital crime has due process right to counsel that includes right to consult with counsel and prepare a defense).

[50] C. NORRIS & S. WASHINGTON, *supra* note 48.

[51] Chastity evidence, for example, was treated differently for Black and white defendants, see *infra* text accompanying notes 145-155.

[52] McQuirter v. State, 36 Ala. App. 707, 709, 63 So. 2d 388, 390 (1953) (citations omitted). In this case, the defendant, a Black man who had never before been arrested, was found guilty of an "attempt to commit an assault with intent to rape." *Id.* at 708, 63 So. 2d at 388. He was accused of muttering something unintelligible and walking within six feet of Mrs. Ted Allen, a white woman. *Id.* at 708, 63 So. 2d at 389. *See* Pumphrey v. State, 156 Ala. 103, 107-08, 47 So. 156, 158 (1908); Kelley v. State, 1 Ala. App. 133, 135, 56 So. 15, 15-16 (1911).

[53] *See supra* notes 33-35. Many opinions graphically illustrate this assumption, for example: "[T]he accused, a negro, under the excitement of lust and with the intention of gratifying it by force, entered the bedroom of Mrs. Crimm, a white woman.... There was nothing in the evidence to indicate that Mrs. Crimm was not virtuous...." Pumphrey v. State, 156 Ala. 103, 107, 47 So. 156, 158 (1908). Note the significance to the court, even in this situation, that "Mrs. Crimm" is "virtuous." *See* Barnett v. State, 83 Ala. 40, 3 So. 612 (1878); Kelley v. State, 1 Ala. App. 133, 56 So. 15 (1911); Dorsey v. State, 108 Ga. 477, 34 S.E. 135 (1899). *See infra* text accompanying notes 140-155.

[54] *See, e.g.*, Story v. State, 178 Ala. 98, 5 So. 480 (1912), discussed *infra* text accompanying notes 149-150.

The Georgia Supreme Court of 1899 was even more explicit about the significance of race in the context of attempted rape, and particularly about the motivations of Black men. It held that race may properly be considered "to rebut any presumption that might otherwise arise in favor of the accused that his intention was to obtain the consent of the female, upon failure of which he would abandon his purpose to have sexual intercourse with her."[55] Such a rebuttal denied to Black defendants procedural protection that was accorded white defendants.

Judicial attitudes toward the rape of white women by Black men are also manifested in the factual descriptions of the crime in opinions. Courts sometimes created pornographic images of the events of the rape.[56] One court, for example, wrote, "[The victim,] while clad only in her pajamas was forced to a remote spot some two blocks from her home, where battered, bruised, bleeding and exhausted she was overpowered. . . ."[57] The sense of disgusted fascination that such opinions convey is not paralleled in cases where offender and victim are both white.[58]

The outcome of this disparate treatment of Black men by the legal system was often the same as lynching—death.[59] Between 1930 and 1967, thirty-six percent of the Black men who were convicted of raping a white woman were executed.[60] In stark contrast, only two percent

[55] Dorsey v. State, 108 Ga. 477, 480, 34 S.E. 135, 136–37 (1899). This rule was not used where both parties were Black. *See* Washington v. State, 138 Ga. 370, 75 S.E. 253 (1912); *see infra* text accompanying notes 106–108.

[56] That the descriptions were pornographic was pointed out to the author by Karen Getman.

[57] Maxwell v. State, 236 Ark. 694, 697, 370 S.W. 2d 113, 115 (1963); *see* Vanleeward v. State, 220 Ga. 135, 136, 137 S.E. 2d 452, 453 (1964).

[58] For example, in Rice v. State, 35 Fla. 236, 17 So. 286 (1895), the court drily notes "the plaintiff in error was convicted of the crime of rape upon one Helen Smith, his stepdaughter."

[59] In 1965, 18 American jurisdictions allowed the death penalty for rape. Wolfgang & Reidel, *Race, Judicial Discretion and the Death Penalty* 407 ANNALS 120 (1973). Hugo Bedau has written that most criminologists think capital punishment for rape was "introduced in order to *Keep the Nigras in line*" and "had nothing to do with its deterrent effect." Bailey, *Rape and the Death Penalty: A Neglected Area of Deterrence Research*, in CAPITAL PUNISHMENT IN THE UNITED STATES 336 (H. Bedau & C. Pierce eds. 1975) (citing unpublished letter) (emphasis in the original).

[60] Wolfgang, *Racial Discrimination in the Death Sentence for Rape*, in EXECUTIONS IN AMERICA, *supra* note 13, at 116. A systematic analysis of 1238 convictions for rape between 1945 and 1965 examined many variables in addition to race, such as presence of a weapon and prior record of the defendant, to attempt to account for the disparate numbers of executions. The study concluded that race was the only factor that accounted for the disparities. *Id.* at 114–20. The Wolfgang study is unique in its methodology and conclusiveness. It supports a larger body of prior research summarized in *id.* at 110–11.

of all defendants convicted of rape involving other racial combinations were executed.[61] As a result of such disparate treatment, eighty-nine percent of the men executed for rape in this country were Black.[62] While execution rates for all crimes were much higher for Black men than for white men, the differential was most dramatic when the crime was the rape of a white woman.[63]

The Legacy Today

The patterns that began in slavery and continued long afterwards have left a powerful legacy that manifests itself today in several ways. Although the death penalty for rape has been declared unconstitutional,[64] the severe statutory penalties for rape[65] continue to be applied in a discriminatory manner. A recent study concluded that Black men convicted of raping white women receive more serious sanctions than all other sexual assault defendants.[66] A recent attitudinal study found that white potential jurors treated Black and white defendants similarly when the victim was Black. However,

---

[61] *Id.* at 110–13; *see* Mann & Selva, *supra* note 5.

[62] Wolfgang & Reidel, *supra* note 59.

[63] Wolfgang, *supra* note 60, at 110–13. The NAACP-LDEF challenged the constitutionality of the death penalty partly on the grounds that the execution rate disparities for rape constituted racial discrimination. M. Meltsner, Cruel and Unusual 73–105 (1973). This argument was not accepted by the Supreme Court in its decision limiting the circumstances in which the death penalty could constitutionally be imposed. *See* Furman v. Georgia, 408 U.S. 238, 92 S. Ct. 2726 (1972). A striking example of opposition to this type of argument is the response of the Supreme Court of Arkansas in 1962 to evidence that over a recent 47 year period, 95% of the executions for rape had been of Black men (19 out of 20) and 72.9% of the executions for murder had been of Black men or women (108 out of 148). *See* Maxwell v. State, 236 Ark. 694, 370 S.W.2d 113 (1963). The court rejected the idea that such statistics proved discrimination, concluding:

> Certainly there was no evidence offered even remotely suggesting that the ratio of violent crimes by Negroes and Whites was different from the ratio of the executions. There was no testimony suggesting that the State's attorneys in the various judicial districts had not been asking for the death penalty in their prosecutions for rape, whether the accused be black or white.

Id. at 701. This demonstrates an acceptance of the stereotypes of Black male criminality, *see supra* note 34, and rapaciousness, *see supra* note 35.

[64] Coker v. Georgia, 433 U.S. 584 (1977).

[65] In almost half the states today, the maximum punishment for rape is life imprisonment. Jurors, *supra* note 16, at 207–458.

[66] LaFree, *The Effect of Sexual Stratification by Race on Official Reactions to Rape*, 45 Amer. Soc. Rev. 842, 852 (1980).

Black defendants received more severe punishment than white defendants when the victim was white.[67]

The rape of white women by Black men is also used to justify harsh rape penalties. One of the few law review articles written before 1970 that takes a firm position in favor of strong rape laws to secure convictions begins with a long quote from a newspaper article describing rapes by three Black men, who at 3 a.m. on Palm Sunday "broke into a West Philadelphia home occupied by an eighty-year-old widow, her forty-four-year-old daughter and fourteen-year-old granddaughter," brutally beat and raped the white women, and left the grandmother unconscious "lying in a pool of blood."[68] This introduction presents rape as a crime committed by violent Black men against helpless white women. It is an image of a highly atypical rape—the defendants are Black and the victims white, the defendants and victims are strangers to each other, extreme violence is used, and it is a group rape. Contemporaneous statistical data on forcible rapes reported to the Philadelphia police department reveals that this rape case was virtually unique.[69] Use of this highly unrepresentative image of rape to justify strict rape laws[70] is consistent with recent research showing that it is a prevalent, although false, belief about rape that the most common racial combination is Black offender and white victim.[71]

---

[67] JURORS, *supra* note 16, at 117–18. This difference is not solely attributable to the type of crime at issue, since many studies show that Black defendants usually receive stricter sentences than white defendants for crimes committed against whites other than rape, *id.* at 117, and that white jurors are generally lenient on Black defendants who commit crimes against Blacks. Note, *The Case for Black Jurors*, 79 YALE L.J. 531, 534 (1970). But the degree of misinformation and sensationalism associated with the accusation of rape is unique. *See infra* note 71.

[68] Schwartz, *The Effect in Philadelphia of Pennsylvania's Increased Penalties for Rape and Attempted Rape*, 59 J. CRIM. L., CRIMINOLOGY, & POLICE BEHAVIOR 509 (1968). The author concludes that the increased penalties for rape did not reduce the incidence of rape.

[69] M. AMIR, *infra* note 116. Out of 343 rapes reported to the Philadelphia police, 3.3% involved Black defendants accused of raping white women, *id.* at 44; 42% involved complaints of stranger rape, *id.* at 250; 20.5% involved brutal beatings, *id.* at 155–56; 43% involved group rapes, *id.* at 200.

[70] In October 1969, *The Thunderbolt*, the newspaper of the National States Rights Party, carried a strikingly similar image. At the bottom of the page was a drawing of the FBI's crime time clock, with a caption proclaiming: "Every thirty minutes, a woman is RAPED somewhere in the U.S.A." Dominating the top of the page was the phrase "THE BLACK PLAGUE," next to a drawing of a large unkempt Black man with a knife, running toward the reader and away from a tangled pile of grass. On close examination, what appeared initially as grass was revealed as the virtually subliminal image of a partly disrobed, prone blonde white woman. This image is reproduced in L. CURTIS, CRIMINAL VIOLENCE 22 (1974).

[71] In answer to the question, "Among which racial combination do most rapes occur?" 48% of respondents stated Black males and white females, 3% stated white males and Black females, 16% stated Black males and Black females, 33% stated white males and white females. JURORS,

Charges of rapes committed by Black men against white women are still surrounded by sensationalism[72] and public pressure for prosecution. Black men seem to face a special threat of being unjustly prosecuted or convicted.[73] One example is Willie Sanders.[74] Sanders is a Black Boston man who was arrested and charged with the rapes of four young white women after a sensational media campaign and intense pressure on the police to apprehend the rapist. Although the rapes continued after Sanders was incarcerated, and the evidence against him was extremely weak, the state subjected him to a vigorous twenty-month prosecution. After a lengthy and expensive trial, and an active public defense, he was eventually acquitted.[75] Although Sanders was clearly innocent, he could have been convicted; he and his family suffered incalculable damage despite his acquittal.

Another recent example is the Alabama case of Thomas Lee Hines.[76] Hines is a young mentally retarded Black man who was accused of raping several white women. The trial judge granted a change of venue, noting, "the facts of the race of the defendant and victims have so overpowered the case as to make it appear to the community as a racial incident."[77] Hines' trial was transferred to a nearby county, where he was convicted by an all-white jury in proceedings marked by frequent outbursts from spectators, sensationalist press coverage,

supra note 16, at 80. Recent victim survey data contradicts this prevalent belief; more than four-fifths of illegal rapes reported to researchers were between members of the same race, and white/Black rapes roughly equaled Black/white rapes. Bowker, *supra* note 2, at 172. In that text, there is a misprint so that the sentence reads: "nearly four-fifths of all rapes were interracial." *Id.* While the context makes clear that "intraracial" is intended, it is fascinating that this particular typographical error slipped past all proofreaders. For a discussion of rape statistics, see *supra* note 2.

[72] *See* Abbott & Calonico, *Black Man, White Woman—The Maintenance of a Myth: Rape and the Press in New Orleans*, in CRIME AND DELINQUENCY: DIMENSIONS OF DEVIANCE 141 (M. Riedel & T. Thornberry eds. 1974); Evans, *supra* note 13, at 75; Stern, *The Right of the Accused to a Public Defense*, 18 HARV. C.R.-C.L. L. REV. (forthcoming 1983).

[73] Several commentators have noted recent rape convictions of Black men accused of raping white women that seem to be based on inadequate evidence. *See* A. DAVIS, WOMEN, RACE AND CLASS, 172–75 (1981); SOCIALIST WOMEN'S CAUCUS OF LOUISVILLE, THE RACIST USE OF RAPE AND THE RAPE CHARGE (July 1975) (on file at the HARV. WOMEN'S L.J.); BRADEN, *A Second Open Letter to Southern White Women*, 4 SOUTHERN EXPOSURE 50 (Winter 1977); Evans, *supra* note 13, at 80.

[74] Suffolk Superior Court Indictment No. 025027-36, 025077 (1980).

[75] *See* Stern, *supra* note 72; Sands, *Rape and Racism in Boston: An Open Letter to White Feminists*, OFF OUR BACKS, Jan. 1980, at 16–17; THE WILLIE SANDERS DEFENSE COMMITTEE, FROM SCOTTSBORO 1930 TO BOSTON 1980: THE FRAME-UP CONTINUES (1980).

[76] Hines v. State, 384 So. 1171 (Ala. Crim. App. 1980). This case was brought to the attention of the author by Stephanie Y. Moore.

[77] *Id.* at 1183.

and extensive security to protect the courtroom participants.[78] The appellate court granted a new trial because police behavior coupled with the degree of Hines' retardation called into question the voluntariness of his statements to the police, and stated that the court found that the racially charged trial conditions justified a second change of venue.[79] Hines was eventually declared incompetent for trial and committed to a state institution.[80]

Conclusion

From slavery to the present day, the legal system has consistently treated the rape of white women by Black men with more harshness than any other kind of rape. The punishment for Black offender/white victim rape has ranged historically from castration, to death by torture and lynching, to executions. Today Black men convicted of raping white women receive longer prison sentences than other rape defendants. Innocent Black men also face the threat of racially motivated prosecutions.

This selective focus is significant in several ways. First, since tolerance of coerced sex has been the rule rather than the exception, it is clear that the rape of white women by Black men has been treated seriously not because it is coerced sex and thus damaging to women, but because it is threatening to white men's power over both "their" women and Black men.[81] Second, in treating Black offender/white

[78] *Id.* at 1183.

[79] *Id.* at 1181, 1183.

[80] N.Y. Times, Nov. 22, 1980, at A17, col. 4.

[81] Part of the reason for this social meaning of rape is that laws against rape originate in the conception of women as property. *See* S. Brownmiller, *supra* note 13, at 7-10, 201; L. Clark & D. Lewis, Rape: The Price of Coercive Sexuality 115-32 (1977); The Second Assault, *supra* note 3, at 24; Comment, *supra* note 2, at 924-25.

In nineteenth century cases and literature, this notion sometimes took the form of discussing women as "goods." For example, in one rape case where a slave was accused of raping a white woman, force was an element of the crime, but since there was no evidence of force, the Alabama Supreme Court wrote:

> There was, in this case, at least some evidence tending to show that the act of the prisoner was an attempt to accomplish his object by fraudulent personation of the husband.... [W]e depart from our usual course, for the purpose of inviting the attention of the legislature to this subject. Under our penal laws, one who obtains the goods of another under false and fradulent pretenses, is held guilty...as if he had feloniously stolen them. He who contaminates female purity under like fraudulent pretenses, goes unwhipped of justice.

victim illegal rape much more harshly than all coerced sex experienced by Black women and most coerced sex experienced by white women, the legal system has implicitly condoned the latter forms of rape. Third, this treatment has contributed to a paradigmatic but false concept of rape as being primarily a violent crime between strangers where the perpetrator is Black and the victim white. Finally, this pattern is perverse and discriminatory because rape is painful and degrading to both Black and white victims[82] regardless of the attacker's race.[83]

PART II: THE DENIAL OF THE RAPE OF BLACK WOMEN

Who knows what the black woman thinks of rape? Who has asked her? Who cares? —ALICE WALKER[84]

The selective acknowledgement of the existence and seriousness of the rape of white women by Black men has been accompanied by a denial of the rape of Black women that began in slavery and continues today. Because of racism and sexism, very little has been written about this denial. Mainstream American history has ignored the role of Black people to a large extent; systematic research into Black history has been published only recently.[85] The experiences of Black women have yet to be fully recognized in those histories,[86] although this is beginning to change.[87] Indeed, very little has been written about rape from the perspective of the victim, Black or white,

---

Lewis, a slave, v. State, 30 Ala. 54, 56–57 (1857). For explanations of how the conception of women as property links with the creation of myths about the Black male as rapist, see A. DWORKIN, RIGHT-WING WOMEN 124 (1983); Mann & Selva, *supra* note 5, at 170.

[82] Powerful poems about the effects of rape on its victims have been published in the last decade, by both Black and white women. *See, e.g.*, Jordan, *Poem About My Rights*, AEGIS, March-Apr. 1979, at 31; M. PIERCY, *Rape Poem*, in LIVING IN THE OPEN (1976); Shange, *is not so gd to be born a girl*, 10 THE BLACK SCHOLAR, May–June 1979, at 8–9. This is not to assert that Black and white women's experiences have been identical. *See* Part II, *infra* text accompanying notes 84–124.

[83] Evans, *supra* note 13, at 81.

[84] A. WALKER, *Advancing Luna—and Ida B. Wells*, in YOU CAN'T KEEP A GOOD WOMAN DOWN 85, 93 (1981).

[85] Beale, *Slave of a Slave No More: Black Women in Struggle*, 12 THE BLACK SCHOLAR, Nov.–Dec. 1981, at 16.

[86] *Id.*

[87] G. LERNER, *supra* note 28; BUT SOME OF US ARE BRAVE: BLACK WOMEN'S STUDIES (G. Hull, P. Scott & B. Smith eds. 1982); CONDITIONS: FIVE, Autumn 1979 (The Black Women's Issue); 2 HERESIES, Fall 1979 (Third World Women: The Politics of Being Other); 8 SOJOURNER,

until quite recently.[88] Research about Black women rape victims encounters all these obstacles.

Slavery

The rape of Black women by white men during slavery was commonplace and was used as a crucial weapon of white supremacy.[89] White men had what one commentator called "institutionalized access" to Black women.[90] The rape of Black women by white men cannot be attributed to unique Southern pathology, however, for numerous accounts exist of northern armies raping Black women while they were "liberating" the South.[91]

The legal system rendered the rape of Black women by any man, white or Black, invisible. The rape of a Black woman was not a crime.[92] In 1859 the Mississippi Supreme Court dismissed the indictment of a male slave for the rape of a female slave less than 10 years old, saying:

> [T]his indictment can not be sustained, either at common law or under our statutes. It charges no offense known to either system. [Slavery] was unknown to the common law...and hence its provisions are inapplicable.... There is no act (of our legislature on this subject) which embraces either the attempted or actual commission of a rape by a slave on a female slave.... Masters and slaves can not be governed by the same system or laws; so different are their positions, rights and duties.[93]

Jan. 1983 (Special Issue: Women of Color); Jones, *My Mother was Much of a Woman: Black Women, Work and the Family Under Slavery*, 8 FEMINIST STUDIES 235 (1982); 9 THE BLACK SOCIOLOGIST, Spring/Summer 1982 (special issue entitled *New Thoughts on Feminism, Race Relations and Social Change*); Reagon, *My Black Mothers and Sisters or On Beginning a Cultural Autobiography*, 8 FEMINIST STUDIES 81 (1982); Smith, *Racism and Women's Studies*, 5 FRONTIERS, Winter 1980, at 48; Spelman, *The Erasure of Black Women* 5 QUEST 36 (1982).

[88] *See infra* note 212.

[89] S. BROWNMILLER, *supra* note 13, at 165; A. DAVIS, *supra* note 73, at 24-27 (1981); B. HOOKS, AIN'T I A WOMAN: BLACK WOMEN AND FEMINISM 24-27 (1981); G. LERNER, *supra* note 28, at 149-50; J. NOBLE, BEAUTIFUL ALSO ARE THE SOULS OF MY BLACK SISTERS 35 (1978); *see* DuBois, *Divine Right*, in DOCUMENTARY HISTORY, *supra* note 26, at 53.

[90] L. CURTIS, *supra* note 70, at 22.

[91] H. GUTMAN, THE BLACK FAMILY IN SLAVERY AND FREEDOM 1750-1925, at 386-87 (1978).

[92] *See supra* text accompanying notes 13-14.

[93] George, a slave, v. State, 37 Miss. 306 (1859). The following year the state legislature, evidently shocked by the decision, outlawed attempted or actual rape of a Black or mulatto female under 12 by a Black or mullato male, and made it punishable by death or whipping. 1860 Miss. Laws 62. The legislature refused to recognize the rape of adult Black females and the rape of any Black females by white men.

This decision is illuminating in several respects. First, Black men are held to lesser standards of sexual restraint with Black women than are white men with white women.[94] Second, white men are held to lesser standards of restraint with Black women than are Black men with white women.[95] Neither white nor Black men were expected to show sexual restraint with Black women.[96]

The Post-Civil War Period

After the Civil War, the widespread rape of Black women by white men persisted.[97] Black women were vulnerable to rape in several ways that white women were not. First, the rape of Black women was used as a weapon of group terror by white mobs and by the Ku Klux Klan during Reconstruction.[98] Second, because Black women worked outside the home,[99] they were exposed to employers' sexual aggression as white women who worked inside the home were not.[100]

The legal system's denial that Black women experienced sexual abuse by both white and Black men also persisted,[101] although

[94] "Whites, perhaps originally to perpetuate breeding, encouraged the identity of Black males in terms of uninhibited sexuality.... It seems clear that the Black male was given sexual license by the White patriarchy in exchange for his economic and political autonomy." THE SECOND ASSAULT, *supra* note 3, at 30-31; *see* B. HOOKS, *supra* note 89, at 35; G. LERNER, *supra* note 28, at 194. The "sexual license" of course did not extend to white women. *Id.* at 31-33.

The comparison between masters and slaves in George v. State, 37 Miss. 306 (1859), implies that real standards of sexual restraint were applied to white men's behavior toward white women, an assumption questioned in Part III of this Note, *infra* text accompanying notes 138-180.

[95] *See supra* text accompanying notes 5-17.

[96] R. STAPLES, THE BLACK WOMAN IN AMERICA 40 (1973); B. HOOKS, *supra* note 89, at 32-34.

[97] *See* H. GUTMAN, *supra* note 91, at 390; B. HOOKS, *supra* note 89, at 52, 56-59; G. LERNER, *supra* note 28, at 173-93.

[98] *See* G. LERNER, *supra* note 28, at 172-81.

[99] *See* B. HOOKS, *supra* note 89, at 22, 71-72; G. LERNER, *supra* note 28, at xxiv; J. NOBLE, *supra* note 89, at 46; Beckett, *Working Women: A Historical Review of Racial Differences*, 9 THE BLACK SOCIOLOGIST 5 (1982). Analyses of women's situations which assume the "traditional women's role" to be that of housewife, and treat "women's" introduction into the workforce as a relatively recent phenomena, effectively deny the existence of Black women. While this denial has been pointed out in many publications, recent examples of it exist. *See, e.g.*, Taub & Schneider, *Perspectives on Women's Subordination and the Role of Law*, in THE POLITICS OF LAW, *supra* note 8, at 125-26.

[100] *See* B. HOOKS, *supra* note 89, at 56-59. The myths concerning Black women's promiscuity probably contributed to the sexual abuse of Black women by white employers.

[101] Bell Hooks discusses newspaper articles urging the public to take action in opposition to the rape of Black women, B. HOOKS, *supra* note 89, at 56-59. The author of this Note has been unable to find any legal literature on the rape of Black women either during or after slavery.

statutes had been made race-neutral.[102] Even if a Black victim's case went to trial—in itself highly unlikely[103]—procedural barriers and prejudice against Black women protected any man accused of rape or attempted rape.[104] The racist rule which facilitated prosecutions of Black offender/white victim attempted rapes by allowing the jury to consider the defendant's race as evidence of his intent,[105] for instance, was not applied where both persons were "of color and there was no evidence of their social standing."[106] That is, the fact that a defendant was Black was considered relevant only to prove intent to rape a white woman; it was not relevant to prove intent to rape a Black woman. By using disparate procedures, the court implicitly makes two assertions. First, Black men do not want to rape Black women with the same intensity or regularity that Black men want to rape white women.[107] Second, Black women do not experience coerced sex in the sense that white women experience it.[108]

These attitudes reflect a set of myths about Black women's supposed promiscuity which were used to excuse white men's sexual abuse

---

[102] *See supra* note 18.

[103] The process that white rape victims must go through in pursuing a rape complaint has been shown to be arduous and taxing. *See* L. HOLMSTROM & A. BURGESS, THE VICTIM OF RAPE: INSTITUTIONAL REACTIONS 30-62 (1978) [hereinafter cited as THE VICTIM OF RAPE]; Note, *supra* note 17, at 347-51; Comment, *supra* note 2, at 937-38; Comment, *The Rape Victim: A Victim of Society and the Law*, 11 WILLAMETTE L.J. 36, 43-49 (1974) [hereinafter cited as Comment, *The Rape Victim*]. The treatment by the legal system of a Black rape victim in the first half of this century was incalculably worse. *See* S. GRIFFIN, RAPE: THE POWER OF CONSCIOUSNESS 14 (1979) (description of the treatment Billie Holiday received after having been raped at age 10).

[104] Traditional common-law rules which made rape generally a difficult crime to prove protected the defendant. *See infra* note 159. In addition, Black women's claims were not taken seriously regardless of the offender's race. In a 1971 study on judges' attitudes towards rape victims, a judge was quoted as saying: "with the Negro community, you really have to redefine rape. You never know about them." Bohmer, *Judicial Attitudes Towards Rape Victims*, 57 JUDICATURE 303 (1974). A vivid example of the judicial system's response to Black women's claims of sexual harassment is the account by a nurse published in 1912:

> I remember well the first and last work place from which I was dismissed. I lost my place because I refused to let the madam's husband kiss me.... I didn't know then what has been a burden to my mind and heart ever since; that a colored woman's virtue in this part of the country has no protection. When my husband went to the man who had insulted me, the man...had him arrested! I...testified on oath to the insult offered me. The white man, of course, denied the charge. The old judge looked up and said: 'This court will never take the word of a nigger against the word of a white man.'

More Slavery at the South, 72 THE INDEPENDENT, Jan. 25, 1912, at 197-200, *reprinted in* G. LERNER, *supra* note 28, at 155-56.

[105] *See supra* text accompanying notes 52-55.

[106] Washington v. State, 38 Ga. 370, 75 S.E. 253 (1912).

[107] *See supra* note 35.

[108] *See* B. HOOKS, *supra* note 89, at 52.

of Black women.[109] An example of early twentieth century assumptions about Black women's purported promiscuity was provided by the Florida Supreme Court in 1918. In discussing whether the prior chastity of the victim in a statutory rape case should be presumed subject to defendant's rebuttal or should be an element of the crime which the state must prove, the court explained that:

> What has been said by some of our courts about an unchaste female being a comparatively rare exception is no doubt true where the population is composed largely of the Caucasian race, but we would blind ourselves to actual conditions if we adopted this rule where another race that is largely immoral constitutes an appreciable part of the population.[110]

Cloaking itself in the mantle of legal reasoning, the court states that most young white women are virgins, that most young Black women are not, and that unchaste women are immoral. The traditional law of statutory rape at issue in the above-quoted case provides that women who are not "chaste" cannot be raped.[111] Because of the way the legal system considered chastity,[112] the association of Black women with unchastity meant not only that Black women could not be victims of statutory rape, but also that they would not be recognized as victims of forcible rape.

The Legacy Today

The criminal justice system continues to take the rape of Black women less seriously than the rape of white women. Studies show that judges generally impose harsher sentences for rape when the victim is white than when the victim is Black.[113] The behavior of white

[109] *Id.* at 54–85; G. Lerner, *supra* note 28, at 163–71; J. Noble, *supra* note 89, at 47.

[110] Dallas v. State, 76 Fla. 358, 79 So. 690 (1918), quoted in Note, *Statutory Rape: Previous Chaste Character in Florida*, 13 U. Fla. L. Rev. 201, 203–04 (1960).

[111] Jurors, *supra* note 16, at 167; Bienen, *supra* note 8, at 192.

[112] The operation of traditional laws and conceptions of rape that depend on victims' prior chastity is discussed in greater detail at *infra* text accompanying notes 140–155.

[113] LaFree, *supra* note 66, at 847–48. A 1968 study of rape sentencing in Maryland revealed that in *all* 55 cases where the death penalty was imposed the victim had been white, and that between 1960 and 1967, 47% of all Black men convicted of criminal assaults on Black women were immediately released on probation. The average sentence received by Black men, exclusive of cases involving life imprisonment or death, was 4.2 years if the victim was Black, 16.4 years if the victim was white. Howard, *Racial Discrimination in Sentencing*, 59 Judicature 121, 123 (1975).

jurors shows a similar bias. A recent study found that sample white jurors imposed significantly lighter sentences on defendants whose victims were Black than on defendants whose victims were white.[114] Black jurors exhibited no such bias.[115]

Evidence concerning police behavior also documents the fact that the claims of Black rape victims are taken less seriously than those of whites.[116] A 1968 study of Philadelphia police processing decisions concluded that the differential in police decisions to charge for rape "resulted primarily from a lack of confidence in the veracity of Black complainants and a belief in the myth of Black promiscuity."[117]

The thorough denial of Black women's experiences of rape by the legal system is especially shocking in light of the fact that Black women are much more likely to be victims of rape than are white women.[118] Based on data from national surveys of rape victims,[119] "the profile of the most frequent rape victim is a young woman, divorced or separated, Black and poverty stricken."[120]

Recent victim survey data shows that of the roughly one-fifth of illegal rapes that are interracial, Black men were as likely to rape white women as white men were to rape Black women.[121] The statistics concerning Black women's rape by white men, however, may be too low. Black women apparently underreport illegal rape to the police—especially rape by white men[122]—and may do the same with

---

[114] JURORS, *supra* note 16, at 106.

[115] *Id.* at 119.

[116] *See* M. AMIR, PATTERNS IN FORCIBLE RAPE 11 (1971); Peters, *The Philadelphia Rape Survey*, in VICTIMOLOGY: A NEW FOCUS, VOL. III, CRIMES, VICTIMS AND JUSTICE 186 (I. Drapkin & E. Viano eds. 1975) [hereinafter cited as VICTIMOLOGY III]; Note, *supra* note 17, at 343. The relatively high credibility accorded white women's accusations of rape against Black men was mitigated if the woman was known to socialize with Blacks.

[117] Comment, *Police Discretion and the Judgment that a Crime Has Been Committed—Rape in Philadelphia*, 117 U. PA. L. REV. 277, 304 (1968).

[118] Recent data from random citizen interviews suggest that Black women are much more likely to be victims of illegal rape than are white women. Bowker, *supra* note 2, at 164; *see* Karmen, *Women Victims of Crime: Introduction* 185, 188, in THE CRIMINAL JUSTICE SYSTEM AND WOMEN: OFFENDERS, VICTIMS, WORKERS (B. Price & N. Sokoloff eds. 1982).

[119] *See supra* note 2.

[120] Karmen, *supra* note 118, at 188.

[121] Bowker, *supra* note 2, at 172.

[122] There is conflicting commentary as to whether Black women are more or less likely than white women to report rape to the police. Lee Bowker explains that the National L.E.A.A. Survey published in 1976 found that, "[w]hite rape victims were much more likely to report the crime to the police (59%) than were Black rape victims (36%)." Bowker, *supra* note 2, at 173. Allen Johnson, however, claims, "the available evidence suggests that nonwhites are more likely than whites to report their assaults." Johnson, *On the Prevalence of Rape in the*

victim survey interviewers. Even if the victim survey data were accurate, the type of forced sex it studies is only a small fraction of the various kinds of sexual subordination to which women are subjected,[123] some of which are available disproportionately to white men.[124]

Conclusion

From slavery to the present time, the rape of Black women has been denied by the legal system. During slavery, the rape of Black women by Black men was legal. The rape of Black women by white men was frequent, legal, and a crucial weapon of white supremacy. After the Civil War, the legal system's continued denial of the rape of Black women was manifested in discriminatory doctrinal rules and judicial language. Today Black women continue to suffer rape in disproportionate numbers, while the criminal justice system still takes the claims of Black rape victims less seriously than the claims of white victims.

PART III: THE DENIAL OF THE SIGNIFICANCE OF SEXUAL COERCION

The legal system and American society have acknowledged the existence and seriousness of one racial combination of rape—that

United States, 6 SIGNS 136, 145 (1980). See *infra* notes 116 and 117, suggesting that police behavior may be an especial deterrent to Black women's reporting. When the race of the assailant is taken into account, there is agreement that Black women tend not to report rapes by white men. In a 1971 study of rape in Oakland, California, few Black women reported being raped by white men. One respondent told the questioners: "No Black woman would report being raped by a white man to the police in Oakland. They might report it to the Panthers, but never the police." Agopian, Chappell & Geis, *Black Offender and White Victim: A Study of Forcible Rape in Oakland, California*, in VICTIMOLOGY III, *supra* note 116, at 101 [hereinafter cited as *Black Offender*]. *See* L. CURTIS, *supra* note 70; *see also* THE RACIST USE OF RAPE AND THE RAPE CHARGE, *supra* note 73, at 5-6 (discussion of the rape of Black women by Alabama police during the Civil Rights movement); A. DAVIS, *supra* note 73, at 173 (the rape of Black women by Chicago police in 1974).

[123] *See infra* text accompanying notes 171-178.

[124] The opportunity for sexual harassment of women employees by their employers or supervisors is disproportionately available to white men, who disproportionately hold such positions of power. *See* A. DAVIS, *supra* note 73, at 197-200. To acknowledge this is not to claim that Black men do not sexually harass women; both Black and white women have complained of sexual harassment by Black men. C. MACKINNON, SEXUAL HARASSMENT OF WORKING WOMEN 30-31 (1979).

of white women by Black men.[125] Courts and commentators justified this focus by exaggerating the trauma white women face when raped by Black men.[126] This chacterization allowed the crime of rape to be narrowly defined and treated in a way that denied to all women an effective legal shield against rape.[127] Moreover, the myth that rape is only a crime committed by Black men against white women has obscured and deflected attention from the varied nature, pervasiveness, and influence of the sexual subordination to which all women are subjected.[128]

Characterizing White Women's Experiences

Part of the justification given by white men for treating Black offender/white victim rape with special severity was that rape by a Black man felt worse, was worse, than rape by a white man. An 1889 law review note on lynching bid its readers to "consider how profoundly humiliated any woman must feel who has been the victim of an outrage of this character, and how, under existing social conditions, this humiliation must be greatly intensified by the wrong having been committed by a negro."[129]

White men also told white women that death was preferable to rape by a Black man. In one of the Scottsboro opinions[130] the Alabama Supreme Court wrote, "some things may happen to one worse than death by an assassin. One of those things happened to this defenseless woman."[131] Thirty years later, in 1964, the Georgia

[125] *See* Part I, *supra* text accompanying notes 1-83.

[126] *See infra* text accompanying notes 129-132.

[127] *See infra* text accompanying notes 140-175.

[128] While there has been virtually no recognition that Black women experience any kind of sexual coercion, the illegal rape of white women has been recognized to some extent, albeit within the limits discussed in this Part.

[129] Reynolds, *supra* note 31, at 21. Note that, although the author refers to the humiliation of "any woman," he means only white women. The notion that a Black woman could have been humiliated by a rape would have been virtually inconceivable. *See* notes 92-112 and accompanying text. To the extent that the definition "woman" was limited by the helpless white woman image, Black women were excluded. The stereotype of the delicate, helpless white woman has never applied and has never been applied to Black women. Part of the reason for this is that Black women have been workers outside their households from slavery to the present. *See supra* note 99. But even with the recent recognition of the introduction of women into the workforce, the notion that Black women are not feminine persists, *see* B. Hooks, *supra* note 89, at 83.

[130] *See supra* text accompanying notes 43-50.

[131] Powell v. State, 224 Ala. 540, 551, 141 So. 201, 211 (1932).

Supreme Court described the rape of a white woman by a Black man as "a crime more horrible than death[,]...the forcible sexual invasion of her body, the temple of her soul," which "soil[ed] for life her purity, the most precious attribute of all mankind."[132] In fostering racism, these characterizations presented a rationalization for the brutal murder of Black men.[133] Yet they also created fear in white women and thus helped maintain their powerlessness[134]—both by encouraging white women's physical dependence on white men, and by robbing women of the power to define their own sexual experiences.[135]

The unstated converse of these characterizations is that for white women, rape by white men is better than death and not nearly as bad as rape by Black men. Indeed, the criminal justice system in practice has virtually denied the seriousness of the rape of white women other than in the rare circumstances where the offender is a violent Black man who is a stranger to the "virtuous" victim.

The Legal System's Denial of Rape

The 1897 law review article on lynching demonstrates great sympathy for the rape complainant[136] and does not explicitly doubt her

[132] Sims v. Balkcom, 220 Ga. 7, 136 S.E. 2d 766, 769 (1964).

[133] *See* Part I *supra* text accompanying notes 1-83.

[134] It is important to acknowledge that to say that something furthers racism is not to deny that it can also be sexist. Likewise, to say that something contributes to sexism is not to deny that it can also be racist. Racism and sexism are complementary, not contradictory. For further discussion, *see* Part IV, *infra* text accompanying notes 181-233.

[135] These characterizations embody two types of disempowerment. First is the disempowerment involved simply in having one's own experience defined by someone else. Second is the disempowering content of the definitions imposed. Here, the treatment of the rape victim after the rape is that of a stigmatized, ruined woman. An early description of the purported effect of rape on a virgin is Camp v. State, 3 Ga. 417, 422 (1847), which stated that after the loss of her virginity, "all is gone: her love of justice, sense of character, and regard for truth." This extreme stigmatization is perhaps decreasing, Sagarin, *Forcible Rape and the Problem of the Rights of the Accused*, FORCIBLE RAPE, *supra* note 2, at 142, but it nonetheless persists in powerful forms. The stigma is often internalized, which is also disempowering. *See* J. BARKAS, VICTIMS 126 (1978); Peters, *supra* note 116, at 197.

[136] *See supra* note 129 and accompanying text. Reynolds argues that society's desire to spare the white woman the extreme humiliation she suffers from public cross-examination is the force behind lynching. Reynolds, *supra* note 31, at 21. This characterization of the causes of lynching is obviously incorrect. It uses false stereotypes of white women's extreme delicacy and the false idea that society sincerely aimed to protect white women from rape (this idea is refuted in Part III, *supra* text accompanying notes 125-180) to make lynching seem understandable and even noble.

veracity.[137] These "feminist" attitudes are anomalous in the pre-1970s legal literature.[138] Except for the lynching article, the legal literature on rape shows concern solely for the defendant and invariably implicitly or explicitly favors acquittal.[139]

Until recently various rules and attitudes made rape an extremely difficult crime to prosecute. The issue of chastity, or virginity, was one such barrier. Chastity was legally relevant in rape cases for three reasons. First, in many jurisdictions it was an element of the crime of statutory rape that the victim be chaste.[140] Second, in most jurisdictions the chastity of the rape complainant was considered probative on the issue of consent, the assumption being that a sexually experienced woman was likely to have consented to this particular act of intercourse regardless of her words or actions to the contrary.[141] Third, evidence as to a rape complainant's chastity was thought to bear on the woman's general character, and, hence, on her credibility. A woman's propensity for falsehood was assumed to increase proportionately to her sexual experience.[142]

The concept of chastity was not race-neutral.[143] According to governing sterotypes, chastity could not be possessed by Black women.[144] Thus, Black women's rape charges were automatically

---

[137] *See* Reynolds, *supra* note 31, at 20–21.

[138] It should be noted that lynching played a strikingly minor role in legal literature, as did rape, until recently. The INDEX TO LEGAL PERIODICALS lists a total of 39 entries for lynching between 1791 and 1949 (the last year containing an entry on lynching). During the same time period there were 53 entries for rape. By comparison, there were 775 entries under murder and homicide during those years. From 1949 until 1970 there were 51 articles about rape compared to 511 about murder or homicide. Between 1970 and February 1982 there were 187 articles about rape and 362 about murder/homicide.

[139] Rife, *Scientific Evidence in Rape Cases*, 31 J. CRIM. L. & CRIMINOLOGY 232 (1940) is an exception. Recognizing the difficulties in proving rape, Rife details methods of obtaining evidence to corroborate victims' testimony.

[140] JURORS, *supra* note 16, at 168. For a discussion of statutory rape roughly contemporaneous with the *Patterson* decision, see Comment, *Criminal Law: Rape* 19 KY. L.J. 339 (1931). *See generally*, Note, *Statutory Rape: Previous Chaste Character in Florida*, 13 U. FLA. L. REV. 201 (1960); Note, *Statutory Rape—Previous Chaste Character*, 57 W. VA. L. REV. 199 (1955); Comment, *Recent Decisions—Criminal Law—No Defense To Statutory Rape That Victim Is Married Woman Below The Age Of Consent*, 21 MD. L. REV. 84 (1961).

[141] *See, e.g.*, *Evidence—Specific Acts of Unchastity by Prosecutrix*, 14 GA. B.J. 362 (1953). For a detailed and critical discussion, see Berger, *supra* note 17, at 15–22; *see also* J. BARKAS, *supra* note 135, at 104; Holmstrom & Burgess, *Rape: The Victim Goes on Trial* in VICTIMOLOGY III, *supra* note 116, at 37–38; Note, *supra* note 17, at 338; Comment, *The Rape Victim*, *supra* note 103, at 41; Comment, *supra* note 2, at 935, 938.

[142] Berger, *supra* note 17, at 16; Note, *supra* note 17, at 335; Comment, *supra* note 2, at 931; Comment, *The Rape Victim*, *supra* note 103, at 39, 40.

[143] *See supra* text accompanying notes 109–112.

[144] *See supra* note 103.

discounted, and the issue of chastity was contested only in cases where the rape complainant was a white woman.

For white women, evidence of unchastity was given less weight when the defendant was Black.[145] A blatant example of the courts' willingness to ignore victims' lack of chastity appeared in the Scottsboro opinions. The Alabama Supreme Court demonstrated its determination to affirm the defendants' convictions by its vigorous protection of the reputation and credibility of the white woman who claimed she was raped. It ruled that evidence pertaining to her marital status,[146] her previous chastity,[147] and her general reputation[148] had been properly excluded as irrelevant.

A less famous but equally vivid case also illustrates this dynamic. In *Story v. State*,[149] where a Black man was charged with the rape of a white prostitute, the Court found that her unchastity with white men was not relevant to her unchastity with Black men, commenting that: "The consensus of public opinion, unrestricted to either race, is that a white woman prostitute is yet, though lost of virtue, above the even greater sacrifice of the voluntary submission of her person to the embraces of the other race."[150]

These rulings shielding the victim's reputation were contrary to the weight of authority at that time.[151] Indeed, the debate in the legal literature prior to the 1970s concerned not whether evidence of the complainant's sexual history should be admissible, but rather the type of evidence that should be admissible—specific sexual acts or only the victim's general reputation.[152]

Many feminists favor excluding evidence of the rape complainant's sexual history because the admission of such evidence reflects and

---

[145] In the 19th century, evidence of a white woman's lack of chastity sometimes convinced courts to treat Black defendants with relative leniency. *See, e.g.*, Cato, a slave, v. State, 9 Fla. 163 (1860) (rape conviction of slave based on partly contradicted testimony of white prostitute set aside and new trial granted). *But see* Barnett v. State, 83 Ala. 40, 3 So. 612 (1888) (rape conviction of Black defendant on uncorroborated testimony of white prostitute upheld).

[146] Weems v. State, 224 Ala. 524, 527, 141 So. 215, 217 (1932).

[147] Patterson v. State, 224 Ala. 531, 536, 141 So. 195, 197 (1932).

[148] Powell v. State, 224 Ala. 540, 550–51, 141 So. 201, 210 (1932).

[149] 178 Ala. 98, 59 So. 480 (1912).

[150] *Id.* at 104, 59 So. at 482.

[151] 1 WIGMORE, EVIDENCE § 200 (2d ed. 1923).

[152] *See Recent cases—Evidence—Admissability of Prior Acts of Unchastity Upon Issue of Consent of Prosecutrix in a Rape Prosecution*, 9 TEX. L. REV. 98 (1930). The author argued that the better practice was to admit evidence of prior acts rather than general reputation "in view of the gross injustice which might result from placing an innocent man at the mercy of a lewd and unscrupulous woman." *See Cross-examination of Prosecutrix in Rape Prosecution*, 19 GA. B.J. 95 (1956); 14 GA. B.J., *supra* note 141.

reinforces misogynistic views of women[153] and allows defendants to discredit easily the victim's testimony.[154] Yet, in the *Scottsboro* context, other considerations are also important. The complainant was allowed to testify without being cross-examined as to her sexual history only because the defendants were Black. Had they been white, such evidence would have been admitted, the reputation of the witness discredited, and the defendants probably freed.[155]

Another barrier to successful rape prosecutions has been the statutory requirements that the testimony of a rape complainant be corroborated by other evidence.[156] The corroboration requirement was introduced "for the purpose of protecting against false accusations."[157] To justify the stricter standards of proof required in rape cases than for other crimes, commentators claimed women

---

[153] These include stereotypes that women are especially likely to lie and to be deluded, *see supra* note 142; that sexually experienced women are likely to have actually consented to sex with the man they now are accusing, *see* Note, *supra* note 17, at 41; Comment, *supra* note 2, at 932; Comment, *The Rape Victim*, *supra* note 103, at 41; that sexually experienced women are apt to lie, *see* Berger, *supra* note 17, at 16; Note, *supra* note 17, at 345; and that sexually experienced women cannot be raped, Comment, *supra* note 103, at 44.

[154] *See infra* text accompanying notes 209-210.

[155] Susan Brownmiller notes sexist attitudes manifested in the case, since the white women were threatened with vagrancy and prostitution charges, S. BROWNMILLER, *supra* note 13, at 257-58, and since defense counsel tried to destroy the complainant's credibility by claiming she was a prostitute, *id.* at 254. Brownmiller's discussion of the cases is misleading and disturbing because of its singleminded focus on sexism with its attendant sympathy for the white women, its belittlement of racism, and its lack of sympathy for the Black defendants sentenced to death. Her distortions are well discussed in A. EDWARDS, RAPE, RACISM AND THE WHITE WOMEN'S MOVEMENT: AN ANSWER TO SUSAN BROWNMILLER, 8-15 (2d printing 1979) and A. DAVIS, *supra* note 73, at 198-99. Although Brownmiller is correct that white women were under pressure to cry rape because they were often stigmatized or ostracized if they were discovered in a voluntary relationship with a Black man, A. ROSE, *supra* note 26, at 305, these hardships on women do not justify false rape charges. Susan Griffin claims, without citation, that if a white woman discovered with a Black man did not cry rape, "she herself would be subject to lynching." S. GRIFFIN, *supra* note 103, at 18. This is refuted by the NAACP study cited *supra* at note 28, that found that only 16 out of the 4951 people lynched between 1882 and 1927 were white women. (The reasons for the lynchings were not given.) The number is so small that it is highly unlikely that lynching could have posed a meaningful threat to white women who refused to claim that sexual contact with Black men was rape.

[156] *See, e.g.*, Comment, *Corroborating Charges of Rape*, 67 COLUM. L. REV. 1137 (1967); Comment, *Nebraska's Corroboration Rule*, 54 NEB. L. REV. 93 (1975); Comment, *The Corroboration Rule and Crimes Accompanying a Rape*, 118 U. PA. L. REV. 458 (1970); *Criminal Law—Attempted Rape—Merger and Corroboration*, 14 BROOKLYN L. REV. 122 (1948); *Recent Criminal Cases—Rape—Corroboration of Prosecutrix*, 26 J. CRIM. L. & CRIMINOLOGY 463 (1935-36); *Recent cases*, 18 OR. L. REV. 264 (1939).

[157] 26 J. CRIM. L. & CRIMINOLOGY, *supra* note 156, at 463. It was incorrectly thought that the number of reported rapes exceeded the number of actual rapes due to false accusations brought by deluded or malicious women. *See* Comment, *supra* note 2, 919, 931; *infra* note 158. It is now well known that rape is underreported, *see supra* note 2. The justifications for the corroboration requirement became more complex, far-fetched, and misogynist in the late 1960s, apparently through the influence of Freudian psychology, *see* S. BROWNMILLER, *supra*

frequently made malicious rape charges and easily duped juries into awarding convictions.[158]

One result of the chastity and corroboration rules was that rape was often a very difficult crime to prove.[159] Rapes where the woman made her report too soon or not soon enough,[160] rapes where the woman knew her assailant,[161] rapes where the woman did not resist enough,[162] rapes where the woman was sexually experienced,[163] were all difficult to prosecute successfully.

The attitudes manifested in the rape laws and expressed in the legal literature extend to other areas of the criminal justice system. Police have often been extremely insensitive to rape victims.[164] Rape com-

---

note 13, at 415-20; Berger, *supra* note 17, at 28. For example, a 1970 comment claimed that "[w]omen often falsely accuse men of sexual attacks to extort money, to force marriage, to satisfy a childish desire for notoriety, or to attain personal revenge. Their motives include hatred, a sense of shame after consenting to illicit intercourse, especially when pregnancy results, and delusion." Comment, 118 U. PA. L. REV., *supra* note 156, at 460; *see* Comment, 67 COLUM. L. REV., *supra* note 156, at 1138-39.

[158] *See, e.g.*, Note, *Criminal Law—Rape—Evidence—Corroboration of Female—Pregnancy*, 13 NEB. L. BULL. 184, 185 (1934-35) ("Because of the difficulty of refuting the testimony of the prosecutrix, because of the tendency of juries to convict without weighing carefully the evidence, and further, because the crime is one which is often maliciously prosecuted"). A 1967 commentator stressed the "inordinate danger that innocent men will be convicted." Comment, 67 COLUM. L. REV., *supra* note 156, at 1137. For a more thorough discussion of this notion *see* Berger, *supra* note 17, at 22. Feminist writers had responded that the conviction rate for rape was actually extremely low. *See* Note, *supra* note 17, at 338; Comment, *supra* note 2, at 931, 935; *see also infra* note 187.

[159] JURORS, *supra* note 16, at 100-01; Berger, *supra* note 17, at 29-32; Comment, *The Rape Victim*, *supra* note 103, at 38-40.

[160] Holmstrom & Burgess, *supra* note 141, at 41, report that a victim must make a "fresh complaint" but if she does it is assumed by the police that she reported promptly merely in order to get back in her husband's or boyfriend's good graces, not because the claim is real.

[161] *See* Note, *supra* note 17, at 343-45; Comment, *The Rape Victim*, *supra* note 103, at 41. The incidence of illegal rape by acquaintances is high; in victim survey data for 1973-1976, approximately half the sexual assaults were by men their victims knew; Bowker, *supra* note 2, at 166, 169.

[162] The resistance requirements for rape are an excellent example of the ways that the legal system fails to protect women from rape. On the one hand, modern rape statutes require that the victim's resistance be overcome by force or by violence or by threats of imminent bodily harm. *See, e.g.*, N.Y. PENAL LAW § 130.00(8) (McKinney Supp. 1981); WASH. REV. CODE ANN. § 9A. 44.010(5) (West Supp. 1981). On the other hand, rape victims who do resist are more likely to be seriously injured than are victims who do not. *See* NATIONAL INSTITUTE FOR LAW ENFORCEMENT AND CRIMINAL JUSTICE, LEAA, FORCIBLE RAPE: FINAL PROJECT REPORT (1978) cited in Field, *Rape*, in ENCYCLOPEDIA OF CRIME AND JUSTICE (S. Kadish ed. forthcoming 1983); *Black Offender*, *supra* note 122, at 134; Note, *supra* note 17, at 345-47.

[163] *See infra* text accompanying notes 209-210.

[164] S. BROWNMILLER, *supra* note 13, at 408; S. GRIFFIN, *supra* note 103, at 13-14; Note, *supra* note 17, at 348; *see* York v. Story, 324 F.2d 450 (9th Cir. 1963), *cert. denied*, 376 U.S. 939 (1964). Traditionally police were trained to expect that rape was one of the most falsely reported crimes. G. PAYTON, PATROL PROCEDURE 283 (1967), cited in Comment, *supra* note 117, at 277 n.6. Several recent studies claim that police have become more sensitive. *See, e.g.*, THE VICTIM OF RAPE, *supra* note 103, at 38-41; W. SANDERS, RAPE AND WOMAN'S IDENTITY

plainants have been disbelieved by police more frequently than complainants of other crimes.[165]

Women's Actual Experiences

While denial of any experience is a significant indication of powerlessness, the widespread denial of women's experiences of coerced sex is the denial of a phenomenon which deeply affects every woman's life.

The crime of illegal rape is a terrifying, traumatic experience which often has long-term damaging effects on its victims.[166] Illegal rape is much more widespread than is reported to police. A recent study concluded that twenty to thirty percent of girls currently aged twelve will suffer a sexual attack during their lifetimes.[167] A recent random survey of San Francisco households revealed that forty-four to forty-six percent of women in that city had been victims of rape or attempted rape.[168]

Additionally, the fear and threat of rape influences many women who are never actually raped.[169] It restricts movement and forces

---

82 (1980). The accounts of negative treatment experienced by many women become notorious and thus have a disproportionately large impact on victims' reluctance to report and on the image of the police, THE VICTIM OF RAPE, *supra* note 103, at 53-55. These studies do not indicate whether police sensitivity towards women of color has increased; *see supra* note 122.

[165] In one study, the "unfounding" determination by the police for forcible rape was 18%, while for larceny it was only two percent. G. NETTLER, EXPLAINING CRIME 45 (1974), cited in Robin, *Forcible Rape: Institutionalized Sexism in the Criminal Justice System* in THE CRIMINAL JUSTICE SYSTEM AND WOMEN, *supra* note 118, at 246.

[166] *See* J. BARKAS, *supra* note 135, 107-29; S. BROWNMILLER, *supra* note 13, 404-07; E. HILBERMAN, THE RAPE VICTIM 17-19, 33-40 (1976); T. MCCAHILL, L. MEYER & A. FISCHMAN, THE AFTERMATH OF RAPE (1979); THE VICTIM OF RAPE, *supra* note 103; Burgess & Holmstrom, *Rape Trauma Syndrome*, in FORCIBLE RAPE, *supra* note 2 at 315 [hereinafter cited as *Rape Trauma*]; Note, *supra* note 17.

[167] Johnson, *supra* note 122, at 145.

[168] Russell & Howell, *Revisions/Reports: The Prevalence of Rape in the United States Revisited*, 8 SIGNS (forthcoming Summer 1983). The researchers concluded that there is a 26% probability that a woman will be a victim of a completed rape at some point in her lifetime, and that there is a 46% probability that a woman will be a victim of a completed or attempted rape at some point in her life, *see* Russell, *Sexual Assault: The Prevalence and Incidence of Forcible Rape and Attempted Rape of Females*, 7 VICTIMOLOGY (forthcoming 1983).

[169] "I have never been free of the fear of rape. From a very early age I, like most women, have thought of rape as part of my natural environment—something to be feared and prayed against like fire or lightning." S. GRIFFIN, *supra* note 103, at 3; *see* S. BROWNMILLER, *supra* note 13, at 449; Riger, Gordon & LeBailly, *Women's Fear of Crime: From Blaming to Restricting the Victim*, 3 VICTIMOLOGY 274, 278-80 (1978) [hereinafter cited as *Women's Fear of Crime*].

women to maintain a special wariness about the situations in which they place themselves.[170]

Illegal rape is neither the only nor necessarily the most harmful kind of coerced sex for women.[171] Although the definition of rape has been expanded in many statutes,[172] the requirement of penetration remains in some states.[173] Spousal rape is legal in most states,[174] and its incidence is widespread.[175] Other forms of sexual coercion are also pervasive. The incidence of incest is difficult to calculate, but it is certainly widespread; whatever the exact incidence, there is unanimity among researchers that the victims are overwhelmingly female, the perpetrators male.[176] A large proportion of working

---

[170] A recent study found that women feared crime more than men, and that their greater fear was rooted in a fear of rape. 93% of women expressed fear of the thought of rape. The major practical effect on women of the fear of rape is a restriction of freedom of action. *Women's Fear of Crime*, *supra* note 169, at 282-83. The researchers concluded: "The effect of women's greater fear of crime is to produce social constraints upon them; women not heeding those constraints may be punished not only by direct victimization, but also by being blamed for their own victimization. The irony of course, is that these restrictions do not guarantee that safety." *Id.* at 282-83; *see* Reynolds, *Rape as Social Control*, 8 CATALYST 62 (Winter 1974).

[171] An essential element of the traditional common-law definition of rape is sexual intercourse including penetration by the penis, *see* S. BROWNMILLER, *supra* note 13, at 424-25; L. CLARK & D. LEWIS, *supra* note 81, at 130-32, 160; Bienen, *supra* note 8, at 174-75; MacKinnon, *supra* note 2, at 15-16; Comment, *supra* note 2, at 83. Ignored by such a definition are forced oral sex, fondling, and penetration with an object, for example.

[172] *E.g.*, acts other than sexual intercourse, N.J. STAT. ANN. § 2C:14-1 (West Supp. 1982); sexual assaults with an object, S.D. CODIFIED LAWS ANN. § 22-22-2 (Supp. 1982).

[173] *E.g.*, IDAHO CODE 18-6101, 6103 (1979); MISSOURI REV. STAT. § 566.040 (1979).

[174] The spousal rape exemption has been abolished in only three states (New Jersey, Nebraska, Oregon). JURORS, *supra* note 16, at 196. All other states retain some version of it, based on a notion that the decision to marry implies continual consent to sexual intercourse. *Id.* at 165. The exemption originated in a conception of the wife as the sexual property of the husband. Lord Hale explained, "[The] husband cannot be guilty of a rape committed by himself upon his lawful wife, for by their mutual matrimonial consent and contract the wife hath given up herself in this kind into her husband, which she cannot retract," Bienen, *supra* note 8, at 184, quoting M. HALE, THE HISTORY OF THE PLEAS OF THE CROWN 629 (S. Emlyn ed. 1778).

[175] The incidence of spousal rape is difficult to estimate, partly because it is legal in most states. JURORS, *supra* note 16, at 163-66; *see* note 174. However, estimates of wife-battering run as high as 50% of marriages, R. LANGLEY & R. LEVY, WIFE BEATING 4 (1977); and most battered wives are apparently also victims of rape by their husbands, S. SCHECTER, WOMEN AND MALE VIOLENCE: THE VISIONS AND STRUGGLES OF THE BATTERED WOMEN'S MOVEMENT 17, 223 (1982); L. WALKER, THE BATTERED WOMAN 108 (1979).

[176] One estimate is that at least 200,000 girls a year are sexually molested, overwhelmingly by men. L. SANFORD, THE SILENT CHILDREN: A PARENT'S GUIDE TO THE PREVENTION OF CHILD ABUSE 83 (1980). Another source estimates the number of incest victims at one million a year. F. RUSH, THE BEST KEPT SECRET: THE SEXUAL ABUSE OF CHILDREN, 2, 4-5 (1980). An estimate by the Children's Division of the American Humane Association is that a minimum of 80,000 to 100,000 children are sexually molested each year. The pattern appears to be 97% male offenders, 92% female victims. In the majority of the cases the molester is well-known to the child; in one quarter, the molester is a relative. The Humane Association's figures were

women are sexually harassed on the job.[177] Women also face harassment on the street.[178]

Very little is done about these forms of sexual abuse, and what has been done has largely been done by women themselves, in the last decade.[179] Widespread societal ignorance and general denial of sexual coercion by the legal system persist.[180]

Conclusion

The legal system's treatment of rape is not designed to protect women from sexual coercion. Through discriminatory punishment, the language of opinions, scholarly writing, and the manipulation of doctrine, the legal system has implicitly defined rape so as to limit it to the rape of white women by Black men. The social meaning of rape is thus limited to a Black offender and white victim. In addition, because of the legal system's traditionally narrow definition of rape, coupled with the widespread acceptance of other forms of sexual coercion, the legal system has also implied that illegal rape is the only form of sexual abuse. In fact, both of these implications are false. The great majority of rapes of white women are committed by white men; and women are subjected to a range of sexual coercion in addition to illegal rape.

Because of the specific social meaning of rape, sole responsibility for the coerced sex of white women has been placed on the shoulders of Black men, and Black women have been ignored as rape victims.

---

based on poor and disorganized families who came to the attention of social service agencies. Most incest, however, probably occurs in intact families which escape social service agencies' attention; thus the actual incest incidence is probably much higher. Herman & Hirschman, *Father-Daughter Incest*, 2 SIGNS 735, 736 (1977); *see* S. BROWNMILLER, *supra* note 13, at 307–12. For personal analyses, see VOICES IN THE NIGHT: WOMEN SPEAKING ABOUT INCEST (T. McNaron & Y. Morgan eds. 1982); and Cottom, *Resistance to Incestuous Assault*, in FIGHT BACK! 26–27 (F. Delacoste & F. Newman eds. 1981).

177 C. MACKINNON, *supra* note 124, at 26–55.

178 Despite its ubiquitousness, very little has been published concerning street harassment. *See* L. WALKER, *supra* note 175, 107–08; Benard & Schlaffer, *The Man in the Street: Why He Harasses*, Ms., May 1981, at 18; di Leonardo, *Political Economy of Street Harassment*, AEGIS, Summer 1981, at 51–56.

179 *See, e.g.*, FIGHT BACK!, *supra* note 176.

180 The problems of sexual harassment, incest, and spousal abuse have received very little attention and action until very recently. For examples of recent discussions of these problems, see C. MACKINNON, *supra* note 124 at 158–74 (1979) (sexual harassment); F. RUSH, *supra* note 176, at 137–38 (incest); L. WALKER, *supra* note 175, at 212–13 (spousal abuse).

Those who work against rape and other forms of sexual coercion must be vigilant not to support this racist social meaning. Activists must realize that the false image of rape sustained by the legal system fosters fear and resentment between white women and Black people. It is not true that efforts to fight racist abuses of rape charges necessarily deny the reality of women's experiences of sexual coercion. Nor is it correct that efforts to fight sexist denials of women's experiences of sexual coercion necessarily deny the reality of racist abuses of rape charges.

PART IV: RECASTING THE FORM OF THE DEBATE–BEYOND LEGAL REFORM

The Master's Tools Will Never Dismantle the Master's House
–AUDRE LORDE[181]

The pervasiveness of racism and its historical connection to rape raise complex issues for those who oppose sexual coercion. As leaders of the movement against rape,[182] feminists are responsible for examining closely the implications of their actions and proposals.[183] The foregoing analysis raises considerations often neglected in feminist writing[184] and thus leads to some conclusions about strategies to fight sexual coercion that differ in emphasis from other feminist work.

---

[181] Lorde, *The Master's Tools Will Never Dismantle the Master's House*, in THIS BRIDGE CALLED MY BACK 98 (C. Moraga & G. Anzaldua eds. 1981).

[182] *See* Rose, *Rape as a Social Problem: A By-Product of the Feminist Movement* 25 SOC. PROBS. 75, 75–77 (1977).

[183] Various commentators have noted that white feminists often demonstrate ignorance of the racist uses of the rape charge, and have pointed out the limitations of anti-rape theories and strategies that fail to deal with issues of racism. *See, e.g.*, A. DAVIS, *supra* note 73, at 178–82, 196–99; A. EDWARDS, *supra* note 155; THE RACIST USE OF RAPE AND THE RAPE CHARGE, *supra* note 73; Braden, *supra* note 73; *Does the Women's Movement Compromise the Struggle of Minorities?* 4 WOMEN'S RTS. L. REP. 27, 31 (1977); Friedman, *Rape, Racism and Reality*, AEGIS, Summer 1981, at 14; Hare, *Revolution Without A Revolution: The Psychology of Sex and Race* 13, THE BLACK SCHOLAR, Summer 1982, at 14; Sagarin, *supra* note 135, at 146; Sands, *supra* note 75.

[184] A fairly common analogy in feminist literature is between lynching and rape. S. BROWNMILLER, *supra* note 13, at 281 ("Rape is to women what lynching was to blacks: the ultimate physical threat by which all men keep all women in a state of psychological intimidation."); D. RUSSELL, THE POLITICS OF RAPE 231 (1974) ("Just as lynching may be seen as the supreme political act of whites against blacks, so rape may be seen as the supreme political act of men against women."); Karmen, *supra* note 118, at 196 ("Rapes serve, as other crimes against women, to remind them of their 'appropriate' place in society–beneath men, just as the lynchings of blacks by whites in the south carried the message–accept your lot in life–

The legal system has historically ignored or denied the claims of women who have been victims of rape.[185] At the same time, women have been traumatized by the criminal justice system,[186] few men have been convicted of rape,[187] and women continue to be victimized by rape in appalling numbers.[188]

Feminist strategies to combat rape have included encouraging self-defense and protection,[189] improving the treatment rape victims receive after their attack,[190] and reforming rape laws so as to increase the conviction rate.[191]

Improving the Treatment of Rape Victims

One of the most degrading aspects of rape for victims has been the treatment they receive from the criminal justice system.[192] One

---

don't step out of line."); MacMillan & Klein, *FAAR Editorial*, AEGIS, Summer 1981, at 5 ("Rape is a mechanism used to terrorize and subjugate women in much the same way that lynching has been used against blacks.").

This comparison between the functions of rape and lynching is problematic in several respects. First, it suggests that it is simple to compare racism and sexism, and in fact implies that they function in the same way. Actually, the two operate in complex and different, but related ways, as this Note demonstrates. Second, the comparison in itself is ill-chosen. Rapes rarely end in murder while lynchings by definition *are* murder, so from the potential victim's perspective, the terror created by the threats of lynching and rape must be different. Third, the comparison ignores the fact that the usual excuse for lynching Black men was actually the rape of white women, so that to glibly compare the two is insensitive at best.

Certain aspects of lynching and rape may be meaningfully analogous. For example, the fact that lynching was illegal but socially acceptable, Reynolds, *supra* note 170, at 64, is also true of rape. Also, the seemingly random nature of both crimes and the attendant fear and denial by potential victims that the randomness makes possible may make them comparable in that respect. But much more historical analysis is needed before such parallels can be constructively drawn. Works that begin this process include Aptheker, *Woman Suffrage and the Crusade Against Lynching 1890-1920*, in WOMAN'S LEGACY 53 (1982); Hall, *supra* note 30.

[185] *See* Parts II and III, *supra* text accompanying notes 84-180.

[186] *See supra* notes 164, 192 and accompanying text.

[187] NATIONAL INSTITUTE FOR LAW ENFORCEMENT AND CRIMINAL JUSTICE, LEAA, FORCIBLE RAPE: FINAL PROJECT REPORT (1978) (one in 50 chance that a conviction will result if the rape is reported).

[188] *See supra* note 168.

[189] D. RUSSELL, *supra* note 184, at 284-86; Note, *supra* note 17, at 352. The philosophy and implications of the women's self-defense movement are beyond the scope of this Note; for a discussion of the movement, see Telsey, *Karate and the Feminist Resistance Movement* in FIGHT BACK!, *supra* note 176, at 184; *see also* James, *Do It Yourself Self-Defense* in *id.* at 201; and Telsey, *Some Facts on Self-Defense* in *id.* at 197.

[190] *See* THE VICTIM OF RAPE, *supra* note 103, at 264-65; D. RUSSELL, *supra* note 184, at 287-88; Bienen, *supra* note 8, at 171; Rose, *supra* note 182, at 75-76; Note, *supra* note 17, at 351-54.

[191] *See* S. BROWNMILLER, *supra* note 13, at 436; J. MARSH, A. GEIST & N. CAPLAN, RAPE AND THE LIMITS OF LAW REFORM 22-23 (1982) [hereinafter cited as RAPE AND THE LIMITS OF LAW REFORM]; BIENEN, *supra* note 8, at 171; Comment, *The Rape Victim*, *supra* note 103, at 54.

[192] *See* S. BROWNMILLER, *supra* note 13, at 408-10; THE VICTIM OF RAPE, *supra* note 103, at 1-4; Berger, *supra* note 17, at 23-24; Note, *supra* note 17, at 347-51.

of the critical contributions of feminist anti-rape work has been to increase public awareness of this unsympathetic treatment. One proposal to improve the treatment rape victims receive has been to increase the representation of women who deal with rape victims within the criminal justice system.[193] A second proposal has been to exclude evidence of a complainant's prior sexual experiences at trial.[194]

The first proposal is a positive one as far as it goes, but placing more women in law enforcement is not in itself adequate to improve the treatment victims receive. If the women participants are all white, or have little understanding of racism, many of the problems pointed out in this Note will remain.[195] Black women's rape claims will continue to lack credibility because white women share with white men notions of Black people's promiscuity and untrustworthiness.[196] The special harshness reserved for Black men who are accused of raping white women will also continue.[197]

---

[193] *See* S. BROWNMILLER, *supra* note 13, at 434-37; Note, *supra* note 17, at 352.

[194] *See* RAPE AND THE LIMITS OF LAW REFORM, *supra* note 191, at 22-23; THE VICTIM OF RAPE, *supra* note 103, at 279; Rose, *supra* note 182, at 80; Note, *supra* note 17, at 353.

[195] Howard, *Battered and Raped: The Physical/Sexual Abuse of Women*, in FIGHT BACK!, *supra* note 176, at 80-81.

[196] *See* THIS BRIDGE CALLED MY BACK, *supra* note 181 (especially pp. 61-101 including *And When You Leave, Take Your Pictures With You*). *See generally* TOP RANKING (J. Gibbs & S. Bennett eds. 1980) (especially Cornwall, *Notes From a Third World Woman* 61; Gwendolyn, *Righteous Anger in Three Parts: Racism in the Lesbian Community—One Black Lesbian's Perspective* 70; Calderone & Charoula, *The Personal is Political Revisited: An Exploration of Racism in the Lesbian Community* 79); Bethel, *What chou mean* we, *white girl?* 86 CONDITIONS: FIVE, Autumn 1979 (The Black Women's Issue); Smith, *supra* note 87.

[197] Both men and women were included in the studies of beliefs about rape, *supra* note 71, which showed that most people incorrectly believed the most common racial combination in rape cases was Black offender/white victim. Similarly, the study of white jurors which showed that the heaviest sentences were given to Black men accused of raping white women, *supra* note 67, was based on a sample of both female and male jurors. Many white feminists have been reluctant or have refused to support Black men falsely accused of raping white women. *See* Braden, *supra* note 73; Sands, *supra* note 75. Angela Davis eloquently exposes the contributions of several white feminists' work to the perpetuation of racism with respect to rape. A. DAVIS, *supra* note 73, 178-82, 198-99. Even more recent writings which have ideological roots in feminism contain inaccurate statements which perpetuate racism. A most striking example appears in WOMEN AND CRIME IN AMERICA, *supra* note 1. This book, published in 1981, is intended to fill the need for a text on women in the criminal justice system, *id.* at v.

> When an interracial rape occurs today, it is most likely to be a black rapist and a white victim, which is a reversal of the historical situation that existed in the United States during the days of slavery and the decades that followed its termination. During this period, it was black women who were constantly in danger of being sexually assaulted by white men.

If increasing the number of women involved in the legal and criminal justice systems is to create a system more sympathetic to all women, it is imperative that substantial numbers of these women be Black and that all individuals working with rape victims are keenly aware of, and strongly opposed to, racism.[198]

Another proposal for improving the legal system's treatment of rape victims has been the reform of rape statutes to exclude evidence of rape victims' sexual history from trial.[199] Cross-examination on the details of one's sexual history, a common defense technique, is one of the victim's most traumatic contacts with the legal system.[200] Another rationale for this proposal is that the introduction of the rape victim's sexual history as evidence reflects and reinforces misogynistic attitudes about women and sexuality.[201]

In Michigan, where the law has forbidden the introduction of evidence of past sexual behavior since 1975,[202] the overall experiences of victims, as reported by rape crisis center workers and criminal justice participants, seem to have improved markedly.[203] It does not appear from the Michigan study, however, that attitudes about the right of women to be free from sexual coercion have changed as a result of the statutory change.[204]

Id. at 182. First, this statement is empirically false, as is acknowledged several pages earlier: "[Based on the 1975 LEAA crime survey data] Blacks were about as likely to rape whites as whites were to rape blacks in the limited proportion of rapes that were interracial." *Id.* at 172. Second, even if it were true that the number of illegal rapes committed by Black men against white women outnumbered white rapist/Black victim rapes, the vulnerability of white women would not be analogous to the vulnerability of Black women to white masters during slavery. To suggest such a comparison is offensive because it denies the seriousness of Black women's sexual victimization. *See* Part II, *supra* notes 89-124 and accompanying text. In addition, the analogy resonates with a mythology that defines Black men as rapists of white women. *See supra* note 35.

[198] In one recent study only about three percent of the rape victims commented specifically on the sex of the police officers who investigated their cases, although all were male; most of the victims' responses about the police were positive, although 10% had serious complaints about their treatment by police. The Victim of Rape, *supra* note 103, at 51, 53-54.

[199] *See supra* note 194.

[200] The Victim of Rape, *supra* note 103, at 179-83; Note, *supra* note 17, at 350-51; Comment, *The Rape Victim*, *supra* note 103, at 45-46.

[201] *See* note 153.

[202] Michigan's sexual assault statute, which took effect in 1975, is widely considered one of the nation's most innovative and comprehensive rape laws and has served as the model for many states. Bienen, *supra* note 8, at 172. The most detailed published research on the impact of rape laws deals with Michigan. *See* Rape and the Limits of Law Reform, *supra* note 191. For these reasons, the discussion on reforming rape laws is limited to Michigan.

[203] Rape and the Limits of Law Reform, *supra* note 191, at 68-71.

[204] *Id.* at 106-107.

Increasing the Conviction Rate

Another major goal of feminists has been to increase rape convictions.[205] Law reform proposals offered to accomplish this have included limiting the admissibility of evidence of a victim's sexual history,[206] reducing the penalties allowed for rape,[207] and introducing degrees of rape.[208]

In Michigan, the conviction rate for sexual assaults has increased markedly since the passage of its law making sexual history inadmissible as evidence and introducing degrees of rape.[209] Apparently the increase is largely due to the provision limiting admissibility of prior sexual activities.[210]

It is understandable that many white feminists initially perceive an increased rape conviction rate as a victory. Rape has been denied so consistently by the criminal justice system[211] until so recently[212] that any type of recognition of it by the legal system seems positive. Also, upperclass white women until recently have been fairly isolated in a private sphere in which their subordination to men has been furthered by the law's absence,[213] so that the prospect of the law's presence in an area, seemingly acting on behalf of women, is attractive.

However, the subordination of other groups has been furthered by the law's presence,[214] and rape laws in particular have functioned

---

[205] *See* note 191.

[206] RAPE AND THE LIMITS OF LAW REFORM, *supra* note 191, at 23.

[207] Many reformers favor reducing penalties for rape because they think the severity of traditional penalties deters juries from convicting. Bienen, *supra* note 8, at 173.

[208] S. BROWNMILLER, *supra* note 13, at 425; Note, *supra* note 17, at 353.

[209] RAPE AND THE LIMITS OF LAW REFORM, *supra* note 191, at 29-33, 62.

[210] *Id.* at 57-62.

[211] *See supra* text accompanying notes 138-165.

[212] The anti-rape movement began scarcely more than a decade ago, *see* Rose, *supra* note 182, at 76. Susan Griffin's essay *Rape: The All-American Crime* in RAMPARTS, September 1971, was one of the first major pieces published. The essay is reprinted in FORCIBLE RAPE, *supra* note 2, at 47. The first law review pieces that had roots in the movement against rape also appeared in the early 1970s, *e.g.*, Note, *supra* note 17; Comment, *supra* note 2.

[213] *See* Taub & Schneider, *supra* note 99, at 117, 121-24. Examples cited by the authors include tort law's family immunity provisions, the marital rape exemption, and contract law's failure to deal with financial commitments relating to marriage, *id.* at 121-22. "For example, when the police do not respond to a battered woman's call for assistance or when a civil court refuses to evict her husband, the woman is relegated to self-help, while the man who beats her receives the law's tacit encouragement.... By declining to punish a man for inflicting injuries on his wife, for example, the law implies she is his property and he is free to control her as he sees fit." *Id.* at 122.

[214] The criminal justice system allows women to be victimized in their homes and actively victimizes people of color. A recent survey of seven geographically diverse U.S. cities found

to further white supremacy.[215] In light of the racist history surrounding the legal system's treatment of rape, the goal of increasing the rape conviction rate must be examined in more detail.

Working to increase the conviction rate for rape is not necessarily a constructive tactic in the struggle against sexual coercion for several reasons. First, most pragmatically, raising the conviction rate has not been shown to have any impact on the incidence of rape, although long-term data are not yet available.[216] Second, given the existing disparities in punishments between whites and Blacks, an across-the-board increase would simply reproduce these disparities.[217] Third, the increasingly racist political climate,[218] and the Supreme Court's destruction of various constitutional procedures to protect defendants,[219] suggest that the punishment disparities are likely to increase. Fourth, to the extent these disparities implicitly indicate that men are being punished on racial grounds and not because they committed rape, the credibility of the underlying claim of sexual abuse is undermined.[220] Fifth, to press for convictions under rape laws suggests that women accept the narrow definitions and limited conceptions of sexual abuse that underlie those laws. Finally, to say that rape should be treated like other crimes is problematic in that it implicitly validates the way other crimes have been and are treated. The criminal justice system has radical shortcomings—the treatment,[221]

---

that 78% of persons fatally shot by police during 1973 and 1974 were Black. C. MILTON, J. HALLECK, J. LARDNER & G. ALBRECHT, POLICE USE OF DEADLY FORCE 19, 22 (1975). Black women are not immune from police violence. *See* R. KNOOHUIZEN, R. FAHEY & D. PALMER, THE POLICE AND THEIR USE OF FATAL FORCE IN CHICAGO 20 (1972); Los Angeles Board of Police Commissioners, *Concerning the Shooting of Eula Love*, reprinted in 14 CRIME & SOC. JUST., Winter 1980, at 2. *See generally* D. BELL, *supra* note 18; A. L. HIGGINBOTHAM, *supra* note 13; Burns, *supra* note 8.

215 *See* Parts I and II, *supra* text accompanying notes 1-124.

216 F 'E AND THE LIMITS OF LAW REFORM, *supra* note 191, at 27.

217 *See supra* note 67.

218 *See* Braden, *The Ku Klux Klan Mentality—A Threat in the 1980's*, 20 FREEDOMWAYS 7 (1980).

219 For example, for limitations on federal habeas corpus rights, see Engle v. Isaac, 102 S. Ct. 1558 (1982), *reh. den.*, 102 S. Ct. 2286 (1982); Rose v. Lundy, 102 S. Ct. 1198 (1982); Wainwright v. Sykes, 433 U.S. 72 (1977), *reh. den.*, 434 U.S. 880 (1977); Stone v. Powell, 428 U.S. 465 (1976), *reh. den.*, 429 U.S. 874 (1976).

220 Williams and Holmes claim that "To a great extent, the lack of credibility given the charge of rape today is attributable to the interwoven history of rape and racism where all involved *know* from their own experience (whether that of White male oppressor, White female, or Black male) that rape has been a technique of social control to maintain the White Patriarchy." THE SECOND ASSAULT, *supra* note 3, at 35.

221 *See* Rudovsky, *The Criminal Justice System and the Role of the Police*, THE POLITICS OF LAW, *supra* note 8, at 242-52. For example, the shooting of civilians by police officers,

definition,[222] and punishment[223] of many other crimes should be deplored rather than endorsed. It has refused to protect and indeed has consistently worked against the interests of Black men, Black women, and white women.[224]

The *Sanders* and *Hines* cases discussed earlier[225] illustrate the risks of pressuring the criminal justice system to "do something" about specific rapes, especially rapes committed by Black men against white women. Rather than leading to apprehension of the actual rapist,[226] such pressure can lead police to scapegoat an innocent Black man. This is not to argue that Black men never rape white women; but rather that, where such a rape claim is being prosecuted, white feminists must not overlook the circumstances surrounding the event in order to be certain that the prosecution is not a racial act against the wrong man in an attempt to defuse community pressures.[227] Such prosecutions not only hurt Black people,[228] they also divide women along color lines, and do nothing to halt rape.

Conclusion

Attempting to reform rape laws to increase convictions thus has numerous shortcomings as a feminist strategy. Improving the criminal

---

see supra note 214, almost invariably goes unpunished – out of 1500 killings of civilians by police from 1960-1970, only three resulted in criminal punishment, according to a study by A. Kobler, *Police Homicide in a Democracy*, 31 J. OF SOC. ISSUES, Winter 1975, at 163-64.

[222] The illegality of consensual sexual acts other than penis-vagina intercourse between unmarried persons is an excellent example. *See* People v. Onofre, 51 N.Y.2d 476 (1980), *cert. denied*, 101 S. Ct. 2323 (1981) (New York's prohibition against consensual sodomy held unconstitutional on privacy and equal protection grounds); Note, *The Constitutionality of Laws Forbidding Private Homosexual Conduct*, 72 MICH. L. REV. 1613 (1974).

[223] Strong evidence suggests that Black defendants generally receive longer sentences than do white defendants for most crimes. *See* JURORS, *supra* note 16, at 117; Owens, *Looking Back Black* in BLACKS AND CRIMINAL JUSTICE, *supra* note 13, 7 at 11.

[224] *See* Rudovsky, *supra* note 221, at 244; Taub & Schneider, *supra* note 99, at 117. Janet Howard notes that "given the history and nature of the 'justice' system, [using the legal system] can only bring small concessions to women's safety, and is more likely to strengthen the repressive, racist power of the police, the courts, and the prisons." Howard, *supra* note 195, at 82.

[225] *See supra* text accompanying notes 74-80.

[226] *See* Sands, *supra* note 75.

[227] Sagarin, *supra* note 135, at 148.

[228] The targetting of Black men for punishment also affects Black women. Alice Walker writes, "Whenever interracial rape is mentioned, a black woman's first thought is to protect the lives of her brothers, her father, her sons, her lover. A history of lynching has bred this in her." A. WALKER, *supra* note 84, at 93; *see* A. DAVIS, *supra* note 73, at 173-74.

justice system's treatment of the victim is a positive goal but does not change the fact of women's victimization. A problem with both approaches is that they only address the problems of women who are known victims of illegal rape. This focus is insufficient. First, even if the activity forbidden by rape laws stopped, other powerful forms of women's sexual subordination would persist.[229] Second, given the racist content of the social meaning of rape, struggles limited to illegal rape are likely to have the racist repercussion of targeting Black men.[230]

A response must be devised which goes beyond the formulation of rape as an extraordinary crime to which only some unlucky women fall victim, to a conception that the sexual coercion of women is pervasive, multivariate, and wholly unacceptable in every form.[231] If women go beyond the formulation given by the legal system they may be able to escape some of the traps of racism, and claim their own lives and sexuality.

This means linking rape issues with other issues of sexual coercion such as incest,[232] spousal abuse, and sexual harassment. It also means recognizing that rape will be treated by the criminal justice system in a racist way as long as this society is racist.

CONCLUSION

. . . *Eyes that only see the bruises inflicted by men miss seeing other bruises and deep scars.* —JANET HOWARD[233]

The legal system's treatment of rape both has furthered racism and has denied the reality of women's sexual subordination. It has disproportionately targetted Black men for punishment and made Black women both particularly vulnerable and particularly without

[229] *See supra* notes 171–178 and accompanying text.

[230] *See* Part I, *supra* text accompanying notes 1-83.

[231] *See supra* notes 171–178 and accompanying text; *see also* Hoagland, *Violence, Victimization, Violation*, 15 SINISTER WISDOM, Fall 1980, at 70.

[232] Susan Brownmiller observes that "If protection of the bodily integrity of all children is to be genuinely reflected in the law, and not simply the protection of patriarchal interests, then the current division of offenses (statutory rape for outsiders; incest for a member's family) must be erased." S. BROWNMILLER, *supra* note 13, at 429.

[233] Howard, *supra* note 195, at 80.

redress. It has denied the reality of women's sexual subordination by creating a social meaning of rape which implies that the only type of sexual abuse is illegal rape and the only form of illegal rape is Black offender/white victim. Because of the interconnectedness of rape and racism, successful work against rape and other sexual coercion must deal with racism. Struggles against rape must acknowledge the differences among women and the different ways that groups other than women are disempowered. In addition, work against rape must go beyond the focus on illegal rape to include all forms of coerced sex, in order to avoid the racist historical legacy surrounding rape and to combat effectively the subordination of women.

Sexual Assault Prosecution: An Examination of Model Rape Legislation in Michigan

Susan Caringella-MacDonald

ABSTRACT. Since the mid-1970s virtually every state has altered its rape legislation in an effort to rectify problems in the prosecution of such crimes. Because implementation of rape reform statutes can affect the success of these efforts, and because prosecutors play a decisive role in the process, this study assesses one aspect of the effectiveness of reform rape legislation by measuring attrition and conviction rates in the prosecution of sexual assault. Attrition rates in one Michigan jurisdiction operating under the model Criminal Sexual Conduct Code are discussed and then compared to other research data. This comparative examination indicates that the law can be productively employed to combat problems, such as high attrition and low conviction rates, historically associated with prosecution of sexual assault offenses. It is also noted that problems may persist despite reform legislation. For instance, while attrition and conviction rates in this research jurisdiction compared favorably to all other available data, almost two-thirds (64%) of the criminal sexual conduct cases brought to prosecutors were lost at some stage in the criminal justice system. While legislative alterations represent a step in the direction of progress, such measures alone will fall short of generating the encompassing social change necessary to rectify the inequitable treatment of rape victims.

INTRODUCTION

A recent concern in the literature on rape has centered on the problems surrounding prosecution of this crime. Both the carnal

---

Department of Sociology, Western Michigan University, Kalamazoo, Michigan 49008.
Gratitude is expressed to James Gregart, Prosecuting Attorney of Kalamazoo County, for his continued support via data access, but more importantly, for his commitment to the victims of sexual assault.

knowledge statutes and the myths underscoring such laws have been challenged.[1] Critics have commented on the double victimization of rape victims by first the sexual assault and then the criminal justice system. The definition of rape as carnal knowledge of a female, forcibly and against her will, has brought about unique case treatment evidenced in corroboration requirements, consent and resistance standards, and the admissibility of victim character evidence. The misguided beliefs which serve as justification for unique standards and treatment of rape revolve around notions of false accusation, victim precipitation, consent, and the predilection of the judicial system to sympathize with victims and thereby convict allegedly innocent men.[2]

These types of beliefs have contributed to high attrition and low conviction rates at all stages of the criminal justice system. Rape is the most underreported offense in the country.[3] Additionally, 15% of the cases coming to the authorities' attention are declared unfounded by police.[4] Of cases reported and founded, 52% are not cleared;[5] and of those reported, founded and cleared, 48% result in the accused rapists' release through acquittals.[6] Other sources indicate that the attrition of rape cases is in fact as high as a 97% loss between report and conviction.[7]

Attrition presents problems other than low conviction rates. It both originates in and leads to the perpetuation of myths and differential treatment of rape cases as compared to all other crimes. For example, beliefs that victims frequently ask for the assault, falsely accuse men, and so forth, relate historically to attrition and acquittal. Conversely, dropping cases has often been viewed as proof that rape victims deserved or consented to the sexual attack. Attrition and nonconviction have, then, operated to sustain myths and to justify strict and unique legal requirements. Because of this circumstance, victims of rape deciding to pursue cases through legal channels have faced discrimination by and trauma from excessive scrutiny of their behavior, credibility, demeanor, resistance, and provocation. The net effect has been to shift the burden in rape cases from demonstrating the offender's guilt to demonstrating the victim's innocence.

By 1980, in direct response to these problems, most states reformed their rape laws.[8] Much of this legislation was meant to eliminate unjust and discriminatory treatment of rape victims. A brief discussion of the specific changes will highlight the various kinds of reform efforts.[9]

Contributing to high attrition and low conviction rates, significant obstacles in the prosecution of rape cases were corroboration requirements, resistance and consent standards, and the admissability of victim reputation evidence. A number of states, such as Michigan, New Mexico and Florida, have repealed corroboration requirements. Traditionally, a rape defendant could not be convicted on the sole basis of victim testimony: Requiring additional evidence or witness statements is related to stereotypes of frequent false reports and victim consent. One dimension of the new rape laws is the removal of this unique feature of rape statutes, making prosecution and conviction more tenable as an outcome.

The redefinition of rape as a graduated series of offenses is a second aspect of reform. Objective criteria upon which to judge the existence as well as the severity of the sexual assault are specified. Reliance on utmost resistance for duration of the attack is removed as the standard for non-consent. Several stages, e.g., Michigan, Minnesota and Ohio, have abolished their resistance requirements in favor of the more objective criteria of absence/presence of force or threat thereof. The specification of objective criteria additionally addresses the problems traditionally surrounding consent: If certain elements are present, e.g., force, injury or weapons, regardless of victim resistance a crime is deemed to have occurred.[10]

A third feature of reform legislation concerns evidence about the victim's past sexual activity. As of 1980, 40 states have limited the admissibility of character/reputation evidence in the courtroom.[11] Most states now "simply require a pre-trial hearing on relevance before evidence regarding the victim's sex conduct with persons other than the defendant can be admitted."[12] A few other states, such as Michigan, have placed rigid limitations on the admissibility of such evidence, essentially admitting evidence only to show the origin of semen, disease or pregnancy.[13]

Other types of reform over the past decade redefine rape as sexual assault, criminal sexual conduct, or sexual battery, and include a wider range of victims (e.g., males, spouses), and a wider range of behaviors in sexual assault statutes (e.g., oral and anal conduct and forced sexual contact, in addition to penetration). Given the different types of legislative changes aimed at abating the discriminatory treatment of rape victims, one might expect a significant decrease in attrition and acquittal rates associated with this offense. This paper will examine the success of these legislative solutions by investigating the attrition or loss of cases before, during and after trial.

MICHIGAN'S MODEL REFORM LAW

In 1974 the state of Michigan passed reform legislation addressing many of the problems with rape prosecution. Michigan's comprehensive statute, the Criminal Sexual Conduct Code, has been referred to as model rape legislation.[14] This code attempted to abolish the de facto corroboration requirement by specifying the lack of its de jure existence. This was accomplished by stating that "the testimony of a victim need not be corroborated in prosecutions."[15] The code eliminates the resistance requirement, stipulating that "a victim need not resist the actor."[16] Instead of using the word consent, the code established criminal sexual conduct in the first, second, third and fourth degrees. These offenses are graduated along objective criteria, such as the absence/presence of weapons, aiders and abettors, and victim injury.[17] The Michigan statute further employed sex-neutral terminology and covered a wide range of sexual acts. The code additionally permitted reputation/character evidence only:

> (1) to the extent that the judge finds that the following proposed evidence is material to a fact at issue in the case and that its inflammatory or prejudicial nature does not outweigh its probative value:
> a. Evidence of the victim's past sexual conduct with the actor.
> b. Evidence of specific instances of sexual activity showing the source of origin of semen, pregnancy or disease.[18]

The Study

One measure of the success of model legislation will be found in attrition and conviction rates. Because the code reformed the major elements contributing to case mortality, the new code might be expected to bring about low attrition and high conviction rates. Not only is the shift in scrutiny meant to lessen victim trauma, but also the encouragement of higher conviction rates is designed to rectify the inequitable treatment of rape. High conviction or low attrition and acquittal rates would be one indicator of implementation meeting the law's objectives.

This study assesses Michigan's legislative act of 1974 by examining attrition and conviction. The implementation of statutory enactments renders legislation successful in impact. Sexual assault prosecutions were scrutinized for a three year period subsequent to the 1974 enactment in order to examine the impact of the model law.

Prosecutorial decision making was singled out in this investigation for two reasons: first, prosecutors are traditionally neglected in the theoretical and research literature. This least studied official is said nonetheless to be the most powerful agent in the administration of justice.[19] Second, the prosecutor alone "activates the judicial machinery,"[20] determines whether to charge, which charges to levy, and whether to plea bargain and nolle cases. The discretionary powers exercised by prosecutors have tremendous impact on rape case treatment. The prosecutor plays a critical role in shaping outcomes.

In examining prosecutorial discretion, the attempt was to discern the types of decisions rendered in sexual assault cases, as well as to specify the stages and extent of attrition. Attrition refers to where and how often charges do not proceed through complete adjudication. The data for this study include all criminal sexual conduct cases in Kalamazoo County, Michigan, between 1975 to 1977, beginning with the first full year of implementation of the 1974 code and continuing through the next two years of operation. Kalamazoo County is a medium sized, relatively urban area, with a population of approximately one/quarter million inhabitants. Data were made available for this project by the county's prosecuting attorney. The attrition rates calculated in this study are discussed, then compared to comparable data in the few similar studies. These comparisons shed light on the use of rape reform law as a means to combat problems such as attrition in rape prosecutions.

APPLICATION AND RESULTS OF THE 1974 MICHIGAN RAPE LAW

Two primary types of attrition rates are pertinent to this investigation. One concerns prosecution, the other convictions. At the first stage of prosecution, cases may drop out of the system after police make an arrest decision. In Kalamazoo, as in most other jurisdictions, police must seek prosecutorial approval by submitting an arrest warrant request before or after a crime suspect is arrested. At this point, prosecutors decide their "causes, cases and targets for prosecution,"[21] either denying or authorizing warrant requests. Warrant denial by prosecutors means that the suspect cannot be picked up/arrested, or if the arrest has already been effected, the suspect must be released because prosecution of the case has been declined. Warrant authorization means that the case will proceed through the criminal justice system. The *prosecution rate* in this study was calculated to reflect the proportion of authorizations given all police requests. The *non-prosecution rate* indicates the percentage of warrant denials given all requests, or the attrition of cases at the charging stage of prosecution.

Once cases are accepted for prosecution they do not automatically terminate with conviction. The *acquittal rate*, reflects the loss of cases due to acquittal/dismissal by juries and judges, or to nolles by prosecutors. One acquittal rate was calculated for authorized cases only, and another for all sexual assault cases based on all warrant requests.

The nonprosecution and acquittal rates comprise the focus of this study, but several other rates were calculated for interpretative purposes. A *conviction rate* indicates the percentage of cases which terminated in guilty verdicts or guilty pleas. One convicton rate was calculated based on all authorized cases—i.e., the proportion of accepted cases which ended in a finding/pleading of guilt—and another on all criminal sexual conduct cases which came to the prosecutor's attention through warrant requests. The latter indicates the overall prosecution and conviction ratio of sexual assault cases.

Finally, the *plea bargaining rate* reflects the percentage of cases involving plea negotiations. Ascertaining guilty pleas assures convictions, which enhance the conviction rates when determined on an overall or an authorized case basis.

The most direct means to assess the effectiveness of Michigan's law would entail a comparison of attrition and acquittal rates before and after the 1974 Code was implemented. Such data were available only for Detroit, and only for the conviction rate based on accepted/authorized cases. Data on warrant requests and authorization/denial were not available for the pre-1974 period in Kalamazoo or any other state jurisdiction. The Detroit data are therefore drawn on for authorized-case comparisons, but are not amenable to interpretations concerning the charging stage of prosecution. Data for the calculation of prosecution rates were available only in the few prosecution studies conducted in other cities in other states. The Michigan law's impact on attrition at the charging stage can be assessed by comparing the prosecution rate in a jurisdiction such as Kalamazoo, operating under model legislation, to prosecution rates in jurisdictions operating under traditional rape statutes.

The acquittal rate—nonconviction of accepted or all cases—can also be compared for the model and traditional legislation jurisdictions. Michigan's law should have led to less attrition/more conviction of attackers if implementation led to a positive impact. This would be reflected in a lower (nonprosecution and) acquittal rate in the Kalamazoo and Detroit data as contrasted to other jurisdictions where such reform laws had not been enacted.

Site Findings

The Kalamazoo data offer some insight into the effectiveness of the law once implemented. Table I summarizes the various rates for Kalamazoo County.

The findings in Kalamazoo County show that prosecutors authorized police-requested charges 46% of the time, while they denied requests or dropped cases at intake in over one/half (54%) the cases. The acquittal rate for authorized cases was 22%, indicating that

TABLE I: ATTRITION AND NON-CONVICTION IN CRIMINAL SEXUAL CONDUCT CASES, KALAMAZOO, MICHIGAN

Rate	1975-77
Prosecution Rate (authorized/requested warrants)	46%
Non-Prosecution Rate (denials/requested warrants)	54%
Acquittal Rate for Authorized Cases (acquittal, dismissal, and nolle/authorized warrants)	22%
Plea Bargaining Rate (plea bargains/authorized warrants)	58%
Conviction Rate for Authorized Cases (guilty pleas and verdicts/authorized warrants)	73%
Overall Conviction Rate (guilty pleas and verdicts/requested warrants)	34%
Overall Non-Conviction Rate (warrant denials, acquittals, dismissals, and nolles/requested warrants)	64%*

*The overall conviction and attrition rates add to 98 rather than 100% due to missing data.

almost one/quarter of all cases accepted for prosecution were either acquitted/dismissed by judges or juries or nolled by prosecutors. Another way to look at these authorized cases is to examine the conviction rate. Almost three/quarters (73%) of the cases accepted at intake by prosecutors resulted in convictions, either through guilty verdicts or guilty pleas. Over half (58%) of these convictions in the authorized cases were the result of plea negotiations as opposed to trial.

Examination of overall nonconviction rates, those based on all police requested cases rather than on cases accepted by prosecutors, shows that approximately two/thirds (64%) of all criminal sexual conduct cases dropped out at some point in the criminal justice process. This means that prosecutors were able to accept and successfully complete about one/third (34%) of all sexual assaults that came within the purview of their office over the first three years of the new law's operation.

While additional types of data are required to understand the implications of these findings, several preliminary comments about the Michigan Criminal Sexual Code and its implementation can be made. Taken at face value, the various rates in Kalamazoo County appear to indicate limited success with the model code in the first three years of its implementation.

Consideration of what happened in the authorized cases points to a measure of success as a result of implementation process. Once prosecutors decided to proceed with cases at the intake charging stage, they followed through on the cases with a degree of efficacy, as demonstrated by the 73% conviction rate. In other words, prosecutors were able to secure guilty verdicts/pleas in almost three/quarters of all accepted criminal sexual conduct cases. The objective of enhancing prosecution, by making convictions more tenable as an outcome, can be viewed as having met with some success.

The finding that 58% of the authorized cases were plea bargained is amenable to two interpretations. On the one hand, because of plea bargaining, prosecutors ensured convictions and simultaneously saved victims the time and trauma of public court and trial. On the other hand, prosecutors reduced the severity of the charges and/or recommended lighter sentences than allowed by the statute as a part of plea negotiations in more than one/half (58%) of all accepted cases.

From a victim advocate point of view, the warrant denials, acquittals and nolle prosequis can be viewed with disfavor. Slightly over one/half of the sexual assault cases police deemed founded and therefore worthy of pursuit were totally rejected by prosecutors. Aside from denying over one/half of the cases at the outset, prosecutors lost almost an additional quarter of accepted cases through acquittals/dismissals by judges and juries or by their own nolles of charges. The fact that almost two/thirds of all cases coming to the prosecutor's attention were lost at some stage clearly indicates that the phenomena of attrition and nonconviction persisted. Because the new law was enacted to address problems of case mortality and low convictions, and to make easier the prosecution of rape, these findings can be interpreted as unfavorable.

Rate Comparisons Within State

Comparison of these rates with other Michigan data provides one basis for decisive, in-depth interpretation. While only Detroit data were available for comparative assessment, these data were available for the pre- and post-reform law years (1973[22] and 1975-1979[23] respectively). Table II presents these Michigan data.

As Table II indicates, during 1973, the year preceding the passage of the Criminal Sexual Conduct Code, only 10% of all reported rapes in Detroit resulted in arrest warrant authorizations. Of these authorized cases slightly over one/half (55%) resulted in conviction. Overall, only 5% of all reported rapes terminated with convictions by guilty pleas/verdicts. Data on plea bargaining as a means employed to sustain these convictions were unavailable for this pre-1974 period in Detroit.

The only available data for Detroit relevant to rates after the model code was enacted concern nonconviction and plea bargaining for authorized cases. Data on warrant requests and dispositions for Detroit in the post-1974 period were not available. Between 1975 and 1979 approximately 30% of the criminal sexual conduct cases accepted for prosecution in Detroit did not terminate with guilty pleas or verdicts. Almost three/quarters (70.1% to 73.2%, varying by year) of the accepted cases wound up in convictions. Of these convictions, 77% were obtained through guilty pleas entered by defendants.

The pattern demonstrated in Table II with a measure of consistency is the success of the model code in Michigan in the reduction of attrition and enhancement of conviction. Specifically, the percentage of cases accepted for prosecution appears to have increased

TABLE II: ATTRITION AND NON-CONVICTION IN SEXUAL ASSAULT CASES, KALAMAZOO AND DETROIT, MICHIGAN 1973, 1975-79, 1975-77

	Detroit		Kalamazoo
	1973	1975-79	1975-77
Prosecution Rate	10%	-	46%
Non-Prosecution Rate	90%	-	54%
Acquittal Rate for Authorized Cases	45%	26.8-29.9%*	22%
Plea Bargaining Rate	-	77%	58%
Conviction Rate for Authorized Cases	55%	70.1-73.2%*	73%
Overall Conviction Rate	5%	-	34%
Overall Non-Conviction Rate	95%	-	64%

*Range of variation given over the time period 1975-79.

after the Criminal Sexual Conduct Code was implemented (10% in 1973 Detroit vs. 46%, 1975-1977, in Kalamazoo).[24] The loss of these accepted cases through findings of nonguilt, dismissals, and nolles additionally decreased, from 45% in 1973 in Detroit to approximately 20% in both Detroit and Kalamazoo after the code was enacted, indicating the reduction of nonconviction.[25] The nonattrition or conviction rates for these authorized cases can similarly be interpreted as a measure of the law's success, because there was almost a 20% increase in convictions once prosecutors had accepted cases (the change from a 55% conviction rate in 1973 in Detroit to a 70.1%-73.2% conviction rate between 1975-1979, with Kalamazoo's post model code conviction rate directly paralleling the Detroit experience).[26]

The similarity of authorized case acquittal and conviction rates in Kalamazoo and Detroit indicates that the 1973 Detroit figure of 95% overall nonconviction of rape cases dropped after enactment of the Criminal Sexual Conduct Code, i.e., that the law had a favorable impact on overall case mortality and convictions. The 64% loss of cases overall in Kalamazoo in the post-1974 period compares favorably to the 95% figure. Between 1975-1977, the overall nonattrition or conviction rate of one/third (34%) of all requested cases in Kalamazoo similarly indicates an improvement over the 1973 Detroit figure of 5%.

Data were not available on plea bargaining in Michigan for the time preceding the model code. After the law's enactment, however, both the Detroit and Kalamazoo jurisdictions plea bargained over one/half of their sexual assault cases, with figures of 77% and 58% respectively. The new law at least facilitated the use of plea bargaining, a process which enhanced convictions in both locations.

Comparisons with Traditional Law Jurisdictions

The effectiveness of the Michigan Criminal Sexual Conduct Code in abating attrition and low convictions in sexual assault prosecutions can be further assessed through comparative data from other communities.[27] There were two research projects which presented relevant data. The first study to provide data on attrition in rape was conducted in Washington, D.C.[28] The second covered Kansas City, Missouri and Seattle, Washington.[29]

The kind of rape legislation existing in these locations differed. Washington, D.C., has a traditional rape statute which dichotomizes rape into forcible and statutory offenses and stipulates that the crime involves carnal knowledge of a female, forcibly and against her will.[30] Although minor alterations were enacted in the 1970s,[31] Kansas City, Missouri, also has an essentially traditional rape law. Seattle, Washington, incorporates some reform measures, but not the type of model legislation enacted in Michigan.[32]

Table III shows the attrition for the different jurisdictions. As can be seen, the prosecution rates vary from a low of one/fourth to a high of almost three/fourths of all cases charged by prosecutors. The rank order of the prosecution rates most favorable to a victim advocate would be Washington, D.C. (70%), Kalamazoo (46%), and Kansas City/Seattle (25%). Given the different codes operating in these jurisdictions, this result is not the expected one. The model legislation jurisdiction (Kalamazoo) would presumably have had the highest prosecution rate, because the law was designed to encourage prosecution.

To understand the implications of this finding it is necessary to examine the other attrition and nonconviction rates. Scrutiny of ad-

TABLE III. ATTRITION AND NON-CONVICTION IN SEXUAL ASSAULT CASES KALAMAZOO, WASHINGTON, D.C., AND KANSAS CITY/SEATTLE

	Kalamazoo (1975-77)	Washington, D.C. (1973)	Kansas City/ Seattle (1978)
Prosecution Rate	46%	70%	25%
Non-Prosecution Rate	54%	30%	75%
Acquittal Rate for Authorized Cases	22%	65%	27%
Plea Bargaining Rate	58%	22%	-
Convicted Rate for Authorized Cases	73%	33%	45%
Overall Conviction Rate	34%	23%	14%
Overall Non-Conviction Rate	64%	76%	86%

ditional rates indicates that not only is it misleading to examine the prosecution rate alone, but further that a very different summary interpretation, such as a ranking of favorable rates by city, can be reached.

The misleading nature of judging success by nonattrition at only one stage of prosecution becomes evident when attention is directed to the overall conviction and nonconviction rates. The overall nonconviction rate was lowest in Kalamazoo and highest in Kansas City/Seattle. Similarly, the highest overall conviction rate pertained to the Kalamazoo jurisdiction and the lowest to Kansas City/Seattle. Given the model legislation it would be anticipated that the Kalamazoo jurisdiction would experience the least attrition. Moreover, this pattern denotes a realization of the objective to minimize case losses. Further inquiry needs to be made, because the Washington, D.C., data might have been expected to exhibit the worst rather than middle ground figures on attrition. Traditional legislation operates in the District of Columbia jurisdiction, as compared to the basically traditional but slightly mixed laws in Kansas City and Seattle.

An explanation for the figures in Washington, D.C., relative to those for Kansas City and Seattle, can be found by re-examining the prosecution rates. The Washington, D.C., figures on overall conviction and nonconviction were better than Kansas City and Seattle figures, because prosecutors authorized such a high percentage of cases at the initial in-take screening stage. Washington, D.C., experienced the least attrition early on in the criminal justice process, yielding a more favorable overall conviction rate than Kansas City and Seattle.[33]

Authorizing a high percentage of cases does not necessarily result in optimal net gains such as high conviction rates. The evidence for this proposition is derived from the Washington, D.C., results where the highest prosecution rate did not yield the highest conviction or the lowest acquittal rates. What happens to cases after the charges have been levied by prosecutors? Two/thirds (65%) of the cases accepted for prosecution in Washington, D.C., did not result in findings or pleadings of guilt, contributing to a relatively high overall nonconviction or low conviction rate. The lowest acquittal and nonconviction rates were associated with the Kalamazoo jurisdiction, which authorized approximately one/half (45%) as opposed to over two/thirds (70%) of the sexual assault cases.

Plea bargaining presents an important consideration in relation to these rates. The Kalamazoo data displayed both the highest conviction (73%) and plea bargaining (58%) rates. The frequent use of plea bargaining in Kalamazoo is directly related to the large proportion of convictions for authorized cases. It can be argued that the success evident in the Kalamazoo rates is partly due to the model legislation. Flexibility in plea bargaining is enhanced by the Criminal Sexual Conduct Code which permits four degrees of sexual assault as opposed to strictly forcible and statutory rape categories. The model code allows prosecutors greater discretionary latitude in plea negotiations because of the wider variety of charges on which guilty pleas can be accepted, and because of the broad range of sentences and thus sentence recommendations possible.[34] These may be offered in exchange for guilty pleas. This increased flexibility in plea bargaining facilitates guilty pleas and hence convictions. The Detroit data showing a 77% plea bargaining rate and approximately 70% conviction rate for accepted cases (Table II) supports this interpretation.

Higher plea bargaining rates are not necessarily desirable from a victim advocate point of view. When plea bargaining rates are low, yielding a lower conviction rate (as in the Washington D.C., study), a gain may, in fact, be made in terms of more severe sentencing for those cases that result in guilt at trial. This sort of trade-off should be borne in mind when discussing attrition.

In terms of acquittal and conviction rates, the Michigan jurisdictions fared most favorably. Both jurisdictions operating under model legislation had the lowest acquittal and highest conviction rates. The implementation of the code appears to have met with some measure of success by rendering sexual assault case prosecution and conviction more feasible than before the legislation's enactment.

Nonetheless, attrition and nonconviction in sexual assault cases remain a problem. Even in the Michigan jurisdictions, acquittal was the outcome in roughly one/quarter of accepted cases (22% Kalamazoo, 26.8%-29.9% Detroit). And, because over one/half of the cases never get beyond the warrant authorization stage (54% Kalamazoo), almost two/thirds (64% Kalamazoo) of all cases brought to prosecutors suffered.

While the law may be radically altered, requirements and practices for prosecuting rape suspects remain problematic. Prosecutors may not (be able to) authorize criminal sexual conduct cases because the cases are too weak to take to trial or even too weak to have any leverage for plea bargaining. The Criminal Sexual Conduct Codes stipulates criteria for the various degrees; but many cases the police believe founded apparently do not meet the standard necessary for prosecution, if the prosecution rate, even under the new code, is an indication. Lack of evidence such as injuries in addition to the sexual assault, or weak evidence such as a small number of witnesses, influence prosecutors' charging and plea bargaining decisions in criminal sexual conduct cases.[35]

It is tenable that the persisting de facto need for more evidence, etc., is due to a lack of change in prosecutorial attitudes. It is also tenable that prosecutors, as the victim's representative, have aligned themselves with the attitude change as manifest in reform statutes, yet are thwarted in practice. If their views have changed, their anticipations about judicial/juror attitudes may preclude authorizations and/or necessitate plea bargains for lesser charges and/or sentences.[36]

Regardless of the explanation entertained, a conclusion of success is questionable. Despite the findings that the two model code cities compared favorably to the traditional law jurisdictions, these cities still experienced attrition, as evidenced by the acquittal and overall nonconviction rates.

CONCLUSIONS

In examining whether the model rape reform statute was effective in Kalamazoo County, attrition and lack of convictions were found to be continuing problems with the prosecution of criminal sexual conduct cases. The findings indicated an overall loss of 64% of the cases which came to the attention of the prosecutor. Approximately one half of the cases were denied for prosecution at intake and 58% were plea bargained to lesser charges or for lesser sentences than allowed by the Criminal Sexual Conduct statute. Of those cases accepted, 22% resulted in judicial acquittal or prosecutor nolles.

Comparison of the Kalamazoo data to pre-reform rates from Detroit suggested that the law was effective in reducing the magnitude of these problems. Further comparisons of the two Michigan jurisdiction rates after reform to three basically traditional rape law jurisdictions (Washington, D.C., and Kansas City/Seattle) strengthened the viability of such an interpretation. A measure of success in the implementation of the model code was evident in lower attrition of cases. In addition, the removal of unique and discriminatory requirements and standards in the 1974 Michigan statute can be seen as effective, because higher conviction rates were achievable. The degree structure of sexual assault offenses in Michigan is also beneficial, not only because it covers a broad range of criminal behaviors, but also because it facilitates plea bargaining.

Several additional considerations require elaboration. The use of plea bargaining in sexual assault cases may advantageously sustain convictions, but may also have deleterious effects. Two frequent types of plea negotiation agreements are prosecutorial recommendations for relatively lenient sentencing by judges and agreements to permit the accused to plead guilty to a lesser related offense—by definition carrying lesser penalties—in exchange for the guilty plea. Rapists who are convicted by plea bargained guilty pleas serve shorter sentences than those convicted at trial. Sexual assault victims, thus, see the men who raped them receive light(er) penalties and obtain release from institutions in short(er) amounts of time than those adjudicated guilty at trial. The trade-off between high conviction rates and more lenient sentences (even ranging to probation) must be considered in the evaluation of differential rates of prosecution. Future research might productively examine the relationship between trial and plea bargaining dispositions and sentencing outcomes with the use of sentencing data.

That legislation alone can abate the double burden for rape victims is doubtful. It is asserted here that while attempts at reform legislation represent a step in the right direction, alone they seem to fall short of meeting stated goals. Even positively altered legislation has pitfalls, as evidenced in this paper. For example, a 64% rate of overall nonconviction was found to exist in Kalamazoo, Michigan, even after model legislation was implemented. Further evidence that legislative reform represents insufficient change can be found in the de facto corroboration requirements in most jurisdictions throughout the country, despite the nonexistence or removal of de jure requirements.[37] Michigan sought to eliminate this de facto requirement by specifying its lack of de jure standing; whether this legislative solution was successful remains to be seen.[38]

Implementation of legislation cannot be assumed to mirror legislative objectives.[39] The passage of legislation should be viewed as only a first measure. Laws as well as the beliefs, perceived vested interests, and power structure must all be addressed jointly if real change is to come about. If myths are not dispelled, and attitudes about sexual assault and its victims are not changed, they will likely permeate the implementation of even model legislation and operate to preclude the amelioration of problems attending the prosecution of this crime. The alteration of legal codes by itself seems to be only partially successful. Misguided, erroneous beliefs and historically grounded discriminatory tactics must be replaced with new awareness, realistic attitudes and humane practices.

ENDNOTES

1. See for example Carol Bohmer and Audrey Blumberg, "Twice Traumatized: The Rape Victim and the Court," 58 *Judicature* 341 (1975); Susan Brownmiller, *Against Our Will: Men, Women and Rape* (New York: Simon & Schuster, 1975); Lynda Lytle Holmstrom and Ann Wolbert Burgess, "Rape: The Victim Goes on Trial," in *Victimology: A New Focus*, ed. Israel Drapkin and Emilio Viano (Lexington, Massachusetts: D. C. Heath, 1975); David Luginbill, "Repeal of the Corroboration Requirement: Will It Tip the Scales of Justice?" 24 *Drake Law Review* 669 (1975); Helene Sasko and Deborah Sesek, "Rape Reform Legislation: Is It the Solution?" 24 *Cleveland State Law Review* 463 (1975); Julia R. and Herman Schwendinger, *Rape and Inequality* (Beverly Hills: Sage, 1983).

2. Camile E. LeGrand, "Rape and Rape Laws: Sexism in Society and the Law," 61 *California Law Review* 919 (1973); Gerald D. Robin, "Forcible Rape: Institutionalized Sexism in the Criminal Justice System,"[26] *Crime and Delinquency* 136 (1977); Martin D. Schwartz and Todd R. Clear, "Toward a New Law on Rape," 26 *Crime and Delinquency* 129 (1980); Julia and Herman Schwendinger, *Rape and Inequality*, pp. 170-31.

3. Federal Bureau of Investigation, *Uniform Crime Reports: Crime in the United States* (Washington, D.C.: U.S. Government Printing Office, 1973), p. 15; U.S., Department of

Justice, Bureau of Justice Statistics, *Criminal Victimization in the United States* (Washington, D.C.: U.S. Government Printing Office, 1979), p. 15; Susan Brownmiller, *Against Our Will*, p. 190; Lynn A. Curtis, "Present and Future Measures of Victimization in Forcible Rape," in *Sexual Assault: The Victim and the Rapist*, ed. Marcia J. Walker and Stanley Brodsky (Lexington, Massachusetts: Lexington Books, 1979), pp. 61-68.

4. Federal Bureau of Investigation, *Uniform Crime Reports* (Washington, D.C.: U.S. Government Printing Office, 1979), p. 15.

5. Federal Bureau of Investigation, *Uniform Crime Reports* (Washington, D.C.: U.S. Government Printing Office, 1980), p. 178.

6. Federal Bureau of Investigation, *Uniform Crime Reports* (Washington, D.C.: U.S. Government Printing Office, 1975), p. 24.

7. National Institute of Law Enforcement and Criminal Justice, Law Enforcement Assistance Administration, *Forcible Rape: Final Project Report* (Washington, D.C.: U.S. Government Printing Office, March 1978), pp. ix, 57.

8. Herbert S. Field and Leigh B. Bienen, *Jurors and Rape: A Study in Psychology and Law* (Lexington, Massachusetts: Lexington Books, 1980), p. 153.

9. See *ibid.* for an inventory of state statutes and changes.

10. See for example *The Michigan Criminal Sexual Conduct Code*, P.A. 226 (1974).

11. Herbert Field and Leigh Bienen, *Jurors and Rape*, p. 171.

12. *Ibid.*

13. P.A. 226, Section 520(j).

14. Jan BenDor, "Justice After Rape: Legal Reform in Michigan," in *Sexual Assault*, ed. Marcia Walker and Stanley Brodsky, pp. 149-60; Charles W. Dean and Mary deBruyn-Kops, *The Crime and Consequences of Rape* (Springfield, Illinois: Charles C. Thomas, 1982); Herbert Field and Leigh Bienen, *Jurors and Rape;* National Institute of Law Enforcement and Criminal Justice, *Forcible Rape.*

15. P.A. 266, Section 520(h).

16. *Ibid.*, Section 520(i).

17. *Ibid.*, Sections 520(b)(c).

18. *Ibid.*, Section 520(j).

19. George Cole, *The American System of Criminal Justice* (North Sciturate, Massachusetts: Duxbery Press, 1975); Abraham S. Blumberg, *Criminal Justice: Issues and Ironies* (New York: New Viewpoints, 1979), p. 227.

20. Delmar Karlen and T. Laurence Schultz, "Justice in the Accusation," in *The Rights of the Accused: In Law and Action*, ed. Stuart S. Nagel (Beverly Hills, California: Sage Publications, 1975), p. 13.

21. Abraham Blumberg, *Criminal Justice*, p. 123.

22. Jan BenDor, "Justice After Rape," in *Sexual Assault: The Victim and the Rapist*, ed. Marcia Walker and Stanley Brodsky.

23. Jeanne C. Marsh, Alison Geist and Nathan Caplan, *Rape and the Limits of Law Reform* (Boston: Auburn House Publishing Company, 1982).

24. The difference in the prosecution rate of Detroit in the pre- and Kalamazoo in the post-Criminal Sexual Conduct Code periods is not a direct measure of change because of the different research sites; it may, however, be taken as indicative of success with the model code. As the problem of attrition before rape reform statutes was pervasive nation-wide, there is no reason to suspect that Kalamazoo's pre-1974 prosecution rate was higher than Detroit's.

25. This comparison is based on the same logic described above. Support of this reasoning is additionally found in the similarity between Detroit and Kalamazoo data over a period of years subsequent to the reform legislation (1975-1979 Detroit, 1975-1977 Kalamazoo).

26. The pre- and post-conviction rates reported for Michigan in Jeanne Marsh, Alison Geist and Nathan Caplan, *Rape and the Limits of Law Reform*, are consistent with these data and this interpretations.

27. Because data on prosecutors' charging decisions are unavailable for other Michigan jurisdictions, and because they are little available on plea bargaining and convictions in

Michigan and elsewhere, it must be cautioned that generalizations to Michigan or to national patterns, based upon the data and discussion in this paper, would be unwarranted. The findings and comparisons described herein are instructive for heuristic purposes in pointing to implications for legal reform and sexual assault prosecutions.

28. Kristen M. Williams, *The Prosecution of Sexual Assault* (Washington, D.C.: Institute for Law and Policy Research, 1978), pp. 23-28.

29. National Institute of Law Enforcement and Criminal Justice, *Forcible Rape*, p. 49.

30. See Herbert Field and Leigh Bienen, *Jurors and Rape*, for state statistics.

31. *Ibid.*

32. *Ibid.* Unfortunately the data from Kansas City and Seattle were not provided separately. One state has traditional legislation and the other, minor types of reform. Because of the need to interpret findings in an aggregate manner, the jurisdictions studied by the National Institute of Law enforcement of Criminal Justice will be treated as having essentially traditional legislation.

33. It should be noted that Washington, D.C., has a well organized anti-rape group which may help to account for the high prosecution rate despite the traditional rape legislation operating in this jurisdiction.

34. P.A. 266.

35. Susan Caringella-MacDonald, "Factors Influencing Prosecutorial Discretion in Criminal Sexual Conduct Cases," paper presented to annual meeting of the American Psychological Association, Montreal, 1980.

36. The results of interview data reported in Jeanne Marsh, Alison Geist and Nathan Caplan, *Rape and the Limits of Legal Reform*, support the latter interpretation, that criminal justice officials' attitudes have not kept pace with legal change.

37. Richard A. Hibey, "The Trial of a Rape Case: An Advocate's Analysis of Corroboration, Consent, and Character," in *Rape Victimology*, ed. Leroy Schultz (Springfield: Charles C. Thomas, 1975); Note, "The Rape Corroboration Requirement: Repeal Not Reform," 81 *Yale Law Journal* 1365 (1975); H.S. Shapo, "Recent Statutory Developments in the Definition of Forcible Rape," 61 *Virginia Law Review* 1500 (1975).

38. The author has research of this nature presently underway.

39. See for example Piers Bierne and Richard Quinney, ed., *Marxism and Law* (New York: Wiley, 1982); W.G. Carson, "The Sociology of Crime and the Emergence of Criminal Laws," in *Deviance and Social Control*, ed. Paul Rock and Mary McIntosh (London: Tavistock Publications, 1974); David Greenberg, ed., *Crime and Capitalism: Readings in Marxist Criminology* (Palo Alto, California: Mayfield Publishing, 1981); Richard Quinney, *Class, State and Crime* (New York: Longman, 1980).

Policing Woman Battering*

KATHLEEN J. FERRARO, *Arizona State University*

In the 1980s, many states and cities mandated police officers to arrest men who batter women in family disputes. This observational study of a large metropolitan police department shows that in spite of the presumptive arrest policy, officers made arrests in only 18 percent of assaults involving intimate partners. Case material illustrates how legal, ideological, practical, and political factors led police to ignore the presumptive arrest policy when responding to family disputes.

The definition of woman battering as a social problem in the 1970s initiated debate about how to control and prevent violence between intimates. Feminists have argued that the control of intimate violence depends on fundamental restructuring of gender relations and the empowerment of women. Mentai health professionals have promoted therapeutic intervention for offenders and victims of domestic violence. Most experts agreed that battered women need more legal protection (Hart et al., 1984; Schechter, 1981; Stanko, 1985; Taub, 1983; Walker, 1985; U.S. Commission on Civil Rights, 1978). The police are the "front line" of the official response to battering. Past research shows that police did not arrest men who battered their wives, even when victims were in serious danger and directly asked officers to arrest (Berk and Loseke, 1981; Black, 1980; Brown, 1984; Davis, 1983; Parnas, 1967). Activists in the battered women's movement saw failure to arrest as tacit support for battering, contributing to the inability of women to escape violent relationships and in the escalation of abuse to domestic homicides (Police Foundation, 1976).

Since 1976, civil suits, legislation, and policy initiatives have challenged police inaction (Ferraro, 1989). In 1984, the U.S. Attorney General's Task Force on Family Violence recommended that "family violence should be recognized and responded to as a criminal activity" and law enforcement agencies should "establish arrest as the preferred response in cases of family violence" (Hart et al., 1984:10, 17). Advocates for battered women insist that police should arrest men who use violence against their wives and lovers (Ferraro, 1989). This "get tough" stance is supported by legislative changes that expand police power to arrest.

By 1986, six states passed laws *requiring* arrests when probable cause exists and the offender is on the scene. Probable cause is established by the presence of witnesses, visible injuries, or property damage that indicate a crime has been committed. Forty-seven large city police departments had adopted a policy of mandatory or presumptive arrests for family fights by 1986 (Crime Control Institute, 1986). In 28 other states and the District of Columbia, police *may* arrest for a misdemeanor spousal assault on the basis of probable cause (Lerman and Livingston, 1983). Officers cannot arrest for misdemeanor assaults between unmarried people unless the assault is observed by the officer, an arrest warrant has been issued, or a citizen signs a complaint. The changes in the statutes are a response to the fact that most assaults against wives occur in private settings and fall in the misdemeanor category. Without ex-

* Earlier versions of this paper were presented at the annual meetings of the American Sociological Association, Washington, DC, 1985 and the American Society of Criminology, San Diego, California, 1985. This research was supported in part by grants from the Arizona State Women's Studies Summer Grant program and the Arizona State University Research Fund. David Altheide and John M. Johnson were co-researchers on this project and have made significant contributions to this article. Kim Bauman, Nancy Jurik, Gerri Klein, and Kathy Seeley helped in completing this research. I appreciate the cooperation of Chief Ruben Ortega and all the officers who generously allowed us to observe their work. Thanks also to Malcolm Spector and the anonymous *Social Problems* reviewers for their comments.
Correspondence to: School of Justice Studies, Arizona State University, Tempe, AZ 85287.

panded arrest powers, police cannot arrest batterers unless the assault is felonious or witnessed by an officer. Eighteen states require officers to provide information on legal options and services, and in eleven states police must transport victims to hospitals or shelters. Twenty-nine states also provide for temporary restraining orders, in which courts order abusers to stay away from their victims (Buzawa and Buzawa, 1985).

The push to arrest batterers enhances police power to arrest, but mandatory arrest policies limit the discretion of police officers to dismiss woman battering as a "civil matter." Policies that require arrest also limit discretion of complainants in that they ignore the wishes of the victim. Many battered women experience ambivalence about pressing criminal charges or fear retribution if they do so (Ferraro, 1988). Yet academic research purports to demonstrate the superior effect of arrest. Sherman and Berk (1984) found that violence was less frequently repeated when arrests were made than when battering incidents were mediated or resolved through physically separating the couple. Their findings have gained widespread recognition in police culture.

While laws and policies regarding woman battering have changed, the police response to battering relies heavily on extra-legal factors in police decision making (Bell, 1985; Berk and Loseke, 1981; Black, 1980; Davis, 1983; Smith and Klein, 1984; Waaland and Keeley, 1985). Observational studies of police work have consistently supported Black's (1971) early finding that the closer the relationship between victim and assailant, the less likely police are to arrest. Thus, even when departmental policies instruct police to arrest, officers continue to rely on victim and offender characteristics in deciding whether a law has been broken.

The response of police in the field to formal rules and policy about battering is embedded in a social context. As Manning (1971:162) notes, a police officer "moves in a dense web of social action and social meanings, burdened by a problematic, complex array of ever-changing laws." To better understand how these extra-legal considerations reduce protection of battered women, we must look at how police work is done. The purpose of this paper is to examine the web of actions, meanings, and changing laws through which police construct their response to battering. I begin with a description of the emergence of new laws and policies about policing domestic disputes in Phoenix, Arizona. I then outline four dimensions of police response to battering and conclude by summarizing the difficulties of implementing the presumptive arrest policy for domestic violence.

Arizona's Domestic Violence Law and Policy

Most misdemeanors in Arizona result in a citation and release of the offender. In 1980, the state legislature passed a domestic violence bill that: (1) prohibits officers from citing and releasing domestic violence offenders; (2) expands police power to arrest on the basis of probable cause and requires officers to provide information to victims about procedures and available services; and (3) provides for orders of protection that can be obtained through any court, without filing for divorce. The orders provide grounds for arrest if a batterer goes near his victim. Two local judges drafted the bill. They were responding to two county coalitions on domestic violence that were putting pressure on police and courts to do more to protect battered women. In addition, police and lower court judges had complained that their hands were tied by constraints on arrests and by unwilling victims. The authors of the bill were fully aware of the practical limitations of controlling intimate violence through court orders.

The new law went into effect in July 1980. It had very little impact on law enforcement in Arizona. The police departments did not change their arrest policies. Officers had available one more tool for dealing with domestic violence, but did not view the law as an indication that arrests should increase. By 1983, the Maricopa County Task Force Against Domestic Violence, composed primarily of shelter and mental health workers, convinced a state representative that more legislation was required to force police to arrest batterers. A committee formed to draft a bill mandating arrest for domestic violence. The Phoenix Chief of Police, Ruben Ortega, discouraged the group from pressing for the law, promising that he would adopt a mandatory arrest policy and would encourage other chiefs to do so. Police administrators said that the superior court judge heading the family court had made several complaints to Chief Ortega about failure to arrest violent husbands. At the same time, Chief Ortega was appointed to the U.S. Attorney General's Task Force on Family Violence. After traveling around the country listening to testimony about the need to crack down on wife abuse, he returned to Arizona to help implement the recommendations of the Attorney General's Task Force. In May 1984, the Phoenix police department adopted a presumptive arrest policy. It stated that:

> Officers *should* arrest domestic violence violators even if the victim does not desire prosecution. When probable cause exists, an arrest should be made even if a misdemeanor offense did not occur in the officer's presence (Ortega, 1984:1, emphasis added).

The policy was publicized in the local papers and on television. All police officers received training on the new policy from their sergeants and from members of the domestic violence coalition.

The Phoenix presumptive arrest policy represented only one minor change in an extensive city and county criminal justice system. Other cities in the county did not immediately alter their policies regarding domestic violence, although some since have done so. The city and county prosecutors did not increase prosecutions, and judges did not sentence batterers to jail. The Phoenix police were not supported in their policy shift by correlative changes in other parts of the system.

The police department figures indicate that the rate of arrest at the scene for family fights more than doubled in the second month after the policy was implemented. In 1983, the average monthly arrest rate was 33 percent. In June 1984, it was 67 percent, at which time a clarifying statement emphasized that probable cause was still a requirement for arrest. Officers told us that "ridiculous" arrests were annoying the judges who, in turn, complained to the chief. The chief reminded the officers that the policy did not override the constitutional requirement of reasonable grounds for arrest. This clarification created some confusion among officers. Some told us things were back to normal; others said they were only supposed to arrest in cases where there was serious injury and witnesses. This apparent hedging by the administration undermined the policy's initial forcefulness about the importance of arrest. In July 1984, the official arrest rate dropped to 52 percent, and by August it was 42 percent.

Methods

The Phoenix presumptive arrest policy offered an opportunity to observe the street level response to an administrative crackdown on battering. I asked Chief Ortega for permission to study the Phoenix police, and after some prodding from my college dean, he agreed to grant me entree. I interviewed Chief Ortega, four assistant chiefs, and the detective in charge of family fights to gather administrative perceptions of the policy before beginning ridealongs. Our team of six field observers entered the field in May 1984, three weeks after the presumptive arrest policy was adopted. Two male professors, one female professor, and three female graduate students conducted the observations. The observers rode with officers on ten-hour weekend evening shifts for 44 nights. Phoenix is divided into five districts with separate stations in each. The districts are divided into beats. Officers do not cross district boundaries but may enter unassigned beats within their districts. Three districts were observed. The two districts with the highest concentration of low income and transient individuals were selected because they represented the highest proportion of domestic violence calls. One district primarily composed of middle income whites was also observed. Officers were told that we were studying domestic violence and were instructed to respond to as many family fight calls as possible. On many evenings we were assigned to "roving cars," which had no beat boundaries and that could respond to family fight calls anywhere in the district.

During the ten-hour shifts, we accompanied officers on every aspect of their duties. During periods in which there was no activity, we questioned officers about the new presumptive arrest policy, their experiences with family fights, and their opinions about the appropriate response. Observers carried yellow pads for recording information and verbatim quotes. Information about police work in general was outlined, but officers' statements about and actions at family fights were recorded in as much detail as possible on the day following observations. At family fight calls we observed the police intervention and spoke with victims whenever possible. When arrests were made, we sometimes went to the station to observe the booking process. In one case, an observer was called to court as a witness to an assault.

In most cases, observers did not attempt to influence police behavior, even when they disagreed with decisions. Observers did not suggest arrest or nonarrest at the scene. When officers signalled completion of the call by saying good-by to the victim and walking toward their car, I sometimes suggested—consistent with the new statute—that they provide victims with information about services and orders of protection. In several cases I also suggested officers request the services of the on-call mental health team, but only after they began to leave the scene.

We observed the police respond to 69 reports of family fights. Of these, 34 involved married or formerly married couples, 15 involved cohabitees or former lovers, 13 involved neighbors or other relatives, and 7 were false reports. Although twenty of the cases do not involve woman battering, they were dispatched and referred to as family fights by the officers.

Police Response Under the New Policy

The intent of mandatory and presumptive arrest policies is to treat domestic violence "as a crime." Thus, officers are supposed to arrest batterers regardless of other characteristics of the situation. That was not what we observed. Out of 69 family fight calls, 49 involved spouses, cohabitants, estranged lovers, or current lovers and fit the definition of battering. Officers made no arrests in 40 of these cases (82%); arrests were made in only 9 (18%) of the battering incidents, in spite of the presumptive arrest policy. In 25 (51%) cases, police used conciliation, which means talking to the people and emphasizing the importance of the relationship over the dispute. Very few cases involved a therapeutic style of social control, and none could be classified as compensatory, in which the officer would attempt to gain redress for the violence inflicted on the victim.

These results are similar to those reported by Black (1980:156) in cases involving married and common law couples: 70 percent conciliatory, 26 percent penal, 2 percent therapeutic, and 2 percent preventative. Black (1980:158) found that for those cases where penal action was taken, 26 percent were arrests. This is quite striking in that Black's observations were conducted prior to the emergence of the battered women's movement and statutory and policy changes in policing battering. The consistency over time attests to the complexity of the police response to battering and the difficulty of altering it.

Department policy is only one factor influencing police decision making at family fights. As Berk and Loseke (1981:342) note, police responses are "rife with situationally determined contingencies." In their research, using police reports, presence of both disputants on the scene, women's willingness to sign complaints, victims' allegations of violence, and male alcohol consumption were all positively correlated with the decision to arrest (Berk and Loseke, 1981:341-42). Our observations suggest that these factors continue to play a major role in decision making even when arrest is the preferred policy.

Officers evaluate each call to decide whether it is really a "family fight." A set of behaviors in one context might lead one officer to arrest, while similar behaviors in another context might lead another officer to take no action. Most of the time officers rejected arrest as an option after weighing certain considerations. However, when they did arrest, they often invoked some of the same considerations. The following categories summarize the considerations impinging on the decision making process at family fights: legal, ideological, practical, and political.

Legal

By legal considerations I mean to emphasize how police think about and use their understandings of the laws and statutes they are officially charged with enforcing. The most obvious instances of these laws being "applied" might be the 9 arrests we observed.

There were two arrests the police classified as misdemeanor spousal assaults that seemed consistent with the intent of the new policy. In the first case, the couple was married the day before the assault. A neighbor called the police after she saw the husband assault his wife. All three people were sitting quietly at the apartment when we arrived. The couple was Hispanic and lived in a low-income neighborhood. The woman had a deep cut on her forehead and said she wanted to press charges. Police called paramedics to treat the cut, took photographs for evidence of injury, and took the man to jail. With all legal and policy criteria met and a compliant offender, officers did not hesitate to make an arrest.

A second case where the wife was the only victim involved an argument in the presence of a female friend who called the police when the husband threatened his wife with a knife. When police arrived, all three people denied any conflict. Police searched the husband and found a knife. The presence of a weapon satisfied the legal criterion of assault even though the victim and witness said no assault or threat occurred. The officer perceived danger and arrested the man.

In two cases, men were violent in the presence of officers and both were arrested. In the first case, a 65-year-old man was drunk and wrestling with his son. Two male police officers grabbed the man, cuffed him, and loaded him into a back-up police car. In the second case, a man spit on his girlfriend and punched a male neighbor in the mouth. When the officer arrived, the man greeted him at the front door with a raised ball bat. The officer drew his gun, and the man slammed the door in this face. Police subsequently chased and captured the offender, threw him to the floor, tightly cuffed his hands and feet and carried him to the car.

This case was the only instance where police asked the victim to make a "citizen's arrest." The charges against him were simple assault against a male bystander and spitting at his girlfriend. The officer perceived him as a dangerous character and one who showed a lack of respect for the law. The officer told the observer the assault charge might not hold because the bystander was trespassing; the spitting charge was obviously weak. He therefore instructed the girlfriend to place her foot on the "hog-tied" man's back and say, "I place you under citizen's arrest."

Most of the time, however, the police did not arrest anyone when called to the site of reported domestic violence. One legal ground for this decision is that, at the time of the research, the domestic violence statute did not extend to cohabitants, although the law now has been changed to include them. Of the 15 cases observed involving cohabitants, lovers or ex-lovers, three resulted in arrests. Arrests involving violence in nonmarried couples did not fall within the purview of the new policy. Presumptive arrest relied on enhanced power to arrest in misdemeanor domestic violence cases. When couples were not married, officers did not consider arrest, even if there were legal grounds for it. For example, it is always possible to arrest if a citizen signs a complaint, but that option was used only once in 69 cases. In that case, the offender was violent to a male neighbor, threatened a police officer, and attempted to escape. In this and the other two cases where an unmarried person was arrested, the high level of danger was more significant to officers than the fact that the new policy did not formally apply. In most cases observed, however, officers did not consider arresting unmarried cohabitees.

In one case, for example, a live-in boyfriend broke down the front door when his girlfriend refused to let him in. He was very drunk, and she did not want to see him, as they were both recovering alcoholics. He tore up their apartment, breaking and destroying her personal belongings. He also hit her in the face, and she had a small cut where her glasses bridged her nose. Three officers arrived at the scene, and the two patrolmen asked their sergeant what to "make" the call. He told them no crime had been committed, except against the landlady for destruction of the apartment door.

Several crimes could have been constructed from these facts, including assault, criminal damage, endangerment, and threatening or intimidating. The officers might have encouraged the woman to sign a citizen's complaint. Either a stranger or a husband committing identical acts would have been defined differently, but the sergeant focused on the cohabitant status of the relationship and decided that no crime had been committed.

Another legal consideration was seen when officers searched for probable cause for arrest. The detective in charge of family fights told us that the presence of visible injuries, property damage, weapons, or witnesses establishes probable cause. The statute permitting misdemeanor arrests based on probable cause authorizes officers to determine whether the situation permits a reasonable conclusion that a crime has been committed. But this determination is, of course, discretionary. For most officers, severe visible injuries or the use of weapons constituted probable cause, but minor injury, property damage, and the presence of child witnesses did not. Officers' interpretations of probable cause undermined the policy because they used a level of evidence high enough for felony arrests. Administrative directives that emphasized the importance of probable cause led many officers to conclude that they had wide discretion in this area.

After receiving the directive about probable cause, one officer said that "things are back to normal." He made no arrests in the three family fights we responded to in one night of observations. In one case, for example, a woman fled her home after her husband beat and choked her. She had taken one child with her, but the other remained at her mother's home where her husband had gone and subsequently assaulted her brother. The husband was drunk and violent, and the woman was afraid he would either hurt the baby or take it away where she could not find them. She had bruises on her neck from the choking, and her mother had witnessed the assault on the brother. They lived in a housing project, and she had to walk three blocks to use a phone to call the police. It was 2:00 A.M. when we arrived on the scene. The officer told her there was nothing he could do. He said the baby was not in danger and that everything was okay. He told her to call if anything else happened. The victim was frightened and believed her husband was "crazy" and capable of serious violence. The officer did not agree and offered her no information or advice except to "call back."

This incident could have met the standards of probable cause. The victim was anxious to press charges, had visible signs of injury, and there were witnesses to the assault on her brother. The man was a few blocks away at his mother-in-law's home, but the officer made no attempt to contact him. He did not suggest that the victim sign a complaint. Legally, his decision not to arrest could be justified by the absence of probable cause as no serious injury or weapons were present. His interpretation of the new policy required these elements for an arrest. But the officer's actions in this case are not what would be expected based on the "get tough" rhetoric or the presumptive arrest policy.

The domestic violence statute specifies the destruction of property, or criminal damage, as a crime. In several cases, women were not physically attacked, but their property was destroyed. These cases included tire slashing, smashed windshields, a waterbed punctured with an ice pick, doors kicked in, and the two cases described above. In all but one case, officers told victims that nothing could be done. The officers said that Arizona is a community property state. Therefore, everything belongs to both people, and one cannot be charged for destroying one's own property. Yet the legislature and courts have recognized that community property means half, not total, ownership. When jointly held property is destroyed, the half not owned is destroyed as well as the half that is. The one case of arrest for criminal damage indicates that it was a legitimate charge if officers wanted to use it.

Legal criteria are not the most salient in police decision making. Presumptive arrest implies that legal standards are the most important consideration for family fights, but in the cases we observed the legal interpretation of events were strongly influenced by other considerations.

Ideological

Ideological considerations are those background beliefs and ideas about battered women and family fights that police officers use to evaluate specific incidents. They include general ideas police have about the people they encounter, specific ideas about family fights, and images of danger. These ideas emerge through police practice, although officers may be predisposed to interpret other people as adversaries. As Manning (1971:156) emphasizes, the occupational culture of police sets the standards for a "good policeman" and prompts the assumptions police officers use in shaping their work.

Police tend to dichotomize the community into normal and deviant citizens (Ferraro, 1989). Normal citizens abide by society's rules through maintaining employment, sobriety, a family, and a modestly clean home. They are heterosexual, white, and speak English. Deviants serve as the "other" for police officers; they are publicly intoxicated or high, homeless, involved in crime, live in run-down houses, have atypical family structures, and/or speak foreign languages. Habitual problems are endemic to their lifestyle.

According to this view, a normal citizen who violates a law responds to police intervention with shame and anxiety. A "normal" wife beater is perceived as situationally deviant, his behavior the product of particular strain or a response to a threatened divorce. Such a man, officers believe, may be deterred by arrest because both violence and arrest are extraordinary and undesirable events for such people. On the other hand, arrest and violence are viewed as routine events for deviant men. Officers on patrol often referred to Mexicans, Indians, gay men, and people in the housing projects as "low lifes," "scum," or "these kind of people." Officers believed arrests were a waste of time and meaningless for these people because violence is a way of life for them. Empirically, middle income, professional men do engage in repetitive wife beating (Weller, 1988). However, representative surveys find higher rates of wife beating among low-income and unemployed men (Gelles and Straus, 1988; Straus et al., 1980). Police ideology about the types of situations in which violence occurs may be grounded in experience.

In one case, a Hispanic woman who spoke little English approached us at 3:00 A.M. for help as we responded to another call. She complained, through a 14-year-old neighbor, that her husband was drunk, violent, and threatening to take her children away. We found the man intoxicated, sitting among a pile of beer cans. Three small boys sat nearby. The officers (one man and one woman) resolved the problem by walking the woman and children to an apartment a few doors away. They told the woman to call the police if there was any more trouble although she had no telephone or money. The residents were not friends of the woman and were not happy to have her. We left the woman sitting on the porch and walked past the husband who waved good-by to us. The low level of protection provided by this arrangement and the imposition on neighbors did not concern the officers. The male officer expressed frustration at dealing with Spanish speakers and people in the projects.

Police also held stereotypes about battered women. One repeatedly expressed idea was that battered women were likely to drop any charges that might be filed. They often asked for arrest at night when they were angry and then refused to testify or lied about the abuse when later contacted by detectives or prosecutors. The presumptive arrest policy is supposed to take the burden of prosecution off the victim. Still, it is difficult to prosecute an assault when the victim denies it occurred. One officer argued that the policy would lead to more homicides because once women knew arrests would be made they would stop calling the police for help. He said,

> A lot of these people, especially in this district, just want you to do something to stop it for the night. They want us to get somebody to leave. They could do that for themselves, but they want us to do it. If they can't call us, because we'll arrest, then they don't have anybody to help them, and instead of somebody leaving for the night, somebody's going to get killed.

Several officers thought there were fewer reports of family fights because the word had gone out about arrests. However, department figures indicated an increase in calls. Police statistics showed an average of 83 reports a month in 1983. In the first month of the policy, 327 family violence reports were received. The number steadily dropped over the first five months of the policy, but in September there were still 157 calls.

The police believe battered women choose to remain in abusive situations. Most officers believed adult women could leave violent situations if they wanted to. If they stayed with a violent man, it was not the responsibility of police to try to control the violence. An officer expressed this belief in a case involving a young, black woman staying in a run-down motel in a low-income section of town. Her boyfriend hit her, took all her clothes, and left in their car. They had recently moved to town, and she had nowhere to go and no money or clothes. Officers arranged for her to spend the night with others in the motel. On leaving, one officer commented, "This is your typical family fight. They don't really want to do anything." He did not empathize with the woman's lack of alternatives, but rather typified her as willfully choosing an abusive situation.

Officers expressed a range of attitudes toward battered women. At the sympathetic end of the continuum, a female officer, herself a formerly battered woman, strongly supported the new policy. She said,

> What is a woman really supposed to do if she has no job skills and a couple of kids, and he's been tellin' her he'll kill her if she leaves? What is she gonna' do? A lot of people can't understand why she stays, but I can really empathize with that. Sure there are a few dingbats that are just so stupid they don't know enough to leave. But I think most women who get beat up really don't have anyplace else to go and they're afraid.

This woman was the only officer who expressed sympathy with the battered woman's situation. Three other female officers mentioned appreciation for the new policy, but the other female officers (15) were either neutral or antagonistic toward the policy. Several female officers openly expressed disdain for family fight calls, citing the danger involved and unwillingness of victims to follow through. One female officer said she believed women who dropped charges should be held in contempt of court.

Male officers also expressed a range of attitudes about woman battering and the policy, but the negative evaluations were more extreme. At the critical end of the continuum, one male officer expressed the belief that a man's home is his castle where he should be allowed to do what he wants. He believed most wife beating was provoked by the woman. He had recently punched a whole in his own living room wall during an argument with his wife. From his perspective, arresting men for destroying their own property was an outrageous infringement on liberty. For officers who view arrests as a waste of time or an illegitimate infringement on private life, presumptive arrest is an illogical policy.

Officers also held implicit images of dangerous situations. For two nights we drove down alleys and kept watch for a man wearing women's clothing who was suspected of rape. Officers believed he was dangerous. Reports of "drive-by" shootings by gangs and gang conflicts were also perceived as dangerous and worth investigating. Certain bars and neighborhoods were described as extremely dangerous, and one bar was singled out for intervention "before somebody gets killed."

Battered women, on the other hand, were usually not perceived as being in dangerous situations. Women cried and shook with fear as they told officers their husbands or lovers were going to hurt them. But repeatedly officers responded with a "call if anything happens," rather than giving them the immediate protection they sought. Everything appeared to officers to be "under control" because they could see no visible signs of danger. To women who were battered and were experienced with their assailants' patterns of violence, the danger was real and frightening, and easy to see. The divergent perceptions of danger held by battered women and police resulted in a minimal effort to intervene in cases which appeared to officers as stable.

Practical

The statute and policy did not specify the degree of inconvenience and probing required of officers at family fights. So if both husband and wife denied the existence of a fight, or if both accused the other of violence, it was left to the officer's discretion whether intervention of any kind was appropriate.

The policy did not specifically state that offenders had to be on the scene for arrests to be made. Neither did it encourage officers to search for men who had fled. In order for us to observe an arrest, the offender had to have been on or near the scene. In 28 cases (40%) the man was not on the scene at the time of police arrival. Either he had left, or the woman had called from a location other than that of the dispute. In these cases, the officers were supposed to write detective's reports that would allow a detective to follow up the next day. It was not always apparent whether reports were written because several police units were on the scene. Officers with whom we were not riding did not commonly share information about the calls. In cases where our assigned officer was the primary respondent to the call, it was possible to determine whether detective's reports were written. In most cases, they were not.

Although failure to file a report is not a technical violation of the presumptive arrest policy, it does undermine the intent to "get tough." In practice, if the batterer is not on the scene, no punitive action will be taken, even if the woman has left her home to seek safety while her abuser remains at home. In one case a woman called police from her friend's home after her drunken husband smashed her car windshield with a ball and chain and threatened to kill her and her children. She asked the officers to go to her home and arrest him. The officers said they could not do that without a warrant or unless she accompanied them because her home was in another district. The officer told me the woman would not accompany them, but I heard her tell him that she would. They left her at her friend's home, telling her to call if he came around. Whether the policy only applied to cases where the offender was on the scene was irrelevant for the officers. In their view, there was no danger of the violence continuing that night and so the policy was not invoked. The officer said it was a typical family fight and that, although the woman was angry that night, she would cool down the next day and forget about charges. As Davis (1983:275) notes, the police at family fights are concerned with achieving a situational "semblance of order" rather than finding a solution to the larger relational problem.

Arizona domestic violence statute 13-3601 D includes the requirement for officers to inform victims of the procedures and resources available for the protection of victims, namely orders of protection, emergency telephone numbers of the police, and telephone numbers of emergency services in the area. Officers were supplied with domestic violence cards that listed magistrates, shelters, and hotlines along with their phone numbers. In only two of the 69 cases we observed did officers provide this information to victims without being prompted by the observers. Officers did not see providing the victim with information as relevant to restoring order in the situation and so they seldom did it (see Davis, 1983).

Police also had access to a special mental health team on weekend nights. The Family Stress Team was made up of mental health professionals who were on call to respond to mental health problems. Officers stated that the team did good work and was a good resource, but they called them only four times in the 69 cases we observed. When arrests were made, they did not see a need for mental health assistance. As long as the immediate problem was resolved, and order was restored, officers did not consider relevant those options for more long term solutions, such as calling the stress team or providing the victim with community service information.

In four cases (6%) the problem was defined as "resolved prior to arrival." In these cases either no one answered the door, or someone appeared at the door and told police everything was under control. Officers did not insist on entering the home when the resident requested them to leave. In these situations, there was no complainant, no apparent violence, and thus no problem for the police to handle. In domestic violence situations this response is disturbing, as it is unknown whether the victim is being forced to keep quiet or ask the police to leave.

Officers also spoke about cases they called "mutual combat," where there was aggressive interaction rather than explicit violence. A man physically assaulting a woman who was screaming and yelling at him could be construed by officers as mutual combat, particularly in cases where the woman was intoxicated. Officers said they would not arrest in these cases because it was not possible to determine who was at fault. Directives from the Assistant Chief of the Patrol Division discouraged arrest when both parties were violent at a misdemeanor level. In such cases, it was difficult to get testimony from either party, as they could not talk without incriminating themselves.

Arresting both spouses could also create practical problems of placing children. The police could use local social services to foster children temporarily. This is difficult and time consuming and may be as frightening to children as their father's violence. While some officers explicitly stated that the presence of children would not inhibit them from making an arrest, others recounted instances in which arrests had not been made because they would have had to foster children out.

Although the presumptive arrest policy was intended to remove the decision to arrest from the victim, establishing probable cause is more difficult if a woman refuses to testify to her abuse. Some battered women do not press charges because they love their husbands. But there may be other reasons why arrest would not be in a woman's best interests. In follow-up interviews conducted during a second stage of this research, one victim said she did not want her husband arrested because he had recently obtained a job after six months of unemployment. He might lose his job if he missed a day of work or if his employer learned he had been arrested. Other women worried about immigration authorities and did not want to get too close to the law. Why a woman does not want to press charges may not be clear to the responding officer. But if she unequivocally states that she does not want to press charges, officers may recognize her competence and knowledge of what is best for her. Although the intent of presumptive arrest policies is to shift the responsibility for arrest from the woman to the police, some officers continued to consider the practical consequences of arrest for the victim and her children.

Finally, time is a practical consideration. Since it takes at least an hour to process an arrest, officers are less likely to arrest when they are about to finish their shifts. Moreover, officers view time as a resource to be saved for "important" cases. An arrest makes officers unavailable for other activities during the booking procedure. During this time, officers are off the street, unable to respond to other calls. One officer lamented that once she had been unable to respond to an armed robbery call because she was transporting a woman to a shelter. She implied that the armed robbery was more important and exciting. This was cited by other officers in explaining why they would not transport victims to a safe place. Although time is never sufficient to account for arrest/nonarrest decisions, it combines and probably interacts with legal, ideological and other practical considerations in shaping an officer's response to a given incident.

Internal and External Politics

In the police department, there is a tension between administrative policy makers and street level actors. Administrators are attuned to professional and community level politics, while patrol officers are attuned to the politics of the street. The presumptive arrest policy was interpreted by officers through their perceptions of administrative motives.

Traditionally, domestic violence is a low status offense. The presumptive arrest policy tried to elevate its importance. But without clear-cut rewards or incentives, officers doubted the political significance of the policy. Some officers believed the policy was just for show, and some said it came from pressure from judges. But most did not know why they were suddenly urged to alter their responses in these cases. Family fights remain low status, undesirable calls for most officers.

One final consideration is the political organization of the housing projects. The projects have committees that officers perceive as "really powerful" and having "a direct line to the chief's office." Officers believe that project residents despise them and that the committees are eager to complain about police misconduct. Graffiti in these neighborhoods suggest that the contempt is not entirely imaginary. Two officers explained that they had been transferred from the projects because of fabricated complaints brought to the chief by the project committee. The belief that the committees had influence with the chief and that people are more than willing to complain about police misconduct was not conducive to a presumptive arrest policy. Officers were hesitant to arrest without sufficient evidence or victim cooperation when they feared retribution from the committees.

Legal, ideological, practical, and political considerations do not exhaust the factors that influenced police decision making at family fights. Sometimes legal considerations voiced in one context were contradicted by actions in another. The process of police responses to domestic violence situations is not entirely rational or accessible to observers. Still, seeing how police took these factors into account in their work helps us to understand how the new law and policy were in fact enacted.

Discussion

The officers in this study did not implement the presumptive arrest policy in a uniform way. The observational data show that discretion persists in spite of well publicized policy changes and training on domestic violence. In part, lack of adherence to the policy can be traced to the confusion produced by policy clarifications after the fact, which was evidence that the chief was "backing off." Publicly, Chief Ortega maintains a "get tough" stance on arresting batterers. Training on the policy did not resolve questions about its political meaning within the department. Officers were free to guess how much importance they should attach to a policy that drastically altered their traditional approach to domestic violence. No explicit incentives were offered for compliance, and no penalties were attached to evasion of the new policy. These were situational problems that may be remedied by a more vigorous, explicit administrative plan to increase arrests. The level of tension and conflict between administrators and patrol officers varies by locale. A department with strong leadership and morale may have more success at implementing a presumptive arrest policy.

On the other hand, these data indicate that each case is evaluated in terms of its relationship to a web of considerations, including legal, ideological, practical, and political issues. Officers can be encouraged to interpret situations in a given manner, but the interpretive process remains tied to these influences. For example, officers may be told to arrest regardless of the victim's wishes, yet still evaluate her recalcitrance in light of the perceived power of the housing project committees or the time taken away from other work. Policy directives did alter police behavior in this study, as evidenced by the two arrests for misdemeanor wife assaults. They did not, however, eliminate the impact of the web of considerations on police decision making.

Information on the factors that discouraged arrests is useful in designing programs to enhance arrests. The legal and political considerations described reflect officers' concerns with what will happen if arrests are made. If they perceive that high standards of evidence are required for prosecution and observe low rates of prosecution, they are likely to see most arrests as a waste of time. Mandatory and presumptive arrest policies implemented in the absence of change in other parts of the legal system will probably have little lasting impact on how police respond to domestic violence. If the official rhetoric about "treating domestic violence as a crime" embodied in the task force recommendations is genuine, changes must occur at the prosecutorial, judicial, and correctional levels in tandem with changes in law enforcement practices.

Concerns about the power of housing project committees suggest that police officers recognize the impact of citizen complaints on their work lives. The recent surge in law suits against police departments may have some impact on street level decision making (Woods, 1986). At the local level, the relationship between police officials and battered women's advocacy groups could have a positive impact on police response. If officers view policies as rhetoric to quiet the "women's libbers," they are not likely to be concerned about the consequences of their street level decisions. However, if they believe that failure to provide adequate protection will result in complaints that include their name and badge number and may lead to disciplinary action, they may be more thorough in their response to victims' complaints. Education and organizing by battered women's advocates can likely influence police perceptions of the power of battered women.

References

Bell, Daniel J.

1985 "A multiyear study of Ohio urban, suburban, and rural police dispositions of domestic disputes." Victimology 10:301-10.

Berk, Sarah F. and Donileen R. Loseke

1981 " 'Handling' family violence: Situational determinants of police arrest in domestic disturbances." Law and Society Review 15:317-46.

Black, Donald

1971 "The social organization of arrest." Stanford Law Review 23:1087-1111.

1980 The Manners and Customs of the Police. New York: Academic Press.

Brown, Stephen
1984 "Police responses to wife beating: neglect of a crime of violence." Journal of Criminal Justice 12:277-88.

Buzawa, Eva and Carl C. Buzawa
1985 "Legislative trends in the criminal justice response to domestic violence." Pp. 124-47 in Alan J. Lincoln and Murray A. Straus (eds.), Crime and the Family. Springfield, IL: Charles C. Thomas.

Crime Control Institute
1986 "Police domestic violence policy change." Response 9:16.

Davis, Philip W.
1983 "Restoring the semblance of order: police strategies in the domestic disturbance." Symbolic Interaction 6:216-74.

Ferraro, Kathleen J.
1988 "Prosecution of felony assaults against women." Paper given at the annual meeting of the American Society of Criminology, Chicago, IL.
1989 "The legal response to battering in the United States." Pp. 155-84 in Jalna Hanmer, Jill Radford, and Elizabeth Stanko (eds.), Women, Policing, and Male Violence. London: Tavistock.

Gelles, Richard J. and Murray A. Straus
1988 Intimate Violence. New York: Simon and Schuster.

Hart, William L., John Ashcroft, Ann Burgess, Newman Flanagan, Ursula Meese, Catherine Milton, Clyde Narramore, Ruben Ortega, and Frances Seward
1984 Attorney General's Task Force on Family Violence. Washington, DC: U.S. Department of Justice.

Lerman, Lisa G. and Franci Livingston
1983 "State legislation on domestic violence." Response 6:1-28.

Manning, Peter K.
1971 "The police: mandate, strategies, and appearances." Pp. 149-93 in Jack Douglas (ed.), Crime and Justice in American Society. Indianapolis, IN: Bobbs-Merrill.

Ortega, Ruben B.
1984 Operations Digest No. 84-85:1-2.

Parnas, Raymond
1967 "The police response to the domestic disturbance." Wisconsin Law Review 2:914-60.

Police Foundation
1976 Domestic Violence and the Police: Studies in Detroit and Kansas City. Washington, DC: The Police Foundation.

Schechter, Susan
1981 Women and Male Violence: The Visions and Struggles of the Battered Women's Movement. Boston, MA: South End.

Sherman, Lawrence W. and Richard A. Berk
1984 "The specific deterrent effects of arrest for domestic assault." American Sociological Review 49:261-72.

Smith, Douglas A. and Jody R. Klein
1984 "Police control of interpersonal disputes." Social Problems 31:466-81.

Stanko, Elizabeth A.
1985 Intimate Intrusions: Women's Experience of Male Violence. London: Routledge and Kegan Paul.

Straus, Murray, Suzanne K. Steinmetz, and Richard J. Gelles
1980 Behind Closed Doors. Garden City, NY: Anchor.

Taub, Nadine
1983 "Adult domestic violence: the law's response." Victimology 8:152-171.

U.S. Commission on Civil Rights
1978 Battered Women: Issues of Public Policy. Washington, DC: U.S. Government Printing Office.

Waaland, Pam and Stuart Keeley
1985 "Police decision making in wife abuse: the impact of legal and extralegal factors." Law and Human Behavior 9:355-66.

Walker, Lenore E.
1985 "Psychological impact of the criminalization of domestic violence on victims. Victimology 10:281-300.

Weller, Sheila
1988 "Middle-class murder." Ms. May:56-61.

Woods, Laurie
1986 Resource List: Battered Women: Litigation. New York: National Center on Women and Family Law.

RETHINKING BATTERED WOMAN SYNDROME: A BLACK FEMINIST PERSPECTIVE

Sharon Angella Allard*

Introduction

The plight of battered women gained national attention when Farrah Fawcett portrayed a battered spouse in the television movie *The Burning Bed*.[1] The program depicted the physical and psychological torture that leads a battered woman to take the life of her batterer, and the subsequent legal challenges she faces when claiming self-defense in response to a murder charge. Viewers observed a woman in the throes of a psychological breakdown and in fear of losing her life. But viewers never saw her anger. The lack of any hostility in the act of killing her husband made her actions appear justifiable, excusable, or at least sympathetic.

This perception of battered women as psychologically impaired and lacking hostility is not limited to the confines of television programs or movies. Consider, for example, the real-life stories of Hedda Nussbaum and Geraldine Mitchell. Each woman claimed to have been battered by her companion, and each woman was charged with the battering death of the child in her care. The charges against Nussbaum were dropped because "she was so beaten down — emotionally and physically — that she had been

* J.D., UCLA School of Law, 1991; B.A., Wesleyan University, 1985. This Essay was conceived in Professor Kimberlé Crenshaw's seminar, "Race and Gender in the Law," given at UCLA School of Law in the spring of 1990. The seminar provided the unique opportunity to develop theory through application. In addition to Professor Crenshaw, I would like to thank Callie Glanton, Victor Cannon, and Laura Reece for their time, comments, and encouragement. I am especially grateful to Elvina and Lincoln Allard who taught me that knowledge opens doors others would rather leave closed.

1. *The Burning Bed* (NBC television broadcast, Oct. 10, 1984).

powerless to stop [her companion]."[2] Mitchell, in contrast, "was not given a chance to testify in return for the dropping of charges"[3] and pleaded guilty to manslaughter. Despite almost identical factual situations, Mitchell's story was silenced while Nussbaum's was publicized and accepted. According to Mitchell's attorney, Mitchell was treated more harshly than Nussbaum because Mitchell was Black and poor while Nussbaum was white and middle class.[4] The courts' different treatments of these cases perpetuate a view in the public that the impact of battering on a woman's life varies, depending on whether a woman is Black or white.[5]

The relatively recent exposure of the plight of battered women led to a general theory of how a battered woman responds to her situation. In an effort to educate the court about why a battered woman might respond by killing, battered woman syndrome is often introduced at trials. As articulated by Lenore Walker, the syndrome is characterized by a cyclical pattern of psychological and physical abuse which can be broken down into three phases.[6] The first phase is marked by minor battering incidents, when tension builds and the woman exhibits complacent behavior to appease the batterer. The second phase is marked by an acute battering incident, when the woman feels completely isolated and helpless. The third phase is marked by a period of conciliation (the "honeymoon" period), when the batterer expresses his remorse and the woman is forgiving and understanding. Battered woman syndrome theory rests on the notion that a battered woman may suffer from "learned helplessness," whereby the psychological pressures of living in a constant state of fear limit her responses to coping with each individual attack rather than focusing on a way to escape her circumstances.[7] Expert witnesses testify to educate the jury about the reasonableness of the battered woman's conduct. In a homicide

2. Tumulty & Drogin, *Steinberg Convicted In Girl's Death; Jury Returns Manslaughter Verdict, Rejects Murder Count*, L.A. Times, Jan. 31, 1989, at A4, col. 1.

3. Fried, *Queens Mother Pleads Guilty in Fatal Battering of Boy, 3,* N.Y. Times, Jan. 24, 1991, at B2, col. 5.

4. *Id.*

5. The Essay will capitalize "Black" while not capitalizing "white." I mean to distinguish between Black as a cultural group as opposed to a skin color. "Blacks, like Asians, Latinos, and other 'minorities,' constitute a specific cultural group and, as such, require denotation as a proper noun." Crenshaw, *Race, Reform, and Retrenchment: Transformation and Legitimation in Antidiscrimination Law*, 101 HARV. L. REV. 1331, 1332 n.2 (1988). Inherent devaluation is communicated by the term "black," and so the capitalization also seeks to empower the cultural group.

6. *See generally* L. WALKER, THE BATTERED WOMAN (1979).

7. *See id.* at 42–70.

case, expert testimony on battered woman syndrome can comprise an essential part of a battered woman's case for self-defense.

To claim self-defense, a defendant must show that she "reasonably" believed that she was in "imminent" danger of serious bodily harm or death. For a belief to be reasonable, the threatened harm must be imminent. The prevailing definitions of reasonableness and imminence, however, exclude a battered woman. Without testimony on battered woman syndrome, the court will not admit evidence of prior abuses against the woman by her batterer on the grounds of irrelevance to the homicide. Consequently, a jury is unlikely to find that a battered woman's use of deadly force was based on a reasonable belief that she was in danger of imminent death or serious bodily harm. Yet, the circumstances under which a battered woman kills her batterer often do not reflect standard notions of imminent danger: a battered woman might strike out against her batterer when his back is turned, or when he is asleep or is inattentive in some other way. Such an action may be perceived as unreasonable because the woman was not necessarily in imminent harm. The classic, male orientation of the law of self-defense, coupled with gender stereotypes, limits the ability of judges and jurors to perceive a battered woman's conduct as reasonable.[8] Testimony on battered woman syndrome, therefore, makes an enormous difference in convincing juries that a battered woman's response was, in fact, a reasonable exercise of self-defense.

While battered woman's syndrome furthers the interest of some battered women, the theory incorporates stereotypes of limited applicability concerning how a woman would and, indeed, should react to battering. To successfully defend herself, a battered woman needs to convince a jury that she is a "normal" woman —

---

8. The chief criticism of the law of self-defense has been that it is inapplicable to the sociological experiences of women. In this context, as well as in the area of battered woman syndrome, the analysis employed is not wholly transferable to the experiences of Black women. Discussions on the sex biases in the law of self-defense point to the differences in the socialization of men and women with regard to the use of physical force and violence.

> A woman who has spent twenty, thirty or fifty years absorbing the message that she is, and ought to be, gentle, weak and helpless; that she needs to be protected from pain and injury; that she cannot really rely on her own strength to save her from danger . . . is bound to view a violent assault differently than a man whose own training in these matters is likely to have been so very different.

C. GILLESPIE, JUSTIFIABLE HOMICIDE: BATTERED WOMEN, SELF-DEFENSE, AND THE LAW 115–16 (1989). This characterization applies to all women to some degree. However, the dominant perception of Black women, coupled with their actual socialization, may render the above characterization inapplicable. *See infra* Part III.

weak, passive, and fearful. If the battered woman deviates from these characteristics, the jury may not associate her situation with that of the stereotypical battered woman. Therefore, it is possible that the difference in perception as to the reality of Nussbaum's and Mitchell's experiences with battering was shaped by cultural notions of who are "good" women and "bad" women.[9] Race certainly plays a major role in the cultural distinction between the "good" and "bad" woman. The passive, gentle white woman is automatically more like the "good" fairy tale princess stereotype than a Black woman, who as the "other" may be seen as the "bad" witch. White women have the benefit of this dual stereotype of "good" and "bad" women. If a woman is perceived as being a "good" woman, she can expect greater protection, while Black women are seen as "bad" and as deserving victims.[10]

This Essay demonstrates that while theories such as battered woman syndrome explain why a battered woman's behavior is reasonable, the definition of "woman" which guides such theories is based upon limited societal constructs of appropriate behavior for white women. This mythological standard, however, does not apply to the historical experiences of women of color, particularly Black women. Part I of the Essay addresses the need for an intersectional analysis of battered woman syndrome based upon race and gender. Such an analysis is needed to free all women from subordinating stereotypes. Part II compares the different historical legal treatment of Black and white women. The fact that Black and white women have been subordinated in different ways has resulted in distinct normative definitions of their roles as women. Finally, Part III explores media portrayals and images generated by the historical experiences of Black women. These images define Black wo-

---

9. Feminist scholars have developed the idea of "good" as opposed to "bad" women in the context of gender stereotypes. *See, e.g.*, A. DWORKIN, WOMAN HATING 17–46 (1974). The racial component of this concept, however, has not been widely explored.

I am expanding upon the concept set forth by Kimberlé Crenshaw that "Racist ideology . . . arrang[es] oppositional categories in a hierarchical order; historically, whites represented the dominant antinomy while Blacks came to be seen as separate and subordinate." Crenshaw, *supra* note 5, at 1373.

10. *See* Murray & Stahly, *Some Victims are Derogated More than Others*, 11 W.J. BLACK STUD. 177 (1987). The results of this study confirm that "the derogation of Black women relative to white women seems to be both a general and a pervasive phenomenon." *Id. See also* McClain, *Cause of Death — Homicide: A Research Note on Black Females as Homicide Victims*, 7 VICTIMOLOGY 204, 205 (1986). Although this Essay focuses on the experiences of Black women, the underlying arguments apply to all women who fall outside of the standard gender definitions described by current battered woman syndrome theory.

men in a manner which excludes them from the "feminist" critiques of either self-defense or battered woman syndrome. This Essay concludes that theories such as battered woman syndrome provide, at best, only a partial solution for explaining the conduct of battered women. By relying on prevailing definitions of "women," the theory does not address the law's refusal to recognize a battered woman's conduct as reasonable unless her conduct falls within a very narrow set of stereotypical behaviors and circumstances.

I. The Need for an Intersectional Analysis of Battered Woman Syndrome

An intersectional approach — one which incorporates a gender and race analysis — of battered woman syndrome is needed if the law is to address adequately the needs of all battered women.[11] Existing studies on the sexual biases in the law of self-defense and battered woman syndrome include little, if any, analysis as to how race and gender shape women's experiences of violence. Ideally, theories about battered woman syndrome should not marginalize any group of women, but should incorporate those experiences shaped by race and gender.[12] Racism alone does not cause the disproportionate conviction of Black women who kill their batterers. We must expose why stories about battered Black women are less credible to a jury than stories about battered white women.

Battered woman syndrome relies on prevailing gender characterizations of dominant, white society. A recent study identified

---

11. See Crenshaw, *Demarginalizing the Intersection of Race and Sex: A Black Feminist Critique of Antidiscrimination Doctrine, Feminist Theory and Antiracist Politics*, 1989 U. Chi. Legal F. 139, for an analysis of how race and gender are viewed as exclusive of one another and are treated as such in antidiscrimination law, feminist theory, and antiracist politics. This exclusive analysis results in the exclusion of Black women's legal claims.

12. *See* B. hooks, Ain't I a Woman: Black Women and Feminism (1981); P. Giddings, When and Where I Enter: The Impact of Black Women On Race and Sex in America (1984). Both works offer an historical analysis of the impact of Black women on race and gender in American society. Hooks's introduction presents the problem:

> No other group in America has so had their identity socialized out of existence as have black women. . . . When black people are talked about, sexism militates against the acknowledgement of the interests of black women; when women are talked about, racism militates against a recognition of black female interests. When black people are talked about the focus tends to be on black *men*; and when women are talked about the focus tends to be on *white* women.

B. hooks, *supra*, at 7.

forty-one sex role stereotypes.[13] A number of these stereotypes about women can be found in the battered woman syndrome characterization of women: very emotional, very submissive, very excitable in a minor crisis, very passive, very uncomfortable about being aggressive, very dependent, very gentle.[14] Each of these characterizations reflects traditional notions of what society considers appropriate behavior for "normal" women.

In contrast to these stereotypes, both the stereotypical images and the historical reality of Black women's experiences in the United States are interpreted by the dominant society as a manifestation of Black women's deviance from "normal" women. This deviance is reflected in the omnipresent images of the hostile Sapphire,[15] the wanton Jezebel,[16] and the strong and assertive Sojourner Truth.[17] The characterizations of the antagonistic yet subordinated Sapphire and the promiscuous Jezebel reaffirm society's belief that Blacks are less human and less individualistic than whites, while the strength found in the characterization of Sojourner is a direct challenge to the prevailing definitions of "pas-

---

13. *See* C. GILLESPIE, *supra* note 8, at 106.

14. *Id.*

15. Sapphire is the name of the Black female character in the television comedy *Amos 'n' Andy* about two Black males. Sapphire was the loud and sassy wife of one of the men. She regularly fought with her husband about his annoying behavior. The show was eventually discontinued after civil rights organizations complained about the stereotypical and derogatory depiction of Blacks. Today the term "Sapphire" conjures up images of a shrill, nagging, hostile, and aggressive Black woman. *See* Austin, *Sapphire Bound!*, 1989 WIS. L. REV. 539, 540 n.1; B. ANDREWS & A. JULLIARD, HOLY MACKEREL! THE AMOS 'N' ANDY STORY 15–16 (1986); NEW DICTIONARY OF AMERICAN SLANG 368 (R. Chapman ed. 1986).

16. Jezebel is defined as a woman who is "impudent, shameless, or abandoned." WEBSTER'S NEW COLLEGIATE DICTIONARY 616 (150th ed. 1981). "Jezebel was the wanton, libidinous black woman whose easy ways excused white men's abuse of their slaves as sexual partners." Austin, *supra* note 15, at 570; D. WHITE, AR'N'T I A WOMAN? FEMALE SLAVES IN THE PLANTATION SOUTH 46, 61 (1985).

17. Sojourner Truth freed herself from slavery to become an active abolitionist and suffragist. Her bold spirit and unswaying convictions became a touchstone within the 1970s women's rights movement. Truth is widely known for her response to a heckler at a women's rights convention in 1871:

> Truth asserted that women were not inherently weak and helpless. Raising herself to her full height of six feet, flexing a muscled arm, and bellowing with a voice one observer likened to the apocalyptic thunders, Truth informed the audience that she could outwork, outeat, and outlast any man. Then she challenged: "Ain't I a woman?"

P. GIDDINGS, *supra* note 12, at 54; BLACK WOMEN IN NINETEENTH-CENTURY AMERICAN LIFE: THEIR WORDS, THEIR THOUGHTS, THEIR FEELINGS 234 (B. Loewenberg & R. Bogin 3d ed. 1981).

sive" womanhood. Consequently, Black women must overcome the demeaning stereotypes of both race and gender.

To the extent that battered woman syndrome theory is based on stereotypes of white women, the theory is inapplicable to women of color. For instance, Black women's exclusion is evident in Lenore Walker's discussion of battered women and anger.[18] Walker stresses that for a battered woman to present a successful defense to a charge of killing her batterer, the woman must not appear angry. If the jury perceives that a woman killed out of anger, rather than fear, the jury is likely to give her a harsher penalty. This has disturbing implications for Black women, who Walker acknowledges are subject to the stereotype that all Black women are "angry."[19] Given that the legal system legitimizes these perceptions,[20] there is a greater likelihood that a jury would believe a prosecutor's story that a battered Black woman acted out of revenge and anger, as opposed to fear, in taking the life of her batterer.

While Walker recognizes that such perceptions greatly affect a Black woman's chances for acquittal when she kills her batterer, Walker does not offer an analysis of how battered woman syndrome, by its own terms, fails to address this problem. Consider the story of Sarah Smith, a Black woman who shot and killed her abusive husband to save her own life. Smith was convicted of second degree murder.[21] When asked by the prosecution if she considered leaving her husband when he was lying down, Smith responded: "Not without chancing that he would catch me at the door and blow my brains out[,] no."[22] Smith's story arguably would have

---

18. *See* L. WALKER, TERRIFYING LOVE: WHY BATTERED WOMEN KILL AND HOW SOCIETY RESPONDS 201–22 (1989).

19. The ratio of Black women to white women convicted of killing their abusive husbands is nearly two to one in one of my studies. My feeling is that this is the result of our society's misperceptions of Black people in general, of women in general, and of Black women in particular. The "angry Black woman" is a common stereotype in many white minds; subtly, but no less powerfully, white society in America fears "Black anger."

Id. at 206.

20. The courts have permitted prosecutors to use peremptory challenges to strike prospective Black jurors on the basis that such persons appeared to be hostile. *See* Johnson, *Black Innocence and the White Jury*, 83 MICH. L. REV. 1611 (1985). Similarly, it is unlikely that a potential employer will be found to have discriminated on the basis of race if she can point to specific deficiencies in an applicant's interview even when these deficiencies may reflect cultural biases.

21. Golden, *Abused Wife Is Found Guilty of Murder; Self-Defense Plea Rejected*, N.Y. Times, Jan. 24, 1991, at A16, col. 4. One juror commented, "We didn't believe her."

22. *Id.*

been accepted by the jury if battered woman syndrome did not limit a battered woman's motivation to a response based solely on a woman's fear. Moreover, Smith's story would have been more "believable" to a jury under a theory which legitimized a battered woman who acted from a position of strength rather than of weakness. Such a theory does not now exist; such a theory is needed.

II. The Historical Legal View of "Women" Is Race-Based

The Anglo-American legal tradition initially viewed women as property. This view was based on the patriarchal gender stereotypes of active, masculine, powerful, and authoritative men and passive, feminine, powerless, and deferential women.[23] In 1897, British jurist William Blackstone held that men were responsible for the actions of their wives and therefore authorized to control them.[24] Included within men's responsibility was a duty to protect their wives. Therefore, "good" women were not expected to have to defend themselves in any fashion. Women were certainly not permitted to kill their protectors for any reason.[25]

Feminist theorists criticize these traditional laws as reflecting the "origin of law as a form of male authority and power."[26] These theorists argue that the adoption of sexist images results in paternalistic laws designed to protect women.[27] But such critiques ignore

23. D. Wareha & R. Castillo, Afro-American and Mexican-American Women Who Have Been Victims of Domestic Violence (Battered) in Los Angeles County Shelters (June 1985) (Thesis, Graduate School of Social Welfare, UCLA); L. Gilbert & P. Webster, Bound By Love: The Sweet Trap of Daughterhood, xvi (1982).

24. Husband and wife, in the language of the law, are styled *baron* and *feme*. . . . [I]f the baron kills his feme it is the same as if he had killed a stranger, or any other person; but if the feme kills her baron, it is regarded by the laws as a much more atrocious crime, as she not only breaks through the restraints of humanity and conjugal affection, but throws off all subjection to the authority of her husband. And therefore the law denominates her crime a species of treason, and condemns her to the same punishment as if she had killed the king. And for every species of treason . . . the sentence of women was to be drawn and burnt alive.

Schneider, *Equal Rights to Trial For Women: Sex Bias in the Law of Self-Defense*, 15 Harv. C.R.-C.L. L. Rev. 623, 629 (1980) (quoting 1 W. Blackstone, Commentaries on the Laws of England 418 n.103 (R. Welsh & Co. ed. 1897)).

25. *Id.*

26. Rifkin, *Toward a Theory of Law and Patriarchy*, 3 Harv. Women's L.J. 83, 87 (1980).

27. The conventional policy wisdom of the eighteenth and nineteenth centuries regarded women as appropriately dependent on men. Women were thought incapable of determining important matters for themselves, too virtuous to be exposed to the rough and tumble of the larger world.

the distinct impact of race in the assignment of gender definitions. Sexist as these protectionist images may have been, they were not meant for Black women. Throughout history, Black women's experiences with patriarchy differed from those of white women.[28]

Black women's historical and social experiences under slavery and thereafter resulted in images which define Black women as deviant. While the Victorian notion of "true womanhood" defined white women as possessing unquestionable moral character, Black women were defined as immoral.[29] This race-based difference in stereotypes made it easier for white men to justify the sexual exploitation of Black women. Such stereotypes also made it easier for white women to accept the exploitation of Black women. Because exploitation was ignored or justified, Black women were not perceived as deserving of male protection.[30] For example, the law historically denied that Black slave women could be raped because they were regarded as immoral. This perception continues to influence the investigation and prosecution of rape charges brought by Black women today.[31]

The difference between how Black and white women are treated and perceived also stems from the fact that Blacks as a group have not received the protection of the law and have histori-

---

D. KIRP, M. YUDOF & M. FRANKS, GENDER JUSTICE 30 (1986).

28. Family life during slavery presents but one example of this difference. While white women's experiences were marked by a paternalistic protection in the domestic sphere, Black women were subjected to the sexual and economic desires of their captors.

29. P. GIDDINGS, *supra* note 12, at 46–48. Giddings discusses how economic expansion in the 1830s resulted in the growth of a new middle class seeking to reach upper class status.

> For women, the vehicle for these aspirations was what became known as the "cult of the lady" or the "cult of true womanhood." . . . [A] woman had to be true to the cult's cardinal tenets of domesticity, submissiveness, piety, and purity in order to be good enough for society's inner circles. Failing to adhere to any of these tenets — which the overwhelming number of Black women could hardly live up to — made one less than a moral, "true" woman.

Id. at 47.

30. *See infra* Part III for a discussion of the masculine characterization of Black women.

31. See Wriggins, *Rape, Racism and the Law*, 6 HARV. WOMEN'S L. J. 103, 117–23, for a discussion of the law's failure to address the rape of Black women. Wriggins traces this denial through slavery (rape of Black women by both Black and white men legal) and the Post-Civil War Period (fact of Black defendant only relevant to prove intent to rape a white woman). She notes recent studies showing both that white judges and juries impose harsher sentences when the victim is white and that decisions to prosecute for rape are based on differences in the perceptions of chastity based on race.

cally been denied all rights.[32] While laws formally changed, recent statistics continue to reflect that crimes committed against whites have higher prosecution rates and result in longer sentences than crimes committed against Blacks.[33] Again, Black women are saddled with dual stereotypes of race and gender. As women, they have to overcome the presumption that the law provides sufficient protection for them. As Black women, they must further prove that they are deserving of such protection.

This difference in stereotyping is what makes battered woman syndrome all the more damaging; not only does the theory perpetuate dominant gender role stereotypes, but it does so to the exclusion of Black women. Therefore, when a jury hears a story of a downtrodden woman completely overwrought by the circumstances of her situation and in fear for her life, it is less likely that they will accept this story as applied to women whose history and present day images deny their need for protection. It is true that white women may face this risk due to the "good" woman/"bad" woman dichotomy. However, while white battered women have to transcend one set of stereotypes to achieve the "good" woman status, Black women, who are in a sense twice removed from this status, have a far heavier burden.

III. Media Images and Social Perceptions of Black Women: The Impact of Race and Gender in the Law of Self-Defense and Battered Woman Syndrome

Black women generally fall outside the dominant gender definitions upon which battered woman syndrome and feminist analyses of self-defense rely. The media provides much of the information about persons outside of the majority population.[34] Deviant images of Black women abound in society. Images which accurately repre-

32. Both during and after slavery, Blacks were subjected to white discipline and control as a matter of law; first through the use of slavery codes and then through "Black" codes. For a more expansive treatment of these issues, see A. Higgenbotham, In the Matter of Color (1978); D. Bell, Race, Racism and American Law 85 (1980).

33. *See* McCleskey v. Kemp, 481 U.S. 279, 312 (1987) (statistics show that the race of the defendant and the victim are often factors which lead to disparities in death penalty sentencing); Bureau of Justice Statistics, U.S. Dep't of Justice, Sourcebook of Criminal Justice Statistics 692 table 6.70 (1984) (data indicates that a larger number of nonwhites than whites are executed).

34. Mass media contributes to the "public's conceptions of reality, the 'facts', concepts, and definitions from which people construct their beliefs about the world in general and about social reality in particular." Discourse and Discrimination 24 (G. Smitherman-Donaldson & T. Van Dijk ed. 1988).

sent the experiences of Black women exist, but nonetheless remain outside the dominant view of who is a "real" woman.

One image of the Black woman is that of an immoral, promiscuous being.[35] This image arose from a perverted reversal of the historical sexual exploitation of Black women. Current media images perpetuate this perversion. For example, in a commercial for an automobile, Tina Turner appears in shorn clothing while her counterpart, Lindsay Wagner, appears in long, light, and airy ensembles. Actress/singer Grace Jones will never run out of material to continue her public persona as strange yet enticing and seemingly masochistic.[36] These commercial images do not exactly replicate the extreme degradation of Black women found in the Black exploitation films[37] of the 1970s. Many contemporary images of Black women, however, may be derived from these films. Black exploitation films portrayed Black women as mindless sex objects "to be used and abused without rationale by white and black males

---

35. After slavery ended, the sexual exploitation of black women continued, in both the North and the South. . . . To sustain it, in the face of the nominal freedom of black men, a complex system of supportive mechanisms and sustaining myths was created. One of these was the myth of the "bad" black woman. By assuming a different level of sexuality for all Blacks than that of whites and mythifying their greater sexual potency, the black woman could be made to personify sexual freedom and abandon. A myth was created that all black women were eager for sexual exploits, voluntarily "loose" in their morals and, therefore, deserved none of the consideration and respect granted to white women.

G. LERNER, BLACK WOMEN IN WHITE AMERICA: A DOCUMENTARY HISTORY 163 (1973).

36. Grace Jones is a Jamaican-born Black woman who is a singer, model, and actress. Her hairstyle, attire, and performance style have earned her a myriad of images including: "jungle cat," Rosemberg, *Guillotines, Sheep Chopped From French Revolution Parade*, Reuters, Feb. 11, 1989 (LEXIS, Nexis); "androgynous," Wrong, *French Impresario Plans Surrealist Bastille Day Parade*, Reuters, Feb. 11, 1989 (LEXIS, Nexis); "erotic menace — she once appeared in a tiger cage gnawing raw meat," *The Stars, The Sounds, The Screens of June*, LIFE, June 1985, at 139; "an image either sexless or voraciously sexy, depending on your point of view," *Jungle Fever; by Jean-Paul Goude*, PEOPLE, Oct. 25, 1982, at 12. Grace Jones "once wore a dress so tight she had to be carried up the stairs to the stage by a bodyguard," O'Malley & Gratteau, *No Biz Like Show Biz*, Chi. Tribune, Mar. 11, 1987, § 1, at 16, col. 1.

The purpose of sketching this contrast is simply to identify the fact that the public images which we observe reflect a historical construction which labels Black women as "other."

37. The term refers to a genre of film from the 70s which depicted streetwise Black men (and sometimes women) as the central characters in action adventure stories. The films were widely criticized as derogatory for their portrayal of Blacks as pimps, drug dealers, hustlers, or other criminal types. *See* Mills, *Blaxploitation 101: A Brief Film History of Sticking It to the Man*, Wash. Post, Nov. 4, 1990, at G1, col. 2.

in films."[38] Black women's sexuality continues to be portrayed as deviant. Black women are represented as sex objects and as comparatively more sexually aggressive and available than white women.

The media has since moved away from the extreme caricatures of Pam Grier as a "female superspade"[39] in the movie *Foxy Brown*[40] or the role played by Diana Sands as the adulterous wife who seduces her white landlord while her husband is imprisoned in the movie *The Landlord*.[41] Nonetheless, when they appear in current films, Black women are vividly portrayed as sexually immoral. In the movie *Coming to America,*[42] for example, there is no need to juxtapose a Black woman's sexual immorality against the virtuousness of a white woman's, because the contrast between the portrayals of the darker-skinned sister's sexual exploits as compared to the angelic existence of her older fair-complexioned sister is obvious. In the movie *48 Hours,*[43] the only Black woman depicted is a prostitute.

The overall image of Black women on prime time television is still in conflict with the normative definition of womanhood. For

---

38. BLACK FILMS AND FILMAKERS: A COMPREHENSIVE ANTHOLOGY FROM STEREOTYPE TO SUPERHERO 199 (Patterson ed. 1975) [hereinafter BLACK FILMS AND FILMAKERS]. In an interview, Donald Bogle, a historian of Blacks in television and film, discussed the troubling images in Black exploitation films, including those of Black women,

> who were often "thrown in and out of bed" by the ever-ready hero. Even when a black woman was the star, playing a tough, assertive character, as Pam Grier did in "Coffy" and "Foxy Brown," the viewer still knew "she was going to get tied up, the blouse was going to pop open, the breasts were going to surface."

See Mills, *supra* note 37, at G6, col. 5.

39. A superspade was the characterization given to the Black heroes of the Black exploitation films of the 1970s. "Typical is the main character of the 1971 MGM movie *Shaft*. Indestructible, flippant, romantic and triumphant . . . . Superspade is just another caricature." D. LEAB, FROM SAMBO TO SUPERSPADE: THE BLACK EXPERIENCE IN MOTION PICTURES 4, 237 (1975).

40. A newspaper review of the 1974 American International release described the movie.

> Before femme might makes right, Grier and callgirl Juanita Brown have a brawl in a lesbian bar . . . doxy Sally Ann Stroud has her throat slashed, two degenerate white thugs who've raped Grier are burned to death, and white Brown is castrated. Tasteful finale has Grier delivering Brown's private parts in a pickle jar to leader Loder before driving off with neighborhood vigilante leader . . . .

Variety, Apr. 17, 1974, at 16, col. 5.

41. *See* BLACK FILMS AND FILMAKERS, *supra* note 38, at 199.

42. *Coming To America* (Paramount 1988).

43. *48 Hours* (Paramount 1988).

example, the television program *Miami Vice*[44] attempts to justify the scantily clad Olivia Brown ("Trudy") by making her an undercover detective. As an "undercover detective," she mostly poses as a prostitute. The image of sexual aggressiveness is again depicted on the television show *227*[45] in which Black actress Jackee plays the role of Sandra, whose sole purpose in life is to obtain as many male companions as possible.[46]

Very few Black female television characters are likely to be depicted as passive or demure. In fact, it is more likely that their assertiveness would be interpreted as reflective of some element of a "Sapphire."[47] Recent examples include the younger sisters on *Family Matters*,[48] who spend a great deal of their time verbally abusing their older brother and finding ways to ingratiate themselves with their parents, and Robin Givens's role in *Head of the Class* as a self-centered domineering high school student.[49]

Moreover, the women of the *Cosby Show*[50] and *A Different World*[51] challenge prevailing notions about the traditional role of women by occupying equal, if not domineering positions, with respect to their male counterparts on the shows.[52] The fact that the majority of Black female characters on television appear in situation

---

44. *Miami Vice* (NBC television broadcast, 1984).

45. *227* (NBC television broadcast, 1985).

46. It is interesting to compare the character of Chrissie, a white woman, on the television program *Three's Company* (ABC television broadcast, 1977) with the character of Sandra on *227*. While Chrissie's dress is at least as suggestive as Sandra's, she is portrayed as having no sexual interests outside of marriage. She shares her room with another female, and the two regularly rebuff their male roommate's sexual advances. Sandra, on the other hand, lives alone and cannot wait until her next "hot date." A comparison of the two characters provides a stark contrast in imagery.

47. *See supra* note 15 and accompanying text.

48. *Family Matters* (ABC television broadcast, 1989).

49. *Head of the Class* (ABC television broadcast, 1986). In one episode involving a competition for high school queen, Givens threatened the white male student chair of the program to obtain a promise that she would be queen while her white counterparts cajoled him with flattery and flirts to obtain the same promise.

50. *Cosby Show* (NBC television broadcast, 1984).

51. *A Different World* (NBC television broadcast, 1987).

52. Other illustrations abound. Take, for example, the women of *227* (NBC television broadcast, 1985). All of the characters are domineering and aggressive: Pearl the elderly grandmother reigns over her teenage grandson; Rose is the single landlady of the building; Mary, though a loving mother and wife, nonetheless frequently challenges her husband. Similarly, on the television show *Amen* (NBC television broadcast, 1986), Thelma, the daughter of a deacon, is anything but demure and obedient. She is always ready to assert her quick tongue, fierce eyes, and aggressive posture anytime another woman threatens her relationship with her husband.

comedies further challenges their legitimacy.[53] While these characters' assertiveness may be considered a positive attribute by feminists, this potential positive effect is substantially weakened by the fact that these characters are not meant to be taken seriously by the viewer.

All of the above images deviate from or directly challenge those of the traditional passive woman. Because battered woman syndrome is based on the traditional view of the "normal," passive woman, the theory does little to help Black women who are excluded from this stereotype. The dominant images of Black women as domineering, assertive, hostile, and immoral may hinder a judge's or juror's ability to comprehend a Black woman's act of self-defense as based on "learned helplessness"[54] in much the same way that gender definitions of white women serve as an obstacle in the law of self-defense. While a white woman's conduct in killing may be viewed as inapposite to traditional gender roles, the same conduct by a Black woman may be viewed as typical of her character.

The historical acceptance of wife beating[55] also makes it less likely that a jury will perceive any present or prior beating as indicative of bodily harm sufficient to justify the use of deadly harm by any woman. This is particularly likely to be the case for Black women who are considered "strong and suffering."[56] The perception that Black women possess more physical strength than white women may decrease the likelihood that a Black woman reasonably believed that she was in danger of serious bodily harm.[57] This per-

53. STEENLAND, UNEQUAL PICTURE: BLACK, HISPANIC, ASIAN AND NATIVE AMERICAN CHARACTERS ON T.V. (1989) (National Commission on Working Women, Washington, D.C.). Additionally, Black sitcoms in syndication such as *The Jeffersons* (CBS television broadcast, 1975); *Good Times* (CBS television broadcast, 1974); *What's Happening* (ABC television broadcast, 1976); and *Sanford and Son* (NBC television broadcast, 1972) provide even more extreme images of Black women as Sapphires.

54. *See supra* note 7 and accompanying text.

55. *See* Schneider, *supra* note 24, at 627–30 (discussing the legal origins of the sanctioning of woman abuse based on a notion that women were property to be protected by men).

56. Gloria Naylor in an essay on the myth of the strong Black woman also traces the roots of this imagery to the role of Black women during slavery: "They were stronger creatures; they didn't feel pain in childbirth; they didn't have tear ducts."

Naylor, *The Myth of the Matriarch*, LIFE, Spring 1988, at 65. Naylor also points out that Black women themselves may have adopted this perception at great cost to their personal well-being by feeling that if they are not able to withstand all things they are somehow inadequate. This observation provides an interesting perspective from which to evaluate the experiences of Black women who are battered. *Id.*

57. The image of the strong Black woman arose during slavery to justify the disparate treatment of Black women and white women with regard to labor. "To explain the black female's ability to survive without the direct aid of a male and her ability to

ception of Black women is further perpetuated today in theories which assert either implicitly or explicitly that Black women are emasculating or matriarchal. For example, the current policy debate concerning the status of the "underclass" tends to focus on the plight of Black men, which implies that Black female-headed households are the real problem for the underclass.[58] Moreover, the moralistic overtones of this debate contributes to the perception that Black women are sexually immoral.[59]

The relevance of the differences in the normative definitions of Black women and white women may not be significant with regard to self-defense if neither woman's behavior is considered reasonable. The distinction is significant, however, in the context of battered woman syndrome theory. The theory's use of characterizations which reflect traditional gender role stereotypes appears to be an attempt to restore the battered woman's image to reflect society's normative definition of a normal woman. But this definition does not apply to women who are considered "other." "Black men and women live in a society that creates sex-based norms and expectations which racism operates simultaneously to deny; Black men are not viewed as powerful, nor are Black women seen as passive."[60] Thus, battered woman syndrome essentially excludes Black women.

CONCLUSION

Battered woman syndrome presents a troubling paradox. For some battered women, the theory is a viable tool for satisfying the legal standard of self-defense and for explaining their behavior as reasonable. For others, the theory's use of standard gender definitions may not only exclude some battered women but may actually

---

perform tasks that were culturally defined as 'male' work, white males argued that black slave women were not 'real' women but were masculinized sub-human creatures." B. HOOKS, *supra* note 12, at 71.

58. "Anti-feminists argue that changing sex role patterns have threatened males so that they are demonstrating their anger by domestic brutality. As supporters of male dominance they assert that violent acts against women will continue until society returns to the good old-fashioned days of sharply delineated sex roles." *Id.* at 105. *See also* W. WILSON, THE TRULY DISADVANTAGED: THE INNER CITY, THE UNDERCLASS AND PUBLIC POLICY (1987); D. MOYNIHAN, *The Tangle of Pathology* in THE NEGRO FAMILY: A CASE FOR NATIONAL ACTION (1965) (This controversial report asserted the existence of a matriarchal family structure among Black households was the reason for the low socio-economic progress of Blacks in America.)

59. McGrory, *Moynihan Was Right 21 Years Ago*, Wash. Post, Jan. 26, 1986, at B1, col. 1; Will, *Voting Rights Won't Fix It*, Wash. Post, Jan. 23, 1986, at A23, col. 5. Both articles point to irresponsible sexual conduct as the primary cause of the underclass.

60. *See* Crenshaw, *supra* note 11, at 155.

impose an additional obstacle. To the extent that battered woman syndrome restores a battered woman's image to that of a "good" woman, the theory implicitly embraces the notion that there are "good" women and "bad" women. This dichotomy necessarily implies there is an "other" who can be pointed to as lacking in the characteristics of "true womanhood." Therefore, to assert battered woman syndrome successfully, a woman must avoid association with any of the images of "other."[61] Such avoidance is especially difficult for a Black woman, who is viewed as "other" simply by virtue of her skin color. Thus, battered woman syndrome fails as a viable theory for *all* battered women.

While it may be possible to expand the characterizations or terminology upon which battered woman syndrome relies, this would also be a limited solution. The problems which spawned the need for theories such as battered woman syndrome still remain. The law of self-defense is a narrow vehicle for accommodating the specific circumstances in which women may find it necessary to take defensive action. Battered woman syndrome explains the behavior of battered women within fairly strict categories, i.e. that a woman is fearful, weak, and submissive. Yet, the theory provides no means for assessing the reasonableness of the woman's act of killing unless she is given the "excuse" of learned helplessness. "Excuse connotes personal weakness and implies that the defendant could not be expected to function as would a 'normal' person."[62]

Even an analysis that criticizes battered woman syndrome for pigeonholing the battered women's behavior as unreasonable relies on dominant gender-based experiences.[63] Gender-based theories that do not incorporate race and class will be as problematic as battered woman syndrome. As long as such theories rely on majority gender definitions, the majority will marginalize the experiences of the minority.

---

61. Such images include those based on ethnicity, class, and sexual orientation as well as race.

62. Sagaw, *A Hard Case for Feminists: People v. Goetz*, 10 HARV. WOMEN'S L.J. 253, 256 n.21 (1987).

63. *See* Littleton, *Women's Experience and the Problem of Transition: Perspectives on Male Battering of Women*, 1989 U. CHI. LEGAL F. 23. While this work provides a legitimate critique of battered woman syndrome, it is nonetheless a gender-based analysis; it is suggested that another explanation for why a battered woman remains in an abusive relationship is the connection thesis which describes women as connected to others (materially in the context of pregnancy), and as fearing abandonment and isolation.

Measures must be taken to isolate and redefine established gender norms. The lack of a comprehensive analysis incorporating the effects of race, class, and gender on the legal system reinforces the necessity of "multiple consciousness as jurisprudential method."[64] This is not to suggest that the existing studies and theories are without merit. Rather, it is a call to recognize the harm which will continue in the absence of an intersectional analysis of feminist legal principles.

64. Matsuda, *When the First Quail Calls: Multiple Consciousness as Jurisprudential Method*, 11 WOMEN'S RTS. L. REP. 7 (1989).

Mapping the Margins: Intersectionality, Identity Politics, and Violence Against Women of Color

Kimberle Crenshaw*

Introduction

Over the last two decades, women have organized against the almost routine violence that shapes their lives.[1] Drawing from the strength of shared experience, women have recognized that the political demands of millions speak more powerfully than the pleas of a few isolated voices. This politicization in turn has transformed the way we understand violence against women. For example, battering and rape, once seen as private (family matters) and aberrational (errant sexual aggression), are now largely recognized as part of a broad-scale system of domination that affects women as a class.[2] This process of recognizing as social and systemic what was for-

---

* © 1993 by Kimberle Crenshaw. Professor of Law, University of California, Los Angeles. B.A. Cornell University, 1981; J.D. Harvard Law School, 1984; LL.M. University of Wisconsin, 1985.

I am indebted to a great many people who have pushed this project along. For their kind assistance in facilitating my field research for this article, I wish to thank Maria Blanco, Margaret Cambrick, Joan Creer, Estelle Cheung, Nilda Rimonte and Fred Smith. I benefitted from the comments of Taunya Banks, Mark Barenberg, Darcy Calkins, Adrienne Davis, Gina Dent, Brent Edwards, Paul Gewirtz, Lani Guinier, Neil Gotanda, Joel Handler, Duncan Kennedy, Henry Monaghan, Elizabeth Schneider and Kendall Thomas. A very special thanks goes to Gary Peller and Richard Yarborough. Jayne Lee, Paula Puryear, Yancy Garrido, Eugenia Gifford and Leti Volpp provided valuable research assistance. I gratefully acknowledge the support of the Academic Senate of UCLA, Center for Afro-American Studies at UCLA, the Reed Foundation and Columbia Law School. Earlier versions of this article were presented to the Critical Race Theory Workshop and the Yale Legal Theory Workshop.

This article is dedicated to the memory of Denise Carty-Bennia and Mary Joe Frug.

1. Feminist academics and activists have played a central role in forwarding an ideological and institutional challenge to the practices that condone and perpetuate violence against women. *See generally* SUSAN BROWNMILLER, AGAINST OUR WILL: MEN, WOMEN AND RAPE (1975); LORENNE M.G. CLARK & DEBRA J. LEWIS, RAPE: THE PRICE OF COERCIVE SEXUALITY (1977); R. EMERSON DOBASH & RUSSELL DOBASH, VIOLENCE AGAINST WIVES: A CASE AGAINST THE PATRIARCHY (1979); NANCY GAGER & CATHLEEN SCHURR, SEXUAL ASSAULT: CONFRONTING RAPE IN AMERICA (1976); DIANA E.H. RUSSELL, THE POLITICS OF RAPE: THE VICTIM'S PERSPECTIVE (1974); ELIZABETH ANNE STANKO, INTIMATE INTRUSIONS: WOMEN'S EXPERIENCE OF MALE VIOLENCE (1985); LENORE E. WALKER, TERRIFYING LOVE: WHY BATTERED WOMEN KILL AND HOW SOCIETY RESPONDS (1989); LENORE E. WALKER, THE BATTERED WOMAN SYNDROME (1984); LENORE E. WALKER, THE BATTERED WOMAN (1979).

2. *See, e.g.*, SUSAN SCHECHTER, WOMEN AND MALE VIOLENCE: THE VISIONS AND STRUGGLES OF THE BATTERED WOMEN'S MOVEMENT (1982) (arguing that battering is a means of maintaining women's subordinate position); S. BROWNMILLER, *supra* note 1 (arguing that rape is a

merly perceived as isolated and individual has also characterized the identity politics of African Americans, other people of color, and gays and lesbians, among others. For all these groups, identity-based politics has been a source of strength, community, and intellectual development.

The embrace of identity politics, however, has been in tension with dominant conceptions of social justice. Race, gender, and other identity categories are most often treated in mainstream liberal discourse as vestiges of bias or domination—that is, as intrinsically negative frameworks in which social power works to exclude or marginalize those who are different. According to this understanding, our liberatory objective should be to empty such categories of any social significance. Yet implicit in certain strands of feminist and racial liberation movements, for example is the view that the social power in delineating difference need not be the power of domination; it can instead be the source of social empowerment and reconstruction.

The problem with identity politics is not that it fails to transcend difference, as some critics charge, but rather the opposite—that it frequently conflates or ignores intragroup differences. In the context of violence against women, this elision of difference in identity politics is problematic, fundamentally because the violence that many women experience is often shaped by other dimensions of their identities, such as race and class. Moreover, ignoring difference *within* groups contributes to tension *among* groups, another problem of identity politics that bears on efforts to politicize violence against women. Feminist efforts to politicize experiences of women and antiracist efforts to politicize experiences of people of color have frequently proceeded as though the issues and experiences they each detail occur on mutually exclusive terrains. Although racism and sexism readily intersect in the lives of real people, they seldom do in feminist and antiracist practices. And so, when the practices expound identity as woman or person of color as an either/or proposition, they relegate the identity of women of color to a location that resists telling.

My objective in this article is to advance the telling of that location by exploring the race and gender dimensions of violence against women of color.[3] Contemporary feminist and antiracist discourses have failed to con-

---

patriarchal practice that subordinates women to men); Elizabeth Schneider, *The Violence of Privacy*, 23 CONN. L. REV. 973, 974 (1991) (discussing how "concepts of privacy permit, encourage and reinforce violence against women"); Susan Estrich, *Rape*, 95 YALE L.J. 1087 (1986) (analyzing rape law as one illustration of sexism in criminal law); *see also* CATHARINE A. MACKINNON, SEXUAL HARASSMENT OF WORKING WOMEN: A CASE OF SEX DISCRIMINATION 143-213 (1979) (arguing that sexual harassment should be redefined as sexual discrimination actionable under Title VII, rather than viewed as misplaced sexuality in the workplace).

3. This article arises out of and is inspired by two emerging scholarly discourses. The first is critical race theory. For a cross-section of what is now a substantial body of literature, see PATRICIA J. WILLIAMS, THE ALCHEMY OF RACE AND RIGHTS (1991); Robin D. Barnes, *Race Consciousness: The Thematic Content of Racial Distinctiveness in Critical Race Scholarship*, 103 HARV. L. REV. 1864 (1990); John O. Calmore, *Critical Race Theory, Archie Shepp, and Fire Music: Securing an Authentic Intellectual Life in a Multicultural World*, 65 S. CAL. L. REV. 2129 (1992); Anthony E. Cook, *Beyond Critical Legal Studies: The Reconstructive Theology of Dr. Martin Luther King*, 103 HARV. L. REV. 985 (1990); Kimberle Williams Crenshaw, *Race, Reform and Retrenchment: Transformation and Legitimation in Antidiscrimination Law*, 101 HARV. L. REV. 1331 (1988); Richard

sider intersectional identities such as women of color.[4] Focusing on two dimensions of male violence against women—battering and rape—I consider how the experiences of women of color are frequently the product of intersecting patterns of racism and sexism,[5] and how these experiences tend not

---

Delgado, *When a Story is Just a Story: Does Voice Really Matter?*, 76 VA. L. REV. 95 (1990); Neil Gotanda, *A Critique of "Our Constitution is Colorblind,"* 44 STAN. L. REV. 1 (1991) Mari J. Matsuda, *Public Response to Racist Speech: Considering the Victim's Story*, 87 MICH. L. REV. 2320 (1989); Charles R. Lawrence III, *The Id, the Ego, and Equal Protection: Reckoning with Unconscious Racism*, 39 STAN. L. REV. 317 (1987); Gerald Torres, *Critical Race Theory: The Decline of the Universalist Ideal and the Hope of Plural Justice—Some Observations and Questions of an Emerging Phenomenon*, 75 MINN. L. REV. 993 (1991). For a useful overview of critical race theory, see Calmore, *supra*, at 2160-2168.

A second, less formally linked body of legal scholarship investigates the connections between race and gender. *See, e.g.*, Regina Austin, *Sapphire Bound!*, 1989 WIS. L. REV. 539; Crenshaw, *supra*; Angela P. Harris, *Race and Essentialism in Feminist Legal Theory*, 42 STAN. L. REV. 581 (1990); Marlee Kline, *Race, Racism and Feminist Legal Theory*, 12 HARV. WOMEN'S L.J. 115 (1989); Dorothy E. Roberts, *Punishing Drug Addicts Who Have Babies: Women of Color, Equality and the Right of Privacy*, 104 HARV. L. REV. 1419 (1991); Cathy Scarborough, *Conceptualizing Black Women's Employment Experiences*, 98 YALE L.J. 1457 (1989) (student author); Peggie R. Smith, *Separate Identities: Black Women, Work and Title VII*, 14 HARV. WOMEN'S L.J. 21 (1991); Judy Scales-Trent, *Black Women and the Constitution: Finding Our Place, Asserting Our Rights*, 24 HARV. C.R-C.L. L. REV. 9 (1989); Judith A. Winston, *Mirror, Mirror on the Wall: Title VII, Section 1981, and the Intersection of Race and Gendeɪ ɪn the Civil Rights Act of 1990*, 79 CAL. L. REV. 775 (1991). This work in turn has been informed oy a broader literature examining the interactions of race and gender in other contexts. *See, e.g.*, PATRICIA HILL COLLINS, BLACK FEMINIST THOUGHT: KNOWLEDGE, CONSCIOUSNESS, AND THE POLITICS OF EMPOWERMENT (1990); ANGELA DAVIS, WOMEN, RACE AND CLASS (1981); BELL HOOKS, AIN'T I A WOMAN? BLACK WOMEN AND FEMINISM (1981); ELIZABETH V. SPELMAN, INESSENTIAL WOMAN: PROBLEMS OF EXCLUSION IN FEMINIST THOUGHT (1988); Frances Beale, *Double Jeopardy: To Be Black and Female*, in THE BLACK WOMAN 90 (Toni Cade ed. 1970); Kink-Kok Cheung, *The Woman Warrior versus The Chinaman Pacific: Must a Chinese American Critic Choose between Feminism and Heroism?*, in CONFLICTS IN FEMINISM 234 (Marianne Hirsch & Evelyn Fox Keller eds. 1990); Deborah H. King, *Multiple Jeopardy, Multiple Consciousness: The Context of a Black Feminist Ideology*, 14 SIGNS 42 (1988); Diane K. Lewis, *A Response to Inequality: Black Women, Racism and Sexism*, 3 SIGNS 339 (1977); Deborah E. McDowell, *New Directions for Black Feminist Criticism*, in THE NEW FEMINIST CRITICISM: ESSAYS ON WOMEN, LITERATURE AND THEORY 186 (Elaine Showalter ed. 1985); Valerie Smith, *Black Feminist Theory and the Representation of the "Other"*, in CHANGING OUR OWN WORDS: ESSAYS ON CRITICISM, THEORY AND WRITING BY BLACK WOMEN 38 (Cheryl A. Wall ed. 1989).

4. Although the objective of this article is to describe the intersectional location of women of color and their marginalization within dominant resistance discourses, I do not mean to imply that the disempowerment of women of color is singularly or even primarily caused by feminist and antiracist theorists or activists. Indeed, I hope to dispell any such simplistic interpretations by capturing, at least in part, the way that prevailing structures of domination shape various discourses of resistance. As I have noted elsewhere, "People can only demand change in ways that reflect the logic of the institutions they are challenging. Demands for change that do not reflect . . . dominant ideology . . . will probably be ineffective." Crenshaw, *supra* note 3, at 1367. Although there are significant political and conceptual obstacles to moving against structures of domination with an intersectional sensibility, my point is that the effort to do so should be a central theoretical and political objective of both antiracism and feminism.

5. Although this article deals with violent assault perpetrated by men against women, women are also subject to violent assault by women. Violence among lesbians is a hidden but significant problem. One expert reported that in a study of 90 lesbian couples, roughly 46% of lesbians have been physically abused by their partners. Jane Garcia, *The Cost of Escaping Domestic Violence: Fear of Treatment in a Largely Homophobic Society May Keep Lesbian Abuse Victims from Calling for Help*, L.A. Times, May 6, 1991, at 2; *see also* NAMING THE VIOLENCE: SPEAKING OUT ABOUT LESBIAN BATTERING (Kerry Lobel ed. 1986); Ruthann Robson, *Lavender Bruises: Intralesbian Violence, Law and Lesbian Legal Theory*, 20 GOLDEN GATE U.L. REV. 567 (1990). There are clear parallels between violence against women in the lesbian community and violence against women in

to be represented within the discourses of either feminism or antiracism. Because of their intersectional identity as both women *and* of color within discourses that are shaped to respond to one *or* the other, women of color are marginalized within both.

In an earlier article, I used the concept of intersectionality to denote the various ways in which race and gender interact to shape the multiple dimensions of Black[6] women's employment experiences.[7] My objective there was to illustrate that many of the experiences Black women face are not subsumed within the traditional boundaries of race or gender discrimination as these boundaries are currently understood, and that the intersection of racism and sexism factors into Black women's lives in ways that cannot be captured wholly by looking at the race or gender dimensions of those experiences separately. I build on those observations here by exploring the various ways in which race and gender intersect in shaping structural, political, and representational aspects of violence against women of color.[8]

I should say at the outset that intersectionality is not being offered here as some new, totalizing theory of identity. Nor do I mean to suggest that violence against women of color can be explained only through the specific frameworks of race and gender considered here.[9] Indeed, factors I address

---

communities of color. Lesbian violence is often shrouded in secrecy for similar reasons that have suppressed the exposure of heterosexual violence in communities of color—fear of embarassing other members of the community, which is already stereotyped as deviant, and fear of being ostracized from the community. Despite these similarities, there are nonetheless distinctions between male abuse of women and female abuse of women that in the context of patriarchy, racism and homophobia, warrants more focused analysis than is possible here.

6. I use "Black" and "African American" interchangeably throughout this article. I capitalize "Black" because "Blacks, like *A*sians, *L*atinos, and other 'minorities,' constitute a specific cultural group and, as such, require denotation as a proper noun." Crenshaw, *supra* note 3, at 1332 n.2 (citing Catharine MacKinnon, *Feminism, Marxism, Method, and the State: An Agenda for Theory*, 7 SIGNS 515, 516 (1982)). By the same token, I do not capitalize "white," which is not a proper noun, since whites do not constitute a specific cultural group. For the same reason I do not capitalize "women of color."

7. Kimberle Crenshaw, *Demarginalizing the Intersection of Race and Sex*, 1989 U. CHI. LEGAL F. 139.

8. I explicitly adopt a Black feminist stance in this survey of violence against women of color. I do this cognizant of several tensions that such a position entails. The most significant one stems from the criticism that while feminism purports to speak *for* women of color through its invocation of the term "woman," the feminist perspective excludes women of color because it is based upon the experiences and interests of a certain subset of women. On the other hand, when white feminists attempt to include other women, they often add our experiences into an otherwise unaltered framework. It is important to name the perspective from which one constructs her analysis; and for me, that is as a Black feminist. Moreover, it is important to acknowledge that the materials that I incorporate in my analysis are drawn heavily from research on Black women. On the other hand, I see my own work as part of a broader collective effort among feminists of color to expand feminism to include analyses of race and other factors such as class, sexuality, and age. I have attempted therefore to offer my sense of the tentative connections between my analysis of the intersectional experiences of Black women and the intersectional experiences of other women of color. I stress that this analysis is not intended to include falsely nor to exclude unnecessarily other women of color.

9. I consider intersectionality a provisional concept linking contemporary politics with postmodern theory. In mapping the intersections of race and gender, the concept does engage dominant assumptions that race and gender are essentially separate categories. By tracing the categories to their intersections, I hope to suggest a methodology that will ultimately disrupt the tendencies to see race and gender as exclusive or separable. While the primary intersections that I explore here are

only in part or not at all, such as class or sexuality, are often as critical in shaping the experiences of women of color. My focus on the intersections of race and gender only highlights the need to account for multiple grounds of identity when considering how the social world is constructed.[10]

I have divided the issues presented in this article into three categories. In Part I, I discuss structural intersectionality, the ways in which the location of women of color at the intersection of race and gender makes our actual experience of domestic violence, rape, and remedial reform qualitatively different than that of white women. I shift the focus in Part II to political intersectionality, where I analyze how both feminist and antiracist politics have, paradoxically, often helped to marginalize the issue of violence against women of color. Then in Part III, I discuss representational intersectionality, by which I mean the cultural construction of women of color. I consider how controversies over the representation of women of color in popular culture can also elide the particular location of women of color, and thus become yet another source of intersectional disempowerment. Finally, I address the implications of the intersectional approach within the broader scope of contemporary identity politics.

I. Structural Intersectionality

A. *Structural Intersectionality and Battering*

I observed the dynamics of structural intersectionality during a brief field study of battered women's shelters located in minority communities in Los Angeles.[11] In most cases, the physical assault that leads women to these shelters is merely the most immediate manifestation of the subordination they experience. Many women who seek protection are unemployed or underemployed, and a good number of them are poor. Shelters serving these women cannot afford to address only the violence inflicted by the batterer; they must also confront the other multilayered and routinized forms of domination that often converge in these women's lives, hindering their ability to create alternatives to the abusive relationships that brought them to shelters in the first place. Many women of color, for example, are burdened by poverty, child care responsibilities, and the lack of job skills.[12] These burdens,

---

between race and gender, the concept can and should be expanded by factoring in issues such as class, sexual orientation, age, and color.

10. Professor Mari Matsuda calls this inquiry "asking the other question." Mari J. Matsuda, *Beside My Sister, Facing the Enemy: Legal Theory Out of Coalition,* 43 STAN. L. REV. 1183 (1991). For example, we should look at an issue or condition traditionally regarded as a gender issue and ask, "Where's the racism in this?"

11. During my research in Los Angeles, California, I visited Jenessee Battered Women's Shelter, the only shelter in the Western states primarily serving Black women, and Everywoman's Shelter, which primarily serves Asian women. I also visited Estelle Chueng at the Asian Pacific Law Foundation, and I spoke with a representative of La Casa, a shelter in the predominantly Latino community of East L.A.

12. One researcher has noted, in reference to a survey taken of battered women's shelters, that "many Caucasian women were probably excluded from the sample, since they are more likely to have available resources that enable them to avoid going to a shelter. Many shelters admit only women with few or no resources or alternatives." MILDRED DALEY PAGELOW, WOMAN-BAT-

largely the consequence of gender and class oppression, are then compounded by the racially discriminatory employment and housing practices women of color often face,[13] as well as by the disproportionately high unemployment among people of color that makes battered women of color less able to depend on the support of friends and relatives for temporary shelter.[14]

Where systems of race, gender, and class domination converge, as they do in the experiences of battered women of color, intervention strategies based solely on the experiences of women who do not share the same class or race backgrounds will be of limited help to women who because of race and class face different obstacles.[15] Such was the case in 1990 when Congress amended the marriage fraud provisions of the Immigration and Nationality Act to protect immigrant women who were battered or exposed to extreme cruelty by the United States citizens or permanent residents these women

---

TERING: VICTIMS AND THEIR EXPERIENCES 97 (1981). On the other hand, many middle- and upper-class women are financially dependent upon their husbands and thus experience a diminution in their standard of living when they leave their husbands.

13. Together they make securing even the most basic necessities beyond the reach of many. Indeed one shelter provider reported that nearly 85 percent of her clients returned to the battering relationships, largely because of difficulties in finding employment and housing. African Americans are more segregated than any other racial group, and this segregation exists across class lines. Recent studies in Washington, D.C., and its suburbs show that 64% of Blacks trying to rent apartments in white neighborhoods encountered discrimination. Tracy Thompson, *Study Finds 'Persistent' Racial Bias in Area's Rental Housing,* Wash. Post, Jan. 31, 1991, at D1. Had these studies factored gender and family status into the equation, the statistics might have been worse.

14. More specifically, African Americans suffer from high unemployment rates, low incomes, and high poverty rates. According to Dr. David Swinton, Dean of the School of Business at Jackson State University in Mississippi, African Americans "receive three-fifths as much income per person as whites and are three times as likely to have annual incomes below the Federally defined poverty level of $12,675 for a family of four." *Urban League Urges Action,* N.Y. Times, Jan. 9, 1991, at A14. In fact, recent statistics indicate that racial economic inequality is "higher as we begin the 1990s than at any other time in the last 20 years." David Swinton, *The Economic Status of African Americans: "Permanent" Poverty and Inequality,* in THE STATE OF BLACK AMERICA 1991, at 25 (1991).

The economic situation of minority women is, expectedly, worse than that of their male counterparts. Black women, who earn a median of $7,875 a year, make considerably less than Black men, who earn a median income of $12,609 a year, and white women, who earn a median income of $9,812 a year. *Id.* at 32 (Table 3). Additionally, the percentage of Black female-headed families living in poverty (46.5%) is almost twice that of white female-headed families (25.4%). *Id.* at 43 (Table 8). Latino households also earn considerably less than white households. In 1988, the median income of Latino households was $20,359 and for white households, $28,340—a difference of almost $8,000. HISPANIC AMERICANS: A STATISTICAL SOURCEBOOK 149 (1991). Analyzing by origin, in 1988, Puerto Rican households were the worst off, with 34.1% earning below $10,000 a year and a median income for all Puerto Rican households of $15,447 per year. *Id.* at 155. 1989 statistics for Latino men and women show that women earned an average of $7,000 less than men. *Id.* at 169.

15. *See* text accompanying notes 61-66 (discussing shelter's refusal to house a Spanish-speaking woman in crisis even though her son could interpret for her because it would contribute to her disempowerment). Racial differences marked an interesting contrast between Jenesee's policies and those of other shelters situated outside the Black community. Unlike some other shelters in Los Angeles, Jenessee welcomed the assistance of men. According to the Director, the shelter's policy was premised on a belief that given African American's need to maintain healthy relations to pursue a common struggle against racism, anti-violence programs within the African American community cannot afford to be antagonistic to men. For a discussion of the different needs of Black women who are battered, see Beth Richie, *Battered Black Women: A Challenge for the Black Community,* BLACK SCHOLAR, Mar./Apr. 1985, at 40.

immigrated to the United States to marry. Under the marriage fraud provisions of the Act, a person who immigrated to the United States to marry a United States citizen or permanent resident had to remain "properly" married for two years before even applying for permanent resident status,[16] at which time applications for the immigrant's permanent status were required of both spouses.[17] Predictably, under these circumstances, many immigrant women were reluctant to leave even the most abusive of partners for fear of being deported.[18] When faced with the choice between protection from their batterers and protection against deportation, many immigrant women chose the latter.[19] Reports of the tragic consequences of this double subordination put pressure on Congress to include in the Immigration Act of 1990 a provision amending the marriage fraud rules to allow for an explicit waiver for hardship caused by domestic violence.[20] Yet many immigrant women, par-

16. 8 U.S.C. § 1186a (1988). The Marriage Fraud Amendments provide that an alien spouse "shall be considered, at the time of obtaining the status of an alien lawfully admitted for permanent residence, to have obtained such status on a conditional basis subject to the provisions of this section." § 1186a(a)(1). An alien spouse with permanent resident status under this conditional basis may have her status terminated if the Attorney General finds that the marriage was "improper," § 1186a(b)(1), or if she fails to file a petition or fails to appear at the personal interview. § 1186a(c)(2)(A).

17. The Marriage Fraud Amendments provided that for the conditional resident status to be removed, "the alien spouse and the petitioning spouse (if not deceased) *jointly* must submit to the Attorney General . . . a petition which requests the removal of such conditional basis and which states, under penalty of perjury, the facts and information." § 1186a(b)(1)(A) (emphasis added). The Amendments provided for a waiver, at the Attorney General's discretion, if the alien spouse was able to demonstrate that deportation would result in extreme hardship, or that the qualifying marriage was terminated for good cause. § 1186a(c)(4). However, the terms of this hardship waiver have not adequately protected battered spouses. For example, the requirement that the marriage be terminated for good cause may be difficult to satisfy in states with no-fault divorces. Eileen P. Lynsky, *Immigration Marriage Fraud Amendments of 1986: Till Congress Do Us Part,* 41 U. MIAMI L. REV. 1087, 1095 n.47 (1987) (student author) (citing Jerome B. Ingber & R. Leo Prischet, *The Marriage Fraud Amendments,* in THE NEW SIMPSON-RODINO IMMIGRATION LAW OF 1986, at 564-65 (Stanley Mailman ed. 1986)).

18. Immigration activists have pointed out that "[t]he 1986 Immigration Reform Act and the Immigration Marriage Fraud Amendment have combined to give the spouse applying for permanent residence a powerful tool to control his partner." Jorge Banales, *Abuse Among Immigrants; As Their Numbers Grow So Does the Need for Services,* Wash. Post, Oct. 16, 1990, at E5. Dean Ito Taylor, executive director of Nihonmachi Legal Outreach in San Francisco, explained that the Marriage Fraud Amendments "bound these immigrant women to their abusers." Deanna Hodgin, *'Mail-Order' Brides Marry Pain to Get Green Cards,* Wash. Times, Apr. 16, 1991, at E1. In one egregious instance described by Beckie Masaki, executive director of the Asian Women's Shelter in San Francisco, the closer the Chinese bride came to getting her permanent residency in the United States, the more harshly her Asian-American husband beat her. Her husband, kicking her in the neck and face, warned her that she needed him, and if she did not do as he told her, he would call immigration officials. *Id.*

19. As Alice Fernandez, head of the Victim Services Agency at the Bronx Criminal Court, explained, " 'Women are being held hostage by their landlords, their boyfriends, their bosses, their husbands. . . . The message is: If you tell anybody what I'm doing to you, they are going to ship your ass back home. And for these women, there is nothing more terrible than that . . . . Sometimes their response is: I would rather be dead in this country than go back home.' " Vivienne Walt, *Immigrant Abuse: Nowhere to Hide; Women Fear Deportation, Experts Say,* Newsday, Dec. 2, 1990, at 8.

20. Immigration Act of 1990, Pub. L. No. 101-649, 104 Stat. 4978. The Act, introduced by Representative Louise Slaughter (D-N.Y.), provides that a battered spouse who has conditional permanent resident status can be granted a waiver for failure to meet the requirements if she can show that "the marriage was entered into in good faith and that after the marriage the alien spouse was

ticularly immigrant women of color, have remained vulnerable to battering because they are unable to meet the conditions established for a waiver. The evidence required to support a waiver "can include, but is not limited to, reports and affidavits from police, medical personnel, psychologists, school officials, and social service agencies."[21] For many immigrant women, limited access to these resources can make it difficult for them to obtain the evidence needed for a waiver. And cultural barriers often further discourage immigrant women from reporting or escaping battering situations. Tina Shum, a family counselor at a social service agency, points out that "[t]his law sounds so easy to apply, but there are cultural complications in the Asian community that make even these requirements difficult. . . . Just to find the opportunity and courage to call us is an accomplishment for many."[22] The typical immigrant spouse, she suggests, may live "[i]n an extended family where several generations live together, there may be no privacy on the telephone, no opportunity to leave the house and no understanding of public phones."[23] As a consequence, many immigrant women are wholly dependent on their husbands as their link to the world outside their homes.[24]

Immigrant women are also vulnerable to spousal violence because so many of them depend on their husbands for information regarding their legal status.[25] Many women who are now permanent residents continue to suffer abuse under threats of deportation by their husbands. Even if the threats are unfounded, women who have no independent access to information will still be intimidated by such threats.[26] And even though the domes-

---

battered by or was subjected to extreme mental cruelty by the U.S. citizen or permanent resident spouse." H.R. REP. No. 723(I), 101st Cong., 2d Sess. 78 (1990), *reprinted in* 1990 U.S.C.C.A.N. 6710, 6758; *see also* 8 C.F.R. § 216.5(3) (1992) (regulations for application for waiver based on claim of having been battered or subjected to extreme mental cruelty).

21. H.R. REP. No. 723(I), *supra* note 20, at 79, *reprinted in* 1990 U.S.C.C.A.N. 6710, 6759.

22. Hodgin, *supra* note 18.

23. *Id.*

24. One survey conducted of battered women "hypothesized that if a person is a member of a discriminated minority group, the fewer the opportunities for socioeconomic status above the poverty level and the weaker the English language skills, the greater the disadvantage." M. PAGELOW, *supra* note 12, at 96. The 70 minority women in the study "had a double disadvantage in this society that serves to tie them more strongly to their spouses." *Id.*

25. A citizen or permanent resident spouse can exercise power over an alien spouse by threatening not to file a petition for permanent residency. If he fails to file a petition for permanent residency, the alien spouse continues to be undocumented and is considered to be in the country illegally. These constraints often restrict an alien spouse from leaving. Dean Ito Taylor tells the story of "one client who has been hospitalized—she's had him arrested for beating her—but she keeps coming back to him because he promises he will file for her . . . . He holds that green card over her head." Hodgin, *supra* note 18. Other stories of domestic abuse abound. Maria, a 50-year-old Dominican woman, explains that " 'One time I had eight stitches in my head and a gash on the other side of my head, and he broke my ribs . . . . He would bash my head against the wall while we had sex. He kept threatening to kill me if I told the doctor what happened.' " Maria had a "powerful reason for staying with Juan through years of abuse: a ticket to permanent residence in the United States." Walt, *supra* note 19.

26. One reporter explained that "Third-world women must deal with additional fears, however. In many cases, they are afraid of authority, government institutions and their abusers' threat of being turned over to immigration officials to be deported." Banales, *supra* note 18.

tic violence waiver focuses on immigrant women whose husbands are United States citizens or permanent residents, there are countless women married to undocumented workers (or who are themselves undocumented) who suffer in silence for fear that the security of their entire families will be jeopardized should they seek help or otherwise call attention to themselves.[27]

Language barriers present another structural problem that often limits opportunities of non-English-speaking women to take advantage of existing support services.[28] Such barriers not only limit access to information about shelters, but also limit access to the security shelters provide. Some shelters turn non-English-speaking women away for lack of bilingual personnel and resources.[29]

These examples illustrate how patterns of subordination intersect in women's experience of domestic violence. Intersectional subordination need not be intentionally produced; in fact, it is frequently the consequence of the imposition of one burden that interacts with preexisting vulnerabilities to create yet another dimension of disempowerment. In the case of the marriage fraud provisions of the Immigration and Nationality Act, the imposition of a policy specifically designed to burden one class—immigrant spouses seeking permanent resident status—exacerbated the disempowerment of those already subordinated by other structures of domination. By failing to take into account the vulnerability of immigrant spouses to domestic vio-

---

27. Incidents of sexual abuse of undocumented women abound. Marta Rivera, director of the Hostos College Center for Women's and Immigrant's Rights, tells of how a 19-year-old Dominican woman had "arrived shaken . . . after her boss raped her in the women's restroom at work." The woman told Rivera that "70 to 80 percent of the workers [in a Brooklyn garment factory] were undocumented, and they all accepted sex as part of the job . . . . She said a 13-year-old girl had been raped there a short while before her, and the family sent her back to the Dominican Republic." Walt, *supra* note 19. In another example, a "Latin American woman, whose husband's latest attack left her with two broken fingers, a swollen face and bruises on her neck and chest, refused to report the beating to police." She returned to her home after a short stay in a shelter. She did not leave the abusive situation because she was "an undocumented, illiterate laborer whose children, passport and money are tightly controlled by her husband." Although she was informed of her rights, she was not able to hurdle the structural obstacles in her path. Banales, *supra* note 18.

28. For example, in a region with a large number of Third-World immigrants, "the first hurdle these [battered women's shelters] must overcome is the language barrier." Banales, *supra* note 18.

29.

> There can be little question that women unable to communicate in English are severely handicapped in seeking independence. Some women thus excluded were even further disadvantaged because they were not U.S. citizens and some were in this country illegally. For a few of these, the only assistance shelter staff could render was to help reunite them with their families of origin.

M. Pagelow, *supra* note 12, at 96-97. Non-English speaking women are often excluded even from studies of battered women because of their language and other difficulties. A researcher qualified the statistics of one survey by pointing out that "an unknown number of minority group women were excluded from this survey sample because of language difficulties." *Id.* at 96. To combat this lack of appropriate services for women of color at many shelters, special programs have been created specifically for women from particular communities. A few examples of such programs include the Victim Intervention Project in East Harlem for Latina women, Jenesee Shelter for African American women in Los Angeles, Apna Gar in Chicago for South Asian women, and, for Asian women generally, the Asian Women's Shelter in San Francisco, the New York Asian Women's Center, and the Center for the Pacific Asian Family in Los Angeles. Programs with hotlines include Sakhi for South Asian Women in New York, and Manavi in Jersey City, also for South Asian women, as well as programs for Korean women in Philadelphia and Chicago.

lence, Congress positioned these women to absorb the simultaneous impact of its anti-immigration policy and their spouses' abuse.

The enactment of the domestic violence waiver of the marriage fraud provisions similarly illustrates how modest attempts to respond to certain problems can be ineffective when the intersectional location of women of color is not considered in fashioning the remedy. Cultural identity and class affect the likelihood that a battered spouse could take advantage of the waiver. Although the waiver is formally available to all women, the terms of the waiver make it inaccessible to some. Immigrant women who are socially, culturally, or economically privileged are more likely to be able to marshall the resources needed to satisfy the waiver requirements. Those immigrant women least able to take advantage of the waiver—women who are socially or economically the most marginal—are the ones most likely to be women of color.

B. *Structural Intersectionality and Rape*

Women of color are differently situated in the economic, social, and political worlds. When reform efforts undertaken on behalf of women neglect this fact, women of color are less likely to have their needs met than women who are racially privileged. For example, counselors who provide rape crisis services to women of color report that a significant proportion of the resources allocated to them must be spent handling problems other than rape itself. Meeting these needs often places these counselors at odds with their funding agencies, which allocate funds according to standards of need that are largely white and middle-class.[30] These uniform standards of need ignore the fact that different needs often demand different priorities in terms of resource allocation, and consequently, these standards hinder the ability of counselors to address the needs of nonwhite and poor women.[31] A case in point: women of color occupy positions both physically and culturally marginalized within dominant society, and so information must be targeted directly to them in order to reach them.[32] Accordingly, rape crisis centers

---

30. For example, the Rosa Parks Shelter and the Compton Rape Crisis Hotline, two shelters that serve the African-American community, are in constant conflict with funding sources over the ratio of dollars and hours to women served. Interview with Joan Greer, Executive Director of Rosa Parks Shelter, in Los Angeles, California (April 1990).

31. One worker explained:

> For example, a woman may come in or call in for various reasons. She has no place to go, she has no job, she has no support, she has no money, she has no food, she's been beaten, and after you finish meeting all those needs, or try to meet all those needs, then she may say, by the way, during all this, I was being raped. So that makes our community different than other communities. A person wants their basic needs first. It's a lot easier to discuss things when you are full.

Nancy Anne Matthews, Stopping Rape or Managing its Consequences? State Intervention and Feminist Resistance in the Los Angeles Anti-Rape Movement, 1972-1987, at 287 (1989) (Ph.D dissertation, University of California, Los Angeles) (chronicling the history of the rape crisis movement, and highlighting the different histories and dilemmas of rape crisis hotlines run by white feminists and those situated in the minority communities).

32.

> Typically, more time must be spent with a survivor who has fewer personal resources.

must earmark more resources for basic information dissemination in communities of color than in white ones.

Increased costs are but one consequence of serving people who cannot be reached by mainstream channels of information. As noted earlier, counselors in minority communities report spending hours locating resources and contacts to meet the housing and other immediate needs of women who have been assualted. Yet this work is only considered "information and referral" by funding agencies and as such, is typically underfunded, notwithstanding the magnitude of need for these services in minority communities.[33] The problem is compounded by expectations that rape crisis centers will use a significant portion of resources allocated to them on counselors to accompany victims to court,[34] even though women of color are less likely to have their cases pursued in the criminal justice system.[35] The resources expected to be set aside for court services are misdirected in these communities.

The fact that minority women suffer from the effects of multiple subordination, coupled with institutional expectations based on inappropriate nonintersectional contexts, shapes and ultimately limits the opportunities for meaningful intervention on their behalf. Recognizing the failure to consider intersectional dynamics may go far toward explaining the high levels of failure, frustration, and burn-out experienced by counselors who attempt to meet the needs of minority women victims.

II. Political Intersectionality

The concept of political intersectionality highlights the fact that women

---

> These survivors tend to be ethnic minority women. Often, a non-assimilated ethnic minority survivor requires translating and interpreting, transportation, overnight shelter for herself and possibly children, and counseling to significant others in addition to the usual counseling and advocacy services. So, if a rape crisis center serves a predominantly ethnic minority population, the "average" number of hours of service provided to each survivor is much higher than for a center that serves a predominantly white population.

Id. at 275 (quoting position paper of the Southern California Rape Hotline Alliance).

33. *Id.* at 287-88.

34. The Director of Rosa Parks reported that she often runs into trouble with her funding sources over the Center's lower than average number of counselors accompanying victims to court. Interview with Joan Greer, *supra* note 30.

35.

> Even though current statistics indicate that Black women are more likely to be victimized than white women, Black women are less likely to report their rapes, less likely to have their cases come to trial, less likely to have their trials result in convictions, and, most disturbing, less likely to seek counseling and other support services.

Patricia Hill Collins, Black Feminist Thought: Knowledge, Consciousness and the Politics of Empowerment 178-79 (1990); *accord* Hubert S. Feild & Leigh B. Bienen, Jurors and Rape: A Study in Psychology and Law 141 (1980) (data obtained from 1,056 citizens serving as jurors in simulated legal rape cases generally showed that "the assailant of the black woman was given a more lenient sentence than the white woman's assailant"). According to Fern Ferguson, an Illinois sex abuse worker, speaking at a Women of Color Institute conference in Knoxville, Tennessee, 10% of rapes involving white victims end in conviction, compared with 4.2% for rapes involving non-white victims (and 2.3% for the less-inclusive group of Black rape victims). UPI, July 30, 1985. Ferguson argues that myths about women of color being promiscuous and wanting to be raped encourage the criminal justice system and medical professionals as well to treat women of color differently than they treat white women after a rape has occurred. *Id.*

of color are situated within at least two subordinated groups that frequently pursue conflicting political agendas. The need to split one's political energies between two sometimes opposing groups is a dimension of intersectional disempowerment that men of color and white women seldom confront. Indeed, their specific raced *and* gendered experiences, although intersectional, often define as well as confine the interests of the entire group. For example, racism as experienced by people of color who are of a particular gender—male—tends to determine the parameters of antiracist strategies, just as sexism as experienced by women who are of a particular race—white—tends to ground the women's movement. The problem is not simply that both discourses fail women of color by not acknowledging the "additional" issue of race or of patriarchy but that the discourses are often inadequate even to the discrete tasks of articulating the full dimensions of racism and sexism. Because women of color experience racism in ways not always the same as those experienced by men of color and sexism in ways not always parallel to experiences of white women, antiracism and feminism are limited, even on their own terms.

Among the most troubling political consequences of the failure of antiracist and feminist discourses to address the intersections of race and gender is the fact that, to the extent they can forward the interest of "people of color" and "women," respectively, one analysis often implicitly denies the validity of the other. The failure of feminism to interrogate race means that the resistance strategies of feminism will often replicate and reinforce the subordination of people of color, and the failure of antiracism to interrogate patriarchy means that antiracism will frequently reproduce the subordination of women. These mutual elisions present a particularly difficult political dilemma for women of color. Adopting either analysis constitutes a denial of a fundamental dimension of our subordination and precludes the development of a political discourse that more fully empowers women of color.

A. *The Politicization of Domestic Violence*

That the political interests of women of color are obscured and sometimes jeopardized by political strategies that ignore or suppress intersectional issues is illustrated by my experiences in gathering information for this article. I attempted to review Los Angeles Police Department statistics reflecting the rate of domestic violence interventions by precinct because such statistics can provide a rough picture of arrests by racial group, given the degree of racial segregation in Los Angeles.[36] L.A.P.D., however, would not release the statistics. A representative explained that one reason the statistics were not released was that domestic violence activists both within and

36. Most crime statistics are classified by sex or race but none are classified by sex *and* race. Because we know that most rape victims are women, the racial breakdown reveals, at best, rape rates for Black women. Yet, even given this head start, rates for other non-white women are difficult to collect. While there are some statistics for Latinas, statistics for Asian and Native American women are virtually non-existent. *Cf.* G. Chezia Carraway, *Violence Against Women of Color,* 43 STAN. L. REV. 1301 (1993).

outside the Department feared that statistics reflecting the extent of domestic violence in minority communities might be selectively interpreted and publicized so as to undermine long-term efforts to force the Department to address domestic violence as a serious problem. I was told that activists were worried that the statistics might permit opponents to dismiss domestic violence as a minoirty problem and, therefore, not deserving of aggressive action.

The informant also claimed that representatives from various minority communities opposed the release of these statistics. They were concerned, apparently, that the data would unfairly represent Black and Brown communities as unusually violent, potentially reinforcing stereotypes that might be used in attempts to justify oppressive police tactics and other discriminatory practices. These misgivings are based on the familiar and not unfounded premise that certain minority groups—especially Black men—have already been stereotyped as uncontrollably violent. Some worry that attempts to make domestic violence an object of political action may only serve to confirm such stereotypes and undermine efforts to combat negative beliefs about the Black community.

This account sharply illustrates how women of color can be erased by the strategic silences of antiracism and feminism. The political priorities of both were defined in ways that suppressed information that could have facilitated attempts to confront the problem of domestic violence in communities of color.

1. *Domestic violence and antiracist politics.*

Within communities of color, efforts to stem the politicization of domestic violence are often grounded in attempts to maintain the integrity of the community. The articulation of this perspective takes different forms. Some critics allege that feminism has no place within communities of color, that the issues are internally divisive, and that they represent the migration of white women's concerns into a context in which they are not only irrelevant but also harmful. At its most extreme, this rhetoric denies that gender violence is a problem in the community and characterizes any effort to politicize gender subordination as itself a community problem. This is the position taken by Shahrazad Ali in her controversial book, *The Blackman's Guide to Understanding the Blackwoman.*[37] In this stridently antifeminist tract, Ali draws a positive correlation between domestic violence and the

37. SHAHRAZAD ALI, THE BLACKMAN'S GUIDE TO UNDERSTANDING THE BLACKWOMAN (1989). Ali's book sold quite well for an independently published title, an accomplishment no doubt due in part to her appearances on the Phil Donahue, Oprah Winfrey, and Sally Jesse Raphael television talk shows. For public and press reaction, see Dorothy Gilliam, *Sick, Distorted Thinking*, Wash. Post, Oct. 11, 1990, at D3; Lena Williams, *Black Woman's Book Starts a Predictable Storm*, N.Y. Times, Oct. 2, 1990, at C11; *see also* PEARL CLEAGUE, MAD AT MILES: A BLACK WOMAN'S GUIDE TO TRUTH (1990). The title clearly styled after Ali's, *Mad at Miles* responds not only to issues raised by Ali's book, but also to Miles Davis's admission in his autobiography, *Miles: The Autobiography* (1989), that he had physically abused, among other women, his former wife, actress Cicely Tyson.

liberation of African Americans. Ali blames the deteriorating conditions within the Black community on the insubordination of Black women and on the failure of Black men to control them.[38] Ali goes so far as to advise Black men to physically chastise Black women when they are "disrespectful."[39] While she cautions that Black men must use moderation in disciplining "their" women, she argues that Black men must sometimes resort to physical force to reestablish the authority over Black women that racism has disrupted.[40]

Ali's premise is that patriarchy is beneficial for the Black community,[41] and that it must be strengthened through coercive means if necessary.[42] Yet

38. Shahrazad Ali suggests that the "[Blackwoman] certainly does not believe that her disrepect for the Blackman is destructive, *nor* that her opposition to him has deteriorated the Black nation." S. ALI, *supra* note 37, at viii. Blaming the problems of the community on the failure of the Black woman to accept her "real definition," Ali explains that "[n]o nation can rise when the natural order of the behavior of the male and the female have been altered against their wishes by force. No species can survive if the female of the genus disturbs the balance of her nature by acting other than herself." *Id.* at 76.

39. Ali advises the Blackman to hit the Blackwoman in the mouth, "[b]ecause it is from that hole, in the lower part of her face, that all her rebellion culminates into words. Her unbridled tongue is a main reason she cannot get along with the Blackman. She often needs a reminder." *Id.* at 169. Ali warns that "if [the Blackwoman] ignores the authority and superiority of the Blackman, there is a penalty. When she crosses this line and becomes viciously insulting it is time for the Blackman to soundly slap her in the mouth." *Id.*

40. Ali explains that, "[r]egretfully some Blackwomen want to be physically controlled by the Blackman." *Id.* at 174. "The Blackwoman, deep inside her heart," Ali reveals, "wants to surrender but she wants to be coerced." *Id.* at 72. "[The Blackwoman] wants [the Blackman] to stand up and defend himself even if it means he has to knock her out of the way to do so. This is necessary whenever the Blackwoman steps out of the protection of womanly behavior and enters the dangerous domain of masculine challenge." *Id.* at 174.

41. Ali points out that "[t]he Blackman being number 1 and the Blackwoman being number 2 is another absolute law of nature. The Blackman was created first, he has seniority. And the Blackwoman was created 2nd. He is first. She is second. The Blackman is the beginning and all others come from him. Everyone on earth knows this except the Blackwoman." *Id.* at 67.

42. In this regard, Ali's arguments bear much in common with those of neoconservatives who attribute many of the social ills plaguing Black America to the breakdown of patriarchal family values. *See, e.g.*, William Raspberry, *If We Are to Rescue American Families, We Have to Save the Boys*, Chicago Trib., July 19, 1989, at C15; George F. Will, *Voting Rights Won't Fix It*, Wash. Post, Jan. 23, 1986, at A23; George F. Will, *"White Racism" Doesn't Make Blacks Mere Victims of Fate*, Milwaukee J., Feb. 21, 1986, at 9. Ali's argument shares remarkable similarities to the controversial "Moynihan Report" on the Black family, so called because its principal author was now-Senator Daniel P. Moynihan (D-N.Y.). In the infamous chapter entitled "The Tangle of Pathology," Moynihan argued that

> the Negro community has been forced into a matriarchal structure which, because it is so out of line with the rest of American society, seriously retards the progress of the group as a whole, and imposes a crushing burden on the Negro male and, in consequence, on a great many Negro women as well.

OFFICE OF POLICY PLANNING AND RESEARCH, U.S. DEPARTMENT OF LABOR, THE NEGRO FAMILY: THE CASE FOR NATIONAL ACTION 29 (1965), *reprinted in* LEE RAINWATER & WILLIAM L. YANCEY, THE MOYNIHAN REPORT AND THE POLITICS OF CONTROVERSY 75 (1967). A storm of controversy developed over the book, although few commentators challenged the patriarchy embedded in the analysis. Bill Moyers, then a young minister and speechwriter for President Johnson, firmly believed that the criticism directed at Moynihan was unfair. Some 20 years later, Moyers resurrected the Moynihan thesis in a special television program, *The Vanishing Family: Crisis in Black America* (CBS television broadcast, Jan. 25, 1986). The show first aired in January 1986 and featured several African-American men and women who had become parents but were unwilling to marry. Arthur Unger, *Hardhitting Special About Black Families*, Christian Sci. Mon., Jan. 23, 1986,

the violence that accompanies this will to control is devastating, not only for the Black women who are victimized, but also for the entire Black community.[43] The recourse to violence to resolve conflicts establishes a dangerous pattern for children raised in such environments and contributes to many other pressing problems.[44] It has been estimated that nearly forty percent of all homeless women and children have fled violence in the home,[45] and an estimated sixty-three percent of young men between the ages of eleven and twenty who are imprisoned for homicide have killed their mothers' batterers.[46] And yet, while gang violence, homicide, and other forms of Black-on-Black crime have increasingly been discussed within African-American politics, patriarchal ideas about gender and power preclude the recognition of domestic violence as yet another compelling incidence of Black-on-Black crime.

Efforts such as Ali's to justify violence against women in the name of Black liberation are indeed extreme.[47] The more common problem is that

---

at 23. Many saw the Moyers show as a vindication of Moynihan. President Reagan took the opportunity to introduce an initiative to revamp the welfare system a week after the program aired. Michael Barone, *Poor Children and Politics*, Wash. Post, Feb. 10, 1986, at A1. Said one official, "Bill Moyers has made it safe for people to talk about this issue, the disintegrating black family structure." Robert Pear, *President Reported Ready to Propose Overhaul of Social Welfare System*, N.Y. Times, Feb. 1, 1986, at A12. Critics of the Moynihan/Moyers thesis have argued that it scapegoats the Black family generally and Black women in particular. For a series of responses, see *Scapegoating the Black Family*, NATION, July 24, 1989 (special issue, edited by Jewell Handy Gresham and Margaret B. Wilkerson, with contributions from Margaret Burnham, Constance Clayton, Dorothy Height, Faye Wattleton, and Marian Wright Edelman). For an analysis of the media's endorsement of the Moynihan/Moyers thesis, see CARL GINSBURG, RACE AND MEDIA: THE ENDURING LIFE OF THE MOYNIHAN REPORT (1989).

43. Domestic violence relates directly to issues that even those who subscribe to Ali's position must also be concerned about. The socioeconomic condition of Black males has been one such central concern. Recent statistics estimate that 25% of Black males in their twenties are involved in the criminal justice systems. *See* David G. Savage, *Young Black Males in Jail or in Court Control Study Says*, L.A. Times, Feb. 27, 1990, at A1; Newsday, Feb. 27, 1990, at 15; *Study Shows Racial Imbalance in Penal System*, N.Y. Times, Feb. 27, 1990, at A18. One would think that the linkages between violence in the home and the violence on the streets would alone persuade those like Ali to conclude that the African-American community cannot afford domestic violence and the patriarchal values that support it.

44. A pressing problem is the way domestic violence reproduces itself in subsequent generations. It is estimated that boys who witness violence against women are ten times more likely to batter female partners as adults. *Women and Violence: Hearings Before the Senate Comm. on the Judiciary on Legislation to Reduce the Growing Problem of Violent Crime Against Women*, 101st Cong., 2d Sess., pt. 2, at 89 (1991) [hereinafter *Hearings on Violent Crime Against Women*] (testimony of Charlotte Fedders). Other associated problems for boys who witness violence against women include higher rates of suicide, violent assault, sexual assault, and alcohol and drug use. *Id.*, pt. 2, at 131 (statement of Sarah M. Buel, Assistant District Attorney, Massachusetts, and Supervisor, Harvard Law School Battered Women's Advocacy Project).

45. *Id.* at 142 (statement of Susan Kelly-Dreiss) (discussing several studies in Pennsylvania linking homelessness to domestic violence).

46. *Id.* at 143 (statement of Susan Kelly-Dreiss).

47. Another historical example includes Eldridge Cleaver, who argued that he raped white women as an assault upon the white community. Cleaver "practiced" on Black women first. ELDRIDGE CLEAVER, SOUL ON ICE 14-15 (1968). Despite the appearance of misogyny in both works, each professes to worship Black women as "queens" of the Black community. This "queenly subservience" parallels closely the image of the "woman on a pedestal" against which white feminists have railed. Because Black women have been denied pedestal status within dominant society, the image of the African queen has some appeal to many African-American women. Although it is not a

the political or cultural interests of the community are interpreted in a way that precludes full public recognition of the problem of domestic violence. While it would be misleading to suggest that white Americans have come to terms with the degree of violence in their own homes, it is nonetheless the case that race adds yet another dimension to why the problem of domestic violence is suppressed within nonwhite communities. People of color often must weigh their interests in avoiding issues that might reinforce distorted public perceptions against the need to acknowledge and address intracommunity problems. Yet the cost of suppression is seldom recognized in part because the failure to discuss the issue shapes perceptions of how serious the problem is in the first place.

The controversy over Alice Walker's novel *The Color Purple* can be understood as an intracommunity debate about the political costs of exposing gender violence within the Black community.[48] Some critics chastised Walker for portraying Black men as violent brutes.[49] One critic lambasted Walker's portrayal of Celie, the emotionally and physically abused protagonist who finally triumphs in the end. Walker, the critic contended, had created in Celie a Black woman whom she couldn't imagine existing in any Black community she knew or could conceive of.[50]

The claim that Celie was somehow an unauthentic character might be read as a consequence of silencing discussion of intracommunity violence. Celie may be unlike any Black woman we know because the real terror experienced daily by minority women is routinely concealed in a misguided (though perhaps understandable) attempt to forestall racial stereotyping. Of course, it is true that representations of Black violence—whether statistical or fictional—are often written into a larger script that consistently portrays Black and other minority communities as pathologically violent. The problem, however, is not so much the portrayal of violence itself as it is the absence of other narratives and images portraying a fuller range of Black experience. Suppression of some of these issues in the name of antiracism imposes real costs. Where information about violence in minority communi-

---

feminist position, there are significant ways in which the promulgation of the image directly counters the intersectional effects of racism and sexism that have denied African-American women a perch in the "gilded cage."

48. ALICE WALKER, THE COLOR PURPLE (1982). The most severe criticism of Walker developed after the book was filmed as a movie. Donald Bogle, a film historian, argued that part of the criticism of the movie stemmed from the one-dimensional portrayal of Mister, the abusive man. *See* Jacqueline Trescott, *Passions Over Purple; Anger and Unease Over Film's Depiction of Black Men*, Wash. Post, Feb. 5, 1986, at C1. Bogle argues that in the novel, Walker linked Mister's abusive conduct to his oppression in the white world—since Mister "can't be himself, he has to assert himself with the black woman." The movie failed to make any connection between Mister's abusive treatment of Black women and racism, and thereby presented Mister only as an "insensitive, callous man." *Id.*

49. *See, e.g.*, Gerald Early, *Her Picture in the Papers: Remembering Some Black Women*, ANTAEUS, Spring 1988, at 9; Daryl Pinckney, *Black Victims, Black Villains*, N.Y. REVIEW OF BOOKS, Jan. 29, 1987, at 17; Trescott, *supra* note 48.

50. Trudier Harris, *On the Color Purple, Stereotypes, and Silence*, 18 BLACK AM. LIT. F. 155, 155 (1984).

ties is not available, domestic violence is unlikely to be addressed as a serious issue.

The political imperatives of a narrowly focused antiracist strategy support other practices that isolate women of color. For example, activists who have attempted to provide support services to Asian- and African-American women report intense resistance from those communities.[51] At other times, cultural and social factors contribute to suppression. Nilda Rimonte, director of Everywoman's Shelter in Los Angeles, points out that in the Asian community, saving the honor of the family from shame is a priority.[52] Unfortunately, this priority tends to be interpreted as obliging women not to scream rather than obliging men not to hit.

Race and culture contribute to the suppression of domestic violence in other ways as well. Women of color are often reluctant to call the police, a hesitancy likely due to a general unwillingness among people of color to subject their private lives to the scrutiny and control of a police force that is frequently hostile. There is also a more generalized community ethic against public intervention, the product of a desire to create a private world free from the diverse assaults on the public lives of racially subordinated people. The home is not simply a man's castle in the patriarchal sense, but may also function as a safe haven from the indignities of life in a racist society. However, but for this "safe haven" in many cases, women of color victimized by violence might otherwise seek help.

There is also a general tendency within antiracist discourse to regard the problem of violence against women of color as just another manifestation of racism. In this sense, the relevance of gender domination within the community is reconfigured as a consequence of discrimination against men. Of

---

51. The source of the resistance reveals an interesting difference between the Asian-American and African-American communities. In the African-American community, the resistance is usually grounded in efforts to avoid confirming negative stereotypes of African-Americans as violent; the concern of members in some Asian-American communities is to avoid tarnishing the model minority myth. Interview with Nilda Rimonte, Director of the Everywoman Shelter, in Los Angeles, California (April 19, 1991).

52. Nilda Rimonte, *A Question of Culture: Cultural Approval of Violence Against Women in the Pacific-Asian Community and the Cultural Defense,* 43 STAN. L. REV. 1311 (1991); *see also* Nilda Rimonte, *Domestic Violence Against Pacific Asians,* in MAKING WAVES: AN ANTHOLOGY OF WRITINGS BY AND ABOUT ASIAN AMERICAN WOMEN 327, 328 (Asian Women United of California ed. 1989) ("Traditionally Pacific Asians conceal and deny problems that threaten group pride and may bring on shame. Because of the strong emphasis on obligations to the family, a Pacific Asian woman will often remain silent rather than admit to a problem that might disgrace her family."). Additionally, the possibility of ending the marriage may inhibit an immigrant woman from seeking help. Tina Shum, a family counselor, explains that a " 'divorce is a shame on the whole family. . . . The Asian woman who divorces feels tremendous guilt.' " Of course, one could, in an attempt to be sensitive to cultural difference, stereotype a culture or defer to it in ways that abandon women to abuse. When—or, more importantly, how—to take culture into account when addressing the needs of women of color is a complicated issue. Testimony as to the particularities of Asian "culture" has increasingly been used in trials to determine the culpability of both Asian immigrant women and men who are charged with crimes of interpersonal violence. A position on the use of the "cultural defense" in these instances depends on how "culture" is being defined as well as on whether and to what extent the "cultural defense" has been used differently for Asian men and Asian women. See Leti Volpp, (Mis)Identifying Culture: Asian Women and the "Cultural Defense," (unpublished manuscript) (on file with the *Stanford Law Review*).

course, it is probably true that racism contributes to the cycle of violence, given the stress that men of color experience in dominant society. It is therefore more than reasonable to explore the links between racism and domestic violence. But the chain of violence is more complex and extends beyond this single link. Racism is linked to patriarchy to the extent that racism denies men of color the power and privilege that dominant men enjoy. When violence is understood as an acting-out of being denied male power in other spheres, it seems counterproductive to embrace constructs that implicitly link the solution to domestic violence to the acquisition of greater male power. The more promising political imperative is to challenge the legitimacy of such power expectations by exposing their dysfunctional and debilitating effect on families and communities of color. Moreover, while understanding links between racism and domestic violence is an important component of any effective intervention strategy, it is also clear that women of color need not await the ultimate triumph over racism before they can expect to live violence-free lives.

2. *Race and the domestic violence lobby.*

Not only do race-based priorities function to obscure the problem of violence suffered by women of color; feminist concerns often suppress minority experiences as well. Strategies for increasing awareness of domestic violence within the white community tend to begin by citing the commonly shared assumption that battering is a minority problem. The strategy then focuses on demolishing this strawman, stressing that spousal abuse also occurs in the white community. Countless first-person stories begin with a statement like, "I was not supposed to be a battered wife." That battering occurs in families of all races and all classes seems to be an ever-present theme of anti-abuse campaigns.[53] First-person anecdotes and studies, for example, consistently assert that battering cuts across racial, ethnic, economic, educational, and religious lines.[54] Such disclaimers seem relevant only in the presence of an

53. *See, e.g., Hearings on Violent Crime Against Women, supra* note 44, pt. 1, at 101 (testimony of Roni Young, Director of Domestic Violence Unit, Office of the State's Attorney for Baltimore City, Baltimore, Maryland) ("The victims do not fit a mold by any means."); *Id.* pt. 2, at 89 (testimony of Charlotte Fedders) ("Domestic violence occurs in all economic, cultural, racial, and religious groups. There is not a typical woman to be abused."); *Id.* pt. 2 at 139 (statement of Susan Kelly-Dreiss, Executive Director, Pennsylvania Coalition Against Domestic Violence) ("Victims come from a wide spectrum of life experiences and backgrounds. Women can be beaten in any neighborhood and in any town.").

54. *See, e.g.*, LENORE F. WALKER, TERRIFYING LOVE: WHY BATTERED WOMEN KILL AND HOW SOCIETY RESPONDS 101-02 (1989) ("Battered women come from all types of economic, cultural, religious, and racial backgrounds. . . . They are women like you. Like me. Like those whom you know and love."); MURRAY A. STRAUS, RICHARD J. GELLES, SUZANNE K. STEINMETZ, BEHIND CLOSED DOORS: VIOLENCE IN THE AMERICAN FAMILY 31 (1980) ("Wife-beating is found in every class, at every income level."); Natalie Loder Clark, *Crime Begins At Home: Let's Stop Punishing Victims and Perpetuating Violence,* 28 WM. & MARY L. REV. 263, 282 n.74 (1987) ("The problem of domestic violence cuts across all social lines and affects 'families regardless of their economic class, race, national origin, or educational background.' Commentators have indicated that domestic violence is prevalent among upper middle-class families.") (citations omitted); Kathleen Waits, *The Criminal Justice System's Response to Battering: Understanding the Problem, Forging the Solutions,* 60 WASH. L. REV. 267, 276 (1985) ("It is important to emphasize that wife abuse is prevalent

initial, widely held belief that domestic violence occurs primarily in minority or poor families. Indeed some authorities explicitly renounce the "stereotypical myths" about battered women.[55] A few commentators have even transformed the message that battering is not *exclusively* a problem of the poor or minority communities into a claim that it *equally* affects all races and classes.[56] Yet these comments seem less concerned with exploring domestic abuse within "stereotyped" communities than with removing the stereotype as an obstacle to exposing battering within white middle- and upper-class communities.[57]

Efforts to politicize the issue of violence against women challenge beliefs that violence occurs only in homes of "others." While it is unlikely that advocates and others who adopt this rhetorical strategy intend to exclude or ignore the needs of poor and colored women, the underlying premise of this seemingly univeralistic appeal is to keep the sensibilities of dominant social

---

throughout our society. Recently collected data merely confirm what people working with victims have long known: battering occurs in all social and economic groups.") (citations omitted); Liza G. Lerman, *Mediation of Wife Abuse Cases: The adverse Impact of Informal Dispute Resolution on Women,* 7 HARV. WOMEN'S L.J. 57, 63 (1984) ("Battering occurs in all racial, economic, and religious groups, in rural, urban, and suburban settings.") (citation omitted); Steven M. Cook, *Domestic Abuse Legislation in Illinois and Other States: A Survey and Suggestions for Reform,* 1983 U. ILL. L. REV. 261, 262 (1983) (student author) ("Although domestic violence is difficult to measure, several studies suggest that spouse abuse is an extensive problem, one which strikes families regardless of their economic class, race, national origin, or educational background.") (citations omitted).

55. For example, Susan Kelly-Dreiss states:

> The public holds many myths about battered women—they are poor, they are women of color, they are uneducated, they are on welfare, they deserve to be beaten and they even like it. However, contrary to common misperceptions, domestic violence is not confined to any one socioeconomic, ethnic, religious, racial or age group.

Hearings on Violent Crime Against Women, supra note 44, pt. 2, at 139 (testimony of Susan Kelly-Dreiss, Executive Director, Pa. Coalition Against Domestic Violence). Kathleen Waits offers a possible explanation for this misperception:

> It is true that battered women who are also poor are more likely to come to the attention of governmental officials than are their middle- and upper-class counterparts. However, this phenomenon is caused more by the lack of alternative resources and the intrusiveness of the welfare state than by any significantly higher incidence of violence among lower-class families.

Waits, *supra* note 54, at 276-77 (citations omitted).

56. However, no reliable statistics support such a claim. In fact, some statistics suggest that there is a greater frequency of violence among the working classes and the poor. *See* M. STRAUS, R. GELLES, & S. STEINMETZ, *supra* note 54, at 31. Yet these statistics are also unreliable because, to follow Waits's observation, violence in middle- and upper-class homes remains hidden from the view of statisticians and governmental officials alike. *See* note 55 *supra*. I would suggest that assertions that the problem is the same across race and class are driven less by actual knowledge about the prevalence of domestic violence in different communities than by advocates' recognition that the image of domestic violence as an issue involving primarily the poor and minorities complicates efforts to mobilize against it.

57. On January 14, 1991, Senator Joseph Biden (D-Del.) introduced Senate Bill 15, the Violence Against Women Act of 1991, comprehensive legislation addressing violent crime confronting women. S. 15, 102d Cong., 1st Sess. (1991). The bill consists of several measures designed to create safe streets, safe homes, and safe campuses for women. More specifically, Title III of the bill creates a civil rights remedy for crimes of violence motivated by the victim's gender. *Id.* § 301. Among the findings supporting the bill were "(1) crimes motivated by the victim's gender constitute bias crimes in violation of the victim's right to be free from discrimination on the basis of gender" and "(2) current law [does not provide a civil rights remedy] for gender crimes committed on the street or in the home." S. REP. NO. 197, 102d Cong., 1st Sess. 27 (1991).

groups focused on the experiences of those groups. Indeed, as subtly suggested by the opening comments of Senator David Boren (D-Okla.) in support of the Violence Against Women Act of 1991, the displacement of the "other" as the presumed victim of domestic violence works primarily as a political appeal to rally white elites. Boren said,

> Violent crimes against women are not limited to the streets of the inner cities, but also occur in homes in the urban and rural areas across the country.
>
> Violence against women affects not only those who are actually beaten and brutalized, but indirectly affects all women. Today, our wives, mothers, daughters, sisters, and colleagues are held captive by fear generated from these violent crimes—held captive not for what they do or who they are, but solely because of gender.[58]

Rather than focusing on and illuminating how violence is disregarded when the home is "othered," the strategy implicit in Senator Boren's remarks functions instead to politicize the problem only in the dominant community. This strategy permits white women victims to come into focus, but does little to disrupt the patterns of neglect that permitted the problem to continue as long as it was imagined to be a minority problem. The experience of violence by minority women is ignored, except to the extent it gains white support for domestic violence programs in the white community.

Senator Boren and his colleagues no doubt believe that they have provided legislation and resources that will address the problems of all women victimized by domestic violence. Yet despite their universalizing rhetoric of "all" women, they were able to empathize with female victims of domestic violence only by looking past the plight of "other" women and by recognizing the familiar faces of their own. The strength of the appeal to "protect our women" must be its race and class specificity. After all, it has always been someone's wife, mother, sister, or daughter that has been abused, even when the violence was stereotypically Black or Brown, and poor. The point here is not that the Violence Against Women Act is particularistic on its own terms, but that unless the Senators and other policymakers ask why violence remained insignificant as long as it was understood as a minority problem, it is unlikely that women of color will share equally in the distribution of resources and concern. It is even more unlikely, however, that those in power will be forced to confront this issue. As long as attempts to politicize domestic violence focus on convincing whites that this is not a "minority" problem but *their* problem, any authentic and sensitive attention to the

---

58. 137 Cong. Rec. S611 (daily ed. Jan. 14, 1991) (statement of Sen. Boren). Senator William Cohen (D-Me.) followed with a similar statement, noting that rapes and domestic assaults

> are not limited to the streets of our inner cities or to those few highly publicized cases that we read about in the newspapers or see on the evening news. Women throughout the country, in our Nation's urban areas and rural communities, are being beaten and brutalized in the streets and in their homes. It is our mothers, wives, daughters, sisters, friends, neighbors, and coworkers who are being victimized; and in many cases, they are being victimized by family members, friends, and acquaintances.

Id. (statement of Sen. Cohen).

experiences of Black and other minority women probably will continue to be regarded as jeopardizing the movement.

While Senator Boren's statement reflects a self-consciously political presentation of domestic violence, an episode of the CBS news program *48 Hours*[59] shows how similar patterns of othering nonwhite women are apparent in journalistic accounts of domestic violence as well. The program presented seven women who were victims of abuse. Six were interviewed at some length along with their family members, friends, supporters, and even detractors. The viewer got to know something about each of these women. These victims were humanized. Yet the seventh woman, the only nonwhite one, never came into focus. She was literally unrecognizable throughout the segment, first introduced by photographs showing her face badly beaten and later shown with her face electronically altered in the videotape of a hearing at which she was forced to testify. Other images associated with this woman included shots of a bloodstained room and blood-soaked pillows. Her boyfriend was pictured handcuffed while the camera zoomed in for a close-up of his bloodied sneakers. Of all the presentations in the episode, hers was the most graphic and impersonal. The overall point of the segment "featuring" this woman was that battering might not escalate into homicide if battered women would only cooperate with prosecutors. In focusing on its own agenda and failing to explore why this woman refused to cooperate, the program diminished this woman, communicating, however subtly, that she was responsible for her own victimization.

Unlike the other women, all of whom, again, were white, this Black woman had no name, no family, no context. The viewer sees her only as victimized and uncooperative. She cries when shown pictures. She pleads not to be forced to view the bloodstained room and her disfigured face. The program does not help the viewer to understand her predicament. The possible reasons she did not want to testify—fear, love, or possibly both—are never suggested.[60] Most unfortunately, she, unlike the other six, is given no epilogue. While the fates of the other women are revealed at the end of the episode, we discover nothing about the Black woman. She, like the "others" she represents, is simply left to herself and soon forgotten.

I offer this description to suggest that "other" women are silenced as much by being relegated to the margin of experience as by total exclusion. Tokenistic, objectifying, voyeuristic inclusion is at least as disempowering as complete exclusion. The effort to politicize violence against women will do little to address Black and other minority women if their images are retained simply to magnify the problem rather than to humanize their experiences. Similarly, the antiracist agenda will not be advanced significantly by forcibly suppressing the reality of battering in minority communities. As the *48 Hours* episode makes clear, the images and stereotypes we fear are readily

59. *48 Hours: Till Death Do Us Part* (CBS television broadcast, Feb. 6, 1991).

60. *See* Christine A. Littleton, *Women's Experience and the Problem of Transition: Perspectives on Male Battering of Women*, 1989 U. CHI. LEGAL F. 23.

available and are frequently deployed in ways that do not generate sensitive understanding of the nature of domestic violence in minority communities.

3. *Race and domestic violence support services.*

Women working in the field of domestic violence have sometimes reproduced the subordination and marginalization of women of color by adopting policies, priorities, or strategies of empowerment that either elide or wholly disregard the particular intersectional needs of women of color. While gender, race, and class intersect to create the particular context in which women of color experience violence, certain choices made by "allies" can reproduce intersectional subordination within the very resistance strategies designed to respond to the problem.

This problem is starkly illustrated by the inaccessibility of domestic violence support services to many non-English-speaking women. In a letter written to the deputy commissioner of the New York State Department of Social Services, Diana Campos, Director of Human Services for Programas de Ocupaciones y Desarrollo Económico Real, Inc. (PODER), detailed the case of a Latina in crisis who was repeatedly denied accomodation at a shelter because she could not prove that she was English-proficient. The woman had fled her home with her teenaged son, believing her husband's threats to kill them both. She called the domestic violence hotline administered by PODER seeking shelter for herself and her son. Because most shelters would not accommodate the woman with her son, they were forced to live on the streets for two days. The hotline counselor was finally able to find an agency that would take both the mother and the son, but when the counselor told the intake coordinator at the shelter that the woman spoke limited English, the coordinator told her that they could not take anyone who was not English-proficient. When the woman in crisis called back and was told of the shelter's "rule," she replied that she could understand English if spoken to her slowly. As Campos explains, Mildred, the hotline counselor, told Wendy, the intake coordinator

> that the woman said that she could communicate a little in English. Wendy told Mildred that they could not provide services to this woman because they have house rules that the woman must agree to follow. Mildred asked her, "What if the woman agrees to follow your rules? Will you still not take her?" Wendy responded that all of the women at the shelter are required to attend [a] support group and they would not be able to have her in the group if she could not communicate. Mildred mentioned the severity of this woman's case. She told Wendy that the woman had been wandering the streets at night while her husband is home, and she had been mugged twice. She also reiterated the fact that this woman was in danger of being killed by either her husband or a mugger. Mildred expressed that the woman's safety was a priority at this point, and that once in a safe place, receiving counseling in a support group could be dealt with.[61]

61. Letter of Diana M. Campos, Director of Human Services, PODER, to Joseph Semidei,

The intake coordinator restated the shelter's policy of taking only English-speaking women, and stated further that the woman would have to call the shelter herself for screening. If the woman could communicate with them in English, she might be accepted. When the woman called the PODER hotline later that day, she was in such a state of fear that the hotline counselor who had been working with her had difficulty understanding her in Spanish.[62] Campos directly intervened at this point, calling the executive director of the shelter. A counselor called back from the shelter. As Campos reports,

> Marie [the counselor] told me that they did not want to take the woman in the shelter because they felt that the woman would feel isolated. I explained that the son agreed to translate for his mother during the intake process. Furthermore, that we would assist them in locating a Spanish-speaking battered women's advocate to assist in counseling her. Marie stated that utilizing the son was not an acceptable means of communication for them, *since it further victimized the victim.* In addition, she stated that they had similar experiences with women who were non-English-speaking, and that the women eventually just left because they were not able to communicate with anyone. I expressed my extreme concern for her safety and reiterated that we would assist them in providing her with the necessary services until we could get her placed someplace where they had bilingual staff.[63]

After several more calls, the shelter finally agreed to take the woman. The woman called once more during the negotiation; however, after a plan was in place, the woman never called back. Said Campos, "After so many calls, we are now left to wonder if she is alive and well, and if she will ever have enough faith in our ability to help her to call us again the next time she is in crisis."[64]

Despite this woman's desperate need, she was unable to receive the protection afforded English-speaking women, due to the shelter's rigid commitment to exclusionary policies. Perhaps even more troubling than the shelter's lack of bilingual resources was its refusal to allow a friend or relative to translate for the woman. This story illustrates the absurdity of a feminist approach that would make the ability to attend a support group without a translator a more significant consideration in the distribution of resources than the risk of physical harm on the street. The point is not that the shelter's image of empowerment is empty, but rather that it was imposed without regard to the disempowering consequences for women who didn't match the kind of client the shelter's administrators imagined. And thus they failed to accomplish the basic priority of the shelter movement—to get the woman out of danger.

Deputy Commissioner, New York State Department of Social Services (Mar. 26, 1992) [hereinafter *PODER Letter*].

62. The woman had been slipping back into her home during the day when her husband was at work. She remained in a heightened state of anxiety because he was returning shortly and she would be forced to go back out into the streets for yet another night.

63. *PODER Letter, supra* note 61 (emphasis added).

64. *Id.*

Here the woman in crisis was made to bear the burden of the shelter's refusal to anticipate and provide for the needs of non-English-speaking women. Said Campos, "It is unfair to impose more stress on victims by placing them in the position of having to demonstrate their proficiency in English in order to receive services that are readily available to other battered women."[65] The problem is not easily dismissed as one of well-intentioned ignorance. The specific issue of monolingualism and the monistic view of women's experience that set the stage for this tragedy were not new issues in New York. Indeed, several women of color reported that they had repeatedly struggled with the New York State Coalition Against Domestic Violence over language exclusion and other practices that marginalized the interests of women of color.[66] Yet despite repeated lobbying, the Coalition did not act to incorporate the specific needs of nonwhite women into its central organizing vision.

Some critics have linked the Coalition's failure to address these issues to the narrow vision of coalition that animated its interaction with women of color in the first place. The very location of the Coalition's headquarters in Woodstock, New York—an area where few people of color live—seemed to guarantee that women of color would play a limited role in formulating policy. Moreover, efforts to include women of color came, it seems, as something of an afterthought. Many were invited to participate only after the Coalition was awarded a grant by the state to recruit women of color. However, as one "recruit" said, "they were not really prepared to deal with us or our issues. They thought that they could simply incorporate us into their organization without rethinking any of their beliefs or priorities and that we would be happy."[67] Even the most formal gestures of inclusion were not to be taken for granted. On one occasion when several women of color attended a meeting to discuss a special task force on women of color, the group debated all day over including the issue on the agenda.[68]

The relationship between the white women and the women of color on the Board was a rocky one from beginning to end. Other conflicts developed over differing definitions of feminism. For example, the Board decided to hire a Latina staffperson to manage outreach programs to the Latino community, but the white members of the hiring committee rejected candidates favored by Latina committee members who did not have recognized feminist

---

65. *Id.*

66. Roundtable Discussion on Racism and the Domestic Violence Movement (April 2, 1992) (transcript on file with the *Stanford Law Review*). The participants in the discussion—Diana Campos, Director, Bilingual Outreach Project of the New York State Coalition Against Domestic Violence; Elsa A. Rios, Project Director, Victim Intervention Project (a community-based project in East Harlem, New York, serving battered women); and Haydee Rosario, a social worker with the East Harlem Council for Human Services and a Victim Intervention Project volunteer—recounted conflicts relating to race and culture during their association with the New York State Coalition Against Domestic Violence, a state oversight group that distributed resources to battered women's shelters throughout the state and generally set policy priorities for the shelters that were part of the Coalition.

67. *Id.*

68. *Id.*

credentials. As Campos pointed out, by measuring Latinas against their own biographies, the white members of the Board failed to recognize the different circumstances under which feminist consciousness develops and manifests itself within minority communities. Many of the women who interviewed for the position were established activists and leaders within their own community, a fact in itself suggesting that these women were probably familiar with the specific gender dynamics in their communities and were accordingly better qualified to handle outreach than other candidates with more conventional feminist credentials.[69]

The Coalition ended a few months later when the women of color walked out.[70] Many of these women returned to community-based organizations, preferring to struggle over women's issues within their communities rather than struggle over race and class issues with white middle-class women. Yet as illustrated by the case of the Latina who could find no shelter, the dominance of a particular perspective and set of priorities within the shelter community continues to marginalize the needs of women of color.

The struggle over which differences matter and which do not is neither an abstract nor an insignificant debate among women. Indeed, these conflicts are about more than difference as such; they raise critical issues of power. The problem is not simply that women who dominate the antiviolence movement are different from women of color but that they frequently have power to determine, either through material or rhetorical resources, whether the intersectional differences of women of color will be incorporated at all into the basic formulation of policy. Thus, the struggle over incorporating these differences is not a petty or superficial conflict about who gets to sit at the head of the table. In the context of violence, it is sometimes a deadly serious matter of who will survive—and who will not.[71]

B. *Political Intersectionalities in Rape*

In the previous sections, I have used intersectionality to describe or frame various relationships between race and gender. I have used intersectionality as a way to articulate the interaction of racism and patriarchy generally. I have also used intersectionality to describe the location of women of color both within overlapping systems of subordination and at the margins of feminism and antiracism. When race and gender factors are examined in the context of rape, intersectionality can be used to map the ways in which racism and patriarchy have shaped conceptualizations of rape, to describe the unique vulnerability of women of color to these converging sys-

---

69. *Id.*

70. Ironically, the specific dispute that led to the walk-out concerned the housing of the Spanish-language domestic violence hotline. The hotline was initially housed at the Coalition's headquarters, but languished after a succession of coordinators left the organization. Latinas on the Coalition board argued that the hotline should be housed at one of the community service agencies, while the board insisted on maintaining control of it. The hotline is now housed at PODER. *Id.*

71. Said Campos, "It would be a shame that in New York state a battered woman's life or death were dependent upon her English language skills." *PODER Letter, supra* note 61.

tems of domination, and to track the marginalization of women of color within antiracist and antirape discourses.[72]

1. *Racism and sexism in dominant conceptualizations of rape.*

Generations of critics and activists have criticized dominant conceptualizations of rape as racist and sexist. These efforts have been important in revealing the way in which representations of rape both reflect and reproduce race and gender hierarchies in American society.[73] Black women, as both women and people of color, are situated within both groups, each of which has benefitted from challenges to sexism and racism, respectively, and yet the particular dynamics of gender and race relating to the rape of Black women have received scant attention. Although antiracist and antisexist assaults on rape have been politically useful to Black women, at some level, the monofocal antiracist and feminist critiques have also produced a political discourse that disserves Black women.

Historically, the dominant conceptualization of rape as quintessentially Black offender/white victim has left Black men subject to legal and extralegal violence. The use of rape to legitimize efforts to control and discipline the Black community is well established, and the casting of all Black men as potential threats to the sanctity of white womanhood was a familiar construct that antiracists confronted and attempted to dispel over a century ago.

Feminists have attacked other dominant, essentially patriarchal, conceptions of rape, particularly as represented through law. The early emphasis of rape law on the property-like aspect of women's chastity resulted in less solicitude for rape victims whose chastity had been in some way devalued. Some of the most insidious assumptions were written into the law, including the early common-law notion that a woman alleging rape must be able to show that she resisted to the utmost in order to prove that she was raped, rather than seduced. Women themselves were put on trial, as judge and jury scrutinized their lives to determine whether they were innocent victims or women who essentially got what they were asking for. Legal rules thus functioned to legitimize a good woman/bad woman dichotomy in which women who lead sexually autonomous lives were usually least likely to be vindicated if they were raped.

---

72. The discussion in following section focuses rather narrowly on the dynamics of a Black/white sexual hierarchy. I specify African Americans in part because given the centrality of sexuality as a site of racial domination of African Americans, any generalizations that might be drawn from this history seem least applicable to other racial groups. To be sure, the specific dynamics of racial oppression experienced by other racial groups are likely to have a sexual componant as well. Indeed, the repertoire of racist imagery that is commonly associated with different racial groups each contain a sexual stereotype as well. These images probably influence the way that rapes involving other minority groups are perceived both internally and in society-at-large, but they are likely to function in different ways.

73. For example, the use of rape to legitimize efforts to control and discipline the Black community is well established in historical literature on rape and race. *See* JOYCE E. WILLIAMS & KAREN A. HOLMES, THE SECOND ASSAULT: RAPE AND PUBLIC ATTITUDES 26 (1981) ("Rape, or the threat of rape, is an important tool of social control in a complex system of racial-sexual stratification.").

Today, long after the most egregious discriminatory laws have been eradicated, constructions of rape in popular discourse and in criminal law continue to manifest vestiges of these racist and sexist themes. As Valerie Smith notes, "a variety of cultural narratives that historically have linked sexual violence with racial oppression continue to determine the nature of public response to [interracial rapes]."[74] Smith reviews the well-publicized case of a jogger who was raped in New York's Central Park[75] to expose how the public discourse on the assault "made the story of sexual victimization inseparable from the rhetoric of racism."[76] Smith contends that in dehumanizing the rapists as "savages," "wolves," and "beasts," the press "shaped the discourse around the event in ways that inflamed pervasive fears about black men."[77] Given the chilling parallels between the media representations of the Central Park rape and the sensationalized coverage of similar allegations that in the past frequently culminated in lynchings, one could hardly be surprised when Donald Trump took out a full page ad in four New York newspapers demanding that New York "Bring Back the Death Penalty, Bring Back Our Police."[78]

Other media spectacles suggest that traditional gender-based stereotypes that are oppressive to women continue to figure in the popular construction of rape. In Florida, for example, a controversy was sparked by a jury's acquittal of a man accused of a brutal rape because, in the jurors' view, the woman's attire suggested that she was asking for sex.[79] Even the press cov-

---

74. Valerie Smith, *Split Affinities: The Case of Interracial Rape*, in CONFLICTS IN FEMINISM 271, 274 (Marianne Hirsch & Evelyn Fox Keller eds. 1990).

75. On April 18, 1989, a young white woman, jogging through New York's Central Park, was raped, severely beaten, and left unconscious in an attack by as many as 12 Black youths. Craig Wolff, *Youths Rape and Beat Central Park Jogger*, N.Y. Times, Apr. 21, 1989, at B1.

76. Smith, *supra* note 74, at 276-78.

77. Smith cites the use of animal images to characterize the accused Black rapists, including descriptions such as: " 'a wolfpack of more than a dozen young teenagers' and '[t]here was a full moon Wednesday night. A suitable backdrop for the howling of wolves. A vicious pack ran rampant through Central Park. . . . This was bestial brutality.' " An editorial in the *New York Times* was entitled "The Jogger and the Wolf Pack." *Id.* at 277 (citations omitted).

Evidence of the ongoing link between rape and racism in American culture is by no means unique to media coverage of the Central Park jogger case. In December 1990, the George Washington University student newspaper, *The Hatchet*, printed a story in which a white student alleged that she had been raped at knifepoint by two Black men on or near the campus. The story caused considerable racial tension. Shortly after the report appeared, the woman's attorney informed the campus police that his client had fabricated the attack. After the hoax was uncovered, the woman said that she hoped the story "would highlight the problems of safety for women." Felicity Banger, *False Rape Report Upsetting Campus*, N.Y. Times, Dec. 12, 1990, at A2; *see also* Les Payne, *A Rape Hoax Stirs Up Hate*, Newsday, Dec. 16, 1990, at 6.

78. William C. Troft, *Deadly Donald*, UPI, Apr. 30 1989. Donald Trump explained that he spent $85,000 to take out these ads because "I want to hate these muggers and murderers. They should be forced to suffer and, when they kill, they should be executed for their crimes." *Trump Calls for Death to Muggers*, L.A. Times, May 1, 1989, at A2. *But cf. Leaders Fear 'Lynch' Hysteria in Response to Trump Ads*, UPI, May 6, 1989 (community leaders feared that Trump's ads would fan "the flames of racial polarization and hatred"); Cynthia Fuchs Epstein, *Cost of Full-Page Ad Could Help Fight Causes of Urban Violence*, N.Y. Times, May 15, 1989, at A18 ("Mr. Trump's proposal could well lead to further violence.").

79. Ian Ball, *Rape Victim to Blame, Says Jury*, Daily Telegraph, Oct. 6, 1989, at 3. Two months after the acquittal, the same man pled guilty to raping a Georgia woman to whom he said,

erage of William Kennedy Smith's rape trial involved a considerable degree of speculation regarding the sexual history of his accuser.[80]

The racism and sexism written into the social construction of rape are merely contemporary manifestations of rape narratives emanating from a historical period when race and sex hierarchies were more explicitly policed. Yet another is the devaluation of Black women and the marginalization of their sexual victimizations. This was dramatically shown in the special attention given to the rape of the Central Park jogger during a week in which twenty-eight other cases of first-degree rape or attempted rape were reported in New York.[81] Many of these rapes were as horrific as the rape in Central Park, yet all were virtually ignored by the media. Some were gang rapes,[82] and in a case that prosecutors described as was "one of the most brutal in recent years," a woman was raped, sodomized and thrown fifty feet off the top of a four-story building in Brooklyn. Witnesses testified that the victim "screamed as she plunged down the air shaft. . . . She suffered fractures of both ankles and legs, her pelvis was shattered and she suffered extensive internal injuries."[83] This rape survivor, like most of the other forgotten victims that week, was a woman of color.

In short, during the period when the Central Park jogger dominated the headlines, many equally horrifying rapes occurred. None, however, elicited the public expressions of horror and outrage that attended the Central Park rape.[84] To account for these different responses, Professor Smith suggests a

---

"It's your fault. You're wearing a skirt." Roger Simon, *Rape: Clothing is Not the Criminal,* L.A. Times, Feb. 18, 1990, at E2.

80. *See* Barbara Kantrowitz, *Naming Names,* NEWSWEEK, Apr. 29, 1991, at 26 (discussing the tone of several newspaper investigations into the character of the woman who alleged that she was raped by William Kennedy Smith). There were other dubious assumptions animating the coverage. One article described Smith as an "unlikely candidate for the rapist's role." *Boy's Night Out in Palm Beach,* TIME, Apr. 22, 1991, at 82. *But see* Hillary Rustin, *Letters: The Kennedy Problem,* TIME, May 20, 1991, at 7 (criticizing authors for perpetuating stereotypical images of the who is or is not a "likely" rapist). Smith was eventually acquitted.

81. The New York Times pointed out that "[n]early all the rapes reported during that April week were of black or Hispanic women. Most went unnoticed by the public." Don Terry, *In Week of an Infamous Rape, 28 Other Victims Suffer,* N.Y. Times, May 29, 1989, at B25. Nearly all of the rapes occurred between attackers and victims of the same race: "Among the victims were 17 blacks, 7 Hispanic women, 3 whites, and 2 Asians." *Id.*

82. In Glen Ridge, an affluent New Jersey suburb, five white middle-class teenagers allegedly gang-raped a retarded white woman with a broom handle and a miniature baseball bat. *See* Robert Hanley, *Sexual Assault Splits a New Jersey Town,* N.Y. Times, May 26, 1989, at B1; Derrick Z. Jackson, *The Seeds of Violence,* Boston Globe, June 2, 1989, at 23; Bill Turque, *Gang Rape in the Suburbs,* NEWSWEEK, June 5, 1989, at 26.

83. Robert D. McFadden, *2 Men Get 6 to 18 Years for Rape in Brooklyn,* N.Y. Times, Oct. 2, 1990, at B2. The woman "lay, half naked, moaning and crying for help until a neighbor heard her" in the air shaft. *Community Rallies to Support Victim of Brutal Brooklyn Rape,* N.Y. Daily News, June 26, 1989, at 6. The victim "suffered such extensive injuries that she had to learn to walk again. . . . She faces years of psychological counseling . . . ." McFadden, *supra.*

84. This differential response was epitomized by public reaction to the rape-murder of a young Black woman in Boston on October 31, 1990. Kimberly Rae Harbour, raped and stabbed more than 100 times by eight members of a local gang, was an unwed mother, an occasional prostitute, and a drug-user. The Central Park victim was a white, upper-class professional. The Black woman was raped and murdered intraracially. The white woman was raped and left for dead interracially. The Central Park rape became a national rallying cause against random (read Black male) violence; the

sexual hierarchy in operation that holds certain female bodies in higher regard than others.[85] Statistics from prosecution of rape cases suggest that this hierarchy is at least one significant, albeit often overlooked factor in evaluating attitudes toward rape.[86] A study of rape dispositions in Dallas, for example, showed that the average prison term for a man convicted of raping a Black woman was two years,[87] as compared to five years for the rape of a Latina and ten years for the rape of an Anglo woman.[88] A related issue is the fact that African-American victims of rape are the least likely to be believed.[89] The Dallas study and others like it also point to a more subtle problem: neither the antirape nor the antiracist political agenda has focused on the Black rape victim. This inattention stems from the way the problem of rape is conceptualized within antiracist and antirape reform discourses. Although the rhetoric of both agendas formally includes Black women, racism is generally not problematized in feminism, and sexism, not problematized in antiracist discourses. Consequently, the plight of Black women is relegated to a secondary importance: The primary beneficiaries of policies supported by feminists and others concerned about rape tend to be white women; the primary beneficiaries of the Black community's concern over racism and rape, Black men. Ultimately, the reformist and rhetorical strategies that have grown out of antiracist and feminist rape reform movements have been ineffective in politicizing the treatment of Black women.

2. *Race and the antirape lobby.*

Feminist critiques of rape have focused on the way rape law has reflected

---

rape of Kimberly Rae Harbour was written into a local script highlighted by the Boston Police Department's siege upon Black men in pursuit of the "fictional" Carol Stuart murderer. *See* John Ellement, *8 Teen-agers Charged in Rape, Killing of Dorchester Woman,* Boston Globe, Nov. 20, 1990, at 1; James S. Kunen, *Homicide No. 119,* PEOPLE, Jan. 14, 1991, at 42. For a comparison of the Stuart and Harbour murders, see Christopher B. Daly, *Scant Attention Paid Victim as Homicides Reach Record in Boston,* Wash. Post, Dec. 5, 1990, at A3.

85. Smith points out that "[t]he relative invisibility of black women victims of rape also reflects the differential value of women's bodies in capitalist societies. To the extent that rape is constructed as a crime against the property of privileged white men, crimes against less valuable women—women of color, working-class women, and lesbians, for example—mean less or mean differently than those against white women from the middle and upper classes." Smith, *supra* note 74, at 275-76.

86. "Cases involving black offenders and black victims were treated the least seriously." GARY D. LAFREE, RAPE AND CRIMINAL JUSTICE: THE SOCIAL CONSTRUCTION OF SEXUAL ASSAULT (1989). LaFree also notes, however, that "the race composition of the victim-offender dyad" was not the only predictor of case dispositions. *Id.* at 219-20.

87. *Race Tilts the Scales of Justice. Study: Dallas Punishes Attacks on Whites More Harshly,* Dallas Times Herald, Aug. 19, 1990, at A1. A study of 1988 cases in Dallas County's criminal justice system concluded that rapists whose victims were white were punished more severely than those whose victims were Black or Hispanic. The Dallas Times Herald, which had commissioned the study, reported that "[t]he punishment almost doubled when the attacker and victim were of different races. Except for such interracial crime, sentencing disparities were much less pronounced . . . ." *Id.*

88. *Id.* Two criminal law experts, Iowa law professor David Baldus and Carnegie-Mellon University professor Alfred Blumstein "said that the racial inequities might be even worse than the figures suggest." *Id.*

89. *See* G. LAFREE, *supra* note 86, at 219-20 (quoting jurors who doubted the credibility of Black rape survivors); *see also* H. FEILD & L. BIENEN, *supra* note 35, at 117-18.

dominant rules and expectations that tightly regulate the sexuality of women. In the context of the rape trial, the formal definition of rape as well as the evidentiary rules applicable in a rape trial discriminate against women by measuring the rape victim against a narrow norm of acceptable sexual conduct for women. Deviation from that norm tends to turn women into illegitimate rape victims, leading to rejection of their claims.

Historically, legal rules dictated, for example, that rape victims had to have resisted their assailants in order for their claims to be accepted. Any abatement of struggle was interpreted as the woman's consent to the intercourse under the logic that a real rape victim would protect her honor virtually to the death. While utmost resistance is not formally required anymore, rape law continues to weigh the credibility of women against narrow normative standards of female behavior. A woman's sexual history, for example, is frequently explored by defense attorneys as a way of suggesting that a woman who consented to sex on other occasions was likely to have consented in the case at issue. Past sexual conduct as well as the specific circumstances leading up to the rape are often used to distinguish the moral character of the legitimate rape victim from women who are regarded as morally debased or in some other way responsible for their own victimization.

This type of feminist critique of rape law has informed many of the fundamental reform measures enacted in antirape legislation, including increased penalties for convicted rapists[90] and changes in evidentiary rules to preclude attacks on the woman's moral character.[91] These reforms limit the tactics attorneys might use to tarnish the image of the rape victim, but they operate within preexisting social constructs that distinguish victims from nonvictims on the basis of their sexual character. And so these reforms, while beneficial, do not challenge the background cultural narratives that undermine the credibility of Black women.

Because Black women face subordination based on both race and gender, reforms of rape law and judicial procedures that are premised on narrow conceptions of gender subordination may not address the devaluation of Black women. Much of the problem results from the way certain gender expectations for women intersect with certain sexualized notions of race, no-

90. For example, Title I of the Violence Against Women Act creates federal penalties for sex crimes. *See* 137 CONG. REC. S597, S599-600 (daily ed. Jan. 14, 1991). Specifically, section 111 of the Act authorizes the Sentencing Commission to promulgate guidelines to provide that any person who commits a violation after a prior conviction can be punished by a term of imprisonment or fines up to twice of what is otherwise provided in the guidelines. S. 15, *supra* note 57, at 8. Additionally section 112 of the Act authorizes the Sentencing Commission to amend its sentencing guidelines to provide that a defendant convicted of rape or aggravated rape, "shall be assigned a base offense . . . that is at least 4 levels greater than the base offense level applicable to such offenses." *Id.* at 5.

91. Title I of the Act also creates new evidentiary rules for the introduction of sexual history in criminal and civil cases. *Id.* Sections 151 and 152 amend Fed. R. Evid. 412 by prohibiting "reputation or opinion evidence of the past sexual behavior of an alleged victim" from being admitted, and limiting other evidence of past sexual behavior. *Id.* at 39-44. Similarly, section 153 amends the rape shield law. *Id.* at 44-45. States have also either enacted or attempted to enact rape shield law reforms of their own. *See* Harriet R. Galvin, *Shielding Rape Victims in the State and Federal Courts: A Proposal for the Second Decade,* 70 MINN. L. REV. 763 (1986); Barbara Fromm, *Sexual Battery: Mixed-Signal Legislation Reveals Need for Further Reform,* 18 FLA. ST. U. L. REV. 579 (1991).

tions that are deeply entrenched in American culture. Sexualized images of African Americans go all the way back to Europeans' first engagement with Africans. Blacks have long been portrayed as more sexual, more earthy, more gratification-oriented. These sexualized images of race intersect with norms of women's sexuality, norms that are used to distinguish good women from bad, the madonnas from the whores. Thus Black women are essentially prepackaged as bad women within cultural narratives about good women who can be raped and bad women who cannot. The discrediting of Black women's claims is the consequence of a complex intersection of a gendered sexual system, one that constructs rules appropriate for good and bad women, and a race code that provides images defining the allegedly essential nature of Black women. If these sexual images form even part of the cultural imagery of Black women, then the very representation of a Black female body at least suggests certain narratives that may make Black women's rape either less believable or less important. These narratives may explain why rapes of Black women are less likely to result in convictions and long prison terms than rapes of white women.[92]

Rape law reform measures that do not in some way engage and challenge the narratives that are read onto Black women's bodies are unlikely to affect the way cultural beliefs oppress Black women in rape trials. While the degree to which legal reform can directly challenge cultural beliefs that shape rape trials is limited,[93] the very effort to mobilize political resources toward addressing the sexual oppression of Black women can be an important first step in drawing greater attention to the problem. One obstacle to such an effort has been the failure of most antirape activists to analyze specifically the consequences of racism in the context of rape. In the absence of a direct attempt to address the racial dimensions of rape, Black women are simply presumed to be represented in and benefitted by prevailing feminist critiques.

3. *Antiracism and rape.*

Antiracist critiques of rape law focus on how the law operates primarily to condemn rapes of white women by Black men.[94] While the heightened

---

92. *See* note 35 *supra*.

93. One can imagine certain trial-based interventions that might assist prosecutors in struggling with these beliefs. For example, one might consider expanding the scope of voir dire to examine jurors' attitudes toward Black rape victims. Moreover, as more is learned about Black women's response to rape, this information may be deemed relevant in evaluating Black women's testimony and thus warrant introduction through expert testimony. In this regard, it is worth noting that the battered women's syndrome and the rape trauma syndrome are both forms of expert testimony that frequently function in the context of a trial to counter stereotypes and other dominant narratives that might otherwise produce a negative outcome for the woman "on trial." These interventions, probably unimaginable a short while ago, grew out of efforts to study and somehow quantify women's experience. Similar interventions that address the particular dimensions of the experiences of women of color may well be possible. This knowledge may grow out of efforts to map how women of color have fared under standard interventions. For an example of an intersectional critique of the battered women's syndrome, see Sharon A. Allard, *Rethinking Battered Woman Syndrome: A Black Feminist Perspective,* 1 U.C.L.A. WOMEN'S L.J. 191 (1991) (student author).

94. *See* Smith, *supra* note 74 (discussing media sensationalization of the Central Park jogger case as consistent with historical patterns of focusing almost exclusively on Black male/white female

concern with protecting white women against Black men has been primarily criticized as a form of discrimination against Black men,[95] it just as surely reflects devaluation of Black women.[96] This disregard for Black women results from an exclusive focus on the consequences of the problem for Black men.[97] Of course, rape accusations historically have provided a justification for white terrorism against the Black community, generating a legitimating power of such strength that it created a veil virtually impenetrable to appeals based on either humanity or fact.[98] Ironically, while the fear of the Black rapist was exploited to legitimate the practice of lynching, rape was not even alleged in most cases.[99] The well-developed fear of Black sexuality served primarily to increase white tolerance for racial terrorism as a prophylactic measure to keep Blacks under control.[100] Within the African-American community, cases involving race-based accusations against Black men have stood as hallmarks of racial injustice. The prosecution of the Scottsboro boys[101] and the Emmett Till[102] tragedy, for example, triggered African-

---

dyads.); *see also* Terry, *supra* note 81 (discussing the 28 other rapes that occurred during the same week, but that were not given the same media coverage). Although rape is largely an intraracial crime, this explanation for the disparate coverage given to nonwhite victims is doubtful, however, given the findings of at least one study that 48% of those surveyed believed that most rapes involved a Black offender and a white victim. *See* H. FEILD & L. BIENEN, *supra* note 35, at 80. Ironically, Feild and Bienen include in their book-length study of rape two photographs distributed to the subjects in their study depicting the alleged victim as white and the alleged assailant as Black. Given the authors' acknowledgment that rape was overwhelmingly intraracial, the appearance of these photos was particularly striking, especially because they were the only photos included in the entire book.

95. *See, e.g.*, G. LAFREE, *supra* note 86, at 237-39.

96. For a similar argument that race-of-victim discrimination in the administration of the death penalty actually represents the devalued status of Black victims rather than discrimination against Black offenders, see Randall L. Kennedy, *McCleskey v. Kemp: Race, Capital Punishment, and the Supreme Court*, 101 HARV. L. REV. 1388 (1988).

97. The statistic that 89% of all men executed for rape in this country were Black is a familiar one. Furman v. Georgia, 408 U.S. 238, 364 (1972) (Marshall, J., concurring). Unfortunately, the dominant analysis of racial discrimination in rape prosecutions generally does not discuss whether any of the rape *victims* in these cases were Black. *See* Jennifer Wriggins, *Rape, Racism, and the Law*, 6 HARV. WOMEN'S L.J. 103, 113 (1983) (student author).

98. Race was frequently sufficient to fill in facts that were unknown or unknowable. As late as 1953, the Alabama Supreme Court ruled that a jury could take race into account in determining whether a Black man was guilty of "an attempt to commit an assault with an attempt to rape." *See* McQuirter v. State, 63 So. 2d. 388, 390 (Ala. 1953). According to the "victim's" testimony, the man stared at her and mumbled something unintelligible as they passed. *Id.* at 389.

99. Ida Wells, an early Black feminist, investigated every lynching she could for about a decade. After researching 728 lynchings, she concluded that "[o]nly a third of the murdered Blacks were even *accused* of rape, much less guilty of it." PAULA GIDDINGS, WHEN AND WHERE I ENTER: THE IMPACT OF BLACK WOMEN ON RACE AND SEX IN AMERICA 28 (1984) (quoting Wells).

100. *See* Jacquelyn Dowd Hall, *"The Mind That Burns in Each Body": Women, Rape, and Racial Violence*, in POWERS OF DESIRE: THE POLITICS OF SEXUALITY 328, 334 (Ann Snitow, Christine Stansell, & Sharon Thompson eds. 1983).

101. Nine Black youths were charged with the rape of two white women in a railroad freight car near Scottsboro, Alabama. Their trials occurred in a heated atmosphere. Each trial was completed in a single day, and the defendants were all convicted and sentenced to death. *See* DAN T. CARTER, SCOTTSBORO: A TRAGEDY OF THE AMERICAN SOUTH (1976). The Supreme Court reversed the defendants' convictions and death sentences, holding that they were unconstitutionally denied the right to counsel. Powell v. Alabama, 287 U.S. 45, 65 (1932). However, the defendants were retried by an all-white jury after the Supreme Court reversed their convictions.

102. Emmett Till was a 14-year-old Black boy from Chicago visiting his relatives near Money,

American resistance to the rigid social codes of white supremacy.[103] To the extent rape of Black women is thought to dramatize racism, it is usually cast as an assault on Black manhood, demonstrating his inability to protect Black women. The direct assault on Black womanhood is less frequently seen as an assault on the Black community.[104]

The sexual politics that this limited reading of racism and rape engenders continues to play out today, as illustrated by the Mike Tyson rape trial. The use of antiracist rhetoric to mobilize support for Tyson represented an ongoing practice of viewing with considerable suspicion rape accusations against Black men and interpreting sexual racism through a male-centered frame. The historical experience of Black men has so completely occupied the dominant conceptions of racism and rape that there is little room to squeeze in the experiences of Black women. Consequently, racial solidarity was continually raised as a rallying point on behalf of Tyson, but never on behalf of Desiree Washington, Tyson's Black accuser. Leaders ranging from Benjamin Hooks to Louis Farrakhan expressed their support for Tyson,[105] yet no established Black leader voiced any concern for Washington. The fact that Black men have often been falsely accused of raping white women underlies the antiracist defense of Black men accused of rape even when the accuser herself is a Black woman.

As a result of this continual emphasis on Black male sexuality as the core issue in antiracist critiques of rape, Black women who raise claims of rape against Black men are not only disregarded but also sometimes vilified within the African-American community. One can only imagine the alienation experienced by a Black rape survivor such as Desiree Washington when the accused rapist is embraced and defended as a victim of racism while she is, at best, disregarded, and at worst, ostracized and ridiculed. In contrast, Tyson was the beneficiary of the longstanding practice of using antiracist rhetoric to deflect the injury suffered by Black women victimized by Black men. Some defended the support given to Tyson on the ground that all Afri-

---

Mississippi. On a dare by local boys, he entered a store and spoke to a white woman. Several days later, Emmett Till's body was found in the Tallahatchie River. "The barbed wire holding the cotton-gin fan around his neck had became snagged on a tangled river root." After the corpse was discovered, the white woman's husband and his brother-in-law were charged with Emmett Till's murder. JUAN WILLIAMS, EYES ON THE PRIZE 39-43 (1987). For a historical account of the Emmett Till tragedy, see STEPHEN J. WHITFIELD, A DEATH IN THE DELTA (1988).

103. Crenshaw, *supra* note 7, at 159 (discussing how the generation of Black activists who created the Black Liberation Movement were contemporaries of Emmett Till).

104.

> Until quite recently, for example, when historians talked of rape in the slavery experience they often bemoaned the damage this act did to the Black male's sense of esteem and respect. He was powerless to protect his woman from white rapists. Few scholars probed the effect that rape, the threat of rape, and domestic violence had on the psychic development of the female victims.

Darlene Clark Hine, *Rape and the Inner Lives of Black Women in the Middle West: Preliminary Thoughts on the Culture of Dissemblance,* in UNEQUAL SISTERS: A MULTI-CULTURAL READER IN U.S. WOMEN'S HISTORY (Ellen Carol Dubois & Vicki L. Ruiz eds. 1990).

105. Michael Madden, *No Offensive from Defense,* Boston Globe, Feb. 1, 1992, at 33 (Hooks); *Farrakhan Backs Calls for Freeing Tyson,* UPI, July 10, 1992.

can Americans can readily imagine their sons, fathers, brothers, or uncles being wrongly accused of rape. Yet daughters, mothers, sisters, and aunts also deserve at least a similar concern, since statistics show that Black women are more likely to be raped than Black men are to be falsely accused of it. Given the magnitude of Black women's vulnerability to sexual violence, it is not unreasonable to expect as much concern for Black women who are raped as is expressed for the men who are accused of raping them.

Black leaders are not alone in their failure to empathize with or rally around Black rape victims. Indeed, some Black women were among Tyson's staunchest supporters and Washington's harshest critics.[106] The media widely noted the lack of sympathy Black women had for Washington; Barbara Walters used the observation as a way of challenging Washington's credibility, going so far as to press Washington for a reaction.[107] The most troubling revelation was that many of the women who did not support Washington also doubted Tyson's story. These women did not sympathize with Washington because they believed that Washington had no business in Tyson's hotel room at 2:00 a.m. A typical response was offered by one young Black woman who stated, "She asked for it, she got it, it's not fair to cry rape."[108]

Indeed, some of the women who expressed their disdain for Washington acknowledged that they encountered the threat of sexual assault almost daily.[109] Yet it may be precisely this threat—along with the relative absence of rhetorical strategies challenging the sexual subordination of Black women—that animated their harsh criticism. In this regard, Black women who condemned Washington were quite like all other women who seek to distance themselves from rape victims as a way of denying their own vulnerability. Prosecutors who handle sexual assault cases acknowledge that they often exclude women as potential jurors because women tend to empathize the least with the victim.[110] To identify too closely with victimization may reveal their own vulnerability.[111] Consequently, women often look for evi-

---

106. *See* Megan Rosenfeld, *After the Verdict, The Doubts: Black Women Show Little Sympathy for Tyson's Accuser,* Wash. Post, Feb. 13, 1992, at D1; Allan Johnson, *Tyson Rape Case Strikes a Nerve Among Blacks,* Chicago Trib., Mar. 29, 1992, at C1; Suzanne P. Kelly, *Black Women Wrestle with Abuse Issue: Many Say Choosing Racial Over Gender Loyalty Is Too Great a Sacrifice,* Star Trib., Feb. 18, 1992, at A1.

107. *20/20* (ABC television broadcast, Feb. 21, 1992).

108. *Id.*

109. According to a study by the Bureau of Justice, Black women are significantly more likely to be raped than white women, and women in the 16-24 age group are 2 to 3 times more likely to be victims of rape or attempted rape than women in any other age group. *See* Ronald J. Ostrow, *Typical Rape Victim Called Poor, Young,* L.A. Times, Mar. 25, 1985, at 8.

110. *See* Peg Tyre, *What Experts Say About Rape Jurors,* Newsday, May 19, 1991, at 10 (reporting that "researchers had determined that jurors in criminal trials side with the complainant or defendant whose ethnic, economic and religious background most closely resembles their own. The exception to the rule . . . is the way women jurors judge victims of rape and sexual assault."). Linda Fairstein, a Manhattan prosecutor, states, "(T)oo often women tend to be very critical of the conduct of other women, and they often are not good jurors in acquaintance-rape cases." Margaret Carlson, *The Trials of Convicting Rapists,* TIME, Oct. 14, 1991, at 11.

111. As sex crimes prosecutor Barbara Eganhauser notes, even young women with contemporary lifestyles often reject a woman's rape accusation out of fear. "To call another woman the victim

dence that the victim brought the rape on herself, usually by breaking social rules that are generally held applicable only to women. And when the rules classify women as dumb, loose, or weak on the one hand, and smart, discriminating, and strong on the other, it is not surprising that women who cannot step outside the rules to critique them attempt to validate themselves within them. The position of most Black women on this issue is particularly problematic, first, because of the extent to which they are consistently reminded that they are the group most vulnerable to sexual victimization, and second, because most Black women share the African-American community's general resistance to explicitly feminist analysis when it appears to run up against long-standing narratives that construct Black men as the primary victims of sexual racism.

C. *Rape and Intersectionality in Social Science*

The marginalization of Black women's experiences within the antiracist and feminist critiques of rape law are facilitated by social science studies that fail to examine the ways in which racism and sexism converge. Gary LaFree's *Rape and Criminal Justice: The Social Construction of Sexual Assault*[112] is a classic example. Through a study of rape prosecutions in Minneapolis, LaFree attempts to determine the validity of two prevailing claims regarding rape prosecutions. The first claim is that Black defendants face significant racial discrimination.[113] The second is that rape laws serve to regulate the sexual conduct of women by withholding from rape victims the ability to invoke sexual assault law when they have engaged in nontraditional behavior.[114] LaFree's compelling study concludes that law constructs rape in ways that continue to manifest both racial and gender domination.[115] Although Black women are positioned as victims of both the racism and the sexism that LaFree so persuasively details, his analysis is less illuminating than might be expected because Black women fall through the cracks of his dichotomized theoretical framework.

1. *Racial domination and rape.*

LaFree confirms the findings of earlier studies that show that race is a significant determinant in the ultimate disposition of rape cases. He finds that Black men accused of raping white women were treated most harshly, while Black offenders accused of raping Black women were treated most leniently.[116] These effects held true even after controlling for other factors

---

of rape is to acknowledge the vulnerability in yourself. They go out at night, they date, they go to bars, and walk alone. To deny it is to say at the trial that women are not victims." Tyre, *supra* note 110.

112. G. LaFree, *supra* note 86.

113. *Id.* at 49-50.

114. *Id.* at 50-51.

115. *Id.* at 237-40.

116. LaFree concludes that recent studies finding no discriminatory effect were inconclusive because they analyzed the effects of the defendant's race independently of the race of victim. The differential race effects in sentencing are often concealed by combining the harsher sentences given to

such as injury to the victim and acquaintance between victim and assailant.

> Compared to other defendants, blacks who were suspected of assaulting white women received more serious charges, were more likely to have their cases filed as felonies, were more likely to receive prison sentences if convicted, were more likely to be incarcerated in the state penitentiary (as opposed to a jail or minimum-security facility), and received longer sentences on the average.[117]

LaFree's conclusions that Black men are differentially punished depending on the race of the victim do not, however, contribute much to understanding the plight of Black rape victims. Part of the problem lies in the author's use of "sexual stratification" theory, which posits both that women are differently valued according to their race and that there are certain "rules of sexual access" governing who may have sexual contact with whom in this sexually stratified market.[118] According to the theory, Black men are discriminated against in that their forced "access" to white women is more harshly penalized than their forced "access" to Black women.[119] LaFree's analysis focuses on the harsh regulation of access by Black men to white women, but is silent about the relative subordination of Black women to

---

Black men accused of raping white women with the more lenient treatment of Black men accused of raping Black women. *Id.* at 117, 140. Similar results were found in another study. *See* Anthony Walsh, *The Sexual Stratification Hypothesis and Sexual Assault in Light of the Changing Conceptions of Race,* 25 CRIMINOLOGY 153, 170 (1987) ("sentence severity mean for blacks who assaulted whites, which was significantly in excess of mean for whites who assaulted whites, was masked by the lenient sentence severity mean for blacks who assaulted blacks").

117. G. LAFREE, *supra* note 86, at 139-40.

118. Sexual stratification, according to LaFree, refers to the differential valuation of women according to their race and to the creation of "rules of sexual access" governing who may have contact with whom. Sexual stratification also dictates what the penalty will be for breaking these rules: The rape of a white woman by a Black man is seen as a trespass on the valuable property rights of white men and is punished most severely. *Id.* at 48-49.

The fundamental propositions of the sexual stratification thesis have been summarized as follows:

> (1) Women are viewed as the valued and scarce property of the men of their own race.
>
> (2) White women, by virtue of membership in the dominant race, are more valuable than black women.
>
> (3) The sexual assault of a white by a black threatens both the white man's "property rights" and his dominant social position. This dual threat accounts for the strength of the taboo attached to interracial sexual assault.
>
> (4) A sexual assault by a male of any race upon members of the less valued black race is perceived as nonthreatening to the status quo and therefore less serious.
>
> (5) White men predominate as agents of social control. Therefore, they have the power to sanction differentially according to the perceived threat to their favored social position.

Walsh, *supra* note 116, at 155.

119. I use the term "access" guardedly because it is an inapt euphemism for rape. On the other hand, rape is conceptualized differently depending on whether certain race-specific rules of sexual access are violated. Although violence is not explicitly written into the sexual stratification theory, it does work itself into the rules, in that sexual intercourse that violates the racial access rules is presumed to be coercive rather that voluntary. *See, e.g.,* Sims v. Balkam, 136 S.E. 2d 766, 769 (Ga. 1964) (describing the rape of a white woman by a Black man as "a crime more horrible than death"); Story v. State, 59 So. 480 (Ala. 1912) ("The consensus of public opinion, unrestricted to either race, is that a white woman prostitute is yet, though lost of virtue, above the even greater sacrifice of the voluntary submission of her person to the embraces of the other race."); Wriggins, *supra* note 97, at 125, 127.

white women. The emphasis on differential access to women is consistent with analytical perspectives that view racism primarily in terms of the inequality between men. From this prevailing viewpoint, the problem of discrimination is that white men can rape Black women with relative impunity while Black men cannot do the same with white women.[120] Black women are considered victims of discrimination only to the extent that white men can rape them without fear of significant punishment. Rather than being viewed as victims of discrimination in their own right, they become merely the means by which discrimination against Black men can be recognized. The inevitable result of this orientation is that efforts to fight discrimination tend to ignore the particularly vulnerable position of Black women, who must both confront racial bias *and* challenge their status as instruments, rather than beneficiaries, of the civil rights struggle.

Where racial discrimination is framed by LaFree primarily in terms of a contest between Black and white men over women, the racism experienced by Black women will only be seen in terms of white male access to them. When rape of Black women by white men is eliminated as a factor in the analysis, whether for statistical or other reasons, racial discrimination against Black women no longer matters, since LaFree's analysis involves comparing the "access" of white and Black men to white women.[121] Yet Black women are not discriminated against simply because white men can rape them with little sanction and be punished less than Black men who rape white women, or because white men who rape them are not punished the same as white men who rape white women. Black women are also discriminated against because intraracial rape of white women is treated more seriously than intraracial rape of Black women. But the differential protection that Black and white women receive against intraracial rape is not seen as racist because intraracial rape does not involve a contest between Black and white men. In other words, the way the criminal justice system treats rapes of Black women by Black men and rapes of white women by white men is not seen as raising issues of racism because Black and white men are not involved with each other's women.

In sum, Black women who are raped are racially discriminated against because their rapists, whether Black or white, are less likely to be charged with rape, and when charged and convicted, are less likely to receive significant jail time than the rapists of white women. And while sexual stratification theory does posit that women are stratified sexually by race, most applications of the theory focus on the inequality of male agents of rape rather than on the inequality of rape victims, thus marginalizing the racist

120. This traditional approach places Black women in a position of denying their own victimization, requiring Black women to argue that it is racist to punish Black men more harshly for raping white women than for raping Black women. However, in the wake of the Mike Tyson trial, it seems that many Black women are prepared to do just that. *See* notes 106-109 *supra* and accompanying text.

121. In fact, critics and commentators often use the term "interracial rape" when they are actually talking only about Black male/white female rape.

treatment of Black women by consistently portraying racism in terms of the relative power of Black and white men.

In order to understand and treat the victimization of Black women as a consequence of racism and sexism, it is necessary to shift the analysis away from the differential access of men and more toward the differential protection of women. Throughout his analysis, LaFree fails to do so. His sexual stratification thesis—in particular, its focus on the comparative power of male agents of rape—illustrates how the marginalization of Black women in antiracist politics is replicated in social science research. Indeed, the thesis leaves unproblematized the racist subordination of less valuable objects (Black women) to more valuable objects (white women), and it perpetuates the sexist treatment of women as property extensions of "their" men.

2. *Rape and gender subordination.*

Although LaFree does attempt to address gender-related concerns of women in his discussion of rape and the social control of women, his theory of sexual stratification fails to focus sufficiently on the effects of stratification on women.[122] LaFree quite explicitly uses a framework that treats race and gender as separate categories, giving no indication that he understands that Black women may fall in between or within both. The problem with LaFree's analysis lies not in its individual observations, which can be insightful and accurate, but in his failure to connect them and develop a broader, deeper perspective. His two-track framework makes for a narrow interpretation of the data because it leaves untouched the possibility that these two tracks may intersect. And it is those who reside at the intersection of gender and race discrimination—Black women—that suffer from this fundamental oversight.

LaFree attempts to test the feminist hypothesis that "the application of law to nonconformist women in rape cases may serve to control the behavior of all women."[123] This inquiry is important, he explains, because "if women who violate traditional sex roles and are raped are unable to obtain justice through the legal system, then the law may be interpreted as an institutional arrangement for reinforcing women's gender-role conformity."[124] He finds that "acquittals were more common and final sentences were shorter when nontraditional victim behavior was alleged."[125] Thus LaFree concludes that the victim's moral character was more important than victim injury, and was second only to the defendant's character. Overall, 82.3 percent of the traditional victim cases resulted in convictions and average sentences of

122. G. LaFree, *supra* note 86, at 148. LaFree's transition between race and gender suggests that the shift might not loosen the frame enough to permit discussion of the combined effects of race and gender subordination on Black women. LaFree repeatedly separates race from gender, treating them as wholly distinguishable issues. *See, e.g., id.* at 147.

123. *Id.*

124. *Id.* at 151. LaFree interprets nontraditional behavior to include drinking, drug use, extramarital sex, illegitimate children, and "having a reputation as a 'partier,' a 'pleasure seeker' or someone who stays out late at night." *Id.* at 201.

125. *Id.* at 204.

43.38 months.[126] Only 50 percent of nontraditional victim cases led to convictions, with an average term of 27.83 months.[127] The effects of traditional and nontraditional behavior by Black women are difficult to determine from the information given and must be inferred from LaFree's passing comments. For example, LaFree notes that Black victims were evenly divided between traditional and nontraditional gender roles. This observation, together with the lower rate of conviction for men accused of raping Blacks, suggests that gender role behavior was not as significant in determining case disposition as it was in cases involving white victims. Indeed, LaFree explicitly notes that "the victim's *race* was . . . an important predictor of jurors' case evaluations."[128]

> Jurors were less likely to believe in a defendant's guilt when the victim was black. Our interviews with jurors suggested that part of the explanation for this effect was that jurors . . . were influenced by stereotypes of black women as more likely to consent to sex or as more sexually experienced and hence less harmed by the assault. In a case involving the rape of a young black girl, one juror argued for acquittal on the grounds that a girl her age from 'that kind of neighborhood' probably wasn't a virgin anyway.[129]

---

126. *Id.*

127. *Id.*

128. *Id.* at 219 (emphasis added). While there is little direct evidence that prosecutors are influenced by the race of the victim, it is not unreasonable to assume that since race is an important predictor of conviction, prosecutors determined to maintain a high conviction rate might be less likely to pursue a case involving a Black victim than a white one. This calculus is probably reinforced when juries fail to convict in strong cases involving Black victims. For example, the acquittal of three white St. John's University athletes for the gang rape of a Jamaican schoolmate was interpreted by many as racially influenced. Witnesses testified that the woman was incapacitated during much of the ordeal, having ingested a mixture of alcohol given to her by a classmate who subsequently initiated the assault. The jurors insisted that race played no role in their decision to acquit. "There was no race, we all agreed to it," said one juror; "They were trying to make it racial but it wasn't," said another. *Jurors: 'It Wasn't Racial,'* Newsday, July 25, 1991, at 4. Yet it is possible that race did influence on some level their belief that the woman consented to what by all accounts, amounted to dehumanizing conduct. *See, e.g.,* Carole Agus, *Whatever Happened to 'The Rules',* Newsday, July 28, 1991, at 11 (citing testimony that at least two of the assailants hit the victim in the head with their penises). The jury nonetheless thought, in the words of its foreman, that the defendants' behavior was "obnoxious" but not criminal. *See* Sydney H. Schanberg, *Those 'Obnoxious' St. John's Athletes,* Newsday, July 30, 1991, at 79. One can imagine a different outcome had the races of the parties only been reversed.

Representative Charles Rangel (D-N.Y.) called the verdict "a rerun of what used to happen in the South." James Michael Brodie, *The St. John's Rape Acquittal: Old Wounds That Just Won't Go Away,* BLACK ISSUES IN HIGHER EDUC., Aug. 15, 1991, at 18. Denise Snyder, executive director of the D.C. Rape Crisis Center, commented:

> It's a historical precedent that white men can assault black women and get away with it. Woe be to the black man who assaults white women. All the prejudices that existed a hundred years ago are dormant and not so dormant, and they rear their ugly heads in situations like this. Contrast this with the Central Park jogger who was an upper-class white woman.

Judy Mann, *New Age, Old Myths,* Wash. Post, July 26, 1991, at C3 (quoting Snyder); *see* Kristin Bumiller, *Rape as a Legal Symbol: An Essay on Sexual Violence and Racism,* 42 U. MIAMI L. REV. 75, 88 ("The cultural meaning of rape is rooted in a symbiosis of racism and sexism that has tolerated the acting out of male aggression against women and, in particular, black women.").

129. *Id.* at 219-20 (citations omitted). Anecdotal evidence suggests that this attitude exists among some who are responsible for processing rape cases. Fran Weinman, a student in my seminar on race, gender, and the law, conducted a field study at the Rosa Parks Rape Crisis Center. During

LaFree also notes that "[o]ther jurors were simply less willing to believe the testimony of black complainants."[130] One white juror is quoted as saying, "Negroes have a way of not telling the truth. They've a knack for coloring the story. So you know you can't believe everything they say."[131]

Despite explicit evidence that the race of the victim is significant in determining the disposition of rape cases, LaFree concludes that rape law functions to penalize nontraditional behavior in women.[132] LaFree fails to note that racial identification may itself serve as a proxy for nontraditional behavior. Rape law, that is, serves not only to penalize actual examples of nontraditional behavior but also to diminish and devalue women who belong to groups in which nontraditional behavior is perceived as common. For the Black rape victim, the disposition of her case may often turn less on her behavior than on her identity. LaFree misses the point that although white and Black women have shared interests in resisting the madonna/whore dichotomy altogether, they nevertheless experience its oppressive power differently. Black women continue to be judged by who they are, not by what they do.

3. *Compounding the marginalizations of rape.*

LaFree offers clear evidence that the race/sex hierarchy subordinates Black women to white women, as well as to men—both Black and white. However, the different effects of rape law on Black women are scarcely mentioned in LaFree's conclusions. In a final section, LaFree treats the devaluation of Black women as an aside—one without apparent ramifications for rape law. He concludes: "The more severe treatment of black offenders who rape white women *(or, for that matter, the milder treatment of black offenders who rape black women)* is probably best explained in terms of racial discrimination within a broader context of continuing social and physical segregation between blacks and whites."[133] Implicit throughout LaFree's

---

her study, she counseled and accompanied a 12-year-old Black rape survivor who became pregnant as a result of the rape. The girl was afraid to tell her parents, who discovered the rape after she became depressed and began to slip in school. Police were initially reluctant to interview the girl. Only after the girl's father threatened to take matters into his own hands did the police department send an investigator to the girl's house. The City prosecutor indicated that the case wasn't a serious one, and was reluctant to prosecute the defendant for statutory rape even though the girl was underage. The prosecutor reasoned, "After all, she looks 16." After many frustrations, the girl's family ultimately decided not to pressure the prosecutor any further and the case was dropped. *See* Fran Weinman, Racism and the Enforcement of Rape Law, 13-30 (1990) (unpublished manuscript) (on file with the *Stanford Law Review*).

130. G. LaFree, *supra* note 86, at 220.

131. *Id.*

132. *Id.* at 226.

133. *Id.* at 239 (emphasis added). The lower conviction rates for those who rape Black women may be analogous to the low conviction rates for acquaintance rape. The central issue in many rape cases is proving that the victim did not consent. The basic presumption in the absence of explicit evidence of lack of consent is that consent exists. Certain evidence is sufficient to disprove that presumption, and the quantum of evidence necessary to prove nonconsent increases as the presumptions warranting an inference of consent increases. Some women—based on their character, identity, or dress—are viewed as more likely to consent than other women. Perhaps it is the combination of the sexual stereotypes about Black people along with the greater degree of familiarity presumed to

study is the assumption that Blacks who are subjected to social control are Black *men*. Moreover, the social control to which he refers is limited to securing the boundaries between Black males and white females. His conclusion that race differentials are best understood within the context of social segregation as well as his emphasis on the interracial implications of boundary enforcement overlook the intraracial dynamics of race and gender subordination. When Black men are leniently punished for raping Black women, the problem is *not* "best explained" in terms of social segregation but in terms of both the race- and gender-based devaluation of Black women. By failing to examine the sexist roots of such lenient punishment, LaFree and other writers sensitive to racism ironically repeat the mistakes of those who ignore race as a factor in such cases. Both groups fail to consider directly the situation of Black women.

Studies like LaFree's do little to illuminate how the interaction of race, class and nontraditional behavior affects the disposition of rape cases involving Black women. Such an oversight is especially troubling given evidence that many cases involving Black women are dismissed outright.[134] Over 20 percent of rape complaints were recently dismissed as "unfounded" by the Oakland Police Department, which did not even interview many, if not most, of the women involved.[135] Not coincidentally, the vast majority of the complainants were Black and poor; many of them were substance abusers or prostitutes.[136] Explaining their failure to pursue these complaints, the police remarked that "those cases were hopelessly tainted by women who are transient, uncooperative, untruthful or not credible as witnesses in court."[137]

---

exist between Black men and Black women that leads to the conceptualization of such rapes as existing somewhere between acquaintance rape and stranger rape.

134. *See, e.g.*, Candy J. Cooper, *Nowhere to Turn for Rape Victims: High Proportion of Cases Tossed Aside by Oakland Police*, S.F. Examiner, Sept. 16, 1990, at A1 [hereinafter Cooper, *Nowhere to Turn*]. The most persuasive evidence that the images and beliefs that Oakland police officers hold toward rape victims influence the disposition of their cases is represented in two follow-up stories. *See* Candy J. Cooper, *A Rape Victim Vindicated*, S.F. Examiner, Sept. 17, 1990, at A1; Candy J. Cooper, *Victim of Rape, Victim of the System*, S.F. Examiner, Sept. 17, 1990, at A10. These stories contrasted the experiences of two Black women, both of whom had been raped by an acquaintance after smoking crack. In the first case, although there was little physical evidence and the woman was initially reluctant to testify, her rapist was prosecuted and ultimately convicted. In the second case, the woman was severely beaten by her assailant. Despite ample physical evidence and corroboration, and a cooperative victim, her case was not pursued. The former case was handled by the Berkeley, California, police department while the latter was handled by the Oakland police department. Perhaps the different approaches producing these disparate results can best be captured by the philosophies of the investigators. Officers in Berkeley "take every woman's case so seriously that not one [in 1989] was found to be false." *See* Candy J. Cooper, *Berkeley Unit Takes All Cases as Legitimate*, S.F. Examiner, Sept. 16, 1990, at A16. The same year, 24.4% of Oakland's rape cases were classified as "unfounded." Cooper, *Nowhere to Turn*, *supra*.

135. Cooper, *Nowhere to Turn*, *supra* note 134, at A10.

136. *Id.* ("Police, prosecutors, victims and rape crisis workers agree that most of the dropped cases were reported by women of color who smoked crack or were involved in other criminal, high-risk behavior, such as prostitution.").

137. *Id.* Advocates point out that because investigators work from a profile of the kind of case likely to get a conviction, people left out of that profile are people of color, prostitutes, drug users and people raped by acquaintances. This exclusion results in "a whole class of women . . . systematically being denied justice. Poor women suffer the most." *Id.*

The effort to politicize violence against women will do little to address the experiences of Black and other nonwhite women until the ramifications of racial stratification among women are acknowledged. At the same time, the antiracist agenda will not be furthered by suppressing the reality of intraracial violence against women of color. The effect of both these marginalizations is that women of color have no ready means to link their experiences with those of other women. This sense of isolation compounds efforts to politicize sexual violence within communities of color and permits the deadly silence surrounding these issues.

D. *Implications*

With respect to the rape of Black women, race and gender converge in ways that are only vaguely understood. Unfortunately, the analytical frameworks that have traditionally informed both antirape and antiracist agendas tend to focus only on single issues. They are thus incapable of developing solutions to the compound marginalization of Black women victims, who, yet again, fall into the void between concerns about women's issues and concerns about racism. This dilemma is complicated by the role that cultural images play in the treatment of Black women victims. That is, the most critical aspects of these problems may revolve less around the political agendas of separate race- and gender-sensitive groups, and more around the social and cultural devaluation of women of color. The stories our culture tells about the experience of women of color present another challenge—and a further opportunity—to apply and evaluate the usefulness of the intersectional critique.

III. Representational Intersectionality

With respect to the rape of Black women, race and gender converge so that the concerns of minority women fall into the void between concerns about women's issues and concerns about racism. But when one discourse fails to acknowledge the significance of the other, the power relations that each attempts to challenge are strengthened. For example, when feminists fail to acknowledge the role that race played in the public response to the rape of the Central Park jogger, feminism contributes to the forces that produce disproportionate punishment for Black men who rape white women, and when antiracists represent the case solely in terms of racial domination, they belittle the fact that women particularly, and all people generally, should be outraged by the gender violence the case represented.

Perhaps the devaluation of women of color implicit here is linked to how women of color are represented in cultural imagery. Scholars in a wide range of fields are increasingly coming to acknowledge the centrality of issues of representation in the reproduction of racial and gender hierarchy in the United States. Yet current debates over representation continually elide the intersection of race and gender in the popular culture's construction of images of women of color. Accordingly, an analysis of what may be termed "representational intersectionality" would include both the ways in which these images are produced through a confluence of prevalent narratives of race and gender, as well as a recognition of how contemporary critiques of racist and sexist representation marginalize women of color.

In this section I explore the problem of representational intersectionality—in particular, how the production of images of women of color and the contestations over those images tend to ignore the intersectional interests of women of color—in the context of the controversy over 2 Live Crew, the Black rap group that was the subject of an obscenity prosecution in Florida in 1990. I oppose the obscenity prosecution of 2 Live Crew, but not for the same reasons as those generally offered in support of 2 Live Crew, and not without a sense of sharp internal division, of dissatisfaction with the idea that the "real issue" is race or gender, inertly juxtaposed. An intersectional analysis offers both an intellectual and political response to this dilemma. Aiming to bring together the different aspects of an otherwise divided sensibility, an intersectional analysis argues that racial and sexual subordination are mutually reinforcing, that Black women are commonly marginalized by a politics of race alone or gender alone, and that a political response to each form of subordination must at the same time be a political response to both.

A. *The 2 Live Crew Controversy*

In June 1990, the members of 2 Live Crew were arrested and charged under a Florida obscenity statute for their performance in an adults-only club in Hollywood, Florida. The arrests came just two days after a federal court judge ruled that the sexually explicit lyrics in 2 Live Crew's album, *As Nasty As They Wanna Be*,[138] were obscene.[139] Although the members of 2 Live Crew were eventually acquitted of charges stemming from the live performance, the federal court determination that *Nasty* is obscene still stands. This obscenity judgment, along with the arrests and subsequent trial, prompted an intense public controversy about rap music, a controversy that merged with a broader debate about the representation of sex and violence in popular music, about cultural diversity, and about the meaning of freedom of expression.

Two positions dominated the debate over 2 Live Crew. Writing in *Newsweek*, political columnist George Will staked out a case for the prosecu-

138. 2 LIVE CREW, AS NASTY AS THEY WANNA BE (Luke Records 1989).

139. In June 1990, a federal judge ruled that 2 Live Crew's lyrics referring to sodomy and sexual intercourse were obscene. Skywalker Records, Inc. v. Navarro, 739 F. Supp. 578, 596 (S.D. Fla. 1990). The court held that the recording appealed to the prurient interest, was patently offensive as defined by state law, and taken as a whole, lacked serious literary, artistic or political value. *Id.* at 591-96. However, the court also held that the sheriff's office had subjected the recording to unconstitutional prior restraint and consequently granted 2 Live Crew permanent injunctive relief. *Id.* at 596-604. Two days after the judge declared the recording obscene, 2 Live Crew members were charged with giving an obscene performance at a club in Hollywood, Florida. *Experts Defend Live Crew Lyrics*, UPI, Oct. 19, 1990. Deputy sheriffs also arrested Charles Freeman, a merchant who was selling copies of the *Nasty* recording. *See* Gene Santoro, *How 2 B Nasty*, NATION, July 2, 1990, at 4. The 11th Circuit reversed the conviction, Luke Records, Inc. v. Navarro, 960 F.2d 134 (11th Cir. 1992).

tion.[140] Will argued that *Nasty* was misogynistic filth and characterized 2 Live Crew's performance as a profoundly repugnant "combination of extreme infantilism and menace" that objectified Black women and represented them as suitable targets of sexual violence.[141] The most prominent defense of 2 Live Crew was advanced by Henry Louis Gates, Jr., Harvard professor and expert on African-American literature. In a *New York Times* op-ed piece and in testimony at the criminal trial, Gates contended that 2 Live Crew's members were important artists operating within and inventively elaborating upon distinctively African-American forms of cultural expression.[142] According to Gates, the characteristic exaggeration featured in 2 Live Crew's lyrics served a political end: to explode popular racist stereotypes in a comically extreme form.[143] Where Will saw a misogynistic assault on Black women by social degenerates, Gates found a form of "sexual carnivalesque" with the promise to free us from the pathologies of racism.[144]

Unlike Gates, there are many who do not simply "bust out laughing" upon first hearing 2 Live Crew.[145] One does a disservice to the issue to describe the images of women in *Nasty* as simply "sexually explicit."[146] Listening to *Nasty*, we hear about "cunts" being "fucked" until backbones are cracked, "asses" being "busted," "dicks" rammed down throats, and semen

---

140. *See* George F. Will, *America's Slide into the Sewer,* NEWSWEEK, July 30, 1990, at 64.

141. *Id.*

142. Henry Louis Gates, *2 Live Crew, Decoded,* N.Y. Times, June 19, 1990, at A23. Professor Gates, who testified on behalf of 2 Live Crew in the criminal proceeding stemming from their live performance, pointed out that the members of 2 Live Crew were expressing themselves in coded messages, and were engaging in parody. "For centuries, African-Americans have been forced to develop coded ways of communicating to protect them from danger. Allegories and double meanings, words redefined to mean their opposites . . . have enabled blacks to share messages only the initiated understood." *Id.* Similarly, parody is a component of "the street tradition called 'signifying' or 'playing the dozens,' which has generally been risqué, and where the best signifier or 'rapper' is the one who invents the most extravagant images, the biggest 'lies,' as the culture says." *Id.*

143. Testifying during 2 Live Crew's prosecution for obscenity, Gates argued that, "[o]ne of the brilliant things about these four songs is they embrace that stereotype [of blacks having overly large sexual organs and being hypersexed individuals]. They name it and they explode it. You can have no reaction but to bust out laughing. The fact that they're being sung by four virile young black men is inescapable to the audience." Laura Parker, *Rap Lyrics Likened to Literature; Witness in 2 Live Crew Trial Cites Art, Parody, Precedents,* Wash. Post, Oct. 20, 1990, at D1.

144. *Compare* Gates, *supra* note 142 (labeling 2 Live Crew's braggadocio as "sexual carnivalesque") *with* Will, *supra* note 140 (characterizing 2 Live Crew as "lower animals").

145. *See* note 143 *supra*.

146. Although I have elected to print some of the actual language from *Nasty,* much of the debate about this case has proceeded without any specific discussion of the lyrics. There are reasons one might avoid repeating such sexually explicit material. Among the more compelling ones is the concern that presenting lyrics outside of their fuller musical context hampers a complex understanding and appreciation of the art form of rap itself. Doing so also essentializes one dimension of the art work—its lyrics—to stand for the whole. Finally, focusing on the production of a single group may contribute to the impression that that group—here, 2 Live Crew—fairly represents all rappers.

Recognizing these risks, I believe that it is nonetheless important to incorporate excerpts from the Crew's lyrics into this analysis. Not only are the lyrics legally relevant in any substantive discussion of the obscenity prosecution, but also their inclusion here serves to reveal the depth of misogyny many African-American women must grapple with in order to defend 2 Live Crew. This is particularly true for African-American women who have been sexually abused by men in their lives. Of course, it is also the case that many African-American women who are troubled by the sexual degradation of Black women in some rap music can and do enjoy rap music generally.

splattered across faces. Black women are "cunts," "bitches," and all-purpose "hos."[147]

This is no mere braggadocio. Those who are concerned about high rates of gender violence in our communities must be troubled by the possible connections between these images and the tolerance for violence against women. Children and teenagers are listening to this music, and one cannot but be concerned that the range of acceptable behavior is being broadened by the constant propagation of misogynistic imagery. One must worry as well about young Black women who, like young men, are learning that their value lies between their legs. But the sexual value of women, unlike that of men, is a depletable commodity; boys become men by expending theirs, while girls become whores.

Nasty is misogynist, and an intersectional analysis of the case against 2 Live Crew should not depart from a full acknowledgement of that misogyny. But such an analysis must also consider whether an exclusive focus on issues of gender risks overlooking aspects of the prosecution of 2 Live Crew that raise serious questions of racism.

B. *The Obscenity Prosecution of 2 Live Crew*

An initial problem with the obscenity prosecution of 2 Live Crew was its apparent selectivity.[148] Even the most superficial comparison between 2 Live Crew and other mass-marketed sexual representations suggests the likelihood that race played some role in distinguishing 2 Live Crew as the first group ever to be prosecuted for obscenity in connection with a musical recording, and one of a handful of recording artists to be prosecuted for a live performance. Recent controversies about sexism, racism, and violence in popular culture point to a vast range of expression that might have provided targets for censorship, but was left untouched. Madonna has acted out masturbation, portrayed the seduction of a priest, and insinuated group sex on stage,[149] but she has never been prosecuted for obscenity. While 2 Live Crew was performing in Hollywood, Florida, Andrew Dice Clay's recordings were being sold in stores and he was performing nationwide on HBO.

---

147. *See generally* 2 LIVE CREW, *supra* note 138; N.W.A., STRAIGHT OUTTA COMPTON (Priority Records, Inc. 1988); N.W.A., N.W.A. & THE POSSE (Priority Records, Inc. 1989).

148. There is considerable support for the assertion that prosecution of 2 Live Crew and other rap groups is a manifestation of selective repression of Black expression which is no more racist or sexist than expression by non-Black groups. The most flagrant example is Geffen Records' decision not to distribute an album by the rap act, the Geto Boys. Geffen explained that "the extent to which the Geto Boys album glamorizes and possibly endorses violence, racism, and misogyny compels us to encourage Def American (the group's label) to select a distributor with a greater affinity for this musical expression." Greg Ket, *No Sale, Citing Explicit Lyrics, Distributor Backs Away From Geto Boys Album,* Chicago Trib., Sept. 13, 1990, § 5, at 9. Geffen apparently has a greater affinity for the likes of Andrew Dice Clay and Guns 'N Roses, non-Black acts which have come under fire for racist and sexist comments. Despite criticism of Guns 'N Roses for lyrics which include "niggers" and Clay's "joke" about Native Americans (see note 150 *infra*), Geffen continued to distribute their recordings. *Id.*

149. *See* Derrick Z. Jackson, *Why Must Only Rappers Take the Rap?,* Boston Globe, June 17, 1990, at A17.

Well-known for his racist "humor," Clay is also comparable to 2 Live Crew in sexual explicitness and misogyny. In his show, for example, Clay offers, "Eenie, meenie, minee, mo / Suck my [expletive] and swallow slow," and "Lose the bra, bitch."[150] Moreover, graphic sexual images—many of them violent—were widely available in Broward County where the performance and trial took place. According to the testimony of a Broward County vice detective, "nude dance shows and adult bookstores are scattered throughout the county where 2 Live Crew performed."[151] Given the availability of other forms of sexually explicit "entertainment" in Broward County, Florida, one might wonder how 2 Live Crew could have been seen as uniquely obscene by the lights of the "community standards" of the county.[152] After all, patrons of certain Broward County clubs "can see women dancing with at least their breasts exposed," and bookstore patrons can "view and purchase films and magazines that depict vaginal, oral and anal sex, homosexual sex and group sex."[153] In arriving at its finding of obscenity, the court placed little weight on the available range of films, magazines, and live shows as evidence of the community's sensibilities. Instead, the court apparently accepted the sheriff's testimony that the decision to single out *Nasty* was based on the number of complaints against 2 Live Crew "communicated by telephone calls, anonymous messages, or letters to the police."[154]

Evidence of this popular outcry was never substantiated. But even if it

---

150. *Id.* at A20. Not only does Clay exhibit sexism comparable to, if not greater than, that of 2 Live Crew, he also intensifies the level of hatred by flaunting racism: " 'Indians, bright people, huh? They're still livin' in [expletive] tepees. They deserved it. They're dumb as [expletive].' " *Id.* (quoting Clay).

One commentator asked, "What separates Andrew Dice Clay and 2 Live Crew? Answer: Foul-mouthed Andrew Dice Clay is being chased by the producers of 'Saturday Night Live.' Foul-mouthed 2 Live Crew are being chased by the police." *Id.* at A17. When Clay did appear on Saturday Night Live, a controversy was sparked because cast member Nora Dunn and musical guest Sinead O'Connor refused to appear. Jean Seligmann, *Dicey Problem,* NEWSWEEK, May 21, 1990, at 95.

151. Jane Sutton, *Untitled, 2 Live Crew,* UPI, Oct. 18, 1990.

152. Prosecuting 2 Live Crew but not Clay might be justified by the argument that there is a distinction between "obscenity," defined as expressions of prurient interests, and "pornography" or "racist speech," defined as expressions of misogyny and race hatred, respectively. 2 Live Crew's prurient expressions could be prosecuted as constitutionally unprotected obscenity while Clay's protected racist and misogynistic expressions could not. Such a distinction has been subjected to critical analysis. *See* Catharine A. MacKinnon, *Not A Moral Issue,* 2 YALE L. & POL'Y REV. 321 (1984). The distinction does not explain why other expressions which appeal more directly to "prurient interests" are not prosecuted. Further, 2 Live Crew's prurient appeal is produced, at least in part, through the degradation of women. Accordingly, there can be no compelling distinction between the appeal Clay makes and that of 2 Live Crew.

153. Sutton, *supra* note 151.

154. Skywalker Records, Inc. v. Navarro, 739 F. Supp. 578, 589 (S.D. Fla 1990). The court rejected the defendants' argument that "admission of other sexually explicit works" is entitled to great weight in determining community standards and held that "this type of evidence does not even have to be considered even if the comparable works have been found to be nonobscene." *Id.* (citing Hamling v. United States, 418 U.S. 82, 126-27 (1974)). Although the court gave "some weight" to sexually explicit writings in books and magazines, Eddie Murphy's audio tape of *Raw,* and Andrew Dice Clay's tape recording, it did not explain why these verbal messages "analogous to the format in the *Nasty* recording" were not obscene as well. *Id.*

were, the case for selectivity would remain.[155] The history of social repression of Black male sexuality is long, often violent, and all too familiar.[156] Negative reactions to the sexual conduct of Black men have traditionally had racist overtones, especially where that conduct threatens to "cross over" into the mainstream community.[157] So even if the decision to prosecute did reflect a widespread community perception of the purely prurient character of 2 Live Crew's music, that perception itself might reflect an established pattern of vigilante attitudes directed toward the sexual expression of Black men.[158] In short, the appeal to community standards does not undercut a

155. One report suggested that the complaint came from a lawyer, Jack Thompson. Thompson has continued his campaign, expanding his net to include rap artists the Geto Boys and Too Short. Sara Rimer, *Obscenity or Art? Trial on Rap Lyrics Opens,* N.Y. Times, Oct. 17, 1990, at A1. Despite the appearance of selective enforcement, it is doubtful that any court would be persuaded that the requisite racial motivation was proved. Even evidence of racial disparity in the heaviest of criminal penalties—the death sentence—is insufficient to warrant relief absent specific evidence of discrimination in the defendant's case. *See* McClesky v. Kemp, 481 U. S. 279 (1987).

156. *See* notes 101-104 *supra* and accompanying text.

157. Some critics speculate that the prosecution of 2 Live Crew has less to do with obscenity than with the traditional policing of Black males, especially as it relates to sexuality. Questioning whether 2 Live Crew is more obscene than Andrew Dice Clay, Gates states, "Clearly, this rap group is seen as more threatening than others that are just as sexually explicit. Can this be completely unrelated to the specter of the young black male as a figure of sexual and social disruption, the very stereotypes that 2 Live Crew seems determined to undermine?" Gates, *supra* note 142. Clarence Page makes a similar point, speculating that "2 Live Crew has become the scapegoat for widespread frustration shared by many blacks and whites over a broad range of social problems that seem to have gotten out of control." Clarence Page, *Culture, Taste and Standard-Setting,* Chicago Trib., Oct. 7, 1990, § 4, at 3. Page implies, however, that this explanation is something more than or different from racism. "Could it be (drumroll, please) racism? *Or* could it be fear?" *Id.* (emphasis added). Page's definition of racism apparently does not include the possibility that it is racist to attach one's societal fears and discomforts to a subordinated and highly stigmatized "other." In other words, scapegoating, at least in this country, has traditionally been, and still is, considered racist, whatever the source of the fear.

158. Even in the current era, this vigilantism is sometimes tragically expressed. Yusef Hawkins became a victim of it in New York on August 23, 1989, when he was killed by a mob of white men who believed themselves to be protecting "their" women from being taken by Black men. UPI, May 18, 1990. Jesse Jackson called Hawkins's slaying a "racially and sexually motivated lynching" and compared it to the 1955 murder of black Mississippi youth Emmett Till, who was killed by men who thought he whistled at a white woman. *Id.* Even those who denied the racial overtones of Hawkins's murder produced alternative explanations that were part of the same historical narrative. Articles about the Hawkins incident focused on Gina Feliciano as the cause of the incident, attacking her credibility. *See, e.g.,* Lorrin Anderson, *Cracks in the Mosaic,* NAT'L REV., June 25, 1990, at 36. "Gina instigated the trouble . . . . Gina used drugs and apparently still does. She dropped out of a rehabilitation program before testifying for the prosecution at trial" and was later picked up by the police and "charged with possession of cocaine—15 vials of crack fell out of her purse, police said, and she had a crack pipe in her bra." *Id.* at 37. At trial, defense attorney Stephen Murphy claimed that Feliciano "lied, . . . perjured herself . . . . She divides, polarizes eight million people . . . . It's despicable what she did, making this a racial incident." *Id.* (quoting Murphy). But feminists attacked the "scapegoating" of Feliciano, one stating, "Not only are women the victims of male violence, they're blamed for it." Alexis Jetter, *Protesters Blast Scapegoat Tactics,* Newsday, Apr. 3, 1990, at 29 (quoting Francoise Jacobsohn, president of the New York chapter of the National Organization for Women). According to Merle Hoffman, founder of the New York Pro-Choice Coalition, "Gina's personal life has nothing to do with the crime, . . . [b]ut rest assured, they'll go into her sexual history. . . . It's all part of the 'she made me do it' idea." *Id.* (quoting Hoffman). And New York columnist Ilene Barth observed that

> Gender . . . has a role in New York's race war. Fingers were pointed in Bensonhurst last week at a teenage girl . . . [who] never harmed anyone . . . . Word of her invitation offended local studs, sprouting macho-freaks determined to own local turf and the young

concern about racism; rather, it underscores that concern.

A second troubling dimension of the case brought against 2 Live Crew was the court's apparent disregard for the culturally rooted aspects of 2 Live Crew's music. Such disregard was essential to a finding of obscenity given the third prong of the *Miller* test requiring that material judged obscene must, taken as a whole, lack literary, artistic, or political value.[159] 2 Live Crew argued that this criterion of the *Miller* test was not met in the case of *Nasty* since the recording exemplified such African-American cultural modes as "playing the dozens," "call and response," and "signifying."[160] The court denied each of the group's claims of cultural specificity, recharacterizing in more generic terms what 2 Live Crew contended was distinctly African American. According to the court, "playing the dozens" is "commonly seen in adolescents, especially boys, of all ages"; "boasting" appears to be "part of the universal human condition"; and the cultural origins of "call and response"—featured in a song on *Nasty* about fellatio in which competing groups chanted "less filling" and "tastes great"—were to be found in a Miller beer commercial, not in African-American cultural tradition.[161] The possibility that the Miller beer commercial may have itself evolved from an African-American cultural tradition was apparently lost on the court.

In disregarding the arguments made on behalf of 2 Live Crew, the court denied that the form and style of *Nasty* and, by implication, rap music in general had any artistic merit. This disturbing dismissal of the cultural attributes of rap and the effort to universalize African-American modes of expression are a form of colorblindness that presumes to level all significant racial and ethnic differences in order to pass judgment on intergroup conflicts. The court's analysis here also manifests a frequently encountered strategy of cultural appropriation. African-American contributions that have been accepted by the mainstream culture are eventually absorbed as

---

> females in their ethnic group. . . . [W]omen have not made the headlines as part of marauding bands intent on racial assault. But they number among their victims."

Ilene Barth, *Let the Women of Bensonhurst Lead Us in a Prayer Vigil,* Newsday, Sept. 3, 1989, at 10.

159. The Supreme Court articulated its standard for obscenity in Miller v. California, 413 U.S. 15 (1973), *reh'g denied,* 414 U.S. 881 (1973). The Court held that the basic guidelines for the trier of fact were (a) "whether the 'average person, applying contemporary community standards' would find that the work, taken as a whole, appeals to the prurient interest"; (b) "whether the work depicts or describes, in a patently offensive way, sexual conduct specifically defined by the applicable state law"; and (c) "whether the work, taken as a whole, lacks serious literary, artistic, political, or scientific value." *Id.* at 24 (citations omitted).

160. *See* Gates, *supra* note 142.

161. Skywalker Records, Inc., v. Navarro, 739 F. Supp. 578, 595 (S.D. Fla. 1990). The commercial appropriation of rap is readily apparent in pop culture. Soft drink and fast food commercials now feature rap even though the style is sometimes presented without its racial/cultural face. Dancing McDonald's french fries and the Pillsbury Doughboy have gotten into the rap act. The crossover of rap is not the problem; instead, it is the tendency, represented in *Skywalker,* to reject the cultural origins of language and practices which are disturbing. This is part of an overall pattern of cultural appropriation that predates the rap controversy. Most starkly illustrated in music and dance, cultural trailblazers like Little Richard and James Brown have been squeezed out of their place in popular consciousness to make room for Elvis Presley, Mick Jagger, and others. The meteoric rise of white rapper Vanilla Ice is a contemporary example.

simply "American" or found to be "universal." Other modes associated with African-American culture that resist absorption remain distinctive and are either neglected or dismissed as "deviant."

The court apparently rejected as well the possibility that even the most misogynistic rap may have political value as a discourse of resistance. The element of resistance found in some rap is in making people uncomfortable, thereby challenging received habits of thought and action. Such challenges are potentially political, as are more subversive attempts to contest traditional rules by becoming what is most feared.[162] Against a historical backdrop in which the Black male as social outlaw is a prominent theme, "gangsta' rap" might be taken as a rejection of a conciliatory stance aimed at undermining fear through reassurance, in favor of a more subversive form of opposition that attempts to challenge the rules precisely by becoming the very social outlaw that society fears and attempts to proscribe. Rap representations celebrating an aggressive Black male sexuality can be easily construed as discomforting and oppositional. Not only does reading rap in this way preclude a finding that *Nasty* lacks political value, it also defeats the court's assumption that the group's intent was to appeal solely to prurient interests. To be sure, these considerations carry greater force in the case of other rap artists, such as N.W.A., Too Short, Ice Cube, and The Geto Boys, all of whose standard fare includes depictions of violent assault, rape, rape-murder, and mutilation.[163] In fact, had these other groups been targeted rather than the comparatively less offensive 2 Live Crew, they might have successfully defeated prosecution. The graphic violence in their representations militate against a finding of obscenity by suggesting an intent not to appeal to prurient interests but instead to more expressly political ones. So long as violence is seen as distinct from sexuality, the prurient interest requirement may provide a shield for the more violent rap artists. However, even this somewhat formalistic dichotomy may provide little solace to such rap artists given the historical linkages that have been made between Black

---

162. Gates argues that 2 Live Crew is undermining the "specter of the young black male as a figure of sexual and social disruption." Gates, *supra* note 142. Faced with "racist stereotypes about black sexuality," he explains, "you can do one of two things: you can disavow them or explode them with exaggeration." *Id.* 2 Live Crew, Gates suggests, has chosen to burst the myth by parodying exaggerations of the "oversexed black female and male." *Id.*

163. Other rap acts that have been singled out for their violent lyrics include Ice Cube, the Geto Boys, and Too Short. *See, e.g.*, ICE CUBE, KILL AT WILL (Gangsta Boogie Music (ASCAP)/ UJAMA Music, Inc. 1990); GETO BOYS, THE GETO BOYS (N-The-Water Music, Inc. (ASCAP) 1989); TOO SHORT, SHORT DOG'S IN THE HOUSE (RCA Records 1990). Not all rap lyrics are misogynist. Moreover, even misogynist acts also express a political world view. The differences among rap groups and the artistic value of the medium is sometimes overlooked by mainstream critics. *See, e.g.*, Jerry Adler, *The Rap Attitude*, NEWSWEEK, Mar. 19, 1990, at 56, 57 (labeling rap as a "bombastic, self-aggrandizing" by-product of the growing "Culture of Attitude"). Adler's treatment of rap set off a storm of responses. *See, e.g.*, Patrick Goldstein, *Pop Eye: Rappers Don't Have Time For Newsweek's Attitude*, L.A. Times, Mar. 25, 1990, at 90 (Magazine). Said Russell Simmons, chairman of Def-Jam Records, rap's most successful label, "Surely the moral outrage in [Adler's] piece would be better applied to contemporary American crises in health care, education, homelessness . . . . Blaming the victims—in this case America's black working class and underclass—is never a very useful approach to problem-solving." *Id.* (quoting Simmons).

male sexuality and violence. Indeed, it has been the specter of violence that surrounds images of Black male sexuality that presented 2 Live Crew as an acceptable target of an obscenity prosecution in a field that included Andrew Dice Clay and countless others.

The point here is not that the distinction between sex and violence should be rigorously maintained in determining what is obscene or, more specifically, that rap artists whose standard fare is more violent ought to be protected. To the contrary, these more violent groups should be much more troubling than 2 Live Crew. My point instead is to suggest that obscenity prosecutions of rap artists do nothing to protect the interests of those most directly implicated in rap—Black women. On the one hand, prevailing notions of obscenity separate out sexuality from violence, which has the effect of shielding the more violently misogynistic groups from prosecution; on the other, historical linkages between images of Black male sexuality and violence permit the singling out of "lightweight" rappers for prosecution among all other purveyors of explicit sexual imagery.

C. *Addressing the Intersectionality*

Although Black women's interests were quite obviously irrelevant in the 2 Live Crew obscenity judgment, their images figured prominently in the public case supporting the prosecution. George Will's *Newsweek* essay provides a striking example of how Black women's bodies were appropriated and deployed in the broader attack against 2 Live Crew. Commenting on "America's Slide into the Sewers," Will laments that

> America today is capable of terrific intolerance about smoking, or toxic waste that threatens trout. But only a deeply confused society is more concerned about protecting lungs than minds, trout than black women. We legislate against smoking in restaurants; singing "Me So Horny" is a constitutional right. Secondary smoke is carcinogenic; celebration of torn vaginas is "mere words."[164]

Lest one be misled into thinking that Will has become an ally of Black women, Will's real concern is suggested by his repeated references to the Central Park jogger assault. Will writes, "Her face was so disfigured a friend took 15 minutes to identify her. 'I recognized her ring.' Do you recognize the relevance of 2 Live Crew?"[165] While the connection between the threat of 2 Live Crew and the image of the Black male rapist was suggested subtly in the public debate, it is blatant throughout Will's discussion. Indeed, it bids to be the central theme of the essay. "Fact: Some members of a particular age and societal cohort—the one making 2 Live Crew rich—stomped and raped the jogger to the razor edge of death, for the fun of it."[166] Will directly indicts 2 Live Crew in the Central Park jogger rape through a fictional dialogue between himself and the defendants. Responding to one de-

---

164. *See* Will, *supra* note 140.
165. *Id.*
166. *Id.*

fendant's alleged confession that the rape was fun, Will asks, "Where can you get the idea that sexual violence against women is fun? From a music store, through Walkman earphones, from boom boxes blaring forth the rap lyrics of 2 Live Crew."[167] Since the rapists were young Black males and *Nasty* presents Black men celebrating sexual violence, 2 Live Crew was in Central Park that night, providing the underlying accompaniment to a vicious assault. Ironically, Will rejected precisely this kind of argument in the context of racist speech on the ground that efforts to link racist speech to racist violence presume that those who hear racist speech will mindlessly act on what they hear.[168] Apparently, the certain "social cohort" that produces and consumes racist speech is fundamentally different from the one that produces and consumes rap music.

Will invokes Black women—twice—as victims of this music. But if he were really concerned with the threat of 2 Live Crew to Black women, why does the Central Park jogger figure so prominently in his argument? Why not the Black woman in Brooklyn who was gang-raped and then thrown down an airshaft? In fact, Will fails even to mention Black victims of sexual violence, which suggests that Black women simply function for Will as stand-ins for white women. Will's use of the Black female body to press the case against 2 Live Crew recalls the strategy of the prosecutor in Richard Wright's novel *Native Son*. Bigger Thomas, Wright's Black male protagonist, is on trial for killing Mary Dalton, a white woman. Because Bigger burned her body, it cannot be established whether Bigger had sexually assaulted her, so the prosecutor brings in the body of Bessie, a Black woman raped by Bigger and left to die, in order to establish that Bigger had raped Mary Dalton.[169]

These considerations about selectivity, about the denial of cultural specificity, and about the manipulation of Black women's bodies convince me that race played a significant, if not determining, role in the shaping of the case against 2 Live Crew. While using antisexist rhetoric to suggest a concern for women, the attack on 2 Live Crew simultaneously endorses traditional readings of Black male sexuality. The fact that the objects of these violent sexual images are Black women becomes irrelevant in the representation of the threat in terms of the Black rapist/white victim dyad. The Black male becomes the agent of sexual violence and the white community becomes his potential victim. The subtext of the 2 Live Crew prosecution thus becomes a re-reading of the sexualized racial politics of the past.

---

167. *Id.*

168. *See* George F. Will, *On Campuses, Liberals Would Gag Free Speech*, Newsday, Nov. 6, 1989, at 62.

169. RICHARD WRIGHT, NATIVE SON 305-08 (Perennial Library ed. 1989) (1940). Wright wrote,

> Though he had killed a black girl and a white girl, he knew that it would be for the death of the white girl that he would be punished. The black girl was merely "evidence." And under it all he knew that white people did not really care about Bessie's being killed. White people never searched for Negroes who killed other Negroes.

Id. at 306-07.

While concerns about racism fuel my opposition to the obscenity prosecution of 2 Live Crew, the uncritical support for, and indeed celebration of, 2 Live Crew by other opponents of the prosecution is extremely troubling as well. If the rhetoric of antisexism provided an occasion for racism, so, too, the rhetoric of antiracism provided an occasion for defending the misogyny of 2 Live Crew. That defense took two forms, one political, the other cultural, both advanced prominently by Henry Louis Gates. Gates's political defense argues that 2 Live Crew advances the antiracist agenda by exaggerating stereotypes of Black male sexuality "to show how ridiculous [they] are."[170] The defense contends that by highlighting to the extreme the sexism, misogyny, and violence stereotypically associated with Black male sexuality, 2 Live Crew represents a postmodern effort to "liberate" us from the racism that perpetuates these stereotypes.[171]

Gates is right to contend that the reactions of Will and others confirm that the racial stereotypes still exist, but even if 2 Live Crew intended to explode these stereotypes, their strategy was misguided. Certainly, the group wholly miscalculated the reaction of their white audience, as Will's polemic amply illustrates. Rather than exploding stereotypes, as Gates suggests, 2 Live Crew, it seems most reasonable to argue, was simply (and unsuccessfully) trying to be funny. After all, trading in sexual stereotypes has long been a means to a cheap laugh, and Gates's cultural defense of 2 Live Crew recognizes as much in arguing the identification of the group with a distinctly African-American cultural tradition of the "dozens" and other forms of verbal boasting, raunchy jokes, and insinuations of sexual prowess, all of which were meant to be laughed at and to gain for the speaker respect for his word wizardry, and not to disrupt conventional myths of Black sexuality.[172] Gates's cultural defense of 2 Live Crew, however, recalls similar efforts on behalf of racist humor, which has sometimes been defended as antiracist—an effort to poke fun at or to show the ridiculousness of racism.

---

170. Gates, *supra* note 142. Gates's defense of 2 Live Crew portrayed the group as engaging in postmodern guerrilla warfare against racist stereotypes of Black sexuality. Says Gates, "2 Live Crew's music exaggerates stereotypes of black men and women to show how ridiculous those portrayals are. One of the brilliant things about these songs is that they embrace the stereotypes . . . . It's ridiculous. That's why we laugh about them. That is one of the things I noticed in the audience's reaction. There is no undertone of violence. There's laughter, there's joy." *Id.* Gates repeats the celebratory theme elsewhere, linking 2 Live Crew to Eddie Murphy and other Black male performers because

> they're saying all the things that we couldn't say even in the 1960's about our own excesses, things we could only whisper in dark rooms. They're saying we're going to explode all these sacred cows. It's fascinating, and it's upsetting everybody—not just white people but black people. But it's a liberating moment.

John Pareles, *An Album is Judged Obscene; Rap: Slick, Violent, Nasty and, Maybe Hopeful,* N. Y. Times, June 17, 1990, at 1 (quoting Gates). For a cogent intersectional analysis of Eddie Murphy's popular appeal, see Herman Beavers, The Cool Pose: Intersectionality, Masculinity and Quiescence in the Comedy and Films of Richard Pryor and Eddie Murphy (unpublished manuscript) (on file with the *Stanford Law Review*).

171. Gates and others who defend 2 Live Crew as postmodern comic heroes tend to dismiss or downplay the misogyny represented in their rap. Said Gates, "Their sexism is so flagrant, however, that it almost cancels itself out in a hyperbolic war between the sexes." Gates, *supra* note 142.

172. *See* note 142 *supra*.

More simply, racist humor has often been excused as "just joking"—even racially motivated assaults have been defended as simple pranks. Thus the racism of an Andrew Dice Clay could be defended in either mode as an attempt to explode racist stereotypes or as simple humor not meant to be taken seriously. Implicit in these defenses is the assumption that racist representations are injurious only if they are intended to injure, or to be taken literally, or are devoid of some other nonracist objective. It is highly unlikely that this rationale would be accepted by Blacks as a persuasive defense of Andrew Dice Clay. Indeed, the Black community's historical and ongoing criticism of such humor suggests widespread rejection of these arguments.

The claim that a representation is meant simply as a joke may be true, but the joke functions as humor within a specific social context in which it frequently reinforces patterns of social power. Though racial humor may sometimes be intended to ridicule racism, the close relationship between the stereotypes and the prevailing images of marginalized people complicates this strategy. And certainly, the humorist's positioning vis-á-vis a targeted group colors how the group interprets a potentially derisive stereotype or gesture. Although one could argue that Black comedians have broader license to market stereotypically racist images, that argument has no force here. 2 Live Crew cannot claim an in-group privilege to perpetuate misogynist humor against Black women: the members of 2 Live Crew are not Black women, and more importantly, they enjoy a power relationship over them.

Humor in which women are objectified as packages of bodily parts to serve whatever male-bonding/male-competition needs men please subordinates women in much the same way that racist humor subordinates African Americans. Claims that incidences of such humor are just jokes and are not meant to injure or to be taken literally do little to blunt their demeaning quality—nor, for that matter, does the fact that the jokes are told within an intragroup cultural tradition.

The notion that sexism can serve antiracist ends has proponents ranging from Eldridge Cleaver[173] to Shahrazad Ali,[174] all of whom seem to expect Black women to serve as vehicles for the achievement of a "liberation" that functions to perpetuate their own subordination.[175] Claims of cultural specificity similarly fail to justify toleration of misogyny.[176] While the cultural

173. *See* note 47 *supra*.

174. *See* notes 37-42 *supra* and accompanying text.

175. Gates occasionally claims that both Black male and Black female images are exploded by 2 Live Crew. Even if Gates's view holds true for Black male images, the strategy does not work—and was not meant to work—for Black women. Black women are not the actors in 2 Live Crew's strategy; they are acted upon. To challenge the images of Black women, Black women themselves would have to embrace them, not simply permit Black men to "act out" on them. The only Black female rap groups that might conceivably claim such a strategy are Bytches With Problems and Hoes With Attitudes. Yet, having listened to the music of these Black female rap groups, I am not sure that exploding racist images is either their intent or effect. This is not to say, of course, that all Black female rap is without its strategies of resistance. *See* note 179 *infra*.

176. It is interesting that whether those judging the 2 Live Crew case came out for or against,

defense of 2 Live Crew has the virtue of recognizing merit in a form of music common to the Black community, something George Will and the court that convicted 2 Live Crew were all too glib in dismissing, it does not eliminate the need to question both the sexism within the tradition it defends and the objectives to which the tradition has been pressed. The fact that playing the dozens, say, is rooted in the Black cultural tradition, or that themes represented by mythic folk heroes such as "Stackolee" are African American does not settle the question of whether such practices oppress Black women.[177] Whether these practices are a distinctive part of the African-American cultural tradition is decidedly beside the point. The real question is how subordinating aspects of these practices play out in the lives of people in the community, people who share the benefits as well as the burdens of a common culture. With regard to 2 Live Crew, while it may be true that the Black community has accepted the cultural forms that have evolved into rap, that acceptance should not preclude discussion of whether the misogyny within rap is itself acceptable.

With respect to Gates's political and cultural defenses of 2 Live Crew, then, little turns on whether the "word play" performed by the Crew is a postmodern challenge to racist sexual mythology or simply an internal group practice that crossed over into mainstream America. Both defenses are problematic because they require Black women to accept misogyny and its attendant disrespect and exploitation in the service of some broader group objective, whether it be pursuing an antiracist political agenda or maintaining the cultural integrity of the Black community. Neither objective obligates Black women to tolerate such misogyny.

Likewise, the superficial efforts of the anti-2 Live Crew movement to link

---

all seemed to reject the notion that race has anything to do with their analysis. *See* Skywalker Records, Inc. v. Navarro, 739 F. Supp. 578, 594-96 (S.D. Fla 1990) (rejecting defense contention that 2 Live Crew's *Nasty* had artistic value as Black cultural expression); *see also* Sara Rimer, *Rap Band Members Found Not Guilty in Obscenity Trial,* N.Y. Times, Oct. 21, 1990, at A30 ("Jurors said they did not agree with the defense's assertion that the 2 Live Crew's music had to be understood in the context of black culture. They said they thought race had nothing to do with it."). Clarence Page also rejects the argument that 2 Live Crew's NASTY must be valued as Black cultural expression: "I don't think 2 Live Crew can be said to represent black culture any more than, say, Andrew Dice Clay can be said to represent white culture. Rather, I think both represent a lack of culture." *See* Page, *supra* note 157.

177. Gay men are also targets of homophobic humor that might be defended as culturally specific. Consider the homophobic humor of such comedians as Eddie Murphy, Arsenio Hall, and Damon Wayans and David Alan Grier, the two actors who currently portray Black gay men on the television show *In Living Color.* Critics have linked these homophobic representations of Black gay men to patterns of subordination within the Black community. Black gay filmmaker Marlon Riggs has argued that such caricatures discredit Black gay men's claim to Black manhood, presenting them as "game for play, to be used, joked about, put down, beaten, slapped, and bashed, not just by illiterate homophobic thugs in the night, but by black American culture's best and brightest." Marlon Riggs, *Black Macho Revisited: Reflections of a SNAP! Queen,* in BROTHER TO BROTHER: NEW WRITINGS BY BLACK GAY MEN 253, 254 (Essex Hemphill ed. 1991); *see also* Blair Fell, *Gayface/Blackface: Parallels of Oppression,* NYQ, Apr. 5, 1992, at 32 (drawing parallels between gayface and blackface and arguing that "gayfaced contemporary comedy . . . serves as a tool to soothe the guilty consciences and perpetuate the injustices of gay-bashing America. After all, laughing at something barely human is easier than dealing with flying bullets, split skulls, dying bodies and demands for civil rights.").

the prosecution of the Crew to the victimization of Black women had little to do with Black women's lives. Those who deployed Black women in the service of condemning 2 Live Crew's misogynist representations did not do so in the interest of empowering Black women; rather, they had other interests in mind, the pursuit of which was racially subordinating. The implication here is not that Black feminists should stand in solidarity with the supporters of 2 Live Crew. The spirited defense of 2 Live Crew was no more about defending the entire Black community than the prosecution was about defending Black women. After all, Black women whose very assault is the subject of the representation can hardly regard the right to be represented as bitches and whores as essential to their interest. Instead, the defense primarily functions to protect 2 Live Crew's prerogative to be as misogynistic as they want to be.[178]

Within the African-American political community, Black women will have to make it clear that patriarchy is a critical issue that negatively affects the lives not only of Black women, but of Black men as well. Doing so would help reshape traditional practices so that evidence of racism would not constitute sufficient justification for uncritical rallying around misogynistic politics and patriarchal values. Although collective opposition to racist practice has been and continues to be crucially important in protecting Black interests, an empowered Black feminist sensibility would require that the terms of unity no longer reflect priorities premised upon the continued marginalization of Black women.

---

178. Although much of the sexism that is voiced in rap pervades the industry, Black female rappers have gained a foothold and have undertaken various strategies of resistance. For some, their very presence in rap challenges prevailing assumptions that rap is a Black male tradition. *See* Tricia Rose, *One Queen, One Tribe, One Destiny*, VILLAGE VOICE ROCK & ROLL QUARTERLY, Spring 1990, at 10 (profiling Queen Latifah, widely regarded as one of the best female rappers). Although Latifah has eschewed the head-on approach, her rap and videos are often women-centered, as exemplified by her single, "Ladies First." QUEEN LATIFAH, ALL HAIL THE QUEEN (Tommy Boy 1989). The "Ladies First" video featured other female rappers, "showing a depth of women's solidarity never seen before." Rose, *supra*, at 16. Rappers like Yo-Yo, "hip-hop's first self-proclaimed feminist activist," take a more confrontational line; for example, Yo-Yo duels directly with rapper Ice Cube in "It's a Man's World." Joan Morgan, *Throw the 'F'*, Village Voice, June 11, 1991, at 75.

Some female rappers, such as Bytches With Problems, have attempted to subvert the categories of bitches and whores by taking on the appellations and infusing them with power. As Joan Morgan observes,

> It's common practice for oppressed peoples to neutralize terms of disparagement by adopting and redefining them. Lyndah McCaskill and Tanisha Michelle Morgan's decision to define *bitch* "as a strong woman who doesn't take crap from anyone, male or female" and to encourage women to "wear the title as a badge of honor and keep getting yours" does not differ significantly from blacks opting to use the word *nigger* or gays embracing *queer*.

Id. However in the case of the Bytches, Joan Morgan ultimately found the attempt unsuccessful, in part because the subversion operated merely as an exception for the few ("Lynda and Tanisha Michelle are the only B-Y-T-C-H's here; all the other women they speak about, including the menstrual accident, the woman whose boyfriend Lyndah screws, and anyone else who doesn't like their style, are B-I-T-C-H's in the very male sense of the word") and because ultimately, their world view serves to reinscribe male power. Said Morgan, "It's a tired female rendition of age-old sexist, patriarchal thinking: the power is in the pistol or the penis." *Id.*

CONCLUSION

This article has presented intersectionality as a way of framing the various interactions of race and gender in the context of violence against women of color. Yet intersectionality might be more broadly useful as a way of mediating the tension between assertions of multiple identity and the ongoing necessity of group politics. It is helpful in this regard to distinguish intersectionality from the closely related perspective of antiessentialism, from which women of color have critically engaged white feminism for the absence of women of color on the one hand, and for speaking for women of color on the other. One rendition of this antiessentialist critique—that feminism essentializes the category woman—owes a great deal to the postmodernist idea that categories we consider natural or merely representational are actually socially constructed in a linguistic economy of difference.[179] While the descriptive project of postmodernism of questioning the ways in which meaning is socially constructed is generally sound, this critique sometimes misreads the meaning of social construction and distorts its political relevance.

One version of antiessentialism, embodying what might be called the vulgarized social construction thesis, is that since all categories are socially constructed, there is no such thing as, say, Blacks or women, and thus it makes no sense to continue reproducing those categories by organizing around them.[180] Even the Supreme Court has gotten into this act. In *Metro Broadcasting, Inc. v. FCC*,[181] the Court conservatives, in rhetoric that oozes vulgar constructionist smugness, proclaimed that any set-aside designed to increase the voices of minorities on the air waves was itself based on a racist assumption that skin color is in some way connected to the likely content of one's broadcast.[182]

But to say that a category such as race or gender is socially constructed is not to say that that category has no significance in our world. On the contrary, a large and continuing project for subordinated people—and indeed, one of the projects for which postmodern theories have been very helpful—is

179. I follow the practice of others in linking antiessentialism to postmodernism. *See generally* LINDA NICHOLSON, FEMINISM/POSTMODERNISM (1990).

180. I do not mean to imply that all theorists who have made antiessentialist critiques have lasped into vulgar constructionism. Indeed, antiessentialists avoid making these troubling moves and would no doubt be receptive to much of the critique set forth herein. I use the term vulgar constructionism to distinguish between those antiessentialist critiques that leave room for identity politics and those that do not.

181. 110 S. Ct. 2997 (1990).

182.

> The FCC's choice to employ a racial criterion embodies the related notions that a particular and distinct viewpoint inheres in certain racial groups and that a particular applicant, by virtue of race or ethnicity alone, is more valued than other applicants because the applicant is "likely to provide [that] distinct perspective." The policies directly equate race with belief and behavior, for they establish race as a necessary and sufficient condition of securing the preference. . . . The policies impermissibly value individuals because they presume that persons think in a manner associated with their race.

Id. at 3037 (O'Connor, J., joined by Rehnquist, C.J., and Scalia and Kennedy, J.J., dissenting) (internal citations omitted).

thinking about the way power has clustered around certain categories and is exercised against others. This project attempts to unveil the processes of subordination and the various ways those processes are experienced by people who are subordinated and people who are privileged by them. It is, then, a project that presumes that categories have meaning and consequences. And this project's most pressing problem, in many if not most cases, is not the existence of the categories, but rather the particular values attached to them and the way those values foster and create social hierarchies.

This is not to deny that the process of categorization is itself an exercise of power, but the story is much more complicated and nuanced than that. First, the process of categorizing—or, in identity terms, naming—is not unilateral. Subordinated people can and do participate, sometimes even subverting the naming process in empowering ways. One need only think about the historical subversion of the category "Black" or the current transformation of "queer" to understand that categorization is not a one-way street. Clearly, there is unequal power, but there is nonetheless some degree of agency that people can and do exert in the politics of naming. And it is important to note that identity continues to be a site of resistance for members of different subordinated groups. We all can recognize the distinction between the claims "I am Black" and the claim "I am a person who happens to be Black." "I am Black" takes the socially imposed identity and empowers it as an anchor of subjectivity. "I am Black" becomes not simply a statement of resistance but also a positive discourse of self-identification, intimately linked to celebratory statements like the Black nationalist "Black is beautiful." "I am a person who happens to be Black," on the other hand, achieves self-identification by straining for a certain universality (in effect, "I am first a person") and for a concommitant dismissal of the imposed category ("Black") as contingent, circumstantial, nondeterminant. There is truth in both characterizations, of course, but they function quite differently depending on the political context. At this point in history, a strong case can be made that the most critical resistance strategy for disempowered groups is to occupy and defend a politics of social location rather than to vacate and destroy it.

Vulgar constructionism thus distorts the possibilities for meaningful identity politics by conflating at least two separate but closely linked manifestations of power. One is the power exercised simply through the process of categorization; the other, the power to cause that categorization to have social and material consequences. While the former power facilitates the latter, the political implications of challenging one over the other matter greatly. We can look at debates over racial subordination throughout history and see that in each instance, there was a possibility of challenging either the construction of identity or the system of subordination based on that identity. Consider, for example, the segregation system in *Plessy v. Ferguson*.[183] At issue were multiple dimensions of domination, including cate-

183. 163 U.S. 537 (1896).

gorization, the sign of race, and the subordination of those so labeled. There were at least two targets for Plessy to challenge: the construction of identity ("What is a Black?"), and the system of subordination based on that identity ("Can Blacks and whites sit together on a train?"). Plessy actually made both arguments, one against the coherence of race as a category, the other against the subordination of those deemed to be Black. In his attack on the former, Plessy argued that the segregation statute's application to him, given his mixed race status, was inappropriate. The Court refused to see this as an attack on the coherence of the race system and instead responded in a way that simply reproduced the Black/white dichotomy that Plessy was challenging. As we know, Plessy's challenge to the segregation system was not successful either. In evaluating various resistance strategies today, it is useful to ask which of Plessy's challenges would have been best for him to have won—the challenge against the coherence of the racial categorization system or the challenge to the practice of segregation?

The same question can be posed for *Brown v. Board of Education*.[184] Which of two possible arguments was politically more empowering—that segregation was unconstitutional because the racial categorization system on which it was based was incoherent, or that segregation was unconstitutional because it was injurious to Black children and oppressive to their communities? While it might strike some as a difficult question, for the most part, the dimension of racial domination that has been most vexing to African Americans has not been the social categorization as such, but the myriad ways in which those of us so defined have been systematically subordinated. With particular regard to problems confronting women of color, when identity politics fail us, as they frequently do, it is not primarily because those politics take as natural certain categories that are socially constructed but rather because the descriptive content of those categories and the narratives on which they are based have privileged some experiences and excluded others.

Along these lines, consider the Clarence Thomas/Anita Hill controversy. During the Senate hearings for the confirmation of Clarence Thomas to the Supreme Court, Anita Hill, in bringing allegations of sexual harassment against Thomas, was rhetorically disempowered in part because she fell between the dominant interpretations of feminism and antiracism. Caught between the competing narrative tropes of rape (advanced by feminists) on the one hand and lynching (advanced by Thomas and his antiracist supporters) on the other, the race and gender dimensions of her position could not be told. This dilemma could be described as the consequence of antiracism's essentializing Blackness and feminism's essentializing womanhood. But recognizing as much does not take us far enough, for the problem is not simply linguistic or philosophical in nature. It is specifically political: the narratives of gender are based on the experience of white, middle-class women, and the narratives of race are based on the experience of Black men. The solution does not merely entail arguing for the multiplicity of identities or

184. 397 U.S. 483 (1954).

challenging essentialism generally. Instead, in Hill's case, for example, it would have been necessary to assert those crucial aspects of her location that were erased, even by many of her advocates—that is, to state what difference her difference made.

If, as this analysis asserts, history and context determine the utility of identity politics, how then do we understand identity politics today, especially in light of our recognition of multiple dimensions of identity? More specifically, what does it mean to argue that gender identities have been obscured in antiracist discourses, just as race identities have been obscured in feminist discourses? Does that mean we cannot talk about identity? Or instead, that any discourse about identity has to acknowledge how our identities are constructed through the intersection of multiple dimensions? A beginning response to these questions requires that we first recognize that the organized identity groups in which we find ourselves in are in fact coalitions, or at least potential coalitions waiting to be formed.

In the context of antiracism, recognizing the ways in which the intersectional experiences of women of color are marginalized in prevailing conceptions of identity politics does not require that we give up attempts to organize as communities of color. Rather, intersectionality provides a basis for reconceptualizing race as a coalition between men and women of color. For example, in the area of rape, intersectionality provides a way of explaining why women of color have to abandon the general argument that the interests of the community require the suppression of any confrontation around intraracial rape. Intersectionality may provide the means for dealing with other marginalizations as well. For example, race can also be a coalition of straight and gay people of color, and thus serve as a basis for critique of churches and other cultural institutions that reproduce heterosexism.

With identity thus reconceptualized, it may be easier to understand the need for and to summon the courage to challenge groups that are after all, in one sense, "home" to us, in the name of the parts of us that are not made at home. This takes a great deal of energy and arouses intense anxiety. The most one could expect is that we will dare to speak against internal exclusions and marginalizations, that we might call attention to how the identity of "the group" has been centered on the intersectional identities of a few. Recognizing that identity politics takes place at the site where categories intersect thus seems more fruitful than challenging the possibility of talking about categories at all. Through an awareness of intersectionality, we can better acknowledge and ground the differences among us and negotiate the means by which these differences will find expression in constructing group politics.

Discrediting Victims' Allegations of Sexual Assault: Prosecutorial Accounts of Case Rejections*

LISA FROHMANN, *University of California, Los Angeles and American Bar Foundation*

Complaint filing is a critical stage in the prosecution of a case, for here prosecutors decide which cases will go on for adjudication by the courts. A significant percentage of sexual assault cases never get beyond this stage in the criminal justice process. This paper examines prosecutorial accounts for sexual assault case rejection. A central feature of these accounts is discrediting the victim's rape allegation with the techniques of finding discrepancies in the victim's story and assuming ulterior motives for reporting the assault. The resources that prosecutors use to develop these techniques are official reports and records, typifications of rape-relevant behavior, and knowledge of the victim's personal life and criminal connections. Prosecutors' accounts reveal the indigenous logic of prosecutors' decisions to reject cases and the organizational structure in which these decisions are situated.

Case screening is the gateway to the criminal court system. Prosecutors, acting as gatekeepers, decide which instances of alleged victimization will be passed on for adjudication by the courts. A recent study by the Department of Justice (Boland et al. 1990) suggests that a significant percentage of felony cases never get beyond this point, with only cases characterized as "solid" or "convictable" being filed (Stanko 1981, 1982; Mather 1979). This paper will examine how prosecutors account for the decision to reject sexual assault cases for prosecution and looks at the centrality of discrediting victims' rape allegations in this justification.

A number of studies on sexual assault have found that victim credibility is important in police decisions to investigate and make arrests in sexual assault cases (LaFree 1981; Rose and Randall 1982; Kerstetter 1990; Kerstetter and Van Winkle 1990). Similarly, victim credibility has been shown to influence prosecutors' decisions at a number of stages in the handling of sexual assault cases (LaFree 1980, 1989; Chandler and Torney 1981; Kerstetter 1990).

Much of this prior research has assumed, to varying degrees, that victim credibility is a phenomenon that exists independently of prosecutors' interpretations and assessments of such credibility. Particularly when operationalized in terms of quantitative variables, victim credibility is treated statistically as a series of fixed, objective features of cases. Such approaches neglect the processes whereby prosecutors actively assess and negotiate victim credibility in actual, ongoing case processing.

An alternative view examines victim credibility as a phenomenon constructed and maintained through interaction (Stanko 1980). Several qualitative studies have begun to identify and analyze these processes. For example, Holmstrom and Burgess's (1983) analysis of a victim's experience with the institutional handling of sexual assault cases discusses the importance of victim credibility through the prosecutor's evaluation of a complainant as a "good witness." A "good witness" is someone who, through her appearance and demeanor, can convince a jury to accept her account of "what happened." Her testimony is "consistent," her

* An earlier version of this paper was presented at the American Sociological Association, August 1990. I want to thank Jack Katz, Janet A. Gilboy, Elizabeth A. Stanko, Nancy A. Matthews, James A. Holstein, Timothy Diamond, Kate Gilbert, and the anonymous reviewers of *Social Problems* for their comments on earlier drafts. I am indebted to Robert M. Emerson for his reading of numerous drafts, ever insightful comments, and continuing guidance and support. Correspondence to: Frohmann, American Bar Foundation, 750 N. Lake Shore Dr., Chicago, IL 60611.

behavior "sincere," and she cooperates in case preparation. Stanko's (1981, 1982) study of felony case filing decisions similarly emphasizes prosecutors' reliance on the notion of the "stand-up" witness—someone who can appear to the judge and jury as articulate and credible. Her work emphasizes the centrality of victim credibility in complaint-filing decisions.

In this article I extend these approaches by systematically analyzing the kinds of accounts prosecutors offer in sexual assault cases to support their complaint-filing decisions. Examining the justifications for decisions provides an understanding of how these decisions appear rational, necessary, and appropriate to decision-makers as they do the work of case screening. It allows us to uncover the inner, indigenous logic of prosecutors' decisions and the organizational structures in which those decisions are embedded (Garfinkel 1984).

I focus on prosecutorial accounting for case rejection for three reasons. First, since a significant percentage of cases are not filed, an important component of the case-screening process involves case rejection. Second, the organization of case filing requires prosecutors to justify case rejection, not case acceptance, to superiors and fellow deputies. By examining deputy district attorneys' (DDAs') reasons for case rejection, we can gain access to what they consider "solid" cases, providing further insight into the case-filing process. Third, in case screening, prosecutors orient to the rule—when in doubt, reject. Their behavior is organized more to avoiding the error of filing cases that are not likely to result in conviction than to avoiding the error of rejecting cases that will probably end in conviction (Scheff 1966). Thus, I suggest that prosecutors are actively looking for "holes" or problems that will make the victim's version of "what happened" unbelievable or not convincing beyond a reasonable doubt, hence unconvictable (see Miller [1970], Neubauer [1974], and Stanko [1980, 1981] for the importance of conviction in prosecutors' decisions to file cases). This bias is grounded within the organizational context of complaint filing.

Data and Methods

The research was part of an ethnographic field study of the prosecution of sexual assault crimes by deputy district attorneys in the sexual assault units of two branch offices of the district attorney's offices in a metropolitan area on the West Coast.[1] Research was conducted on a full-time basis in 1989 for nine months in Bay City and on a full-time basis in 1990 for eight months in Center Heights. Three prosecutors were assigned to the unit in Bay City, and four prosecutors to the unit in Center Heights. The data came from 17 months of observation of more than three hundred case screenings. These screenings involved the presentation and assessment of a police report by a sexual assault detective to a prosecutor, conversations between detectives and deputies regarding the "filability"/reject status of a police report, interviews of victims by deputies about the alleged sexual assault, and discussions between deputies regarding the file/reject status of a report. Since tape recordings were prohibited, I took extensive field notes and tried to record as accurately as possible conversation between the parties. In addition, I also conducted open-ended interviews with prosecutors in the sexual assault units and with investigating officers who handled these cases. The accounts presented in the data below include both those offered in the course of negotiating a decision to reject or file a case (usually to the investigating officer [IO] but sometimes with other prosecutors or to me as an insider), and the more or less fixed accounts offered for a decision already made (usually to me). Although I will indicate the context in which the account occurs, I will not emphasize the differences between accounts in the analysis.

The data were analyzed using the constant comparison method of grounded theory (Glaser and Strauss 1967.) I collected all accounts of case rejection from both offices. Through

1. To protect the confidentiality of the people and places studied, pseudonyms are used throughout this article.

constant comparison of the data, I developed coding schema which provide the analytic framework of the paper.

The two branches of the district attorney's office I studied cover two communities differing in socioeconomic and racial composition. Bay City is primarily a white middle-to-upper-class community, and Center Heights is primarily a black and Latino lower-class community. Center Heights has heavy gang-drug activity, and most of the cases brought to the district attorney were assumed to involve gang members (both the complainant and the assailant) or a sex-drug or sex-money transaction. Because of the activities that occur in this community, the prior relationships between the parties are often the result of gang affiliation. This tendency, in connection with the sex-drug and sex-money transactions, gives a twist to the "consent defense" in "acquaintance" rapes. In Bay City, in contrast, the gang activity is much more limited and the majority of acquaintance situations that came to the prosecutors' attention could be categorized as "date rape."

The Organizational Context of Complaint Filing

Several features of the court setting that I studied provided the context for prosecutors' decisions. These features are prosecutorial concern with maintaining a high conviction rate to promote an image of the "community's legal protector," and prosecutorial and court procedures for processing sexual assault cases.

The promotion policy of the county district attorney's (DA) office encourages prosecutors to accept only "strong" or "winnable" cases for prosecution by using conviction rates as a measure of prosecutorial performance. In the DA's office, guilty verdicts carry more weight than a conviction by case settlement. The stronger the case, the greater likelihood of a guilty verdict, the better the "stats" for promotion considerations. The inducement to take risks—to take cases to court that might not result in conviction—is tempered in three ways: First, a pattern of not-guilty verdicts is used by the DA's office as an indicator of prosecutorial incompetency. Second, prosecutors are given credit for the number of cases they reject as a recognition of their commitment to the organizational concern of reducing the case load of an already overcrowded court system. Third, to continually pursue cases that should have been rejected outright may lead judges to question the prosecutor's competence as a member of the court.

Sexual assault cases are among those crimes that have been deemed by the state legislature to be priority prosecution cases. That is, in instances where both "sex" and "nonsex" cases are trailing (waiting for a court date to open), sexual assault cases are given priority for court time. Judges become annoyed when they feel that court time is being "wasted" with cases that "should" have been negotiated or rejected in the first place, especially when those cases have been given priority over other cases. Procedurally, the prosecutor's office handles sexual assault crimes differently from other felony crimes. Other felonies are handled by a referral system; they are handed from one DDA to another at each stage in the prosecution of the case. But sexual assault cases are vertically prosecuted; the deputy who files the case remains with it until its disposition, and therefore is closely connected with the case outcome.

Accounting for Rejection because of "Discrepancies"

Within this organizational context, a central feature of prosecutorial accounts of case rejection is the discrediting of victims' allegations of sexual assault. Below I examine two techniques used by prosecutors to discredit victim's complaints: discrepant accounts and ulterior motives.

Using Official Reports and Records to Detect Discrepancies

In the course of reporting a rape, victims recount their story to several criminal justice officials. Prosecutors treat consistent accounts of the incident over time as an indicator of a victim's credibility. In the first example two prosecutors are discussing a case brought in for filing the previous day.

> DDA Tamara Jacobs: In the police report she said all three men were kissing the victim. Later in the interview she said that was wrong. It seems strange because there are things wrong on major events like oral copulation and intercourse . . ., for example whether she had John's penis in her mouth. Another thing wrong is whether he forced her into the bedroom immediately after they got to his room or, as the police report said, they all sat on the couch and watched TV. This is something a cop isn't going to get wrong, how the report started. (Bay City)

The prosecutor questions the credibility of the victim's allegation by finding "inconsistencies" between the complainant's account given to the police and the account given to the prosecutor. The prosecutor formulates differences in these accounts as "discrepancies" by noting that they involve "major events"—events so significant no one would confuse them, forget them, or get them wrong. This is in contrast to some differences that may involve acceptable, "normal inconsistencies" in victims' accounts of sexual assault. By "normal inconsistencies," I mean those that are expected and explainable because the victim is confused, upset, or shaken after the assault.

The DDA also discredited the victim's account by referring to a typification of police work. She assumes that the inconsistencies in the accounts could not be attributed to the incorrect writing of the report by the police officer on the grounds that they "wouldn't get wrong how the report started." Similarly, in the following example, a typification of police work is invoked to discredit the victim's account. Below the DDA and IO are discussing the case immediately after the victim interview.

> DDA Sabrina Johnson: [T]he police report doesn't say anything about her face being swollen, only her hand. If they took pictures of her hand, wouldn't the police have taken a picture of her face if it was swollen? (Bay City)

The prosecutor calls the credibility of the victim's complaint into question by pointing to a discrepancy between her subsequent account of injuries received during the incident and the notation of injuries on the police reports taken at the time the incident was reported. Suspicion of the complainant's account is also expressed in the prosecutor's inference that if the police went to the trouble of photographing the victim's injured hand they would have taken pictures of her face had it also shown signs of injury.

In the next case the prosecutor cites two types of inconsistencies between accounts. The first set of inconsistencies is the victim's accounts to the prosecutor and to the police. The second set is between the account the victim gave to the prosecutor and the statements the defendants gave to the police. This excerpt was obtained during an interview.

> DDA Tracy Timmerton: The reason I did not believe her [the victim] was, I get the police report first and I'll read that, so I have read the police report which recounts her version of the facts but it also has the statement of both defendants. Both defendants were arrested at separate times and give[n] separate independent statements that were virtually the same. Her story when I had her recount it to me in the DA's office, the number of acts changed, the chronological order of how they happened has changed. (Bay City)

When the prosecutor compared the suspects' accounts with the victim's account, she interpreted the suspects' accounts as credible because both of their accounts, given separately to police, were similar. This rests on the assumption that if suspects give similar accounts when arrested together, they are presumed to have colluded on the story, but if they give similar accounts independent of the knowledge of the other's arrest, there is presumed to be a degree of truth to the story. This stands in contrast to the discrepant accounts the complainant gave to law enforcement officials and the prosecutor.

Using Official Typifications of Rape-Relevant Behavior

In the routine handling of sexual assault cases prosecutors develop a repertoire of knowledge about the features of these crimes.[2] This knowledge includes how particular kinds of rape are committed, post-incident interaction between the parties in an acquaintance situation, and victims' emotional and psychological reactions to rape and their effects on victims' behavior. The typifications of rape-relevant behavior are another resource for discrediting a victim's account of "what happened."

Typifications of rape scenarios. Prosecutors distinguish between different types of sexual assault. They characterize these types by the sex acts that occur, the situation in which the incident occurred, and the relationship between the parties. In the following excerpt the prosecutor discredits the victim's version of events by focusing on incongruities between the victim's description of the sex acts and the prosecutor's knowledge of the typical features of kidnap-rape. During an interview a DDA described the following:

> DDA Tracy Timmerton: [T]he only act she complained of was intercourse, and my experience has been that when a rapist has a victim cornered for a long period of time, they engage in multiple acts and different types of sexual acts and very rarely do just intercourse. (Bay City)

The victim's account is questioned by noting that she did not complain about or describe other sex acts considered "typical" of kidnap-rape situations. She only complained of intercourse. In the next example the DDA and IO are talking about a case involving the molestation of a teenage girl.

> DDA William Nelson: Something bothers me, all three acts are the same. She's on her stomach and has her clothes on and he has a "hard and long penis." All three times he is grinding his penis into her butt. It seems to me he should be trying to do more than that by the third time. (Center Heights)

Here the prosecutor is challenging the credibility of the victim's account by comparing her version of "what happened" with his typification of the way these crimes usually occur. His experience suggests there should be an escalation of sex acts over time, not repetition of the same act.

Often the typification invoked by the prosecutor is highly situational and local. In discussing a drug-sex-related rape in Center Heights, for example, the prosecutor draws on his knowledge of street activity in that community and the types of rapes that occur there to question whether the victim's version of events is what "really" happened. The prosecutor is describing a case he received the day before to an investigating officer there on another matter.

> DDA Kent Fernome: I really feel guilty about this case I got yesterday. The girl is 20 going on 65. She is real skinny and gangly. Looks like a cluckhead [crack addict]—they cut off her hair. She went to her uncle's house, left her clothes there, drinks some beers and said she was going to visit a friend in Center Heights who she said she met at a drug rehab program. She is not sure where this friend Cathy lives. Why she went to Center Heights after midnight, God knows? It isn't clear what she was doing between 12 and 4 a.m. Some gang bangers came by and offered her a ride. They picked her up on the corner of Main and Lincoln. I think she was turning a trick, or looking for a

2. The use of practitioners' knowledge to inform decision making is not unique to prosecutors. For example, such practices are found among police (Bittner 1967; Rubinstein 1973), public defenders (Sudnow 1965), and juvenile court officials (Emerson 1969).

> rock, but she wouldn't budge from her story. . . . There are lots of conflicts between what she told the police and what she told me. The sequence of events, the sex acts performed, who ejaculates. She doesn't say who is who. . . . She's beat up, bruises on face and a laceration on her neck. The cop and doctor say there is no trauma—she's done by six guys. That concerns me. There is no semen that they see. It looks like this to me—maybe she is a strawberry, she's hooking or looking for a rock, but somewhere along the line it is not consensual. . . . She is [a] real street-worn woman. She's not leveling with me—visiting a woman with an unknown address on a bus in Center Heights—I don't buy it. . . . (Center Heights)

The prosecutor questioned the complainant's reason for being in Center Heights because, based on his knowledge of the area, he found it unlikely that a woman would come to this community at midnight to visit a friend at an unknown address. The deputy proposed an alternative account of the victim's action based on his knowledge of activities in the community—specifically, prostitution and drug dealing—and questioned elements of the victim's account, particularly her insufficiently accounted for activity between 12 and 4 a.m., coming to Center Heights late at night to visit a friend at an unknown address, and "hanging out" on the corner.

The DDA uses "person-descriptions" (Maynard 1984) to construct part of the account, describing the complainant's appearance as a "cluckhead" and "street-worn." These descriptions suggested she was a drug user, did not have a "stable" residence or employment, and was probably in Center Heights in search of drugs. This description is filled in by her previous "participation in a drug rehab program," the description of her activity as "hanging out" and being "picked up" by gang bangers, and a medical report which states that no trauma or semen was found when she was "done by six guys." Each of these features of the account suggests that the complainant is a prostitute or "strawberry" who came to Center Heights to trade sex or money for drugs. This alternative scenario combined with "conflicts between what she told the police and what she told me" justify case rejection because it is unlikely that the prosecutor could get a conviction.

The prosecutor acknowledges the distinction between the violation of women's sexual/physical integrity—"somewhere along the line it wasn't consensual"—and prosecutable actions. The organizational concern with "downstream consequences" (Emerson and Paley, forthcoming) mitigate against the case being filed.

Typifications of post-incident interaction. In an acquaintance rape, the interaction between the parties after the incident is a critical element in assessing the validity of a rape complaint. As implied below by the prosecutors, the typical interaction pattern between victim and suspect after a rape incident is not to see one another. In the following cases the prosecutor challenges the validity of the victims' allegations by suggesting that the complainants' behavior runs counter to a typical rape victim's behavior. In the first instance the parties involved in the incident had a previous relationship and were planning to live together. The DDA is talking to me about the case prior to her decision to reject.

> DDA Sabrina Johnson: I am going to reject the case. She is making it very difficult to try the case. She told me she let him into her apartment last night because she is easily influenced. The week before this happened [the alleged rape] she agreed to have sex with him. Also, first she says "he raped me" and then she lets him into her apartment. (Bay City)

Here the prosecutor raises doubt about the veracity of the victim's rape allegation by contrasting it to her willingness to allow the suspect into her apartment after the incident. This "atypical" behavior is used to discredit the complainant's allegation.

In the next excerpt the prosecutor was talking about two cases. In both instances the parties knew each other prior to the rape incident as well as having had sexual relations after the incident. As in the previous instance, the victims' allegations are discredited by referring to their atypical behavior.

DDA Sabrina Johnson: I can't take either case because of the women's behavior after the fact. By seeing these guys again and having sex with them they are absolving them of their guilt. (Bay City)

In each instance the "downstream" concern with convictability is indicated in the prosecutor's talk—"She is making it very difficult to try the case" and "By seeing these guys again and having sex with them they are absolving them of their guilt." This concern is informed by a series of common-sense assumptions about normal heterosexual relations that the prosecutors assume judges and juries use to assess the believability of the victim: First, appropriate behavior within ongoing relationships is noncoercive and nonviolent. Second, sex that occurs within the context of ongoing relationships is consensual. Third, if coercion or violence occurs, the appropriate response is to sever the relationship, at least for a time. When complainants allege they have been raped by their partner within a continuing relationship, they challenge the taken-for-granted assumptions of normal heterosexual relationships. The prosecutors anticipate that this challenge will create problems for the successful prosecution of a case because they think that judges and jurors will use this typification to question the credibility of the victim's allegation. They assume that the triers of fact will assume that if there is "evidence" of ongoing normal heterosexual relations—she didn't leave and the sexual relationship continued—then there was no coercive sex. Thus the certitude that a crime originally occurred can be retrospectively undermined by the interaction between complainant and suspect after the alleged incident. Implicit in this is the assumed primacy of the normal heterosexual relations typification as the standard on which to assess the victim's credibility even though an allegation of rape has been made.

Typifications of rape reporting. An important feature of sexual assault cases is the timeliness in which they are reported to the police (see Torrey, forthcoming). Prosecutors expect rape victims to report the incident relatively promptly: "She didn't call the police until four hours later. That isn't consistent with someone who has been raped." If a woman reports "late," her motives for reporting and the sincerity of her allegation are questioned if they fall outside the typification of officially recognizable/explainable reasons for late reporting. The typification is characterized by the features that can be explained by Rape Trauma Syndrome (RTS). In the first excerpt the victim's credibility is not challenged as a result of her delayed reporting. The prosecutor describes her behavior and motives as characteristic of RTS. The DDA is describing a case to me that came in that morning.

DDA Tamara Jacobs: Charlene was in the car with her three assailants after the rape. John (the driver) was pulled over by the CHP [California Highway Patrol] for erratic driving behavior. The victim did not tell the officers that she had just been raped by these three men. When she arrived home, she didn't tell anyone what happened for approximately 24 hours. When her best friend found out from the assailants (who were mutual friends) and confronted the victim, Charlene told her what happened. She then reported it to the police. When asked why she didn't report the crime earlier, she said that she was embarrassed and afraid they would hurt her more if she reported it to the police. The DDA went on to say that the victim's behavior and reasons for delayed reporting were symptomatic of RTS. During the trial an expert in Rape Trauma Syndrome was called by the prosecution to explain the "normality" and commonness of the victim's reaction. (Bay City)

Other typical motives include "wanting to return home first and get family support" or "wanting to talk the decision to report over with family and friends." In all these examples, the victims sustained injuries of varying degrees in addition to the trauma of the rape itself, and they reported the crime within 24 hours. At the time the victims reported the incident, their injuries were still visible, providing corroboration for their accounts of what happened.

In the next excerpt we see the connection between atypical motives for delayed reporting and ulterior motives for reporting a rape allegation. At this point I focus on the prosecutors' use of typification as a resource for discrediting the victim's account. I will examine ulterior motives as a technique of discrediting in a later section. The deputy is telling me about a case she recently rejected.

> DDA Sabrina Johnson: She doesn't tell anyone after the rape. Soon after this happened she met him in a public place to talk business. Her car doesn't start, he drives her home and starts to attack her. She jumps from the car and runs home. Again she doesn't tell anyone. She said she didn't tell anyone because she didn't want to lose his business. Then the check bounces, and she ends up with VD. She has to tell her fiance so he can be treated. He insists she tell the police. It is three weeks after the incident. I have to look at what the defense would say about the cases. Looks like she consented, and told only when she had to because of the infection and because he made a fool out of her by having the check bounce. (Bay City)

The victim's account is discredited because her motives for delayed reporting—not wanting to jeopardize a business deal—fall outside those considered officially recognizable and explicable.

Typifications of victim's demeanor. In the course of interviewing hundreds of victims, prosecutors develop a notion of a victim's comportment when she tells what happened. They distinguish between behavior that signifies "lying" versus "discomfort." In the first two exchanges the DDA and IO cite the victim's behavior as an indication of lying. Below, the deputy and IO are discussing the case immediately after the intake interview.

> IO Nancy Fauteck: I think something happened. There was an exchange of body language that makes me question what she was doing. She was yawning, hedging, fudging something.
>
> DDA Sabrina Johnson: Yawning is a sign of stress and nervousness.
>
> IO Nancy Fauteck: She started yawning when I talked to her about her record earlier, and she stopped when we finished talking about it. (Bay City)

The prosecutor and the investigating officer collaboratively draw on their common-sense knowledge and practical work experience to interpret the yawns, nervousness, and demeanor of the complainant as running counter to behavior they expect from one who is "telling the whole truth." They interpret the victim's behavior as a continuum of interaction first with the investigating officer and then with the district attorney. The investigating officer refers to the victim's recurrent behavior (yawning) as an indication that something other than what the victim is reporting actually occurred.

In the next excerpt the prosecutor and IO discredit the victim's account by referencing two typifications—demeanor and appropriate rape-victim behavior. The IO and prosecutor are telling me about the case immediately after they finished the screening interview.

> IO Dina Alvarez: One on one, no corroboration.
>
> DDA William Nelson: She's a poor witness, though that doesn't means she wasn't raped. I won't file a one-on-one case.
>
> IO Dina Alvarez: I don't like her body language.
>
> DDA William Nelson: She's timid, shy, naive, virginal, and she didn't do all the right things. I'm not convinced she is even telling the truth. She's not even angry about what happened to her. . . .
>
> DDA William Nelson: Before a jury if we have a one on one, he denies it, no witnesses, no physical evidence or medical corroboration they won't vote guilty.
>
> IO Dina Alvarez: I agree, and I didn't believe her because of her body language. She looks down, mumbles, crosses her arms, and twists her hands.
>
> DDA William Nelson: . . . She has the same mannerisms and demeanor as a person who is lying. A jury just won't believe her. She has low self-esteem and self-confidence. . . . (Center Heights)

The prosecutor and IO account for case rejection by characterizing the victim as unbelievable and the case as unconvictable. They establish their disbelief in the victim's account by citing the victim's actions that fall outside the typified notions of believable and expected behavior—"she has the same mannerisms and demeanor as a person who is lying," and "I'm not convinced she is even telling the truth. She isn't even angry about what happened." They assume that potential jurors will also find the victim's demeanor and post-incident behavior problematic. They demonstrate the unconvictability of the case by citing the "holes" in the case—a combination of a "poor witness" whom "the jury just won't believe" and "one on one, [with] no corroboration" and a defense in which the defendant denies anything happened or denies it was nonconsensual sex.

Prosecutors and investigating officers do not routinely provide explicit accounts of "expected/honest" demeanor. Explicit accounts of victim demeanor tend to occur when DDAs are providing grounds for discrediting a rape allegation. When as a researcher I pushed for an account of expected behavior, the following exchange occurred. The DDA had just concluded the interview and asked the victim to wait in the lobby.[3]

> IO Nancy Fauteck: Don't you think he's credible?
>
> DDA Sabrina Johnson: Yes.
>
> LF: What seems funny to me is that someone who said he was so unwilling to do this talked about it pretty easily.
>
> IO Nancy Fauteck: Didn't you see his eyes, they were like saucers.
>
> DDA Sabrina Johnson: And [he] was shaking too. (Bay City)

This provides evidence that DDAs and IOs are orienting to victims' comportment and could provide accounts of "expected/honest" demeanor if necessary. Other behavior that might be included in this typification are the switch from looking at to looking away from the prosecutor when the victim begins to discuss the specific details of the rape itself; a stiffening of the body and tightening of the face as though to hold in tears when the victim begins to tell about the particulars of the incident; shaking of the body and crying when describing the details of the incident; and a lowering of the voice and long pauses when the victim tells the specifics of the sexual assault incident.

Prosecutors have a number of resources they call on to develop typification related to rape scenarios and reporting. These include how sexual assaults are committed, community residents and activities, interactions between suspect and defendants after a rape incident, and the way victims' emotional and psychological responses to rape influence their behavior. These typifications highlight discrepancies between prosecutors' knowledge and victims' accounts. They are used to discredit the victims' allegation of events, justifying case rejection.

As we have seen, one technique used by prosecutors to discredit a victim's allegations of rape as a justification of case rejection is the detection of discrepancies. The resources for this are official documents and records and typifications of rape scenarios and rape reporting. A second technique prosecutors use is the identification of ulterior motives for the victim's rape allegation.

Accounting for Rejection by "Ulterior Motive"

Ulterior motives rest on the assumption that a woman consented to sexual activity and for some reason needed to deny it afterwards. These motives are drawn from the prosecutor's knowledge of the victim's personal history and the community in which the incident occurred. They are elaborated and supported by other techniques and knowledge prosecutors use in the accounting process.

I identify two types of ulterior motives prosecutors use to justify rejection: The first type

3. Unlike the majority of rape cases I observed, this case had a male victim. Due to lack of data, I am unable to tell if this made him more or less credible in the eyes of the prosecutor and police.

suggests the victim has a reason to file a false rape complaint. The second type acknowledges the legitimacy of the rape allegation, framing the motives as an organizational concern with convictability.

Knowledge of Victim's Current Circumstances

Prosecutors accumulate the details of victims' lives from police interviews, official documents, and filing interviews. They may identify ulterior motives by drawing on this information. Note that unlike the court trial itself, where the rape incident is often taken out of the context of the victim's life, here the DDAs call on the texture of a victim's life to justify case rejection. In an excerpt previously discussed, the DDA uses her knowledge of the victim's personal relationship and business transactions as a resource for formulating ulterior motives. Drawing on the victim's current circumstances, the prosecutor suggests two ulterior motives for the rape allegation—disclosure to her fiance about the need to treat a sexually transmitted disease, and anger and embarrassment about the bounced check. Both of these are motives for making a false complaint. The ulterior motives are supported by the typification for case reporting. Twice unreported sexual assault incidents with the same suspect, a three-week delay in reporting, and reporting only after the fiance insisted she do so are not within the typified behavior and reasons for late reporting. Her atypical behavior provides plausibility to the alternative version of the events—the interaction was consensual and only reported as a rape because the victim needed to explain a potentially explosive matter (how she contracted venereal disease) to her fiance. In addition she felt duped on a business deal.

Resources for imputing ulterior motives also come from the specifics of the rape incident. Below, the prosecutor's knowledge of the residents and activities in Center Heights supply the reason: the type of activity the victim wanted to cover up from her boyfriend. The justification for rejection is strengthened by conflicting accounts between the victim and witness on the purpose for being in Center Heights. The DDA and IO are talking about the case before they interview the complainant.

> DDA William Nelson: A white girl from Addison comes to buy dope. She gets kidnapped and raped.
>
> IO Brandon Palmer: She tells her boyfriend and he beats her up for being so stupid for going to Center Heights. . . . The drug dealer positively ID'd the two suspects, but she's got a credibility problem because she said she wasn't selling dope, but the other two witnesses say they bought dope from her. . . .
>
> LF: I see you have a blue sheet [a sheet used to write up case rejections] already written up.
>
> IO Brandon Palmer: Oh yes. But there was no doubt in my mind that she was raped. But do you see the problems?
>
> DDA William Nelson: Too bad because these guys really messed her up. . . . She has a credibility problem. I don't think she is telling the truth about the drugs. It would be better if she said she did come to buy drugs. The defense is going to rip her up because of the drugs. He is going to say, isn't it true you had sex with these guys but didn't want to tell your boyfriend, so you lied about the rape like you did about the drugs, or that she had sex for drugs. . . . (Center Heights)

The prosecutor expresses doubt about the victim's account because it conflicts with his knowledge of the community. He uses this knowledge to formulate the ulterior motive for the victim's complaint—to hide from her boyfriend the "fact" that she trading sex for drugs. The victim, "a white woman from Addison," alleges she drove to Center Heights "in the middle of the night" as a favor to a friend. She asserted that she did not come to purchase drugs. The DDA "knows" that white people don't live in Center Heights. He assumes that whites who come to Center Heights, especially in the middle of the night, are there to buy drugs or trade sex for drugs. The prosecutor's scenario is strengthened by the statements of the victim's two friends who accompanied her to Center Heights, were present at the scene, and admitted buying drugs. The prosecutor frames the ulterior motives as an organizational concern with defense arguments and convictability. This concern is reinforced by citing conflicting accounts between witnesses and the victim. He does not suggest that the victim's allegation was false— "there is no doubt in my mind she was raped"; rather, the case isn't convictable—"she has a credibility problem" and "the defense is going to rip her up."

Criminal Connections

The presence of criminal connections can also be used as a resource for identifying ulterior motives. Knowledge of a victim's criminal activity enables prosecutors to "find" ulterior motives for her allegation. In the first excerpt the complainant's presence in an area known by police as "where prostitutes bring their clients" is used to formulate an ulterior motive for her rape complaint. This excerpt is from an exchange in which the DDA was telling me about a case he had just rejected.

> DDA William Nelson: Young female is raped under questionable circumstances. One on one. The guy states it is consensual sex. There is no corroboration, no medicals. We ran the woman's rap sheet, and she has a series of prostitution arrests. She's with this guy in the car in a dark alley having sex. The police know this is where prostitutes bring their customers, so she knew she had better do something fast unless she is going to be busted for prostitution, so, lo and behold, she comes running out of the car yelling "he's raped me." He says no. He picked her up on Long Beach Boulevard, paid her $25 and this is "where she brought me." He's real scared, he has no record. (Center Heights)

Above, the prosecutor, relying on police knowledge of a particular location, assumes the woman is a prostitute. Her presence in the location places her in a "suspicious" category, triggering a check on her criminal history. Her record of prostitution arrests is used as the resource for developing an ulterior motive for her complaint: To avoid being busted for prostitution again, she made a false allegation of rape. Here the woman's record of prostitution and the imminent possibility of arrest are used to provide the ulterior motive to discredit her account. The woman's account is further discredited by comparing her criminal history—"a series of prostitution arrests" with that of the suspect, who "has no record," thus suggesting that he is the more credible of the two parties.

Prosecutors and investigating officers often decide to run a rap sheet (a chronicle of a person's arrests and convictions) on a rape victim. These decisions are triggered when a victim falls into certain "suspicious" categories, categories that have a class/race bias. Rap sheets are not run on women who live in the wealthier parts of town (the majority of whom are white) or have professional careers. They are run on women who live in Center Heights (who are black and Latina), who are homeless, or who are involved in illegal activities that could be related to the incident.

In the next case the prosecutor's knowledge of the victim's criminal conviction for narcotics is the resource for formulating an ulterior motive. This excerpt was obtained during an interview.

> DDA Tracy Timmerton: I had one woman who had claimed that she had been kidnapped off the street after she had car trouble by these two gentlemen who locked her in a room all night and had repeated intercourse with her. Now she was on a cocaine diversion [a drug treatment program where the court places persons convicted of cocaine possession instead of prison], and these two guys' stories essentially were that the one guy picked her up, they went down and got some cocaine, had sex in exchange for the cocaine, and the other guy comes along and they are all having sex and all doing cocaine. She has real reason to lie, she was doing cocaine, and because she has then violated the terms of her diversion and is now subject to criminal prosecution for her possession of cocaine charge. She is also supposed to be in a drug program which she has really violated, so this is her excuse and her explanation to explain why she has fallen off her program. (Bay City)

The prosecutor used the victim's previous criminal conviction for cocaine and her probation conditions to provide ulterior motives for her rape allegation—the need to avoid being violated on probation for the possession of cocaine and her absence from a drug diversion program. She suggests that the allegation made by the victim was false.

Prosecutors develop the basis for ulterior motives from the knowledge they have of the victim's personal life and criminal connections. They create two types of ulterior motives, those that suggest the victim made a false rape complaint and those that acknowledge the legitimacy of the complaint but discredit the account because of its unconvictability. In the accounts prosecutors give, ulterior motives for case rejection are supported with discrepancies in victims' accounts and other practitioners' knowledge.

Conclusion

Case filing is a critical stage in the prosecutorial process. It is here that prosecutors decide which instances of alleged victimization will be forwarded for adjudication by the courts. A significant percentage of sexual assault cases are rejected at this stage. This research has examined prosecutorial accounts for case rejection and the centrality of victim discreditability in those accounts. I have elucidated the techniques of case rejection (discrepant accounts and ulterior motives), the resources prosecutors use to develop these techniques (official reports and records, typifications of rape-relevant behavior, criminal connections, and knowledge of a victim's personal life), and how these resources are used to discredit victims' allegations of sexual assault.

This examination has also provided the beginnings of an investigation into the logic and organization of prosecutors' decisions to reject/accept cases for prosecution. The research suggests that prosecutors are orienting to a "downstream" concern with convictability. They are constantly "in dialogue with" anticipated defense arguments and anticipated judge and juror responses to case testimony. These dialogues illustrate the intricacy of prosecutorial decision-making. They make visible how prosecutors rely on assumptions about relationships, gender, and sexuality (implicit in this analysis, but critical and requiring of specific and explicit attention) in complaint filing of sexual assault cases. They also make evident how the processes of distinguishing truths from untruths and the practical concerns of trying cases are central to these decisions. Each of these issues, in all its complexity, needs to be examined if we are to understand the logic and organization of filing sexual assault cases.

The organizational logic unveiled by these accounts has political implications for the prosecution of sexual assault crimes. These implications are particularly acute for acquaintance rape situations. As I have shown, the typification of normal heterosexual relations plays an important role in assessing these cases, and case conviction is key to filing cases. As noted by DDA William Nelson: "There is a difference between believing a woman was assaulted and being able to get a conviction in court." Unless we are able to challenge the assumptions on which these typification are based, many cases of rape will never get beyond the filing process because of unconvictability.

References

Bittner, Egon A.

1967 "The police on skid-row: A study of peace keeping." American Sociological Review 32:699-715.

Boland, Barbara, Catherine H. Conly, Paul Mahanna, Lynn Warner, and Ronald Sones.
1990 The Prosecution of Felony Arrests, 1987. Washington, D.C.: Bureau of Justice Statistics, U.S. Department of Justice.

Chandler, Susan M., and Martha Torney
1981 "The decision and the processing of rape victims through the criminal justice system." California Sociologist 4:155-69.

Emerson, Robert M.
1969 Judging Delinquents: Context and Process in Juvenile Court. Chicago: Aldine Publishing Co.

Emerson, Robert M., and Blair Paley
Forthcoming "Organizational horizons and complaint-filing." In The Uses of Discretion, ed. Keith Hawkins. Oxford: Oxford University Press.

Garfinkel, Harold
1984 Studies in Ethnomethodology. Cambridge, Eng.: Polity Press.

Glaser, Barney, and Anselm Strauss
1967 The Discovery of Grounded Theory. Chicago: Aldine Publishing Co..

Holmstrom, Lynda Lytle, and Ann Wolbert Burgess
1983 The Victim of Rape: Institutional Reactions. New Brunswick, N.J.: Transaction Books.

Kerstetter, Wayne A.
1990 "Gateway to justice: Police and prosecutorial response to sexual assaults against women." Journal of Criminal Law and Criminology 81:267-313.

Kerstetter, Wayne A., and Barrik Van Winkle
1990 "Who decides? A study of the complainant's decision to prosecute in rape cases." Criminal Justice and Behavior 17:268-83.

LaFree, Gary D.
1980 "Variables affecting guilty pleas and convictions in rape cases: Toward a social theory of rape processing." Social Forces 58:833-50.
1981 "Official reactions to social problems: Police decisions in sexual assault cases." Social Problems 28:582-94.
1989 Rape and Criminal Justice: The Social Construction of Sexual Assault. Belmont, Calif.: Wadsworth Publishing Co.

Mather, Lynn M.
1979 Plea Bargaining or Trial? The Process of Criminal-Case Disposition. Lexington, Mass.: Lexington Books.

Maynard, Douglas W.
1984 Inside Plea Bargaining: The Language of Negotiation. New York: Plenum Press.

Miller, Frank
1970 Prosecution: The Decision to Charge a Suspect with a Crime. Boston: Little, Brown.

Neubauer, David
1974 Criminal Justice in Middle America. Morristown, N.J.:General Learning Press.

Rose, Vicki M., and Susan C. Randall
1982 "The impact of investigator perceptions of victim legitimacy on the processing of rape/sexual assault cases." Symbolic Interaction 5:23-36.

Rubinstein, Jonathan
1973 City Police. New York: Farrar, Straus & Giroux.

Scheff, Thomas
1966 Being Mentally Ill: A Sociological Theory. Chicago: Aldine Publishing Co.

Stanko, Elizabeth A.
1980 "These are the cases that try themselves: An examination of the extra-legal criteria in felony case processing." Presented at the Annual Meetings of the North Central Sociological Association, December. Buffalo, N.Y.
1981 "The impact of victim assessment on prosecutor's screening decisions: The case of the New York District Attorney's Office." Law and Society Review 16:225-39.
1982 "Would you believe this woman? Prosecutorial screening for "credible" witnesses and a problem of justice." In Judge, Lawyer, Victim, Thief, ed. Nicole Hahn Rafter and Elizabeth A. Stanko, 63-82. Boston: Northeastern University Press.

Sudnow, David

1965 "Normal crimes: Sociological features of the penal code in a public defenders office." Social Problems 12:255-76.

Torrey, Morrison

Forth-coming "When will we be believed? Rape myths and the idea coming of a fair trial in rape prosecutions." U.C. Davis Law Review.

Waegel, William B.

1981 "Case routinization in investigative police work." Social Problems 28:263-75.

Williams, Kristen M.

1978a The Role of the Victim in the Prosecution of Violent Crimes. Washington D.C.: Institute for Law and Social Research.

1978b The Prosecution of Sexual Assaults. Washington D.C.: Institute for Law and Social Research.

LEGAL IMAGES OF BATTERED WOMEN: REDEFINING THE ISSUE OF SEPARATION

*Martha R. Mahoney**

TABLE OF CONTENTS

---

* Associate Professor of Law, University of Miami School of Law. B.A. 1981, Regents College; M.A. 1985, Tulane University; J.D. 1989, Stanford Law School. — Ed. Glynda Avilla, Heather Bell, Donna Coker, Mary Dunlap, Bryan Ford, Mark Kelman, Christine Littleton, and Stephanie Wildman made suggestions and comments on earlier drafts. Ken Casebeer and Lynne Henderson offered extraordinary support, helping preserve and develop my argument. Kim Hanson, Esq., J.D. Stanford Law School 1987, set an example of intellectual and emotional courage ("tell my story and use my name") and would not let me stop working on battered women's issues. All errors are my own. This article is dedicated, with gratitude, to Kim and the other women who talked with me about their experiences.

. . . /I found an
announcement/not the woman's
bloated body in the river/floating
not the child bleeding in the
59th street corridor/not the baby
broken on the floor/
"there is some concern
that alleged battered women
might start to murder their
husbands and lovers with no
immediate cause"[1]

INTRODUCTION

I am writing about women's lives. Our lives, like everyone's, are lived within particular cultures that both reflect legal structures and affect legal interpretation. Focusing on domestic violence, this article describes an interrelationship between women's lives, culture, and law. This relationship is not linear (moving from women's lives to law, or from law to life) but interactive: cultural assumptions about domestic violence affect substantive law and methods of litigation in ways that in turn affect society's perceptions of women; both law and societal perceptions affect women's understanding of our own lives, relationships, and options; our lives are part of the culture that affects legal interpretation and within which further legal moves are made. Serious harm to women results from the ways in which law and culture distort our experience.

The courtroom is the theater in which the dramas of battered women have been brought to public attention. Trials like that of Francine Hughes, whose story became the book and movie *The Burning Bed,*[2] create a cultural and legal spotlight that has in some ways benefited women by increasing public knowledge of the existence of domestic violence. However, the press has emphasized sensational cases that have a high level of terrorism against women and a gro-

1. Ntozake Shange, *With No Immediate Cause, in* FAMILY VIOLENCE: POEMS ON THE PATHOLOGY 66, 67 (Mary McAnally ed., 1982).

2. FAITH MCNULTY, THE BURNING BED (1980).

tesque quality of abuse.[3] These cases come to define a cultural image of domestic violence, and the women in these cases define an image of battered women.

These images disguise the commonality of violence against women. Up to one half of all American women — and approximately two thirds of women who are separated or divorced — report having experienced physical assault in their relationships.[4] However, litigation and judicial decisionmaking in cases of severe violence reflect implicit or explicit assumptions that domestic violence is rare or exceptional.[5]

For actors in the courtroom drama, the fiction that such violence is exceptional allows denial of the ways in which domestic violence has touched their own lives.[6] Perhaps most damagingly, the fiction of exceptionality also increases the capacity of women to deny that the stories told in the publicized courtroom dramas have anything to do with our own lives. Therefore, it limits the help we may seek when we encounter trouble, the charges we are willing to file, our votes as jurors when charges have been filed by or against others, and our consciousness of the meaning of the struggles and dangers of our own experience.

Although domestic violence is important in many areas of legal doctrine, including family law and torts, the criminal justice system places the greatest pressures on cultural images of battered women. The self-defense cases in which women kill their batterers are small in number compared to the overall universe of domestic violence,[7] yet they are highly emotionally charged as well as highly publicized. In many states, the right to expert testimony on behalf of these defendants has been won through much dedicated feminist litigation.[8] The justification for admitting expert testimony is determined in large part by cultural perceptions of women and of battering; therefore, many points made by experts respond to just these cultural perceptions.[9]

3. *See* Julie Blackman, *Emerging Images of Severely Battered Women and the Criminal Justice System*, 8 BEHAVIORAL SCI. & L. 121 (1990). Women who kill their batterers are likely to have experienced extremely severe violence during the course of their marriages. *See* ANGELA BROWNE, WHEN BATTERED WOMEN KILL (1987).

4. For discussion of the estimates of the incidence of domestic violence in the United States, see *infra* text accompanying notes 36-44.

5. *See, e.g.*, quotations given in text and cases cited at notes 153-69 *infra*.

6. *See infra* notes 58-61 and accompanying text (discussing influence on courtroom participants of their own experiences of violence).

7. *See infra* note 140 and accompanying text.

8. *See, e.g.*, State v. Kelly: *Amicus Briefs*, 9 WOMEN'S RTS. L. REP. 245 (1986).

9. *See, e.g.*, State v. Kelly, 478 A.2d 364, 378 (N.J. 1984) ("[Expert testimony] is aimed at an area where the purported common knowledge of the jury may be very much mistaken . . . an area where expert knowledge would enable the jurors to disregard their prior conclusions as being common myths rather than common knowledge."); *see infra* text accompanying notes 153-69

Yet the expert testimony on battered woman syndrome and learned helplessness can interact with and perpetuate existing oppressive stereotypes of battered women.[10]

Academic expertise on women has thus become crucial to the legal explanation of women's actions and the legal construction of women's experience. Psychological analysis, in particular, has responded to the sharp demand for explanation of women's actions in the self-defense cases.[11] Yet the sociological and psychological literature still reflect some of the oppressive cultural heritage that has shaped legal doctrines.[12] Even when expertise is developed by feminists who explain that women act rationally under circumstances of oppression, courts and the press often interpret feminist expert testimony through the lens of cultural stereotypes, retelling a simpler vision of women as victims too helpless or dysfunctional to pursue a reasonable course of action.[13] These retold stories affect other areas of law, such as custody cases, which share the problems of professional evaluation of women and the incorporation of cultural stereotypes.[14] The portrait of battered women as pathologically weak — the court's version of what feminists have told them — therefore holds particular dangers for battered women with children.

Legal pressures thus distort perceptions of violence in ways that

(expert testimony based on issue being beyond jury's ken). A telling example of the relationship between the *need* for expert testimony and the *points* made by experts is the issue of women's "failure" to leave violent relationships. Many cases review the jury's common-sense belief that women can and will leave violent relationships freely. The experts explain the women's incapacity and failure as a function of many factors, especially the psychology of abused women and traditionalism about the family. *See, e.g.,* People v. Torres, 488 N.Y.S.2d 358, 361-62 (Sup. Ct. 1985); State v. Kelly, 478 A.2d 364, 370-73.

10. *See* Elizabeth M. Schneider, *Describing and Changing: Women's Self-Defense Work and the Problem of Expert Testimony on Battering,* 9 WOMEN'S RTS. L. REP. 195 (1986); Lenore Walker, *A Response to Elizabeth M. Schneider's* Describing and Changing, 9 WOMEN'S RTS. L. REP. 223-25 (1986).

11. For example, see three recent books on this subject: JULIE BLACKMAN, INTIMATE VIOLENCE (1989); CYNTHIA GILLESPIE, JUSTIFIABLE HOMICIDE (1989); LENORE WALKER, TERRIFYING LOVE (1989).

12. *Compare* R. EMERSON DOBASH & RUSSELL DOBASH, VIOLENCE AGAINST WIVES 193-99 (1979) (describing traditional psychological approaches) *and* EDWARD GONDOLF & ELLEN FISHER, BATTERED WOMEN AS SURVIVORS: AN ALTERNATIVE TO TREATING LEARNED HELPLESSNESS 13-15 (1988) (describing psychological views of women as masochistic) *with* DOBASH & DOBASH, *supra,* at 211-26 (criticizing the legal system).

13. Schneider, *supra* note 10, at 198.

14. In contested custody decisions, for example, women are also at risk that either too little strength *or* too much strength may be held against them. *See generally* PHYLLIS CHESLER, MOTHERS ON TRIAL: THE BATTLE FOR CHILDREN AND CUSTODY (1986). Therefore, the portrait of battered women as pathologically weak — the courts' version of what feminists have told them — may disserve battered mothers seeking custody. Myra Sun & Elizabeth Thomas, *Custody Litigation on Behalf of Battered Women,* 21 CLEARINGHOUSE REV. 563, 570 (1987); Laura Crites & Donna Coker, *What Therapists See That Judges May Miss,* JUDGES J., Spring 1988, at 8, 13 (1988). *See infra* text accompanying notes 223-25.

create real problems for women. Many of us cannot recognize our experience in the cultural picture that develops under the influence of legal processes. The consequence is that we understand ourselves less, our society less, and our oppression less, as our capacity to identify with battered women diminishes ("I'm not like *that*"). Before the feminist activism of the early 1970s brought battering to public attention, society generally denied that domestic violence existed.[15] Now, culturally, we know what it is, and we are sure it is not us.

Recent feminist work on battering points to the struggle for power and control — the *batterer's quest for control* of the woman — as the heart of the battering process.[16] Case law and the popular consciousness that grows from it have submerged the question of control by psychologizing the recipient of the violence[17] or by equating women's experience of violence with men's experience.[18] We urgently need to develop legal and social explanations of women's experience that illuminate the issue of violence as part of the issue of power, rather than perpetuating or exacerbating the images that now conceal questions of domination and control.

As one example of a strategic effort to change both law and culture, this article proposes that we seek to redefine in both law and popular culture the issue of women's separation from violent relationships.[19] The question "why didn't she leave?" shapes both social and legal inquiry on battering; much of the legal reliance on academic expertise on battered women has developed in order to address this question. At the moment of separation or attempted separation — for many women, the first encounter with the authority of law[20] — the batterer's quest for control often becomes most acutely violent and

15. *See infra* text accompanying note 94 (discussing the role of feminist activists in bringing national attention to domestic violence).

16. *See infra* text accompanying notes 131-35.

17. *See* GONDOLF & FISHER, *supra* note 12, at 1-3 (describing "psychologizing" of domestic violence).

18. *See* Phyllis Crocker, *The Meaning of Equality for Battered Women Who Kill in Self-Defense*, 8 HARV. WOMEN'S L.J. 121 (1985); *see also* GILLESPIE, *supra* note 11, at 115-17 (discussing women's and men's differing experiences of violence in layperson's terms).

19. Redefining separation must include rethinking many assumptions — that it is the woman's job to separate from a battering relationship, that separation is the appropriate choice for all women when violence first occurs within a relationship, that appropriate separation is an immediate and final break rather than the process of repeated temporary separations made by many women — as well as identifying the violent assault on women's attempts to separate.

20. These encounters may take many forms, including the attempt to have a violent partner arrested, the filing of a temporary restraining order or legal separation, or the rush to find legal counsel because the partner has threatened to take custody of the children. *See, e.g., infra* text accompanying notes 200-01 (discussing custody litigation).

potentially lethal.[21] Ironically, although the proliferation of shelters[22] and the elaboration of statutory structures facilitating the grant of protective orders[23] vividly demonstrate both socially and legally the dangers attendant on separation, a woman's "failure" to permanently separate from a violent relationship is still widely held to be mysterious and in need of explanation, an indicator of *her* pathology rather than her batterer's. We have had neither cultural names nor legal doctrines specifically tailored to the particular assault on a woman's body and volition that seeks to block her from leaving, retaliate for her departure, or forcibly end the separation. I propose that we name this attack "separation assault."

Separation assault is the common though invisible thread that unites the equal protection suits on enforcement of temporary restraining orders, the cases with dead women that appear in many doctrinal categories,[24] and the cases with dead men — the self-defense cases. As with other assaults on women that were not cognizable until the feminist movement named and explained them,[25] separation assault must be identified before women can recognize our own experience and before we can develop legal rules to deal with this particular sort of violence. Naming one particular aspect of the violence then illuminates the rest: for example, the very concept of "acquaintance rape" moves consciousness away from the stereotype of rape (assault by a stranger)[26] and toward a focus on the woman's volition (violation of her will, "consent"). Similarly, by emphasizing the urgent control moves that seek to prevent the woman from ending the relationship,

21. *See* Desmond Ellis, *Post-Separation Woman Abuse: The Contribution of Lawyers as "Barracudas," "Advocates," and "Counsellors,"* 10 INTL. J.L. & PSYCHIATRY 403, 408 (1987). Many authors note the dangers of this period. *See, e.g.*, GILLESPIE, *supra* note 11, at 150-52; ANN JONES, WOMEN WHO KILL 298-99 (1980).

22. GONDOLF & FISHER, *supra* note 12, at 1.

23. *Id.*

24. These cases are often concerned with the mental state or sentences of the murderer. *See, e.g., infra* text accompanying notes 325-26, 351-57 (discussing provocation and manslaughter). Another example appears in several Ninth Circuit cases on competency to plead guilty, including Darrow v. Gunn, 594 F.2d 767, 771 n.6 (9th Cir.), *cert. denied*, 444 U.S. 849 (1979) (wife murder); Sailer v. Gunn, 548 F.2d 271, 273 (9th Cir. 1977) (attempted murder of estranged wife); de Kaplany v. Enomoto, 540 F.2d 975 (9th Cir. 1976), *cert denied*, 429 U.S. 1075 (1977) (wife murder).

25. The example I discuss below is "date rape." *See infra* text accompanying notes 304-05. Sexual harassment is another such example. In her book *Sexual Harassment of Working Women*, Catharine MacKinnon defined sexual harassment in terms of power and inequality ("sexual harassment . . . refers to the unwanted imposition of sexual requirements in the context of a relationship of unequal power") and argued that sexual harassment was sex discrimination. CATHARINE MACKINNON, SEXUAL HARASSMENT OF WORKING WOMEN 1, 4 (1979). Within a decade, this argument had transformed both sex discrimination law and cultural understanding of sexual harassment.

26. SUSAN ESTRICH, REAL RAPE 3-4 (1987).

the concept of separation assault raises questions that inevitably focus additional attention on the ongoing struggle for power and control in the relationship.

Because of the interactive relationships between law and culture in this area, law reform requires such an approach to simultaneously reshape cultural understanding. Separation assault is particularly easy to grasp because it responds to prevailing cultural and legal inquiry ("why didn't she leave") with a twist emphasizing the batterer's violent quest for control. However, meaningful change requires rethinking the entire relationship of law and culture in the field of domestic violence and developing many approaches to revealing power and control. Otherwise, since separation assault is so resonant with existing cultural stereotypes, it may be understood as justifying or excusing the woman's failure to leave rather than challenging and reshaping legal and social attitudes that now place this burden on the woman.

To illustrate the contrast between women's lives and legal and cultural stereotypes, and to accomplish a translation between women's lives and law, this article offers narratives and poems from the lives of survivors of domestic violence, and a few from the stories of non-survivors, as part of its analysis and argument.[27] Seven women's stories have come to me through their own accounts.[28] Five of these have

27. Conversations with women are cited several times in the footnotes of this article. Particularly thoughtful input has come from Kim Hanson and Donna Coker. This citation form is deliberately chosen and consistent with the method of the article. Each citation credits the woman with an original thought or contribution that has not appeared in a form suitable for conventional citation as this article goes to press.

There are three reasons for my choice of citation form. The first is honesty: when other women who have not yet published scholarly work have offered me so much of their best thought — and it has become so deeply part of my own best thought — I must either falsely claim their ideas as my own or credit them as they spoke. The second reason is methodological: much of feminist theory, and much of the strength women draw upon for survival, grows out of conversations with each other. This is, for example, the fundamental method of consciousness-raising. *See, e.g.*, Ronnie Lichtman, *Consciousness Raising — 1970, in* The Female Experience 456 (Gerda Lerner ed., 1977). For a discussion of consciousness-raising and its role in feminist method, see, *e.g.*, Christine A. Littleton, *Feminist Jurisprudence: The Difference Method Makes*, 41 Stan. L. Rev. 751 (1989) (reviewing Catharine MacKinnon, Feminism Unmodified (1987)).

Finally, the third reason for citing women's conversations is political: women may not have published their thoughts because of constraints on their time and effort imposed by uniquely womanly responsibilities. This article had its roots in conversations between Kim Hanson and myself, neighbors in family student housing, when I was a first-year and she a third-year law student at Stanford. Our children played together, and we talked around them over the back fence, encountering each other while hanging laundry, while carrying groceries in from the car. This work is in part the product of that shared work and thought. Since then, Kim has litigated for a major law firm, started her own firm, become known as a battered women's advocate, and remarried. She has had two more babies since we first met. I hope some day she writes her own articles. Until then, I acknowledge her thought in my work as a way of acknowledging her *work* as part of my own.

28. These are women who talked with me or sought me out for help over the past several years. One was my next-door neighbor at Stanford; another sought me out during my second

at some time identified themselves as battered women.[29] Three of these women were Stanford Law School students or graduates; another was an undergraduate student at Stanford. One was an acquaintance in a support group. One is black, the rest are white. All but two were mothers when the violence occurred. Though our class backgrounds vary, only one was a highly educated professional before the battering incidents described, but several have acquired academic degrees since the marriages ended. The other women's voices in this paper are drawn from identified published sources.

One of these stories is my own. I do not feel like a "battered woman."[30] Really, I want to say that I am not, since the phrase conjures up an image that fails to describe either my marriage or my sense of myself. It is a difficult claim to make for several reasons: the gap between my self-perceived competence and strength and my own image of battered women, the inevitable attendant loss of my own denial of painful experience, and the certainty that the listener cannot hear such a claim without filtering it through a variety of derogatory stereotypes.[31] However, the definitions of battered women have broad contours,[32] at least some of which encompass my experience and the experiences of the other strong, capable women whose stories are included here.

In fact, women often emphasize that they do not fit their own stereotypes of the battered woman:

> The first thing I would tell you is that very little happened. I am not one of those women who stayed and stayed to be beaten. It is very important to me not to be mistaken for one of them, I wouldn't take it. Besides, I never wanted to be the one who tells you what it was really like.

The rejection of stereotypes, the fear of being identified with these ste-

---

year of law school, six months after I gave a talk for incoming women students about emotional reactions to the materials in casebooks. When I relate these women's stories, I do not include specific citations.

29. Most did not generally use the term when describing themselves.

30. *See infra* text accompanying notes 86-92 (this term labels the woman instead of the process or the man), and *infra* note 93. I would prefer some term that lets us discuss stereotyping without hopelessly dooming the discourse from the start. However, I think it is important to overcome our fear of the stigma and stereotype that come with the term "battered woman," so I accept it for this paper.

31. I fear derogatory stereotypes of myself and of my ex-husband and of that marriage. *See generally infra* text accompanying notes 86-93; *see also* Liz Kelly, *How Women Define Their Experiences of Violence, in* FEMINIST PERSPECTIVES ON WIFE ABUSE 114, 116 (Kersti Yllo & Michele Bograd eds., 1988) (meaning of terms like "rape" and "battering" often taken for granted).

32. *See infra* text accompanying notes 110-36 (critique of definitions of battering and battered women).

reotypes, is expressed by lesbian women as well as heterosexual women:

> First I want you to know that I am an assertive and powerful woman. I do not fit my stereotype of a battered woman. I am telling you this because I *never* thought it could happen to me. Most lesbians I know who have been battered impress me with their presence and strength. None of them fit my stereotype. Do not think that what happened to me could not happen to you.[33]

Although there is relatively little published material on lesbian battering, this literature can shed light on the ways in which we conceptualize the battering process. Although lesbian battering is similar to heterosexual battering, the analysis of lesbian battering is unique in two ways that are significant for this paper: it has been generated entirely by feminist activists, and it has developed in isolation from the legal system. Therefore, it provides one clue to the question, "[W]hat would this . . . landscape look like if women had constructed it for ourselves?"[34]

Part I of this article discusses violence in the ordinary lives of women, describing individual and societal denial that pretends domestic violence is rare when statistics show it is common,[35] and describing the ways in which motherhood shapes women's experience of violence and choices in response to violence. Part II examines definitions of battering and evaluates their effectiveness at disguising or revealing the struggle for control at the heart of the battering process. I then describe in Part III the pressures that self-defense and custody cases place on legal and cultural images of battered women and contrast the development of an analysis of lesbian battering, an analysis generated outside the legal system. In Part IV, I discuss battering as a struggle for power and control and show how legal analysis can help reveal the control issue by naming separation assault and building litigation

---

33. Arlene Istar, *The Healing Comes Slowly, in* NAMING THE VIOLENCE: SPEAKING OUT ABOUT LESBIAN BATTERING 163, 164 (Kerry Lobel ed., 1986) [hereinafter NAMING THE VIOLENCE].

34. Christine A. Littleton, *Women's Experience and the Problem of Transition: Perspectives on Male Battering of Women,* 1989 U. CHI. LEGAL F. 23, 30 (1989) (paraphrasing Heather R. Wishik, *To Question Everything: The Inquiries of Feminist Jurisprudence,* 1 BERKELEY WOMEN'S L.J. 64, 75 (1985) ("In an ideal world, what would this woman's life situation look like, and what relationship, if any, would the law have to this future life situation?")).

35. Denial is a potent force that operates on at least four levels: at a broad societal level that shields the institution of marriage (we do not recognize the pervasiveness of violence and its normal occurrence within marriage), among men who wish to protect their privilege or deny their own battering, among individual women who are not currently battered or who believe they are not ("I wouldn't be like that"), and in women who admit experiencing domestic violence but minimize their estimates of its harm to themselves as part of survival and coping mechanisms. *See generally infra* text accompanying notes 47-73.

strategies to redefine the issue separation. Finally, in Part V, I identify separation assault in the cases where women have been killed or harmed, as well as cases in which women killed in self-defense, and explain how the concept of separation assault is consistent with the particular needs of expert testimony in the self-defense cases. I demonstrate how naming separation assault can intervene in the interrelationship between law and culture in the field of domestic violence to change both the questions asked and the answers found by courts in several areas of law.

I. Violence and the Ordinary Lives of Women

A. *The Prevalence of Violence and the Phenomenon of Denial*

> Most people I have known who have been abused in marriage have come out — once burned, twice shy. But that doesn't mean fire's not hot. But people treat marriage and relationships and love, in our society, as if fire's not hot.

Statistics show that domestic violence is extremely widespread in American society. Exact figures on its incidence are difficult to come by. Some studies have counted incidents of violence by or against either spouse regardless of context and found a nearly equal incidence of violence by men and women.[36] Other studies show that women are far more frequently victimized than men,[37] and that women's violence is almost always in self-defense and generally less severe than their partner's.[38] The most conservative figures estimate that women are physically abused in twelve percent of all marriages,[39] and some scholars estimate that as many as fifty percent[40] or more[41] of all women will

36. Murray A. Straus et al., Behind Closed Doors: Violence in the American Family (1980).

37. In New Jersey, wives or girlfriends were victims in 85% of all reported domestic violent offenses. Gail A. Goolkasian, *Confronting Domestic Violence: A Guide for Criminal Justice Agencies, in* U.S. Dept. of Justice Rep. (1986).

38. Daniel G. Saunders, *Wife Abuse, Husband Abuse, or Mutual Combat? A Feminist Perspective on the Empirical Findings, in* Feminist Perspectives on Wife Abuse, *supra* note 31, at 90, 103-08.

39. Straus et al., *supra* note 36, at 36.

40. Lenore Walker, The Battered Woman 19 (1979) [hereinafter Lenore Walker]. The 50% estimate is weighed and accepted by Christine A. Littleton. Littleton, *supra* note 34, at 28 n.19. For the reasons articulated by Littleton, and from the stories told to me by women, the 50% figure seems reasonable to me as well.

41. Jennifer B. Fleming, Stopping Wife Abuse 155 (1979), *quoted in Achieving Equal Justice for Victims of Domestic Violence, in* Advisory Comm. on Gender Bias in the Courts, California Judicial Council, Achieving Equal Justice for Women and Men in the Courts pt. 6, at 3 (draft Mar. 23, 1990) [hereinafter *Achieving Equal Justice*] (estimating 60% of married women experience domestic violence at some time during their marriages); Sisterhood Is Global, 703 (Robin Morgan ed., 1984) (50%-70% of women experience battering during marriage).

be battering victims at some point in their lives. Accurate estimates are difficult,[42] in part because of the likelihood of underreporting.[43] However, using any of these estimates, marriages that include violence against the woman represent a relatively widespread phenomenon in our society.[44]

Although these statistics are widely reproduced, there is little social or legal recognition that domestic violence has touched the lives of many people in this society and must be known to many people. Judicial opinions, for example, treat domestic violence as aberrant and unusual: "a unique and almost mysterious area of human response and behavior,"[45] "beyond the ken of the average lay [person]."[46] This radical discrepancy between the "mysterious" character of domestic violence and repeatedly gathered statistics reflects massive denial throughout society and the legal system.

Denial is a defense mechanism well recognized in psychology that protects people from consciously knowing things they cannot bear to reckon with at the time.[47] A powerful if undiscussed force affecting

---

42. The incidence of domestic violence is hard to determine, in part because it takes place within the home, and in part because the many studies in the field present statistical information that is not directly comparable with that in other studies. Some focus on the number of women who are victims of spouse abuse: estimates of women physically abused by husbands or boyfriends in the United States range from 1.5 million, BROWNE, *supra* note 3, at 5, to 3-4 million, Mary Pat Bryger, *Domestic Violence: The Dark Side of Divorce*, FAM. ADVOCATE, Summer 1990, at 48. Straus, Gelles, and Steinmetz studied violence against spouses of either gender and found that more than 1.7 million Americans at some time faced a spouse wielding a knife or gun. STRAUS ET AL., *supra* note 36, at 34.

43. BROWNE, *supra* note 3, at 4-5 (citing studies by Straus, Gelles, and Steinmetz and the Louis Harris organization). Self-reports may undercount significantly. *See generally* DIANA E. RUSSELL, RAPE IN MARRIAGE 96-101 (1982) (reviewing statistical techniques and results of several surveys on domestic violence).

44. Stating violence is normal does not mean it is normative or culturally accepted, as it once was. See DOBASH & DOBASH, *supra* note 12, at 48-74, for a discussion of violence that was historically part of control of women within marriage. Violence against women was an early focus of feminist protest and efforts at reform. By the mid-nineteenth century, contrary to some popular stereotypes, wifebeating was already considered "a disreputable, seamy practice"; it was illegal in most states by the 1870s. LINDA GORDON, HEROES OF THEIR OWN LIVES: THE POLITICS AND HISTORY OF FAMILY VIOLENCE 255 (1988). Although today domestic violence is indeed "disreputable," that does not mean that it has disappeared in fact — only that the commonality of its occurrence in normal marriage is widely denied.

45. *See, e.g.*, Sinns v. State, 283 S.E.2d 479, 481 (Ga. 1981) (explaining Smith v. State, 277 S.E.2d 678 (Ga. 1980)).

46. *See, e.g.*, Ibn-Tamas v. United States, 407 A.2d 626, 634 (D.C. 1983).

47. The American Psychiatric Association defines denial as "[a] defense mechanism operating unconsciously used to resolve emotional conflict and allay anxiety by disavowing thoughts, feelings, wishes, needs, or external reality factors that are consciously intolerable." AMERICAN PSYCHIATRIC ASSN., A PSYCHIATRIC GLOSSARY 28 (5th ed. 1980). The emphasis here is on what is *consciously* tolerable for an individual. This is the sense in which I use the term "individual denial." I use the term "societal denial" to mean an ideology that protects us from knowing that which our culture finds intolerable. *Cf.* David M. Trubek, *Where the Action Is: Critical Legal Studies and Empiricism*, 36 STAN. L. REV. 575, 607 (1984) ("Legal thought is a form of

the evolution of the law and litigation on battered women, denial exists at both the societal and individual levels. Societal denial amounts to an ideology[48] that protects the institution of marriage by perpetuating the focus on individual violent actors, concealing both the commonality of violence in marriage and the ways in which state and society participate in the subordination of women.

"Societal" denial — albeit within a smaller, more consciously self-defined society — also slowed recognition of lesbian battering. Although many lesbian activists helped start the battered women's movement, battering did not emerge as an internal problem in the consciousness of the lesbian community until years after the movement had begun.[49] This collective denial of internal violence was based, in part, on the reluctance to let go of an ideal of lesbian relationships and community, a "lesbian utopia — a nonviolent, fairly androgynous, often separatist community struggling for social justice and freedom for ourselves and other oppressed people."[50]

However, there are important differences between the ideological defense of marriage and the defense of lesbian utopia. The differences lie in the way power is vested in one partner of a marriage at the time of marriage by society, law, and tradition, fitting heterosexual battering into a historic framework of oppression and domination *of* women *by* men. Marriage is an institution which underlies many — perhaps most — other social, political, and economic relations, and to that end many elements of society have a stake in defending it. Because of oppression of lesbians and exclusion from many social structures — for example, lesbians *cannot* marry in the United States — the dream at stake was less central to the surrounding society but, poignantly, at least equally central to lesbian self-definition and community.

The ideology that protects the institution of marriage and the state's participation in subordinating women is consistent with the findings of James Ptacek's study of batterers.[51] Ptacek found that

---

denial, a way to deal with perceived contradictions that are too painful for us to hold in consciousness.").

48. JURGEN HABERMAS, KNOWLEDGE AND HUMAN INTERESTS 311 (Jeremy J. Shapiro trans., 1971), *quoted in* James Ptacek, *Why Do Men Batter Their Wives?, in* FEMINIST PERSPECTIVES ON WIFE ABUSE, *supra* note 31, at 155 ("From everyday experiences we know that ideas serve often enough to furnish our actions with justifying motives in place of the real ones. What is called rationalization at this level is called ideology at the level of collective action.").

49. *See, e.g.,* Lydia Walker, *Battered Women's Shelters and Work with Battered Lesbians, in* NAMING THE VIOLENCE, *supra* note 33, at 73 (describing her work in a battered women's project, her work with battered lesbians, and her difficulty in facing the violence she had experienced in her own relationships with women).

50. Barbara Hart, *Preface* to NAMING THE VIOLENCE, *supra* note 33, at 9, 13.

51. *See generally* Ptacek, *supra* note 48. A New York judge told the state's Task Force on Women in the Courts that, when a woman gives up an attempt to separate, judges either smile

both batterers and the criminal justice system tended to blame women for their abuse and deny or trivialize the violence involved.[52] These excuses and justifications are ideological in nature: "At the individual level, they obscure the batterer's self-interest in acting violently; *at the societal level, they mask the male domination underlying violence against women.* Clinical and criminal justice responses to battering are revealed as ideological in the light of their collusion with batterers' rationalizations."[53]

This ideology pervades the courtroom as well as other areas of the criminal justice system. It shapes legal events in several ways: it affects the individual consciousness of the actors in the courtroom,[54] the doctrinal questions that are the legal framework of each action,[55] and the options to avoid legal confrontation and the resources individuals bring into the courtroom.[56] Especially troublesome, this ideology which denies oppression has had a profound impact on the development of explanations of women's experience and behavior that can fit within the conceptual structure of the law.[57]

It is likely that a number of people present in any court will have some personal experience of domestic violence.[58] Using the conservative estimate that domestic violence occurs in one quarter of house-

---

(thinking they have brought the couple back together), or snicker. The snickering response is based on their perception "that the woman who accepts this violent behavior and reconciles with the man[,] even if she reconciles in a split but doesn't pursue the case, isn't worthy of our respect because she does not respect herself . . . ." New York Task Force on Women in the Courts, *Report of the New York Task Force on Women in the Courts,* 15 FORDHAM URB. L.J. 11, 36-37 (1986-1987) [hereinafter *New York Task Force Report*].

52. Ptacek, *supra* note 48, at 141-49 (batterers), 154-55 (criminal justice system).

53. *Id.* at 155 (emphasis added).

54. *See infra* text accompanying notes 58-61 (discussing experience of battering among courtroom participants).

55. *See, e.g., infra* text accompanying notes 371-78, 410-24 (discussing the question of the imminent danger of death or grave bodily harm in cases in which women assert they have killed their batterers in self-defense).

56. *See, e.g., infra* text accompanying notes 195-210 (discussing the relative power of men and women in custody actions).

57. For example, if the batterers' position is essentially identical with the perspective of the criminal justice system, and both fit with an ideology that protects marriage, then the "commonsense" position in any courtroom will tend to favor men. Therefore, women will need experts to explain their lives; men will not. *See, e.g.,* Littleton, *supra* note 34, at 35 (all women, not only battered women, may appear alien from a male perspective).

58. Violence in our personal lives has existed for everyone in varying degrees. The magnitude of the damage and turmoil is the real crux of the problem. If individuals on the panel are afraid of their own feelings about having been battered, then perhaps they will not be open to the battered woman's feelings. Some will have battered someone themselves and will struggle to justify their own actions.

Roberta K. Thyfault et al., *Battered Women in Court: Jury and Trial Consultants and Expert Witnesses, in* DOMESTIC VIOLENCE ON TRIAL: PSYCHOLOGICAL AND LEGAL DIMENSIONS OF FAMILY VIOLENCE 55, 62 (Daniel J. Sonkin ed., 1987) [hereinafter DOMESTIC VIOLENCE ON TRIAL].

holds,[59] at least four of the fifteen or more actors in an average criminal action — jurors, judge, and attorneys — probably will have experienced or committed at least one domestic assault.[60] Similarly, in custody suits, the judge and the attorneys — *and* the social workers and psychologists who are performing evaluations of the parents — have this statistical likelihood of having experienced or committed violence. Therefore, the atmosphere in the courtroom will not reflect mere ignorance, nor merely the broad social stereotypes which courts generally recognize can be a problem.[61] Rather, the response to and evaluation of the case before them will also include the unseen and unspoken ties that bind these participants to the fabric of their own lives, their parents' lives, and their children's.

Social workers and psychologists play an important role in this process. Our legal system — like the rest of society — has to a large extent entrusted these professionals with the definition of what is normal and functional.[62] Despite the statistics on the epidemic incidence of domestic violence, there is almost no legal or social science scholarship that describes an author's experience of violence[63] or even indicates that the author has had any such experience.[64] It is unlikely that a disinterested body of social scientists is doing all this research. However, scholars may be reluctant to indicate their own experience because they fear intellectual marginalization[65] or familial repercussions. Scholarly fears of marginalization probably reflect some acceptance of stereotypes of battered women; certainly, they reflect caution about the power and danger of stereotyping by others.

This silence among professionals and scholars is one intersection between individual denial and an ideology of societal denial. This is where one of the lenses through which we see the world is constructed:

---

59. *See supra* notes 36-44 and accompanying text.

60. Overrepresentation of the middle class in the courtroom would not change this estimate. Domestic violence occurs across class lines. LENORE WALKER, *supra* note 40, at 19.

61. *See, e.g.*, State v. Kelly, 478 A.2d 364, 378 (N.J. 1984) (jurors may hold "common myths").

62. *See, e.g.*, *infra* text accompanying notes 213-22 (discussing the role of social workers in custody disputes).

63. The exceptions here are Robin West, who discusses her own experience of battering, Robin L. West, *The Difference in Women's Hedonic Lives: A Phenomenological Critique of Feminist Legal Theory*, 3 WIS. WOMEN'S L.J. 81, 98-99 (1987); and Terry Davidson, who discusses being the child of a wife beater, TERRY DAVIDSON, CONJUGAL CRIME: UNDERSTANDING AND CHANGING THE WIFEBEATING PATTERN 14-15, 131-54 (1978).

64. *But see* Jan E. Stets' preface to her excellent study, JAN E. STETS, DOMESTIC VIOLENCE AND CONTROL v (1988) (research on domestic violence brought understanding of violence she witnessed and experienced while growing up).

65. *See, e.g.*, West, *supra* note 63, at 99 (describes grappling with this anxiety but goes on to discuss her own experience).

if scholars are silent for "personal" reasons, their "professional" silence then perpetuates the social stereotypes that construct battered women as different, exceptional, "other." Ultimately, the denial of personal experience of domestic violence in social science literature and forensic testimony permits continued societal blindness to the implications of the statistics these same experts gather and employ.[66]

Individual denial protects the images of self and marriage held by individual women and men, as well as being the mechanism through which much societal denial operates. This is true elsewhere as it is in the courtroom: people need to know that their own marriages are sound, therefore it is important to know that they (or their wives) do not "stay" in the relationship; they "are" in the relationship. Their own relationships define what is normal and appropriate; it is appropriate for their own relationships to continue. The battered woman *must* be different. Therefore, the question "why did she stay?" commonly finds answers that attempt to explain difference: "because she had children" or "because she was frightened" or "because she became pathologically helpless" — not, significantly, because I/you/we "stayed" too.

Do we "stay," or are we simply married? Writing this article forced me to grapple with my own image of battered women, my "credentials" in claiming this identity, and my experience of marriage. As I worked, I found similar conceptions of self and marriage in several of the women who spoke with me. These women described their marriages as "bad" or "unhappy" and then went on to recount attacks that were almost murderous — threats with guns and knives, partial strangling, deliberately running into a woman with a car:

> I tried to nurse John [her colicky baby], but Ed screamed that I was trying to poison him. I said, "OK, I'll get you a bottle." I had to kneel down by the microwave, and Ed pushed me over, so that I fell over. So I put the bottle in the micro and stood up, and finished microwaving the bottle, put the nipple on, and gave it to Ed. . . . Ed began screaming almost incoherently, and grabbed John, and started to storm back out to the car with him.
>
> At this point I got worried. The first time [earlier that night, when her husband first stormed out and drove around with the baby] I thought he was angry because I had yelled, and I felt guilty . . . it didn't seem that aberrant. But screaming about poison when I tried to nurse him, knocking me over . . . it just seemed like there was something wrong. I said, "You're welcome to leave, but you can't take John. I don't think you're all there."

66. Conversation with Kim Hanson, 1989 ("As long as you don't speak out, you're part of the conspiracy of silence.").

> He pushed past. I stood in front of the car. He drove into me. I tried to go over the hood of the car, hit the pavement quite hard, and blacked out for a minute. When I came to, he had turned the car around, he was like a foot from me, and he was saying "get up, or I'll drive over you."
>
> [Her husband had "scared himself . . . realized he had gone too far" and gave her the baby to nurse. They finally fell asleep.] Next morning, Ed had gone to work. I couldn't move, I couldn't move my legs. I remember thinking, I'm going to die. [The baby] is going to wake up next to a corpse . . . . When I look back, there was so much rage in that thought [at the colicky baby as well as the husband] . . . . I had a very hard time functioning. I was able to make it to the bathroom, but the tunnel vision seemed worse.

Women often discussed the relationship at length before they mentioned any violence. Finally, I began to understand that the violence against these women seemed shocking to me — and the violence against me seemed shocking to them — precisely because we heard each others' reports of violence isolated from the context of the marriages. For ourselves, on the other hand, the daily reality of the marriages — none of which included daily or even weekly violent episodes — defined most of our memories and retrospective sense of the relationship: these were "bad" marriages, not ordeals of physical torture. We resisted defining the entire experience of marriage by the episodes of violence that had marked the relationship's lowest points. Our understanding of marriage, love, and commitment in our own lives — as well as our stereotypes of battered women — shaped our discussion.

This question of the line between "normal" marriage and violent marriage is a common one. One activist social worker recounts that when she speaks on domestic violence in any forum, someone *always* asks why women "stay." She says, "When should she have left? At what point? Maybe the time she watched while he smashed up the furniture?" A silence, a shock of recognition, falls over the audience. It is, relatively speaking, *normal* for a woman to watch a man smash up the furniture. Many of the women in the room have seen something like it — and called it "marriage," and not "staying."[67]

Denial conditions women's perceptions of our own relationships and need for assistance. An extreme example is a woman who founded a shelter for battered women; although her husband was beating her during this period, she never identified with the women she sought to help:

> I just thought that the incidents of violence that I — in order to be a

67. Conversation with Donna Coker, 1989 (discussing four years of activist feminist social work with battered women in Honolulu).

> battered woman you had to be really battered. I mean OK, I had a couple of bad incidents, but mostly it was pretty minor, in inverted commas, "violence." I didn't see myself in that category, as a battered woman at all.[68]

Similarly, women may fail to perceive armed attacks that do not result in injury as physical abuse — or indeed fail to so perceive anything other than an archetypal brutal beating:

> I don't know what I'd have done if I had to live with what [I assume] you did. My marriage wasn't physically abusive, but there was emotional abuse. My husband had a pistol . . . he did pull his gun on me . . . .

This may happen even when the woman calls for help:

> When I finally called the Battered Women's Center for help, I was just looking for advice — my husband had threatened to move back in without my consent while I was recovering from a Cesarian section . . . . He said "you can't stop me" . . . . I told the counselor that I was just looking for a referral, as I didn't qualify for their help because my marriage had not been violent, although I had left after he attacked me with a loaded shotgun. There was a tiny pause, and then she said gently: "We classify that as extreme violence."

Other aspects of women's denial of oppression within ordinary marriage also affect our perception of battered women. Battered women interviewed by social workers often say they felt a responsibility to support their children's relationship with their father because "he's really good with the children."[69] This is not dissimilar to statements by women in nonviolent relationships — or relationships they do not perceive as violent. Women often admit when pressed that they are actually describing a father who is loving with a child when he chooses to interact with it, even if that interaction happens seldom, yet insist on the value of his presence in the children's lives. However, this is a parallel that makes many women uncomfortable: how could a batterer be like their husband? Similarly, although sexual abuse is often a part of domestic violence, many battered women who did not experience sexual abuse describe sex as having been "the only good thing about the marriage."[70] Women who are in relationships of unequal power that are not violent must also find sexual pleasure under conditions of inequality, yet they may not wish to recognize the similarity in experience.

---

68. Kelly, *supra* note 31, at 114, 123-24.

69. Conversation with Donna Coker, *supra* note 67.

70. *Id.; see also* Lenore Walker's discussion of her difficulty understanding the reports of sexual pleasure among the battered women she interviewed. LENORE WALKER, *supra* note 40, at 108-12.

The literature on battering notes, clinically and sometimes with condescending undertones, that women tend to "perceive" the onset of violence as atypical.[71] Of course, the *onset* of violence *is* atypical, and therefore our perceptions are in many ways appropriate.[72] Yet we may ignore danger signals and early attacks because we believe that the "battered-ness" is a characteristic of the woman — a characteristic we do not have — rather than a characteristic of her partner or a symptom of a dynamic in the relationship. Denial creates and reinforces the perceptions (1) that battered women are weak, (2) that we are not weak, and (3) that therefore we are safe.

Finally, individual denial leads women to minimize the pain and oppressiveness of our experiences while we continue to live with them. This is also a familiar dynamic in women's relationships; yet if violence is what we are minimizing, we face great costs and dangers.

> That session in the hospital when I had been married one month, and the nurse came and sat on the bed and said she had heard I didn't care if I went home for Christmas . . . . The truth was, I couldn't face what I was going home to. I instinctively knew it was very bad to lie about this but I couldn't bear to tell the truth. It was too humiliating. I didn't tell her anything. To my friends, I said I fell down. I did not intend to cover for him but for myself . . . for the confusion and humiliation . . . for finding myself in this unbelievable position.

This woman's images of battered women and herself make her position "unbelievable." Her response, based on these images, is to disguise her experience. She allows her husband to avoid the censure of family and friends in order to protect *herself* from their opinions, setting up the possibility of more such lies in the future because the image itself has not been confronted, and making it likely that she will minimize her own pain in order to maintain silence.[73]

The cumulative effect of this denial has been very destructive for women. We have difficulty recognizing ourselves and our experience on the continuum of violence and power in which we actually live. To the extent that we cannot recognize ourselves, we are hindered in for-

---

71. BROWNE, *supra* note 3, at 85.

72. The initial violent episode is not treated as though it signals the beginning of a violent relationship. It is treated as an isolated, exceptional event, which is what one would expect it to be treated as. Only in retrospect does the woman begin to examine the first violent act more broadly, seeking signs that "she should have noticed. . . . " The evidence is that there has never been any violence before, that the husband rejects this behavior in principle. . . . There is no reason to expect the violence to be repeated.

DOBASH & DOBASH, *supra* note 12, at 95-96.

73. Battered women tend to minimize the history of assault against them and the pain they have suffered. *See* Julie Blackman, *Potential Uses for Expert Testimony: Ideas Toward the Representation of Battered Women Who Kill*, 9 WOMEN'S RTS. L. REP. 227, 228-29 (1986).

mulating an affirmative vision in which our integrity is protected. Although much of this article emphasizes legal aspects of the related forces of law, society, and academia at work in the field of battered women, I believe that the ways in which women are divided from each other — and deprived of the capacity to understand our own experience in relation to other women — are ultimately most important.

B. *Motherhood: Connectedness and Violence Against Women*

> Look at me, a voodoo doll,
> stuffed with hair, toenails, and fear,
> stuck with pins radiating like hatred
> from my pincushion body.
> You've held me in your hands,
> a wooden fetish —
> female figure carved out of heartwood
> and studded with nails.
> Each nail driven in is a desire, a wish,
> is somebody's want driven into me.[74]

One of the most pervasive fictions in the case law is that women with children are individual actors. Even much feminist legal literature has tended to pretend all women's notions of self and autonomy will be the same.[75] In fact, mothers continually make decisions on the basis of extended, collective, multiple self-interest (their children's as well as their own, their husbands' as well as their children's).[76] The connectedness of mothers is not simply biological — it is existential, social, and extremely practical. Most simply, what makes my children's lives harder makes my life harder. If they are ill or sleepless, I do not sleep.[77] It goes both ways: what hurts me, or terrorizes me, often hurts them as well. Also, anything that made their father's life harder made my life harder, in both emotional and economic dimensions. Finally, as the safest outlet for emotional expression and the source of consolation for our unequal loved ones of greater or lesser

---

74. Harryette Mullen, *Veteran of Domestic Wars, in* FAMILY VIOLENCE: POEMS ON THE PATHOLOGY, *supra* note 1, at 51.

75. *See generally* Stephanie Wildman, *The Power of Women,* 2 YALE J.L. & FEMINISM 435 (1990) (book review) (criticizing Catharine MacKinnon and other feminist scholars for their inattention to the particular situations of women with children).

76. On women's intimate connection with our families, and the identity built on this connection, see generally Robin West, *Jurisprudence and Gender,* 55 U. CHI. L. REV. 1, 18-22, 40 (1988).

77. I do not mean that these roles are purely biologically defined. To the extent that some men fill this role with children, they can be seen as also engaged in mothering. Christine Littleton has pointed out that gender is in many ways socially constituted. Christine A. Littleton, *Reconstructing Sexual Equality,* 75 CAL. L. REV. 1279 (1987). Men who interact at this primal caregiving level with their children are carrying out conduct Littleton calls "socially female." *Id.* at 1308-09.

power,[78] women are uniquely bound to weighing the needs of others as our own. These needs have, in fact, become our own in many significant ways — our "selves" simply are not single.

The ordinary lives of women leave us vulnerable to violence and oppression both because of our commitments and because of the lack of understanding and protection within the law. Despite the many responsibilities and connections of women's lives, courts and legal scholars widely assume that it is a woman's responsibility to leave the relationship.[79] When women tell the stories of their commitment to relationships, stories which may include love and hope, the legal system often has no way to hear them.[80] In order to recognize women's attempts to forge families and the complex attendant pressures on decisions about domestic violence, we need to increase social understanding of women's commitments as well as of women's fear. In fact, the onset of violence often occurs *after* commitment deepens. This may occur soon after the couple is married:

> He beat me up on our wedding night. I wound up with a black eye, a very bad black eye, and split lip. He was almost arrested that night . . . . I ran out of the house in my nightgown and flagged down a passing car and got them to take me to my father-in-law's house. When my father-in-law came back, the neighbors had called the police and the police were there. My father-in-law talked them out of taking him in.

Pregnancy, which also increases commitment, is also often an onset point for violence.[81] Women who experience this violence have had their emotional and economic needs transformed by the pregnancy itself; it is a very poor time for them to respond. Since mothers bear much of the responsibility for the emotional ties between the fathers and children in our society, the new family structure changes her responsibilities to all parties: if the children are not physically

78. *See* West, *supra* note 76, at 26 (women exist in a web of natural *inequality* that involves continual care for dependent children).

79. This assumption is questioned by Littleton, *supra* note 34, at 29, 53-54 ("Why should the woman leave? It's her home, too — in fact, often it's her home, period.").

80. *Id.* at 43-44, 46-47 (discussing Smith v. State, 277 S.E.2d 678, (Ga. 1981)).

81. The accounts of pregnancy triggering men's violence against women are virtually universal. *See, e.g.*, LENORE WALKER, *supra* note 40, at 105-06. This is generally interpreted as the man's competition with the fetus for his wife's attention and affection. *Id.* It is true that our emotional lives and daily practical lives are transformed by children; men often want this attention, have received it, fear its loss, show resentment and anger. People who have problems with control may react badly to change and stress. *See* RICHARD A. STORDEUR & RICHARD STILLE, ENDING MEN'S VIOLENCE AGAINST THEIR PARTNERS: ONE ROAD TO PEACE 101-03 (1989). Interestingly, pregnancy is not on the list of stressors listed by Stordeur and Stille that therapists see most in treating batterers. This may be a function of the point in the relationship at which men enter treatment: the top stressors (divorce, marital separation, jail term, marital reconciliation) all refer to later points in the relationship than marriage or pregnancy. *Id.*

harmed, the woman may hesitate to deprive the children of his companionship, even at substantial danger to herself.[82] However, our social and legal doctrines increase the cost of her loyalty by viewing her attempt to fulfill this responsibility as problematic "staying" in the relationship.

From the viewpoint of the woman in a violent marriage, "staying" may look very different. One of the women in my support group was strikingly strong and serene. She worked as a legal secretary, earning a good salary for a working woman. She was attractive, intelligent, thoughtful. I simply could not reconcile this woman's presence, composure, and depth with my image of a battered woman. Finally, after a meeting, I took her aside and said, "I know this question must sound just awful, but what on earth are you doing here? You're so strong. . . ." She said:

> Well, my husband is an alcoholic. Things have been really bad these past few years. But we've been married thirteen years. And I have three children. For nine of those years, he was the best husband and father anyone could have asked for. The way I look at it, he has a disease. I *know* that when he's not drinking, he's not like this. I may have to leave. But if I do, I'm giving up on a father for the children, and I'm giving up on him. And I can't just throw away those nine years. So I go to Al-Anon, and I come here. I get the support I need. And I may have to decide to go. But I'm not going to do it lightly.

The wearing, repetitious labor of motherhood becomes part of the cycle of survival in ways we have had trouble recognizing. The constant work and need create a wearing down of the self, an erosion of borders that represents not confusion but exhaustion — a thirst for solace and protection as well as individuation. The constant demands of children, especially in an unstable situation, may prove exhausting. Women experience this blurring of borders, this need to subject their own needs to others, even when violence is not present. Question: Was it a battered or nonbattered wife who wrote this poem?

82. Even after divorce, most women place high value on their children's relationship with the father. Lenore Weitzman, The Divorce Revolution 230 (1985). In fact, the woman is essentially required to be responsible to these broad familial emotional and developmental needs when she goes into court to pursue her claim to custody. Martha Fineman notes that social workers are suspicious of individuals who seek sole custody and seem to want to break ties with the other parent; social workers tend to want to punish these individuals by awarding custody to the other parent. Martha Fineman, *Dominant Discourse, Professional Language, and Legal Change in Child Custody Decisionmaking*, 101 Harv. L. Rev. 727, 766 (1988).

A Woman's Work is Done (on the Run)

Mama, I'm hungry
So get up and feed me
my diapers are dirty
it's your job to clean me.

Mama, I'm happy
and I want to play
Do you really have
something
else to do anyway?

Mama, I'm angry
and I want to fight
Sometimes it seems like
you can't do nothing right.

Mama, I'm hurting
you gotta make me better.
Cure my cold, wipe my
nose
and make me wear a
sweater.

Mama, I'm tired
so rock me off to sleep.
Just give me the best
of your life and don't
weep.

Baby, I'm hungry
you know I got to eat
You've got a way w/cookin
that just can't be beat.

Baby, I'm happy
and I want to play
A little of your love
goes a long way.

Baby, I'm angry
coz you want your "rights"
You know you're *just(!)* a
woman
so go fly a kite.

Baby, I'm hurting
and need your gentle touch
Just hold me close and rock
me
it doesn't take that much

Baby, I'm tired
so let me go to sleep
Don't bother me with your
needs
just make my life complete.

Answer: It was a nineteen-year-old woman in the midst of a battering relationship,[83] but like the furniture smashing example above, there seems little to distinguish this woman's daily concerns from a nonviolent marriage. The skills common to women in dealing with these demands easily convert to battlefield skills of compartmentalization and an emergency mode of coping with only immediate present demands; while extremely functional in times of crisis, these skills are wearing over time and may later cause her to be defined — or to define herself — as dysfunctional.

> Two days after he broke the glass in the door, it was the middle of a hot summer afternoon. My son was asleep in his crib in my room, my daughter was taking a nap in hers. I was lying in bed reading. Suddenly, I heard a popping noise, and glass started crashing to the floor. Someone was shooting through my windows. There were no bullets flying around — I remember wondering if it was an air rifle. The windows kept shattering, and I didn't know what would happen if anything hit the baby.

83. I thank Kim Hanson for sending the poems by J.C. Clark, as well as portions of her own journals I drew on extensively for this article.

> I grabbed him out of the crib, got down toward the floor, and half-crawled out of the room. I took him downstairs. Of course, he was only three-months-old, when he woke up he had to nurse. Then I had to change his diaper. Then my daughter started crying — she had waked up from her nap. Then I had to change her diaper. Then she was hungry. Then I had to change his diaper again. By then he had to nurse again . . . .
>
> At 5:30 when I took them upstairs for their baths, I noticed the glass all over the floor. That was when I remembered what had happened. It was the worst moment of all of it . . . because I couldn't even rely on myself any more. I started crying and I called my mother long-distance. I said, "Mama, it finally got to me, I've finally lost my mind. If your window is shot out and you crawl out of the room with your baby in your arms, you're not supposed to forget about it. It should at least be the main event of the day!"

Ironically, this particular attack ultimately proved to be teenage vandalism, coincidentally following by two days a violent episode in which the woman's ex-husband broke a pane of glass in her door and lay bleeding on her floor until the police arrived. She described an initial unwillingness to call the police again so soon after the previous events, and her conviction at the time that the attacks must be related. The blurring of borders, so frightening at the time, is in fact part of women's experience of motherhood and daily life — of her daily duty to lay aside her own needs for her children's. In many cases, the emotional changes of motherhood may combine with the pressures of violence to push women toward at least temporary compliance with a batterer's demands — while in the long run impelling her toward whatever choice (leaving, staying, seeking family or professional intervention) seems to best protect both herself and her children.

Finally, the sense of physical responsibility to the children — inevitably, economic responsibility — is a major constraint. Women and children suffer severe economic losses upon divorce.[84] Mothers must be very desperate to walk out without knowing how they will all survive. A large number of homeless women and children today have fled violent situations, and women often balance the possible harm to the children through inadequate housing with the harm from maintaining the relationship. Unless the children are threatened directly or indirectly, the woman may well choose for them rather than herself. In a very real way, she is choosing between known and unknown dangers, blurred borders under familiar conditions and those under unfamiliar conditions.

> Our building was very roach-infested. In winter, the children needed

84. Weitzman, *supra* note 82, at x.

real shoes instead of sneakers, and I put together the money to get them good high-tops. My son's shoes had an unusually strong smell of leather. One morning I picked up his shoe and it erupted . . . a volcano of baby roaches, with a few big roaches as well. They loved that shoe. Every night they tried to move in. Powder didn't help. I couldn't afford more shoes.

To me, this is what all of it was like, the marriage and what followed. I just remembered to pick up and hide the baby's shoe every night or . . . remembered to get there first every morning, when he couldn't see me, and shake out the hundreds of nesting roaches. Or, because eventually it happened, I forgot, and heard him scream in terror. And felt terrible because I had failed to protect him from knowing that shoes can explode into insects, that everything can change to nightmare in a second.

Whether the woman is trying to maintain a relationship or trying to leave it, her particular life circumstances will affect the dangers she faces and the choices she makes. Women are entitled, as Christine Littleton says, to "safe connection" — to the measures that protect us in this effort as well as to social recognition of our values and needs.[85] We are also entitled to legal doctrines that respect our circumstances and responsibilities by recognizing that every aspect of our experience of assault and response to it may be shaped by the experience of motherhood, including the times at which we are attacked, the nature of the attacks, the methods by which we cope, and our judgment of whether the pain of relationship outweighs its value.

II. Definitions of Battering and Battered Women

A. *Identification as a "Battered Woman"*

"Battered woman" is not a simple term.[86] It focuses on the woman and defines her through the battering experience. While the term has some value for understanding women and our experience, both of these qualities might also reinforce stereotypical notions of women's experience. This section describes problems women encounter in identifying ourselves as "battered," the ways in which definitions of battered women reflect changing social consciousness, and the way descriptions of battering have moved from a focus on control toward a focus on incidents of violence.

85. *See* Littleton, *supra* note 34, at 49-53. "If battered women seek to maintain connection in the face of enormous danger, perhaps the key to accessing the legal system on their behalf lies in taking seriously *both* the connection they seek *and* the danger they face in that quest." *Id.* at 52. Littleton suggests four basic approaches: changing the batterer, decreasing the costs of rupture to women, increasing the perceived costs of battering, and expanding the options for community. *Id.* at 53-56.

86. *See* Stordeur & Stille, *supra* note 81, at 18-20 (providing brief recent review of many positions on the terminology of "*wife assault, battering, abuse, violence, family violence,* and *domestic violence*" (emphasis in original)).

Women resist applying the term "battered woman" to ourselves. This is often true even when we approach hotlines and shelters,[87] even when we seek temporary restraining orders against our abusers, even when we talk to each other. I believe that we do this *not only* because of the denial discussed above, but because the stereotypical implications of the term fail to correlate with our self-images in ways that reflect *correct* self-assessment on our parts.

It is a deadly combination, this mixture of (negative) denial and (positive) self-respect that makes women reject an image of degradation and incapacitation. As a woman interviewed at a shelter in England said, "It's difficult to accept yourself as a 'battered wife' as the term isn't right. I have had a lot of marital troubles, which have included violence. Despite all my attempts to make the marriage work, I had no choice but to get away."[88] She defines herself as active, working to solve her problems, reaching out for solutions.[89] These actions conflict with her sense of what a "battered wife" is. Yet her story told of frequent beatings and otherwise fit the stereotypical picture of a battering relationship reasonably well.[90] Her self-esteem and insistence on her own competency may have been double-edged: a woman's rejection of the stereotype may slow her perception of her problems or available resources, or postpone her decision to seek help, since she may not turn immediately to agencies targeting "battered women."

Because the term "battered woman" focuses on the woman in a violent relationship rather than the man or the battering process, it creates a tendency to see the woman as the problem. There are other options: at one conference, several women described themselves with the phrase "a woman who used to be married to a battering man."[91] However, many feminists insist on using "battered woman" in preference to terms such as "spouse abuse" which are not gender specific in order to emphasize that women, not men, are almost always the target of intraspousal abuse.[92] The very substantial psychic damage done

87. Conversation with Donna Coker, *supra* note 67 (recounting stories of several clients at a battered woman's program who doubted whether they were "really" battered women).

88. Joy Melville, *Some Violent Families*, *in* VIOLENCE AND THE FAMILY 10 (J.P. Martin ed., 1978).

89. *Id.* at 10-11.

90. This woman had been hit frequently. Her husband did not permit her to leave the house, even to go to social security or the doctor. *Id.* at 11.

91. Conversation with Donna Coker, *supra* note 67.

92. Studies that equated all forms of violence by all actors, whether or not provoked, have generated concern for "battered husbands." This methodology has been extensively criticized. *See* RUSSELL, *supra* note 43, at 102-09. Debate on this point continues. *See generally* 11 RESPONSE TO THE VICTIMIZATION OF WOMEN AND CHILDREN No. 3 (1988); Susan Schechter,

through the experience of violence may be minimized or denied through less woman-focused terminology. Although the term "battered woman" is unfortunate in its potential for stigma, no less specific term can capture this damage; the search for different language may lose a sense of the harm.[93]

B. *Evolution of The Definition of the Problem*

The current debate over terminology reflects differences in the backgrounds and approaches of feminist activists, scholars in sociology and psychology (some feminist, some not), and professionals such as social workers active in the field of domestic violence. Social awareness of violence against women grew out of the activism of the feminist movement of the late 1960s and early 1970s. In *Women and Male Violence,* Susan Schechter traces the evolution of the "women's rights" and "women's liberation" wings of the feminist movement and places the roots of public consciousness of domestic violence in the early women's liberation literature.[94] Other groups were also active in the field. Women from Al-Anon, the organization for families of alcoholics, founded the first shelters for battered women in the 1960s.[95] The first Boston shelter was also a self-help project: two battered women opened their home as a haven and rapidly found support from radical feminists.[96]

Social workers had dealt extensively with battered women since the early days of social service agencies. Over time, historian Linda Gordon has shown, women clients began to create out of their own complaints a right not to be beaten.[97] Until the 1930s, the women were more likely to receive social work assistance for their charges of nonsupport by husbands than for charges of brutality; however, from

---

Building Bridges Between Activists, Professionals, and Researchers, in FEMINIST PERSPECTIVES ON WIFE ABUSE, *supra* note 31, at 299.

93. Conversation with Kim Hanson, *supra* note 66. We need definitions that do not inherently blame women. For the past decade, I have often reluctantly applied the term to myself in order to help break down stereotypes and overcome the strong pressures toward silence. To the extent that I do not "really" feel like a battered woman but like a bit of an imposter, I know this puts me in line with battered women everywhere. For the similar perspective of a woman who chose to use the terms "batterer" and "battered" when she had been violently struck once by her partner, see BELL HOOKS, TALKING BACK: THINKING FEMINIST, THINKING BLACK 88 (1989).

94. SUSAN SCHECHTER, WOMEN AND MALE VIOLENCE 32-33 (1982) (citing the anthology SISTERHOOD IS POWERFUL (Robin Morgan ed., 1970) and the discussion in consciousness-raising groups). Schechter reviews the different ideologies within the women's movement that contributed to the battered women's movement.

95. The Al-Anon women were concerned that women who fled abusive alcoholic husbands were sleeping in cars. *Id.* at 5, 55-57.

96. Schechter, *supra* note 92, at 302.

97. GORDON, *supra* note 44, at 257-61.

the 1930s on, women increasingly insisted on their right to physical integrity.[98] Heavily influenced by Freudian thought, social workers in the 1940s and 1950s were likely to interpret women's complaints as indicating frigidity or a need to undermine their husbands' authority.[99] This victim-blaming mentality contributed to family violence becoming less visible until the new emphasis and political mobilization grew out of the feminist movement of the 1970s.[100]

Recently, several feminists have written about the split between social scientists and feminist activists on domestic violence issues.[101] Some psychological and sociological studies of domestic violence are deeply antiwoman. Most of the early studies focused on the psychopathology of the female victims, not the aggressors;[102] such approaches tended to reinforce batterers' defenses and denial, since the psychiatric problems under consideration appeared outside their control.[103] Although some studies of domestic violence focus on the oppressive societal structures that vest power in men,[104] those written from the family systems perspective most widespread in social work today[105] tend to portray the partners as equally responsible for violence[106] and ask the woman who describes experiencing violent attacks to consider how she provoked them.[107] The gender-neutral approach adopted by many sociologists minimizes the importance of male domination and power. Division between activists and professionals, social scientists and funding sources has also affected how issues were explored and what research was conducted in the field of domestic violence,[108] since

98. *Id.* at 258-59.

99. *Id.* at 282.

100. *Id.* at 22-25.

101. Michele Bograd, *Feminist Perspectives on Wife Abuse: An Introduction, in* FEMINIST PERSPECTIVES ON WIFE ABUSE, *supra* note 31, at 11, 19; Schechter, *supra* note 92, at 299; Kersti Yllo, *Political and Methodological Debates in Wife Abuse Research, in* FEMINIST PERSPECTIVES ON WIFE ABUSE, *supra* note 31; *see also* DOBASH & DOBASH, *supra* note 12, at 193-99; GONDOLF & FISHER, *supra* note 12, at 1-2; Edward W. Gondolf, *The State of the Debate: A Review Essay on Woman Battering,* 11 RESPONSE TO THE VICTIMIZATION OF WOMEN AND CHILDREN No. 3, *supra* note 92, at 3-8; *cf.* Lee Ann Hoff, *Collaborative Feminist Research and the Myth of Objectivity, in* FEMINIST PERSPECTIVES ON WIFE ABUSE, *supra* note 31, at 269.

102. MILDRED D. PAGELOW, WOMAN-BATTERING: VICTIMS AND THEIR EXPERIENCE 20 (1981) (citing several studies).

103. STORDEUR & STILLE, *supra* note 81, at 24-25.

104. *See generally* DOBASH & DOBASH, *supra* note 12 (discussing wife beating that is consistently placed in the context of a critique of both patriarchy and capitalism).

105. Fineman, *supra* note 82, at 744 & n.77.

106. *See generally* Michele Bograd, *Family Systems Approaches to Wife Battering: A Feminist Critique,* 54 AM. J. ORTHOPSYCHIATRY 558-68 (1984) (family systems theories can perpetuate gender bias by blaming the victims of wife abuse).

107. STORDEUR & STILLE, *supra* note 81, at 26; *see also* LEWIS OKUN, WOMAN ABUSE: FACTS REPLACING MYTHS 96-97 (1986) (dicussing Straus' application of systems theory).

108. Feminist activists first raised the issues of wife beating as part of their struggle against

conscious use of feminist methodology in research is rare.[109] Our conceptions of battering reflect this mixed intellectual and political background.

C. *The Attempt To Define the Battered Woman*

The most widely known definitions of battering tend to be incident-focused, looking to the types of assaultive or coercive incidents and the number of times these occurred. This makes it possible to bring a woman and her history into court with objective indicia of her status as a battered woman. However, this type of definition tends to direct attention away from the source of the violence — the struggle for power and control — and has the additional problem of emphasizing the very incidents women tend to minimize and fortifying an image women seek to deny.

Lenore Walker, author of three books and many articles on battered women, is also one of the leading forensic psychologists in the field.[110] By 1986, she had introduced expert testimony on battered woman syndrome in sixty-five cases in which battered women had killed or hurt their abusers.[111] In Walker's first book, her definition of "battered woman" emphasized the batterer's control of the woman: "A battered woman is a woman who is repeatedly subjected to any forceful physical or psychological behavior by a man in order to coerce her to do something he wants her to do without any concern for her rights."[112] However, the very next sentence moves from a focus on control to the issue of repetition of violence and whether the woman has remained in the relationship:

> Battered women include wives or women in any form of intimate

---

the oppression of women; professionals, researchers, and funding sources then recast and transformed the way these issues were seen and developed, casting shelter residents and program participants as "clients" rather than inclusively defining them as experiencing an extreme form of oppression faced by all women. Schechter, *supra* note 92, at 302. Schechter believes the differences between activists and professionals are growing more complicated as "more professionally trained women join the movement at the same time that more battered women try to assume power within it." *Id.* at 309.

109. For a general discussion, see descriptions of applied feminist methodology in Hoff, *supra* note 101, at 270-77 (describing process of developing questions and focus for research through helping and working with the women she would study until they trusted and spoke with her, before developing her questions, thus overcoming severe mistrust of academics and professionals among shelter staff and residents).

110. *See, e.g.*, LENORE WALKER, *supra* note 40; LENORE E. WALKER, THE BATTERED WOMAN SYNDROME (1984) [hereinafter WALKER, SYNDROME]; WALKER, *supra* note 11. Walker's description of a three-stage cycle of battering and application of the psychosocial theory of learned helplessness to battered women had great influence on the field of domestic violence and proved especially significant in law.

111. Walker, *supra* note 10, at 224.

112. LENORE WALKER, *supra* note 40, at xv.

> relationships with men. Furthermore, in order to be classified as a battered woman, the couple must go through the battering cycle at least twice. Any woman may find herself in an abusive relationship with a man once. *If it occurs a second time, and she remains in the situation, she is defined as a battered woman.*[113]

By 1984, in her second book, Walker had elaborated her description of battered women and developed another definition, now also cited by courts. This definition was not related to control but defined by incidents of violence: "A *battered woman* is a woman . . . who is or has been in an intimate relationship with a man who repeatedly subjects or subjected her to forceful physical and/or psychological abuse. . . . 'Repeatedly' means more than one assault [at least two 'acute battering incidents']."[114] Physical abuse is "any form of a coercive physical act, with or without resultant injury."[115]

Walker articulated her first, more control-focused definition of battered women based on an interest in women's lives growing out of her feminist consciousness.[116] However, the elaboration of "battered woman's syndrome" led away from an emphasis on power and toward a focus on incidents and behavior. Even Walker's first study showed some ambivalence about the implications of recognizing the issue of control. Walker found that as her women clients in psychotherapy became more assertive, they encountered more physical and psychological abuse.[117]

> My first fear was that critics of the women's movement might be right. Perhaps violence erupted because women began to make their own decisions to control their lives. Feminism was indeed having a profound impact on the family by changing power relationships. Would strong, assertive women be able to live in harmony and equality with those men whom they loved? Fortunately, a further investigation proved these fears to be groundless; in those relationships where battering was occurring, coercion between the partners had existed from the beginning of the relationship.[118]

Walker flinched from the prospect that changes in power in relationships may generate violence or that men would resist changes in women's empowerment. This distinction between existent "coercion"

---

113. *Id.*

114. WALKER, SYNDROME, *supra* note 110, at 203.

115. *Id.* at 202. Psychological abuse consists of eight elements, including periods of contrite, loving behavior that keep alive hope that the abuse will stop. *Id.*

116. See her account of the commencement of her work in LENORE WALKER, *supra* note 40, at xi-xiii. Walker has also done extensive work to further feminist goals in psychotherapy through the Feminist Therapy Institute, of which she was a co-founder and the first chairperson. Conversation with Jeanne Adleman, Chair, Feminist Therapy Institute, 1988-1990 (1988).

117. LENORE WALKER, *supra* note 40, at xi.

118. *Id.* at xi-xii.

and "strong, assertive women" is somewhat stereotyping and fails to account for the existence of battered feminists.[119] I believe that this psychological approach — not unique to Walker — also reflects white middle-class norms about the family: women are either strong and assertive *or* coerced. Some of us may be both — a lot may depend on the level and type of coercion involved. Especially, women who are not white or middle class may not fit these generalizations;[120] they may have less difficulty reconciling the simultaneous experience of strength and oppression.[121]

However, Walker's definition is useful when women's experience must be described to a court. First, the definition is incident-focused: incidents can be asserted and often proven as objective support for the woman's perceptions and feelings. Second, the "repeatedly" requirement is a sorting mechanism that allows the judge or jury to consider the woman before them without accepting that any woman who has been struck even one time — a figure that may be familiar from their own relationships in ways they still deny — is susceptible to the development of battered woman syndrome.[122]

The various attempts by feminist scholars to define battering show some tension between breadth — reaching to include the many ways women are harmed — and precision in describing particular experience, which generally leads toward focus on incidents. Mary Ann Douglas gives a broad definition:

> A battered woman is any woman who has been the victim of physical, sexual, and/or psychological abuse by her partner. . . . Physical abuse is assault that ranges from hitting or slapping at one end of the continuum to homicide at the other [citing Pagelow]. Physical abuse may or may not be accompanied by physical injury and/or by the victims' attempts

119. Feminists and nontraditional women are also battered, and one author states it is questionable whether feminists have even a diminished tendency to be battered. OKUN, *supra* note 107, at 86.

120. *See* Angela Harris, *Race and Essentialism in Feminist Legal Theory,* 42 STAN. L. REV. 581, 612-13 (1990) ("Feminist theory at present, especially feminist legal theory, tends to focus on women as passive victims. . . . At the individual level, black women have had to learn to construct themselves in a society that denied them full selves.").

121. *See* Schneider, *supra* note 10, at 216 n.146 (discussing the possibility that white women and their perspective have formed the basis for much of the literature on battering). I believe these descriptions poorly capture the discrepancy between how women appear to others and how they appear to themselves. In Walker's later study, *The Battered Woman Syndrome,* she found higher levels of self-esteem than she had in her previous study. WALKER, SYNDROME, *supra* note 110, at 80-82, 114.

122. For further discussion of battered woman syndrome, see *infra* text accompanying notes 148-89. The "repeatedly" requirement also raises the issue of inquiry into the woman's "failure" to leave that expert testimony is designed to address; there may be less expectation that a woman would leave a marriage over only one incident of violence, which then in hindsight becomes *the first* such incident.

to defend themselves.[123]

Douglas' definition has the advantage of being broad and inclusive, and explicitly rejecting any requirement that the woman have suffered physical injury. However, people may see one incident of violence as insufficient to distinguish "battering" from any ordinary relationship.[124] Also, women do not always recognize being physically restrained from moving as a form of physical abuse when it is not mentioned specifically, and therefore this definition lacks some of the inclusiveness of Walker's "any physically coercive act."

Angela Browne's definition of battered women is *more* specific in its attention to incidents of assault:

> "[B]attered women" are those who have been struck repeatedly, often experiencing several different kinds of physically violent actions in one incident, and usually, by the time they are identified, having experienced a series of such incidents, each consisting of a cluster of violent acts.[125]

If closely examined, Browne's definition reveals some of the other problems. It plays into women's denial by its specificity and its focus on "striking." Women who have been threatened with deadly weapons may fail to recognize their experience in this definition if they were not physically injured, as may women who have experienced other types of assault such as sexual abuse.

Mildred Pagelow defines battered women without requiring striking in a way that allows her to reconsider the question of repetition of violence:

> *[B]attered women* refers to adult women who were intentionally physically abused in ways that caused pain or injury, or who were forced into involuntary action or restrained by force from voluntary action by adult men with whom they have or had established relationships, usually involving sexual intimacy, whether or not within a legally married state.[126]

Pagelow separates battering into "primary battering" (the first attack)

---

123. Mary Ann Douglas, *The Battered Woman Syndrome, in* DOMESTIC VIOLENCE ON TRIAL, *supra* note 58, at 39.

124. *See supra* text accompanying note 113 (Lenore Walker stating: "Any woman may find herself in an abusive relationship with a man once.").

125. BROWNE, *supra* note 3, at 13. Since Browne's material was gathered in the Walker study, *id.* at ix, 196 nn.1-2, the works had identical underlying criteria despite the difference in language of their definitions. The emphasis on physical striking and patterns of repetition in Browne's definition is similar to that offered by Deschner: "a series of physically injurious attacks on an intimate or family member that form part of a repeated, habitual pattern." JEANNE P. DESCHNER, THE HITTING HABIT: ANGER CONTROL FOR BATTERING COUPLES 2 (1984), *quoted in* STORDEUR & STILLE, *supra* note 81, at 19. Obviously Deschner goes further than Browne in requiring physical injury.

126. PAGELOW, *supra* note 102, at 33. This definition may screen out women who have experienced such attacks as the pointing of a loaded gun or a knife held against the skin; some women who spoke with me identified such experiences as "emotional" rather than physical abuse. Diana Russell mentions a similar phenomenon in which many women fail to recognize marital rape as rape. RUSSELL, *supra* note 43, at 63.

and "secondary battering" (everything that follows).[127] She views the *woman's* "acceptance" of the primary battering incident as the key to whether secondary battering will develop, because the woman's reaction to the first episode may in some way provide incentives for the man to continue, and thus move the relationship toward secondary battering.[128] In this view, women reinforce battering through compliance with batterers' demands, giving them "feelings of increased control and power."[129] While this description identifies power and control as issues, it obscures them again by indirectly holding the woman responsible for the batterer's continued control efforts;[130] it remains incident-focused with the second incident decisive for categorization.

Most of these definitions are essentially incident-focused, not control-focused. Falling into this conceptualization in describing their experiences, some women describe clear cut control struggles as separate from "battering":

> The way it came out for me was not a battered woman's thing. I wanted to go out with my girlfriends, and that triggered possessive jealousy . . . . He wouldn't let me go do the things I wanted to do, therefore the marriage wouldn't work. The problem didn't start with his beating me up. After I made my stand on that ground, then the violence started. That led to a lot of self-blame — if only I had been a better wife, this wouldn't have happened.

This woman has completed therapy, participated in a battered woman's group, obtained a bachelor's degree in sociology and a law degree. She is doing pro bono work with battered women. I would argue that the information she has been given, and her interpretation of it above, show a functional definition of battering as based on male violence that is *not* about control, and a "battered woman's thing" that is about the *woman's* "thing," rather than the batterer's pursuit of power.

Lesbian battering, in contrast, considers the victim of domestic vi-

---

127. PAGELOW, *supra* note 102, at 42-51.

128. "The responsibility for taking decisive action at the first occurrence of battering appears to fall almost entirely on the woman. If . . . this behavior appears to be accepted by his spouse because of lack of negative feedback, he is most likely to continue it." *Id.* at 44.

129. *Id.* at 45. Pagelow does not explain what actions by women *other than* leaving at the first incident would be sufficient to avoid secondary battering, although she recognizes that in some relationships violence occurs only once.

130. Similarly, Pagelow says she rejects a focus on what "types" of women are battered as opposed to another type who are not. *Id.* at 223. Yet she formulates the "most important question" as "what are the characteristics (social and personal) that distinguish among women who are never battered, never battered a second time, or battered repeatedly?" *Id.* at 42. This is merely another formulation of essentially the same focus.

olence within the framework of continued attempts by the batterer to achieve and maintain dominance and control in the relationship:

> Lesbian battering is that pattern of violent and coercive behaviors whereby a lesbian seeks to control the thoughts, beliefs or conduct of her intimate partner or to punish the intimate for resisting the perpetrator's control over her.
>
> Individual acts of violence, by this definition, do not constitute lesbian battering. Physical violence is not battering unless it results in the enhanced control of the batterer over the recipient. If the assaulted partner becomes fearful of the violator, if she modifies her behavior in response to the assault or to avoid future abuse, or if the victim intentionally maintains a particular consciousness or behavioral repertoire to avoid violence, despite her preference not to do so, she is battered.[131]

Several elements of this definition merit discussion. Battering is a "pattern of violent and coercive behaviors" defined by the batterer's purpose. The state of being battered is defined by the woman's response. This would seem to exclude situations in which someone struck out in anger but did not hit hard, or in which they hit again but there was no effective intimidation; it would seem to include the times the furniture was smashed up and threats uttered, and the nonviolent partner was afraid to move or respond.

At first, the emphasis on the battered woman's response seems superficially similar to Pagelow's definitions of primary and secondary battering. However, the difference is crucial: the lesbian battering definition emphasizes a woman's *experience* of the violence, which may include either her feelings or her behavior; Pagelow targets her *responsive behavior* to emphasize her success or failure at nonrewarding the batterer.[132] In essence, this defines the woman by her success at controlling the partner who is attempting to control her. This focus on the woman's experience does not automatically resolve problems of denial: women may not recognize how much our thoughts, feelings or actions are determined by the violence until a period of time has passed, or until the relationship is over. However, this approach does help the battered woman overcome denial: she need only recognize that she has modified her behavior or "intentionally maintain[ed] a particular consciousness or behavioral repertoire to avoid violence." These elements imply little stigma and help reveal the context of power and control within which the violence took place.

---

131. Barbara Hart, *Lesbian Battering: An Examination, in* NAMING THE VIOLENCE, *supra* note 33, at 173.

132. I believe that this definition is useful and possible in part because lesbian battering is so seldom litigated. As a result, few if any of the power and control moves between lesbians wind up in the courtroom.

Feminist activists writing about heterosexual battering have also defined power and control, rather than incidents of violence, as the heart of the question. Ellen Pence and Michael Paymar's training manual, which grew out of a treatment program for batterers in Minnesota developed by activists, is entitled *Power and Control: Tactics of Men Who Batter.*[133] Pence and Paymar treat violence as *a form of control*[134] and explicitly reject theories that focus on "some flaw in the abuser, the victim, the relationship, or all three of these."[135]

Incident-focused definitions have advantages in court which they lack if we look to them as a way to explain women's experience to ourselves and each other, support women, and fight oppression. For example, Pagelow's emphasis on traditional ideology in women may be very appealing to traditionalism in some jurors or in judges, who are mostly male: this woman was hurt and became so desperate *because* she was so determined to be a good wife and mother. Control-based definitions may be more comprehensible to many women in regard to our own lives. However, women who resist types of control that have general societal acceptance (for example, women who resist traditional roles in their lives) may evoke less sympathy in judges or jurors who hold traditional values. If women are hurt for resisting domination, it may also be more difficult to explain the nature of the struggle in court simply because so many aspects of domination may appear normal and are subsumed under the label "traditionalism."[136] In order to resolve the tensions inherent in the effort to define battering and battered women, we need to understand the pressures of the legal system and create solutions that change cultural consciousness as well as law.

III. Pressures of the Legal System

A. *Self-Defense, the Battered Woman Syndrome, and Learned Helplessness*

On the Defensive

Four a.m.
Watching his headlights
pan across the walls.
Listening to the familiar
engine's drone.

---

133. Ellen Pence & Michael Paymar, Power and Control: Tactics of Men Who Batter (1986).

134. *See, e.g., id.* at 64-83.

135. *Id.* at 64.

136. *See infra* text accompanying notes 250-57.

The car door slam.
His keys.

His footfall on the stair.

I have this baby bottle.
Loaded, cocked, aimed and ready
to dash his skull to bits.[137]

Ironically, the most complete description of women's suffering from domestic violence has entered our case law and legal literature at the point where violence against women finally harms men — when battered women kill in self-defense.[138] These are also the cases that have had the greatest impact on public consciousness of battered women. Francine Hughes, whose story became the book and movie *The Burning Bed,* killed her sleeping husband after years of extremely violent abuse. Although Hughes was acquitted on grounds of temporary insanity rather than on grounds of self-defense, her story became the paradigm for the image of battered women who kill their abusers.[139]

Although only a fraction of battered women kill their abusers,[140] feminists and legal scholars put a great deal of energy into the self-defense cases, which comprise a large portion of the legal literature on battering.[141] Of course, the stakes are terribly high for the women involved in these cases: many women who are jailed for the murders of their abusers have been brutally and repeatedly abused.[142]

137. Linda Bart, *On the Defensive, in* FAMILY VIOLENCE: POEMS ON THE PATHOLOGY, *supra* note 1, at 15.

138. *See* Cynthia L. Coffee, Note, *A Trend Emerges: A State Survey on the Admissibility of Expert Testimony Concerning the Battered Woman Syndrome,* 25 J. FAM. L. 373 (1986-1987).

139. *See, e.g.,* Thyfault et al., *supra* note 58, at 68 (suggesting that attitudes of potential jurors toward battered woman syndrome may be elicited by asking whether they saw *The Burning Bed*).

140. An estimated 1.5 to 4 million women are battered in the United States each year. *See supra* note 42. In 1984, approximately 477 husbands or boyfriends were killed by women. Laurie J. Taylor, Comment, *Provoked Reason in Men and Women: Heat-of-Passion Manslaughter and Imperfect Self-Defense,* 33 UCLA L. REV. 1679, 1680-81 & n.10 (1986).

141. *See* Schneider, *supra* note 10, at 196 n.5 (citing 38 articles and Notes in law reviews and legal journals). Five more articles on the subject appeared in the issue of the *Women's Rights Law Reporter.* A review of the categories covering battered women and self-defense in "Infotrac" reveals that in the ensuing three years, at least a dozen additional pieces appeared, totaling at least 50 to 60 published pieces on the subject. In 1987, two more books on the subject were published: BROWNE, *supra* note 3, and CHARLES P. EWING, BATTERED WOMEN WHO KILL (1987). In 1989, three more new books appeared. *See* BLACKMAN, *supra* note 11; GILLESPIE, *supra* note 11; WALKER, *supra* note 11.

142. Angela Browne's study brought together statistical findings based on a large sample of women and explored in depth the stories of eleven couples. The women in these couples had been severely, even grotesquely, abused over a period of years. Seven of them served sentences from one year to life in prison. Two received suspended sentences or probation. In one case, the district attorney's office finally agreed that the slaying was justifiable and dropped charges. One woman was tried for first-degree murder, pled self-defense, and was acquitted. BROWNE, *supra* note 3, at 187-90.

Last year, the governor of Ohio released 25 women who had been serving prison terms after

When a woman is tried for killing her abuser, she encounters not only the problem of the jury's ability to understand her experience,[143] but the problem of articulating her experience in court in the first place. Lenore Walker argues that the rules of evidence prevent the explanation of women's experience:

> There is a fundamental difference between the way women tell of their battering experiences and what is permitted under the male-identified rules of evidence. Women tend to tell of the events in question rooted in their context, by weaving a tale of patterns of events and feelings in the context of how they happened. Rules of evidence call for the recitation of discrete events separated from feelings or opinions. Facts out of context may be acceptable, but they do not convey the battered woman's experience. Expert witnesses can tie together what the current evidentiary rules do not allow the defendant to say. Until feminist legal scholars argue for and attain reform in the rules of evidence, a battered woman will be constrained from putting her case in front of the trier of fact.[144]

The conditions of women's lives — the children needing sweaters or needing noses wiped,[145] or the constant demands of breastfeeding or diapers[146] — may not be seen as relevant to the explanation of the violent marriage or even to the question of why women "stayed." Similarly, a statement that a husband's drinking problem developed after many happy years is not adequate to capture the keen, passionate consciousness of love and responsibility for *both* husband and children articulated by the woman who was in my support group.[147] Finally, a woman's perception of danger and her decisions to act are dependent on the context of that particular relationship. Therefore, these "male-identified" rules constrain the categories within which the legal image of battered women has evolved.

Expert testimony on battered woman syndrome was developed by feminist litigators and psychologists to explain the experiences of abused women and the way women were affected by abuse.[148] Battered woman syndrome is "a collection of specific characteristics and

---

reviewing their records carefully. The women presented evidence of abuse. More than one hundred women's records were reviewed. Isabel Wilkerson, *Clemency Granted to 25 Women Convicted for Assault or Murder,* N.Y. TIMES, Dec. 22, 1990, at 1, col. 1.

143. *See supra* text accompanying notes 58-60; *see also* Littleton, *supra* note 34, at 35 ("Not only battered women but all women" are alien from a male perspective, and therefore beyond the ken of laymen.).

144. Walker, *supra* note 10, at 223-24.

145. *See supra* discussion of children's needs in poem in text accompanying note 83.

146. *See supra* narrative in text following note 83.

147. *See supra* narrative in text following note 82.

148. Schneider, *supra* note 10, at 198.

effects of abuse on the battered woman."[149] While it does not affect all battered women, it makes women who do suffer from the syndrome unable to respond effectively to violence and therefore entrapped in the violent relationship.[150] Testimony on battered woman syndrome includes a description of Walker's three-stage battering cycle,[151] the concept of "learned helplessness," and may also include descriptions of the objective economic and social difficulties women face in leaving their relationships.[152]

In most states,[153] testimony on battered woman syndrome is admitted under the rule of evidence that allows expert testimony when the jurors could not understand the issue without it.[154] "[A] battering relationship is a subject beyond the understanding of an average juror."[155] Jurors are particularly unable to grasp for themselves why the woman failed to leave the relationship.[156] Judges may have grasped the need for expert testimony through motives of justice, empathy, recognition of the need to cope with prejudices and stereotypes held by jurors, or similar reasons. Yet judges and jurors will inevitably hear this testimony filtered through cultural stereotypes which are *of necessity enforced* by the claim of exceptionality, of incomprehensibility, required by the requirement that the issue be "beyond the layman's ken." The result may often tend to perpetuate stereotypes:

> [T]he expert testified that those who suffer from the battered woman syndrome, *because of certain characteristics in their personalities,* do not leave their husbands, even after numerous beatings, do not inform police or friends of their husbands' violence, and, under certain circumstances, believe that they are in present danger that their husbands will kill them, although some time has elapsed since the husband's last assault against them.[157]

---

149. Douglas, *supra* note 123, at 40.

150. *Id.*

151. Walker divides battery into three stages: the tension building phase, the explosion or acute battering incident, and the calm, loving respite. LENORE WALKER, *supra* note 40, at 55. The periods of loving remorse are essential in cementing bonding between the couple and renewing hope for change.

152. Schneider, *supra* note 10, at 202-03.

153. For a discussion of state and federal rules, see *id.*

154. *See, e.g.,* Smith v. State, 277 S.E.2d 678, 683 (Ga. 1981) ("Expert . . . testimony . . . is admissible where the conclusion of the expert is one which jurors would not ordinarily be able to draw for themselves; i.e., the conclusion is beyond the ken of the average layman").

155. *See, e.g.,* Kansas v. Hodges, 716 P.2d 563, 567 (Kan. 1986).

156. *See, e.g.,* People v. Torres, 488 N.Y.S.2d 358, 362 (Sup. Ct. 1985) ("[T]he proffered expert [testimony] would . . . serve to dispel the ordinary lay perception that [the] woman who remains in a battering relationship is free to leave her abuser at any time . . . . [T]he jury's 'commonsense' conclusions [would be] that the beatings and threats . . . could not have been at all that bad or else she would have left long before.").

157. Chapman v. State, 367 S.E.2d 541, 543 (Ga. 1988) (emphasis added) (reversing for ex-

Feminist litigators grapple with the difficulties presented by portraying women in a complex life situation, both acting and being acted upon — what Elizabeth Schneider has called a contrast between agency (the woman as actor and agent in her own life) and victimization (the woman as acted upon by her batterer).[158] As Schneider points out, however, even if litigators tell a more complex story, the legal and cultural pressures at work in this area contribute to the judges hearing and retelling a story of dysfunctionality.[159] Courts describe a battered woman who is "financially dependent on the batterer," which may cause her to "feel partly responsible for the batterer's violence, [also,] she may believe that her children need a father, or fear reprisal if she leaves."[160] She is powerless, lacks self-esteem, and has few close friends.[161] Her "self-respect is very low and she believes she is a worthless person."[162] Her primary emotion is fear.[163] She undergoes a personality change and is "unable to project her thinking into the future. She lives her life from one beating to the next and her thoughts relate solely to her efforts to avoid the next beating."[164]

Significantly, this description explains her continued presence in the relationship, her failure to separate: her emotional paralysis and inability to think clearly are the reasons she cannot think clearly about escape.[165] She has "traditional beliefs about the sanctity of home and family and . . . false hopes that things will improve."[166] Among the most important aspects of her problem is the condition of "learned helplessness," described with varying degrees of sophistication as a de-

---

clusion of testimony regarding victim's reputation for violence). In another Georgia case the discussion of *Smith* also reinforced this perception of battered women:

> We reasoned that a jury could not ordinarily draw certain conclusions for themselves, such as; "why a person suffering from battered woman's syndrome would not leave her mate, would not inform police or friends, and would fear increased aggression against herself. . . ." [citing Smith v. State, 277 S.E.2d 678, 683 (Ga. 1981)] Testimony regarding the battered woman syndrome assists the jury in understanding the defendant's unusual *behavior and conduct*, which are vital issues in the battered woman's defense. . . . [which is] beyond the ken of the jury . . . .

State v. Butler, 349 S.E.2d 684, 687-88 (Ga. 1986).

158. Schneider, *supra* note 10, at 220-22. Victimization can also include trying to describe the woman's life in the context of a male-dominated system.

159. *Id.* at 198-99.

160. Fennell v. Goolsby, 630 F. Supp. 451, 456 (E.D. Pa. 1985).

161. Ibn-Tamas v. United States, 407 A.2d 626, 634 (D.C. 1983).

162. Smith v. State, 277 S.E.2d 678, 680 (Ga. 1981).

163. *Smith*, 277 S.E.2d at 680.

164. People v. Emick, 103 A.D.2d 643, 654 (N.Y. App. Div. 1984).

165. People v. Torres, 488 N.Y.S.2d 358, 361 (Sup. Ct. 1985) ("Numbed by a dread of imminent aggression, these women are unable to think clearly about the means of escape from this abusive family existence.").

166. *Torres*, 488 N.Y.S.2d at 361.

ficiency in perceiving escape possibilities[167] or a psychological adjustment to economic dependence, love, and the failure of the legal system to respond adequately to the problem.[168]

These opinions present an image of utterly dysfunctional women. "Such testimony generally explains the 'phenomenon' as one in which a regular pattern of spouse abuse creates in the battered spouse low self-esteem and a 'learned helplessness,' *i.e.*, a sense that she cannot escape from the abusive relationship she has become a part of."[169]

> A conversation between two friends who had violent marriages:
> R: They say we have this thing called "learned helplessness" . . . .
> Y: Really? I always thought it was when I was getting too *much* power.

Martin Seligman developed the psychological theory of "learned helplessness" based on laboratory experiments conducted on animals.[170] Caged dogs subjected to repeated random electrical shocks that they could not control eventually "ceased any further voluntary activity and became compliant, passive and submissive."[171] Even when it was possible for dogs to leave the cages, they "remained passive, refused to leave, and did not avoid the shock."[172] In 1979, Lenore Walker applied the theory of learned helplessness to the battered women she studied:

> Once the women are operating from a belief of helplessness, the perception becomes reality and they become passive, submissive, "helpless." They allow things that appear to them to be out of their control actually to get out of their control. When one listens to descriptions of battering incidents from battered women, it often seems as if these women were not actually as helpless as they perceived themselves to be. However, their behavior was determined by their negative cognitive set, or their perceptions of what they could or could not do, not by what actually existed. The battered women's behavior appears similar to that of Selig-

167. "[A] feeling of surrender and a failure to realize or know options available to escape the relationship." State v. Kelly, 685 P.2d 564, 567 (Wash. 1984).

168. "[A] condition in which the woman is psychologically locked into her situation due to economic dependence on the man, an abiding attachment to him, and the failure of the legal system to adequately respond to the problem." State v. Allery, 682 P.2d 312, 315 (Wash. 1984).

169. State v. Leidholm, 334 N.W.2d 811, 819 (N.D. 1983) (footnote omitted).

170. *See, e.g.*, discussion in GONDOLF & FISHER, *supra* note 12, at 13 ("The prevailing notion of learned helplessness is drawn from the extensive laboratory research of Martin Seligman of the University of Pennsylvania . . . . During the late sixties, Dr. Seligman led a team of researchers experimenting with dogs in studies that would raise the ire of today's animal rights activists.") (citation omitted).

171. Walker describes Seligman's experiments in LENORE WALKER, *supra* note 40, at 45-47. The hidden question of captivity in Seligman's experiments and Walker's interpretation is discussed further, *infra* notes 364-66 and accompanying text.

172. LENORE WALKER, *supra* note 40, at 46.

man's dogs, rats, and people.[173]

Although Walker later cautioned against overgeneralizing about women's responses to violence, learned helplessness and its attendant images of submissiveness and passivity underlie much of the expertise on battered woman syndrome and much of the legal literature.[174] Even in Walker's 1984 study, which in some ways revealed a more complex portrait of battered women,[175]the discussion of battered women's "coping skills" revealed the ongoing importance of the concept of learned helplessness:

> [B]attered women develop survival or coping skills that keep them alive with minimal injuries. There is also some evidence that such skills are developed at the expense of escape skills. [It is] consistent with [learned helplessness] theory to narrow one's perceptions and focus only on survival, causing misperception of other important information. . . . I interpret their behavior as a basic coping mechanism, much like Seligman's dogs, who used passivity as their way to stay alive. The analogy is in the failure for both the dogs and the battered woman to develop adequate escape skills.[176]

Feminists have cautiously criticized the way learned helplessness emerges in court both for failing to fully explain the many aspects of battered women's behavior[177] and for creating a double bind in which women must prove helplessness in court after they have killed an abusive partner and therefore do not appear helpless as the term is ordinarily understood:[178] "[A] defendant may be considered a battered woman only if she never left her husband, never sought assistance, and

---

173. *Id.* at 48.

174. For example, the following passage from the *Journal of Family Law* makes passivity and submissiveness an integral part of the syndrome:

> The battered woman syndrome is a term used to describe the stages of a physically and psychologically abusive relationship with a mate and the effects of each stage of the relationship on the battered woman. Three stages of a battering relationship have been identified by Dr. Lenore E. Walker in her book entitled *The Battered Woman.* . . . Due to the repetition of this pattern, the woman develops certain learned responses. The batterer's false promises of reform in the third stage result in repeated disappointments and cause the woman to develop *a learned helplessness evidenced by extreme passivity and submissiveness.*

Coffee, *supra* note 138, at 373 n.1 (emphasis added).

175. In her later work, Walker found battered women often held liberal rather than traditional attitudes and had higher self-esteem than she expected to find. WALKER, SYNDROME, *supra* note 110, at 143.

176. *Id.* at 33.

177. *See generally* Littleton, *supra* note 34; Schneider, *supra* note 10.

178. For example, in Mullis v. State, 282 S.E.2d 334 (Ga. 1981), testimony on battered women was excluded. Although the court offered no specific grounds for excluding the testimony on battered women, the evidence had clearly demonstrated the defendant's ability to fight back and may have made her seem less "helpless." *Mullis,* 282 S.E.2d at 336-37. Georgia courts had earlier accepted testimony on the battered woman's syndrome in a case where the defendant had never resisted. *See* Crocker, *supra* note 18, at 146 (interpreting *Mullis* as showing an implicit requirement that the woman never fight back).

never fought back."[179] To the extent the theory of learned helplessness is based on repeated violence, women may have trouble establishing the appropriateness of expert testimony if they strike back after experiencing one severe prior incident of abuse.[180]

It is difficult to communicate the cumulative effect of a violent marriage. A great deal of the literature on battering develops themes and conclusions through presentation of women's stories. While in part this reflects a feminist methodology of working from women's experience,[181] it also may be the only way to describe a complex reality for which we have few names.[182]

If the woman does need expert testimony, how can her reality be described? Elizabeth Schneider has expressed concern over the tendency of testimony on learned helplessness to promote stereotypes of women and undermine examination of the woman's particular circumstances,[183] as well as the way carefully framed feminist testimony on learned helplessness may be distorted in the courtroom.[184] Some authors find the term "learned helplessness" misleading because "helplessness" is only one coping tactic among many that change over time.[185] Most important, women's stories as well as much social science literature indicate that many battered women seek energetically to protect themselves and their families. In this vein, the most socially situated description of learned helplessness describes it as a product of the interaction of frustrations women meet as they energetically pursue safety.[186]

---

179. Crocker, *supra* note 18, at 144. Crocker points to a conflict with the "reasonable man" standard in self-defense cases: "If the defendant has tried to resist in the past, the court accepts this as evidence that rebuts her status as a battered woman. On the other hand, if the defendant has never attempted to fight back, the prosecution argues that the defendant did not act as a 'reasonable man.' " *Id.* at 145; *see also id.* at 152-53 (discussing the tensions between sex-neutral standards, male definitions of "objectivity," and individualization theories).

180. *See id.* at 147 (discussing State v. Griffiths, 610 P.2d 522 (Idaho 1980)). "[T]he defendant shot her husband after seeing a look in his eyes which she had seen only once before when he choked her to near insensibility." *Id.*

181. *See generally* Littleton, *supra* note 27 (discussing feminist methodology of working from women's experience); *see also* West, *supra* note 63 (discussing need for phenomenological critique based on women's stories of their own experiences, and employing this method).

182. *See generally* Kelly, *supra* note 31, at 114-17 (on importance of naming women's experience).

183. Elizabeth M. Schneider, *Equal Rights to Trial for Women: Sex Bias in the Law of Self-Defense,* 15 HARV. C.R.-C.L. L. REV. 623, 646 (1980).

184. Schneider, *supra* note 10, at 198 ("Even if lawyers are not emphasizing [the woman's learned helplessness rather than the circumstances,] judges are hearing it this way.").

185. *See* Kelly, *supra* note 31, at 114; *see generally* GONDOLF & FISHER, *supra* note 12, at 27-39 (describing many types of helpseeking behavior by battered women).

186.The battered woman who meets with failure in [all her] tactics to create her own safety experiences a series of lessons in the reality that neither her behavior, nor that of any other woman[ ], is able to stop the violence against her . . . she cannot control the actions of her

I do not mean to criticize here the psychological theory underlying battered woman syndrome, or even the particular theory of learned helplessness. First, the collection of experience and perception summed up in battered woman syndrome are descriptively true of many women.[187] Lenore Walker's defense of expert testimony is also correct: it helps women's stories be brought into court by bringing together fragments that women experience as part of a whole relationship.[188] Finally, I would not choose to discard such a major tool in the effort to explain women's experience in court, just because it has proved vulnerable to distortion in culture and law — we need more, not less, explanation. However, as long as explanation emphasizes "helplessness" in the psychology of individual women, it runs into the danger of contributing to stereotyping.

Therefore, a profound irony marks this expert testimony: Domestic violence is beyond the layman's ken (even though we know it is fairly common) because some jurors will interpret their *own* experience through cultural perceptions that distort understanding and make it difficult for all of us to talk about the subject, and because cultural stereotypes will shape the vision of battered women held by jurors who have *no* personal experience of such violence as well. Expert testimony, designed to overcome these stereotypes and help show the context for the woman's actions, has through the pressures of the legal system contributed to a focus on victimization that is understood as passivity or even pathology on the part of the woman.[189] This image further promotes many cultural stereotypes, and may contribute to further stigmatizing of battered women and further denial by women of the dangers they face through domestic violence. In a particular legal action, an individual battered woman's experience is at least partly explained, but the cultural perceptions that limit broader social understanding may remain untouched, and go on to shape legal action again.

> partner. Learned helplessness in battered women refers to the low rate of behaviors that could potentially increase safety, based on her decreased ability or on her judgment that these behaviors are also unsafe. [Since her judgment of the dangers of helpseeking may be realistic,] the presence of certain behaviors associated with learned helplessness is not necessarily irrational or unreasonable. . . . They may be what kept her alive.

Douglas, *supra* note 123, at 42-43.

187. See also the support for battered woman syndrome theory discussed in the amicus briefs of the American Psychological Association and American Civil Liberties Union in *State v. Kelly, reprinted in* 9 WOMEN'S RTS. L. RPTR. 245 (1986).

188. *See supra* notes 143-47 and accompanying text.

189. Schneider, *supra* note 10, at 207 ("[T]he term 'battered woman syndrome' has been heard to communicate an implicit but powerful view that battered women are all the same, that they are suffering from a psychological disability and that this disability prevents them from acting 'normally.' ").

Therefore, one result of the highly publicized legal focus on battered woman syndrome and learned helplessness has been to inappropriately increase cultural attention to the battered woman's psychological makeup. Evidence suggests that the batterer's behavior, rather than the battered woman's characteristics, determines her response and predicts whether she will kill in self-defense.[190] Yet placing courtroom emphasis on the *batterer's conduct* has its own pitfalls: for example, cases in which violence took nonstandard forms may prove confusing, and much domestic violence might not be comprehensible to the jury without a simultaneous exposition of the context and history of the relationship.[191] Also, the explanation of the woman's experience and interpretation of violence may again be lost by too much focus on the batterer.

In the past, we have lacked explanatory language and litigative strategies for exposing the batterer's quest for power and control — the link between the conduct of the batterer and the experience of the woman. Evidentiary rules and courtroom bias therefore continue to skew the image of women in the self-defense cases, and these cases continue to contribute to cultural images that in turn shape law. Below, I propose a collateral attack on this problem. By identifying those violent power and control moves that target the woman's separation, we can begin to bridge the gap between self-defense and other battering cases. Because of the interrelatedness of the legal rules and cultural attitudes in this area, we need law reform that illuminates the nature of power and control in all areas of battering.

B. *Custody and the Professional Evaluation of Women*

> A custody battle is *the* quintessential power struggle between men and women. It's about who controls a woman's mind and body. It's also about who gets to control the future. Children are the future. Men think of children as the necessary chains to keep wives from flying away. If we fly away anyway, they transfer their needs to their children.[192]

Women fear losing our children upon divorce.[193] During mar-

190. BROWNE, *supra* note 3, at 127. Browne found seven predictors of homicide in a battering relationship. Only one of these (the woman's threats of suicide) is based on the woman's behavior; all the other predictors (frequency of abusive incidents, extent of woman's injuries, frequency of forced sexual acts by man, man's drug use, and frequency of his intoxication) are based on actions by the man. *Id.*

191. This problem is symmetrical to the dangers that helplessness theories pose for women who fight back against violence.

192. Anonymous quotations from mothers on custody battles, from the chapter, *Mothers' Voices, Written on the Wind, in* CHESLER, *supra* note 14, at 449.

193. WEITZMAN, *supra* note 82, at 311 (stating that men see custody as part of a total package of divorce issues; women "are more likely to consider custody on an altogether different level

riage, women are usually primary caregivers for children, even when both father and mother work full time.[194] In Lenore Weitzman's study of divorce, one third of the women interviewed reported their husbands threatened to seek custody as a ploy in postseparation negotiations, usually because they sought financial gains.[195] Women routinely sacrificed support to which they would otherwise be entitled in order to avoid even the risk of losing their children.[196] Other studies have observed a dynamic with regard to domestic violence that parallels the financial bargaining Weitzman recounted: rather than face custody suits, women accept mutual orders of protection, which are inappropriate if the woman has not been violent and can hinder the effectiveness of the protective order.[197] In both instances, women lose protection they need and to which they are legally entitled, because they fear the treatment they are likely to receive in court.[198]

These fears are realistic.[199] First, since so many divorcing women report they have experienced violence, the problem is common. Second, violent men will likely seek new means of control when old ones fail. Batterers use the legal system as a new arena of combat when they seek to keep their wives from leaving.[200] Of the women whose stories are in this paper, all but one who had children at the time of divorce have either fought a custody action or were threatened with one.[201]

Men who pursue custody have a better than even chance of gaining

— it is something they simply cannot negotiate about because it is too important — it is worth any price").

194. Fineman, *supra* note 82, at 769 & n.166; *see also* WEITZMAN, *supra* note 82, at 240 (noting that husbands spend even less time with their children when their wives are employed).

195. WEITZMAN, *supra* note 82, at 310.

196. *Id.* at 311-12.

197. *New York Task Force Report, supra* note 51, at 40 n.84.

198. One woman obtained a temporary restraining order when her husband threatened to move back in without her consent or to take away the children if she refused to reconcile. See narrative regarding fear of opinion of therapist, text following *infra* note 217. After being served with the order, her husband offered to drop the threat of a custody suit if she would agree not to obtain a permanent protective order. She agreed and allowed the temporary order to expire without seeking a permanent order. She was pleased, in part because she believed that permanent orders would be difficult to enforce. In actuality, however, she had agreed to less legal protection solely in order to protect her relationship with her infant children.

199. For a discussion of the problem of domestic violence in custody decisions, including cases in which courts awarded custody to violent or even murderous fathers, see Naomi Cohen, *Civil Images of Battered Women: The Impact of Domestic Violence on Child Custody Determinations*, VAND. L. REV. (forthcoming).

200. Lenore E.A. Walker & Glenace E. Edwall, *Domestic Violence and Determination of Visitation and Custody in Divorce, in* DOMESTIC VIOLENCE ON TRIAL, *supra* note 58, at 130.

201. The one woman who reported no such threat had a husband disabled by mental illness who was not working steadily at the time of divorce.

custody.[202] Even violent men are frequently successful in custody suits. In one study, fifty-nine percent of the judicially successful fathers had physically abused their wives; thirty-six percent had kidnapped their children.[203] A recent article estimated that at least one half of all contested custody cases involved families with a history of some form of domestic violence; in approximately forty percent of those cases, fathers were awarded the children irrespective of their history of violence.[204] Another study reported many awards of custody to battering fathers, including one case in which the judge made his decision after walking past the shelter to which the mother and children had fled. The judge found the shelter to be an inappropriate living arrangement and concluded the father provided the better home.[205]

The past two decades have seen major changes in child custody litigation.[206] Martha Fineman has explained how the advent of gender-neutral rules in custody decisionmaking created a situation that actually disfavors women, since factors that would favor women, such as nurturing, are defined as gender-biased.[207] In devaluing past caregiving and seeking decisionmaking factors that would not inherently prefer women, courts have wound up relying on factors such as financial resources that usually favor men.[208]

With the advent of no-fault divorce, fault became relevant only in custody proceedings.[209] This contributes to a critical evaluation of mothering and holds particular problems for women leaving violent marriages. Violence against women is less likely to be raised at all in a no-fault action. It may be dangerous for women to raise the issue of domestic violence, since it invokes stereotypes that judges or social

---

202. Martha L. Fineman & Anne Opie, *The Uses of Social Science Data in Legal Policymaking: Custody Determinations at Divorce*, 1987 WIS. L. REV. 107, 120 & n.37. In one study, 70% of 37 judges ordered children into paternal custody. CHESLER, *supra* note 14, at 80-81. In Weitzman's study, men who requested custody received it 63% of the time in negotiated cases. Weitzman found that in many cases where fathers received custody there was some explicit or implicit agreement by the mother. However, the "agreement" sometimes appeared to have been coerced by threats against the woman's safety, reputation, or financial security. WEITZMAN, *supra* note 82, at 233-34. Men won 33% to 38% of the cases that were fully contested in court. *Id.* at 234.

203. CHESLER, *supra* note 14, at 81.

204. Walker & Edwall, *supra* note 200, at 127, 130.

205. *New York Task Force Report*, *supra* note 51, at 42.

206. *See, e.g.*, Fineman, *supra* note 82, at 738-39; Fineman & Opie, *supra* note 202, at 113-21. Beginning in the 1970s, feminists sought to construct a notion of woman not tied to the idea of mothering. Simultaneously, in a reaction to women's liberation, father's rights groups challenged the assumption of maternal custody that had characterized the preceding period. *See id.*

207. Fineman & Opie, *supra* note 202, at 121.

208. *Id.*

209. WEITZMAN, *supra* note 82, at 223.

workers may hold. It may not even be helpful: in the absence of physical harm to a child, violence against the mother might not be seen as relevant to the welfare of the children.[210] Women therefore must decide whether to describe the violence against them — and risk judicial stereotyping — or keep silent, and allow the violence of their spouse to be judicially invisible.

The difficulties here have been exacerbated by the simultaneous development of several liberal legal reforms. Feminist litigation on battered women's syndrome occurred contemporaneously both with the attempt — as part of some feminist visions of equality — to make motherhood less central to women's identity, and with the advent of no-fault divorce. The evolution of a dysfunctional portrait of battered women therefore occurred simultaneously with the changes wrought by no-fault and joint custody. Indeed, by making violence against women less visible at divorce, no-fault divorce laws may have indirectly contributed to cultural stereotypes of battered women by removing public blame of the perpetrator of the violence. Once the man as bad actor disappears, it is easy to shift the focus to the woman. Rather than asserting his harm to her from the beginning, the woman must raise battering as an issue defensively, while she is being clinically evaluated, with greater attendant risk of stereotyping.

The resulting legal dangers appear in many women's stories. Angela Browne tells of a woman who left her husband after the third "physically assaultive incident" had endangered their infant son. She went into hiding with relatives and consulted an attorney to file protective orders and obtain a divorce. The husband sought custody and claimed that his wife's disappearance from the family home proved her instability. Because the woman had left before the violence became grotesque, she was not treated as having been seriously endangered. The state placed the child with the abuser's family because they were considered stable; his family then fought to restrict the mother's visitation. The welfare department finally recommended the baby remain with its grandparents since they had been taking care of it, noting "the fact that their stories [were] so contradictory makes both parents seem unreliable."[211] Christine Littleton tells a similar story: a

210. Walker & Edwall, *supra* note 200, at 140.

211. BROWNE, *supra* note 3, at 112-13.

This woman's story provides one answer to the question: "Why don't battered women leave?" The woman acted independently and rationally: She left the situation when she began to realize that it would not improve; she refused to tolerate victimization; she sought legal remedies. She escaped her abuser before the violence was serious. She may also have lost her child.

Id. at 113.

woman who had obtained a restraining order against her husband awoke one night to find him wielding a knife in her bedroom; after she fled into the night, he claimed she had abandoned the children, and she was unable to regain custody.[212]

No-fault divorce and the widespread adoption of the "best interest of the child" standard for resolving custody disputes also put more power in the hands of professionals such as social workers.[213] Judges follow the recommendations in evaluations ninety percent of the time.[214] The increased reliance on these professionals created problems for battered women with children. Even before separation, it may be dangerous to place much trust in a counselor who may later be called on to testify regarding the qualities of the parents:

> The problem is, I feel as if the therapist likes him better. She took it seriously the day he had attacked me. But then I decided I wanted a separation, and I asked him to leave. She told me that "the person who wants the separation should be the one who leaves." It's student housing — it's my apartment. But I'm afraid to argue with her. I don't know what she'll do if he tries to take the children.

This woman was right to perceive the marriage counselor as a hazard.[215] Therapists can prove susceptible to the charm of batterers.[216] The battered woman often believes she is a less attractive figure than her spouse. "Who would like me? Can't think straight, crying, depressed . . . ugly . . . tired, twenty years old, with two kids to support. . . ." Therapists may justify the batterer during the counseling process, or break the wife's confidence to inform the batterer of the wife's complaints of violence, as well as posing a danger in the event of later custody disputes.[217]

The woman's unwillingness to compromise may be penalized as well. A woman may manage to drag the man into marriage counseling, yet despair after continued problems and seek a separation. Both

---

212. Littleton, *supra* note 34, at 54.

213. Fineman, *supra* note 82, at 740-44.

214. Sun & Thomas, *supra* note 14, at 573.

215. Family systems theory has great influence in the field of social work today. Fineman, *supra* note 82, at 744-45 & nn.77-81. The family systems approach strongly protects the status quo. When a woman describes her husband's violence, social workers following family systems theory often ask the woman to focus on what she did to provoke the man. STORDEUR & STILLE, *supra* note 81, at 26.

216. Walker & Edwall, *supra* note 200, at 141; *see also* LOUISE ARMSTRONG, THE HOME FRONT: NOTES FROM THE FAMILY WAR ZONE 37-62 (1983) (describing how psychiatrists misconstrue or even ignore the realities of abuse); LENORE WALKER, *supra* note 40, at 248-50 (discussing sexist attitudes among psychotherapists).

217. *See, e.g.*, Anonymous, Letter to the Editor, *Why Battered Wives Don't Leave Home*, N.Y. TIMES, Dec. 29, 1983, at A18 (describing the counselor's violation of confidences in order to establish "trust and communication").

the charm of the batterer and the therapist's desire for an evenhanded, unifying solution may lead to problems.

> My husband threatened to try to take the children from me, to tell the court I was unfit, that my friends were a bad influence. The therapist had always liked him better, and for several months I had been afraid she would be biased against me if she testified. But by the time he made the threat I wasn't as scared as I had been, because I knew I had won. He had finally lost the therapist as an ally — not by pulling a gun on me, not by being proud of it later and scaring her so badly that day — but by failing appointments when I continued to make them.

The battered woman fearing a custody action therefore faces powerful forces that may be hostile or difficult to control. Mothers generally fare poorly in the professional literature used by social workers.[218] Battered women face additional difficulties from court reliance on social workers and other professionals in evaluating contested custody issues, since few evaluators have much training at understanding the impact of battering on the child as well as the woman.[219] Also, the background of Freudian psychology, with its emphasis on women's masochism, still affects some of the psychological and sociological expertise in the field of domestic violence.[220] Feminist scholars have particularly criticized family systems theory, widespread in the field of social work today, for its tendency to equalize responsibility for the violence:[221] the family systems view of battering as an interaction between family members tends to blame the victim for failing to stop the violence, and to define success as reconciling the partners in the relationship rather than as stopping the abuse.[222]

Finally, battered women with children face an image problem. We need to be strong, resourceful, effective as a parent, meeting the needs of the children when we appear in court. On the other hand, if we do that too well, the court may disbelieve our stories because of stereotypes held by judges or psychologists.[223] If the court will consider

218. Fineman, *supra* note 82, at 767 n.161 (noting that in 125 articles studied, mothers were blamed for 72 psychological disorders in children; no mother-child relationships were described as healthy, though some father-child relationships were described as healthy).

219. Walker & Edwall, *supra* note 200, at 140; Sun & Thomas, *supra* note 14, at 573.

220. *See* ARMSTRONG, *supra* note 216, at 16-36.

221. Family systems theory tends to view the divorcing family as a whole rather than looking at individuals and to seek to accommodate the entire family's transition to a new set of relationships. Fineman, *supra* note 82, at 744-45 & nn.77-81.

222. STORDEUR & STILLE, *supra* note 81, at 25-26.

223. Crites & Coker, *supra* note 14, at 13. One such story was recounted by a social worker, whose client had been evaluated by a therapist as too strong to have been a battered woman and too upset about her ex-husband, considering that two years had passed, to be a stable parent. The ex-husband had continued his attacks for two years, including such calculated violence as cutting the brake lines on her car. Conversation with Donna Coker, *supra* note 67.

violence as a factor at all in custody decisions, we may be seen as — or in effect be *required* to appear as — having been weak, helpless, and economically dependent to have "stayed" with the man all these years.

The hazards are obvious. In self-defense claims, we have pressed upon judges and juries a portrait of induced dysfunctionality. In custody cases, we must prove functionality — or at least recovery.[224] The concept of "learned helplessness" is a factor that may influence negative custody decisions.[225] The needs of battered women in custody cases seem almost directly inverse to self-defense cases: women must prove our *subjective* reasonableness for self-defense claims, our *objective* rationality and competence as parents; learned helplessness may "explain" why a woman "stayed" in the self-defense context, but may be interpreted as making her a poor model in childrearing and possibly a poor caregiver as well when custody is in question. The cases may not always be tried before the same judges, but they work within the same legal system and popular culture. To the extent that our psychological literature has been focused on "battered women" rather than the violent power and control moves against these women, it perpetuates stereotypes that damage us in our other encounters with the legal system.

Therefore, fear of the law controls some of the behavior of battered women with children. A woman who leaves her husband may wind up on the defensive regarding custody, subject to rules that disfavor her which are then interpreted through negative cultural images. Through this interaction of the power of the legal system and the man's violent moves for control, women are hindered in simultaneously protecting ourselves and our relationships with our children. In this impossible bind, we may end temporary separations under pressure from social workers[226] or from fear of custody actions,[227] or make concessions over needed financial support or the level of protection we demand or receive from the state. We may also reluctantly accept dangers we can observe and respond to personally — the threat of violent men we know — to avoid the uncertainties of custody suits.

C. *Lesbian Battering: Defining a Problem Outside the Legal System*

Lesbians are excluded from most constraints of the courtroom.

224. Battered women's adjustments to the separation may bring stress and emotions that can harm her on evaluation. Walker & Edwall, *supra* note 200, at 140-41.

225. Sun & Thomas, *supra* note 14, at 569.

226. *See* STORDEUR & STILLE, *supra* note 81, at 26.

227. Sun & Thomas, *supra* note 14, at 574.

This is not a fact that should be idealized; it grows out of oppression. They cannot marry. While they do confront custody litigation by former male partners, lesbians have not historically been able to sue each other for custody of children they coparented.[228] Lesbians may also find it difficult to assert legal rights in shared property on separation.[229] Homophobia in society deters many battered lesbians from invoking the legal system by calling the police for help or attempting to arrest the batterer.[230] Even when lesbians seek protection through law, restraining orders may be unavailable against same-sex partners in some states.[231] Because of this exclusion, the analysis of battered lesbians has developed in less direct relation to legal pressures than has analysis of heterosexual battering.

There are a few reported differences between lesbian and heterosexual battering.[232] Lesbians report physically fighting back more often than women who are battered by men.[233] Since heterosexual women also report fighting back against physical assaults,[234] this difference in reporting may show a difference in what it is acceptable for women to discuss, or it may reflect an actual difference in women's responses to battering.[235] The virtual absence of self-defense killings in lesbian relationships[236] has also helped keep battered lesbians outside the legal system: battered woman syndrome is less emphasized in materials on lesbian battering in part because lesbians have not been raising claims of self-defense in court.

Lesbians have not only been excluded from the courtroom. Their stories *as stories of women's lives* have also often been excluded from

228. In three very recent cases, lesbians sought custody or visitation rights in court; in each case, however, no parental rights were recognized in the partner who was not the biological mother. Nancy S. v. Michele G., 228 Cal. App. 3d 831, 279 Cal. Rptr. 212 (1991); Curiale v. Reagan, 222 Cal. App. 3d 1597, 272 Cal. Rptr. 520 (1990); *In the Matter of* Alison D. v. Virginia M., 572 N.E.2d 27 (N.Y. 1991).

229. Nancy Hammond, *Lesbian Victims and the Reluctance to Identify Abuse, in* NAMING THE VIOLENCE, *supra* note 33, at 190, 196.

230. Hammond, *supra* note 229, at 190, 196.

231. Ruthann Robson, *Lavender Bruises: Intra-Lesbian Violence, Law and Lesbian Legal Theory,* 20 GOLDEN GATE U. L. REV. 567, 576-81 (1990).

232. Walker, *supra* note 49, at 75-76.

233. *Id.*

234. *See generally* Saunders, *supra* note 38, at 90, 103-08 (self-defense is most common reason women exhibit violence).

235. Lydia Walker notes that possible explanations include "less size differential, less acceptance from the community to not fight back, [and] *more permission from the community to talk about fighting back* . . . ." Walker, *supra* note 49, at 76 (emphasis added).

236. Recently, a Florida court allowed the first use of expert testimony on battered woman syndrome in the defense of a lesbian who killed her batterer. *See* Robson, *supra* note 231, at 574-75. The jury convicted Annette Green of first degree murder despite *the prosecution's* acknowledgement that she had been battered and shot at in the past. *Id.* at 575.

the legal,[237] psychological, and sociological literature.[238] Despite the hard work of some lesbians in the battered women's movement, including staffing agencies and shelters, lesbians have often been excluded from shelters and from the support of the battered women's movement.[239] Although this lack of recognition and scarcity of resources has caused harm to many lesbians, it left lesbian battering to be defined within an activist tradition close to the grassroots shelter movement and dedicated to supporting women.

Naming The Violence, the first book on lesbian battering, includes the stories of many battered lesbians. Compared with *published* narratives of heterosexual women's battering relationships, the lesbian narratives place more emphasis on the positive aspects of the relationship; the battered women seem more willing to explain, or possibly more in touch with, the positive feelings that drew them in and kept them involved:

> I look back and can see that there was something good. It didn't start with violence and ugliness. It started with summer nights, two women in their early twenties trying to find a way to see each other. Both lived in households where it wasn't possible to be open about the relationship. Meeting at movies and bars until early in the morning — until finally one left her home. Nights of lovemaking, not enough sleep and feeling fine at work the next day — being relaxed and happy. I had found something that I never even knew existed. I never thought that there would be some one person for me, and I had now found her. I think neither of us doubted that we had found a lifetime relationship. The feeling of rightness was there. . . .
>
> And who is the monster in the next room who did this? She's just a woman like you who is feeling as upset as you are and is temporarily full of remorse. She is the only friend you have, the only one who seems to

---

237. *See generally* Leigh M. Leonard, *The Missing Voice in Feminist Legal Theory: The Heterosexual Presumption,* 12 WOMEN'S RTS. L. REP. 39 (1990).

238. The stories of lesbians have been excluded from most fictional treatment of women's lives as well. In "Listening," the final story in Grace Paley's most recent book, the narrator, Faith, is in a car, stopped at a light, watching a man crossing the street and thinking warmly about his body. She speaks to Cassie, a friend sitting next to her who has not previously appeared in the book of stories, and asks, "He's nice, isn't he?" Cassie refuses to accept Faith's statement that the man is returning to "everyday life":

> To whose everyday life, she said, goddamnit, whose?
>
> She turned to me. . . . Listen, Faith, why don't you tell my story? You've told everybody's story but mine. I don't even mean my whole story, that's my job. You probably can't. But I mean you've just omitted me from the other stories and I was there. In the restaurant and the train, right there. Where is Cassie? Where is *my* life? It's been women and men, women and men, ... Goddamnit, where the hell is my woman and woman, woman-loving life in all this? . . . You let [our other friends] in [to your stories] all the time; it's really strange, why have you left me out of everybody's life?

GRACE PALEY, LATER THE SAME DAY 209-10 (1985).

239. *See* Hammond, *supra* note 229, at 190, 195-96 (on problems for lesbians in shelters and the shelter movement).

> care. The idea of leaving seems worse than if you try to stay and make it work and make sure it doesn't happen again. Bruises heal and resentment fades back into the routines of work, shopping, watching reruns of *All Creatures Great and Small,* and driving her to church on Sunday morning.[240]

In these stories, lesbians seem more willing to face the *current* duality of their memories and feelings. This does not necessarily represent a difference between lesbian and heterosexual battering. These stories are more like those I heard from heterosexuals whose stories are included in this article, which emphasized the complexity of the marriage relationship while trying to analyze the violence, than they are like most of the stories in the published material on heterosexual battering.[241] Lesbians do not seem less hurt by battering relationships than heterosexual women. Rather, it seems likely that the editors simply excised less of this quality than do the editors of most social science research:

> I fell in love with her because she was warm and loving and open. Her brilliance and clear political thinking dazzled me, as did her creativity — her artwork, her cooking, her carpentry, her ideas about raising children. Like me, she was Jewish and radical and understood the importance of making one's home in the country. She was responsive to our class differences in ways that surprised and delighted me. We had similar dreams of family and commitment, and fantasies of how we wanted to live. We often had hot, passionate sex. She bought me flowers, and chocolate, and crystals, and wool socks. She played a mean game of Pac-Man. She sang me love songs, and slow-danced with me in the living room. She did not do these things only at the beginning but throughout our relationship. Even when the violence was most frequent, she also expressed caring tenderness toward me.
>
> I want you to understand that I stayed with her for the same reasons any woman stays with her lover — because I honestly and deeply loved her, and was honestly and deeply loved by her.
>
> I also stayed because I had nowhere else to go . . . .[242]

The second major difference in this lesbian battering literature is the absence of blaming the victim. Historically, lesbians have at least at times shared the cultural stereotype of battered women as weak. Therefore, *Naming the Violence* and articles on lesbian battering recount an initial resistance to recognizing the problem and show early

240. Lisa, *Once Hitting Starts, in* NAMING THE VIOLENCE, *supra* note 33, at 37-39.

241. Donna Coker suggests that battered heterosexual women also tell complex stories that mix love, happiness, pain, and unhappiness, but that professionals working with battered women are often uneasy with the complexity of these stories. Conversation with Donna Coker, 1990.

242. Istar, *supra* note 33, at 164-65.

acceptance of myths about lesbian abuse.[243] Some women initially believed that only "bar dykes" engaged in violence, that feminist lesbians were not involved in battering relationships, and that only couples "strictly locked into butch/femme roles ha[d] a problem with violence."[244]

So stereotypes have indeed existed among lesbians. Yet when these attitudes emerged within activist, feminist communities they were promptly confronted. They do not define the literature, and therefore do not create more ongoing stereotyping of battered lesbians. Traditional stereotypes are largely absent: the voice of the conservative social scientist, the Freudian analyst, and the professional who blames the battered woman for failing to control her batterer, have been left behind. The analysis generated by a grassroots, feminist, activist community presents a more nuanced, less stereotyping, and less victim-blaming view than any other literature in the field.

IV. Power, Control, Autonomy, and Separation

A. *Identifying Domination in Violence Against Women*

Battering is about domination: "Violence is a way of 'doing power' in a relationship,"[245] an effort by the batterer to control the woman who is the recipient of the violence.[246] This is not news. A review of the literature shows that the conception of battering as about power — rather than about incidents of violence or about the psychology of women who experience violence — has been present in some of the psychological and sociological literature for some time.[247] A decade ago, Dobash and Dobash placed battering in the context of patriarchy and described it as domination: "The fact that violence against wives is a form of a husband's domination is irrefutable in the light of historical evidence."[248] However, the emphasis on power comprised only one

243. Barbara Hart reported that when lesbian battering was first brought to light, battered lesbians were perceived as "weak sisters." Hart, *supra* note 50, at 14. This obviously reflects some influence of cultural stereotypes.

244. Ann Strach et al., *Lesbian Abuse: The Process of the Lesbian Abuse Issues Network (LAIN), in* Naming the Violence, *supra* note 33, at 88, 89.

245. Stets, *supra* note 64, at 110 ("The men want to direct and determine how their partner behaves, and the way they do this is through violence. . . . [T]he men use violence to dominate, control, and force the women to conform to what they want."). *Id.* at 109.

246. Lee H. Bowker, Beating Wife-Beating 7-9 (1983) (discussing the balance of power in families); Schechter, *supra* note 94, at 219-24 (describing battering as a way to maintain control).

247. *See generally* Dobash & Dobash, *supra* note 12 (patriarchy and domination key framework of study); Bograd, *supra* note 101, at 559 ("Violence such as rape and battering is a form of male control over women."); *see also* Stordeur & Stille, *supra* note 81, at 20 (noting recent emphasis on power and control in writings of some authors).

248. Dobash & Dobash, *supra* note 12, at ix.

thread in the literature and was intermixed with much work psychologizing battered women.[249] Legal literature, in particular, has often ignored the interplay of power and control, domination and subordination in the battering relationship.

The quest for control underlying the enforcement of women's social roles is often hard to perceive. In a heterosexual marriage, if one partner does all the dishes and the other does all the driving — that is, if one is assigned all responsibility for household work and spends a substantial amount of time on this work, and the other has virtually all the mobility — this may not strike observers as the result of an exercise of power but merely as a "traditional"[250] attitude in the relationship. A researcher describing such a relationship might perceive "traditionalism" on the part of the woman. If the researcher is already looking for indicia of "traditionalism" in the woman's behavior or life circumstances,[251] the terms of the inquiry may construct the findings. The woman's apparent "traditionalism" might mask a more fundamental issue. For example, domestic work, or large numbers of children, will represent "traditionalism" in a *woman* only to the extent that they are not the *man*'s choice. If they are his choice, both factors might indeed represent the man's attempt to control the woman.

Dobash and Dobash treat battering as part of a context and history of patriarchy in which violence and disapproval inflicted by society as a whole, as well as by individual men, enforced women's roles.[252] In fact, batterers often justify their violence with complaints describing

---

249. GONDOLF & FISHER, *supra* note 12, at 1-2; SCHECHTER, *supra* note 94, at 20-24 (discussing theories of victim provocation).

250. In her 1979 study, Lenore Walker called battered women "traditionalists" who "readily accept[] the notion that 'a woman's proper place is in the home.'" LENORE WALKER, *supra* note 40, at 33. Walker stated that battered women give up careers *to make the batterer happy* or accede to his need to possess her. The battered woman turns her money over to her husband, feels that income belongs to her husband, and goes out of her way to make the man feel he is head of the home even while she holds it together. Some women secretly save money and leave when they have enough to go. *Id.* at 33-34. Although Walker describes this as the woman's traditionalism, all these actions except the belief that her income belongs to the husband seem to reflect the *man's* traditionalism and ability to control the woman rather than establishing *her* traditionalism. In her 1984 study, Walker found battered women more liberal and batterers the "traditionalists." WALKER, SYNDROME *supra* note 110, at 148.

251. For example, PAGELOW, *supra* note 102, at 105-44 first hypothesizes "traditionalism" in *both* men and women in battering relationships. She then goes on to interpret even contradictory data as "traditionalism." Variables presumed to show "traditionalism" include: "numbers of children" and "secondary battering cohabitation" (continuing to live with the batterer after the first incident of violence). *Id.* at 127. When Pagelow's data show that women with more children, and especially more young children, stayed in relationships longer than other women, she interprets this as evidence of a belief in the importance of two-parent homes, rather than as a reflection of the difficulties of leaving or the low earning power relative to child care costs of these women. *Id.* at 141-42. The researcher's *hypothesis* of "traditionalism" is subtly transformed to support a *finding* of traditionalism.

252. DOBASH & DOBASH, *supra* note 12, at 47-96.

the woman's insufficient fulfillment of household responsibilities and social role.[253] The energy required to maintain that division of labor may go unnoticed when the expectations are most shared and enforced by social norms, and even by the actions of the state.[254]

> Then we went to get the wedding license.
>
> We took our blood tests and identification down to the big state office building . . . , filled in some forms, and handed them to the clerk. She . . . showed us what the minister would sign and gave us a little pamphlet on the "Louisiana Community Property Law."
>
> Then she turned to me and said, "And these are for you." She handed me a nylon mesh bag with a tag attached that said, "For the Bride." It had samples of Tide, Joy, Spray'n Wash [detergent for clothes, detergent for dishes, stain remover for clothes], Windex, PAM . . . and other household products I don't remember. I said, "You've got to be kidding." And she said, sweetly, "No, these are for the bride."

The congruence of expectation by *heterosexual* batterers and society in general may be one reason *lesbian* battering has been understood as concerned with power. The expenditure of energy that goes into controlling a loved one may be more perceptible as an exercise of power when the control that is sought is less completely in accord with social expectation.[255]

While early studies assumed — and looked for — "traditional" attitudes in battered women, other studies found that battered women were likely to have *less* traditional attitudes regarding women's roles in the family, but that battering men had *more* "traditional" attitudes.[256] Consistent with this, Bowker found that men's participation in male networks increased the likelihood that the men would have rigid attitudes regarding male dominance and enforce these attitudes with

---

253. OKUN, *supra* note 107, at 69-70 (batterers justify assaults with criticisms of wives' household tasks); STETS, *supra* note 64, at 71, 95-98.

254. State actions enforcing women's roles include refusal to enforce TROs and returning women to abusive situations, generations of home economics education for girls and not for boys, and giving out cleaning supplies as in the narrative below. Additional examples are public housing policies that define women fleeing abusive relationships *outside* the category of those homeless "through no fault of [their] own," *see* LEE ANN HOFF, BATTERED WOMEN AS SURVIVORS 195-201 (1990), and public housing policies that give the battering man possession of the apartment if his wife leaves. Conversation with Kim Hanson, 1990.

The following incident took place in Louisiana in 1976. I have heard of other women who were given with their wedding licenses either actual cleaning supplies or coupons for cleaning supplies in California during the late 1970s and in the midwest at various times. (It is not obvious which gift the women considered more offensive).

255. This would not necessarily link "role-playing" in lesbian relationships with violence; in fact, no such correlation emerges in the reports on lesbian battering. Barbara Hart, Violence in Lesbian Relationships 2 (unpublished manuscript in materials on lesbian battering distributed by W.O.M.A.N., Inc.) (on file with author); *id.* at 3 (denial fed by idea that only violent lesbians are those "who hang out in bars or are into playing butch").

256. *See, e.g.*, WALKER, SYNDROME, *supra* note 110, at 8.

violence.[257]

Focusing on the struggle to control the woman that lies at the heart of battering makes sense of many apparently discrepant research findings. Questions of money, status, and education could trigger acute insecurities regarding power in relationships. In many violent relationships the woman has a higher educational level and comes from a higher social status than the man.[258] Kersti Yllo found battering highest in states where women's power and status were *highest* relative to men's.[259] On the other hand, Bowker's study of women in formerly violent marriages showed that women with higher current incomes were less likely to have been severely beaten or beaten while pregnant, and found no correlation of violence with the woman's higher or lower social class.[260] In lesbian relationships, some experts have found that the battered lesbian is more likely to be the breadwinner or primary supporter of the household,[261] however, another commentator observed higher educational and social status among batterers.[262]

If the central question in battering were the woman's acceptance of violence, it would be difficult to explain both the widespread finding of women's higher education and status, and the inconsistency in some of this data. However, if we emphasize the batterer's struggle for control and look at battering as a (violent) point on a continuum of domination in relationships, then these findings make sense in two ways: first, factors that increase the woman's independence and autonomy might

---

257. BOWKER, *supra* note 246, at 54. Bowker had expected to find greater social isolation among battered women — reflecting some assumption that society disapproves violence as well as the assumption that battered women have been isolated from society — but instead found increased social embeddedness among the men, with concomitant support for male dominance.

258. WALKER, SYNDROME, *supra* note 110, at 11, 16, 156, 158, 160; *see also* Molly Chaudhuri & Kathleen Daley, *Do Restraining Orders Help? Battered Women's Experience with Male Violence and Legal Process, in* DOMESTIC VIOLENCE: THE CHANGING CRIMINAL JUSTICE RESPONSE (Eve Buzawa & Carl Buzawa eds., forthcoming 1992) (tentative title) (stating that violent men had fewer years of education than their wives). Walker notes that it is said most women marry at or above their own social class, while most men marry at or below theirs. She therefore finds this a sharp break from the usual pattern in marriage and a noteworthy characteristic of battering relationships. LENORE WALKER, *supra* note 40, at 11, 17.

259. Yllo, *supra* note 101, at 28, 31 (noting that this finding contradicted her assumptions about traditionalism in relationships).

260. Women with higher current income also were less likely to have suffered marital rape. BOWKER, *supra* note 246 at 50-51. None of Bowker's findings permitted a comparison with marriages in which the husbands had higher status. His findings did not support the theory that battering was a form of compensation for other forms of maintaining power in a relationship. *Id.*

261. *Domestic Violence By and Against Women: An Interview About Lesbian Violence,* excerpts from an interview by KALX, Berkeley, California, with Susan Jan Hornstein, Exec. Dir. of Western Center on Domestic Violence, and Naomi Porat, Administrative Coordinator at W.O.M.A.N., Inc. and facilitator of a battered lesbian support group, in materials on lesbian battering collected by W.O.M.A.N., Inc., *supra* note 255, at 2.

262. *See* Hart, *supra* note 255, at 3 (noting battering lesbians of more privileged background).

make additional control moves, including violence, more likely; second, power and control struggles may be triggered by many factors within a relationship and therefore could also be consistent with dominance by the partner with greater resources.

James Ptacek, who worked with batterers, and Jan Stets, who worked with couples, found control an ongoing issue in battering relationships. Both Ptacek and Stets describe men as using violence to control the woman.[263] The instrumental goal of control is made excused or made invisible by the fact that the man appears to be out of control himself: both men and women perceive violence as caused by the man's loss of control over his actions.[264] However, both Stets and Ptacek questioned the man's apparent loss of control. Ptacek emphasized that batterers' actions were selective, and that their descriptions of their own actions reflected conscious choices.[265] Stets found that the men selectively "lost" control *in order to achieve the goal of controlling the women,* but differed from Ptacek in emphasizing the role of the woman's response as minimizing the negative results for the man of his loss of control.[266] Other scholars also have emphasized that "a major reason for the use of marital violence is to increase one's power over a mate."[267]

Recognizing the batterer's attempt at domination as the key to battering relationships allows a focus on his motivations rather than the psychology of the victim. A study of the effectiveness of temporary restraining orders in relation to several different goals[268] found success

263. Ptacek, *supra* note 48, at 147-49; STETS, *supra* note 64, at 101-11, 121-31.

264. To both the man and the woman in the relationship, the man's loss of control over his actions appears to cause his violence. Ptacek, *supra* note 48, at 153-54. *See generally* STETS, *supra* note 64, at 54-68. Indeed, the idea that the man cannot control his anger appears throughout sociological and psychological literature. *Id.* at 11-12 (discussing literature); Ptacek, *supra* note 48, at 152-54 (discussing literature). The man will use this apparent lack of self control to carry out his domination of the woman, and will also use it to "excuse" his domination.

265. Ptacek sees violence as instrumental. "[This] loss of control is substantially contradicted by the batterers' own testimony. While the men claim that their violence is beyond rational control, they simultaneously acknowledge that the violence is deliberate and warranted." Ptacek, *supra* note 48, at 153.

266. *See generally* STETS, *supra* note 64, at 101-11. Stets criticizes Ptacek's instrumentalism for neglecting to ask what makes batterers discontinue particular violent incidents. *Id.* at 61. In her discussion of battering relationships, Stets emphasizes the woman's responses as well as male control goals. *Id.* at 95-100 (emphasizing woman's acts as cues). This brings her somewhat closer to family systems theorists and to Pagelow's emphasis on the woman's response to violence. Stets sees instrumental violence as emerging over time in the course of a battering relationship. *Id.* at 103.

267. BOWKER, *supra* note 246, at 134. Power and control were also central contested issues in the majority of the formerly violent marriages in Bowker's study. The cessation of violence was associated with decreased male dominance in many of the relationships. *Id.*

268. The orders are more effective for some goals than for others. Chaudhuri & Daley, *supra* note 258.

in reducing the likelihood that the man would batter again dependent on the *man's* circumstances and motivation, not the woman's.[269] Similarly, a study of interspousal homicide revealed that the men could not cope with their bondedness with women. Unable to face their dependence on the women they loved, the men struck out against the women when they felt abandoned. Spouse homicide resulted from "individuals attempting to solve by their action the riddles of culture that the events of life force on them."[270] As men, they could not be dependent on their women, yet they could not face abandonment. This finding emphasizes the importance in battering relationships of the *man's* capacity to confront his own feelings and the danger of his need for control.

The focus on the batterer's need for control also reconciles another discrepancy in battering studies. Bowker reports that a threat to leave the batterer may be very effective at ending the violence.[271] However, other studies show that separation often triggers escalated violence.[272] The same behavior — threatening to leave the relationship — might prove extremely effective or tremendously dangerous for women. The difference will depend on the men with whom they are involved. If the key to whether the violence escalates lies in the *man's* capacities, then any system examining the *woman's* behavior and psychology will poorly track the danger she faces — unless we consider her the best judge on this issue.[273] Courts are ill-equipped to measure retrospectively the man's capacity to "solve . . . the riddles of culture" without homicide, or the persuasiveness of his threats to the woman.[274]

A focus on control also makes sense of the particular situations of

269. *Id.* Several attributes made it more likely that the man would abuse the woman again: prior criminal history, unemployment or part-time employment, and drug or alcohol abuse.

270. George Barnard et al., *Till Death Do Us Part: A Study of Spouse Murder,* 10 BULL. AM. ACAD. PSYCHIATRY & L. 271, 279 (1982).

271. BOWKER, *supra* note 246, at 65-67, 123.

272. Ellis, *supra* note 21, at 408.

273. Therefore, we need to vest evaluation of the man's violent potential in the woman. Her understanding of the process of violence and the man's motivation may not be perfect: violence may appear out of control to the women even when men actually retain some ability to control their actions; women also may perceive men's actions after violence as contrition or determination to reform which the men either do not experience or will not admit openly. STETS, *supra* note 64, at 127. However, the instrumental nature of his violence makes her, the target, the closest observer. She has more resources to measure his violent potential than any outside observer and the woman is best placed to assess the man's potential dangerousness, because she is most aware of the times and manner in which violence may occur. Barbara Hart, *Beyond the "Duty to Warn": A Therapist's "Duty to Protect" Battered Women and Children, in* FEMINIST PERSPECTIVES ON WIFE ABUSE, *supra* note 31, at 234, 240.

274. This is true whether the legal issues relate to her injury or death, or his. Barbara Hart has therefore drafted a lethality assessment questionnaire that aims to help professionals elicit from the battered woman information relevant to her informed assessment of her own situation, rather than replacing her assessment with their own. *See id.*

women with children. Women with children often give their children as the reason for their action — whether they have acted to stay, leave, or return to a relationship.[275] With the focus on control, difference makes sense: different male tactics, different types or frequency of violent episodes, might work to keep a woman with no children in a relationship than would work with a woman with children,[276] since women often leave when they perceive either physical or emotional danger to their children from the violence.[277] Controlling a woman with a disability — or whose child has a disability — may also have its own particularities of action within relationships. Fear of custody actions may also facilitate the control of women who believe a court might be unsympathetic to them.

Perhaps most important, identifying power and control as the struggle within a relationship enables women to make sense of our own experiences.

> I don't even talk baby talk to my kid like I did to my first husband. It reduced me — I was not supposed to think. I was not supposed to have any ideas. I was not supposed to be a person.
>
> One thing that made it so difficult was that before hooking up with him, I was a leader in the community. I was doing a lot of anti-war organizing work. I had my own apartment, my own life. I was an independent person, I'd been on my own for years. I had not moved from being dependent on my family to the marriage. I was a person who knew how to take care of myself, who had made it on my own.
>
> To this day, I don't understand it. I'm usually not a person who's lost for words, I'm usually not a person who falls to pieces. I get ambushed by the Klan, and I have the clearest head of anybody around. But that certainly wasn't the case in that marriage.

This woman recognizes her own strength and independence, and finds it hard to reconcile these qualities with the degree of control her husband succeeded in exercising through a few violent episodes followed by explicit and implicit threats. In fact, these could have been the qualities that made her husband feel threatened and turn to violence as a means of control. For years, she described the unhappiness of the marriage to friends without describing her husband's violence. She described personal problems frankly but could not communicate the experience of violence without diminishing her own self-esteem. She

---

275. DOBASH & DOBASH, *supra* note 12, at 148.

276. Pagelow notes that the presence of young children can be a very strong factor that keeps women in their relationships; most women waited to leave until their children were at least past infancy. PAGELOW, *supra* note 102, at 142.

277. "Her decision to terminate the relationship is more often motivated by concern for her children than by any real appreciation of the unacceptability of the abuse she has experienced." Anne McGillivray, *Battered Women: Definition, Models and Prosecutorial Policy*, 6 CAN. J. FAM. L. 15, 22 (1987); *see also* DOBASH & DOBASH, *supra* note 12, at 148.

could have described his actions as inappropriate attempts at controlling her without incurring the same humiliation.

Focusing on control lets women understand our lives without stigma by describing battered women's experience as part of all women's experience. A focus on control places the sensational, severely violent cases on a continuum of violence that makes sense whether the woman or the batterer is the defendant, whether it is a criminal or a civil case, whether or not the case appears likely go to court. Therefore, a focus on control provides the link between the woman's experience in her relationship and the experience of other women she learns of through the press or other media — an essential step toward her informed decisionmaking and toward remaking women's cultural concepts of domestic violence. Finally, by sorting and explaining women's experience in ways that apply across the varied legal postures in which domestic violence comes to public attention, a focus on power and control provides a coherent understanding of the experience of women in different situations: women experiencing varying kinds of attack by batterers in the attempt to exercise power and control; women of varying social status; women with or without children; women perceived as "leaving" or "staying."

To bring women's experience into law and make it more comprehensible to women ourselves, we need litigation strategies aimed at exposing the power and control at the heart of battering. One example of such litigation is the lawsuits brought since the 1970s that expose the failure of police to enforce temporary restraining orders.[278] We need more such creative approaches that expose the complicity of the state and society in the control of women in violent marriages. After being physically threatened and emotionally attacked for my failures at housework, I have often longed to sue the state actor — the clerk processing paperwork for marriage licenses — who by handing me cleaning supplies put the state's imprimatur on my husband's conception that this would be my job. Joyce McConnell describes battering relationships as involuntary servitude in violation of the Thirteenth Amendment — an analysis consistent with an emphasis on power.[279] Below, I develop an example of such a strategy, emphasizing the attacks on women's attempts to separate from violent relationships to help expose issues of power and control in both law and culture.

---

278. *See, e.g.*, Bruno v. Codd, 393 N.E.2d 976 (N.Y. 1979); Balistreri v. Pacifica Police Dept., 855 F.2d 1421 (9th Cir. 1988), *amended on other grounds*, 901 F.2d 696 (9th Cir. 1990); Thurman v. City of Torrington, 595 F. Supp. 1521 (D. Conn. 1984).

279. Joyce McConnell, *Beyond Metaphor: Battered Women and Involuntary Servitude*, 4 YALE J.L. & FEMINISM (forthcoming).

B. *"Who Says She Didn't Leave?":*[280] *Challenging Perceptions of Separation and Autonomy*

The "shopworn question"[281] persists in the cases, legal scholarship, and social science literature. It reveals several assumptions about separation: that the right solution is separation, that it is the woman's responsibility to achieve separation, and that she could have separated. The question "why didn't she leave" is actually an objectifying statement that asserts that the woman did *not* leave. Asking this question often makes actual separations disappear.

If we ask the woman, "What did you do?" the answer very often turns out to be, "I sought help." Edward Gondolf, who studied women's helpseeking behavior, found that women responded to abuse by seeking help from both formal and informal sources.[282] The more apparent it became that the batterer would not change, or the worse the abuse became, the greater diversity the women showed in their efforts to find help.[283] Gondolf concluded that it was the helping professions, rather than battered women, that were afflicted with "helplessness." He described battered women as "survivors" who developed self-transcendence to allow them to go on.[284]

When we ask the woman, "Exactly what did you do in your search for help?" the answer often turns out to be that she left — at least temporarily. In Gondolf's study, more than seventy percent of the women had left home at some time in response to violence, though only fourteen percent had gone to shelters.[285] Of the women Walker studied, about one quarter left temporarily after each battering incident.[286] Walker does not indicate whether the *intention* of these women as they left was temporary or permanent separation or whether they were in fact uncertain when they left.

Some social scientists have criticized the assumption that the woman has a responsibility to — on her own — successfully accomplish a separation in her family on her first attempt to do so.[287] This assump-

280. This is my paraphrase of Lewis Okun's phrase, "Who says she does stay?" OKUN, *supra* note 107, at 56.

281. Ann Jones, *The Burning Bed and Man Slaughter*, 9 WOMEN'S RTS. L. REP. 295, 296 (1986) (book review).

282. GONDOLF & FISHER, *supra* note 12, at 18, 27-28 (describing several studies showing helpseeking); *see also* WALKER, SYNDROME *supra* note 110, at 26 ("As the violence escalated, so did the probability that the battered woman would seek help.").

283. GONDOLF & FISHER, *supra* note 12, at 92-93.

284. *Id.* at 22-23, 99.

285. *Id.* at 77-78.

286. WALKER, SYNDROME, *supra* note 110, at 26.

287. OKUN, *supra* note 107, at 56; GONDOLF & FISHER, *supra* note 12, at 82-83.

tion ignores the woman's substantial ties to her current family structures. Her initial goal in separating may have been to improve her family structure rather than end it. Participation by the batterer in a counseling program is a very significant factor in predicting a woman will end a separation, since his participation tends to increase her hope for safe return.[288] Therefore, some experts recommend the credible threat to leave or attempt to separate as a measure for women who seek to end the violence against them but wish to preserve their relationships.[289] Finally, the assumption that the woman's first separation should be permanent ignores the real dangers that the man will seek actively — and sometimes violently — to end the separation.[290]

When the woman is asked, "what happened to you when you left?" we discover the lack of available resources. Shelters are unable to fill all the women's needs; when shelters make referrals to social service agencies, the agencies are often inadequate. Gondolf therefore identified "learned helplessness" among the helping professionals to whom women turned for assistance.[291] Neighbors, friends, and family may be sources of help, but often they too leave the separated woman without assistance:

> It was a day he was supposed to visit the children, but he didn't come. About nine o'clock at night, I heard a pounding noise downstairs. I heard him shout that he was bleeding, "Help me, help me."
>
> He had broken one of the glass panes in the door and wouldn't stop hitting it. When I opened the door, he fell part way through and lay there on the floor, moaning. He had been in a bar fight around the corner from my house, 10 miles from his own. He had broken a glass door at the bar and come back to the house. He said the police were after him. I thought he was crazy.
>
> I went to the phone — I didn't want to leave the room or take my eyes off him, and called my closest friends, a couple who lived a few blocks away. The man answered the phone. I said urgently that my husband was there and that I needed this friend to come over right away. He said OK and hung up. Fifteen or twenty minutes passed, and then his wife showed up. She said, "Allan wasn't going to come. He didn't see why you were bothering us. But I figured, if you had called, someone ought to check up and see what was going on."
>
> The police arrived. They had traced his car to our house and followed a trail of blood to our door. They weren't going to arrest him.

288. GONDOLF & FISHER, *supra* note 12, at 87.

289. BOWKER, *supra* note 246, at 65-67, 123 (husband's fear of divorce ended violence); *see also* Littleton, *supra* note 34, at 52 (criticizing the current legal system for offering actual separation as the only remedy against violence).

290. *See infra* text accompanying notes 295-302.

291. GONDOLF & FISHER, *supra* note 12, at 22-23.

When I asked, they waited for his brother-in-law to come pick him up. . . . Finally everyone went home.

It was so frightening that a man I had known for five years, who knew how my ex-husband had been, had actually lied to me and said he was coming, then been willing not to show up. They lived four blocks away! My mother told me I should talk to the neighbors, try to line up more help for next time. So I went to my next door neighbor the next day and began, "About the noise last night . . . ." He looked at me very fiercely. "What noise? We didn't hear *anything!*" For a minute, I thought he had been running his air conditioner and really couldn't hear. It was a small quiet street in a family neighborhood. I said, "When the police came . . . ." He glared at me again and interrupted. "We didn't hear a thing!"

Finally, we ask the woman herself about the key behavior of the violent partner whose behavior actually defines her state as a "battered woman." We say, "What did he do when you left?" At that moment, we will hear the story of the attacks on her autonomy; all we need to do is listen. Often, a woman has left several times before she finally ends a marriage.[292] Or, she may have been restrained from leaving by violent or coercive means: by being held prisoner in her home, by being threatened with custody suits, by having her savings taken away before she could depart.[293] One feminist writer in the field recently wrote without apparent irony,

> [He] always found ways to get her to come back. He would come and tell her how sorry he was and how much he loved her; he would promise never to do it again. And she wanted to believe him . . . . When she wavered and it appeared his pleas and promises might not work, he would threaten to kill her if she refused to come home, threats which his past behavior gave her every reason to take seriously.[294]

There are many aspects to redefining separation: we need to comprehend the related power and control issues common to continuing relationships and to separation, rethink the implicit burden on the woman to leave her home and risk losing her family, and change our perceptions of what it means for her to separate. Finally, we need to reckon with the dangers she faces. The rest of this article discusses the assault on women's attempts to separate. The story of the violent pursuit of the separating woman must become part of the way we understand domestic violence to help eliminate the question "Why didn't she leave?" from our common vocabulary.

---

292. *See, e.g.*, Dobash & Dobash, *supra* note 12, at 144-47 (discussing the woman's leaving, returning, and leaving again as a process of pulling away from the commitment of marriage and establishing an autonomous life despite insufficient resources to support a family).

293. *See, e.g.*, Okun, *supra* note 107, at 69 (citing several studies describing women's secret savings to allow them to leave abusive relationships).

294. Gillespie, *supra* note 11, at 2.

C. *Strategies for Change and the Redefinition of Separation*

How can we bring the issues of power and control into the courtroom? Can we explain how differently men and women may perceive control?

> I once told a man in a bar that if I was attacked by a man and could somehow fight him off enough to run away, I would consider that I had won the encounter — that I had beaten him. The man said, "No, no, you had to run away, therefore you lost." I said, "No, I was safe, I was unviolated, and therefore I won, I preserved myself." That's what we have to deal with: the way we cope may be very successful, useful, and good — as women — and you can count that as a success. A man could not count refusal to show fear as success. Because he was able to control you as he saw it, show rage, he may think he was successful in that situation as well.

This reflection on the ways men and women perceive control has important implications for the concept of separation assault. The woman defines successful flight from attack as a victory. The man insists that this is not victory but defeat. The persistent accounts of the difficulty women encounter on separation, especially condemnation from their families and employers, suggest society's perceptions track men's interpretations: leaving a violent relationship is widely perceived as an admission of defeat rather than victory. The ways in which separation is similar to the escape from impliedly sexual assault discussed in the quotation above are generally not cognizable at all in law or social discourse. The dangers women face in the effort to separate make separation a victory. These dangers need a name.

Law assumes — pretends — the autonomy of women. Every legal case that discusses the question "why didn't she leave?" implies that the woman *could* have left. We need to challenge the coercion of women's choices, reveal the complexity of women's experience and struggle, and recast the entire discussion of separation in terms of the batterer's violent attempts at control.

Although it is still focused on successful and final separation as the key event, the recently developed term "postseparation woman abuse" begins to grapple with the problem of revealing the issue of power and control in women's experience of violence.[295] At least half of women who leave their abusers are followed and harassed or further attacked by them.[296] In one study of interspousal homicide,[297] more than half

295. *See, e.g.*, Ellis, *supra* note 21, at 410.

296. BROWNE, *supra* note 3, at 110.

297. Until we begin gathering on a broad scale statistics that speak to separation, we are more likely to know if women kill spouses than if men do, since the status of a woman victim as a former partner of the man may or may not appear in police reports and statistics. Since women

of the men who killed their spouses did so when the partners were separated; in contrast, less than ten percent of women who killed were separated at the time.[298] Power and control are crucial here in several ways. Men who kill their wives describe their feeling of loss of control over the woman as a primary factor; most frequently, the man expresses the fear that the woman was about to abandon him, though in fact this fear may have been unfounded.[299] The fact that marital separation increases the instigation to violence[300] shows that these attacks are aimed at preventing or punishing the woman's autonomy. They are major — often deadly — power moves.

However, the term "postseparation woman abuse" fails to capture the many cases where violence occurs in response to the decision itself: the essential attack is on the woman's autonomy. Barbara Hart notes that "[t]he *decision* by a battered woman to leave is often met with escalated violence by the batterer."[301] When the decision, rather than actual separation, triggers the attack, the circumstances of the violence may not reveal the assault on separation: the couple may still have been living together, and the attack may have taken place inside their mutual home — yet the attack may have been a direct response to her assertion of the will to separate or her first physical moves *toward* separation.

Defining Separation Assault

To expose the struggle for control, we should recognize the assault on the woman's separation as a specific type of attack that occurs at or after the moment she decides on a separation or begins to prepare for one. I propose that we call it "separation assault." The varied violent and coercive moves in the process of separation assault can be termed "separation attacks."

Separation assault is the attack on the woman's body and volition in which her partner seeks to prevent her from leaving, retaliate for the separation, or force her to return. It aims at overbearing her will as to where and with whom she will live, and coercing her in order to enforce connection in a relationship. It is an attempt to gain, retain,

kill partners with whom they are still living, this is more likely to be detected as interspousal violence.

298. Barnard et al., *supra* note 270, at 274; *see also* Franklin Zimring et al., *Intimate Violence: A Study of Intersexual Homicide,* 50 U. CHI. L. REV. 910 (1983).

299. Barnard et al., *supra* note 270, at 224.

300. Ellis, *supra* note 21, at 408.

301. Hart, *supra* note 273, at 240 (emphasis added).

or regain power in a relationship, or to punish the woman for ending the relationship. It often takes place over time.

Attacks on separation pervaded the stories of the women who spoke with me. The announcement of intent to separate may be fraught with grave danger:

> He was on strike for the second time in a year. I was pregnant with the second baby in a row. There was absolutely no money. Every day, he yelled at me for a long time — an hour, two hours — about how awful I was. . . . I remember how desperate I felt and how much I needed it to stop.
>
> [One day, when he seemed receptive, she told him it had to stop.] He wouldn't listen. *I said I couldn't live like that anymore and would leave if he didn't stop. He kept saying I couldn't leave because we didn't have enough money to support two households. I said that only his failure to listen could make me leave — I couldn't live like that anymore* . . . .
>
> Suddenly he lost his temper . . . . He stormed upstairs, and I heard him pushing around in the closet. I thought, "That's funny. It sounds like he's getting the gun." And I didn't sit down or move — I stood in the middle of the living room floor and waited. He came down the stairs shouting and I saw that he really did have the shotgun. I knew it was fully loaded. I remember making the conscious decision that this was different than waiting through other outbursts, and that any argument would be deadly.
>
> I turned around and ran out the front door screaming that I was pregnant and ran up the landlady's front steps. I was going to call the police. But I realized that I had heard the baby crying upstairs. All the noise had wakened her from her nap. I couldn't believe he would shoot his child, but I didn't know why he'd gotten the gun, how well he actually knew what he was doing . . . how irritating her crying might be. I turned around and went back into the house. I could hear him putting the gun away in the closet. We got to the baby at the same moment.
>
> I dressed her, put on my own clothes, and left. I had $1.60 and no more money coming for several days. I took the better car. I drove away without knowing where I was going to go. (Emphasis added.)

Although women's stories recount many attacks triggered by separation, the nature of the attack *on separation itself* generally goes unrecognized. Similarly, women describe coercive violence escalating after separation — violence clearly aimed at denying their autonomy — in terms that show they may internalize self-blame rather than clearly identifying the man's attempt at control:

> We had been separated nine months. I came home late one night with a date. I was sitting in the living room playing backgammon with this man, when I saw the car drive up. I thought of sending [my date] home, but I didn't, maybe because I knew I needed help. Maybe I was just defiant.
>
> He knocked. I kept the chain lock on the door, and I told him to go

> home. He wouldn't leave. He rang the bell for fifteen minutes without stopping. I woke up my roommate, and she disconnected the doorbell.
>
> He started pounding on the door. He broke it in and started a fight with this man. I'm sitting there in horror, watching it — the door broken down, them crashing around the living room . . . . The kids woke up. I sat them on the couch with me.
>
> Then — he was *very* drunk — the fighting stopped. It was pretty short. But it took two hours to try to get him to leave. He ran around with a butcher knife . . . he left the house with it. Finally, I could call the police. Then I don't know if he came back in with the knife — I think he came back after the police were called. The kids were on the couch screaming and crying, I was trying to take care of them.
>
> The police saw the door leaning in the middle of the room, the room trashed and crashed. [They refused to arrest him because "his name is still on the lease."] They told me to get a TRO the next day.
>
> I was left to put the pieces back together. And you know what I did? I went and made love to that guy who was there. I had to — anything to not think. I feel kind of whorish about that — I hardly knew him. I didn't even want to, it was 6 a.m., my whole body hurt, I was just exhausted. It seems bizarre.
>
> So I went and got the TRO. Now when I talk about it, I feel like I should be more upset about it.
>
> No, nobody in the building heard anything. They're afraid to. They didn't hear him break down the door, or even ring the doorbell for fifteen minutes in the middle of the night . . . . None of them heard anything!

This woman's sexual choice seems at least partly explicable as a reassertion of control over her body, over her choice in men, and as a specific denial of power to the ex-husband who had put her through so much pain. Her husband might break down the door, but she could affirm her separation again.

Women describe protracted and inventive attacks on their moves to separate:

> Well, leaving took months. When I first left, I really didn't even know I was leaving the marriage. I was just going to California to get the car that he had left there. But being on my own again, and away from him, I began to regain some of my self-confidence, and I liked it. And people liked me.
>
> But then he came out to California to reclaim me. And totally humiliated me in front of my friends. ["Humiliation" including forcing her to have sex — essentially committing marital rape — in the back of a Volkswagen van while two other men were in the vehicle.] I was scared of him, I was still scared of his violence. As strong as I had been when he wasn't around, as soon as he came around, I would fall back into the baby talk, I would fall back into the patterns.
>
> Then we got back to Michigan, and I left again and went to stay with my friends. I was in Ann Arbor, and I had a fever. And he came to check on me . . . . He got my heirloom ring off my finger that night. The

> ring that all my life I felt separated me from poor white trash. The ring that my great-great-grandmother brought over from Germany when she fled the failed revolution of 1848. I never saw that ring again. He threatened to burn down the house I was staying in, but he was satisfied when I gave him the ring because he knew I would come back for it.
>
> I went back again [because he promised to return the ring]. I never got it. And then when it was time for my friends to leave town, they came to our house in Detroit, en masse, and said it was time to go. And I picked up, and I walked out. "Well, it's time to go, we're leaving." And I went.

Some of these attacks on separation will go unnoticed until we begin identifying them specifically:

> I felt guilty, so I went back. That lasted a month, until Valentine's Day . . . . Finally, on Valentine's Day, he was throwing things. He was throwing glass — I was barefoot — it was totally absurd. I was being held prisoner in my bed by glass!
>
> I picked the kids up, scrunched my feet so they were under the glass, dragged my feet over the floor so they weren't getting cut too much, and made it out of the house.

One of the best-known battered women in America is Francine Hughes, whose story was told in *The Burning Bed.* The trial and movie brought the atrocities against her to public attention, but there was little cultural attention to the lessons of her search for autonomy:

> Hughes' entire marriage — and her life after divorce — was a search for the exit. [Family], in-laws, friends, social services, police, sheriff's office, county prosecutor — she tried them all. And even when Mickey Hughes came within moments of choking her to death or cutting her throat, no one helped.[302]

We already recognize the danger of the attack on separation pragmatically and intuitively. This is a major reason for the existence of shelters, which protect women against attacks while giving them a place to live. It is the main reason that shelter numbers and addresses are not listed in telephone directories. It is the main reason women seek protective orders. It fills the pages of our newspapers with accounts of attacks on women by their separated husbands. Although we see this attack everywhere, we cannot analyze it until it has a name.

Naming Separation Assault and Understanding Battering

Naming women's experience is an important component of feminist struggle for social and legal change.[303] Naming separation assault has the potential to change consciousness in a manner comparable to

302. Jones, *supra* note 281, at 296.

303. Kelly, *supra* note 31, at 114-17.

the concept of "date rape." "Date rape" and "separation assault" name phenomena women know from our own experience, but which remain invisible without names.[304] These terms do more, however, than merely identify hitherto unnamed experience. Each term identifies one aspect of a common attack on women in a way that illuminates the whole picture. Date rape is not all rape; separation assault is not the whole story of battering. Yet in each case, the act of identifying and describing the formerly invisible part transforms our understanding of the formerly misunderstood whole.

"Date rape" was a term women recognized when we heard it. It helped popularize a redefinition of the concept of rape: "Acquaintance rape is forced, manipulated or coerced sexual intercourse by a friend or an acquaintance. It is an act of violence, aggression and power."[305] Naming date rape helped move discussion of rape past its old starting point, an image of sexual violence committed by a stranger. The concept of date rape thereby allowed women to recognize that the assault they had experienced was, in fact, rape.

Naming and recognizing separation assault will make women's experience more comprehensible to ourselves as well as to the legal system: We know it when we hear it. Attacks on our autonomy are one point at which women can — without stereotyping or invoking the likelihood of denial — locate our own experiences and those of our sisters and friends on a continuum of control attempts that includes those extremes of violence that become known through the sensational cases covered by the press. Women may find the current terminology of battering stigmatizing or alienating, yet be willing to admit that they have experienced inappropriate control attempts by their partners, including assaults on their capacity to separate from "bad" marriages. Exposing control attempts reveals the woman's struggle, rather than defining her according to the behavior of her assailant.

The name "separation assault" also helps women understand our own long-term reactions to violence or to the threats accompanying the end of relationships. Shelters and counseling provide short-term separation assistance, but the impact of separation assault goes on: Fear of an ex-husband becomes part of a woman's life.

---

304. That which has no name, that for which we have no words or concepts, is rendered mute and invisible; powerless to inform or transform our consciousness of our experience, our understanding, our vision, powerless to claim its own existence.

Barbara DuBois, *Passionate Scholarship: Notes on Values, Knowing and Method in Feminist Social Sciences*, *in* THEORIES OF WOMEN'S STUDIES 105, 108 (Gloria Bowles & Renate Duelli Klein eds., 1983), *quoted in* Kelly, *supra* note 31, at 114. Another example of an assault we must come to recognize is "sexual harassment." *Id.* at 115.

305. AMERICAN COLLEGE HEALTH ASSOCIATION, ACQUAINTANCE RAPE: IS DATING DANGEROUS? (1987).

> The first year I was at Stanford, I saw *The Burning Bed.* I couldn't *not* watch it, and I couldn't stop watching. I was so scared when it finished. I started calling my ex-husband. It was the middle of the night there. I kept calling him frantically for over an hour. He wasn't home. I became convinced he was on his way there with a gun on a plane. I was sure he would kill me.
>
> I locked the door and got in bed with the kids and shook all night, waiting for him. It was two and a half years later. I was two thousand miles away.

This woman had withstood physical attacks before and after separation, as well as poverty, the indignities inflicted by welfare workers, and the threat of a custody suit. Naming the phenomenon that renewed her fear will allow her to recognize her experience and weigh the dangers of her particular situation.[306] When women blame ourselves for the difficulties we face, this internalized fear becomes part of the culture of women, part of advice mothers give to daughters and friends give each other, as marriages fray and when women are threatened. Naming the assault on separation may begin to pull loose the threads of intimidation from the fabric of feminine wisdom, and to legitimate women's perception of danger while directing our attention toward the resources and support we will need, rather than to our own deficiencies or inadequacies.[307]

Popularizing the concept of separation assault is not without hidden dangers, however. Separation assault is effective in part because, rather than *directly* confronting existing stereotypes of battered women, it provides a partial explanation of women's actions that redirects attention toward the batterer. It works in part through its very resonance with existing stereotypes that ask why the woman didn't leave. Therefore, this concept alone cannot remake our understanding of domestic violence; by itself, separation assault becomes merely another explanation of the woman's apparent "failure" to separate — at worst, subtle reinforcement of existing stereotypes. Without further cultural redefinition of battering as a process of power and control, naming separation assault may not deeply challenge oppressive ideology regarding women and domestic violence. However, on a broader scale, separation assault should help the larger goal of shifting cultural perception because it helps change "objective" judgment — that is, shared cultural perceptions and wisdom — about what is normal in

---

306. Hart, *supra* note 273, at 240-49.

307. Women often blame themselves and internalize responsibility for the violence. DOBASH & DOBASH, *supra* note 12, at 119; OKUN, *supra* note 107, at 73. Gondolf and Fisher report studies showing women most likely to blame themselves for the first incident; after that, they increasingly blame the batterer and seek to change him. GONDOLF & FISHER, *supra* note 12, at 16.

relationships. In the next part of this article, I explain how the redefinition of separation described above can help change legal doctrine in several areas by shifting both cultural expectation and judicial inquiry.

V. The Uses of a Name: Separation Assault and Legal Doctrine

Naming separation assault is an attempt to use a social definition, a cultural concept, to resolve doctrinal problems in law. It should not articulate a new test for women's behavior ("did this woman in fact leave and how shall we judge the energy with which she attempted separation?") but rather promote a new understanding of violence against women. As it intervenes in cultural consciousness, separation assault allows legal actors (including attorneys, prosecutors, judges, jurors, social workers, and legal scholars) to reconceive many legal questions that depend on an understanding of women's lives and experiences. Our understanding of "objective" reasonableness depends on our cultural intuitions about normal experience and normal response. By reflecting a consciousness of power and control, and by emphasizing the dangers attendant on separation, separation assault helps make women's experience comprehensible in law.

In the following sections, I show how separation assault can be identified in cases in many areas of legal doctrine, and then explain how understanding separation assault can help resolve troubled areas in law. My review of the cases and doctrines is necessarily partial and suggestive, rather than comprehensive. It is a beginning. It is intended both to invite more discussion of the ways in which litigation can help expose in both law and culture the power and control at the heart of battering, and to invite further analysis of the particular dangers to women at separation.

A. *Recognizing Separation Assault in the Cases: The Problem of the Dead Woman's Voice*

exit n . . . *1:* a departure from a stage
2a: . . . going away *b:* DEATH[308]

There is a two-layered problem in seeing through the criminal cases involving abuse of women. First, these cases appear in various doctrinal guises, and few explicitly acknowledge that they concern domestic violence at all. Second, on closer examination, many of the "wife-murder" cases turn out to be "ex-wife murder," the most ex-

308. Webster's Ninth New Collegiate Dictionary 435 (1988) (capitalization in original).

treme violence turned against women at separation. Many of the women killed by their husbands are killed after they have separated.[309] Ironically, since those women are not alive to tell their stories, their voices disappear into the narrative voices of the courts, where the women are not usually identified as battered:

> On a day in early September in 1977, the petitioner and his wife of 28 years had a heated argument in their home. During the course of this altercation, the petitioner, who had consumed several cans of beer, threatened his wife with a knife and damaged some of her clothing. At this point, the petitioner's wife declared that she was going to leave him, and departed to stay with relatives. [This was not the first time that he and his wife had been separated as a result of his violent behavior.] That afternoon she went to a Justice of the Peace and secured a warrant charging the petitioner with aggravated assault. A few days later, while still living away from home, she filed suit for divorce. [A court hearing date was set and several efforts to persuade the wife to return home were rebuffed.] At some point during this period, his wife moved in with her mother . . . . [Several angry phone calls were exchanged, while she refused to reconcile.]
>
> At this juncture, the petitioner got out his shotgun and walked with it down the hill from his home to the trailer where his mother-in-law lived. Peering through a window, he observed his wife, his mother-in-law, and his 11-year-old daughter playing a card game. He pointed the shotgun at his wife through the window and pulled the trigger. The charge from the gun struck his wife in the forehead and killed her instantly. He proceeded into the trailer, striking and injuring his fleeing daughter with the barrel of the gun. He then fired the gun at his mother-in-law, striking her in the head and killing her instantly.[310]

Godfrey v. Georgia presents an almost perfect picture of the dangers for women at separation: Mrs. Godfrey had resolutely separated from her husband and energetically sought the protection of the law. However, her story does not enter the criminal law casebook[311] as a domestic violence case. Rather, *Godfrey* is a death penalty case presenting the issue of whether this murder was unambiguously "outrageously or wantonly vile, horrible or inhuman," or whether the case revealed ambiguity and vagueness in the death penalty statute. The Supreme Court essentially found Mrs. Godfrey's death to be quite an

309. No one has counted how many women are killed at the moment they announce that they are leaving. However, the fact that more than half of women who leave their husbands are violently harassed was noted by BROWNE, *supra* note 3, at 110. The tendency for separation to actually *increase* the incidence of violence has also been noted. *See* Ellis, *supra* note 21, at 408 (citing several studies).

310. Godfrey v. Georgia, 446 U.S. 420, 424-25 (1980).

311. See, *e.g.*, JOHN KAPLAN & ROBERT WEISBERG, CRIMINAL LAW (2d ed. 1991), which considers *Godfrey* in its section on capital murder. *Id.* at 412. In fact, most casebooks have no category for domestic violence, though "battered woman's syndrome" may enter discussions of the duty to retreat or of diminished capacity defenses.

ordinary murder.[312] I believe the majority was correct — this *was* an ordinary murder — but the facts were even more ordinary than the majority realized.

Mary McNeill has shown that several torts cases on duty are actually domestic violence cases in disguise.[313] However, once the domestic violence is perceived, separation assault appears to be a further hidden issue in at least one of the cases.[314] In *Jablonski by Pahls v. United States,*[315] Melinda Kimball had repeatedly approached the psychologists who examined the man she lived with, telling his doctors that she was afraid of him.[316] They failed to commit him or to seek his medical records, which would have revealed that he had ten years earlier been diagnosed as schizophrenic and had then had homicidal ideas about his wife.[317] One doctor told Kimball that she should avoid Jablonski if she feared him. Kimball left after a priest also urged her to separate from Jablonski. She was murdered when she returned to the apartment to pick up some baby diapers.[318] Since there is no record of any attempt to kill her before she left, separation appears to be at least a precipitating factor in Kimball's death.

In *Garcia v. Superior Court,* Grace Morales was killed by Napoleon Johnson, Jr., the man from whom she had recently separated.[319] According to the complaint, Johnson's parole officer was aware that Johnson had killed his first wife after she left him.[320] Although he was

---

312. "A person of ordinary sensibility could fairly characterize almost every murder as 'outrageously or wantonly vile, horrible and inhuman.' " 446 U.S. at 428-29.

313. Mary McNeill, *Domestic Violence: The Skeleton in* Tarasoff's *Closet, in* DOMESTIC VIOLENCE ON TRIAL, *supra* note 58, at 197.

314. In one of the cases McNeill describes, Hedlund v. Superior Court, 669 P.2d 41 (Cal. 1983), facts in the opinion are insufficient to reveal whether the couple was together or separated when he shot her. Stephen Wilson and La Nita Wilson had sought counseling and psychotherapy together, though the opinion notes that they were not married and that the identity of their last names was in fact coincidental. 669 P.2d at 42-43 & n.4. Stephen had informed his therapists that he intended to "commit serious bodily injury upon" La Nita. 669 P.2d at 43. When Stephen shot her, La Nita saved her three-year-old son Darryl by throwing her body across the child's. 669 P.2d at 46. The questions in the case were whether the psychologists were negligent in failing to diagnose Stephen's dangerousness and warn La Nita, and whether Darryl should recover because of his close relationship with his mother. 669 P.2d at 46, 46 n.7. Some cases McNeill discusses are ambiguous: in Tarasoff v. Regents of Univ. of Cal., 551 P.2d 334 (Cal. 1976), the dead woman had not in fact been in a relationship with her murderer, but he had imagined that a relationship existed and that she had left him. McNeill, *supra* note 313, at 199. *Tarasoff* is therefore a separation assault from the man's point of view — from the woman's, it is a story of a stranger's obsession, a more general lesson in vulnerability to the male imagination.

315. 712 F.2d 391 (9th Cir. 1983).

316. 712 F.2d at 393-94.

317. 712 F.2d at 393-94. Apparently, this was a first wife, given the long time period and different city in which the first events took place. *See* 712 F.2d at 393.

318. 712 F.2d at 394.

319. 789 P.2d 960, 961-62 (Cal. 1990).

320. 789 P.2d at 962.

notified that Johnson had threatened to kill Morales and that Morales was filing a temporary restraining order, the parole officer advised Morales that Johnson would not come looking for her.[321] Johnson kidnapped Morales and killed her; her children sued.[322] The court distinguished the parole officer's "negligent representations" from a failure to warn for which the officer might have been liable under *Tarasoff v. Regents of the University of California,*[323] and held that the plaintiffs must allege that Morales reasonably relied on the parole officer's advice.[324]

The California case of *People v. Berry,* doctrinally significant for its holding on cooling off periods when killers claim provocation by their victims, also concerns a hidden separation assault.[325] The only account of the marriage is the one Berry gave the police and at trial. According to Berry's story, his wife, Rachel Pessah, had gone to Israel within days of their marriage; on her return, she taunted him about her love for another man and her plans to leave Berry.[326] After repeated arguments and threats or attempts to separate, he tried to strangle her.[327] He called a cab to take her to a hospital, and she later filed a police report that resulted in a warrant for his arrest.[328] He told her he was leaving their home and going to stay with a friend. Two days later, he returned to the apartment and waited overnight. She returned the next day and said she supposed he had come to kill her. He was indecisive, but said he had. She screamed. He strangled her.[329]

Even feminist literature on battering may overlook the particularity of attacks on women's autonomy. For example, the feminist newsletter *Response* cites the 1988 case of *Balistreri v. Pacifica Police Department*[330] in a short article entitled "Court Rules in Favor of Abused Wife." The one-paragraph article describes Balistreri as

> an abused wife who sued police for not protecting her. . . . Police had refused to arrest the batterer when summoned following a beating, failed to offer medical assistance, and did not protect the woman over a 3-year

321. 789 P.2d at 962.

322. 789 P.2d at 961.

323. 551 P.2d 334 (Cal. 1976), *distinguished in Garcia,* 789 P.2d at 963.

324. 789 P.2d at 963.

325. 556 P.2d 777 (Cal. 1976).

326. 556 P.2d at 779. The expert testimony on Rachel's provocative behavior was based entirely on Berry's account of Rachel's words.

327. 556 P.2d at 779.

328. 556 P.2d at 778-79.

329. 556 P.2d at 779. His previous marriage had also ended violently. Reporter's Transcript at 245-53 (on file with the author).

330. 855 F.2d 1421 (9th Cir. 1988), *amended on other grounds,* 901 F.2d 696 (9th Cir. 1990).

period during which she reported incidents to police and obtained a restraining order.[331]

Most of the facts of *Balistreri* concern attacks after separation. When Balistreri's husband beat her severely in February 1982, officers failed to help her.[332] She divorced her husband — apparently promptly, because "throughout 1982" she complained to police of vandalism and harassing phone calls by the husband "from whom she was now divorced."[333] In November that year, her "former husband" crashed his car into her garage, and in March 1983, a firebomb was thrown through the window of her house.[334] From 1983 to 1985, telephone harassment and vandalism continued.[335] Balistreri emerges as a woman of great strength — resisting her ex-husband's repeated attacks and pursuing her complaint within the legal system when her lawyer would go no further.[336] "Abused wife," the term used by *Response,* captures neither her determined resistance nor her separation as the keys to the repeated violence she suffered.

B. *Recognizing the Danger to Women at Separation*

Recognizing the assault on separation can help disentangle a number of complex legal issues in cases in which women have been killed or harmed. In some areas of substantive law, identifying separation assault will change the questions posed by the court in its decisionmaking process. In other doctrinal areas, the shift in time frame made possible by highlighting the assault on separation can change judicial comprehension of the assault on the woman or of the probability that more assaults may occur. Separation assault may also, as in contested custody actions, help reveal underlying motivations in the legal action itself.

Restraining Orders

In some jurisdictions, when women seek orders of protection

331. *Court Rules in Favor of Abused Wife,* 11 RESPONSE TO THE VICTIMIZATION OF WOMEN AND CHILDREN No. 3, 19 (1988).

332. *Balistreri,* 901 F.2d at 698. It seems (from dates given for violent episodes) that the first beating mentioned in the complaint may have taken place in close connection with separation, but the facts in the opinion do not demonstrate this clearly.

333. The second amended opinion in *Balistreri* uses the present tense here — "from whom she is now divorced," 901 F.2d at 698 — but the first opinion used the past tense, 855 F.2d at 1423. The past tense is likely correct here, since both opinions refer to her "former husband" during this period.

334. 901 F.2d at 698.

335. 901 F.2d at 698.

336. Balistreri won her appeal pro se; her lawyer had refused to continue working on the case after the initial dismissal for failure to state a claim. 855 F.2d at 1423.

against violent men, courts routinely grant mutual orders of protection rather than orders specifically protecting the women.[337] Mutual orders of protection direct each party not to assault, endanger, or threaten the other.[338] If mutual orders are violated, police officers believe they must either arrest both parties or do nothing. The New York Task Force on Women in the Courts concluded that a woman with a mutual order of protection is in a worse position than a woman with no order at all, since the mutual order makes her look equally violent in the eyes of the courts, and the husband may not be held responsible if there is another violent incident. Also, it may be harder for her to obtain a more restrictive order if the violence recurs.[339] The Task Force concluded that this was particularly dangerous if the mutual order was granted when the woman had requested protection for herself at the same time she filed an action to end the marriage — an especially dangerous period.[340] Even in jurisdictions that do not routinely grant mutual orders, battering men may make cross-accusations of violence against battered women. While many battered women do fight back against their husbands, their violence is largely defensive and less severe than the men's violence — yet since it is also described as "violence," these allegations can prove troubling and confusing to judges.[341]

If we understood better the particular attacks women face at separation, courts could sort both cross-accusations of violence and requests for mutual orders of protection by examining the nature of current threats and the history of violence in relation to the issue of separation. The question then becomes: "Which of these people needs her [or his] capacity to separate protected?" Answering this question will help sort the dangers and should result in the grant of appropriate protective orders.

Duty to Warn

Recognizing the common occurrence of separation assault may also clarify professionals' duty to warn potential victims. For example, the *Jablonski* court upheld the district court's finding that the psychiatrists committed malpractice in failing to get Jablonski's records and failing to warn Kimball of his potential for violence.[342] Applying

337. *New York Task Force Report, supra* note 51, at 38.

338. *Id.*

339. *Id.* at 39.

340. *Id.* at 40.

341. Saunders, *supra* note 38, at 103-08.

342. Jablonski by Pahls v. United States, 712 F.2d 391, 398 (9th Cir. 1983).

the concept of separation assault does not disturb this holding. Her foreseeability as a victim would be even clearer. However, the clergyman and doctors who advised Kimball to leave Jablonski might also have had a duty to warn her about extra care to be exercised in *separating* from a homicidal man, as well as a duty to warn her of his dangerousness.

In *Garcia v. Superior Court,*[343] Johnson's murder of his first wife was a separation assault of exactly the type that Johnson had threatened against Morales. The parole officer misrepresented Johnson's danger to Morales with respect to the very issue of measures regarding *separation.* Although the parole officer was legally barred from telling anyone the exact crime for which Johnson had previously been imprisoned,[344] the court fails to reckon with the implications of the outright falsehood embodied in the parole officer's statement that Johnson's prior conviction was not for anything that endangered Morales' children.[345]

A telling quote in the *Garcia* dissent shows that judges may inappropriately assume that separation assaults will inevitably culminate in murder: the court below had concluded "it [was] highly speculative to assume that [Morales] could have accomplished any improvement in her security. The frightening reality is that for one in Morales's position there is frequently nothing she can do to protect herself."[346] When courts rely on their own intuitions to state "truths" regarding violence against women, the dangers of cultural stereotyping are severe.[347] A sense of the dangers of separation should have led the court to emphasize the need not to mislead Morales as to her safety and to recognize the implications of consciously identifying the assault on separation.

---

343. 789 P.2d 960 (Cal. 1990).

344. 789 P.2d at 962 n.2.

345. The children are suing for the loss of their mother; both the possibility of her murder and the possibility of harm to themselves in the course of a murderous attack were "danger" shown by Johnson's prior conviction.

346. Garcia v. Superior Court, 249 Cal. Rptr. 449, 454 (Cal. Ct. App. 1988), *quoted in* 789 P.2d 960 (Cal. 1990) (Mosk, J., dissenting). The dissent criticized the majority opinion for essentially adopting the same view the intermediate appellate court had held. 789 P.2d at 970 (Mosk, J., dissenting).

347. *See, e.g.,* Susan Mann, *The Universe and the Library: A Critique of James Boyd White as Writer and Reader,* 41 STAN. L. REV. 959, 1004 (1989) (describing oral argument during which a judge in the Third Circuit Court of Appeals noted that violent couples usually reconciled, regarding a case in which a man killed his *separated* partner). Mann argues for the attempt to reach judges emotionally (through use of narrative). This has some conceptual similarity to my suggested use of a cultural concept to convince judges of the danger to women.

Custody Determinations: Understanding Dominance and Time-Framing Assault

The concept of separation assault provides insight into the difficult bargains women strike during custody determinations. Women may accept mutual orders of protection, rather than orders that specifically protect them against their batterers, in exchange for the husband's agreement not to contest custody.[348] Courts often award joint custody to batterers, and some courts that do not perceive violence against the mother as an aspect of the custody determination may even award them sole custody.[349] The problem is exacerbated for battered women by the professional analyses of the social workers in whom the court vests the power to evaluate women, and by the possibility that the judge will share a stereotypical, stigmatizing image of battered women.

Separation assault provides a link between past violence and current legal disputes by illuminating the custody action as *part of* an ongoing attempt, through physical violence and legal manipulation,[350] to force the woman to make concessions or return to the violent partner. It reveals the potential for continuing danger from a batterer who may not have struck out physically in the recent past. Threats against the woman's separation attempts may reveal that the "domestic" violence has outlasted the marriage. Recognizing separation assault can therefore help judges understand the relevance of past violence and threats, and the relevance of the nature of present attacks, to custody cases. Also, when there is evidence of violent separation assault, a judge could give more intense scrutiny to the motives behind custody disputes and reconsider the appropriateness of joint custody awards or liberal visitation decrees. This would help diminish "legal separation assault" in custody cases. Finally, by remaking the cultural concept of separation, we may hope to affect positively the evaluation of women by the social workers in whom the legal system places so much power.

Judging the Wife-Killer: Time-Framing, Provocation, and the Nature of the Assault

In *Berry,* the defendant's arguments for a jury instruction on provocation depended entirely upon his statements that his wife had taunted him sexually and provoked her own murder.[351] In fact, he did

348. *New York Task Force Report, supra* note 51, at 40 n.84.

349. *Id.* at 41-42; *Achieving Equal Justice, supra* note 41, at 37 (less than half of judges surveyed viewed spousal abuse as a reason not to award joint custody).

350. Batterers may seek custody as part of an overall attempt to continue controlling the woman and to punish her for separating. Walker & Edwall, *supra* note 200, at 140.

351. People v. Berry, 556 P.2d 777, 778-80 (Cal. 1976).

not kill her when she taunted him, but when she left him.[352] Recognizing separation assault expands the relevant time frame to show his behavior was consistent with numerous prior assaults that seem at least as responsive to her departure as to sexual provocation. He had violently assaulted his first wife as well.[353] *Berry* is cited for its holding that twenty hours of waiting in the apartment — some days after his wife's last "provocative" conduct — was not as a matter of law too long a period to permit an instruction on provocation. The court might have viewed the case differently had the assault on separation been as cognizable as his response to her alleged sexual taunts: it is difficult to find "heat-of-passion" in a repeatedly attempted assault carried out over a period of time.[354]

A short time frame favors men in these cases, as it does in many types of cases, by removing violence from a context of power and struggle.[355] Prior attacks on the woman's attempts to separate may essentially be rehearsals for the final killing.[356] Alternatively, the long-term assault on her separation may be perceived as one ongoing attack. If only the final, deadly assault is cognizable, the nature of the assault as an attack on separation, rather than on the woman's sexual provocation, may remain disguised.[357] Separation assault can therefore change the time frame within which the man's mental state is to be evaluated by changing the perception of the ways in which the woman's autonomy is under attack.

C. *Live Women and Dead Men: The Self-Defense Cases*

The self-defense cases, which often have an extraordinarily high level of violence against women, have exercised a powerful influence on the literature on battering. Expert testimony on battered woman syndrome and learned helplessness was first introduced to explain the

352. 556 P.2d at 780-81.

353. He stabbed her with a kitchen knife. Berry's account of his assault on his first wife shows that both sexual jealousy and fear of separation were present in that relationship as well. Reporter's Transcript, at 252-53 (on file with author).

354. In *Terrifying Love,* Lenore Walker describes a case in which the judge found the woman's act of separation to have been provocation for the man's murderous attack. The case was later reversed, however. WALKER, *supra* note 11, at 66-69.

355. *See supra* text accompanying note 350 (custody cases); *infra* notes 371-77 and accompanying text (self-defense cases).

356. I am indebted to Donna Coker for suggesting this possibility. Conversation with Donna Coker, *supra* note 67.

357. This is a similar process to the criticism of sociological studies that only examine an accretion of acts of violence stripped of context and thereby distort the severity and meaning of acts of domestic violence. *See* Hoff, *supra* note 101, at 271-72.

woman's actions and mental state in these cases.[358] The idea that the woman should have left the relationship, and especially the idea that she failed to leave, shapes the courts' analyses of many aspects of self-defense cases, including the reasonableness of the woman's perceptions and reactions, the imminence of the threat of death or great bodily harm, and her duty to retreat from the confrontation. In this section I first examine the relationship between the concepts of separation assault and learned helplessness. I then illustrate the relevance of the concept of separation assault to the issues of imminent danger and the reasonableness of the woman's perception that self-defense is necessary.

Learned Helplessness Revisited: The Bars of the Cage

Expert testimony on battered woman's syndrome often notes the danger of women's moves to separate from violent relationships. In a recent case,[359] a California appellate court summarized Lenore Walker's testimony on battered woman's syndrome, describing the syndrome as the natural result of trauma to women. The court set forth an analysis of why women "stay in the abusive relationship," including some emphasis on the dangers of separation:

> Terminating the relationship usually has adverse economic consequences. Separating from a battering partner may be very dangerous, and the battered woman is aware of the danger. The batterer may have threatened to kill the battered woman or to abscond with the children if she leaves. Many battered women have tried to leave and been unsuccessful. In a battering relationship, the woman loses self-esteem, is terrified, and does not have the psychological energy to leave, resulting in "learned helplessness" and "a kind of psychological paralysis."[360]

The court described a woman's "learned helplessness" as caused by random and unpredictable violence, which led her to believe that she was "incapable of doing anything to prevent the abuse." This court received a sophisticated explanation of the impact battering has on women. Yet, as the court in turn explains the woman's situation, the objective difficulties of leaving and subjective fear and helplessness are both present, but seem unrelated.

---

358. *See, e.g.,* State v. Kelly: *Amicus Briefs, supra* note 8; *supra* notes 138-48 and accompanying text.

359. *People v. Aris,* 264 Cal. Rptr. 167 (Cal. Ct. App. 1989). In *Aris,* the defendant had shot and killed her sleeping husband. She appealed the exclusion of portions of proffered expert testimony on battered women and the refusal to offer jury instructions on perfect self-defense. 264 Cal. Rptr. at 171.

360. 264 Cal. Rptr. at 178. Other factors listed by the court included periodic positive reinforcement during the "loving contrition" stage of the battering cycle, and cultural training of all women to be peacekeepers, playing optimistic and hopeful roles in relationships. 264 Cal. Rptr. at 178.

Despite its generally sympathetic attention to Walker's testimony on battered woman syndrome, the court found harmless error in excluding her further testimony, which would have linked battered woman syndrome with "the psychological symptoms and the psychological impact on the person's state of mind at the time of the homicide."[361] According to the court, no jury could have found that the defendant was in imminent danger of harm from her sleeping husband at the time she shot him.[362] Although separation assaults had occurred,[363] the court did not weigh these past assaults on her capacity to leave when finding no imminent danger from his threat to kill her.

Learned helplessness is in essence a theory of deficiency at perceiving exit. Separation assault confirms the difficulties of exit. Separation assault does not contradict the possibility of developing learned helplessness; the woman's subjective belief could still overestimate the difficulties of leaving. Naming separation assault implies no attempt to measure the accuracy at any particular moment of a particular woman's belief in the possibility or practicality of separation. Rather, by supporting the woman's rational perception of danger, the concept of separation assault supports that aspect of battered woman's syndrome which emphasizes the woman's reasonableness and the normal character of her reaction to violence.

Separation assault is also consistent with the behavioral psychology experiments underlying learned helplessness theory.[364] Walker's discussion of Seligman's dog experiment barely mentions the cages in which the dogs were held.[365] Yet if the dogs had not been trapped, the shocks could not have had the same debilitating effect. Walker also described a less famous learned helplessness experiment in which baby rats were repeatedly held until they ceased struggling: when placed in water, the rats drowned because they sank immediately or gave up swimming soon. The rats were not shocked — it was essentially an experiment in captivity.[366] Captivity is an important though under-

---

361. 264 Cal. Rptr. at 178.

362. 264 Cal. Rptr. at 181. The night of the killing, he said he did not think he would let her live until morning. 264 Cal. Rptr. at 171.

363. The defendant had repeatedly left her husband, but "[b]y a mixture of threats and cajoling, he invariably convinced her to take him back." 264 Cal. Rptr. at 171.

364. LENORE WALKER, *supra* note 40, at 45-47.

365. In derivative descriptions of learned helplessness, the cages may virtually disappear as a factor in creating helplessness. *See, e.g.*, GONDOLF & FISHER, *supra* note 12, at 13 ("The animals after a series of intermittent electric shocks, eventually became immobilized. They could not escape from their cages even when an open route was provided for them.").

366. LENORE WALKER, *supra* note 40, at 46-47.

emphasized component of learned helplessness — not merely the result of a psychological process that makes a woman unable to get out.

The question "why didn't she leave?" reflects a cultural failure to recognize the bars that imprison the woman in a violent marriage. Since separation assault appears in the cases where women are killed or harmed as well as the self-defense cases, the concept of separation assault helps reveal the real and deadly constraints within which learned helplessness develops. The concept of separation assault thus does not challenge the concepts of battered woman's syndrome and learned helplessness. Rather, it explains the experience of many women who may not fit well with the phenomena that distinguish learned helplessness.[367] For example, in *Fennell v. Goolsby,*[368] a federal district court described Karen Anne Fennell as an atypical battered woman because she had obtained a court order to have her husband ejected from the home and had been separated for six months.[369] She had suffered incessant threats and harassment during the separation.[370] The concept of separation assault would have helped refute the court's assumption that typical battered women do not seek court orders and emphasized the need for expert testimony to explain to the jury the link between Karen Anne Fennell's experience and that of other battered women.

Finally, naming separation assault cannot end the need for expert testimony on the subject of battered woman's syndrome and learned helplessness. Collectively, the jury can only "know" what it is possible for them to discuss. Women will still find it impossible to incorporate our own experience in the jury room unless the lens through which we perceive battered women has been entirely transformed. Men will also remain unable to discuss their experience as witnesses to violence against women or their capacity to seek control violently. As long as we have no way to discuss or understand the violence many of us have experienced — or to sort out what we have heard from others — there remains a critical need for expert testimony to explain to the jury things beyond their capacity for collective knowledge and discussion, even if these things are within their individual personal experience.

367. Blackman, *supra* note 3, at 127-28 (noting that even severely battered women may not fit the images described by battered woman syndrome and learned helplessness descriptions).

368. 630 F. Supp. 451 (E.D. Pa. 1985).

369. 630 F. Supp. at 459-60 & n.4.

370. 630 F. Supp. at 457. The court found it had been error to exclude battered woman's syndrome testimony, but not constitutional error for purposes of habeas corpus. 630 F. Supp. at 460-61. Even if it were constitutional error, it was harmless beyond a reasonable doubt because two psychiatrists testified to her mental state. 630 F. Supp. at 461.

Questions of Timing, Captivity, and "Objective" Perception

The concept of "separation assault" brings the ghosts of dead women — women slain by their abusers — into court to stand beside the woman accused of killing an abusive spouse. The facts behind many, perhaps most,[371] self-defense cases reveal that the woman's separation has been repeatedly and successfully attacked before she finally kills her abuser.[372] With its implicit reminder of women killed during separation attacks, the concept of separation assault makes sense of the woman's fear of death and her compliance in the face of the violence that ended her previous separations. Further, by describing an assault that by its nature takes place over time, the concept of separation assault extends the time frame weighed by the court and expands the relevance of past attacks on the woman.[373] Finally, of crucial impor-

---

371. We will not know how many are separation attacks until we ask question designed to elicit information about the various types of assault leveled against the woman's moves to separate. The facts that appear in court opinions may include some — but not all — of the ways the woman's separation was attacked.

372. Ann Jones vividly describes the assaults on the efforts to separate of many women who ultimately killed battering men, either during or after the separation attack, often after being held prisoner or prevented from leaving at all in a variety of ways:

> Homicide is a last resort, and it most often occurs when men simply will not quit. As one woman testified at her murder trial, "It seemed like the more I tried to get away, the harder he beat me." Gloria Timmons left her husband, but he kept tracking her down, raping and beating her; finally when he attacked her with a screwdriver, she shot him. Patricia Evans filed for divorce, but her husband kept coming back to beat her with a dog chain, pistol-whip her, and shoot at her. At last, after she had been hospitalized seven times, she shot him. . . . Janice Strand was forced to return to her husband when he threatened her parents' lives. Patricia Gross' husband tracked her from Michigan to Mississippi and threatened to kill her relatives there to force her to return to him. . . . Mary McGuire's husband, teaching submission, made her watch him dig her grave, kill the family cat, and decapitate a pet horse. When she fled he brought her back with a gun held to her child's head. . . . Agnes Scott's husband found her and cut her up seven years after she left him. There are cases on record of men still harassing and beating their wives twenty-five years after the wives left them and tried to go into hiding. If researchers were not quite so intent upon assigning the pathological behavior to the women, they might see that the more telling question is not "Why do the women stay?" but "Why don't the men let them go?"

JONES, *supra* note 21, at 298-99.

373. Shifting the time frame may also be useful in jurisdictions that impose a duty to retreat before using deadly force in self-defense. Retreat can be reconceptualized as a question of the scope of the attack. First, the prevalence of separation attack means that retreat may only stimulate the man's violence. Second, by expanding the description of the time period involved in the assault on the woman, the concept of separation assault helps move toward dynamic portrayal of the power and control in the relationship. Finally, recognizing separation assault would permit us to argue that a woman need only fulfill her duty to retreat once — that she need not retreat an unlimited number of times from dangerous assaults — and that any woman who has had her separation violently attacked has already fulfilled her duty to retreat. For this question, at least, the proof of past separation assault could itself be taken as the answer to a legal question.

Although only a minority of states impose a duty to retreat when an individual is attacked in the home by another legal resident of that home, see Thomas Katheder, Case Note, *Lovers and Other Strangers: Or, When Is a House a Castle,* 11 FLA. ST. U. L. REV. 465, 473-74 nn.40-41 (1983), the question "why didn't she leave" is, subtextually, a question of retreat any time it is posed in relation to the period directly preceding the assault, rather than to the woman's role in the entire relationship. *See* Walker, Thyfault & Browne, *Beyond the Jurors' Ken: Battered Women,* 7 VT. L. REV. 1, 5 (1982). Retreat is a hidden question in cases like *Stewart* and *Norman,*

tance in women's self-defense claims, this reconceptualization of the assault on the woman helps clarify the existence of imminent danger of death or great bodily harm.

Imminence has proved crucial in cases involving the death of sleeping husbands. Two states have recently held that women who shot sleeping husbands were not entitled to jury instructions on self-defense because the woman faced no *imminent* danger of death or grave bodily harm.[374] This meaning of imminent harm is not universal. "Imminent" is often distinguished from "immediate," and courts and scholars have criticized decisions that confuse the two.[375] The Model Penal Code does not require that the danger actually be immediate: rather, the actor must believe that the defensive action is immediately necessary and that the force against which she defends will be used on the present occasion, "but he [sic] need not apprehend that it will be immediately used."[376] Some states have overturned jury instructions that required that the attack on the woman pose an "immediate" danger of death or great bodily harm, and have upheld statutory standards that require only that the harm be "imminent," a term that broadens the context to include more of the facts and circumstances of the woman's experience in the relationship.[377] Even when a statute required "immediate danger," one court has required an overall consideration of the woman's circumstances and described as "imminent," rather than immediate, the threat necessary to justify the use of deadly force.[378] Therefore, the recent decisions construing imminence as virtually equivalent to immediacy place significant limits on the ability of women to raise claims that they acted in self-defense.

---

in which the woman's ability to leave the house rather than shoot her abuser is explicitly raised by the majority opinions. State v. Stewart, 763 P.2d 572, 578 (Kan. 1988); State v. Norman, 378 S.E.2d 8, 13 (N.C. 1989). By shifting the lens to emphasize prior assaults on separation, women who have fled in the past can be shown to have fulfilled a duty to retreat — whether this duty is explicitly imposed by law or implicitly read into a situation by the way a judge perceived the facts.

374. *Stewart,* 763 P.2d at 573; *Norman,* 378 S.E.2d at 8-9; *see also* People v. Aris, 264 Cal. Rptr. 167 (Cal. Ct. App. 1989).

375. *See, e.g., Norman,* 378 S.E.2d at 13 (noting that interpreting "imminent" to mean "immediate" effectively denies a woman the right to self-defense); GILLESPIE, *supra* note 11, at 64-77, 185-87; *see also* State v. Hodges, 716 P.2d 563, 570-71 (Kan. 1986). *But see* Cathryn Jo Rosen, *The Excuse of Self-Defense: Correcting a Historical Accident on Behalf of Battered Women Who Kill,* 36 AM. U. L. REV. 11, 29 n.107 (common law usually equated imminence with immediacy, though Model Penal Code does not).

376. MODEL PENAL CODE § 3.04 cmt. 2(c)(1985), *quoted in Norman,* 378 S.E.2d at 19 n.1 (Martin, J., dissenting).

377. *See* GILLESPIE, *supra* note 11, at 185-87; *see also Hodges,* 716 P.2d 563; State v. Osbey, 710 P.2d 676 (Kan. 1985), State v. Hundley, 693 P.2d 475 (Kan. 1985).

378. State v. Gallegos, 719 P.2d 1268 (N.M. Ct. App. 1986); *see also* State v. Wanrow, 559 P.2d 548 (Wash. 1977). The jury instruction using an immediacy standard was held to overly restrict the inquiry into the defendant's circumstances. 559 P.2d at 555-56.

State v. Stewart[379] is the latest in a line of Kansas cases to grapple with the meaning of "imminent" and the relevant context for evaluating the woman's action. *Stewart* marks a return to a requirement of immediacy despite a factual background that strongly suggested an expanded contextual approach was relevant. Peggy Stewart married Mike Stewart in 1974.[380] She had two young daughters, Carla and Laura, from previous marriages. Mike was abusive from the beginning. Peggy soon developed severe psychological problems and was treated for schizophrenia.[381] Mike tampered with her medication, forcing her to take too much at times and to do without her medication at other times.[382] Mike severely abused Peggy's daughter Carla. When he ordered Peggy to kill and bury Carla, Peggy filed for divorce,[383] but the case does not indicate that she followed through with the divorce action. When Carla was twelve years old, Mike threw her out of the house with "no coat, no money, and no place to go."[384] He forbade Peggy to have any contact with Carla.[385] Laura left home as soon as she could.[386]

Both the majority and dissenting opinions in *Stewart* chronicle an extraordinarily violent and abusive marriage in which Peggy's life was repeatedly threatened. Mike shot Peggy's cats and then held the gun to Peggy's head, threatening to shoot;[387] another time, he threatened her with a loaded shotgun. She told her friends she believed he would kill her one day.[388] Finally, Peggy ran away to Laura's house in another state.[389] Peggy was suicidal, and Laura had her admitted to a mental hospital, where she was diagnosed as having reacted to an overdose of her medication.[390] Though Peggy told a nurse that she felt like she wanted to shoot Mike, the nurse noted that Peggy's main emotion seemed to be hopelessness.[391] Mike telephoned the hospital

379. 763 P.2d 572 (Kan. 1988).

380. 763 P.2d at 574.

381. 763 P.2d at 574.

382. 763 P.2d at 574 (made her take more than prescribed medication); 763 P.2d at 581 (Herd, J., dissenting) (overdosed her on medication and then cut it off).

383. 763 P.2d at 574.

384. 763 P.2d at 574.

385. 763 P.2d at 574.

386. 763 P.2d at 581 (Herd, J., dissenting).

387. 763 P.2d at 575.

388. 763 P.2d at 575.

389. The court states that this was the first time she left Mike without telling him. 763 P.2d at 575. However, it could not have been her first attempt to separate, since the facts reveal that a divorce action was at least undertaken at some earlier time.

390. 763 P.2d at 575.

391. 763 P.2d at 581 (Herd, J., dissenting).

to say he was coming to get her, and she agreed to leave with him.[392] At trial, she testified that she decided to go with him because the hospital did not provide the medical help she needed.[393]

Mike drove Peggy back to Kansas. He told her that "if she ever ran away again, he would kill her."[394] He "forced Peggy into the house and forced her to have oral sex several times"[395] with such force that the inside of her mouth was bruised[396] — that is, he raped her repeatedly — while telling her how much he preferred other women. She discovered bullets and a loaded gun, which frightened her because he had promised to keep his guns unloaded.[397] She hid the gun.[398] Mike made repeated remarks indicating that "she would not be there long, and could not take her things where she was going," which led her to think that he meant she would soon be dead.[399] He ceased the abuse for a brief period while his parents came over to visit, then forced her to perform oral sex again and demanded that she come to bed with him. As he slept, she heard voices telling her "kill or be killed." Peggy got the gun she had found and hidden earlier, and she shot Mike as he slept.[400]

The Kansas Supreme Court held Peggy was not entitled to a jury instruction on self-defense, since she was in no imminent danger when she shot Mike. "Under such circumstances, a battered woman cannot reasonably fear imminent life-threatening danger from her sleeping spouse."[401] The court distinguished three of its prior cases in which abused women had killed violent husbands. In *State v. Hundley,*[402] *State v. Osbey,*[403] and *State v. Hodges,*[404] the Kansas Supreme Court had held that the statutory requirement of imminence permitted consideration of the history and gradual build-up of violence within a relationship as well as the immediate acts of the batterer. Although

392. 763 P.2d at 581 (Herd, J., dissenting).

393. 763 P.2d at 575.

394. 763 P.2d at 581 (Herd, J., dissenting).

395. 763 P.2d at 575.

396. 763 P.2d at 581 (Herd, J., dissenting).

397. 763 P.2d at 575.

398. 763 P.2d at 575.

399. 763 P.2d at 575.

400. 763 P.2d at 575.

401. 763 P.2d at 578. The court also overruled an earlier holding that measured the reasonableness of perception of harm from the subjective viewpoint of the battered woman. 763 P.2d at 579 (overruling in part State v. Hodges, 716 P.2d 563 (Kan. 1986)). *See infra* text accompanying notes 425-27.

402. 693 P.2d 475 (Kan. 1985).

403. 710 P.2d 676 (Kan. 1985).

404. *Hodges,* 716 P.2d 563.

none of these had directly confronted the question of the propriety of giving a self-defense instruction,[405] they had rejected the use of the term "immediate" in explaining the imminence standard.[406] The *Stewart* court did not directly overrule its prior holdings but distinguished the previous imminence cases as "involv[ing] a threat of death to the wife and a violent confrontation between husband and wife, contemporaneous with the shooting."[407] As the *Stewart* dissent pointed out, however, this holding effectively replaced the state's prior definition of "imminent" with an immediacy standard.[408]

In holding that there was no "imminent" threat to Peggy, the majority ignored the imprisoning effect of Mike's bringing her back from another state after her effort to separate and his threat to kill her if she left again. In contrast, the dissent emphasized Mike's threat to kill Peggy if she separated from him again.[409] The concept of an assault on separation continued over time may help courts appreciate the crucial distinction between imminence and immediacy in self-defense cases such as *Stewart*.

Separation assault can help reveal captivity. In *Hundley*, the Kansas Supreme Court drew an analogy between battered women and hostages or prisoners of war.[410] The *Stewart* dissent repeated this analogy and argued the *Stewart* holding would preclude finding imminence in "a hostage situation where the armed guard inadvertently drops off to sleep and the hostage grabs his gun and shoots him."[411] This could be a persuasive analogy: If a hostage were told, "you will be killed in three days," the danger would still appear imminent even if not immediate.[412] The question of imminence therefore appears to be affected by an assessment of the nature and degree of the hostage's captivity; the persuasive power of the hostage analogy depends on the recognition that the woman in an abusive relationship is not free to leave. At issue is our understanding of the woman's functional autonomy. The key difference between the analysis of the majority and dissent in *Stew-*

---

405. 763 P.2d at 578. *Hodges*, for example, dealt with the language of the self-defense instruction. 716 P.2d at 570-71. The state apparently did not object to the giving of a self-defense instruction in that case.

406. 763 P.2d at 584-85 (Herd, J., dissenting).

407. 763 P.2d at 578.

408. 763 P.2d at 584-85 (Herd, J., dissenting).

409. 763 P.2d at 581 (Herd, J., dissenting).

410. State v. Hundley, 693 P.2d 475, 479 (Kan. 1985).

411. 763 P.2d at 584 (Herd, J., dissenting).

412. I am indebted to Mary Coombs for this discussion. Conversation with Mary Coombs, (Sept. 1990); *see also* M.J. Willoughby, Comment, *Rendering Each Woman Her Due: Can A Battered Woman Claim Self-Defense When She Kills Her Sleeping Batterer?*, 38 U. KAN. L. REV. 169, 184-85 (1990) (comparing battered women to hostages).

art is how seriously each takes the constraints Mike imposed on Peggy's capacity to separate.

Had the *Stewart* majority been able to perceive Mike's successful assault on Peggy's separation, they could have found a common thread of separation assault linking *Stewart* with *Hundley, Osbey,* and *Hodges.*[413] In *Hundley,* the wife shot her husband as he attacked her in the motel room to which she had moved after leaving him.[414] In *Osbey,* the wife had insisted on a separation after a history of substantial abuse.[415] The husband was in the process of moving out when he changed his mind, telling a friend he had put too much time into his wife's house and that "it would be either [him] or her."[416] He had [previously] threatened her with a gun.[417] She shot him when she thought he reached for a weapon as he attempted to return some of his belongings to the apartment.[418] In *Hodges,* the wife had continually left her husband early in their marriage only to have him pursue her and brutally fetch her back. On one such occasion

> [H]e took her to a wooded location where he beat her, broke her jaw, and said she was either going to live with him or she wasn't going to live. He left her there unconscious, but eventually returned, took her to the hospital, and told her to tell the hospital staff she fell down. She returned home with him because he had her children.[419]

She finally succeeded in divorcing him but reunited thirteen years later because he promised he had changed.[420] When the beatings did not stop, she left again; however, when he again brought her back, she gave up trying to leave him. He had also threatened her family if they ever helped her leave him.[421] She shot him as he engaged in yet another bout of violence.[422]

The concept of separation assault thus bridges the difference between cases like *Stewart* that involve sleeping husbands and those like *Hundley, Osbey,* and *Hodges* that involve waking husbands. In

413. Unsuccessful separation attempts are also present in many other cases on self-defense and battered woman's syndrome. For example, in State v. Gallegos, 719 P.2d 1268 (N.M. Ct. App. 1986), the woman told the man in the midst of a long day of violence that she was tired of being hurt and that she would leave him. He "pulled out his gun and threatened to kill her if she left." 719 P.2d at 1272. Similarly, in Smith v. State, 277 S.E.2d 678 (Ga. 1983), Jo Smith tried to flee before her attacker slammed the door on her; finally, she shot him. 277 S.E.2d at 679.

414. 693 P.2d at 476.

415. 710 P.2d at 677-78.

416. 710 P.2d at 678.

417. 710 P.2d at 678.

418. 710 P.2d at 678.

419. 716 P.2d at 566-67.

420. 716 P.2d at 566-67.

421. 716 P.2d at 567.

422. 716 P.2d at 567.

Hodges, expert testimony on battered women was allowed in part to "help dispel the ordinary layperson's perception that a woman in a battering relationship is free to leave at any time."[423] This same "perception" clearly underlies the majority opinion in *Stewart,* which, in deciding that Peggy was not in imminent danger, specifically noted that Peggy had access to the car keys — without reviewing the threat to her life if she used them to escape.[424]

Finally, the *Stewart* opinion emphasized a requirement of objective reasonableness in the battered woman's self-defense claims. In *Hodges,* Kansas had held that "the jury must determine, from the viewpoint of the defendant's mental state, whether defendant's belief in the need to defend herself was reasonable."[425] *Stewart* overruled *Hodges* on this point, holding that after determining whether the defendant subjectively sincerely and honestly believed it necessary to kill in self-defense, "We then use an objective standard to determine whether defendant's belief was reasonable — specifically, whether a reasonable person in defendant's circumstances would have perceived self-defense as necessary."[426] The objective standard to be applied is how a "reasonably prudent battered wife" would have perceived the aggressor's demeanor.[427] Separation assault is important here as well. The cultural redefinition of the dangers of separation goes beyond the individual woman's "subjective" perception of danger; it does not merely bolster her argument that under her particular, individual circumstances, her subjective perceptions (though unreasonable for a "normal person") persuaded her of danger. Rather, separation assault helps shift what judges and jurors "objectively" know as truth: To the extent that objective standards embody in law the shared cultural norms of society, separation assault helps restructure those norms to allow "objective" perception itself to track more closely the painfully accrued understanding of women who have lived with violent partners.

A recent North Carolina self-defense case involving a sleeping husband exemplifies perhaps even more dramatically than *Stewart* the urgent need for a better judicial understanding of separation assault. In *State v. Norman,*[428] a North Carolina court of appeals held that a woman who had shot her sleeping husband was entitled to a jury instruc-

423. 716 P.2d at 567.

424. State v. Stewart, 763 P.2d 572 (Kan. 1988).

425. State v. Hodges, 716 P.2d 563 (Kan. 1985).

426. 763 P.2d at 579.

427. 763 P.2d at 579.

428. 366 S.E.2d 586 (N.C. Ct. App. 1988), *revd.,* 378 S.E.2d 8 (N.C. 1989).

tion on perfect self-defense. The North Carolina Supreme Court reversed, holding that there was no imminent danger to the wife.[429] Judy Norman had been subjected to vicious torture and degradation over a period of twenty years. Her husband, John Thomas (J.T.) Norman, had beaten her, thrown objects at her, put out cigarettes on her skin, and broken glass on her face. He forced her to prostitute herself daily to support him and then ridiculed her to family and friends. He called her a "dog," forced her to bark like a dog, eat pet food out of pet dishes, and sleep on the floor.[430] He deprived her of food for days at a time and had "often stated both to defendant and others that he would kill [her] . . . [and] threatened to cut her heart out."[431] She left him several times, but each time he found her, took her home, and beat her.[432]

The thirty-six hours before Judy Norman shot her husband were marked by incredible violence, which escalated after her husband was arrested for drunken driving. He beat her almost continuously, refused to eat food that her hands had touched, refused to let her eat for a period of days, threatened to cut off her breast and "shove it up her rear end,"[433] and put out a cigarette on her chest.

On the first evening after the drunken driving arrest, Judy called the police for help. An officer told her they could only help if she filed a complaint ("[took] out a warrant on her husband").[434] She replied that "if she did so [her husband] would kill her."[435] An hour later, she swallowed a bottle of "nerve" pills,[436] and her family called for help. Her husband told the paramedics to let her die and repeatedly obstructed their attempts to save her.[437] The police did not arrest him for attempting to block her rescue: "When he refused to respond to the officer's warning that if he continued to hinder the attendants, he would be arrested, the officer was compelled to chase him back into the house."[438] At the hospital, Judy Norman spoke to a therapist and discussed filing charges against her husband and having him committed for treatment.[439] She seemed depressed and said she should kill

429. State v. Norman, 378 S.E.2d 8, 12 (N.C. 1989).

430. 378 S.E.2d at 9-10.

431. 366 S.E.2d at 587.

432. 366 S.E.2d at 589.

433. 366 S.E.2d at 588.

434. 378 S.E.2d at 19 (Martin, J., dissenting).

435. 378 S.E.2d at 19 (Martin, J., dissenting).

436. 366 S.E.2d at 588.

437. 366 S.E.2d at 588.

438. 378 S.E.2d at 19 (Martin, J., dissenting).

439. 378 S.E.2d at 10 (Martin, J., dissenting).

him for what he had done to her. She stayed at her grandmother's that night.[440]

The next day, she went to the mental health center to discuss charges and the possibility of her husband's commitment and "confronted [him] with that possibility."[441] Her husband told her that if he saw them coming to take him away, he would cut her throat before he could be committed.[442] She went to apply for welfare benefits,[443] but her husband followed her there, interrupted her interview, and forced her to return home with him.[444] He continued to beat her and abuse her physically and would not permit her to eat or feed her children.[445] He later lay down to take a nap, but made her lie on the concrete floor next to the bed, because "dogs" couldn't lie on beds.[446] While he slept, her infant grandchild began to cry. She took the baby to her mother's house for fear it would awaken him. Judy's mother had placed a gun in her purse from fear of Judy's husband. At her mother's house, Judy asked for an aspirin, found the gun, returned home, and shot him.[447]

The North Carolina Supreme Court held that

> *all* of the evidence tended to show that the defendant had ample time and opportunity to resort to other means of preventing further abuse by her husband. There was no action underway by the decedent from which the jury could have found that the defendant had reasonable grounds to believe either that a felonious assault was imminent or that it might result in her death or great bodily injury. Additionally, no such action by the decedent had been underway immediately prior to his falling asleep.[448]

It is hard to know where to begin to discuss *Norman*. In the face of all the grave danger and murderous violence the opinion overlooks,[449] it seems presumptuous to claim that the concept of separa-

---

440. 378 S.E.2d at 20 (Martin, J., dissenting).

441. 378 S.E.2d at 11.

442. 378 S.E.2d at 11.

443. 378 S.E.2d at 11. This may have been another separation attempt.

444. 378 S.E.2d at 11.

445. 378 S.E.2d at 11.

446. 378 S.E.2d at 20 (Martin, J., dissenting).

447. 378 S.E.2d at 20 (Martin, J., dissenting).

448. 378 S.E.2d at 13.

449. In *Norman,* so much disappears from *both* the majority and dissenting opinions. Forced prostitution — essentially, third-party rape — must by the terms of the discussion have been considered something other than "great bodily harm." Or, perhaps, since she had experienced this particular bodily harm for many years, it no longer amounted to "great" harm. The *Norman* court indicated that the type of harm required was "life-threatening" injury and denied that her husband had inflicted any such harm on her, "even during the 'reign of terror.' " 378 S.E.2d at 15. In addition, the facts of the case show that he had prevented her from eating for three days and had given no indication of when he might permit her to eat again. Surely this also

tion assault could have remade the *Norman* holding. Yet the idea that Judy Norman was *not* captive is crucial to the majority's finding that she faced no imminent threat. The dissent is clearly groping for just such a concept in its attempt to describe what had happened to her. The dissent first quotes a psychologist, an expert witness, who compared Judy Norman to a brainwashed prisoner of war and described her as "a woman incarcerated by abuse, by fear, and by her conviction that her husband was invincible and inescapable . . .":[450]

> Mrs. Norman didn't leave because she believed, fully believed that escape was totally impossible. There was no place to go . . . . [S]he had left before; he had come and gotten her. She had gone to the Department of Social Services. He had come and gotten her. The law, she believed the law could not protect her, no one could protect her, and I must admit, looking over the records, that there was nothing done that would contradict that belief.[451]

The concept of separation assault addresses a major problem with sleeping husband cases like *Norman* and *Stewart.* These cases look to courts like executions; judges express concern over the specter of homicidal self-help for battered wives.[452] Separation assault replaces this image — as the dissenting judges in *Stewart* urged — with the paradigm of hostages resisting their captors. We believe the danger to a hostage is imminent *both* because the force used to hold them there is apparent *and* because our cultural knowledge includes the memory of the many hostages who have been harmed in the past. Courts might see Judy Norman very differently if they understood that she could as easily be Mrs. Godfrey (shot to death in her mother's trailer), or Rachel Pessah (the dead wife in *Berry*), or Grace Morales (the murdered mother in *Garcia*). By emphasizing the similarities between past and current uses of force, by emphasizing that force which holds the woman captive, and by persuasively invoking the shadow of many past

threatened great bodily harm. Also, the day before he died, her husband had essentially attempted her murder: rather than fulfilling his duty to save her life when she attempted suicide, he had done all he could to cause her to die and prevent others from saving her. He had sworn persuasively to her and to others that he would kill her in the future. Her whole family was convinced that he would kill her, and would kill them if they intervened. 378 S.E.2d at 19-20 (Martin, J., dissenting).

450. 378 S.E.2d at 17 (Martin, J., dissenting).

451. 378 S.E.2d at 17 (Martin, J., dissenting). The dissent concludes that a juror could have found "that defendant believed that her husband's threats to her life were viable, that serious bodily harm was imminent, and that it was necessary to kill her husband to escape that harm . . . [a] juror could find defendant's belief in the necessity to kill her husband not merely reasonable but compelling." 378 S.E.2d at 20 (Martin, J., dissenting).

452. *See, e.g., Norman,* 378 S.E.2d at 15 ("Homicidal self-help would then become a lawful solution, and perhaps the easiest and most effective solution, to this problem."); *see also* State v. Stewart, 763 P.2d 572, 579 (Kan. 1988) ("To hold otherwise in this case would in effect allow the execution of the abuser for past or future acts and conduct.").

assaults that have resulted in the death of women, separation assault helps shift the paradigm from the image of vigilantism to the image of a hostage resisting her own death. Here, at the intersection of legal standards and cultural perception, separation assault helps to reveal that by its very nature battering implicates questions of both violence and power, and to make possible a greater cultural understanding of the lives and experience of women.

Conclusion

Violence is a way of "doing power" in a relationship;[453] battering is power and control marked by violence and coercion. A battered woman is a woman who experiences the violence against her as determining or controlling her thoughts, emotions, or actions, including her efforts to cope with the violence itself. Many, many women experience such violence in our society. The precise response of any woman is likely to be determined by her life circumstances and family situation.

We should know this. Nothing in the preceding paragraph should make women ashamed of being battered. However, the interrelationship among cultural images, legal images, litigation, and substantive law has made it difficult for women to understand our experience of violence. The stereotypical image of a battered woman — dysfunctional, helpless, dependent — is alien to the self-image and self-knowledge of most women who encounter violence from our partners. Attempts to counter these stereotypes have interacted with other contemporary social and legal developments: each block of legal reform (such as the development of expert testimony on battered women) has interacted with the rest of the legal structure (such as the advent of no-fault divorce, or the evidentiary rules governing the admission of expert testimony) to pose continued difficulties in recognizing women's experience in law.

These reciprocal, mutually reinforcing forces of popular perception, law, and litigation have made it difficult for women to identify ourselves and our experience as part of a continuum of power and domination affecting most women's lives. The challenge is to identify legal and social strategies that will allow us to change law and culture simultaneously, by illuminating the context of power and control within which a woman lives and acts. Naming separation assault can help reveal the overall struggle for power that is the heart of the battering process: it describes a particularly dangerous attack hitherto hidden in the phrase "*domestic* violence," emphasizes the assault on

453. Stets, *supra* note 64, at 109.

the woman's autonomy and volition, and offers insights that can help resolve several troubled areas of law. This intervention is both legal and cultural, a way to rewrite legal doctrine by changing the way we understand the questions and categories involved.

I offer the theory of separation assault as part of a feminist approach to law reform in this area: working from women's experience, we must develop legal and cultural strategies that more clearly reveal the struggles we face. We need many such interventions. The key to more widespread change lies in the way transformed legal and social images of women will in turn affect women's experience and understanding of our lives, allowing women to recognize our experience as part of a larger system of subordination so that we can structure our understanding of our needs in relation to those of other women facing oppression. Women's recognition of our own oppression has been slowed by the images that law has helped create. As we come to recognize our experiences as oppression, rather than personal insufficiency, weakness, or "unhappiness" in marriage — for example, recognizing separation assault rather than "failure" to leave a relationship — we will be better able to address the dangers we face and realize our individual and collective capacity for change.

Journal of Social Issues, Vol. 48, No. 1, 1992, pp. 9–22

A Feminist Redefinition of Rape and Sexual Assault: Historical Foundations and Change

Patricia L. N. Donat and John D'Emilio
University of North Carolina at Greensboro

The meanings of sexual assault and women's sexuality have changed significantly since the colonial period. At that time, women were valued for their sexual purity and were viewed as the center of the family. Sexual intercourse was acceptable only within marriage for the purpose of procreation. If a woman engaged in sex outside of marriage, even against her will, she was considered a "fallen" woman and was often blamed for her own victimization. With the feminist movement of the 1960s, rape was reconceptualized as a mechanism for maintaining male control and domination, a violent means of inducing fear in women and reinforcing their subordination to men. This reconceptualization has made a clear difference in the way our culture defines and understands sexual assault, but much still needs to change.

The issues of rape and sexual assault have been major concerns of the feminist movement since its revival in the late 1960s. Because of the work of feminists, the contemporary understanding of rape and sexual assault, and the social response to sexual violence, have undergone significant revision. This paper examines the feminist response to traditional conceptualizations of rape and the impact it has had. It begins by presenting some historical background to set a context for understanding more recent events.

The Colonial Era

During the colonial period, settlers in the English colonies were influenced strongly by the church, which prescribed the behavior of its congregation. The

Correspondence regarding this article should be addressed to Patricia Donat, Department of Psychology, 296 Eberhart Building, University of North Carolina at Greensboro, Greensboro, NC 27412-5001.

family was defined as the central unit in society and sex roles were differentiated rigidly. Men were dominant and women were submissive. The woman was regarded "not as a person . . . but as a sexual 'type'—an inferior, a receptacle, . . . or a simple answer to his needs" (Koehler, 1980, p. 93). Sexuality was channeled into marriage for the procreation of legitimate offspring. Nonmarital sexual intercourse was immoral, an offense against both family and community (D'Emilio & Freedman, 1988).

In order to regulate deviance, the church, courts, and community joined to monitor private sexual behavior and to limit sexual expression to marriage. Colonial society held the entire community responsible for upholding morality, and sexual crimes were punished severely. Women bore the heaviest responsibility for regulating premarital sexual contact. "Church and society dealt more harshly with women . . . [because] female chastity and fidelity assured men of the legitimacy of their children" (D'Emilio & Freedman, 1988). The integrity of the family was critical to the development of community and was guarded with care. For men, the integrity of the family rested on female purity and monogamy.

A woman's value within society was based on her ability to marry and to produce legitimate heirs. The ability to attract a spouse was influenced by the woman's perceived purity. The rape of a virgin was considered a crime against the father of the raped woman rather than against the woman herself. A raped woman could not expect to marry into a respectable family and might very well remain the economic liability of the father.

During the colonial period, the rape cases most likely to come to court were those in which the perpetrator was from a lower social class than the victim or in which the victim was a married woman who physically resisted. "When men of the lower order raped women of a higher social standing, they threatened the prerogatives of other men" (Lindemann, 1984, p. 81).

Women were dependent on the courts and community (i.e., men) for their protection. In order to ensure her safety, a woman who was sexually attacked needed to comply with male standards for her behavior by proving her nonconsent through physical and verbal resistance, and through immediate disclosure of the attack to both family and neighbors. Proof of nonconsent was necessary to verify that the woman had not voluntarily engaged in sexual acts outside of marriage. If a woman could not prove nonconsent, she might be punished for the assault (D'Emilio & Freedman, 1988). Rape was therefore "an expression of male control over women, regulated by law in a way that serves the men who hold political power more than it protects women" (Lindemann, 1984, p. 81).

The 19th Century

Toward the end of the 18th century, sexual meanings began to change. Sexuality no longer was tied so closely to reproductive intentions, and more emphasis was placed on courtship and individual choice rather than on community and family control. The subsequent decline in traditional church and state regulation of morality loosened constraints on nonmarital sex.

During the 19th century, young women from the countryside and from immigrant families began to enter the paid work force and earn their livings outside the family household. Patriarchal controls over women's time, behavior, and sexuality weakened (Stansell, 1986). With increased freedom, however, also came increased vulnerability. Previously, "courtship was one part of a system of barter between the sexes, in which a woman traded sexual favors for a man's promise to marry. Premarital intercourse then became a token of betrothal" (Stansell, 1986, p. 87). Women, however, no longer could assume that a pregnancy would lead to marriage.

Female virtue continued to be important for finding a spouse. In the 19th century women were viewed as pure and virtuous by nature, and as disinterested in sex. Women of all classes were expected to use their natural purity and superior morality to control men's innate lust. The impure woman threatened the delicate moral balance and suggested the "social disintegration that sexuality symbolized" (Freedman, 1981, p. 20). A woman who engaged in sexual intercourse, even against her will, was considered to be depraved—a "fallen" woman—and was often blamed for the man's crime and socially stigmatized as a result of the attack. "As woman falls from a higher point of perfection, so she sinks to a profounder depth of misery than man" (Freedman, 1981, p. 18).

The 20th Century

During the 20th century, the writings of Sigmund Freud and other psychologists and sexologists provided the foundation for reconceptualizing sexual behavior and categorizing sexual deviations. One emerging concern was an interest in understanding the causes of sexual aggression. Many hypotheses were developed, but most theories included the belief that rape was a perversion and that rapists were mentally ill (Amir, 1971). One theory of sexual aggression suggested that the rapist's behavior was the result of socialization by a strong maternal figure and a weak paternal figure. Another theory proposed that the rapist's behavior was the result of a defective superego that left the individual unable to control his sexual and aggressive impulses. Therefore, the rapist was considered to have a "character disorder" and was classified as a "sick" individual. Other theories to explain the rapist's behavior included castration fears, feelings of sexual inferiority and inadequacy, homosexual tendencies, organic factors, and mental deficiencies (Amir, 1971). All of these theories reduced the rapist's responsibility for his actions since he was considered unable to control his pathological impulses. In other words, rape was reconceptualized from the perpetrator's point of view. The focus was on understanding the plight of the man, not the woman. Her victimization was simply a by-product of his pathology.

During the 1930s, the public increasingly became interested in sex crimes committed by men against women. In 1937, the *New York Times* created a new index category of sex crimes, which included 143 articles published that year (Freedman, 1989). Due to the influence of psychoanalytic theories, sex offenders began to be considered more as deviants than as criminals. Between 1935 and 1965, several state commissions to investigate sex crimes were formed; in many places, authority for the treatment and rehabilitation of the sex offender shifted away from the penal system and toward the mental health system (Freedman, 1989). Psychiatrists began to carry more influence concerning treatment of the sex offender. The label "sexual psychopath" was used to describe the violent male offender who was unable to control his sexual impulses and attacked the object of his frustrated desires. Thus rape was conceptualized primarily as an act of sex rather than an act of violence.

As awareness of sex crimes increased, public concern also escalated. Several "sex psychopath laws" were passed that permitted offenders to receive indefinite commitment to state mental hospitals rather than jail sentences. This law reform, initiated by male legislators, was opposed by many women who endorsed stronger criminal penalties for rape and sexual assault. Although sexual psychopath laws were promoted as a measure to protect women, in reality these laws often resulted in White men being labeled as mentally ill and sent to state hospitals, and Black men being found guilty of a crime and sent to jail (Freedman, 1989).

Racial Aspects of Rape

In addition to oppressing women, rape served as a method of racial control. The sexual assault of minority women maintained the supremacy of White men. The experience of the Black female victim was virtually ignored (cf. Wyatt, this issue). White men used

> women as verbs with which to communicate with one another (rape being a means of communicating defeat to the men of a conquered tribe). . . . Rape sent a message to black men, but more centrally, it expressed male sexual attitudes in a culture both racist and patriarchal. (Hall, 1983, p. 322)

In the post-Reconstruction South, White men used the myth of the Black man as sexually uncontrollable and as a threat to all White women as an excuse for violence toward Black men and as a means to control women through fear. Black men who were accused of sexually attacking White women received the harshest penalties. A Black man convicted of rape often was executed or castrated (D'Emilio & Freedman, 1988; Jordon, 1968; Wyatt, this issue). In the 1930s the Association of Southern Women for the Prevention of Lynching stated that the traditions of chivalry and lynching were a form of sexual and racial intimidation rather than protection.

> Lynching, it proclaimed, far from offering a shield against sexual assault, served as a weapon of both racial and sexual terror, planting fear in women's minds and dependency in their hearts. It thrust them in the role of personal property or sexual objects, ever threatened by black men's lust, ever in need of white men's protection. (Hall, 1983, p. 339)

The myth of the Black rapist still lingers in more severe sentencing penalties for Black offenders (Hall, 1983). Thus rape and its legal treatment can be seen as the ultimate demonstration of power in a racist and patriarchal society.

Perceptions of the Rape Victim

In addition to changes in the conceptualization of male offenders, society's perception of the victim's role in the assault also changed during the 20th century. As female nature became sexualized and female desire for sexuality legitimated, rape became redefined as "not only a male psychological aberration, but also an act in which women . . . contributed to their victimization" (Freedman, 1989, p. 211). Many people became skeptical that a woman could be raped if she did not consent. A well-known attorney once began a rape trial by placing a coke bottle on a table, spinning it, and demonstrating to the jury his difficulty in forcing a pencil into the opening (Margolin, 1972). The implication was that a woman would be able to fend off a man attempting to rape her (Schwendinger & Schwendinger, 1983). Therefore, if a woman was raped, she must have "asked for it."

Laws requiring physical evidence of penetration, the need for corroboration, and allowing testimony about the victim's sexual history in court trials had the effect of placing the victim on trial. In addition, juries often still received the traditional instruction that an accusation of rape "is one which is easily made and, once made, difficult to defend against, even if the person accused is innocent" (Berger, 1977, p. 10). The jury was cautioned to be suspicious of the victim's testimony, much more so than in other criminal cases. As a result, prosecution rates for rape remained low.

> In 1972, 3,562 rapes were reported in Chicago; 833 arrests were made, 23 defendants pleaded guilty; and 8 were found guilty and sentenced after a trial . . . fewer than 1 percent of rapes resulted in jail sentences. (Deckard, 1983, p. 433)

The Feminist Redefinition of Sexual Assault

During the 1960s, increasing numbers of women were employed. As the decade began, approximately 36% of women worked outside the home; by its end, over 50% of women were in the paid labor force (Deckard, 1983). Although women's presence in the public sphere was increasing, they rarely held decision and policy-making positions.

With women's increasing involvement in activities outside the home, the opportunity for a woman to be victimized increased (Gardner, 1980). A few men viewed women's new-found assertiveness and involvement in the public sphere as an attack on traditional roles and a defiance of chivalry. To such men, the woman who did not conform to traditional roles was relegated to the role of the "loose woman" and was not entitled to protection under the traditional guidelines for male–female relationships (Griffin, 1971). The following description of rape in the 19th century still applied:

> sexual assault could be conceived of . . . as an exploitation of women's presumed dependence on men. If a woman had herself violated patriarchal norms by straying out of her dependent position—if she had fought off her attacker, asserted her rights alone in court, or behaved in too self-reliant a manner more generally—the term "rape" no longer applied, no matter how forceful the attack visited on her. (Arnold, 1989, p. 49)

Societal definitions of rape demanded adherence to traditionally defined feminine roles and behaviors. The implicit warning to women was to behave (e.g., accept traditional feminine roles) or to suffer the consequence—rape.

Women, however, began to resist traditional definitions of appropriate feminine behavior and expressed their dissatisfaction. Betty Friedan (1963), in *The Feminine Mystique,* and the National Organization for Women (NOW), founded in 1966, expressed women's changing views and interest in public reform. Women's liberationists also began to work toward changing social policies. A process called consciousness raising was used in informal women's groups to begin to empower women and to help them identify sources of sisterhood and oppression. As women began to meet, they realized that individual concerns (e.g., sexual harassment, fear of walking the streets at night) were widely shared. As a result, many women questioned the reasons for their oppression, and they began to recognize that "the personal is political." The dilemmas women were experiencing were not idiosyncratic, but were constructed socially as a result of the hierarchial gender system in our culture (D'Emilio & Freedman, 1988). Kate Millet (1970) in her landmark book, *Sexual Politics,* concluded that within our patriarchal system, force takes "a form of violence particularly sexual in nature and realized most completely in the act of rape" (p. 69).

During the 1970s, rape became an important issue within the feminist movement. Sexual assault was redefined from the victim's perspective. A woman's victimization was an "experience of helplessness and loss of control, the sense of one's self as an object of rage" (Hall, 1983, p. 342). The act of rape was seen not as an end in itself, but as a means of enforcing gender roles in society and maintaining the hierarchy in which men retained control. Feminists refuted the long-held belief that rapists were men who were helplessly controlled by their overwhelming sexual impulses. Rape was recognized as an act of violence, *not* of sex as psychoanalytic theorists had previously held. Rape was a form of domination and control, a weapon used to enforce women's subordinate role to men.

In 1971, an article by Susan Griffin described rape as the "All-American crime." She reported that "forcible rape is the most frequently committed violent crime in America today," and emphasized that all women are victims even if they are not the direct targets of the attack because "rape and the fear of rape are a daily part of every woman's consciousness" (p. 27). She held that women's behavior is shaped by their fear of attack, and as a result, women's movements are restricted. They fear to live alone, walk outside at night, smile at strangers, and leave their windows open. Psychological research has found that women's perceptions of their vulnerability to attack and their fear of being a victim of a violent crime are related to the amount of precautionary behaviors in which they engage. Women, especially those unsure of their ability to protect themselves physically, engage in isolating behavior, such as not going out at night or visiting friends (Riger & Gordon, 1981). This limits women's opportunities to be active participants in the public sphere.

The first rape crisis center was founded in Washington, DC, in 1972, and the number of centers has increased steadily since that time (Deckard, 1983). Now there are more than 550 rape crisis centers across the country, some helping as many as 1100 victims annually (King & Webb, 1981). Rape crisis centers and rape hotlines provide valuable assistance to victims of sexual assault and rape. Victims are provided with information and escorted to the police station and the hospital, and volunteers serve as advocates for the victim after the attack. Many of these centers also have educational programs in the community to help dispel rape myths and change public attitudes about rape (Deckard, 1983). Cuts in governmental funding during the Reagan administration, however, have resulted in the closing of some centers, and in an increased need for volunteers and private funding.

Susan Brownmiller (1975), in her bestselling book, *Against Our Will: Men, Women, and Rape,* reaffirmed the relationship between sexual aggression and women's fear, defining rape as "a conscious process of intimidation by which all men keep all women in a state of fear" (p. 5). Her book was crucial in the definition of rape from a feminist perspective. Brownmiller's analysis formed the foundation for numerous theoretical papers and psychological research. Her book detailed the evolution of rape in our culture and the role it has played throughout history.

Brownmiller began her analysis by considering biology. Women are physiologically vulnerable to sexual attack, and once "men discovered that they could rape, they proceeded to do it" (1975, p. 6). Rape served a critical function of domination and intimidation in primitive societies. "His forcible entry into her body, despite her physical protestations and struggle, became the vehicle of his victorious conquest over her being, the ultimate test of his superior strength, the triumph of his manhood" (p. 5). Rape, therefore, was a purposeful act of control. In some cases, rape was an act of manhood, a rite of passage, or a form of male bonding. This male bonding, on occasion, is exhibited in the form of gang rape. Examining gang rape, Brownmiller concluded that " 'sharing the girl among us fellows' strengthens the notion of group masculinity and power" (p. 28). This bond between men results from their "contempt for women" and thrives in a culture of "forced and exaggerated male/female polarities" (p. 211).

The victims of rape often are portrayed as secretly enjoying their victimization—a depiction particularly common in the media. Movie images often present the woman as resisting only initially and eventually becoming overwhelmed by sexual desire despite her original protests. These images reinforce rape myths, and they prompted many feminists to speak out against the way women are portrayed in the media (Jozsa & Jozsa, 1980; Read, 1989). The images themselves represent women as inferior and as victims rather than agents in their own sexuality. Groth and Birnbaum (1979, p. 27) stated that "pornography is a media equivalent to the crime of rape. It is the sexual expression of power and anger." Women began to speculate about the relationship between the way women were portrayed in the media and the prevalence of rape and sexual assault. As a result, the phrase "pornography is the theory, rape is the practice" became a rallying cry for some radical feminists (Morgan, 1980, p. 134).

The use of coercive authority also is a component of sexual assaults in our culture. Sometimes a mere difference in status provides the necessary tool to force intercourse on an unwilling partner. Date rape, homosexual rape in prisons, and rape by police are just a few examples of this form of manipulation. In reality, however, all rapes involve status differences due to the gender-based distribution of power in our society (Box, 1983, p. 150). A woman's resistance within a dependent relationship often is weakened and she becomes vulnerable to being victimized. In addition, victimization may be facilitated by the institutional structure, which often places men in positions of authority and power over women. "Rape by an authority figure can befuddle a victim who has been trained to respect authority so that she believes herself complicitous. Authority figures emanate an aura of rightness; their actions cannot be challenged" (Brownmiller, 1975, p. 300). The victim is left with feelings of guilt and powerlessness, while the aggressor's behavior is left undisputed. For years, many women blamed themselves and did not define their sexual victimization as rape. Since the advent of feminism, and with increased research and public education, women have begun to define unwanted sexual intercourse, even contact between acquaintances, as rape (Warshaw, 1988).

Acquaintance Rape

As public discourse on sexual violence continued, it became increasingly evident that rapists were not only strangers behind bushes, but also might be dates, acquaintances, neighbors, husbands, friends, and relatives. Feminists made the case that every man is a potential rapist and all women are potential victims. Due to this reconceptualization, date rape became an area of concern. In 1972, *Ms.* magazine discussed the issue of date rape on college campuses across the country. Initial research indicated that rape between acquaintances was much more common than previously believed. Kanin and Parcell (1977) found that approximately 83% of college women had experienced male sexual aggression while dating. Research a decade later confirmed this incidence rate. Koss, Gidycz, and Wisniewski (1987) found that 27.5% of college women reported being victims of rape or attempted rape; 53.7% of women, including those who reported being raped, had experienced some form of unwanted sexual contact and/or sexually assaultive behavior. These results suggest that sexually aggressive behavior is experienced by the majority of women in "normal" dating relationships. This high incidence rate gives credence to the feminist conceptualization of rape as being supported by our culture.

Psychological Research on Rape

The views of feminists, in particular the work of Susan Brownmiller, sparked research within psychology to examine the "rape-supportive culture" that provides the context for sexual assault. Researchers made empirical studies of feminist ideas and combined these feminist views into a theoretical framework to understand and predict sexual aggression. Martha Burt (1980) hypothesized that our culture and the status of women within that culture play a significant role in the attitudes toward sexual violence held by persons, particularly rapists. She hypothesized that myths about rape (e.g., "women ask for it") might act as releasers or facilitators of sexual aggression. These rape myths were proposed as part of a larger attitudinal structure that serves to facilitate sexually aggressive acts in our culture. Attitudinal factors that were found by Burt to predict rape-supportive myths were (a) sex role stereotyping, (b) adversarial sexual beliefs, and (c) acceptance of interpersonal violence.

Sex role stereotyping refers to the appropriateness of familial, work, and social roles being based on the sex of the individual being considered (e.g., "It is acceptable for a woman to have a career, but marriage and family should come first"; Burt, 1980, p. 222). Adversarial sexual beliefs refers to the view that male–female relationships are naturally filled with conflict and competition (e.g., "Most women are sly and manipulating when they are out to attract a man"—p. 222). Acceptance of interpersonal violence refers to the belief that violence is an appropriate way of interacting with others, particularly in male–female relationships (e.g., "Sometimes the only way to get a cold woman turned on is to use force"—p. 222). These attitudes were studied by researchers (Burt & Albin, 1981; Check & Malamuth, 1983; Malamuth, 1983) as a means to understand sexual aggression using a feminist framework.

Koss, Leonard, Beezley, and Oros (1985) developed a theoretical model for characterizing nonstranger sexual aggression that incorporated Burt's findings and feminist views. They proposed a social control/social conflict model of date rape:

> Culturally transmitted assumptions about men, women, violence, sexuality, and myths about rape constitute a rape-supportive belief system. Furthermore, stratified systems such as the American dating situation may legitimate the use of force by those in power and weaken resistance of the less powerful. Finally, acquisition of stereotyped myths about rape may result in a failure to label as rape sexual aggression that occurs in dating situations. (Koss et al., 1985, p. 982)

This view of a culturally based belief system that perpetuates violence against women and oppresses women has been endorsed by several feminist writers (Brownmiller, 1975; Griffin, 1971; Johnson, 1980).

Rape Within the Legal System

In the colonial period, the law conceptualized rape as the violation of a man's property. It was a man's personal privilege to have access to a woman's body. Feminist theorists have rejected traditional legal conceptualizations, which often blame the woman for her own victimization, and have refuted rape myths that women enjoy being raped, and ask and deserve to be raped by dressing provocatively. They refuse to allow women to be blamed for their own victimization. Instead, blame is placed squarely on the attacker.

Feminists have lobbied for changes in rape legislation. Previous laws considered rape an all-or-nothing crime, in which convicted offenders received sentences that ranged from 5 years to life depending on the particular state's statutes. Maximum sentences of 30–50 years in prison were not uncommon for convicted rapists (Babcock, Freedman, Norton, & Ross, 1975). Prior to the 1972 case of *Furman v. Georgia,* which "invalidated arbitrary capital punishment laws, sixteen states permitted imposition of death for rape" (Berger, 1977, p. 8). Some writers hypothesized that the severe penalties for rape may have discouraged juries from convicting a defendant because of a "perceived sense of disproportion between culpability and the prescribed sentence" (Andenaes, 1966, p. 970). Now most states have revised their laws to include several levels of sexual assault with a broader range of penalties. A perpetrator may be charged with first-, second-, or third-degree rape, with each charge varying in the maximum sentence following conviction. First degree rape is defined as forced sexual intercourse under aggravated circumstances. Second degree rape is described as forced sexual intercourse. Third degree rape is defined as nonconsensual intercourse or intercourse with threat to self or property. This calibrated system of offenses and penalties has increased conviction rates, and may therefore enhance the effectiveness of prosecution as a deterrent (Andenaes, 1966, p. 970).

In addition, the criterion of force was determined in the past by examining the victim's behavior rather than the offender's behavior. In the 1970s, women in New York needed the corroboration of a witness who saw or heard the assault to verify that it had indeed been rape, and that the woman had resisted the attack. In addition, some states viewed "no resistance" as consensual intercourse, and required the victim to have verbally said "no" or forcibly resisted or screamed (Margolin, 1972). Unless the woman exhibited these behaviors, the man's behavior was not considered rape.

In 1974, Michigan passed the first comprehensive rape reform legislation in the country (Loh, 1981). Since that time, most states have enacted similar changes. These reforms have focused on the perpetrator's behavior (e.g., use of physical force or threat of force) as the legal criterion rather than the victim's behavior alone. The context of the assault and the interaction between the victim and assailant are becoming increasingly important.

Although rape legislation has changed a great deal, many changes are still sought (see Goldberg-Ambrose, this issue). In about half of the states a man cannot be charged with sexually assaulting his wife unless they are separated legally. In six states, a husband can never be charged with raping his wife (Searles & Berger, 1987). Recently a North Carolina woman was kidnapped and raped by her husband, but since they had been separated less than one year, the separation was not yet legal and she was unable to charge him with rape. In one-fourth of the states, a man cannot be the victim of rape (Searles & Berger, 1987). In states with progressive statutes, sex-neutral terminology is used for both offender and victim. In approximately 70% of states, a victim's past sexual behavior with persons other than the defendant is admissible for determining consent, while only six states prohibit the introduction of the victim's sexual history (Searles & Berger, 1987).

Criticism of Radical Feminist Reconceptualizations

Some feminists have criticized Brownmiller's (1975) conceptualization of rape. Rather than placing all the blame on women as in the past, Brownmiller counterblamed, condemning all men for their innate violence (Benjamin, 1983). In addition, radical feminists have ignored the "history of women's resistance to oppression" and focused on sexuality itself as the enemy—"an unchanging, aggressive male sexuality of which women have been eternally the victims"

(Arnold, 1989, p. 36). Brownmiller's book also has been faulted as "supporting a notion of universal patriarchy and timeless sexual victimization; it leaves no room for understanding the reasons for women's collaboration, their own sources of power, . . . the class and racial differences in their experience of discrimination and sexual danger" (Hall, 1983, p. 341). The radical feminist view also focuses exclusively on the negative. Some writers believe that in order for feminism to persist, women must use their own strength as an energy source for reform.

> Social movements, feminism included, move toward a vision; they cannot operate solely on fear. It is not enough to move women away from danger and oppression; it is necessary to move toward something: toward pleasure, agency, self-definition. Feminism must increase women's pleasure and joy, not just decrease our misery. (Vance, 1984, p. 24)

Areas of Action and Change: Then and Now

Education is still needed to help change society's attitudes about rape. In the recent past, women have been the target for increased awareness, but now men also are being included in the process of consciousness raising (Walsh, 1990). "The anti-rape movement must not limit itself to training women to avoid rape or depending on imprisonment as a deterrent, but must aim its attention at changing the behavior and attitudes of men" (Hall, 1983, p. 346). For example, the University of Florida has introduced a program called FARE (Fraternity Acquaintance Rape Education) to educate men in fraternities and on athletic teams (Walsh, 1990).

Education of women also is needed to empower them to action. In our culture, women are socialized to be submissive, but some feminists have challenged this role. "To be submissive is to defer to masculine strength; is to lack muscular development or any interest in defending oneself" (Griffin, 1971, p. 33). Women can take courses in self-defense to strengthen their bodies, and to gain the ability and the confidence to defend themselves should they be attacked. Ann Sheldon (1972) felt this solution to rape was inescapable: "there is no other way except resistance to be free" (p. 23).

Feminists clearly have made a major difference in the way sexual assault and rape are understood in our culture. Yet considering the long historical tradition of women bearing the guilt for sexual victimization, it is not surprising that much still needs to change. Over 15 years ago, Brownmiller called for action, saying, "the purpose in this book has been to give rape its history. Now we must deny it a future" (1975, p. 454). That need is still true today.

References

Amir, M. (1971). *Patterns in forcible rape*. Chicago: University of Chicago Press.

Andenaes, J. (1966). The general prevention effects of punishment. *Pennsylvania Law Review, 114*, 949–983.

Arnold, M. H. (1989). The life of a citizen in the hands of a woman: Sexual assault in New York City, 1790–1820. In K. Peiss & C. Simmons (Eds.), *Passion and power: Sexuality in history* (pp. 35–56). Philadelphia, PA: Temple University Press.

Babcock, B., Freedman, A., Norton, D., & Ross, S. (1975). *Sex discrimination and the law*. Boston: Little, Brown.

Benjamin, J. (1983). Master and slave: The fantasy of erotic domination. In A. Snitow, C. Stansell, & S. Thompson (Eds.), *Powers of desire: The politics of sexuality* (pp. 280–299). New York: Monthly Review Press.

Berger, V. (1977). Man's trial, woman's tribulation: Rape cases in the courtroom. *Columbia Law Review, 77*, 1–101.

Box, S. (1983). *Power, crime, and mystification*. London: Tavistock.

Brownmiller, S. (1975). *Against our will: Men, women and rape*. Toronto: Bantam.

Burt, M. R. (1980). Cultural myths and supports for rape. *Journal of Personality and Social Psychology, 38*, 217–230.

Burt, M. R., & Albin, R. S. (1981). Rape myths, rape definitions, and probability of conviction. *Journal of Applied Social Psychology, 11*, 212–230.

Check, J. V. P., & Malamuth, N. M. (1983). Sex role stereotyping and reactions to depictions of stranger versus acquaintance rape. *Journal of Personality and Social Psychology, 45*, 344–356.

Deckard, B. S. (1983). *The woman's movement: Political, socioeconomic, and psychological issues* (3rd ed.). New York: Harper & Row.

D'Emilio, J., & Freedman, E. B. (1988). *Intimate matters: A history of sexuality in America*. New York: Harper & Row.

Freedman, E. B. (1981). *Their sisters' keepers: Women's prison reform in America, 1893–1930*. Ann Arbor: University of Michigan Press.

Freedman, E. B. (1989). Uncontrolled desires: The response to the sexual psychopath, 1920–1960. In K. Peiss & C. Simmons (Eds), *Passion and power: Sexuality in history* (pp. 199–225). Philadelphia, PA: Temple University Press.

Friedan, B. (1963). *The feminine mystique*. New York: Dell.

Gardner, T. A. (1980). Racism in pornography and the women's movement. In L. Lederer (Ed.), *Take back the night: Women and pornography* (pp. 105–114). New York: Morrow.

Griffin, S. (1971). Rape: The all-American crime. *Ramparts, 10*, 26–35.

Groth, A., & Birnbaum, H. (1979). *Men who rape: The psychology of the offender*. New York: Plenum.

Hall, J. D. (1983). The mind that burns in each body: Women, rape, and racial violence. In A. Snitow, C. Stansell, & S. Thompson (Eds.), *Powers of desire: The politics of sexuality* (pp. 328–349). New York: Monthly Review Press.

Johnson, A. G. (1980). On the prevalence of rape in the United States. *Signs: Journal of Women in Culture and Society, 6*, 136–146.

Jordon, W. (1968). *White over Black: American attitudes toward the Negro*. Williamsburg, VA: University of North Carolina Press.

Jozsa, B., & Jozsa, M. (1980). Dirty books, dirty films, and dirty data. In L. Lederer (Ed.), *Take back the night: Women on pornography* (pp. 204–217). New York: Morrow.

Kanin, E. J., & Parcell, S. R. (1977). Sexual aggression: A second look at the offended female. *Archives of Sexual Behavior, 6*, 67–76.

King, H. E., & Webb, C. (1981). Rape crisis centers: Progress and problems. *Journal of Social Issues, 37*(4), 93–104.

Koehler, L. (1980). *A search for power: The "weaker sex" in seventeenth-century New England*. Urbana: University of Illinois Press.

Koss, M. P., Gidycz, C. A., & Wisniewski, N. (1987). The scope of rape: Incidence and prevalence of sexual aggression and victimization in a national sample of higher education students. *Journal of Consulting and Clinical Psychology, 55*, 162–170.

Koss, M. P., Leonard, K. E., Beezley, D. A., & Oros, C. J. (1985). Non-stranger sexual aggression: A discriminant analysis of the psychological characteristics of undetected offenders. *Sex Roles, 12*, 981–992.

Lindemann, B. S. (1984). "To ravish and carnally know": Rape in eighteenth-century Massachusetts. *Signs: Journal of Women in Culture and Society, 10*, 63–82.

Loh, W. D. (1981). Q: What has reform of rape legislation wrought? A: Truth in criminal labelling. *Journal of Social Issues, 37*(4), 28–52.
Malamuth, N. M. (1983). Factors associated with rape as predictors of laboratory aggression against women. *Journal of Personality and Social Psychology, 45,* 432–442.
Margolin, D. (1972). Rape: The facts. *Women: A Journal of Liberation, 3,* 19–22.
Millet, K. (1970). *Sexual politics.* New York: Avon.
Morgan, R. (1980). Theory and practice: Pornography and rape. In L. Lederer (Ed.), *Take back the night: Women and pornography* (pp. 134–140). New York: Morrow.
Read, D. (1989). (De)constructing pornography: Feminisms in conflict. In K. Peiss & C. Simmons (Eds.), *Passion and power: Sexuality in history* (pp. 277–292). Philadelphia, PA: Temple University Press.
Riger, S., & Gordon, M. T. (1981). The fear of rape: A study in social control. *Journal of Social Issues, 37*(4), 71–92.
Schwendinger, J. R., & Schwendinger, H. (1983). *Rape and inequality.* Beverly Hills, CA: Sage.
Searles, P., & Berger, R. J. (1987). The current status of rape reform legislation: An examination of state statutes. *Women's Rights Law Reporter, 10,* 25–43.
Sheldon, A. (1972). Rape: The solution. *Women: A Journal of Liberation, 3,* 23.
Stansell, C. (1986). *City of women: Sex and class in New York, 1789–1860.* New York: Knopf.
Vance, C. S. (1984). Pleasure and danger: Toward a politics of sexuality. In C. Vance (Ed.), *Pleasure and danger: Exploring female sexuality* (pp. 1–27). Boston: Routledge & Kegan Paul.
Walsh, C. (1990, April). *FARE: Fraternity acquaintance rape education.* Paper presented at the Southeastern Psychological Association meeting, Atlanta.
Warshaw, R. (1988). *I never called it rape.* New York: Harper & Row.

PATRICIA L. N. DONAT is a social research associate at the University of North Carolina at Greensboro (UNCG) School of Nursing. She earned her master's degree in clinical psychology at UNCG and is currently a doctoral student in social psychology. Her research has focused on acquaintance rape and the attitudinal accessibility of rape supportive attitudes among college men.

JOHN D'EMILIO is Associate Professor of History at the University of North Carolina at Greensboro. He is author of *Sexual Politics, Sexual Communities: The Making of a Homosexual Minority, 1940–1970* (1983) and coauthor of *Intimate Matters: A History of Sexuality in America* (1988).

Journal of Social Issues, Vol. 48, No. 1, 1992, pp. 173–185

Unfinished Business in Rape Law Reform

Carole Goldberg-Ambrose
University of California, Los Angeles

Substantial and widespread changes in federal and state rape laws, designed to advance the concerns of feminists and law enforcement interests, have gone into effect over the past 15 years. Some researchers who have tried to assess the effects of these reforms believe the changes have thwarted feminist goals; others have found little impact on case processing or victims' experiences; still others have pronounced the reform efforts a success. There are many obstacles to measuring and achieving rape reform, the most notable being the need to eliminate juror misconceptions about rape and its victims. Contemporary research and law reform should focus on the trial process, especially on how rules of evidence and methods of constructing a rape case relate to social perceptions about gender, coercion, and sexuality.

As their interests converged in the mid-1970s, feminists and law-and-order forces secured passage of countless state and federal laws broadening the definition of rape and altering the procedures followed in rape trials (for surveys of these laws, see Berger, Searles, & Neuman, 1988; Galvin, 1986; Searles & Berger, 1987). Accompanying these changes was a vast body of feminist literature criticizing traditional rape law for fostering inappropriate conceptions of women and men, for denying legal protection to female victims who failed to adhere to conventional standards of propriety, for disregarding women's experience of sexual violation, and for inflicting emotional distress on rape victims who report and prosecute rape charges (Berger, 1977; Brownmiller, 1975; Clark & Lewis, 1977). Although they sometimes disagreed about the mechanisms at work, these feminist authors all viewed traditional rape law as contributing significantly to a system of male dominance.

For students of the relationship between law and social change, the legal

---

Correspondence regarding this article should be addressed to Carole Goldberg-Ambrose, UCLA School of Law, 405 Hilgard Avenue, Los Angeles, CA 90024-1476.

0022-4537/92/0300-0173$06.50/1

movement to transform these laws invites research. The legal changes were geographically widespread (occurring in almost all of the 50 states, Great Britain, Canada, Australia, and New Zealand), and they touched both substantive and procedural law. Such dramatic change in a legal regime occurs infrequently. Furthermore, the instrumental and symbolic goals spurring legislative changes were well articulated, providing a standard for evaluating the laws' effects. As modern criminologists and sociologists of law debate the efficacy of the criminal law in controlling rates of crime and influencing basic patterns of behavior (e.g., Zimring, 1987), the breadth of legislative changes and the range of goals in rape reform make it an interesting case in point.

In fact, some social scientists have conducted research in this area, and data are now becoming available from which to draw conclusions. Fifteen years after the beginning of the movement to reform our rape laws, it is worth determining what we do and do not know about the effects of this legal change, and what we can say about the success or failure of rape law revision.

Research Findings on Rape Law Reform

Interestingly, the judgments of those researchers prepared to render a verdict run the full gamut. At one extreme are some feminists, such as Bumiller (1987), who view the law as having produced changes, but for the worse. According to Bumiller, these laws (particularly those redefining the crime) did not go far enough in making women's experience of sexual violation the touchstone for rape; consequently, they have delegitimized women's experience, and provided legitimacy for males' claims to sexual access and overall dominance.

Closer to the center of the spectrum are writers who doubt whether the law has had any impact at all, either on attitudes, street crime, or the operation of the criminal justice system. Some of these authors question whether the laws have been implemented as legislators intended them to be. For them, the lack of impact can be chalked up to the lack of real reform outside the law books. Like Adler (1987), who studied English rape trials, they may focus on restrictive judicial interpretations of laws designed to broaden the definition of the crime or to restrict introduction of evidence concerning the victim's sexual history. Studies from Canada, Australia, and the United States have depicted how subjective interpretations of events by a mostly male judiciary override concern with the victim's treatment (Horney & Spohn, 1991; LaFree, 1989; Osborne, 1985; Soshnick, 1987; Tempkin, 1987). Other authors emphasize police and prosecutorial unwillingness to pursue complaints that are clearly within the scope of the law. Chappell (1984), for example, found that one major prosecutor's office did not change its conservative case-filing practices following rape law reform, and Loh's (1980) study of Washington State confirmed those data and also found a slight *decrease* in prison sentences during the period studied.

In five of the six jurisdictions studied by Horney and Spohn (1991) (Chicago, Houston, Washington, DC, Philadelphia, and Atlanta), rape reform did not produce an increase in victim reports and did not affect case processing. In the sixth city (Detroit), reform had only limited effects, and rates of conviction and incarceration remained unchanged. The authors' interviews with criminal justice personnel suggested to them that the explanation for inertia lay in the laws' failure to address broad realms of prosecutorial and judicial discretion. For example, they discovered that the elimination of corroboration and resistance requirements had had little effect on the likelihood of prosecution and conviction, and they hypothesized that the reason for this lack of change was the failure of prosecutors to invoke their discretion to file charges where corroboration or resistance were absent, or to ask for jury instructions explaining the lack of need for corroboration or evidence of resistance.

Another group skeptical about the legal impact of rape reform doubts whether the laws attempted as much as people thought. They express concern that the reform laws became so diluted in going through the legislative process—because of ideological differences between feminists and their law enforcement coalition partners—that the legal changes never truly represented major feminist reform (e.g., Berger et al., 1988). Such a position necessarily assumes that there is widespread agreement among feminists about whether particular rape law reforms advance feminist goals. However, the debates among feminists about whether to abandon the term "rape" in favor of "sexual assault" call that assumption into question.

In contrast with observers who doubt the ambitiousness of law reform are those who contend that reform made little difference because reform-oriented changes had been occurring through court decisions long before formal reform was instituted by statute. For example, judges and lawyers from six states surveyed by Horney and Spohn (1991) could recall few, if any, cases before the advent of rape shield reforms in which attorneys sought to harass victims by introducing evidence of their sexual history. They also claimed that pre-reform case rulings had accomplished much of what rape shield laws and laws eliminating corroboration and resistance requirements were designed to do.

From still another angle, Estrich (1987) discounts the impact of rape law reform because she believes that even the most aggressive state law reform efforts were clumsy or misguided; but if the laws (particularly those defining the crime) had been better formulated, the goals of rape law reform might have been achieved. Her position seems to be that laws defining rape will produce change only if they are drafted to provide a clear and correct symbolic message to those charged with interpreting them.

At the positive end of the spectrum, a number of writers seem more sanguine about realizing the promise of rape reform law. In an exhaustive review of court decisions implementing "rape shield" laws (ones that prohibit the use in trials of certain evidence of the victim's sexual history), Galvin (1986) concluded that the laws and the judges have functioned well in excluding impermissible evidence, even if the laws themselves were not always well drafted. Galvin, it should be noted, believes sexual history *should* be admissible when its admission does not depend on some invidious inference of "unchaste character" (1986, p. 809). Hence, she is less likely than some other commentators to be offended by many court decisions admitting such evidence.

Other researchers have found improvements in arrest, clearing, prosecution, or conviction rates, in the sentences meted out to convicted rapists, or in the experiences of rape victims at trial. For example, in her study of prosecutorial decisions in one Michigan county over a three-year period following the enactment of reform legislation, Caringella-MacDonald (1985) found an increase in the percentage of cases accepted for prosecution (from 10% in 1973 Detroit to 46% in 1975–1977 Kalamazoo). At the same time, the loss of these accepted cases through findings of nonguilt, dismissals, and nolles (refusals to prosecute further) decreased from 45% in 1973 Detroit to approximately 20% in both Detroit and Kalamazoo after passage of rape reform. The conviction rate for authorized cases rose from 55% in 1973 Detroit to 70–73% in 1975–1979 Detroit. Marsh, Geist, and Caplan's (1982) comprehensive study of the impact of Michigan's reform effort indicated that reporting rates had not been affected (they were increasing, but not because of the legal change), arrest rates had increased, both absolutely and relative to other serious crimes, and conviction rates had risen considerably. According to the overwhelming majority of criminal justice personnel, the rape reform law, particularly the rape shield provision, had also made the victim's experience with the criminal justice system less traumatic. Horney and Spohn's (1991) data on Detroit contradicted the findings of Marsh, Geist, and Caplan for Michigan as a whole, but they substituted some positive findings of their own: Reform produced increases in victim reporting rates, indictment rates, and the length of sentences for convicted rapists (an average increase of about 63 months).

One study conducted in California (reported in Marsh et al., 1982, p. 38) found convictions on rape charges had increased in a statistically significant way after California's rape shield law was adopted and the cautionary instruction was eliminated. (The cautionary instruction was a traditional warning that judges gave to jurors, before the jury deliberations, about the vulnerability of rape prosecutions to false accusations by the complaining witness.) Another California study, by Polk (1985), found a modest increase in the percentage of arrests for rape that resulted in the filing of a felony complaint, and hence an increase in the percentage of rape felony convictions per arrest. Polk's most dramatic finding was the increase over time in the probability that a rape offender would be sentenced to a state institution (from 58% in 1975 to 81% in 1982). The significance of these data is tempered, however, by the fact that California created a new sentencing system during the 1970s that resulted in increases in time served for *all* serious felons. Like the researchers who studied Michigan, Loh (1980) found a substantial increase in the number of rape complaints presented to prosecutors for charging following Washington State's rape law form. His findings of no increase in the percentage of cases charged as rape and a slight decrease in prison sentences counter the Michigan and California results, however.

Although aggregate American statistics cannot measure the effect of changes in individual state laws, they do offer some indication that the rate of reporting rape has increased since rape reform legislation was passed. Between 1970 and 1980, reports of rape doubled, from 18.7 to 36.4 per 100,000 population (Bourque, 1989, p. 11). Yet between 1972 and 1980, the National Crime Survey showed a drop in the incidence of rape per 100,000 population over age 11, from 77 to 40 for completed rapes, and from 238 to 120 for attempted rapes (Bourque, 1989, pp. 22–25). These data suggest an increase in the rate of reporting rape, which could possibly be attributable to legal changes designed to ameliorate the experience of the rape victim. National statistics also showed an 18% increase in the number of rape reports cleared by arrest between 1976 and 1980 (Bourque, 1989, pp. 34–35).

Elsewhere in the world, research in New South Wales (Temkin, 1987) found a sizable increase in police acceptance of rape complaints following rape law reform, a stable conviction rate, a marked rise in custodial sentences, and a sharp decline in the number of court cases in which sexual history evidence was admitted. An English study (Lloyd & Walmsley, 1989) supported Polk's findings in California with data showing that, for all convicted rapists between 1973 and 1985, there were significant increases in the likelihood and length of incarceration, even controlling for changes in the characteristics of offenders and the circumstances of crimes.

How Can Reform Success Be Determined?

Any attempt to sort through this tangle of differing assessments must first articulate the goals of reform and the standards for success in achieving them. A list of goals would have to include the following: (1) transformation of public attitudes about women's right to sexual autonomy and about what constitutes coerced sex; (2) changing the criminal justice system so women are no longer unwilling to report rape; (3) increasing the arrest, prosecution, and conviction rates for rape to levels more like those for other serious crimes; (4) eliminating those features of the rape trial that make the woman feel as if she is the defendant, and make the whole experience of testifying painful and degrading; and (5) increasing the amount of jail time served by convicted rapists to make it more comparable to time served by equally serious offenders.

Expressing the standards for success in achieving these goals is not as easy. How quickly must the desired change take place? If effects cannot be documented until 10 or 20 years have passed, has the law failed? How much of an effect qualifies as success? If, for example, the conviction rate for rape approaches but does not equal the rate for assault or robbery, has the law failed? If attitudes remain unchanged, but reporting, arrest, prosecution, and conviction rates improve, has the law failed? Some of the disagreements among writers on this subject stem from differing definitions of success. According to some, anything short of a complete change of attitudes and practices indicates failure. For others, having any effect at all is a major accomplishment.

Even if there were unanimity on the goals and the standards for success, there are still enormous impediments to measuring the legal impact of reform. First, the number and type of legal changes vary tremendously, as does the mode of their adoption. There are changes in the definition of the crime, changes in the legal defenses available (such as misunderstanding about the victim's consent), changes in the grading and sentencing structure (specifying several different levels or "grades" of seriousness of the crime, each with a different penalty), repeal of the cautionary instruction given to the jury, and several alterations in the evidentiary rules applied in rape trials—including the repeal of corroboration requirements, the admission of evidence of rape trauma syndrome, the repeal of requirements that rape victims submit to psychiatric examinations, and restrictions on use of evidence about the victim's sexual history. In most states, these changes were not enacted as a package; instead they dribbled into enactment over a period of years, sometimes decades. States often embraced some of these changes but not others. Furthermore, some changes were adopted by legislation, and others (such as elimination of the cautionary instruction and changes in defenses) were often introduced by court decision (Scutt, 1980).

A result of this variation is that it is difficult to identify the real source of any change in criminal justice outcomes (Chappell, 1984). One can ask the participants in the criminal justice system what they think matters the most, as Marsh et al. (1982) did in their study of the Michigan reform effort; but then one may be learning more about criminal justice personnel than about the criminal justice system. An important question for research is whether the manner and timing of rape reform law enactment are connected with the actual impact of the laws. Research on this question would obviously entail a multistate comparison.

Complicating matters further is that institutional changes often accompany law reform—changes that may make more of a difference than the legal revisions themselves. Two notable illustrations of institutional developments related to rape are the advent of specialized sex-crime units within police departments and prosecutors' offices, and the growth of rape crisis centers. Either type of institution could arise (and in some instances, has arisen) without accompanying legal reform (see the description of Indianapolis politics in LaFree, 1989, p. 94). It may be difficult to discern whether any changes that occur in criminal justice processing are attributable to institutional innovations or to changes in law. Some research, especially that of Handler (1978, 1986), heavily emphasizes the importance of institutional support for policy changes.

Finally, assessments of the legal impact of reform may have to account for delayed effects. Judges are notorious for their conservatism about their own practices. Although most states now regularly provide for continuing judicial education, it remains difficult to get judges to make dramatic changes in their conception of justice and trial process. The area of gender relations may present typical problems in this respect. For example, in 1938, federal courts were given a new set of procedural rules for civil cases, including a novel system by which parties could obtain information from their opponents in advance of trial. The federal judges who were charged with monitoring and enforcing this system, known as pretrial discovery, frequently ignored its scope and implications because it was just too alien to their sense of procedural regularity and fairness. Only when people who had learned this new system in law school ascended to the bench did it receive its most vigorous application. Thus, to the extent that the legal impact of reforms can be thwarted by judicial interpretations, it is important to consider the proper length of time to wait before the full impact of law reform can be fairly tested.

The Special Role of the Jury in Rape Law Reform

Another conservative element in the legal process that suggests the need for delayed assessment is the jury. Jurors play a prominent part in rape cases because defendants are entitled to request a jury and almost always do. At the earliest stages in the criminal justice process and throughout, officials base their decisions (to arrest, to prosecute, to plea bargain) on expectations about jury conduct (Marsh et al., 1982). Yet little is known about the effects of legal changes on juror or jury responses to evidence, and the limited knowledge suggests that change may be slow in coming. The legal system can control the "inputs" to the jury—i.e., evidence, and jury instructions at the close of evidence—but that control is imperfect at best. Constitutional considerations of fairness to defendants may require that certain evidence be admitted, even if feminist goals would dictate its exclusion (e.g., evidence to rebut a victim's claims of virginity or to establish that the victim was having sex with another person at the time of the alleged rape). Furthermore, jurors are transient and untrained participants in the criminal justice system. Whether they will comply with attempts to control them through legal changes depends on the existence of institutions to enforce that control. Yet as it is currently structured, the legal system cannot overturn a jury's decision if the verdict is acquittal.

The most important manifestation of these problems is the phenomenon of juries considering extralegal factors, such as the victim's marital status and her conformity to conservative gender role social practices, in deciding whether to convict the defendant. That juries consider such factors is widely documented (LaFree, Reskin, & Visher, 1985; Scutt, 1980). Rape reform laws do not (and constitutionally *could* not) preclude defense attorneys from introducing much of the evidence of this sort. The "shield" laws merely exclude evidence of the victim's sexual history. Only general evidentiary rules concerning the relevance of testimony are available to prosecutors seeking to exclude evidence of the victim's living arrangements or drinking habits; and usually the defense can demonstrate that testimony about such matters meets a threshold standard of relevance.

The underlying cause of jurors' consideration of extralegal factors seems to be a collection of perceptions, values, and attitudes that jurors hold about gender, sexuality, and what constitutes coercion. Some social science research has begun to probe whether specific evidentiary changes or jury instructions can alter juror perceptions of guilt in rape cases. The results are equivocal. One study (reported in Temkin, 1987) played tapes of real rape trials to simulated jurors, either with or without a subsequent corroboration warning (a traditional jury instruction directing jurors to disregard the victim's testimony unless it is corroborated by other evidence). To the researchers' surprise, the "jurors" were more willing to convict in the condition *with* the warning. In contrast, research using rape vignettes and simulated jurors has suggested that exclusion of sexual history evidence positively affects the likelihood that jurors will vote to convict (Borgida, 1980).

Although the early rape law reform efforts focused on eliminating misogynistic jury instructions and *excluding* prejudicial evidence, some recent legal innovations take a more affirmative approach to reducing jurors' consideration of extralegal factors. Prosecutors, for example, have sought to introduce expert testimony on rape trauma syndrome, a documented condition in which rape victims experience short-term and long-term symptoms such as nausea, sleeplessness, and phobias (Rowland, 1985). Evidence of these postrape symptoms in the victim is used to prove that intercourse was forcible rather than consensual. The value of this evidence to a prosecutor is that it focuses the jurors' attention on the harmful after effects of the sexual encounter rather than on the victim's prior lifestyle or relationship with the perpetrator. It also enables an expert to offer general testimony about the behavior of rape victims, testimony that contradicts a number of documented juror misconceptions. Work in cognitive psychology (e.g., Bennett & Feldman, 1981; Holstein, 1985) suggests that jurors compare the stories they hear at trial with distinct prototypes and specific instances of similar conduct that they have experienced. If rape trauma syndrome evidence makes it possible for jurors to match stories of rape to experiences or models of coercion rather than models of consensual behavior, then jury verdicts may change even without major changes in attitudes and beliefs about rape generally.

A growing legal literature focuses on the admissibility of rape trauma syndrome evidence at trial (Fischer, 1989). Interestingly, however, there seems to be no research on whether such evidence affects or is likely to affect convictions. Frazier and Borgida (1988) have shown that experts on rape trauma syndrome are significantly better informed about the circumstances and sequelae of rape than average citizens. Neither their research nor any other, however, has compared jurors' reactions to simulated or real rape trials with and without rape trauma syndrome evidence.

An even more direct assault on juror misconceptions about rape is the movement by some prosecutors and psychologists to introduce expert testimony about what is called "rape myth acceptance." As one of the advocates for admission of such evidence has written, expert testimony on matters such as the incidence of false accusations of rape, the incidence of acquaintance vs. stranger rape, and the dangers of resistance "may provide jurors with a social framework within which the facts of a particular case could be evaluated" (Tetreault, 1989, p. 243). Substantial research supports the view that jurors hold erroneous beliefs about these matters. Several studies using mock juries have found that the use of such expert testimony increases the incidence of guilty verdicts and improves the quality of jury deliberations (cf. Brekke & Borgida, 1988).

Focusing on the Trial Process: Challenges and New Directions for Research

Because of lessening confidence in the value of substantive changes in the definition of rape, the rape law reform movement seems to be turning its attention to events at trial, and how rules of evidence and methods of constructing a rape case relate to social perceptions about gender, coercion, and sexuality. That change of focus to the trial process suggests the need for much more research about how the race of the victim bears on jurors' perceptions. Data from the *Uniform Crime Reports* and National Crime Surveys, supported by some but not all community studies, show that Black women have a disproportionately higher risk of being raped (Bourque, 1989). Research also demonstrates that jurors are less likely to convict for rape when the victim is Black (Field & Bienen, 1980; LaFree, 1989). Yet surprisingly, no research has examined whether legal reforms are equally effective in rape cases with Black and White victims. The absence of attention to this issue contrasts sharply with the intense scrutiny that has been given to the question of whether Black *men* are treated more harshly than White men charged with raping White women (LaFree, 1989). More emphasis on the race of the victim would be consistent with research on the imposition of the death penalty, which has shown that the race of the victim is more important than the race of the perpetrator in predicting sentencing decisions (Kennedy, 1988). History also suggests the importance of focusing on the victim's race. In the pre-Civil War South, for example, rape of a Black woman carried the sentence of a fine or imprisonment at the court's discretion, while the sentence for rape of a White woman was at least two years in prison, and could be death if the defendant was Black (Kennedy, 1988).

Contemporary feminist theorists have stressed the need for attention to the variety of women's experiences, taking account of differences in race, class, and religion. There is good reason for attention to these differences when studying rape law reform. For example, the history of American race relations suggests that rape myths about Black women may be different from the myths about rape generally (Wyatt, this issue). What implications should that have for the effectiveness of evidence regarding the rape trauma syndrome or rape myth acceptance? Should distinctive testimony be introduced about rape myths concerning Black women? Is more research needed as a basis for such expert testimony?

The goal of rape reform legislation that seems most difficult to achieve is change in knowledge, values, and attitudes about gender and sexuality. Loh (1980), in his study of Washington State's rape law reform, indicated that criminal justice personnel were applying the previous standards to rape cases, regardless of alterations in the law. But changing the perceptions and values of jurors may be most difficult of all; indeed, police and prosecutors often state that they would modify their practices if they perceived a change in jurors' responses at rape trials (Estrich, 1987; Marsh et al., 1982). The evidentiary changes mentioned above may contribute to such a transformation in juror reactions to rape trials, at least if the courts begin to admit expert testimony on rape trauma syndrome and rape myth acceptance.

At the same time, the symbolic or ideological component of rape law reform, be it substantive or evidentiary, may also affect jurors' perceptions and conclusions. Indeed, some notable participants in the rape law reform movement (Bienen, 1983; Chappell, 1984; Nordby, 1980) identify symbolic/educative effects as the most important (and sometimes the *only*) consequences of legal change. Yet little is known about which kinds of legal changes are most effective in inducing attitudinal change. Caringella-MacDonald (1985) suggested that any measure that improves arrest, prosecution, and conviction rates could have a positive effect on attitudes, because attrition in these aspects of rape cases confirms and perpetuates rape myths about false accusations. Yet she also acknowledged that the attitudes she hoped to change were the very source of difficulty in reducing attrition rates. As Field and Bienen (1980) pointed out, "Legislation . . . cannot destroy the social function which the traditional rules [of rape law] performed. As long as large numbers of men and women believe that women are inferior and should be kept in their place through forced submission to sexual acts, the law will reflect that view" (p. 162). Thus, reforms that address the trial process, and hence the attitudes of individual jurors rather than society as a whole, may be more promising as vehicles for achieving feminist goals. Of course, the longer that research waits to assess legal impacts, the more difficult it may become to attribute changes in practice or attitudes to any specific law reforms.

All of these problems and complications suggest the need for careful longitudinal research, comparing complaint and case outcomes, as well as victim experiences and public perceptions of rape, before and after law reform, and using different states to study different types of reform. In fact, given the amount of rape reform legislation that has been enacted, the total amount of before-and-after research is surprisingly limited. Michigan has been the focus of the best and most sustained work (Caringella-MacDonald, 1985; Marsh et al., 1982; Nordby, 1980). Washington State and California have also been studied in this way, as have some foreign countries with British common law traditions, most notably Australia.

However, most research on rape documents a particular condition (be it the victimization rate, the reporting rate, the conviction rate, or the attitudes of jurors or victims) as of a given time, with no attempt to assess change over time generally, let alone to study change as a function of revisions in the law. Sometimes that is not a problem, as when Galvin (1986) studied the practices of state court judges in admitting sexual history evidence. There a safe assumption was that before the law was changed, all such evidence came in at trial, so comparison was possible with just an "after" study. But on other issues, knowing whether the situation has improved would be important. In some instances, commentators may be prepared to say that a given condition is unacceptable even though it constitutes an improvement over the past. But on many topics that judgment would be quite difficult without knowing how much of an improvement occurred and what was required to achieve it. If most of the significant rape law revisions have already been adopted, some of this kind of research may be impossible, for there is no longer a "before" to compare with the "after." However, a number of valuable studies on such topics as victims' experiences and police attitudes toward rape were undertaken in the early years of the rape reform movement. These studies could now be replicated, and comparisons drawn.

With their time-series analyses of six different urban jurisdictions, Horney and Spohn (1991) have made real progress in constructing useful research on rape law reform and suggesting testable hypotheses to explain its general lack of legal impact. Their study fails, however, to examine the full range of rape reforms, particularly those attempting to affect the construction of events at trial.

Ultimately, there are some problems with rape that the legal system cannot hope to fix, at least without compromising bedrock values of fairness to the victim or defendant. For example, to the extent that victims do not report the crime because of concerns with privacy, or to the extent that having to appear at trial under any conditions anguishes victims and deters them from reporting rape, law reform cannot make a difference. Social science research has not yet come up against that brick wall, however. There is still much unfinished business for research in studying problems with rape that the legl system may be able to remedy.

Conclusion

Despite the intense effort that has gone into rape law reform, we have insufficient and conflicting information about the difference that these laws make for victims, for the criminal justice system, and for the treatment of women generally. The variety of law reform approaches and goals in different states both complicates the assessment process and offers opportunities for comparative research. Given the key role of juror values and perceptions in determining how rape complaints will be dealt with, future research could profitably focus on the trial process—especially on how widespread perceptions about gender, sexuality, and coercion interact with legal rules regulating the presentation of a rape case. Such a focus will require greater sensitivity to victims' race and class, as well as other factors that may bear on juror perceptions.

References

Adler, Z. (1987). *Rape on trial.* New York: Routledge & Kegan Paul.

Bennett, L., & Feldman, M. (1981). *Reconstructing reality in the courtroom.* New Brunswick, NJ: Rutgers University Press.

Berger, R., Searles, P., & Newman, W. (1988). The dimensions of rape reform legislation. *Law and Society Review, 22,* 329–349.

Berger, V. (1977). Man's trial, woman's tribulation: Rape cases in the courtroom. *Columbia Law Review, 77,* 1–103.

Bienen, L. (1983). Rape reform legislation in the United States: A look at some practice effects. *Victimology: An International Journal, 8,* 139–151.

Borgida, E. (1980). Evidentiary reform of rape laws: A psycholegal approach. In P. Lipsett & B. Sales (Eds.), *New directions in psycholegal research* (pp. 57–75). New York: Van Nostrand Reinhold.

Bourque, L. (1989). *Defining rape.* Durham, NC: Duke University Press.

Brekke, N., & Borgida, E. (1988). Expert psychological testimony in rape trials: A social-cognitive analysis. *Journal of Personality and Social Psychology, 55,* 372–386.

Brownmiller, S. (1975). *Against our will.* New York: Simon & Schuster.

Bumiller, K. (1987). Rape as a legal symbol: An essay on sexual violence. *University of Miami Law Review, 42,* 75–91.

Caringella-MacDonald, S. (1985). Sexual assault prosecution: An examination of model rape legislation in Michigan. In C. Schweber & C. Feinman (Eds.), *Criminal justice politics and women: The aftermath of legally mandated change* (pp. 65–82). New York: Haworth.

Chappell, D. (1984). The impact of rape legislation reform: Some comparative trends. *International Journal of Women's Studies, 7,* 70–80.

Clark, L., & Lewis, D. (1977). *Rape: The price of coercive sexuality.* Toronto: Women's Educational Press.

Estrich, S. (1987). *Real rape.* Cambridge, MA: Harvard University Press.

Field, H., & Bienen, L. (1980). *Jurors and rape.* Lexington, MA: Heath.

Fischer, K. (1989). Defining the boundaries of admissible expert psychological testimony on rape trauma syndrome. *University of Illinois Law Review,* 691–734.

Frazier, P., & Borgida, E. (1988). Juror common understanding and the admissibility of rape trauma syndrome evidence in court. *Law and Human Behavior, 12,* 101–122.

Galvin, H. (1986). Shielding rape victims in the state and federal courts: A proposal for the second decade. *Minnesota Law Review, 70,* 763–916.
Handler, J. (1978). *Social movements and the legal system: A theory of law reform and social change.* New York: Academic Press.
Handler, J. (1986). *The conditions of discretion.* Beverly Hills, CA: Sage.
Holstein, J. A. (1985). Jurors' interpretations and jury decision-making. *Law and Human Behavior, 9,* 83–100.
Horney, J., & Spohn, C. (1991). Rape law reform and instrumental change in six urban jurisdictions. *Law and Society Review, 25,* 117–153.
Kennedy, R. (1988). *McCleskey v. Kemp:* Race, capital punishment, and the Supreme Court. *Harvard Law Review, 101,* 1388–1443.
LaFree, G. (1989). *Rape and criminal justice.* Belmont, CA: Wadsworth.
LaFree, G., Reskin, B., & Visher, C. (1985). Jurors' responses to victims' behavior and legal issues in sexual assault trials. *Social Problems, 32,* 389–407.
Lloyd, C., & Walmsley, R. (1989). *Changes in rape offenses and sentencing.* London, England: Her Majesty's Stationery Office.
Loh, W. (1980). The impact of common law and reform rape statutes on prosecution: An empirical study. *Washington Law Review, 55,* 543–652.
Marsh, J., Geist, A., & Caplan, N. (1982). *Rape and the limits of law reform.* Boston: Auburn House.
Nordby, V. (1980). Reforming the rape laws: The Michigan experience. In J. Scutt (Ed.), *Rape law reform* (pp. 3–34). Canberra: Australian Institute of Criminology.
Osborne, J. (1985). Rape law reform: The new cosmetic for Canadian women. In C. Schweber & C. Feinman (Eds.), *Criminal justice politics and women: The aftermath of legally mandated change.* New York: Haworth.
Polk, K. (1985). Rape reform and criminal justice processing. *Crime and Delinquency, 31,* 191–205.
Rowland, J. (1985). *The ultimate violation.* Garden City, NJ: Doubleday.
Scutt, J. (1980). Evidence and the role of the jury in trials for rape. In J. Scutt (Ed.), *Rape law reform* (pp. 90–114). Canberra: Australian Institute of Criminology.
Searles, P., & Berger, R. (1987). The current status of rape reform legislation: An examination of state statutes. *Women's Rights Law Reporter, 10,* 25–43.
Soshnick, A. (1987). The rape shield paradox: Complainant protection amidst oscillating trends of state judicial interpretation. *Journal of Criminal Law and Criminology, 78,* 644–698.
Temkin, J. (1987). *Rape and the legal process.* London, England: Sweet & Maxwell.
Tetreault, P. A. (1989). Rape myth acceptance: A case for providing educational expert testimony in rape jury trials. *Behavioral Sciences and the Law, 7,* 243–257.
Zimring, F. (1987). Legal perspectives on family violence. *California Law Review, 75,* 521–539.

CAROLE GOLDBERG-AMBROSE is Professor of Law and Associate Dean at the UCLA School of Law. Her B.A. is from Smith College and her J.D. from Stanford Law School. She has developed and taught courses on rape law, and has lectured extensively on problems of rape and sexual harassment.

During the past 2 decades, the criminal justice system has significantly changed its response to battered women and their assailants. These changes are, in part, being encouraged by newly established community intervention projects (CIPs) across the United States. This study reports the findings of victim interviews and archival data concerning incidents of woman abuse that came to the attention of the Minneapolis police and were referred to a CIP. The results for samples monitored over a 6- to 12-month period tend to support the use of arrest on first police visits to the home and subsequent action by the courts that includes ordering perpetrators into treatment.

The Combined Effects of Coordinated Criminal Justice Intervention in Woman Abuse

MARYANN SYERS
Domestic Abuse Project/Private Practice
JEFFREY L. EDLESON
University of Minnesota/Domestic Abuse Project

Criminal justice interventions in woman abuse have expanded rapidly over the past 2 decades. In particular, the 1980s witnessed a dramatic change in public attitudes toward police intervention in woman abuse. Police departments came under increased pressure to respond to domestic violence in the same manner as they were responding to violence between strangers on the street. Advocates of battered women argued that to do less would imply that women's rights were diminished when an assailant was an intimate partner rather than a stranger. Victim rights advocates were, at the same time, pressuring police to pay greater attention to crime victims, including battered women and children.

Additional pressure was brought to bear by two other events in the early 1980s. First, several battered women succeeded in winning landmark cases

Authors' Note: This study was, in part, funded by a grant from the National Institute of Justice. The authors wish to thank the staff and clients of the Domestic Abuse Project and Dr. Carol Skay for her invaluable assistance. Reprint requests should be sent to Maryann Syers at the Domestic Abuse Project, Inc., 204 West Franklin Avenue, Minneapolis, MN 55404.

JOURNAL OF INTERPERSONAL VIOLENCE, Vol. 7 No. 4, December 1992 490-502

against police departments that did not respond when emergency help was requested (e.g., *Thurman v. City of Torrington*, 1984). Second, Sherman and Berk (1984) released the results of a study that showed arresting perpetrators of woman abuse could reduce recidivism rates by half when compared to other police actions. By mid-decade, these pressures led to an increased use of arrest by police in many parts of the United States.

Increased arrests resulted in large numbers of woman abusers being referred to court systems for the first time, yet prosecution of these cases seldom occurred. Studies by Ford (1983) and Dutton (1987) showed that perpetrators of woman abuse had an extremely small chance of being prosecuted by the courts.

Facing inaction by many police departments and low prosecution rates of woman abusers in court, battered women's advocates designed and established a new type of organization, Community Intervention Projects (CIPs). CIPs are designed to change the responses by the criminal justice and social service systems to battered women and their perpetrators. CIPs have been established across the United States, including Minnesota (Edleson, 1991; Pence, 1983; Pence & Shepard, 1988), Colorado (Domestic Violence Task Force, 1988), California (Soler & Martin, 1983; Soler, 1987), and elsewhere (see Goolkasian, 1986).

To date, very few evaluations of coordinated community interventions have been completed. Gamache, Edleson, and Schock (1988) retrospectively studied system-level activity changes in three communities where CIPs were established. Archival police and court records showed that the CIPs studied had a significant impact on increasing the levels of perpetrator arrests, convictions, and court mandates to treatment. In a series of other studies (see Dutton, 1986; Edleson & Syers, 1991; Pence, Novack, & Galaway, 1982; Shepard, 1987; Tolman & Bhosley, 1989), court-mandated or recommended treatment has been demonstrated to be an effective method both of referring men to treatment and, if treatment is completed, of increasing the likelihood that men will end their use of violence during follow-up periods.

It appears from these results that system activity can be changed and that court involvement in referring men to counseling appears to decrease the likelihood of recidivism. However, few studies are available that take into account the multiple operational factors of CIPs, as will be described later in this article. Two studies by Steinman (1988, 1990) have attempted to do so. In the first study, Steinman evaluated a coordinated community intervention in Lincoln (Nebraska) and found that postarrest sanctions had little influence on recidivism beyond what was achieved through the initial arrest. There were some indications in these data, however, that certain postarrest sanctions, such as fines, might be associated with lower rates of recidivism.

To investigate these possible associations, Steinman (1990) conducted a second study in which he compared those cases that occurred prior to the implementation of the coordinated community effort and those that occurred after it was established. He found that police actions *not* coordinated with other sanctions produced increased violence. Police action, especially arrest, *in coordination* with other criminal justice efforts became a significant deterrent. Steinman also found, however, that coordinated efforts are not consistently effective and that victims who contacted the police on their own initiative and who were not living with their perpetrator tended to be at increased risk of abuse. These findings are somewhat supported by recent studies of police interventions that have generally not found arrest alone to be a strong deterrent (Dunford, Huizinga, & Elliot, 1990; Hirschel, Hutchison, & Dean, 1992; Sherman et al., 1991). Bringing advocates, police, and others into the situation may put some women at a heightened level of risk. However, it may be that these women already live in a high-risk situation and that the violence being committed against them would be increasing regardless of criminal justice efforts.

This article presents the results of a study examining the effect of a CIP on the lives of battered women and their assailants. The study was undertaken to shed greater light on the multiple components of system responses that appear to contribute to lowering perpetrator recidivism rates.

METHOD

Sample

The original sample included 528 incident reports from police. After eliminating the few female perpetrators, repeat incidents of violence, and cases for which minimal data were collected, a total of 358 cases were included as part of this study. The demographic characteristics of this sample are presented in Table 1.

Follow-up data were collected from victims, with the number located and interviewed varying by time period. At the 6-month follow-up, 196 victims (54.8%) were interviewed, and at the 12-month follow-up, 121 (33.8%) were interviewed. As these figures indicate, there were significant missing data in this study. Police incident reports and agency records often contained incomplete information.

Comparisons between those cases for which sufficient initial data were available, those for which initial and 6-month data were available, and those

TABLE 1: **Demographic Characteristics of the Sample** ($N = 358$)

	Victim		*Perpetrator*	
	n	(%)	n	(%)
Annual family income				
No income	124	(34.6)	111	(31.0)
Less than $10,000	95	(26.5)	53	(14.8)
$10,000-$29,999	92	(25.7)	91	(25.4)
$30,000 or more	3	(00.8)	16	(04.5)
Highest education				
Up to high school degree	80	(22.3)	179	(50.0)
More than high school	163	(45.5)	110	(30.7)
Ethnic group				
European-American	211	(58.9)	157	(43.9)
African-American	79	(22.1)	153	(42.7)
Native American	54	(15.1)	32	(08.9)
Asian-American	2	(00.6)	6	(01.7)
Age in years				
Mean age in years	30.1[a]		32.0[b]	
Range of ages	15-70		18-71	
Prior police visits for domestic assault				
No prior visits	168	(46.9)		
Prior visits	190	(53.1)		
	At incident		*At first CIP contact*	
	n	(%)	n	(%)
Relationship status				
Living together	204	(57.0)	100	(27.9)
Not living together	146	(40.8)	232	(64.8)

NOTE: Columns do not total 100% due to missing data.
a. *SD* = 9.14.
b. *SD* = 9.09.

for which data up to and including the 12-month follow-ups were available showed very few differences. Data on men who were better educated (chi-square = 9.94, $df = 4$, $p = .04$) and had higher incomes (chi-square = 9.77, $df = 4$, $p = .04$) were more likely to be gathered during follow-ups. Men and their partners in higher socioeconomic groups may be less transient and thus easier to find than others in the sample.

Intervention Procedures

The Minneapolis Intervention Project (MIP) is one of several CIPs established by the Domestic Abuse Project (DAP) in Minneapolis (see Brygger & Edleson, 1987). When MIP was established in 1983, it focused its early coordination efforts on misdemeanor assault cases in two police precincts of Minneapolis. Felony assaults were then, as now, handled by a different DAP, the Hennepin County Legal Advocacy Project.

In its early stages, MIP had only two advocates for battered women working on individual cases and on systems change. MIP now serves the entire city of Minneapolis with offices located in the City Hall and a satellite office in a predominantly minority area of the city. A total of 8 full-time staff and 30 volunteer advocates now work for the Project.

MIP initially set out to establish a network of new policies and procedures within Minneapolis's criminal justice system and among social service agencies to which men are referred following prosecution. These efforts started with the local police department. Advocates worked with the police administration to adopt policies that required officers to make an arrest when probable cause existed that a domestic assault had occurred or when an order for protection (restraining order) had been violated.

Once an arrest had been made, the police department agreed to immediately notify the MIP office. In order to offer the women increased protection, local jails often agreed to hold the men for several hours or until an arraignment was made the next morning. During this time, trained paid or volunteer advocates visited the victim at her home or talked with her by phone. During such visits or over the telephone, advocates offered support and information about subsequent court proceedings, shelters, and other services available to her. Time permitting, advocates also attempted to contact and provide services to women in homes where police intervened but where an arrest did not occur.

MIP advocates also worked with prosecuting city attorneys in an effort to establish procedures for handling battering cases and to work out agreements whereby prosecutors would aggressively pursue these cases when an arrest occurred or a complaint was filed. With the victim's permission, MIP advocates assisted prosecutors by supplying victim information during the court process. The goal at this point was to obtain judicial outcomes that were seen as helping to end the violence and increase both the victim's safety and her satisfaction with the criminal justice system's response.

Upon entry of a guilty plea by the man or his conviction by the court, judges participated in the coordinated efforts by agreeing to order presentence investigations. During these investigations, probation officers participated by agreeing to incorporate information regarding the history of the man's violence and the battered woman's wishes into their presentence recommendations to the court. Judges and referees were asked to pronounce a sentence that included imprisonment and then to stay part or all of the sentence pending successful completion of a batterers' treatment program as a condition of probation.

Throughout these legal proceedings, advocates worked closely with and on behalf of the battered women. They worked with prosecutors and probation officers and assisted victims to secure or renew orders for protection, temporary custody, and child support agreements. They also helped women link up with shelters, community-based support and education groups, postshelter housing, job training programs, and so on.

Typically, the criminal justice system was asked to mandate men to batterers' treatment programs. A separate program at the Domestic Abuse Project offered group treatment for the violent men and reserved space in the groups for court-mandated members. Support and education groups were also available for the battered women and children. (For full descriptions of programs, see Brygger & Edleson, 1987; Edleson, 1991.)

Data Collection Procedures

Data were collected on all woman abuse cases reported to MIP over a 13-month period from February 1986 to March 1987 in two police precincts of Minneapolis. All women visited by police as the result of a domestic disturbance report where a male partner was suspected of abuse were included in the initial sample. The police reported incidents to advocates working at MIP.

Data were collected from multiple sources including reports filed by police following the incident and records kept by the legal advocates as cases moved through the criminal justice system. In addition, follow-up telephone interviews were conducted with as many female victims as could be reached immediately following a police visit and at both 6 and 12 months after police contact. Attempts to maximize interview response rates included multiple telephone calls to the available telephone number. If this failed to locate the victim, police, court, and perpetrator records were examined to find alternative locations. All victim interviews were, however, strictly voluntary.

Police reports were made shortly after a visit to the location of the incident and copies were sent to MIP staff. These reports included minimal demographic data, a location and description of the incident, the number and gender of victims and perpetrators, and the outcome of the police intervention (arrest or nonarrest). MIP staff kept additional records based on victim reports that provided information about the incident, the perpetrator's past history of assaultive behavior, the court process for past assaults and the current one, and the court outcome for the current incident.

The initial, postpolice visit interview and both 6- and 12-month follow-up interviews provided further demographic information about the woman and her abuser as well as information on the following areas: previous history of police intervention for violence, and specific information about the violence suffered and the resulting injuries.

The 6- and 12-month interviews contained additional questions about the change in the woman's relationship status since the last interview, continued abuse, criminal justice system involvement, and the use of support services (e.g., shelters, support groups, therapy) by the victim.

RESULTS

Findings regarding (a) the number of men who repeated their violence after an initial report of a violent incident and (b) the impact of the various components of the criminal justice response on the men's recidivism rates are reported here. The first subsection reports on the recidivism rate of the perpetrators in the sample and explains how these rates were determined. The second subsection presents the results first of chi-square analyses and then of logistic regression analyses. These procedures were used in an effort to determine the combination of demographic and system response variables that best predicted the variation in perpetrators' continued use of violence.

Repeat Violence

Men were grouped into one of two categories: repeater or nonrepeater of violence. Four data sources were used to determine repeater status. The first source was the police incident report. The 6- and 12-month follow-up interviews constituted two additional sources. During each of these interviews, victims were asked whether the perpetrator had repeated his violence in the 6 months since the initial report. A final source was records that the advocacy staff kept on all perpetrators and victims. These records included information from a variety of sources on perpetrators' repeat offenses and women's further victimization. A man was categorized as a repeater if *any* one of these four sources of data indicated he had committed another act of violence against any victim since the original incident reported to the intervention project by the police.

Analysis of the four data sources indicated that at the 6-month follow-up, 117 (59.7%) of the men for whom data were available had not repeated their violence while 79 (40.3%) had reoffended. At the 12-month follow-up, 74 (61.2%) had not repeated violence while 47 (38.8%) had done so.

The way in which the "repeat violence" variable was created permitted instances in which a man might be placed in the "no repeat" category simply because no further data were available after the initial police contact. As a caution against skewing the sample toward men falsely categorized as nonrepeaters, statistical analyses are reported here only for the subsamples of men for whom complete 6- and/or 12-month follow-up interview data were available. Thus, the results presented below rely heavily on victim reports at follow-up supplemented by information from the other sources mentioned earlier.

Predictors of Recidivism

The categorical nature of the dependent variable dictated the use of crosstabulations and both chi-square and logistic regression analyses. Efforts to identify predictors of repeat violence began with two- and three-way crosstabulations of the dependent variable (repeater status) by independent variables (system response variables) and possible intervening variables (demographic variables). Relationships approaching a generous level of statistical significance ($p < .10$) were included in the logistic regression analysis, as is common practice. Such multivariate analyses produce the combination of variables that most adequately predict variation in the dichotomous dependent variable.

The simple two-way crosstabulation of repeater status by arrest indicated that there were no significant differences between arrest and nonarrest for men on whom both 6- and 12-month follow-up data were obtained. These findings may be the result of the quasi-experimental nature of this study where arrested men represented very different cases than those where no arrest was made.

To clarify the above, further analyses were performed. Men were grouped as follows into three categories representing the outcomes resulting from differing degrees of system intervention: (a) men who were not arrested following the incident (6 months = 72, 12 months = 45); (b) men who were arrested but were not court-ordered to treatment (6 months = 87, 12 months = 51); and (c) men who were arrested and were required to attend treatment as a condition of their sentence (6 months = 37, 12 months = 25). A two-way crosstabulation between the repeater variable and these three categories of men in the 6-month follow-up sample ($N = 196$) showed that those arrested and court-ordered to treatment were the least likely to repeat their violence (n = 12, 32.4%), followed by those who were not arrested (n = 28, 38.9%), and then by those who were arrested but not ordered to treatment (n = 39, 44.8%). These trends were not, however, statistically significant. Slightly stronger trends (chi-square = 5.65, df = 2, p = .06) were found among those men for whom 12-month follow-up data were available (N = 121). At 12 months, those men who were arrested and court-ordered to treatment were again the least likely to be reported as repeating violence (n = 5, 20%), followed this time by those who were arrested but not ordered to treatment (n = 20, 39.2%), and then by those who not arrested (n = 22, 48.9%). It appears that the longer the men in this study were monitored, the stronger the impact of being arrested and mandated to treatment and the weaker the influence of a police visit without an arrest.

Another intervention factor that appears to have distinguished between men who repeated their violence and those who did not was whether there had been previous police visits to the home because of violence. Of those men in the 6-month sample for whom this was the first police visit, 73.1% (n = 76) did not repeat their use of violence as compared to 44.6% (n = 41) who did not repeat among those where police had visited earlier (chi-square = 15.3, df = 1, p < .01). Of those men in the 12-month sample who were first visited by police on this incident, 71.2% (n = 47) did not repeat violence, compared to 49.1% (n = 21) who did not repeat among those having been visited by the police earlier (chi-square = 5.28, df = 1, p = .02).

Logistic regressions were performed, as stated earlier, using variables that achieved a liberal significance level (p < .10) in crosstabulations. Variables meeting this criterion included the system outcome (categorized as nonarrest, arrest without treatment, and arrest with treatment), marital status, race, education, income, and prior police involvement. A variable included in the equation was only removed if it reached p > .15, a commonly used level for removal in logistic regressions.

Analyses were first performed on cases for which 6-month follow-up reports were available (N = 196). Cases where no follow-up data were available were dropped from the analyses. As shown in Table 2, system outcomes, police visits, and perpetrator educational level predicted lower recidivism among those found at the 6-month follow-up. First-time police visits combined with an arrest that is followed by a court order for the perpetrator to receive treatment predict lower recidivism among the men in this subsample. An arrest without a subsequent court order for treatment was the weakest predictor of reduced recidivism. One additional variable, perpetrator's level of education, enters the equation. It appears that the higher a man's education, the lower his likelihood to repeat his use of violence.

TABLE 2: Results of Logistic Regression for Decreased Use of Violence After Intervention Using Sample Located at 6-Month Follow-Up

Term	*Coefficient*	*Standard Error*	*Approximate Chi-Square*	df	p *Value*
System outcomes					
Effect of nonarrest	.30	.27	4.72	2	.09
Effect of arrest only	.45	.25			
Effect of arrest with court-ordered treatment	–.75	.37			
First police visit	–.54	.17	10.63	1	.001
Educational level					
High school or less	.24	.36	5.90	2	.05
Some college	.67	.31			
College degree or more	–.91	.54			
Constant	–1.02	.32	13.76	1	.001

NOTE: Goodness-of-fit chi-square = 15.99, *df* = 11, *p* = .14.

TABLE 3: Results of Logistic Regression for Decreased Use of Violence After Intervention Using Sample Located at 12-Month Follow-Up

Term	*Coefficient*	*Standard Error*	*Approximate Chi-Square*	df	p *Value*
System outcomes					
Effect of nonarrest	.79	.35	7.32	2	.03
Effect of arrest only	.40	.33			
Effect of arrest with court-ordered treatment	–1.19	.53			
First police visit	–.49	.20	6.06	1	.01
Constant	–.85	.29	11.16	1	.001

NOTE: Goodness-of-fit chi-square = 8.24, *df* = 8, *p* = .41.

These three variables—system outcome, police visits, and perpetrator educational level—combined to produce a model of predictive strength.

Next, a logistic regression was performed on data from the 12-month follow-up sample (*N* = 121). Again, if no follow-up was completed at this point, the case was dropped from the analysis. The results of this analysis are presented in Table 3. These findings are similar to the results presented above in Table 2. Again, the strongest predictors of decreased recidivism among the men in this subsample were first-time police visits to the home followed by an arrest with a subsequent court order for the perpetrator to receive treatment. Together, these variables produce a model with a high degree of predictive ability as reflected in the goodness-of-fit chi-square statistic. These data also reveal that men arrested but *not* subsequently ordered by the court to treatment were less likely to reoffend than those who were not arrested.

DISCUSSION

Criminal justice intervention in cases of woman abuse is growing rapidly. The results of this study appear to indicate that the most potent police visit to the home is the first one. These results support Fagan (Fagan, 1989; Fagan, Stewart, & Hansen, 1983) and others who have argued that a first arrest may have a stronger impact on batterers than subsequent arrests.

The results appear to support the combination of police making arrests on first visits with the use of mandated treatment by the courts as a consequence. The strength of this finding appears to increase the longer men are monitored. The results also indicated that, at the 6-month follow-up, the higher a man's education, the less likely it was that he would repeat his violence. It was also true that those more educated and with higher incomes were more likely to be found at follow-up. It may be that those in higher socioeconomic groups will be more likely to respond to social intervention. Other recent studies (Dunford et al., 1990; Hirschel et al., 1992; Saunders & Parker, 1989; Sherman et al., 1991) show that certain case characteristics and types of system response also temper the effectiveness of intervention, particularly by the police.

There are several serious limitations to this study that should be noted. First, this study relied on reporting by a number of informants including police, the victims, and advocates of battered women. Reporting was often incomplete, seriously depleting the number of cases available for the final analyses and limiting the strength of these findings. Second, the dependent variable in this study may tend toward classifying men as nonrepeaters when they are, in fact, repeaters. Analyzing only subsamples found at 6- and 12-month follow-ups partially addressed this possibility. However, even completed follow-ups up to 1 year in length cannot guarantee that all incidents of violence were observed by at least one of the several informants. These findings are thus limited due to these methodological problems.

It appears from this limited study that when police arrest batterers, court system follow-up may be very important. Among those arrested, the men mandated to receive treatment were the least likely to repeat acts of violence. It is this combination of interventions—first visit during which an arrest is made and followed by court-mandated counseling—that is so often promoted by advocates and that appears to be the most consistent model for predicting lower recidivism rates.

This study set out to offer a more systematic examination of criminal justice system efforts to reduce recidivism rates among men who batter. The results for samples monitored over a 6- to 12-month period tend to support the calls of advocates for prompt action by police that includes an arrest *combined with* subsequent action by the courts, including ordering perpetrators of violence into treatment.

REFERENCES

Brygger, M. P., & Edleson, J. L. (1987). The Domestic Abuse Project: A multisystems intervention in woman battering. *Journal of Interpersonal Violence, 2*, 324-336.

Domestic Violence Task Force. (1988). *The Denver domestic violence manual*. Denver, CO: City of Denver.

Dunford, F. W., Huizinga, D., & Elliot, D. S. (1990). The role of arrest in domestic assault: The Omaha police experiment. *Criminology, 28*, 183-206.

Dutton, D. G. (1986). The outcome of court-mandated treatment for wife assault: A quasi-experimental evaluation. *Violence and Victims, 1*, 163-175.

Dutton, D. G. (1987). The criminal justice response to wife assault. *Law and Human Behavior, 11*, 189-206.

Edleson, J. L. (1991). Coordinated community responses to woman battering. In M. Steinman (Ed.), *Woman battering: Policy responses* (pp. 203-219). Cincinnati, OH: Anderson Press.

Edleson, J. L., & Syers, M. (1991). The effects of group treatment for men who batter: An 18-month follow-up study. *Research on Social Work Practice, 1*, 227-243.

Fagan, J. (1989). Cessation of family violence: Deterrence and dissuasion. In L. Ohlin & M. Tonry (Eds.), *Family violence* (pp. 377-425). Chicago: University of Chicago Press.

Fagan, J., Stewart, D. K., & Hansen, K. V. (1983). Violent men or violent husbands? Background factors and situational correlates. In D. Finkelhor, R. J. Gelles, G. T. Hotaling, & M. A. Straus (Eds.), *The dark side of families* (pp. 49-67). Beverly Hills, CA: Sage.

Ford, D. A. (1983). Wife battery and criminal justice: A study of victim decision-making. *Family Relations, 32*, 463-475.

Gamache, D. J., Edleson, J. L., & Schock, M. D. (1988). Coordinated police, judicial and social service response to woman battering: A multi-baseline evaluation across three communities. In G. T. Hotaling, D. Finkelhor, J. T. Kirkpatrick, & M. Straus (Eds.), *Coping with family violence: Research and policy perspectives* (pp. 193-209). Newbury Park, CA: Sage.

Goolkasian, G. A. (1986). *Confronting domestic violence: A guide for criminal justice agencies*. Washington, DC: National Institute of Justice.

Hirschel, J. D., Hutchison, I. W., III, & Dean, C. W. (1992). The failure of arrest to deter spouse abuse. *Journal of Research in Crime and Delinquency, 29*, 7-33.

Pence, E. (1983). The Duluth Domestic Abuse Intervention Project. *Hamline Law Review, 6*, 247-275.

Pence, E., Novack, S., & Galaway, B. (1982). *Domestic Abuse Intervention Project: Six month research report*. Unpublished manuscript from the Duluth (Minnesota) Domestic Abuse Intervention Project.

Pence, E., & Shepard, M. (1988). Integrating feminist theory and practice: The challenge of the battered women's movement. In K. Yllö & M. Bograd (Eds.), *Feminist approaches on wife abuse* (pp. 282-298). Newbury Park, CA: Sage.

Saunders, D., & Parker, J. C. (1989). Legal sanctions and treatment follow-through among men who batter: A multivariate analysis. *Social Work Research & Abstracts, 25*, 21-29.

Sherman, L. W., & Berk, R. A. (1984). The specific deterrent effects of arrest for domestic assault. *American Sociological Review, 49*, 261-272.

Sherman, L. W., Schmidt, J. D., Rogan, D. P., Gartin, P. R., Cohn, E. G., Collins, D. J., & Bacich, A. R. (1991). From initial deterrence to long-term escalation: Short-custody arrest for poverty ghetto domestic violence. *Criminology, 29*, 821-849.

Shepard, M. (1987, July). *Intervention with men who batter: An evaluation of a domestic abuse program.* Paper presented at the Third Family Violence Conference for Researchers, Durham, NH.

Soler, E. (1987). Domestic violence is a crime: A case study—San Francisco Family Violence Project. In D. J. Sonkin (Ed.), *Domestic violence on trial* (pp. 21-35). New York: Springer.

Soler, E., & Martin, S. (1983). *Domestic violence is a crime.* San Francisco: Family Violence Project.

Steinman, M. (1988). Evaluating a system-wide response to domestic violence: Some initial findings. *Journal of Contemporary Criminal Justice, 4*, 172-186.

Steinman, M. (1990). Lowering recidivism among men who batter women. *Journal of Police Science and Administration, 17*, 124-132.

Thurman v. City of Torrington, 595 F. Supp. 1521 (D. Conn. 1984).

Tolman, R. M., & Bhosley, G. (1989, November). *The impact of criminal justice system involvement on the outcome of intervention with men who batter.* Paper presented at the American Society for Criminology, Chicago, IL.

Maryann Syers is in private practice in Minneapolis and is a Research Associate at the Domestic Abuse Project. She has completed and published the results of several studies on battered women and abusive men.

Jeffrey L. Edleson has published extensively on domestic violence, groupwork, and program evaluation. He is a professor in the School of Social Work at the University of Minnesota and has conducted research at the Domestic Abuse Project for almost 10 years, where he is the Director of Evaluation and Research. He also conducts research on and provides technical assistance to domestic violence programs in Israel and Singapore. He coauthored with Dr. Richard Tolman Intervention for Men Who Batter: An Ecological Approach *(Sage, 1992) and is on the editorial boards of the* Journal of Interpersonal Violence, Violence UpDate, *and* Research on Social Work Practice.

LIVING UNDER SIEGE: DO STALKING LAWS PROTECT DOMESTIC VIOLENCE VICTIMS?

INTRODUCTION

Nearly thirty percent of all women murdered in America are killed by their husbands or boyfriends,[1] and as many as ninety percent of them have been stalked.[2] The Commission on the Status of Women revealed:

> [I]t happens too often that a woman who is a victim of battering or other forms of abuse in her home leaves that home, only to be hounded by the battering "husband" wherever she goes. Several cases in which such women have been found and murdered by that person have received notoriety, but many are known only to the families who grieve for them. Many more live in fear for the safety of their families and themselves knowing that a violent person may be lurking about, awaiting the opportunity to do them harm, and that they, the victims, have no one to whom to turn until violence is done.[3]

Traditional civil and criminal remedies have failed to protect domestic violence victims against the pattern of threats and harassment that constitute stalking and that frequently foreshadow more violent acts including assault, rape, and murder.[4] For example, civil remedies impose weak penalties which are poorly enforced[5] and traditional

---

1 FBI UNIFORM CRIME REPORTS, CRIME IN THE UNITED STATES 13 (1988), *quoted in* Caitlin E. Borgmann, Note, *Battered Women's Substantive Due Process Claims: Can Orders of Protection Deflect* DeShaney?, 65 N.Y.U. L. REV. 1280, 1281 n.3 (1990). Domestic violence is the most common form of assault in the United States. FAMILY VIOLENCE: EMERGING ISSUES OF A NATIONAL CRISIS 47 (Leah J. Dickstein, M.D. & Carol C. Nadelson, M.D. eds., 1989) [hereinafter FAMILY VIOLENCE]. It is estimated that the leading cause of injury to women in the United States is abuse inflicted by intimates. Nancy Gibbs, *'Til Death Do Us Part*, TIME, Jan. 18, 1993, at 41.

2 Melinda Beck, *Murderous Obsession*, NEWSWEEK, July 13, 1992, at 61 (statement of Ruth Micklem, co-director of Virginians Against Domestic Violence). A stalker has been legally defined as "[a]ny person who willfully, maliciously, and repeatedly follows or harasses another person and who makes a credible threat with the intent to place that person in reasonable fear of death or great bodily injury . . . ." CAL. PENAL CODE § 646.9(a) (West 1992).

3 Letter from Nina Hull, Chair of Commission on the Status of Woman, to Senator Edward R. Royce (July 23, 1990) (on file with author) [hereinafter Hull Letter].

4 Beck, *supra* note 2, at 60; Ernie Freda, *Stalking A Better Law*, ATLANTA J. & CONST., Dec. 29, 1992, at A7. For example, Olympic skier Patricia Kastle had a restraining order against her former husband when he shot her. Gibbs, *supra*, note 1, at 42.

5 *See infra* text accompanying notes 82-96 (discussing shortcomings of civil protection orders).

criminal remedies do not characterize the seemingly legitimate behavior[6] involved in stalking cases as an offense.[7] Since no actual physical contact or harm may have occurred, victims were left powerless to take legal action.[8]

Most states have now enacted stalking legislation to respond to the need for greater deterrence mechanisms and more efficient intervention.[9] For example, Florida enacted a stalking law because "the traditional protections . . . available under criminal statutes are not always applicable to stalking . . . ."[10] Similarly, Virginia adopted legislation "to permit police and the courts to intervene early in a stalking, to stop the victim from being terrorized and to prevent a violent crime."[11]

Stalking laws have been criticized as being merely a visible instrument for legislatures to respond to the public outcry that accompanies well-publicized cases.[12] Nevertheless, these new laws could play a significant role in improving the legal protection available for victims.

This Note analyzes whether stalking laws provide the needed legal recourse, specifically for domestic violence victims. Part I provides a background of the stalking problem, sets forth three case histories to serve as a framework to analyze and critique the available remedies, and sketches a profile of the stalkers and their victims. Part

---

6 For instance, following another by walking or driving behind them or parking across the street from them are forms of commonplace human interaction that may constitute an offense under the framework of stalking.

7 *See infra* text accompanying notes 102-10 (discussing flaws of traditional criminal remedies available to domestic violence victims).

8 "Unless a specific crime is committed . . . police agencies have historically remained uninvolved . . . leaving the victim to deal with her problem on her own." Lieutenant John C. Lane, *Threat Management Fills Void in Police Services*, POLICE CHIEF, Aug. 1992, at 27. For example, one sergeant explained to a victim who called for help, "We believe you, but we can't [lock-up] someone for something they *might* do." Andy Court, *She Knew The System Would Fail Her*, AM. LAW., June 1992, at 110 (emphasis added). *See generally* Brenda Camp Yarbrough, *Laws Targeting Stalkers Sweep Southern States, New Measures Protect Victims*, ATLANTA J. & CONST., Nov. 4, 1992, at D6. According to Senator Royce, "when our own police are forced to tell a victim, 'Once he attacks you physically, then we can act,' it is clear that our laws need to be changed." Unpublished memorandum from Senator Edward R. Royce (Oct. 1, 1990) (on file with author).

9 *See infra* text accompanying notes 112-33 (discussing legislative history of California stalking statute).

10 FLA. STAT. ANN. § 784.048 note (West 1992).

11 John W. Anderson, *Virginia Targets Stalkers, Bills Would Outlaw Repeated, Fear-Inducing Harassment*, WASH. POST, Feb. 10, 1992, at D1, D5 (statement of State Sen. Glenn Crowshaw, sponsor of Att'y Gen. Mary Sue Terry's bill).

12 *See* Gera-Lind Kolarik, *Stalking Laws Proliferate*, A.B.A. J., Nov. 1992, at 35. Other criticisms include concern that the laws may be unconstitutionally vague and overly broad. *See infra* note 132 (outlining constitutional concerns).

II argues that society has begun to dispel antiquated notions that domestic violence is a nonserious crime, but concludes that the civil and criminal remedies available to protect domestic violence victims and punish offenders fail to effectively provide relief. Part III analyzes the newly enacted stalking legislation. This Part examines the history of the California stalking law, the first statute of its kind to be enacted; evaluates the various elements of the California model stalking law; describes the grading of penalties; and applies the California stalking statute to the case histories presented in Part I. The discussion concludes that the stalking statutes provide recourse not available by traditional civil and criminal remedies, but still come up short for domestic violence victims.

Part IV submits that the stalking laws need to be further developed to account for the sensitive needs of domestic violence victims. Lenore Walker, pioneer in the field of domestic violence, proposed a cycle theory of violence to explain the behavior in battering households.[13] Part A presents Walker's theory and its three recognized phases. Part B advances that stalking often occurs when domestic violence victims attempt to break away from the cycle of violence in the home and proposes that stalking may therefore be viewed as a continuation, or phase-four of the domestic violence cycle.

Based on the analysis developed in Parts III and IV, Part V proposes a model statute which modifies the existing stalking laws so that they adequately respond to the needs of phase-four victims. The proposed statute makes the following changes. It: (1) modifies the "credible threat" language to include implied threats; (2) imposes stronger penalties; (3) uses the domestic violence context as a means to determine the nature of threats made; (4) proposes a reasonable woman standard in place of the reasonable person standard; (5) broadens the definition of harassment to include unconsented contact; and (6) mandates using computerized informational tracking systems. The proposed modifications should significantly increase protection to domestic violence victims.

I. BACKGROUND

Because stalking has only recently been viewed as a serious and prevalent problem, few studies have been done to establish the personality and psychological profile of stalkers or the nature of their behavior.[14] As a result of the lack of research, it has likely been difficult to

---

13 LENORE E. WALKER, BATTERED WOMAN (1979).

14 Most stalking cases fit into one of three categories: domestic violence, stalking of a famous person, or workplace harassment. Elizabeth Ross, *Problem of Men Stalking Women*

evaluate what the most effective sanctions would be to deter stalking. This difficulty is further compounded by the likelihood of substantial underreporting by victims.[15] However, it is estimated that as of 1990, there were more than 200,000 stalkers in the United States[16] and *U.S. News and World Report* has projected that five percent of all adults will be stalked at some point in their lives.[17] Stalkers are typically male,[18] come from all walks of life,[19] cut across all income levels and

Spurs New Laws, CHRISTIAN SCI. MONITOR, June 11, 1992, at 6 (statement of Alana Bowman, deputy city attorney for Los Angeles and supervisor of the city's domestic violence unit). Michael Zona, forensic psychiatrist of the Los Angeles police, estimates that 47% of all stalkers know the target as an ex-spouse, ex-lover, or former acquaintance. Maria Puente, *Legislators Tackling the Terror of Stalking*, USA TODAY, July 21, 1992, at 9A. In comparison, celebrity stalking victims represent only a small fraction of stalking cases and yet the celebrities already gain the lion's share of the media's attention. Gary Spencer, *State Tightens Penalties for Stalking*, N.Y. L.J., Aug. 20, 1992, at 1 (statement of Governor Mario Cuomo of New York). For example, talk show hosts David Letterman and Johnny Carson, actors Clint Eastwood, Michael J. Fox, Jodi Foster, Rebecca Shaeffer, and singer Olivia Newton-John are among the many celebrities who have been stalked at some point in their careers. *See* Puente, *supra*, at 9A; Kathy Swindle, *Dark Shadows*, DALLAS MORNING NEWS, May 24, 1992, at 6F. The stalking problem is not limited to these high profile Hollywood celebrity cases, however; it affects people from all social strata. In fact, the National Organization for Victim Assistance in Washington estimates that 75 to 80% of the stalking cases occur in the domestic violence context. Tamar Lewin, *New Laws Address Old Problem: The Terror of a Stalker's Threats*, N.Y. TIMES, Feb. 8, 1993, at A1, B10. Throughout this Note, the term "stalking" will be used exclusively to describe the domestic violence class of victims.

15 According to government data, only one-third of all crime is reported to the police, and domestic violence is particularly underreported and difficult to document. Borgmann, *supra* note 1, at 1281 *citing* BUREAU OF JUSTICE STATISTICS, U.S. DEP'T OF JUSTICE, SPECIAL REPORT: FAMILY VIOLENCE 4 (1984); PA. ATT'Y GEN. FAMILY VIOLENCE TASK FORCE, DOMESTIC VIOLENCE: A MODEL PROTOCOL FOR POLICE RESPONSE 6 (1989) [hereinafter A MODEL PROTOCOL]. In 1991, approximately 22 million crimes went unreported. BUREAU OF JUSTICE STATISTICS, U.S. DEP'T OF JUSTICE (1993). Underreporting often occurs because victims fear antagonizing their pursuers to the point of retaliation. In addition, victims believe that the police can not, or will not, do anything, and that the crime is not important enough to report. Victims also fear the economic consequences of prosecuting a husband or boyfriend provider. A MODEL PROTOCOL, *supra*, at 6.

16 Puente, *supra* note 14, at 9A (research of Dr. Park Elliot Dietz, clinical psychiatrist and stalking expert).

17 *Id. See also* David Holmstrom, *Efforts to Protect Women from 'Stalkers' Gain Momentum at State, Federal Levels*, CHRISTIAN SCI. MONITOR, Dec. 22, 1992, at 1; Robin Westen, *Stalkers Must Be Stopped*, NEW WOMAN, May 1993, at 122. This estimate is high but realistic given the prevalence of domestic violence in America today. *See* Lauren L. McFarlane, Note, *Domestic Violence Victims v. Municipalities: Who Pays When the Police Will Not Respond?*, 41 CASE W. RES. L. REV. 929, 929 (1991).

18 While stalking is not exclusively a male crime, nearly 80% of the nation's stalkers are men. Scott Bowles, *Stalked by Strangers, Women Seek Protection*, GANNET NEWS SERVICE, Apr. 27, 1992. Furthermore, the National Crime Survey reported that men commit 95% of all assaults on spouses. Laura S. Harper, Note, *Battered Women Suing Police for Failure to Intervene: Viable Legal Avenues after* DeShaney v. Winnebago County Dep't of Social Servs., 75 CORNELL L. REV. 1393, 1424 n.216 (1990). Studies also reveal that victims of spousal abuse are nearly always women. Carolyne R. Hathaway, Comment, *Gender Based Discrimination in Police Reluctance to Respond to Domestic Assault Complaints*, 75 GEO. L.J. 667, 671 (1986).

are both employed and unemployed.[20] Most stalkers have had a relationship with the target and now refuse to let go of the relationship, while others have never had a relationship with the target but have fantasized about establishing one.[21]

The discussion that follows presents three case histories which serve as a framework to highlight several situations and factors involved in stalking cases. In each of these cases, the woman terminated an abusive relationship but was unable to halt eventual violent contact. These examples provide a foundation for understanding phase-four of the cycle of violence discussed in Part IV.

A. *Case Histories*

1. *Case #1*[22]

Geraldine was stalked by her boyfriend. They had a wonderful relationship at first. She characterized him as a "charmer"—"the nicest guy in the world." He moved into her home and helped take care of her children. But the situation changed when the boyfriend suspected that Geraldine was going to leave him. He became obsessed with the idea that she was dating someone else. Overwhelmed with jealousy, he followed her wherever she went, even to work. As a result of his intrusions and accusations, Geraldine withdrew from her friends and all social contact. She later learned that her boyfriend had a history of violent behavior, at which time she tried to terminate the relationship. She changed the locks on her apartment, but he broke into her house, armed with a .38 caliber gun, and threatened, "I'll kill you if you ever leave me!" On numerous occasions, he slashed her tires, destroyed her home, beat and raped her. Geraldine called the police frequently. Despite the evidence of physical abuse, the police did nothing.

In fact, studies show that 75 to 95% of the domestic violence disturbance complaints filed with police are made by women. Amy Eppler, *Battered Women and the Equal Protection Clause: Will the Constitution Help Them When the Police Won't?*, 95 YALE L.J. 788, 799 (1986).

19 "Wife abuse cuts across all social, economic, religious, racial, and ethnic lines according to official records and unofficial studies." WALKER, BATTERED WOMAN, *supra* note 13, at 21-23. *See also* Victoria M. Mather, *The Skeleton in the Closet: The Battered Woman Syndrome, Self-Defense, and Expert Testimony*, 39 MERCER L. REV. 545, 546 (1988).

20 *Twenty-Twenty: I Know He's Out There* (ABC television broadcast, Jan. 10, 1992) (transcript on file with author) [hereinafter *Twenty-Twenty*].

21 This condition has been labeled erotomania. *See* Park Elliot Dietz, *Threatening and Otherwise Inappropriate Letters to Hollywood Celebrities*, J. FORENSIC SCIENCES 185 (1991).

22 This case history is based on the story of a young woman who was stalked and raped by her boyfriend, reported on *Jenny Jones* (WWOR television broadcast, Oct. 23, 1992) (transcript on file with author).

2. *Case #2*[23]

Dawn, a twenty-five year old mother, had been harassed for months by her estranged husband despite a temporary restraining order barring contact. She received a dozen red roses from him but did not acknowledge the contact. In ensuing months, her husband destroyed her car and physically abused her. Although she pressed charges on a number of occasions, he was consistently released on bail. The day before Dawn was to testify against him, she found a bullet lodged in her computer at work. Dawn was too shaken to present her case at trial and the charges were dropped. Subsequently, he shot and killed her.

3. *Case #3*[24]

Joanne felt like a prisoner because in every place where she had lived, her ex-husband had closely watched her. She had been endlessly followed and relentlessly pursued. On one occasion, he cornered Joanne in the drugstore and forcefully threatened her life. She escaped his grasp, ran home and called the police, but the police failed to respond. Later, he parked his car in front of her home for six hours and she did not know what to do. Joanne was too afraid to leave her home, go to work, or send her children to school and her resources were nearly depleted.

4. *Profile of Stalking Violence*

These case histories demonstrate the complex and turbulent nature of stalking violence. They present the typical stalking situations—the jealous lover, the violent husband, or the vengeful ex-husband, respectively. The following discussion uses the case histories as a means to describe the profile of stalkers and to demonstrate weaknesses in the legal system.

The first case history above illustrates that some stalkers who appear to be charming and sensitive may later, deep into the relationship, show their underlying crazed obsession to control their partner and exert power over their every move.[25] The case also depicts that some victims experience such fear and anxiety that they radically alter

---

23 This case history is based on the case of a woman whose husband stalked her, *reported in* Samme Chittum et al., *No Way Out*, LADIES' HOME J., Apr. 1990, at 126.

24 This case history is based on the story of a divorced woman, reported in DEL MARTIN, BATTERED WIVES 77 (1976).

25 For another example, see *Sally Jessy Raphael*: *I Was Stalked Like An Animal* (ABC television broadcast, May 19, 1993), transcript at 5 (transcript on file with author) [hereinafter *Sally Jesse Raphael*].

their lifestyles to avoid further offensive and unwelcome contact with their assailant.[26] In fact, many victims quit their jobs, refrain from answering their telephones, or even relocate in an effort to evade their pursuers.[27] In the first case, Geraldine attempted to terminate the relationship, took steps to prevent contact by changing the locks on her apartment, and notified her partner that further contact was unwelcome. However, her boyfriend continued to frequent her home and make threats. Though the contact was unwelcome, there were no remedies available because such contact had not been characterized as an offense.[28] Moreover, this case shows that the mere decision to leave the relationship is often enough to instigate violence.[29]

The second case history illustrates that some victims rely on more formal legal protections—calling the police, filing a criminal complaint, or seeking a court order of protection. For example, Dawn attempted to use the legal system to protect herself by obtaining a restraining order, filing charges, and going to court to testify. However, her husband continued to harass her despite the court order. The protective order could not guard Dawn from the bullets, nor deter her husband from perpetrating more violence. As her case shows, civil protection orders are not effective shields for deterring unwanted contact or protecting the victim from future violence.[30]

Finally, the third case demonstrates that the legal arsenal lacks tools that can be used to intervene before physical harm occurs. Though Joanne's ex-husband closely watched and followed her and caused her to live in fear, she had no recourse against this disturbing behavior.[31] In addition, this case shows that the police do not always respond to domestic violence complaints.[32] Finally, the third case illustrates that an assailant may instill fear in a victim without using force or making threats. For example, Joanne's ex-husband parked his car outside her home and his presence alone was enough to immo-

---

26 *See generally* Andrea J. Robinson, *A Remedial Approach to Harassment*, 70 VA. L. REV. 507, 507 (1984).

27 Bowles, *supra* note 18, at 1.

28 *See* author's proposal *infra* text accompanying notes 230-31 (expanding definition of harassment to include unconsented contacts).

29 See text accompanying notes 199-215 (discussing separation as the most turbulent and violent stage in the battering cycle).

30 For another example, see *Sally Jesse Raphael*, *supra* note 25, transcript at 6. *See* author's proposal *infra* p. 560 (increasing penalty for crime of stalking from a misdemeanor to a felony offense).

31 *See infra* notes 102-06 and accompanying text (discussing that traditional criminal remedies do not encompass the seemingly legitimate behavior involved in stalking cases).

32 *See infra* notes 51-54 and accompanying text (discussing police inaction).

bilize her.[33]

Other victims may resort to fighting back[34] and then defend their actions on grounds of self-defense.[35] Sandy Gaylord, counselor for battered women in Dallas, explained that some victims reach a point where they have exhausted every legal avenue available and simply can no longer take the abuse.[36] That victims have to take the matter into their own hands suggests that the available legal remedies need to be scrutinized and amended.

The case histories highlight several situations and factors involved in stalking cases. These examples provide a foundation for assessing the legal issues involved in different forms of stalking, while demonstrating that a uniform, rigid solution may not be the answer. The following section provides a brief overview of the civil and criminal remedies and concludes that traditional remedies fail to address the needs of stalking victims.

II. Legal Recourse Prior to Enactment of Stalking Laws

Until 1991 when the first stalking law went into effect, the legal system's response to stalking was feckless. Part A discusses the tran-

33 *See* author's proposal *infra* notes 220-28 and accompanying text (modifying definition of credible threat to include implied threats).

34 For example, one victim divorced her alcoholic and abusive husband and moved away to a small city in Oklahoma to start a new life. There she became involved in the church and cared for her children. But suddenly one night after church, she discovered that the tires of her car had been slashed and suspected that her ex-husband had found her. She was right. He jumped out of the darkness and held a knife to her. He forced her to drive him to her home. Fortunately, his violent energy dissipated and he fell asleep. Thereafter, she purchased a gun and threatened to use it if he ever came near her again. Martin, *supra* note 24, at 78. Although this woman did not actually shoot her ex-husband, she did go through the painstaking efforts of purchasing a gun, learning how to use it, and threatening him. While she successfully frightened her husband, some victims must resort to actually using force.

35 For a review of self-defense claims used by battered women, see, for example, Julie Blackman, Intimate Violence: A Study of Injustice 187-90 (1989); Charles P. Ewing, Battered Women Who Kill: Psychological Self-Defense as Legal Justification (1987); Lee Ann Hoff, Battered Women as Survivors 40-47 (1990); Walker, Battered Woman, *supra* note 13; Lenore E. Walker, The Battered Woman Syndrome 43 (1984); Jennifer Marsh, *Women's Self-Defense Under Washington Law*, 54 Wash. L. Rev. 221 (1978); Mather, *supra* note 19; Marilyn H. Mitchell, *Does Wife Abuse Justify Homicide?*, 24 Wayne L. Rev. 1705, 1720-26 (1978); Jeffrey Robinson, *Defense Strategies for Battered Women Who Assault Their Mates:* State v. Curry, 4 Harv. Women's L.J. 161 (1981); Cathryn J. Rosen, *The Excuse of Self-Defense: Correcting A Historical Accident on Behalf of Battered Women Who Kill*, 36 Am. U. L. Rev. 11 (1986); Richard A. Rosen, *On Self-Defense, Imminence, and Women Who Kill Their Batterers*, 71 N.C. L. Rev. 371 (1993); Richard L. Price, *Battered Woman Syndrome: A Defense Begins to Emerge (pts. 1 & 2)*, N.Y. L.J., Nov. 29, 1985, at 1, N.Y. L.J., Dec. 2, 1985, at 4.

36 Swindle, *supra* note 14, at 6F.

sition from the antiquated presumption that domestic violence was a private matter to a belief that domestic violence warrants attention. Part B analyzes the deficiencies of traditional civil remedies and submits that they are indeed not adequate to protect victims or punish offenders. Finally, Part C assesses the weaknesses of criminal remedies in the stalking context and concludes that criminal statutes fail to recognize stalking as an offense.

A. *Response to Domestic Violence Complaints*

For a long time, domestic violence cases were not treated with the same regard as violence committed between strangers.[37] "When the [perpetrator and the victim] are intimate . . . partners, the legal system transforms the behavior into domestic violence, an implicitly less heinous offense."[38] This attitude of indifference extended to the courts, the police, and to prosecutors, who all tended to assign a low priority to the arrest, prosecution and punishment of spouse abusers.[39] For example, the common law allowed husbands to beat their wives in chastisement, as long as they used a switch no bigger than their thumb.[40] Similarly, marital rape, which has been characterized as the extreme end of domestic violence,[41] was permitted while rape by strangers was proscribed.[42]

Indeed it was not until 1984 that courts began to reject notions that domestic violence was not a serious offense.[43] For example, in *People v. Liberta*, married women were finally granted full legal protection against rape by their husbands.[44] As policymakers, lawmakers

---

37 *See* Helen R. Molden, Comment, *Does the Legal System Batter Women?: Vindicating Battered Women's Constitutional Rights to Adequate Police Protection*, 21 ARIZ. ST. L.J. 705 (1989).

38 *Id.* at 726.

39 Hathaway, *supra* note 18, at 674.

40 WILLIAM L. PROSSER, HANDBOOK OF THE LAW OF TORTS 136 (4th ed. 1971).

41 MILDRED D. PAGELOW, FAMILY VIOLENCE (1984). Many victims of spousal rape explained that they submitted due to actual force, threats, or their own fears. *Id.* at 430. This is the same problem that confronts stalking victims. The victim is subjected to unwanted contact through force, coercion, or intimidation. MARTIN, *supra* note 24, at 77.

42 *See, e.g.*, Commonwealth v. Fogerty, 74 Mass. (8 Gray) 489, 491 (1857); Rene I. Augustine, 29 J. FAM. L. 559, 559 n.2 (1990-91). The theory supporting the spousal rape exemption was that prosecution of a man for raping his wife would destroy marital harmony and obstruct reconciliation efforts. *Id.* at 570.

43 *E.g.*, Weishaupt v. Commonwealth, 315 S.E.2d 847 (Va. 1984) (finding that husband may be convicted of attempted rape if wife revokes consent even while still married).

44 474 N.E.2d 567, 574 (N.Y. 1984), *cert. denied*, 471 U.S. 1020 (1985). The court reasoned that if the marriage had already reached the point where intercourse was accomplished by violent assault, it was doubtful that there was a relationship left to reconcile (citing Trammel v. United States, 445 U.S. 40, 52 (1980)). Similarly, stalking, a component of domestic violence, also signifies that the harmony of the relationship is discordant.

and some courts began to view domestic violence as an offense that deserved protection,[45] new laws were created to establish that domestic violence *is* violence, regardless of whom the victim may be.[46] This development in the law signifies that as the proliferating stalking problem is evaluated in the domestic violence context, then this form of violence may also be treated seriously.

1. *Police Inaction*

The police, who act as gatekeepers and enforcers of the legal system, are an important link to relief for domestic violence victims.[47] When a victim calls the police, it is generally a desperate cry for help: "When we do get a call from a battered wife, it is never the first time that she has been beaten. By the time she gets around to calling us, she's desperate and searching for a way out."[48] However, the police historically have been reluctant to respond to domestic disturbance calls. For example, "[o]f all the women murdered by their ex-husbands or boyfriends, studies indicate that 90% had called the police at least once for protection, and more than half had called five times or more."[49] In 1985, there were 64,443 reports of domestic disputes in Ohio. No action was taken in 41,829 of these.[50] Failure to respond leaves the callers extremely vulnerable to violence.

There are a number of reasons why the police may be reluctant to respond to domestic disturbance calls. Some officers view domestic violence as a nonserious crime.[51] Some officers refrain from enforcing

---

45 For example, the notion of a husband's prerogative to beat his wife is now an outdated misconception. *See* Craig v. Boren, 429 U.S. 190, 198-99 (1976).

46 For example, new laws provide that husbands do not have the right to abuse their wives and that rape is rape. PAGELOW, *supra* note 41, at 448.

47 Mather, *supra* note 19, at 556-57.

48 ROGER LANGLEY & RICHARD C. LEVY, WIFE BEATING: THE SILENT CRISIS (1977) (quoting the director of the New Orleans Crisis Center).

49 Holmstrom, *supra* note 17, at 4.

50 McFarlane, *supra* note 17, at n.18.

51 Police inaction may stem from either written policies, outdated myths such as a belief that the complaints are not serious, or a belief that arrest is inappropriate. For example, the Detroit Police Department had a written policy in the 1950s that directed officers to " 'recognize the sanctity of the home' and diplomatically end the 'disturbance . . . *without making an arrest*.' " Barbara K. Finesmith, *Police Response to Battered Women: A Critique and Proposals for Reform*, 14 SETON HALL L. REV. 74, 84 (1983) (emphasis in original).

Some police officers "think that few domestic disturbances are really violent. They tend to define violence in terms of its effect. Unless blood is drawn and injuries are visible, they are apt to discount the report . . . and call the incident merely a 'family spat.' " MARTIN, *supra* note 24, at 21. Police officers have indicated that "their refusal to intervene was motivated by either an animus toward abused women, or a view that domestic violence is a relatively nonserious crime affecting primarily women." McFarlane, *supra* note 17, at 944.

Other police departments have used "stitch rules" to respond to domestic cases. That is, "a wife who was abused had to require a certain number of surgical sutures before a husband

court orders because they feel that they do not have the authority to do so.[52] Other officers refrain from making an arrest because it is the policy of the district attorney's office that no arrests be made, and the officers comply.[53] Ironically, other officers have treated domestic violence as a low priority because they feared for their own safety in these typically explosive situations.[54]

2. *Liability Imposed for Police Inaction*

The tradition has been that police were not held liable for their inaction. For example, in *Riss v. City of New York*,[55] a young woman was terrorized by a rejected suitor who repeatedly threatened to kill her if she did not yield to him.[56] In fear for her life, she requested police protection but her pleas for assistance were received with indifference.[57] The court held the municipality was not liable for failure to provide police protection to a battered woman who was repeatedly threatened and eventually suffered severe physical harm.[58]

---

could be arrested for assault and battery." RICHARD J. GELLES & CLAIRE P. CORNELL, INTIMATE VIOLENCE IN FAMILIES 124 (2d ed. 1990). Police practices, whether embodied in a formal policy or in established custom, that offer lesser protections for women against domestic assaults than for strangers in other assault situations violate the domestic victims' constitutional right to equal protection of the law. *See* Hathaway, *supra* note 18, at 691. Further, married women who are denied protection simply because their assailants are their husbands are also denied equal protection of the law. *See* Augustine, *supra* note 42, at 587.

52 LANGLEY & LEVY, *supra* note 48, at 177; MARTIN, *supra* note 24, at 105. Failure to arrest may be symbolic that domestic violence is still viewed as a less serious offense. "[I]t has long been established that there is a persistent bias against the use of arrest in [domestic violence] cases. In fact, the closer the relationship between the offender and victim, the less likely it is that an arrest will occur." EVA S. BUZAWA & CARL G. BUZAWA, DOMESTIC VIOLENCE: THE CRIMINAL JUSTICE RESPONSE 43 (1990). However, now that there is a police duty to respond to domestic disturbance calls, this should become less of a problem. *See infra* text accompanying notes 59-66 (discussing police duty to respond to domestic disturbance calls).

53 LANGLEY & LEVY, *supra* note 48, at 178. Police policies towards domestic complaints have taken a variety of forms, "from an outright refusal to arrest the offenders and to recognize domestic violence as a criminal matter, to a practice of giving domestic violence calls lower priority than non-domestic disputes." Eppler, *supra* note 18, at 790.

54 Studies indicate that 33% of all assaults on police officers and 11.5% of police deaths occur when officers respond to domestic disturbance calls. 1980 U.S. DEP'T OF JUSTICE, UNIFORM CRIME REP. FOR THE UNITED STATES 336, 339. Furthermore, officers are aware of "statistics that 'demonstrate' that officers responding to family disturbance calls are the most likely to be killed or injured." BUZAWA & BUZAWA, *supra* note 52, at 29. It has been challenged that the "fear of injury may be overstated, if not totally misplaced." *Id.* at 30. In fact, most police work is inherently dangerous and it would be ridiculous to excuse police action in cases of domestic violence on that basis. Hathaway, *supra* note 18, at 689.

55 240 N.E.2d 860 (N.Y. 1968).

56 The fact pattern in this case, where a relationship was never established, is different from the typical phase-four violence scenario, where an existing relationship is terminated. However, the underlying concept of rejection leading into violence is the same.

57 240 N.E.2d at 862 (Keating, J., dissenting).

58 *Id.* at 861.

Thurman v. City of Torrington[59] broke the tradition: tort liability may now be imposed for negligent failure to provide adequate police protection in domestic violence cases. Tracy Thurman was subjected to repeated threats of violence by her husband, Charles, who was finally arrested for breach of the peace.[60] Despite a court order to stay away,[61] he continued to assault, harass and threaten her.[62] Tracy filed several complaints with the police attempting to enforce the court order and requested that Charles be arrested for violating the terms of his probation, however, the police ignored the requests.[63] On one occasion, Charles appeared at her residence, demanded to speak to her, and stabbed her repeatedly in the neck, throat and chest.[64] The court held that marriage does not give a husband permission to physically abuse his wife and therefore that a police officer may not knowingly refrain from interference in violence merely because the assaulter and his victim are married to each other.[65]

The decision in *Thurman* signifies a literal movement away from the view that domestic violence could be ignored to a view that domestic violence warrants legal attention. Although domestic violence may no longer be viewed as a category of nonserious violence, even when the police do respond to victims' calls, they can only be as effective as the laws allow them to be.[66] Without the proper legal tools, the police, prosecutors, and victims cannot combat the problem. The discussion that follows examines the adequacy of the available legal tools.

B. *Civil Remedies*

Civil remedies available to domestic violence victims[67] may provide victims with greater control over the legal proceedings than the typical criminal prosecution which is conducted by the state[68] and

59 595 F. Supp. 1521 (D. Conn. 1984).

60 *Id.* at 1524-25.

61 *Id.* at 1525.

62 *Id.*

63 *Id.*

64 *Id.*

65 *Id.* at 1528. For a review of this issue of tort liability for the police, see Hathaway, *supra* note 18. *See also* Note, *Police Liability for Negligent Failure to Prevent Crime*, 94 HARV. L. REV. 821, 826 (1981) (noting that courts generally find duty to provide protection where police expressly promise protection to specific individuals).

66 The police must be given the appropriate tools to deal with the stalkers. *See* Art Barnum, *Lawmakers Back Stalker Bill*, CHI. TRIB., Apr. 13, 1992, § 2, at 1.

67 *See* Robinson, *supra* note 26, at 509-10. ("[V]ictims may resort to common-law actions, such as defamation, nuisance, trespass, assault, invasion of privacy, and intentional infliction of emotional distress.").

68 BUZAWA & BUZAWA, *supra* note 52, at 55 ("The decision as to whether to charge,

constrained by limited resources. Some victims find that the litigation process allows them to feel a shift in the balance of power, and to express in a socially accepted manner their anger at having been victimized.[69] It has been argued that the victim has the best knowledge of how to deal with her own danger, and therefore the victim should have control over the arrest decision.[70]

Despite these cited advantages, civil actions are limited by the requirements to prove elements that may be absent from the stalking context.[71] Even if the victim could make a proper showing, civil actions are burdened by tremendous litigation expenses which may only add to the victim's suffering.[72] Further, the filing procedures involved in civil actions may produce substantial time delays which leave the victim vulnerable.[73]

Alternatively, domestic violence victims may obtain civil injunctive relief in the form of an order of protection.[74] To obtain a court

---

which charges to advance, and which charges to later dismiss or settle, does not require the victim's consent.").

69 WALKER, THE BATTERED WOMAN SYNDROME, *supra* note 35, at 143.

70 Eppler, *supra* note 18, at 807 & n.80.

71 *See* Robinson, *supra* note 26. In order for a stalking victim to support a claim for intentional infliction of emotional distress, the victim must show that the stalker's actions were calculated to cause serious emotional disturbance.

72 *See* Janice L. Grau, *Restraining Order Legislation for Battered Women: A Reassessment*, 16 U.S.F. L. REV. 703, 727 (1982).

73 *See id.* at 727-28.

74 An order of protection is sometimes referred to as a civil protection order, a temporary restraining order, a temporary injunction, a stay-away order, or a no-contact order. For example, CAL. CIV. PROC. CODE § 527.6(a) (Deering 1993), provides that:

> (a) A person who has suffered harassment as defined in subdivision (b) may seek a temporary restraining order, and an injunction prohibiting harassment as provided in this section. (b) For the purposes of this section, 'harassment' is a knowing and willful course of conduct directed at a specific person which seriously alarms, annoys, or harasses the person, and which serves no legitimate purpose.

Every civil protection order statute makes protection orders available for spouses. Peter Finn, *Statutory Authority In The Use and Enforcement of Civil Protection Orders Against Domestic Abuse*, 23 FAM. L.Q. 43, 46 (1989). Former spouses, however, are eligible for civil protection orders in forty-six jurisdictions and unmarried persons living as spouses qualify in only thirty-nine jurisdictions. *Id.* For example, a Missouri statute provides that an order of protection terminates "upon the entry of a decree of dissolution of marriage or legal separation." *Id.* at 47 (citing MO. ANN. STAT. § 455.060(4) (Vernon Supp. 1989)). Statutes in Texas and West Virginia specify that no order may be issued if an action for divorce or legal separation is pending. *Id.* (citing TEX. FAM. CODE ANN. § 71.06 (West Supp. 1989); W. VA. CODE § 42-2A-1 (Supp. 1988)). Such a provision denies protection to a large number of vulnerable women who may need the protection most. For example, "[a] study of emergency room records found that 72 percent of the victims of domestic violence . . . were not living with the abuser at the time of the assault." *Id.* These women would be left without the safeguards of a civil protection order. *See supra* note 23 and accompanying text (profiling case #2). In addition, one victim described that her estranged husband stalked and abused her for months after she left him. She recalled that "[o]nce he abducted her from a friend's house, took her to a

order of protection, the victim must file a petition requesting an ex parte order.[75] Within a week or two of the filing of the petition, the court holds an ex parte hearing.[76] If the petitioner demonstrates good cause by showing an immediate and present danger of domestic violence, then a temporary order will be granted,[77] and shall have a duration of not more than three years.[78]

A court generally requires the assailant to stay away from designated territories. For example, an order may mandate the perpetrator to "keep a certain distance between himself and the victim, to stay away from certain places frequented by the victim, or simply to 'stop abusing' the victim."[79] By removing the abusive partner from the victim's personal space, courts intend to provide the victim with a period of separation and thus relief against the harassment, but not to punish the offender.[80] Many victims of domestic violence desire civil protec-

---

secluded area, put a rope around her neck and threatened to drag her from the back of his truck until she died . . . . Another time, he taped her mouth shut and threatened her with a razor blade." Retha Hill, *Victims Urge More Protection Under Maryland Domestic Violence Laws*, WASH. POST., Feb. 25, 1992, at C5. However, "[she] was not eligible for a protective order because she did not live with her abuser at the time of the abuse." *Id.* Thus, protective orders may not be available to all victims.

75 *E.g.*, CAL. CIV. PROC. CODE § 527.6(c) (Deering 1993); CAL. CIV. CODE § 4359 (Deering 1993). *See* Judge Michael J. Voris, *The Domestic Violence Civil Protection Order and the Role of the Court*, 24 AKRON L. REV. 423, 426 (1990). *See also* Lisa Lerman, *A Model State Act: Remedies for Domestic Abuse*, 21 HARV. J. ON LEGIS. 61, 79, 92-93 (1984). The process of filing a complaint and seeking a protection order is often fraught with confusion, resistance, inconsistency and insensitivity. *See* MARTIN, *supra* note 24, at 90; LANGLEY & LEVY, *supra* note 48, at 153. That is, the victim must contact her attorney, sign an affidavit, wait for process to be served on the assailant, wait for the court to be notified, and wait for a hearing. *Id.* at 177. During this delay, the assailant is free to perpetrate more violence.

76 *E.g.*, CAL. CIV. PROC. CODE § 527.6(d) (Deering 1993). *See* Voris, *supra* note 75, at 426. An ex parte hearing is one that is held without both parties present.

77 Voris, *supra* note 75, at 426. *See, e.g.*, FLA. STAT. ANN. § 741.30(6)(a) (West Supp. 1993); MINN. STAT. ANN. § 518B.01, subdiv. 7 (West Supp. 1989); MISS. CODE ANN. § 93-21-13(1) (Supp. 1989); TENN. CODE ANN. § 36-3-605 (Supp. 1991); VA. CODE ANN. § 16.1-253.1 (Michie Supp. 1988).

78 *E.g.*, CAL. CIV. PROC. CODE § 548 (Deering 1993). Most orders are of shorter length and upon their expiration the victim is left vulnerable. For example, one victim who obtained a thirty-day court order to remove her abusive husband from the house explained that when the order expired, he returned home and broke her jaw, sexually violated her, ripped her hair out, kicked her, and even urinated on her. Hill, *supra*, note 74, at C5. Perhaps this abuse could have been avoided by making the civil protection order "permanent." Orders can be made permanent upon a showing of sufficient abuse at an adversarial hearing. Borgmann, *supra* note 1, at 1281.

79 Borgmann, *supra* note 1, at 1280 n.2. The order may also address other pressing concerns including "support and compensation for the woman, child custody and visitation rights, counseling, and disposition of personal property." *Id.*

80 BUZAWA & BUZAWA, *supra* note 52, at 112. A protective order differs from a criminal prosecution in that the hearing "is explicitly designated to separate the parties and prevent future unlawful conduct rather than to punish the past criminal behavior." *Id.* The existence

tion orders because they are only interested in halting the harassment, but not in punishing their partners.[81]

However, these advantages are greatly diminished by inherent drawbacks.[82] First, protection orders place a heavy burden on victims to both obtain and enforce the order.[83] Victim initiation is flawed for a number of reasons. To begin with, the burden of initiation may deter victims who are uncomfortable initiating charges against their current or past partner from seeking help at all.[84] In addition, the victims may not even be aware of the stalker's pursuit, in which case they would be unable to request protection. Further, a complaint brought by a victim may lack credibility because prosecutors and judges may more seriously evaluate the claims brought by the police than by private complainants.[85] Finally, if the order is violated and the abuser returns to the victim's home or other forbidden territories, then the burden shifts back to the victim to call the police to enforce the order. Subsequently, the responding officer may arrest the assailant.[86] However, court orders are also poorly enforced, and thus often fail to provide protection. Generally, the police arrest offenders for a violation of a civil protection order *only* when there are other charges in connection with it, such as destruction of property, disruption of the peace, public intoxication, or violent behavior witnessed by the responding officer.[87]

Even when court orders are issued and enforced, they often fail to deter violent assailants who are determined to inflict harm.[88] For

---

of protective orders appears to be an acknowledgement that separation is a violent time period and that victims require special protection.

81 Finn, *supra* note 74, at 44.

82 Nonetheless, in many cases, "a restraining order is helpful, if for no other reason than to show that you've used the legal tools that are available to you. It usually doesn't stop the stalker, but it serves as further documentation." *Sonya Live* (CNN television broadcast, Oct. 2, 1992) (transcript on file with author). This may be important in order to show a pattern of behavior. *See* text *infra* p. 548 (describing repetitive conduct as an element of the stalking statutes).

83 Finn, *supra* note 74, at 45.

84 Robinson, *supra* note 26, at 512. Some battered women's advocates argue that the burden should not be on the victim because the battered woman should not have to deal with the additional problems of knowing that she sent her husband to jail. Eppler, *supra* note 18, at 807 n.79. For a discussion on how the police should proceed when a battered woman is reluctant to press charges, see LISA LERMAN, PROSECUTION OF SPOUSE ABUSE: INNOVATIONS IN CRIMINAL JUSTICE RESPONSE 24 (1981).

85 Finn, *supra* note 74, at 45.

86 PAGELOW, *supra* note 41, at 265. *See supra* notes 51-54 (discussing reasons police may refrain from making arrests).

87 PAGELOW, *supra* note 41, at 265 n.4.

88 For example, a Baltimore woman testifying before the House Judiciary Committee in Maryland in support of the proposed stalking law explained that she obtained a thirty-day court order requiring her abusive husband to stay away from her home, but that he cornered

example, Governor William F. Weld of Massachusetts declared that:

> The rising tide of violence committed against women by their estranged husbands or boyfriends has made us all painfully aware of the fact that certain individuals are not swayed by restraining orders and that new measures such as are embodied in this [stalking] law must be enacted and utilized.[89]

The deficiencies in deterrence are evidenced by the documented frequent violations of protection orders.[90] For example, Illinois State Police statistics for 1992 showed "35,346 reported violations of orders of protection in a five-month period."[91] Eight thousand of the violations occurred in one month alone.[92] In addition, in Massachusetts, "since September [1992] when a new state record keeping system went into effect, of the 2,000 restraining orders issued, more than one-third had been violated in the first few days."[93] Further, the first violation may even be fatal. Thus, the utility of civil protection orders is limited.[94] The penalties for a violation of an order merely constitute civil contempt in thirty-one states, criminal contempt in twenty states, and civil and criminal contempt in eleven states.[95] However, a civil contempt violation is encumbered by flaws similar to those described above about civil protection orders[96] and a criminal contempt viola-

---

her in the laundromat and set her on fire. Although he was sentenced to thirty years in prison, she was left permanently disfigured. In her testimony, she called on the legislature to change the law because "I got the protection order like I was supposed to, but it didn't help me." Hill, *supra* note 74, at C5.

89 Letter from William F. Weld, Governor of Mass., to Michael J. Connally, Secretary of State of Mass. (May 18, 1992) (on file with author).

90 WALKER, BATTERED WOMAN, *supra* note 13, at 211 ("Many attorneys . . . claim that a restraining order . . . is simply a piece of paper which cannot force a batterer to cease his violent behavior."). For example, one victim, who had a restraining order against her ex-boyfriend who stalked her, explained that "it didn't do any good . . . . [H]e just laughed it off and said he'd never let me really leave him." Kevin Fagan, *New Focus on Deadly Stalkers*, S.F. CHRON., Jan. 11, 1993, at A1, A6.

91 John W. Fountain & Joseph Kirby, *Stalking Victims Find Laws Are Little Help*, CHI. TRIB., Aug. 5, 1992, at 1.

92 *Id.*

93 Holmstrom, *supra* note 17, at 1, 4.

94 *See* LANGLEY & LEVY, *supra* note 48, at 178-79.

95 Finn, *supra* note 74, at 52. *See, e.g.*, People v. Gray, 370 N.E.2d 797 (Ill. 1977) (holding defendant who shot his wife with a gun in contempt for violating a protective order).

96 A civil contempt violation requires the victim to file another petition with the court, then obtain another order, which if granted must be served on the assailant and paid for by the woman. MARTIN, *supra* note 24, at 105. Again, there is a delay before the court hearing and the result is that the assailant will probably only receive a warning. *Id.* at 24. Judges are often reluctant to impose a prison sentence for the first violation of an order. LANGLEY & LEVY, *supra* note 48, at 177; MARTIN, *supra*, at 24. Judges may justify inaction by the fact that most women who make charges fail to prosecute or fail to testify once in court which makes for unnecessary paper work. LANGLEY & LEVY, *supra*, at 179. The effect of enforcement is that the abuser will be evicted from the victim's home, CAL. FAMILY CODE § 5751 (West 1993),

tion only provides minor penalties. Thus, a contempt violation is a weak penalty which further decreases the general and specific deterrent effect of civil protection orders.

This discussion has shown that civil protection orders have the breadth to encompass the behavior involved in stalking, but that the court orders are not that effective.[97] The discussion should make it clear that stronger penalties that are stringently enforced are critical to protect victims of domestic violence. The following discussion highlights the benefits of criminal remedies in general, but concludes that traditional criminal remedies fail to encompass the seemingly legitimate behavior involved in stalking cases, and thus lack the depth to adequately provide a remedy for stalking victims.

C. *Criminal Remedies*

Criminal statutes generally provide more effective relief than civil remedies for victims of domestic violence for two reasons. First, criminal remedies transfer the traditional initiation burden from the victim to the police. Complaints brought by the police carry a notion of credibility that private complaints lack.[98] Because domestic violence in general, and stalking in particular, has only recently been viewed as a serious matter,[99] credibility is still an important objective. Second, criminal statutes are effective because they actually punish the offenders with fines or imprisonment,[100] rather than merely halting the abuse, as is the case with civil protection orders. Not only are the penalties stronger, but the deterrent value is also greater.[101]

---

but will not be fined or incarcerated. Since the remedy is not incarceration and since the abuser may well be outraged or humiliated by the constraints imposed, the offender is likely to perpetrate more violence against the victim in retaliation. LENORE E. WALKER, TERRIFYING LOVE: WHY BATTERED WOMEN KILL AND HOW SOCIETY RESPONDS 241 (1989) [hereinafter WALKER, TERRIFYING LOVE]; Fagan, *supra* note 90, at A6.

97 "Police and restraining orders alone are not enough." Fagan, *supra* note 90, at A6 (statement of Judge John Watson, Orange County Municipal Court). *See infra* notes 112, 116-117, 126 and accompanying text (discussing that the inadequacy of civil protection orders specifically spurred the passing of the first stalking law).

98 Finn, *supra* note 74, at 45.

99 *See supra* notes 37-43 and accompanying text (discussing historical view that domestic violence is a nonserious offense).

100 *See, e.g.*, CAL. PENAL CODE § 243(e) (West 1993) ("When a battery is committed against any noncohabitating former spouse, fiance, fiancee, or a person with whom the defendant currently has, or has previously had, a dating relationship, the battery is punishable by a fine of not exceeding two thousand dollars ($2000), or by imprisonment in a county jail for a period of not more than one year, or by both.").

101 The criminal justice system intends to communicate to society the types of behavior that are so damaging that they are intolerable. FAMILY VIOLENCE, *supra* note 1, at 149. "[A] recent study of police responses to battering . . . indicate[s] that many abusers can be deterred through law enforcement." *Id.*

However, criminal statutes that might apply to stalking cases, battery, assault, menacing and harassment, may not apply to the particular dangers that confront stalking victims. Statutes that prohibit battery, for example, punish the offender for physically harmful contact.[102] Thus, criminal statutes prohibiting battery protect victims suffering only the actual physical contacts involved in stalking, but not other abuses, including intimidation, harassment, and emotional distress.[103] Likewise, statutes that prohibit harassment punish the offender for conduct that alarms the victim, like obscene communication over the phone or through the mail.[104] But the harassment statutes do not protect stalking victims who experience more threatening conduct that places the victim in actual fear for her physical safety. The conduct that tends to occur in stalking cases does not qualify as an offense under the law. For example, one police officer explained to a victim who endured nineteen months of harassment by her ex-husband that she ought to buy a gun "because [the police] cannot do anything unless he rapes you or he kills you."[105] In other words, she would have to wait until she was harmed before the law would recognize the behavior as a legal offense. Although the police now have a duty to respond to domestic disturbance calls,[106] criminal remedies defining as an offense the seemingly innocent behavior involved in stalking are also necessary.

Furthermore, although criminal statutes such as battery and harassment generally provide stronger penalties than civil remedies, the existing statutes typically carry only a misdemeanor conviction.[107] A misdemeanor offense may not be severe enough to punish the violent

---

102 *E.g.*, CAL. PENAL CODE § 242 (West 1993) ("A battery is any willful and unlawful use of force or violence upon the person of another.").

103 Previously, there were no laws that criminalized any domestic violence. Laws have already been developed to protect against battery, which is characteristic of the first and second phases of the cycle theory of violence; now laws need to be developed to protect against the behavior characteristic of phase-four of the cycle theory.

104 *See, e.g.*, COLO. REV. STAT. § 18-9-111 (1992); KY. REV. STAT. ANN. § 525.070 (Michie/Bobbs-Merrill 1992); N.Y. PENAL LAW § 240.25 (McKinney 1993).

105 *Stalker Bill Draws Support*, UPI, Feb. 2, 1992, *available in* LEXIS, Nexis Library, UPI File.

106 *See supra* notes 59-66 and accompanying text (discussing police duty to respond to domestic violence complaints).

107 For example, Jane Fink, senior counsel to the Assembly Codes Committee in Albany, explained that "[o]ur existing menacing law—no matter whether a weapon was used or not, no matter how many times it occurred—it was just a 'B' misdemeanor, which downgrades the conduct." Spencer, *supra* note 14, at 6. Since most misdemeanor penalties carry only a few months of jail time, a misdemeanor conviction will not physically keep a stalker away for very long. Fountain & Kirby, *supra* note 91, at 1. Therefore the traditional criminal laws are insufficient to adequately protect victims. Freda, *supra* note 4, at A7. Furthermore, in some circumstances, only a fine is available, or defendants are released on bail. However, if the

behavior associated with stalkers.[108] On the other hand, a felony charge more effectively communicates to the offender that the behavior will not be condoned.[109] Stalking victims need a criminal remedy that will identify stalking behavior as an offense and punish the offenders with a felony conviction.[110] Merely increasing the penalties of existing statutes is not an adequate solution because those statutes are not broad enough to encompass all of the factual contexts of stalking. Flaws in the current criminal statutes could, however, be cured by felony statutes that specifically address stalking violence.

III. Stalking Legislation

Legislatures in most states have taken a laudatory step in the development and passage of stalking laws. In 1990, California became the first state to enact a stalking law.[111] Because the California statute was the first of its kind and has served as a national model, the following discussions focus on the California legislation.

A. *Legislative History of the California Stalking Statute*

Municipal Court Judge John Watson, of Orange County, initiated the development and passage of California's stalking law because of his frustration over the law's inability to protect four Orange County women who were killed despite the issuance of restraining orders against their assailants.[112] Judge Watson found that restraining orders, safety bonds, and misdemeanor charges were all inadequate means to protect women who knew in advance that their lives were at risk.[113] He proposed that the crime of stalking be cre-

---

offender is not sentenced or incarcerated, the assailant remains free to continue the criminal behavior.

108 For an overview of justifications for punishment, see Wayne R. LaFave & Austin W. Scott, Jr., Criminal Law 306-07 (2d ed. 1986). These theories of punishment suggest that the greater the penalty, the more likely that these goals will be achieved.

109 *See id.* at 307.

110 *See infra* text pp. 563-64 (discussing author's proposal to increase the penalties for a stalking offense).

111 Cal. Penal Code § 646.9 (West 1993). The California stalking law provides in part:

> (a) any person who willfully, maliciously, and repeatedly follows or harasses another person and who makes a credible threat with the intent to place that person in reasonable fear of death or great bodily injury, or to place that person in reasonable fear of the death or great bodily injury of his or her immediate family, is guilty of the crime of stalking, punishable by imprisonment in a county jail for not more than one year or by a fine of not more than one thousand dollars ($1,000), or by both that fine and imprisonment.

112 Letter from Judge John Watson to Senator Edward R. Royce (Jan. 10, 1990) (on file with author) [hereinafter Judge Watson Letter]. *See also* Fagan, *supra* note 90, at A1; Rosalind Resnick, *States Enact 'Stalking' Laws*, Nat'l L.J., May 11, 1992, at 3, 27.

113 *Id.*

ated to cover this conduct which was not yet reached by the Penal Code.[114] Further, Judge Watson suggested that the language of the law be drawn from California Penal Code section 422, which defines terrorism.[115]

On February 26, 1990, California State Senator Edward R. Royce responded to Judge Watson's concern by introducing Senate Bill 2184 to create the crime of "stalking."[116] Royce explained that the bill would "provide law enforcement with the tools necessary to arrest [stalkers] before they can make good their threats."[117] In effect, the legislation would indicate to stalkers that "the people of the State of California will no longer stand for the systematic terrorism of innocent victims."[118]

Senator Royce received strong support from the Conference of Personal Managers,[119] the California State Sheriffs', Police Chiefs', and Police Officers' Associations,[120] the Screen Actors Guild,[121] Women Prosecutors of California,[122] and the Orange County Commission on the Status of Women.[123] For example, in support of Senate Bill 2184, the Women Prosecutors of California revealed that:

> Many domestic violence cases never make it to trial because the victims refuse to testify out of fear for their safety and the safety of their children . . . . [Senate Bill] 2184 is an answer that . . . may

---

114 *Id.*

115 *Id. See* CAL. PENAL CODE § 422 (West 1993) ("Any person who willfully threatens to commit a crime which will result in death or great bodily injury to another person, with the specific intent that the statement is to be taken as a threat, even if there is no intent of actually carrying it out, which, on its face and under the circumstances in which it is made, is so unequivocal, unconditional, immediate, and specific as to convey to the person threatened, a gravity of purpose and an immediate prospect of execution of the threat, and thereby causes that person reasonably to be in sustained fear for his or her safety or for his or her immediate family's safety, shall be punished by imprisonment in the county jail not to exceed one year, or by imprisonment in the state prison."). It is interesting that Judge Watson compared stalking to the crime of terrorism. In both, the threat is defined as an *expressed* statement that places the target in fear. However, there are problems defining credible threat as an explicit threat. *See infra* pp. 561-63.

116 *See* Memorandum from Senator Edward R. Royce to Senate Committee on Constitutional Amendments (Apr. 16, 1990) (on file with author) [hereinafter Royce Memo].

117 *Id.*

118 Unpublished notes from Senator Edward R. Royce (on file with author).

119 Letter from Milton B. Suchin, President of Conference of Personal Managers, Inc., to Senator Edward R. Royce (June 6, 1990) (on file with author).

120 Press Release No. 45 from Senator Edward R. Royce, (July 3, 1990) (on file with author).

121 The Screen Actors Guild endorsed the stalking bill by a unanimous vote in an effort to improve the privacy and personal security of public figures and other state citizens. Screen Actors Guild Press Release (June 19, 1990) (on file with author).

122 Letter from Janet Shaw, Director of Legislation for Women Prosecutors of California, to Senator Edward R. Royce (May 2, 1990) (on file with author) [hereinafter Shaw Letter].

123 Hull Letter, *supra* note 3.

convince [the victims] to testify and put an end to their and other women's victimization.[124]

Moreover, in the hearing before the State Senate Judiciary Committee, Orange County Marshal Mike Carona testified that the bill was essential to empower the police with the tools necessary to combat the alarming number of deaths by stalkers.[125] For example, Carona explained that two of his deputies served a temporary restraining order on an abusive husband; although the deputies suspected that something was wrong and learned through the case tracking system that the husband had a history of threatening his wife, they could not intervene since no crime had been committed.[126] The next morning the husband shot and killed his wife and then killed himself.[127] Citing this as well as other examples, Carona urged the Senate Judiciary Committee to pass Senate Bill 2184 to grant peace officers the ability to intervene.[128]

The California stalking statute's legislative history demonstrates that the statute was created primarily to help victims of domestic violence. The statute advances three interests that orders of protection and other criminal remedies did not. First, the law gives police recourse to intervene before an attack takes place,[129] which takes the onus of enforcement off the victim; second, the law provides greater protection and imposes stiffer penalties;[130] finally, the law allows judges to raise or withhold bail on the basis of the likelihood of a repeat offense, thereby preventing further violence and enabling victims to make arrangements for personal safety.[131]

The bill faced powerful opposition, chiefly on grounds that it was too vague and overly broad.[132] However, as a result of widespread

---

124 Shaw Letter, *supra* note 122. Stronger rules on protecting victims who wish to testify would have also helped Dawn who was too frightened to testify against her husband. *See supra* note 23 and accompanying text (profiling case #2).

125 *Stalking Bill: Hearing on Senate Bill 2184 Before the Senate Judiciary Committee* (Apr. 24, 1990) (statement of Mike Carona, Marshal of Orange County) (on file with author).

126 *Id.*

127 *Id.*

128 *Id.*

129 *See* Donna Hunzeker, *Stalking Laws*, 17 ST. LEGIS. REP. 1 (Oct. 1991) (Hunzeker is manager of the criminal justice program at the National Conference of State Legislatures in Denver, Colorado).

130 *See* unpublished notes from Senator Edward R. Royce (KCBS Stalking Program, Jan. 30, 1991) (on file with author).

131 *Id.* Stronger rules for release on bail would have been particularly helpful for Dawn Jolly, whose husband was continually released on bail and able to perpetrate more violence. *See supra* note 23 and accompanying text (profiling case #2).

132 Letter from David Nagler, Legislative Advocate for Nossaman, Cuthner, Knox & Elliott, to Assembly Member John Burton, Assembly Committee on Public Safety Chair (June 29, 1990) (showing that California Public Defenders Association is troubled by the vagueness of

support and convincing evidence, Senate Bill 2184 passed the Policy Committee without a dissenting vote, passed the Ways and Means Committee by 21-1, passed the Senate by 36-0, and passed the Assembly floor by 66-1.[133] Royce carried the bill to fruition on September 29, 1990, when then Governor George Deukmejian signed the bill into law.

Thirty-five states have followed California's lead in enacting similar legislation[134] and other states are currently discussing the enact-

---

the stalking legislation) (on file with author) [hereinafter Nagler Letter]; Letter from Margaret Pena, Legislative Director, and Francisco Lobaco, Legislative Advocate, American Civil Liberties Union of Northern California to Assembly Members of Public Safety (June 27, 1990) (on file with author) (stating that the American Civil Liberties Union was opposed to Senate Bill 2184 on grounds of vagueness). *See also* Janine Anderson, *Stalking Made a Felony*, ORANGE COUNTY REG., Apr. 16, 1990.

The vagueness doctrine declares a law unconstitutional if persons "of common intelligence must necessarily guess at its meaning." Connally v. Gen. Constr. Co., 269 U.S. 385, 391 (1926) (Oklahoma minimum wage statute struck down because it failed to adequately inform a person subject to the statute's criminal penalties of the wages he had to pay his employees). Courts may find statutes unconstitutional on grounds of vagueness if those statutes are "unduly vague in defining who is affected, what conduct is prohibited, or what punishment may be imposed." Regina O. Matthews, Comment, *The Louisiana Constitution's Declaration of Rights: Post-*Hardwick *Protection for Sexual Privacy?*, 62 TUL. L. REV. 767, 776 (1988).

The vagueness doctrine therefore focuses on the ambiguity or uncertainty of the statutory terms. This precision requirement ensures that individuals are given a fair chance to conform their conduct to the law. The terms of a statute must be sharply defined so that the activities proscribed are knowable. *See* Broderick v. Okla., 413 U.S. 601, 607 (1973); Grayned v. Rockford, 408 U.S. 104, 108 (1972). Without sufficiently clear and definite language any subsequent conviction would be unforeseeable and thus a violation of due process. Osborne v. Ohio, 495 U.S. 103 (1990).

In Palmer v. City of Euclid, 402 U.S. 544, 545-46 (1971), a suspicious person ordinance was held unconstitutionally vague because the language gave insufficient notice to the defendant that his conduct did not show a "visible or lawful business" and the man could not be held criminally responsible "for conduct which he could not reasonably understand to be proscribed." However, stalking laws are distinguishable from the suspicious persons ordinance because stalking laws require the defendant to have formed a specific intent to commit the proscribed result. A specific intent requirement overcomes statutory vagueness because it clarifies the nature of the proscribed conduct. M. Sean Royall, Comment, *Constitutionally Regulating Telephone Harassment: An Exercise in Statutory Precision*, 56 U. CHI. L. REV. 1403, 1407-08 (1989). Innocent victims who do not have the requisite intent will not be mistakenly convicted. Therefore, vagueness challenges with regard to the stalking laws should be dismissed.

For a more in-depth review of the constitutionality of the stalking laws, see Matthew J. Gilligan, Note, *Stalking the Stalker: Developing New Laws to Thwart Those who Terrorize Others*, 27 GA. L. REV. 285, 304-28 (1992).

133 Senate Floor Statement, Unfinished business, file No. 149 at A35 (on file with author).

134 ALA. CODE § 13A-6-90 (1992); 1993 Ark. Acts 388; CAL. PENAL CODE § 646.9 (West Supp. 1993); COLO. REV. STAT. § 18-9-111 (1986); 1992 Conn. Acts 92-237 (Reg. Sess.); DEL. CODE ANN. tit. 11, § 1312A (1992); FLA. STAT. ANN. § 784.048 (West Supp. 1993); 1993 Ga. Laws 560; HAW. REV. STAT. § 711-1106.5 (1992); IDAHO CODE § 18-7905 (1992); ILL. ANN. STAT. ch. 720, para. 12-7.3 (Smith-Hurd 1993); IOWA CODE ANN. § 708.11 (West Supp. 1992); 1992 Kan. Sess. Laws § 95; KY. REV. STAT. ANN. § 508.140 (Michie/Bobbs-Merrill 1992); LA. REV. STAT. ANN. § 14:40.2 (West Supp. 1993); MASS. GEN. LAWS ANN. ch. 265,

ment of such legislation.[135] While some states have included additional or modified provisions,[136] most states have modeled their statutes on the California enactment.[137]

The following section describes the various elements of the California stalking statute, addressing differences in other state statutes where appropriate.

B. *Mechanics*

The California stalking law makes it unlawful for "any person to willfully, maliciously and repeatedly follow or harass another person."[138] By making it unlawful to maliciously follow another,[139] this

§ 43 (West Supp. 1993); MICH. COMP. LAWS ANN. § 750.411h (West Supp. 1993); MISS. CODE ANN. § 532 (1992); NEB. REV. STAT. § 42-903 (1992); N.J. STAT. ANN. § 2C:12-10 (West Supp. 1993); 1993 N.M. Laws 86; N.Y. PENAL LAW § 240.25 (McKinney 1992) (harassment statute); N.C. GEN. STAT. § 14-277.3 (1992); 1993 N.D. Laws 120; OHIO REV. CODE ANN. § 2903.211 (Anderson 1993); OKLA. STAT. ANN. tit. 21, § 1173 (West 1992); R.I. GEN. LAWS § 11-59-2 (1992); S.C. CODE ANN. § 16-3-1070 (Law. Co-op. 1992); S.D. CODIFIED LAWS ANN. § 22-19A-1 (1992); TENN. CODE ANN. § 39-17-315 (1992); 1993 Tex. Gen. Laws 10; UTAH CODE ANN. § 76-5-106.5 (1992); VA. CODE ANN. § 18.2-60.3 (Michie 1992); WASH. REV. CODE ANN. § 9A.46.110 (West Supp. 1993); W. VA. CODE § 61-2-9a (1992); WIS. STAT. § 947.013 (1989-90).

135 Indiana, Minnesota, Missouri, Montana, Pennsylvania, Vermont, and Wyoming have entered into the process of developing stalking laws.

136 For example, Connecticut has passed a law that provides additional protection for children. 1992 Conn. Acts 92-237 (Reg. Sess.). The law provides that a convicted first-time offender would be guilty of a misdemeanor, punishable by up to one year in prison, unless the person he or she stalked was sixteen years old or younger. *Id.* In that case, the crime would be a felony, punishable by up to five years in prison. In addition, West Virginia passed a stalker statute with a limited application. The law applies only to offenders with whom the victim has had an intimate relationship and would therefore not apply to the stalking of celebrities or strangers. W. VA. CODE § 61-2-9a (1992). The law specifically requires that the victim be "any person with whom that person formerly resided or cohabited or with whom that person formerly engaged in a sexual or intimate relationship. . . ." *Id.*

137 CAL. PENAL CODE § 646.9 (West Supp. 1993). *See* the full text of California's stalking statute, *supra* note 111.

138 *Id.* § 646.9(a).

139 This "following" type conduct may not be a mere isolated incident; instead, the statute requires "a pattern of conduct composed of a series of acts over a period of time, however short, evidencing a continuity of purpose." CAL. PENAL CODE § 646.9(e) (West Supp. 1993). *See also* COLO. REV. STAT. § 18-9-111 note (1986) (repeatedly means on more than one occasion); 1992 Conn. Acts 92-237 (Reg. Sess.); DEL. CODE ANN. tit. 11, § 1312A(a) (1992); FLA. STAT. ANN. § 784.048(b) (West Supp. 1993); IOWA CODE ANN. § 708.11(1)(a) (West Supp. 1993); LA. REV. STAT. ANN. § 14:40.2(c)(2) (West Supp. 1993); MASS. GEN. LAWS ANN. ch. 265, § 43(a) (West Supp. 1993); MISS. CODE ANN. § 532 (1992); NEB. REV. STAT. § 42-903(2) (1992); N.J. REV. STAT. ANN. § 2C:12-10(a)(1) (West Supp. 1993); R.I. GEN. LAWS § 11-59-2(a) (1992); S.C. CODE ANN. § 16-3-1070(A)(2) (Law. Co-op. 1992); S.D. CODIFIED LAWS ANN. § 22-19A-1 (1992); TENN. CODE ANN. § 39-17-315(a)(1)(A) (1992); W. VA. CODE § 61-2-9a(a) (1992). The Illinois law is more specific in that it requires the stalker, in furtherance of the credible threat, to follow or put the victim under surveillance on at least two separate occasions. ILL. ANN. STAT. ch. 720, para. 12-7.3(a) (Smith-Hurd 1992).

element of the statute appears to address the situation in which a rejected partner strives for reunion by following and harassing the victim.[140] The statute requires that the following or harassing conduct be repetitive. The purpose of this requirement is to distinguish isolated acts from a series of acts that evince a continuity of purpose and therefore a substantial threat.

In addition to the following or harassing element, the California statute requires that the assailant make a credible threat to be guilty of stalking.[141] According to the statute, a credible threat is one made with the "intent and the apparent ability to carry out the threat."[142] The credible threat requirement therefore establishes whether or not the assailant had the specific intent or purpose of committing the offense.[143]

140 Harassment is further defined by the statute as a course of conduct that serves no legitimate purpose. CAL. PENAL CODE § 646.9(e) (West Supp. 1993). *See also* DEL. CODE ANN. tit. 11, § 1312A(b)(1) (1992); FLA. STAT. ANN. § 784.048(1)(A) (West Supp. 1993); IOWA CODE ANN. § 708.11(B)(2) (West Supp. 1993); OKLA. STAT. ANN. tit. 21, § 1173(E)(1) (West 1992); R.I. GEN. LAWS § 11-59-1(a) (1992); S.C. CODE ANN. § 16-3-1070(A)(1) (Law. Co-op. 1992). Opposition was voiced by the California Association of Licensed Investigators. This organization was concerned that persons such as insurance adjusters, law enforcement officers, private investigators and newspaper reporters, all of whom conduct surveillance for truly legitimate purposes, might be unjustly placed in a position of prosecution. Letter from W. Craig Biddle, Biddle & Hamilton, to Senator Edward R. Royce (Mar. 26, 1990) (on file with author). However, this "no legitimate purpose" provision essentially limits the coverage of the statute to only those defendants who have intent to cause harm. For example, innocent people like journalists and private detectives who repeatedly follow their targets would not fall within the coverage of the statute because they have a legitimate purpose—reporting on an event or discovering facts for a case. Thus, this provision mitigates against the potential challenges of the statute being unconstitutionally overly broad. In a similar fashion, some of the statutes provide exemptions for behavior that is within the language of the laws but has been excluded for policy reasons. *See, e.g.*, DEL. CODE ANN. tit. 11, § 1312A(f) (1992) ("This section shall not apply to conduct which occurs in furtherance of law enforcement or private detective business . . . ."); ILL. STAT. ANN. ch. 720, para. 12-7.3(c) (1992) ("This section does not apply to picketing occurring at the workplace that is otherwise lawful and arises out of a bonafide labor dispute.") *See also* CAL. PENAL CODE § 646.9(g) (West 1992); S.C. CODE ANN. § 16-3-1070(E) (Law. Co-op. 1992). These exemptions may be important to overcome any challenges that the laws are overly broad.

141 CAL. PENAL CODE § 646.9(f) (West Supp. 1993). *See* ALA. CODE § 13A-6-90(a) (1992); COLO. REV. STAT. § 18-9-111 (1986 Repl. Vol.); 1992 Conn. Acts 92-237 (Reg. Sess.); DEL. CODE ANN. tit. 11, § 1312A(a) (1992); FLA. STAT. ch. s.784.048(1)(c) (1992); IOWA CODE ANN. § 708.11(1)(a) (West Supp. 1993); LA. REV. STAT. ANN. § 14:40.2(A) (West Supp. 1993); MASS. GEN. LAWS ANN. ch. 265, § 43(a) (West Supp. 1993); MISS. CODE ANN. § 532 (1992); N.J. STAT. ANN. § 2C:12-10(a)(2) (West Supp. 1993); 1992 R.I. Pub. Laws 201; S.C. CODE ANN. § 16-3-1070(A)(3) (Law. Co-op. 1992); S.D. CODIFIED LAWS ANN. § 22-19A-1 (1992); TENN. CODE ANN. § 39-17-315(a)(1)(A)(2) (1992); UTAH CODE ANN. § 76-5-106.5(1)(b) (1992). *See infra* notes 171, 174 and accompanying text (discussing problems with credible threat language for phase-four victims).

142 CAL. PENAL CODE § 646.9(e) (West 1992).

143 Organizations that opposed the stalking bill were concerned that the language could be misconstrued. For example, the California Public Defenders Association was troubled by the

The California stalking law also requires that the threat create reasonable fear in the target; the threat must "cause the person who is the target of the threat to reasonably fear for his or her safety."[144] States vary in the required level of fear that must be sustained. While the California law requires a victim to "fear . . . death or great bodily injury,"[145] the Connecticut law defines reasonable fear as "fear for his physical safety,"[146] and the Illinois law requires a victim to fear "death, bodily harm, sexual assault, confinement or restraint."[147]

It is not clear what standard will be applied to evaluate the reasonableness of a victim's fear because the California statute uses contradictory language. First, the language of the statute appears to provide for a subjective standard: a "credible threat with the intent to place *that person* in reasonable fear."[148] However, in the definition of harassment, the statute specifies an objective standard: "the course of conduct must be such as would cause a *reasonable person* to suffer substantial emotional distress."[149] This inconsistency is important because the standard used to evaluate whether the fear sustained was reasonable will have a significant impact on the outcome of a case.

An objective standard requires jurors to evaluate evidence in light of what the reasonable person would or would not have done.[150] However, it is often the case that the juror will not have experienced the conduct at issue and thus the conduct may not appear to be reasonable.[151] Evidence regarding the battered woman syndrome and rape trauma syndrome have been admitted into evidence to inform the fact-finder of how people who have been raped or battered actually behave.[152] This subjectivized standard is appropriate in the stalking context because "[b]attered women . . . may perceive danger and imminence differently from men . . . . A subtle gesture or a new method of abuse, insignificant to another person, may create a reason-

---

vagueness of the term stalking. They argued that the bill does not define "follows," or require that repeated attempts be made. Nagler Letter, *supra* note 132. By adding the credible threat language as an additional element, the statute imposed higher standards to ensure that it would pass constitutional muster. *See supra* note 132 (outlining constitutional argument).

144 CAL. PENAL CODE § 646.9(f) (West Supp. 1993). *See, e.g.*, FLA. STAT. ch. s.748.048(1)(c) (1992); 1992 R.I. Pub. Laws 201; N.J. STAT. ANN. § 2C:12-10(a)(2) (West Supp. 1993).

145 CAL. PENAL CODE § 646.9(a) (West Supp. 1993).

146 1992 Conn. Acts 92-237(2)(a) (Reg. Sess.). *See also* W. VA. CODE § 61-2-9a (1992); FLA. STAT. ch. s.784.048(1)(c) (1992).

147 ILL. ANN. STAT. ch. 720, para. 5/12-7.3(a) (Smith-Hurd 1992).

148 CAL. PENAL CODE § 646.9(a) (West Supp. 1993) (emphasis added).

149 *Id.* § 646.9(e) (emphasis added).

150 People v. Day, 2 Cal. Rptr. 2d 916, 924 (Ct. App. 1992).

151 *Id.*

152 People v. Hudson, 6 Cal. Rptr. 2d 690 (Ct. App. 1992).

able fear in a battered woman."[153]

In other contexts, the California courts have held that a victim has sustained reasonable fear when knowledge of prior threats conveys the seriousness of the present threat. For example, in *People v. Hudson*,[154] the court held that evidence of previous obsessive behavior and prior threats was "extremely relevant to the issues of the defendant's specific intent that the statement be taken as a threat, to the nature of the threat, and to the victim's reasonable sustaining of fear."[155] Following this reasoning, a victim who has endured the cycle of abuse may react to conduct by her abusive partner with a heightened level of fear, whereas the reasonable person would not. Although "[i]t's not a crime to make a paranoid person fearful,"[156] a domestic violence victim may be more sensitive than the reasonable person who has not endured years of abuse. Thus, for the purposes of the stalking statute, designed to protect victims of domestic violence, an objective standard appears to be too narrow to take into account the complex and turbulent nature of the cycle theory of domestic violence.

C. *Grading of Penalties*

Under most stalking laws, the first offense is punished as a misdemeanor.[157] Enhanced penalties apply in most states if the crime is committed while a civil protection order is in effect. For example, in Mississippi, an offender not subject to a restraining order "shall be punished by imprisonment for not more than six months or by a fine of not more than one thousand dollars,"[158] whereas an offender who violates the stalking statute "when there is a temporary restraining order or an injunction in effect . . . shall be punished by imprisonment in the county jail for not more than one year or by a fine of not more than one thousand dollars, or by both such fine and imprisonment."[159] Other states provide an even sharper grading of penalties. In Oklahoma, the first offense is a misdemeanor, but if the crime oc-

---

153 People v. Romero, 13 Cal. Rptr. 2d 332, 338 (Ct. App. 1992).

154 6 Cal. Rptr. 2d at 690.

155 *Id.* at 698.

156 Constance L. Hays, *If That Man is Following Her, Connecticut is Going to Follow Him*, N.Y. TIMES, June 5, 1992, at B1, B5 (statement of Thomas S. Luby, a former federal prosecutor).

157 *See, e.g.*, CAL. PENAL CODE § 646.9(a) (West Supp. 1993); UTAH CODE ANN. § 76-5-106.5(3) (1992). Note that in South Dakota, stalking is only a misdemeanor. S.D. CODIFIED LAWS ANN. § 22-19A-1 (1992).

158 MISS. CODE ANN. § 532(1) (1992).

159 *Id.* § 532(2). *See also* COLO. REV. STAT. § 18-9-111(5)(b) (1992); IOWA CODE ANN. § 708.11(2) (West Supp. 1993); MASS. GEN. LAWS ANN. ch. 265, § 43(b) (West Supp. 1993);

curs while a protective order was in effect, the offense rises to a felony offense.[160] The practical consequences of characterizing the offense as a felony rather than a misdemeanor is that it should increase the deterrent value of the law.[161]

Tougher penalties are also provided for second and subsequent offenses. Some states punish the second offense as a misdemeanor but add additional years of imprisonment;[162] others criminalize the subsequent violation as a felony offense.[163] Illinois takes an even stronger approach to punishment. The Illinois law provides that the subsequent offense is a felony and punishes the offender with fines of up to $10,000 and a jail term of up to three years.[164] Similarly, the California law, as amended, provides that once an offender has been convicted of a felony under this section, a subsequent violation "is punishable in the state prison, for 16 months, two or three years and a fine up to ten thousand dollars ($10,000)."[165]

D. *Application of California Statute to Case Histories*

As the preceding discussion shows, although the stalking statutes vary, generally required elements of stalking laws include a pattern of harassing conduct and the making of a credible threat that causes fear. This section applies these elements to each case history

---

S.C. CODE ANN. § 16-3-70(C) (Law. Co-op. 1992); VA. CODE ANN. § 18.2-60.3(B) (Michie 1992); W. VA. CODE § 61-2-9a(b) (1992).

The Colorado statute punishes stalking while a protection order is in effect to an even greater extent. Under the Colorado law, a first offense is punished as a Class 3 misdemeanor (up to 6 months in jail and a fine of up to $750), whereas an offender subject to a restraining order is punished for a Class 1 misdemeanor (up to 24 months in jail and a fine of up to $5,000). COLO. REV. STAT. § 18-9-111 (1992).

160 OKLA. STAT. tit. 21, § 1173(A) & (B) (1992). *See also* 1992 Conn. Acts 92-237(b) (Reg. Sess.); DEL. CODE ANN. tit. 11, § 1312A(f) (1992); KY. REV. STAT. ANN. § 508.140 (Michie/ Bobbs-Merrill 1992); MASS. GEN. LAWS ANN. ch. 265, § 43 (West Supp. 1993).

161 *See supra* notes 107-09 and accompanying text (discussing the purposes of punishment and value of deterrence). The difference between a misdemeanor and felony conviction has important ramifications both substantively and procedurally. *See* LA FAVE & SCOTT, *supra* note 108, at 30.

162 *See, e.g.*, MASS. GEN. LAWS ANN. ch. 265, § 43 (West Supp. 1993); S.C. CODE ANN. § 16-3-1070 (Law. Co-op. 1992); 1992 R.I. Pub. Laws 201.

163 *See* 1992 Conn. Acts 92-237 (Reg. Sess.); DEL. CODE ANN. tit. 11, § 1312A (1992); IDAHO CODE § 18-7905 (1992); IOWA CODE ANN. § 708.11 (West Supp. 1993) (felony for third or subsequent offense); MASS. GEN. LAWS ANN. ch. 265, § 43 (West Supp. 1993); MISS. CODE ANN. § 532 (1992); OKLA. STAT. ANN. tit. 21, § 1173 (West Supp. 1993); S.D. CODIFIED LAWS ANN. §§ 22-19A-1, -3 (1992); TENN. CODE ANN. § 39-17-315 (1992); VA. CODE ANN. § 18.2-60.3 (Michie 1992) (third conviction punished as a felony); *see also* Beck, *supra* note 2, at 60.

164 ILL. ANN. STAT. ch. 720, para. 5/12-7.3 (Smith-Hurd 1993).

165 CAL. PENAL CODE § 646.9(d) (West Supp. 1993).

presented in Part I.A, illustrating the impact of the law on stalking incidents.

1. *Case #1*

The stalking statutes would likely be effective in dealing with the situation presented in case #1.[166] It may not be clear whether following Geraldine to work and confronting her at her home to make accusations of infidelity would constitute harassing conduct.[167] However, Geraldine's boyfriend subsequently broke into her house and threatened her with a gun—such conduct would likely cause distress in the reasonable person and did in fact cause Geraldine to suffer emotional distress. Thus, the harassment element of the statute would be satisfied in this case. In addition, the boyfriend threatened: "I'll kill you if you leave me." His threat suggests that he had the requisite intent to kill Geraldine. Moreover, the fact that he never hesitated to beat her in the past and was armed when he threatened her in this instance showed an apparent ability to carry out the threat. Thus, the courts would probably conclude that the threats were credible. Finally, Geraldine became so frightened by her boyfriend's threats that she withdrew from all social contacts, changed the locks on her door in an attempt to secure herself, and called the police frequently. These reactions to his behavior suggest that the threat caused Geraldine to reasonably fear for her safety.[168] Because the criteria of the statute appear to have been satisfied, it is likely that the boyfriend would have been convicted under the stalking law.[169] Intervention before the boyfriend made good on the threats would have protected Geraldine from the threatening conduct and guarded her against actual confrontation.

---

166 *See supra* text accompanying note 22 (case #1).

167 *But see infra* notes 230-31 and accompanying text (proposing that such unwelcome contacts should be characterized an offense).

168 Since Geraldine had no plans of continuing a relationship with her boyfriend and thus no intention of satisfying his ultimatum to revive the relationship, it was reasonable for her to believe that he would follow through with his plans for murder.

169 In a similar case, a woman filed for divorce from her husband of seventeen years. She alleged that he threatened to kill her at least once. Further, he stalked her home with a video camera on two other occasions in an attempt to gain evidence to use against her in the divorce proceedings. After the stalking law went into effect in Illinois, Lake Forest police were able to arrest the husband. Joseph Kirby, *Stalking Law Sends A New Signal*, CHI. TRIB., Aug. 13, 1992, at C1. Lake County State's Attorney Michael Waller explained that "if it wasn't for the stalking law, we probably wouldn't have been able to charge him with a felony offense since he didn't gain entrance to the home forcibly." James Hill, *First Stalking Charge Filed in Lake County*, CHI. TRIB., July 30, 1992, at L2.

2. *Case #2*

When Dawn received a dozen roses from her husband she was afraid because he violated her decision to terminate contact.[170] It is unlikely that this seemingly innocent contact would constitute a credible threat or that a reasonable person would sustain fear upon the receipt of flowers.[171] However, because her husband subsequently destroyed her car, physically abused her, lodged a bullet in her computer, and showed his access to firearms, he evinced an intent and an ability to cause harm. Therefore, the credible threat element of the statute might well be satisfied. Finally, the fact that Dawn was too shaken to testify in court shows that she sustained reasonable fear for her safety.[172] Thus, it is likely that a court would have found that all of the elements of the statute were satisfied.

3. *Case #3*

While the presence of Joanne's ex-husband outside of her home may not, in itself, seem threatening, the fact that she was too afraid to go to work, go to the market or send her children to school is evidence that his behavior caused Joanne to sustain a heightened level of fear.[173] However, this seemingly innocent behavior does not meet the statutory definition of a credible threat.[174] Thus, intervention would probably not be possible under the stalking laws, leaving Joanne without protection and her husband without punishment.

All of the conditions set forth in the stalking statutes would likely have been satisfied in the first two cases described in Part I.A. If the stalking laws had been in effect at the time of these incidents, Geraldine's boyfriend and Dawn's husband would likely have been convicted and sentenced accordingly. In addition, Geraldine and Dawn would likely have received protection under the law against future violent contact that previously may not have been available. Thus, the stalking statutes are effective in some circumstances. However, victims might not receive legal protection if, as in the third case, the stalker does not make an express declaration to kill or cause bodily injury or use actual force. Given the context of the domestic violence relationship, just waiting in his car outside Joanne's home was

---

170 *See supra* text accompanying note 23 (case #2).

171 *But see infra* notes 230-31 and accompanying text (proposing that stalking laws should respond to this kind of unwelcome contact).

172 *See supra* text accompanying note 23 (discussing refusal to testify).

173 *See supra* text accompanying note 24 (case #3).

174 *See* CAL. PENAL CODE § 646.9(f) (West Supp. 1993).

enough for Joanne to sustain fear. However, the stalking laws do not reach this seemingly legitimate behavior.

The next section sets forth Lenore Walker's theory on violence in battered households and proposes that stalking should be identified as a further, fourth stage within Walker's domestic violence framework. By identifying stalking as phase-four of the domestic violence cycle, lawmakers and others are given a framework within which they may give as much attention to the stalking problem as they have recently been giving the traditional "in-home" domestic violence problem.[175]

IV. Cycle Theory of Violence

Dr. Lenore Walker is one of the leading forensic psychologists in the field of domestic violence and has written three books on battered women. Walker defines a battered woman as a woman "who is or has been in an intimate relationship with a man who repeatedly subjects or subjected her to forceful physical and/or psychological abuse."[176] Walker estimates that as many as fifty percent of all women will be battered at some point in their lives.[177] This alarmingly high figure is a compelling reason to develop laws that more effectively provide needed relief and punishment.

A. *Lenore Walker's Theory*

Walker defined a cycle theory of violence to provide a formula for understanding battering households.[178] According to Walker, wife beating can be explained in three distinct phases.[179] First, Walker defines a tension-building phase, characterized by minor bat-

[175] *See infra* notes 37-66 and accompanying text (discussing transition from view that domestic violence is a private matter to a view that domestic violence is a grave problem that requires legal attention).

[176] Walker, The Battered Woman Syndrome, *supra* note 35, at 203.

[177] *Id.* at 19.

[178] It is helpful for the discussion on battering households to understand the personality profile of battered couples. Characteristics of battering males include personality disorders, easily-threatened masculinity, low self-esteem, lack of assertiveness, a need for power, pathological jealousy, substance abuse, and childhood abuse. *Id.* at 36-40. Similarly, characteristics of battered women include low self-esteem, self-blame, guilt, fear and terror, and learned helplessness. *Id.* at 31-32. These characteristics may explain why, after the woman leaves, the battering male becomes frenzied for reunion. That is, the man's need for power is violated and his low self-esteem is threatened. *See infra* notes 206-15 and accompanying text (discussing the man's drive for reunion). "The presence of the man's excessive *jealousy* has been described as a major component in battering relationships . . . . [T]he batterers' need to control their women leads them to be suspicious and intrusive." Walker, The Battered Woman Syndrome, *supra* note 35.

[179] Walker, Battered Woman, *supra* note 13, at 55.

tering incidents.[180] These minor incidents in which the batterer is suspicious and intrusive are generally the result of the batterer's need to control, his low self-esteem, and his excessive jealousy.[181] Second, there is a phase of acute battery.[182] Finally, there is a period of kindness and loving behavior coupled with promises to reform.[183] Because the woman and man may still love each other, the couple is likely to believe that the violence will never happen again.[184] To be labeled a battered woman or a battering male, the couple must endure the cycle of violence at least twice.[185]

In a subsequent study, Walker confirmed that the three phases tend to repeat in a continuous cycle but concluded that "over time, the first phase of tension building becomes more common and loving contrition, the third phase, declines."[186] Thus, most women who "choose" to remain with their abusive partners[187] endure the repetition of the cycle.

The following case history of a married woman illustrates the distinct phases of the cycle of violence. As to the first cycle: "We were very happy until after the birth of the fourth child . . . . [His drinking] became much more frequent . . . . He was frightening when in this sort of aggressive mood but never made an attempt to hit me until . . . my son's fourth birthday."[188] This first stage of tension developed into more serious threats and assaults. She explained,

> [h]e picked up the bread-knife and threatened to put it through my throat. I told him I had taken my fill of his threats, insults and now assaults. I said I was leaving and taking our children. His reply was that I could get out but if I tried to take the children he would kill me. I grabbed my coat and left the flat.[189]

This phase was followed by a period of contrition. For example, "I stayed away for nearly three weeks, during which time my husband visited us and asked me to return. After he gave me an undertaking

---

180 *Id.* at 56.

181 *Id.* at 57-58; *see* WALKER, THE BATTERED WOMAN SYNDROME, *supra* note 35, at 43.

182 WALKER, BATTERED WOMAN, *supra* note 13, at 60.

183 *Id.* at 65.

184 PAGELOW, *supra* note 41, at 306 ("[T]he couple is likely to 'kiss and make up' . . . .").

185 WALKER, BATTERED WOMAN, *supra* note 13, at xv; WALKER, THE BATTERED WOMAN SYNDROME, *supra* note 35, at 202.

186 Lenore E. Walker, *The Battered Woman Syndrome Study in* THE DARK SIDE OF FAMILIES 31, 43 (David Finkelheur et al. eds., 1983).

187 The phrase "choose to stay" is misleading. There is a perception that women stay in the relationship because the abuse is not that bad. *See* People v. Torres, 488 N.Y.S.2d 358, 362 (Sup. Ct. 1985). *See infra* text accompanying notes 192-96 (discussing reasons why women remain in abusive relationships).

188 ERIN PIZZEY, SCREAM QUIETLY OR THE NEIGHBORS WILL HEAR 26 (1977).

189 *Id.* at 27.

never to touch me again, I went home."[190] However, in accordance with Walker's model, the cycle repeated: "I was back seven months before the next assault."[191] Although in this example the acute battery phase is not fully developed, the cycle of violence is well-illustrated.

Victims may not flee the abusive situation for many reasons, ranging from emotional considerations including hope that the abuse will stop, to practical ones like financial dependence.[192] Fear, however, is the primary reason.[193] "Fear immobilizes them, ruling their actions, their decisions, their very lives."[194] Victims fear the insecurity, the unknown, losing custody of the children, or fear that the abuser will find them and the abuse will escalate.[195] More specifically, as one woman described, "[i]t is the fear of knowing someone is searching for you and will beat you when he finds you."[196]

However, Walker's theory is limited because it rests on the notion that women do not leave the abusive relationship and that as a result, the cycle repeats.[197] However, not all women stay.[198] It is the opinion of this author that Lenore Walker's cycle theory of violence should be extended to include a fourth phase that addresses situations in which women terminate abusive relationships but are unable to escape the abuse.

B. *The Cycle Theory of Violence Extended to Encompass Stalking*

Although some victims remain with their abusive partners and endure the repetition of the cycle of violence, some do not. Lenore Walker did not include women who separated from their abusive

---

190 *Id.*

191 *Id.*

192 Researcher Elizabeth Truninger lists seven reasons why victims stay with their husbands who beat them: "(1) poor self image; (2) beliefs that husbands will reform; (3) economic hardships; (4) the need of their children for the father's economic support; (5) doubt they can get along alone; (6) belief that divorces are stigmatized; and (7) the fact that it is difficult for women with children to find work." LANGLEY & LEVY, *supra* note 48, at 114. For other accounts of why abused women stay with their abuser, see RICHARD J. GELLES, FAMILY VIOLENCE 95-98 (1979). *See also* RICHARD J. GELLES, THE VIOLENT HOME 93-110 (1987) (discussing that the victim has no place to go); HOFF, *supra* note 35, at 40-49; LANGLEY & LEVY, *supra*, at 111-25; MARTIN, *supra* note 24, at 72-86.

193 MARTIN, *supra* note 24, at 76.

194 *Id.*

195 In fact, the woman is most vulnerable to extreme violence when she leaves the abusive relationship. WALKER, TERRIFYING LOVE, *supra* note 96, at 256.

196 MARTIN, *supra* note 24, at 78.

197 HOFF, *supra* note 35, at 40-49; GELLES, THE VIOLENT HOME, *supra* note 192, at 93-110; LANGLEY & LEVY, *supra* note 48, at 111-25; MARTIN, *supra* note 24, at 72-86.

198 *See infra* notes 22-24 and accompanying text (presenting case histories of women who have attempted to terminate the cycle of abuse).

partners in her categorization of domestic violence phases. However, Walker did acknowledge that "[l]eaving the batterer is in many cases, more dangerous than remaining, . . . [as] separation is the time of greatest volatility and peril in battering relationships."[199] Walker thus recognized that women who gather up the strength, courage, and resolution to separate from their abusive partners are unable to simply terminate the cycle of violence. Instead, victims may be haunted by their partner who follows them like a shadow hoping for reunion.

When a battered woman finally attempts to break the cycle of violence by terminating the abusive relationship, her decision to leave is often met with escalated violence, in the form of stalking.[200] For example,

> [i]f the wife does manage to escape [the abuse], her husband often stalks her like a hunted animal. He scours the neighborhood, contacts friends and relatives, goes to all the likely places where she might have sought refuge, and checks with public agencies to track her down . . . . Unless she can afford to leave town and effectively disappear, a woman is never quite safe from a stalking husband.[201]

Many domestic violence victims who do leave their abusive partners, spend the rest of their lives "trying to avoid men fanatically dedicated to pursuing them, harassing them, or even killing them."[202] It is estimated that at least half of the women who leave their abusive partners are followed or harassed as a result.[203] In fact, domestic violence is more common among persons who have separated.[204] Government data also indicates that three-fourths of all domestic violence victims are separated at the time of the incident.[205]

Studies show that the most dangerous time period for an abused woman is when she attempts to separate from her partner.[206] A possible explanation for the escalated violence is the rejected partner's refusal to endure separation; that is, he would "rather kill, or die

---

199 WALKER, TERRIFYING LOVE, *supra* note 96, at 256.

200 *Id.*; *see also* MARTIN, *supra* note 24, at 77.

201 MARTIN, *supra* note 24, at 77.

202 PAGELOW, *supra* note 41, at 318. For example, Sol Wachtler, former Chief Judge of the New York State Court of Appeals, was recently charged with a "campaign against . . . his former lover, after she broke up with him." Associated Press, *Wachtler Asks To Be Released as Trustee*, N.Y. TIMES, Feb. 5, 1993, at L27.

203 ANGELA BROWNE, WHEN BATTERED WOMEN KILL 110 (1987).

204 Ross, *supra* note 14, at 6 (statement of Joan Zorra, senior attorney for the National Battered Women's Law Project in New York).

205 U.S. DEP'T OF JUSTICE, REPORT TO THE NATION ON CRIME AND JUSTICE (1983) *cited in* Finn, *supra* note 74, at 45.

206 PAGELOW, *supra* note 41, at 307; WALKER, TERRIFYING LOVE, *supra* note 96, at 65 ("Separation creates a period of unprecedented danger in battering situations, a danger often not recognized by others.").

himself, than separate from the battered woman."[207] In a state of rejection, "the [partner] resort[s] to intimidation in a desperate attempt to try to regain self-esteem."[208] A typical response from a rejected partner is: "If I can't have you, no one else will have you, and when I get through with you, no one else will want you."[209] Thus, the separation drives the man into a fury to reconcile the divide.[210] The stalker's campaign to force the relationship back together often leads to violent and even bizarre actions resulting in property damage, physical injury, and death.[211]

Fear underlies the rejected partner's efforts to achieve reunion: "The man . . . has a lot to lose if he lets his wife walk out on him. He loses the stability of married life that is so significant to his mental health . . . . He loses 'his' woman, the scapegoat that is living proof of his superiority . . . ."[212]

Moreover, the rejected partner may be unable to watch the woman start anew because of his own low self-esteem. "Some men would rather kill 'their' women than see them make a new life."[213] Consider the example of a couple who entered into a settlement where it was agreed that she would drop the pending criminal charges for assault and battery in return for a quick, uncontested divorce.[214] While she began to consider her new beginning—a new place to live, a new job, new friends—he stormed into her house and snarled,

> You've won for now . . . but don't you ever think that I'm ever going to leave you alone. You're too dumb, too stupid to make it without me. You'll have everything so screwed up in a week you'll be begging me to come back . . . . And I'll be back. Don't you ever forget it. I'll be back, and I'll settle things with you once and for all. You've got a good one coming after this cute trick. Mark my words, lady. You'll live to regret what you've done. You'll pay

---

207 WALKER, TERRIFYING LOVE, *supra* note 96, at 65.

208 Beck, *supra* note 2, at 60 (statement by Stanton Samenow, a Virginia clinical psychologist and author of INSIDE THE CRIMINAL MIND).

209 Riss v. City of New York, 240 N.E.2d 860, 862 (N.Y. 1968) (finding no tort liability in domestic violence cases for failure of police to provide protection).

210 Dr. Park Dietz explained that many stalkers "are after the goal of some union with the person that they stalk, but if they can't have [that] magical and perfect union, second best is this tortured relationship because it's better than no relationship at all." *Twenty-Twenty*, *supra* note 20.

211 MARTIN, *supra* note 24, at 78; WALKER, TERRIFYING LOVE, *supra* note 96, at 65.

212 MARTIN, *supra* note 24, at 78.

213 *Id.*; *see, e.g.*, *supra* note 24 and accompanying text (discussing case history #3 in which Joanne left her husband, and he subsequently searched for her, found her, and was prepared to kill her).

214 LANGLEY & LEVY, *supra* note 48, at 27.

and pay, and you know I mean what I say.[215]

Leaving the relationship does not amount to leaving behind the violence. Instead, what often follows is a phase in which the rejected partner shadows and harasses the woman wherever she goes. I propose that these marital separation cases which have been identified as stalking incidents merely constitute another phase of the domestic violence cycle—what I term phase-four. This characterization is significant for several reasons. First, by labeling the stalking problem as a continuation of the domestic violence cycle, lawmakers, policymakers, and the courts will likely be more prepared to confront the issues seriously.[216] Second, the problem is given social definition by identifying the violence that follows marital or intimate separation as phase-four of the domestic violence cycle. Third, by naming the problem within the framework of the cycle theory of violence, sanctions can be developed to specifically address the idiosyncracies involved in this fourth phase of violence.

V. Proposal

Thus far, the discussion has shown that there is a stronger interest in dealing with domestic violence cases,[217] but that civil remedies are inadequate and traditional criminal remedies are inapplicable to the particularities of phase-four violence. Stalking laws, which were enacted to respond to these deficiencies, may often be effective.[218] However, even the new stalking laws are not effective if the stalker does not overtly communicate a threat. When the victim's fear is based on seemingly legitimate behavior rather than an explicit threat, the laws do not apply. By identifying phase-four of the cycle theory of violence, stalking may be appropriately linked to a history of abusive conduct. That history causes phase-four stalking victims to feel threatened by conduct that an ordinary person who has not endured the violent cycle would not fear. Stalking laws can and ought to be

---

215 *Id.*

216 *See supra* note 43 and accompanying text (discussing view that society is finally prepared to confront the general issues of domestic violence and treat the offenses seriously).

217 For example, in 1991, Senator Joseph R. Biden and Representative Barbara Boxer proposed a federal Violence Against Women Act. The measure would allow women to sue in civil court if they can prove there has been a crime based on their gender, with an intention to commit harm. It is expected that the law will be passed, but that it will offer limited protection against stalkers. Susanne Fowler & Diane Hirth, *Buying Time Legislatures Move to Make Stalking a Crime*, Chi. Trib., Oct. 27, 1991, at C1. Perhaps if phase-four of the cycle theory of violence were recognized, this Act against domestic violence would be able to offer protection against stalkers.

218 *See supra* text accompanying notes 166-69, 173-74 (applying stalking laws to cases #1 and #3).

modified to encompass this otherwise ordinary behavior that threatens phase-four stalking victims.

The following proposed model stalking statute attempts to overcome the shortcomings in the stalking laws outlined above. The statute, as amended, more effectively addresses all stalking cases by accounting for the dynamics of phase-four of domestic violence.

A. *Model Stalking Statute*

The proposed model statute provides:[219]

(1) Stalking Prohibited:

Any person who willfully, maliciously, and repeatedly follows or harasses another person, and who makes a credible threat, *either expressed or implied,* with the intent to place that person or a member of that person's immediate family in fear of death or great bodily injury is guilty of the crime of stalking, punishable by imprisonment in a county jail for not more than one year or by a fine of not more than one thousand dollars ($1,000), or by both that fine and imprisonment.

(2) Aggravated Stalking Prohibited:

(a) Any person who violates subdivision *(1)* when there is a temporary restraining order or an injunction, or both, in effect prohibiting the behavior described in subdivision *(1)* against the same party, is punishable by imprisonment in a county jail for not more than *five years* or by a fine of not more than *ten* thousand dollars (*$10,000*), or by both that fine and imprisonment.

(b) A second or subsequent conviction *of stalking against the same victim*, is punishable by imprisonment in a county jail for not more than *five* years, or by a fine of not more than *ten* thousand dollars (*$10,000*), or by both that fine and imprisonment.

(c) A second or subsequent conviction of aggravated stalking against the same victim shall be punishable by a term of imprisonment of an additional five years of punishment.

(3) Definitions:

(a) For the purposes of this section, "harasses" means a knowing and willful course of conduct directed at a specific person which *includes but is not limited to, unconsented contact,* which seriously alarms, annoys, or *terrorizes* the person, and which serves no legitimate purpose. The course of conduct must actually cause substantial emotional distress to the person. "Course of conduct" means a pattern of conduct composed of a series of acts over a period of time,

---

219 The proposed statute is modeled on the California stalking law. The changes made are highlighted in italics and explained in Part B.

however short, evidencing a continuity of purpose. *"Unconsented contact" means any contact with another individual that is initiated or continued without that individual's consent, or in disregard of that individual's expressed desire that the contact be avoided or discontinued.*

(b) For the purposes of this section, "a credible threat" means a threat, *expressed or implied,* made with the intent and apparent ability to carry out the threat so as to cause the person who is the target of the threat to reasonably fear for his or her safety or the safety of his or her immediate family. *An "implied threat" arises out of any contacts made in the domestic violence context such that the recipient of the contact sustains fear.*

The court, in determining whether the defendant made an implied threat, may consider the following factors: (1) the nature and circumstance of the offense charged; and (2) the history and characteristics of the defendant, including: (a) any evidence of the defendant's prior criminal history indicative of violent, abusive, or assaultive behavior, or lack of that behavior; (b) any evidence of the defendant's psychological, psychiatric, or other similar social history that tends to indicate a violent, abusive, or assaultive nature, or lack of any such history; and (c) whether the defendant is known to possess or have access to any weapon or weapons.

(4) Administrative Mandate:

In accordance with subsections (1) and (2), computerized information tracking systems shall be established to record complaints of domestic violence and violations of protective orders.

(5) Exemptions:

This statute shall not apply to constitutionally protected activity, lawful business activity, or otherwise lawful conduct arising out of a bona fide labor dispute.

B. *Defense of Proposal*

1. *Credible Threat Language Modified*

The California statute requires that a credible threat be made.[220]

---

220 CAL. PENAL CODE § 646.9(a) (West Supp. 1993).

Note that while the California stalking bill was in the Assembly, the Committee on Public Safety questioned whether a credible threat of violence should be required at all. *Stalking: Hearings on S. 2184 Before the Assembly Committee on Public Safety* (1990). Legislative history does not, however, report the Committee's reasoning for answering in the affirmative. Perhaps stalking statutes should not require a credible threat. Although this is a bold approach, if notice were given to the assailant that the conduct is unwanted, then any future contact would constitute an offense. The statute could provide for a notice provision that officially informs the assailant that the victim has withdrawn all consent for contact. Certain crimes are defined in terms of the victim's lack of consent. Rape, for example, is typically

The credible threat language was adopted from the California terrorist statute.[221] Unlike acts of terrorism in which the terrorist makes an express threat, stalking situations are quite different: stalkers frequently circumvent the law by not making an overt threat, whether intentional or not. For instance, Steven McCollum, chief deputy state attorney of Lake County, Illinois, explained that the stalker "could follow [the victim], or go to her house, but that's not stalking, even if he does it 50 times, until there's a threat."[222] Though " 'a lot of times' is very threatening, alarming and obsessive, . . . it is not necessarily criminal."[223]

Joan Zorra, senior attorney for the National Battered Women's Law Project in New York, explained that:

> [M]any of [the stalkers] know what the definition of domestic violence is and officially avoid it. Nevertheless, they are forever following their girlfriends or wives. They block her entrance way to the door, if she wants to leave her home. They follow her around.

---

defined as the "unlawful carnal knowledge of a woman by a man forcibly without her consent." BLACK'S LAW DICTIONARY 1260 (6th ed. 1990). Battery is also defined by lack of consent. Battery is any unwelcome or offensive contact. RESTATEMENT (SECOND) OF TORTS §§ 13, 18 (1965). Thus, it is generally accepted that when a victim makes it clear that consent is denied, the act is unlawful. By providing a notice provision that contact is unwelcome, the seemingly legitimate behavior that occurs in stalking cases would clearly be an offense.

Note that not all states adopted the California "credible threat" language. *See* HAW. REV. STAT. § 711-1106.5 (1992); IDAHO CODE § 18-7905 (1993); ILL. ANN. STAT. ch. 720, para. 5/12-7.3 (Smith-Hurd 1993); 1992 Kan. Sess. Laws 298; KY. REV. STAT. ANN. § 508.140 (Michie/Bobbs-Merrill 1992); MICH. COMP. LAWS ANN. § 750.411(h) (West Supp. 1993); N.C. GEN. STAT. § 14-277.3 (1992); OHIO REV. CODE ANN. § 2903.211-215 (Baldwin 1992); VA. CODE ANN. § 18.2-60.3 (Michie 1992); WASH. REV. CODE ANN. § 9A.46.110 (West Supp. 1993).

For example, the Illinois Code provides that "a person commits stalking when he or she transmits to another person a threat . . . ." ILL. ANN. STAT. ch. 72, para. 5/12-7.3 (Smith-Hurd 1993). Transmits, which means to send from one person to another, addresses how the threat is received, but this language does not overcome the problem that the victim may fear for her safety as a result of the domestic violence context.

The Texas Penal Code provides that the threat can be "either words or acts." 1993 Tex. Gen. Laws 10 (amending TEX. PENAL CODE § 42.07). However, it remains unclear whether "acts" as used in the Texas statute is broad enough to cover the threatening behavior that occurs in phase-four of the cycle of violence.

Other states simply avoided the credible threat language. For example the Kansas statute requires the first element, following or harassing conduct, but does not incorporate the second element, a credible threat. 1992 Kan. Sess. Laws 298; *see also* N.C. GEN. STAT. § 14-277.3 (Supp. 1992); OHIO REV. CODE. ANN. § 2903.211 (Anderson 1993); VA. CODE. ANN. § 18.2-60.3 (Michie Supp. 1992); WASH. REV. CODE ANN. § 9A.46.110(1) (West Supp. 1993).

221 *See* CAL. PENAL CODE § 422 (West 1993).

222 Jennifer Lenhart, *Cops Beginning to Get Handle on Stalking Law*, CHI. TRIB., Nov. 30, 1992, § 2 at 1, 9.

223 Fountain & Kirby, *supra* note 91, at 11 (quoting Lt. John Lane of the Los Angeles Police Department).

They call her repeatedly.[224]

The stalking laws were enacted to make this kind of harassment a crime.[225] That the offenders operate by seemingly legitimate behavior rather than overt threats should not allow them to escape the sanctions of stalking laws, if all other elements of the statute are satisfied.

Assailants often stalk victims merely by following them, staking out their homes, or calling them on the telephone. These actions, which typically are legitimate acts, create grave and well-founded fear in phase-four victims who have endured a history of abuse. For example, sending a dozen red roses in case #2, or parking a car outside the victim's home for six hours in case #3, may not be viewed as express threats that would typically create fear in the average person. But in fact, complaints like these are made almost every day by women whose current or former spouses or boyfriends lurk in buildings or parking lots or watch them leave work and follow them home.[226] One victim explained that she could no longer drive to work without "glancing nervously in the rearview mirror."[227]

The proposed statute provides that the "credible threat be expressed or implied."[228] This modification is based on the recognition that many offenders are careful not to make express threats and not to use force, but are able to achieve the same effect by just driving behind the victim on her way to work, or by parking their car across the street from the victim's home. These acts which are seemingly innocent but calculated to have malevolent effect, in fact have the effect of frightening the victim. Thus, the proposed statute modifies the credible threat language to incorporate this small but significant distinction.

2. *Tougher Penalties Imposed*

Under the proposed statute, offenses that simultaneously violate court orders as well as second and subsequent offenses shall constitute aggravated stalking. The discussion in Part II demonstrated that weak penalties are the principal problem with civil and criminal reme-

---

224 Ross, *supra* note 14, at 6.

225 *Id.*

226 Donald P. Baker, *Wilder Wants Law on Harassment to Take Effect Immediately*, WASH. POST, Apr. 4, 1992, at B8 (statement of Prince William County Magistrate David Burkett, Jr.).

227 *Id.*

228 *See* KY. REV. STAT. ANN. § 508.140(1)(a)(2) (Michie/Bobbs-Merrill 1992). The Kentucky stalking statute provides that a person is guilty of stalking when he intentionally "[m]akes an explicit or implicit threat with the intent to place that person in reasonable fear . . . ." *Id.* By modifying the language in this manner, Kentucky acknowledges that victims are stalked not only by express threats, but also by implied threats.

dies. To overcome this inadequacy, the proposed statute elevates the penalties for aggravated stalking; the penalty imposed for a conviction of aggravated stalking shall be five years and/or a fine of not more than ten thousand dollars. By imposing tougher penalties, the general and specific deterrence should be increased.

3. *Reasonable Woman Standard Applied*

Proposed subsection (3)(a) which defines harassment, provides that "the course of conduct must actually cause *that person* to suffer substantial emotional distress." Therefore, the proposed statute applies a subjective standard to evaluate the fear sustained in the victim. This is important because an objective standard would not be flexible enough to take into account that domestic violence victims may react differently than a person who has not endured the cycle of violence.[229] On the other hand, a subjective standard allows for evidence of prior threats and considers circumstances surrounding the making of the threat to determine the reasonableness of the victim's sustaining of fear.

4. *Harassment Language Expanded*

The proposed statute also expands the definition of "harassment" to include "unconsented contact." Domestic violence victims who try to terminate the abuse generally make it clear to the partner that further contact is unwelcome. Once a victim does so, future acts disrespectful of that wish are offensive. For example, in the first case history, the victim expressed that contact should cease.[230] She even changed the locks on her door to reinforce that further contact should not take place. However, he ignored her decision to be left alone. Because the conduct was seemingly innocent, it would probably not fall within the scope of the California statute. However, the stalking laws were enacted specifically to halt this kind of harassment. The proposed modification expanding the definition of harassment to include "unconsented contacts" is essential because the change characterizes contact as an offense once consent is withdrawn, regardless of whether the behavior is seemingly innocent.

5. *Domestic Violence Context Used to Determine Nature of Threat*

The statute defines a threat in terms of the domestic violence context, referring to implied threats "made in the context of domestic

---

229 *See supra* notes 148-56 and accompanying text (comparing objective and subjective standards).

230 *See supra* note 22 and accompanying text (profiling case #1).

violence." The proposed statute includes a list of factors to be considered in making a determination of the threat to the alleged victim. Illinois attempted to clarify the credible threat language by including a similar list of factors.[231]

The proposed statute would require courts to admit evidence regarding the cycle of abuse endured by the victim. By allowing such evidence into court to help determine whether a threat was made, it is likely that phase-four victims would be able to show that the defendant's conduct was threatening, and thus be able to invoke the protection of the stalking statute.

6. *Computer Tracking System Implemented*

The proposed statute mandates the development of information systems to record complaints of domestic violence and violations of protective orders. Data banks storing this information would enable the police to trace and chronicle incidents of harassment. As a result, police officers, judges, and prosecutors would be able to cross-reference reports of violations to identify repeat offenders.

Currently, many incidents of recurring abuse are viewed as isolated events. For example, one victim's sister described that when the victim went to get a temporary restraining order, the courts were not required to check the defendant's record: "He was out on probation from a similar incident with another girlfriend. He should have been in jail. His attack on her was a violation of that order. The judge didn't look to see his record . . . . And, now she is dead."[232] Perhaps if the judge had examined the defendant's record, he would have seen the defendant's prior history and taken a different course of action that might have saved her life.

Thus, the lack of a computer system that stores information with respect to protective orders and violations of those orders hinders the process of resolving the stalking problem. When the police are called to intervene in situations where the alleged threat appears to be innocent, an accessible database would inform the police as to whether or not the complaint involved a domestic violence situation and whether a restraining order was in effect. In addition, because the stalking statutes specifically require a course of conduct consisting of a series of acts, rather than an isolated incident, it is critical that the states develop a computer system to record and track stalking complaints.

This concept has already gained support. For example, the Con-

231 ILL. ANN. STAT. ch. 720, para. 5/12-7.3(a) (Smith-Hurd 1993).

232 *Sonya Live* (CNN television broadcast, Oct. 2, 1992) (transcript No. 147 on file with author) (statement of Helen Lardner, sister killed by stalker).

ference of Personal Managers, Inc., has donated a computer and the respective organizational software to the Los Angeles Police Department to assist the department in their efforts to track whether a stalking problem actually exists.[233] In addition, Massachusetts has already funded a computerized system to track individuals who violate protective orders.[234]

CONCLUSION

The number of cases of domestic violence, in general, and stalking in particular, is not only alarming but also on the rise. Society no longer views domestic violence as a less heinous offense than violence among strangers. Stalking usually occurs when a domestic violence victim terminates the relationship and the rejected partner strives to reconcile the divide. The rejected partner's attempts to reunite the couple often involve harassing and violent conduct. By labeling this conduct as a component of domestic violence, specifically phase-four of the cycle theory of violence, stalking cases may also be viewed as serious matters that warrant attention.

Given that civil protection orders and traditional criminal remedies are inadequate tools to protect victims, many states have enacted stalking statutes. The stalking laws seek to enlarge the zone of protection afforded stalking victims, and to give the authorities an effective enforcement tool in this area. The state legislatures that have enacted stalking laws have made a laudatory beginning in responding to the stalking problem. It is likely that the use of stalking laws will become a common method to address the problem of stalking. Yet, such laws as they currently exist may not provide protection in all cases, especially in the context of phase-four stalking violence.

The proposed model statute is designed to address all possible factual contexts involved in stalking cases. First, by modifying the language of existing stalking statutes to include credible threats that are implied as well as expressed, the coverage of the statute is broadened to protect phase-four victims who may be threatened by seemingly innocent behavior. Second, by increasing the penalties for stalking offenses, the deterrent value is increased. General deterrence is increased because a message will be sent to society that this conduct will not be tolerated; and the specific deterrence is increased because when the law fails to deter the conduct, at least the offenders will be restrained in jail for longer periods of time. Third, the reasonable

---

233 Letter from Milton B. Suchin, President of Conference of Personal Managers, Inc., to Assemblywoman Carol Bentley (June 27, 1990) (on file with author).

234 Kolarik, *supra* note 12, at 36.

person standard is replaced with a subjective standard so that the reasonableness of a victim's fear may be evaluated in light of the history of domestic abuse. Fourth, the definition of harassment is expanded to include unconsented contacts. By characterizing contact that occurs after consent has been withdrawn as harassment, such behavior is deemed offensive, and appropriately punished. Fifth, a list of factors to be considered in determining whether a threat was made is provided. By allowing evidence of the defendant's prior abusive conduct, the alleged threat will be evaluated in terms of the domestic violence context, which will increase the breadth of the statute so as to apply to cases involving phase-four violence. Finally, the statute mandates the use of computerized information systems to allow for more effective tracking of offenders, and hence, more effective protection and enforcement.

As more states enact stalking statutes and public awareness and sensitivity to the stalking problem increases, the shortcomings of existing stalking statutes will hopefully come to light. The measures proposed above should address those shortcomings, for they treat the stalking problem as an extension of the domestic violence cycle.

Susan E. Bernstein

Responding to Domestic Violence Against Women

Loretta J. Stalans
Arthur J. Lurigio

This year, the public is reminded that domestic violence against women has no racial or social class boundaries. Nicole Brown Simpson knew firsthand that wealthy Caucasian women are beaten and psychologically abused. The O. J. Simpson trial dramatically portrays the terror of a battered woman's life and considers the question of whether Nicole Brown Simpson is yet another victim of domestic murder—a fatal consequence that happens all too often in America. According to the National Crime Victimization Survey (NCVS), women are 10 times more likely than men to be victims of violence inflicted by their intimate partners (Zawitz 1994). Based on a national survey of reported incidents of violence (from slapping to choking or using a weapon), Straus (1991) estimated that "over 6 million women are beaten every year in the United States. This is a lower bound estimate and the true figure easily could be double that" (p. 30).

About 1.8 million women experience at least one of the more serious forms of violence, such as being kicked, punched, choked, or attacked with a weapon. These numbers, of course, are just estimates because all data sources either underestimate or overestimate certain forms of violence. Women experience similar risks of violence in urban, suburban, and rural areas. Ethnic or racial background is unrelated to rates of violence in the home, but age and social class do place women at a higher risk for violent attacks: younger women with less education and lower incomes have much higher rates of victimizations by intimates than do older women and women with more education and higher incomes (Zawitz 1994).

Women are more likely than men to be seriously injured in domestic violence incidents, as documented by police records (Bell and Bell 1991) and victimization surveys such as Brush's (1993) nationwide survey of 5,474

LORETTA J. STALANS: Assistant Professor, Department of Criminal Justice, Loyola University. **ARTHUR J. LURIGIO**: Associate Professor, Department of Criminal Justice, Loyola University.

CRIME & DELINQUENCY, Vol. 41 No. 4, October 1995 387-398

U.S. households in 1988. Brush asked males and females in married couples the following: "Have you ever been cut, bruised, or seriously injured in a fight with your partner?" "Has your partner ever been cut, bruised, or seriously injured?" Women reported that they were hurt more often than their partners. Moreover, in situations where both partners were violent, women were more likely to be seriously injured (also see Straus 1991). Data from emergency rooms, police reports, and court records also support the conclusion that in domestic disputes women receive more serious injuries than men (for a review, see Kurz 1993). However, men are less likely to report victimization experiences, and many incidents of domestic violence, whether women or men are victims, never come to the attention of police or physicians.

As the above findings clearly suggest, women are susceptible to repeat victimizations in the home and may become hopelessly entangled in abusive relationships. They fear not only the consequences of staying but also, and even more, the consequences of leaving those relationships (Barnett and LaViolette 1993). In the NCVS, 20% of women reported that they had been victims of intimate violence at least three times in the prior 6 months (Zawitz 1994). Many women do not react passively and helplessly when faced with repeat abuse. Most seek help from family, friends, or government agencies (Frieze and Browne 1989). In the NCVS, about 80% attempted to defend themselves: 40% reasoned with the offenders and 40% used physical force (Zawitz 1994). More than one half of the women who attempted to protect themselves thought that their tactics had helped, whereas one fourth believed that their tactics had worsened the situations (Zawitz 1994). Faced with repeated abuse, women often begin to anticipate the next violent episode and may engage in behaviors to actually trigger the violence; for them, the anticipation of abuse is often worse than the abuse itself. Victims of violent street crimes typically do not have contact with offenders after the crime; in contrast, domestic violence victims and their perpetrators often share children, property, insurance, and homes. Even if victims leave their homes, courts often force them to allow offenders to visit their children. Victims of domestic violence are particularly vulnerable to repeat abuse because their children make it difficult to sever all contacts with offenders.

The most fatal consequence of domestic violence frequently happens after escalating incidents of repeat violence (see Frieze and Browne 1989). The exact number of homicides that occur because of the actions of intimates is difficult to estimate because the nature of the relationships between victims and offenders is often unknown (e.g., 39% of the relationships were unknown in FBI data for 1992; see Zawitz 1994). Based on FBI data from 1977 to 1992, an estimated 1,432 women and 657 men were killed by intimates in 1992 (Zawitz 1994). The ratio of women to men who kill their intimate partners varies by race. In 1977, a greater number of African American women killed their husbands compared to African American men who killed their wives, but by 1992 a greater number of African American men killed their wives. "Among Whites, wives have always outnumbered husbands as victims of intimate murder" (Zawitz 1994, p. 3). More than half of the victims and offenders were drinking alcohol at the time of the murders (Zawitz 1994). Several studies report that in instances where wives killed their husbands, the husbands were the first to use physical force or to threaten the use of a weapon (see Frieze and Browne 1989). In 1991, 70% of women prisoners incarcerated for intimate violence were first-time offenders, compared to only 30% of men incarcerated for intimate violence. Of those incarcerated for intimate violence, men with previous convictions for violent crimes outnumbered women almost 3 to 1 (Zawitz 1994).

TWO PERSPECTIVES ON DOMESTIC VIOLENCE

Why does domestic violence occur and what can society and the criminal justice system do about it? Kurz (1993) described two theoretical perspectives that have dominated domestic violence research: the family violence perspective (e.g., Straus, Gelles, and Steinmetz 1980) and the feminist perspective (e.g., Dobash and Dobash 1979; Hanmer, Radford, and Stanko 1989). For the family violence perspective, the unit of analysis is the family (Kurz 1993). For the feminist perspective, the unit of analysis is the relationship between men and women; it encompasses all forms of violence against women from sexual harassment in the workplace to physical, verbal, and sexual abuse in the home (Kurz 1993). Both perspectives urge the legal system to focus on violence against women, but they do so for different reasons, which lead to different solutions to the problem.

The family violence perspective maintains that women and men are equally likely to engage in violence, as evidenced by survey data showing that women and men report similar incidences of physical violence against their partners (Straus et al. 1980). Straus and colleagues (1980) found that about 12% of men and women in their study sample engaged in violence and that in 49% of the homes where violence occurred, both men and women were perpetrators. Other surveys have replicated the finding that men and women report similar levels of violence (Brush 1993; for a review, see Straus 1991). Feminists criticize these results by pointing out that many of women's acts of physical aggression are actually attempts to defend themselves from men's attacks (Dobash and Dobash 1979). According to NCVS data, twice as many women physically attacked intimate assailants to protect themselves than attacked stranger assailants for self-protection (40% vs. 20%, respectively; see Zawitz 1994). Feminists point to the higher percentages of women victims of violence (as opposed to women perpetrators) in police and court records, emergency room data, and victimization surveys to underscore the fact that women are much more likely to be victims of domestic violence.

The family violence perspective suggests that women and men learn from childhood experiences and from media portrayals and societal norms that violence is an acceptable way to resolve disputes. In the family violence perspective, therefore, domestic violence is no different from other forms of violence such as stranger-on-stranger violence and violence against children, the elderly, and other social groups—all of which are seen to result from faulty socialization. The family violence perspective focuses on women victims because men engage in more dangerous forms of violence that lead to more serious injuries (Straus et al. 1980).

Feminists argue that male dominance is a central component in understanding why domestic violence occurs and in finding solutions to it. Feminists assert that men and women do not have equal positions in society. Men have had privileged positions in society for centuries and have acquired and maintained these positions by keeping women subordinate (see Dobash and Dobash 1979). According to this viewpoint, organized religion has perpetuated the attitudes and beliefs that lead to violence against women and children (Dobash and Dobash 1979). As Kurz (1993) observed:

> Feminists believe that the decontextualized family violence perspective denies a central element of women's experience by deflecting attention from one of the key places where women's oppression occurs—in the family. For feminists, family violence is a direct outcome of men's attempt to maintain control over the powerless members of the family—women and children. (pp. 262-3)

Because it ignores variables such as social structure and gender, the family violence perspective places great importance on psychological problems of individuals and families. Fine (1993) discussed the implications of concentrating on individuals rather than on the gender-based nature of violence:

> To focus on the individual . . . contributes to a discourse that finally blames individual survivors, for the source of social inequity is sought inside their bodies and minds. Not only does such an approach decontextualize a woman from her political, social, and personal worlds, but it systematically renders oblique the structure of patriarchy, racism, and classism, and advanced capitalism that have sculpted what appear to be the "conditions" or "choices" of her life. (pp. 280-1)

HISTORICAL TREATMENT OF DOMESTIC VIOLENCE

History supports the feminists' position that laws and community norms perpetuate violence against women. The U.S. Constitution declares that "all men are created equal," but did not extend human and civil rights to women until several decades after its passage. In the 17th and 18th centuries, women were property that could be bought and sold, and they were disciplined through physical punishment. Women did not have the right to own property, to vote, or to manage their wages:

> Married women had always been controlled and abused by legal loss of their property upon marriage and by the husband's right to exploit their labor and to appropriate their wages, but the Married Women's Property Act of 1857 forbade a husband to "seize his wife's earnings and neglect her and allowed her to keep her own wages after the desertion of her lord." (Dobash and Dobash 1979, pp. 67-8)

Until the 19th century, husbands who beat their wives could use the defense of chastisement (Dobash and Dobash 1979). In the latter part of the 19th century, domestic violence was considered a crime and laws were created to punish offenders at the whipping post. "Courts declared that 'the rule of love superseded the rule of force' and 'the moral sense of the community revolts at the idea that the husband may inflict personal chastisement upon his wife, even for the most outrageous conduct.' " (Dobash and Dobash 1979, p. 63) These laws, however, were rarely enforced.

At the turn of the 20th century, domestic violence was viewed once again as a "private matter" that should be kept out of public view. Many states created statutes that did not allow police officers to arrest perpetrators for domestic violence misdemeanors where a neutral third party did not witness the episode. Courts and prosecutors believed that formal prosecution was not appropriate and that rehabilitation was the goal (Buzawa and Buzawa 1990). Historically, legal statutes, criminal justice authorities, and community members have regarded violence against women in the home as a "private matter of the family," best handled through advice or mediation.

CHANGES WITHIN THE LEGAL SYSTEM TO HANDLE DOMESTIC VIOLENCE

During the last two decades, the legal system has faced inside and outside pressure to protect women from violence. The women's movement in the 1970s focused on violence against women and characterized the problem as a public concern. Civil liability suits filed against police departments for failing to provide equal protection to women injured in domestic violence incidents signaled to all law enforcement agencies that ignoring battered women can lead to litigation and financial losses. Academic research (for a review, see Buzawa and Buzawa 1990) also called attention to the problems of existing domestic violence policies. For example, research shows that the likelihood of future domestic violence is lower when police arrest batterers in domestic disputes (Sherman and Berk 1984); however, other research suggests that the effectiveness of arrest is contingent on a number of situational factors and batterer characteristics. Together, feminism, court cases, and empirical findings have helped to change state laws to give police officers more power to arrest suspects in domestic violence incidents.

Several states have changed their laws to allow police officers to arrest suspects without victims' consent when there is probable cause (Hirschel and Hutchison 1991). Despite these statutory changes, only a few states actually require officers to arrest suspects under specific circumstances, such as when there are injured victims (Hirschel and Hutchison 1991). Officers still exercise a lot of discretion when deciding to arrest suspects, even in states with laws mandating arrest, because the concept of probable cause is quite ambiguous (Ferraro 1993). Officers have especially difficult times interpreting domestic violence situations where the wife and husband offer conflicting accounts of how the injuries occurred. To handle these situations, some states have passed laws requiring officers to determine who is the primary aggressor in an incident. In one state with a primary aggressor clause, experienced officers are rarely able to untangle the past to assess blameworthiness; instead, they base their decisions to arrest on the respective credibility and dangerousness of wives and husbands. Their "disinterested objectivity," however, has still created a bias toward less formal processing of cases involving women who violate social norms by exhibiting symptoms of mental illness or alcoholism (Stalans and Finn 1995). Moreover, mandatory and presumptive arrest policies have not resulted in equal protection under the law (e.g., Ferraro 1989).

Early evaluations of how legislative changes influenced local criminal justice practices suggested that gatekeepers (i.e., police officers and prosecutors) often fail to process domestic violence cases through the formal criminal justice system and prefer alternatives such as court-ordered mediation. Moreover, evaluations showing higher rates of arrest after the implementation of presumptive arrest policies (see Hirschel and Hutchison 1991) did not examine several key issues, for example, victims' satisfaction with how the police and system treated them, whether certain groups of women obtained less protection, whether states' attorneys lessened or dropped the charges, and how the courts deal with convicted batterers.

Preferred arrest policies do result in significantly more arrests when they are part of a coordinated response involving the legal system and community agencies (for a review, see Hirschel and Hutchison 1991). Key criminal justice institutions (i.e., police, the prosecutor's office, courts, and defense attorneys), community services (i.e., battered women's shelters, children's services, welfare agencies, and mental health services), and public support can change officers' decisions about using arrest as a solution to domestic violence incidents.

Researchers have paid relatively little attention to how domestic violence cases are prosecuted (Cahn and Lerman 1991; Ford and Regoli 1993). In the past, prosecutors typically required victims of domestic violence to sign complaints against batterers, whereas prosecutors themselves signed complaints in other crimes. Prosecutors' offices are changing their procedures so that they now sign complaints against defendants, and victims serve as key witnesses in those cases; this change sends the message that domestic violence is a crime against the state (Cahn and Lerman 1991). Prosecutors' offices also have adopted policies to prevent victims from dropping charges and regularly use subpoena power to force victims to appear in court. Subpoena power may prevent victims from becoming targets of retaliatory violence because victims can show that they were forced to participate in court proceedings (Cahn and Lerman 1991). Prosecutors also have been successful at prosecuting cases without the participation of victims (Cahn and Lerman 1991).

Research on the effectiveness of different prosecution strategies has been sparse. Ford and Regoli (1993) concluded that

> the limited evidence on the effectiveness of alternative prosecution policies for preventing wife assault suggests that no single policy commonly advocated is better than another. The chance of a man assaulting his partner again in the short term is essentially unaffected by whether he is prosecuted under policies calling for harsh punishment or for rehabilitative treatment. What matters is that he faces treatment. (p. 157)

When victims initiate complaints, they are less likely to be harmed by offenders when prosecutors allow the victims to drop charges than when other strategies such as diversion or "no-drop" policies are used (Ford and Regoli 1993). This effectiveness, however, remains to be documented more thoroughly and may not generalize to police-initiated charges.

Many jurisdictions, thanks largely to the feminist perspective, have created victims' programs that help victims with their decisions to participate in the legal process and to leave domestic batterers. Several studies have found that these programs increase victims' willingness to participate in the criminal justice process as well as increase their satisfaction with the process (Cahn and Lerman 1991). Few studies, however, have examined whether victim advocate programs reduce the risk that victims will experience retaliatory violence, increase their knowledge about the system and community-based programs, and empower them to take control over their lives. Research is sorely needed to better understand how interventions can assist victims' recovery and readjustment. In addressing these issues, researchers should explore the independent and combined effects of victims' programs, civil protection orders, and prosecution and sentencing strategies on victims' satisfaction, safety, recovery, and control over their lives.

The family violence perspective is more likely than the feminist perspective to pay attention to the perpetrators of domestic violence. The family violence perspective, for example, encourages researchers to classify offenders into different profiles based on backgrounds and personality characteristics. Saunders (1993) identified three prominent risk factors for wife assault. Men are more likely to batter women if the men were abused as children. The risk of wife assault increases when both partners were abused or witnessed abuse as children. Alcohol abuse and low income are also prominent risk factors. Other risk factors include offender deficits in communication skills, rigid stereotypes of male and female roles, personality disorders, and problems with anger control. These risk factors have been used to customize treatments for batterers. Many criminal justice systems now impose court-mandated treatment at both pre- and postsentencing (Hamberger and Hastings 1993). In pretrial diversion programs, for example, offenders who successfully complete treatment have their arrest records cleared. Court-mandated treatment also can be part of sentences for convicted offenders.

CHANGES WITHIN THE COMMUNITY TO HANDLE DOMESTIC VIOLENCE

A variety of community services and treatment programs exist to assist victims of domestic violence and to treat domestic violence offenders. Feminists have focused on the task of empowering women to control their own lives and have created social services that allow women with limited financial means to leave abusive partners and to find havens from retaliatory violence. Feminists were volunteers for the first battered women's shelters and have fought to limit the amount of funds that are diverted away from abused women to treat abusive men (Ferraro 1989). Shelters provide a safe place to live and offer supportive counseling, child care, and advocacy services (Dutton-Douglas and Dionne 1991). The number of shelters has grown from 0 in 1970 to more than 1,300 in 1989 (Ferraro 1989); nonetheless, there are not enough shelters to meet the demand for services.

The effectiveness of shelters as a means of allowing women to leave violent relationships is uncertain. Research indicates that each additional step that a victim takes to seek help reduces the number of subsequent victimization incidents (for a review, see Dutton-Douglas and Dionne 1991). Battered women can also receive counseling services from outpatient community mental health treatment programs, clergy, private counseling agencies, and women's groups, the latter of which battered women rate as more effective than the other types of counseling services (Dutton-Douglas and Dionne 1991).

OVERVIEW OF THE CONTENTS OF THIS SPECIAL ISSUE

This volume examines how the public, victims, and the legal system are responding to domestic violence against women both in the United States and in Great Britain. The two lead articles explore how persons outside the legal system make decisions about using court resources. In the first contribution, Stalans and Lurigio study how adult residents of Atlanta prefer the court to handle their domestic violence situations, specifically, whether individuals prefer their spouses to receive counseling and probation instead of jail sentences and whether past and current victim injuries, and the intent of batterers to inflict harm change public preferences about sentences. They find much more support for probation and counseling than for jail—although this preference changes as a function of victim status, gender, and situational features. Stalans and Lurigio report that the public's reluctance to use jail time is based in part on a desire to restore harmony in domestic relationships.

In the second contribution, Fischer and Rose report on their use of qualitative interviews with battered women seeking orders of protection. Their findings demonstrate that victims also believe that seeking a court order signals their own and their partners' failures to bring harmony to the relationship and communicates to the court that they have had "enough" of the violence. Furthermore, Fischer and Rose illustrate how economic and social resources, emotional considerations, and perceptions of the legal system contribute to women's decisions to pursue protection orders. They also show how women derive feelings of safety and control from orders of protection, which they believe will shield them from future harm.

Against this backdrop of the public's and victims' mixed feelings about the formal handling of domestic violence cases, the next two articles evaluate mandatory or presumptive arrest policies. Each of them addresses a couple of common questions: Do officers base their arrest decisions on evidentiary and efficiency considerations? What criteria do police officers consider in making arrest decisions? Mignon and Holmes evaluate a mandatory arrest policy in Massachusetts, using police reports from 24 departments. They report that arrest rates increased, especially in cases where the batterer violated a restraining order. The next article, by Buzawa, Austin, and Buzawa, further investigates a topic of considerable debate and research: whether police handle domestic assault cases different from the way they handle assaults involving strangers. After controlling for offenders' presence at the scenes and victim preferences, they find that police were indeed less likely to arrest in incidents of domestic assault. In addition, they report that victim preferences for arrest were ignored by police in nearly twice as many domestic cases when compared to stranger cases.

Whereas many studies have investigated how police officers make decisions about arrest, few have explored how they make referral decisions. In the fifth contribution, Finn and Stalans study how novice and experienced officers make decisions about referring victims to shelters and to outpatient treatment programs. They use a new statistical technique, univariate optimal discriminant analysis, which maximizes classification accuracy to provide a clearer test of whether experienced and novice officers share referral criteria. Finn and Stalans find that inferences about control over actions and responsibility better predict experienced officers' decisions than novice officers' decisions regarding referrals to mental health treatment. Both experienced and novice officers make referrals to battered shelters based on the presence of injuries and inferences concerning responsibility and intentions.

In the sixth contribution, Tolman and Weisz examine a coordinated community intervention designed to reduce domestic violence in an Illinois county just west of Chicago. Specifically, they study the effects of arrest and prosecution on subsequent police calls and arrests. They find that arrests significantly deterred subsequent domestic violence incidents, especially for offenders with previous histories of police involvement for domestic violence.

The seventh article in the issue provides a sobering reminder of the individual and social costs of intimate violence. Block and Christakos present risk patterns for intimate homicide and discuss recent trends in these homicides, using archival data containing every intimate homicide committed in Chicago in the last 29 years. They discuss how such incidents vary according to factors, such as the gender and race of victims and offenders, the existence of weapons, and the use of alcohol and drugs.

In the eighth article, Dwyer takes us across the Atlantic to describe how the legal system in Great Britain responds to domestic violence. Her research provides a relevant comparison to the criminal justice system in the United States. Despite a lower level of stranger-on-stranger violence and a more progressive feminist movement, Great Britain has a similar rate of domestic violence. This cross-cultural comparison suggests that the family violence model cannot account completely for violence against women in Great Britain or the United States.

In the final contribution to this volume, Davis and Smith review research on major criminal justice reforms for handling domestic violence incidents, including restraining orders, mandatory arrests, and court-mandated treatment for batterers. They conclude that there are no simple or universally applicable responses to domestic violence cases.

REFERENCES

Barnett, Ola W. and Alyce D. LaViolette. 1993. *It Could Happen to Anyone: Why Battered Women Stay*. Newbury Park, CA: Sage.

Bell, Daniel J. and Susan L. Bell. 1991. "The Victim Offender Relationship as a Determinant in Police Dispositions of Family Violence Incidents: A Replication Study." *Policing and Society* 1:225-34.

Brush, Lisa D. 1993. "Violent Acts and Injurious Outcomes in Married Couples: Methodological Issues in the National Survey of Families and Households." Pp. 237-51 in *Violence Against Women: The Bloody Footprints*, edited by P. B. Bart and E. G. Moran. Newbury Park, CA: Sage.

Buzawa, Eva S. and Carl G. Buzawa. 1990. *Domestic Violence: The Criminal Justice Response*. Newbury Park: Sage.

Cahn, Naomi R. and Lisa G. Lerman. 1991. "Prosecuting Woman Abuse." Pp. 95-112 in *Woman Battering: Policy Responses*, edited by M. Steinman. Cincinnati, OH: Anderson.

Dobash, R. Emerson and Russell Dobash. 1979. *Violence Against Wives*. New York: Macmillan.

Dutton-Douglas, Mary Anne and Dorothy Dionne. 1991. "Counseling and Shelter Services for Battered Women." Pp. 113-30 in *Woman Battering: Policy Responses*, edited by M. Steinman. Cincinnati, OH: Anderson.

Ferraro, Kathleen J. 1989. "The Legal Response to Woman Battering in the United States." Pp. 155-84 in *Women, Policing, and Male Violence*, edited by J. Hanmer, J. Radford, and E. A. Stanko. New York: Routledge.

———. 1993. "Cops, Courts, and Woman Battering." Pp. 278-87 in *Violence Against Women: The Bloody Footprints*, edited by P. B. Bart and E. G. Moran. Newbury Park, CA: Sage.

Fine, Michelle. 1993. "The Politics of Research and Activism: Violence Against Women." Pp. 278-87 in *Violence Against Women: The Bloody Footprints*, edited by P. B. Bart and E. G. Moran. Newbury Park, CA: Sage.

Ford, David A. and Mary Jean Regoli. 1993. "The Criminal Prosecution of Wife Assaults: Process, Problems, and Effects." Pp. 163-218 in *Legal Responses to Wife Assault: Current Trends and Evaluations*, edited by N. Z. Hilton. Newbury Park, CA: Sage.

Frieze, Irene Hanson and Angela Browne. 1989. "Violence in Marriage." Pp. 163-218 in *Family Violence*, edited by L. Ohlin and M. Tonry. Chicago: University of Chicago Press.

Hamberger, L. Kevin and James E. Hastings. 1993. "Court-Mandated Treatment of Men Who Assault Their Partner." Pp. 188-229 in *Legal Responses to Wife Assault: Current Trends and Evaluations*, edited by N. Z. Hilton. Newbury Park, CA: Sage.

Hanmer, Jalna, Jill Radford, and Elizabeth A. Stanko. 1989. "Policing Men's Violence: An Introduction." Pp. 1-12 in *Women, Policing, and Male Violence*, edited by J. Hanmer, J. Radford, and E. A. Stanko. New York: Routledge.

Hirschel, David J. and Ira Hutchison. 1991. "Police-Preferred Arrest Policies." Pp. 49-72 in *Woman Battering: Policy Responses*, edited by M. Steinman. Cincinnati, OH: Anderson.

Kurz, Demie. 1993. "Social Science Perspectives on Wife Abuse: Current Debates and Future Directions." Pp. 252-69 in *Violence Against Women: The Bloody Footprints*, edited by P. B. Bart and E. G. Moran. Newbury Park, CA: Sage.

Saunders, Daniel G. 1993. "Husbands Who Assault Multiple Profiles Requiring Multiple Responses." Pp. 9-34 in *Legal Responses to Wife Assault: Current Trends and Evaluation*, edited by N. Z. Hilton. Newbury Park, CA: Sage.

Sherman, Lawrence W. and Richard A. Berk. 1994. "The Specific Deterrent Effects of Arrest for Domestic Assault." *American Sociological Review* 49:261-72.

Stalans, Loretta J. and Mary A. Finn. 1995. "How Novice and Experienced Officers Interpret Wife Assaults: Normative and Efficiency Frames." *Law & Society Review* 29:301-55.

Straus, Murray. 1991. "Conceptualization and Measurement of Battering: Implications for Public Policy." Pp. 19-47 in *Woman Battering: Policy Responses*, edited by M. Steinman. Cincinnati, OH: Anderson.

Straus, Murray, Richard Gelles, and S. Steinmetz. 1980. *Behind Closed Doors: Violence in the American Family*. Garden City, NY: Doubleday.

Zawitz, Marianne W. 1994. "Violence Between Intimates." *Bureau of Justice Statistics Selected Findings*, NCJ-149259. Washington, DC: U.S. Government Printing Office.

Acknowledgments

Wriggins, Jennifer. "Rape, Racism, and the Law." *Harvard Women's Law Journal* 6 (1983): 103–41. Reprinted with the permission of the *Harvard Women's Law Journal.*

Caringella-MacDonald, Susan. "Sexual Assault Prosecution: An Examination of Model Rape Legislation in Michigan." *Women and Politics* 4 (1985): 65–82. Reprinted with the permission of Haworth Press, Inc. Copyright 1985.

Ferraro, Kathleen J. "Policing Woman Battering." *Social Problems* 36 (1989): 61–74. Reprinted with the permission of the University of California Press. Copyright (1989) by the Society for the Study of Social Problems.

Allard, Sharon Angella. "Rethinking Battered Woman Syndrome: A Black Feminist Perspective." *UCLA Women's Law Journal* 1 (1991): 191–207. Reprinted with the permission of the *UCLA Women's Law Journal.*

Crenshaw, Kimberle. "Mapping the Margins: Intersectionality, Identity Politics, and Violence Against Women of Color." *Stanford Law Review* 43 (1991): 1241–99. Reprinted with the permission of the Board of Trustees of the Leland Stanford Junior University. Copyright (1991).

Frohmann, Lisa. "Discrediting Victims' Allegations of Sexual Assault: Prosecutorial Accounts of Case Rejections." *Social Problems* 38 (1991): 213–26. Reprinted with the permission of the University of California Press. Copyright (1991) by the Society for the Study of Social Problems.

Mahoney, Martha R. "Legal Images of Battered Women: Redefining the Issue of Separation." *Michigan Law Review* 90 (1991): 1–94. Reprinted with the permission of the Michigan Law Review Association.

Donat, Patricia L.N. and John D'Emilio. "A Feminist Redefinition of Rape and Sexual Assault: Historical Foundations and Change." *Journal of Social Issues* 48 (1992): 9–22. Reprinted with the permission of The Society for the Psychological Study of Social Issues.

Goldberg-Ambrose, Carole. "Unfinished Business in Rape Law Reform." *Journal of Social Issues* 48 (1992): 173–85. Reprinted with the permission of The Society for the Psychological Study of Social Issues.

Syers, Maryann and Jeffrey L. Edleson. "The Combined Effects of Coordinated Criminal Justice Intervention in Woman Abuse." *Journal of Interpersonal*

Violence 74 (1992): 490–502. Reprinted with the permission of Sage Publications, Inc.

Bernstein, Susan E. "Living Under Siege: Do Stalking Laws Protect Domestic Violence Victims?" *Cardozo Law Review* 15 (1993): 525–67. Reprinted with the permission of the *Cardozo Law Review*.

Stalans, Loretta J. and Arthur J. Lurigio. "Responding to Domestic Violence Against Women." *Crime and Delinquency* 41 (1995): 387–98. Reprinted with the permission of Sage Publications.